124	01111100	157	10011101	190	10111110	223	11011111
125	01111101	158	10011110	191	10111111	224	11100000
126	01111110	159	10011111	192	11000000	225	11100001
127	01111111	160	10100000	193	11000001	226	11100010
128	10000000	161	10100001	194	11000010	227	11100011
129	10000001	162	10100010	195	11000011	228	11100100
130	10000010	163	10100011	196	11000100	229	11100101
131	10000011	164	10100100	197	11000101	230	11100110
132	10000100	165	10100101	198	11000110	231	11100111
133	10000101	166	10100110	199	11000111	232	11101000
134	10000110	167	10100111	200	11001000	233	11101001
135	10000111	168	10101000	201	11001001	234	11101010
136	10001000	169	10101001	202	11001010	235	11101011
137	10001001	170	10101010	203	11001011	236	11101100
138	10001010	171	10101011	204	11001100	237	11101101
139	10001011	172	10101100	205	11001101	238	11101110
140	10001100	173	10101101	206	11001110	239	11101111
141	10001101	174	10101110	207	11001111	240	11110000
142	10001110	175	10101111	208	11010000	241	11110001
143	10001111	176	10110000	209	11010001	242	11110010
144	10010000	177	10110001	210	11010010	243	11110011
145	10010001	178	10110010	211	11010011	244	11110100
146	10010010	179	10110011	212	11010100	245	11110101
147	10010011	180	10110100	213	11010101	246	11110110
148	10010100	181	10110101	214	11010110	247	11110111
149	10010101	182	10110110	215	11010111	248	11111000
150	10010110	183	10110111	216	11011000	249	11111001
151	10010111	184	10111000	217	11011001	250	11111010
152	10011000	185	10111001	218	11011010	251	11111011
153	10011001	186	10111010	219	11011011	252	11111100
154	10011010	187	10111011	220	11011100	253	11111101
155	10011011	188	10111100	221	11011101	254	11111110
156	10011100	189	10111101	222	11011110	255	11111111

Cisco CCNP Routing Exam Certification Guide

Clare Gough

CISCO SYSTEMS

CISCO PRESS

Cisco Press
201 W 103rd Street
Indianapolis, IN 46290

Cisco CCNP Routing Exam Certification Guide

Clare Gough

Copyright © 2001 Cisco Press

Cisco Press logo is a trademark of Cisco Systems, Inc.

Published by:
Cisco Press
201 West 103rd Street
Indianapolis, IN 46290 USA

Printed in the United States of America 1 2 3 4 5 6 7 8 9 0

Library of Congress Cataloging-in-Publication Number: 00-105173

ISBN: 1-58720-001-5

Warning and Disclaimer

This book is designed to provide information about Cisco routing. Every effort has been made to make this book as complete and as accurate as possible, but no warranty or fitness is implied.

The information is provided on an "as is" basis. The author, Cisco Press, and Cisco Systems, Inc., shall have neither liability nor responsibility to any person or entity with respect to any loss or damages arising from the information contained in this book or from the use of the discs or programs that may accompany it.

The opinions expressed in this book belong to the author and are not necessarily those of Cisco Systems, Inc.

Trademark Acknowledgments

All terms mentioned in this book that are known to be trademarks or service marks have been appropriately capitalized. Cisco Press or Cisco Systems, Inc., cannot attest to the accuracy of this information. Use of a term in this book should not be regarded as affecting the validity of any trademark or service mark.

Feedback Information

At Cisco Press, our goal is to create in-depth technical books of the highest quality and value. Each book is crafted with care and precision, undergoing rigorous development that involves the unique expertise of members from the professional technical community.

Readers' feedback is a natural continuation of this process. If you have any comments regarding how we could improve the quality of this book, or otherwise alter it to better suit your needs, you can contact us through e-mail at cisco-press@mcp.com. Please make sure to include the book title and ISBN in your message.

We greatly appreciate your assistance.

Publisher	John Wait
Editor-in-Chief	John Kane
Executive Editor	Brett Bartow
Cisco Systems Program Manager	Bob Anstey
Managing Editor	Patrick Kanouse
Acquisitions Editor	Amy Lewis
Development Editor	Andrew Cupp
Production Editor	Marc Fowler
Copy Editor	Krista Hansing
Technical Editors	Jorge Aragon
	Steve Gifkins
	Martin Walshaw
	Steve Wisniewski
CD-ROM Question Authors	David Barnes
	Martin Walshaw
CD-ROM Technical Editors	Steve Gifkins
	Mike Truett
Team Coordinator	Tammi Ross
Book Designer	Gina Rexrode
Cover Designer	Louisa Klucznik
Production Team	Octal Publishing, Inc.
Indexer	Lisa Stumpf

CISCO SYSTEMS

Corporate Headquarters
Cisco Systems, Inc.
170 West Tasman Drive
San Jose, CA 95134-1706
USA
http://www.cisco.com
Tel: 408 526-4000
   800 553-NETS (6387)
Fax: 408 526-4100

European Headquarters
Cisco Systems Europe
11 Rue Camille Desmoulins
92782 Issy-les-Moulineaux
Cedex 9
France
http://www-europe.cisco.com
Tel: 33 1 58 04 60 00
Fax: 33 1 58 04 61 00

Americas Headquarters
Cisco Systems, Inc.
170 West Tasman Drive
San Jose, CA 95134-1706
USA
http://www.cisco.com
Tel: 408 526-7660
Fax: 408 527-0883

Asia Pacific Headquarters
Cisco Systems Australia,
Pty., Ltd
Level 17, 99 Walker Street
North Sydney
NSW 2059 Australia
http://www.cisco.com
Tel: +61 2 8448 7100
Fax: +61 2 9957 4350

Cisco Systems has more than 200 offices in the following countries. Addresses, phone numbers, and fax numbers are listed on the Cisco Web site at www.cisco.com/go/offices

Argentina • Australia • Austria • Belgium • Brazil • Bulgaria • Canada • Chile • China • Colombia • Costa Rica • Croatia • Czech Republic • Denmark • Dubai, UAE • Finland • France • Germany • Greece • Hong Kong • Hungary • India • Indonesia • Ireland Israel • Italy • Japan • Korea • Luxembourg • Malaysia • Mexico • The Netherlands • New Zealand • Norway • Peru • Philippines Poland • Portugal • Puerto Rico • Romania • Russia • Saudi Arabia • Scotland • Singapore • Slovakia • Slovenia • South Africa • Spain Sweden • Switzerland • Taiwan • Thailand • Turkey • Ukraine • United Kingdom • United States • Venezuela • Vietnam • Zimbabwe

About the Author

Clare Gough is a Cisco Certified Internetworking Engineer(CCIE #2893) and was a Cisco Certified Systems Instructor for the ICRC, ACRC, CIT, CLSC, and CID courses. She holds a master's degree in education and a master's degree in information systems. Over the last 15 years, she has developed and taught a variety of networking and internetworking courses throughout the world for Digital Equipment Co. and various Cisco training partners. She moved from England in 1991 and now lives in San Francisco with her family.

About the Technical Reviewers

Jorge Aragon (CCIE #5567) is a network engineer with Perot Systems Corporation (PSC) in Dallas, Texas. He holds a bachelor of science degree in electrical engineering from the National Polytechnic Institute in Mexico, and has a master of science degree in telecommunications from the University of Pittsburgh. He also holds an MCSE certification and several of Cisco's specializations. Jorge is part of the PSC Global Infrastructure team, where he designs, implements, and troubleshoots LAN and WAN networks for clients in multiple industries across the globe. He enjoys spending time with his wife and children, reading, jogging, and practicing martial arts. Jorge can be reached at jorge.aragon@ps.net.

Steve Gifkins is a CCIE and CCSI of four and five years, respectively. He is based in the United Kingdom, where he runs his own independent Cisco-only consulting and training business. He is married with no children, and his hobbies include anything to do with outdoor life. Having retired with a knee injury from playing active sports such as squash, rugby, and soccer, he has taken up new hobbies in horse eventing and show jumping. In addition, he enjoys skiing and hill scrambling.

Martin Walshaw is a CCIE (#5629), CCNP, and CCDP. He is a systems engineer working for Cisco Systems in the enterprise line of business in South Africa. His areas of specialty are multiservice (voice and video) as well as security, which keeps him busy both night and day. During the last 12 years or so, Martin has dabbled in many aspects of the IT industry, ranging from programming in RPG III and Cobol to PC sales. When Martin is not working, he likes to spend all his available time with his wife, Val, and his son, Joshua. Without their patience, understanding, and support, projects such as this would not be possible.

Steve Wisniewski is CCNP certified and has a master of science degree from Stevens Institute of Technology in Telecom Management. Steve works for Lehmqan Brothers as a senior implementation specialist implementing Cisco switches and routers. He has also previously edited several other Cisco books and recently authored a book entitled *Network Administration*. Steve lives in East Brunswick, New Jersey, with his wife, Ellen.

Dedications

This book is dedicated to David and Jack, who make everything worthwhile.

Acknowledgments

All books are the product of a team, and I have been blessed with a dedicated and professional team, whose expertise in their given areas have made this book. Over the course of writing this book and its predecessor, I have come to think of members of this team as friends as well as colleagues. In particular, I would like to thank John Kane, the editor in chief, and Drew Cupp, the development editor, who were always there with solutions and support. My thanks go also to Amy Lewis for her understanding and flexibility. Of course, I thank all the members of the Cisco Press team helping to bring this book together, including the project editor, Marc Fowler, and the copy editor, Krista Hansing.

The technical editors, Steve Gifkins, Martin Walshaw, Jorge Aragon, and Steve Wisniewski, were extremely thorough. Their careful attention to detail and constructive advice improved this book immeasurably. I would particularly like to thank Jorge Aragon and Steve Wisniewski who went the extra mile by testing configurations and producing output screens.

I would also like to thank Wendell Odom, who led me into the art of book writing and has ever generously shared his expertise.

Of course, I am immensely grateful to my husband, David, for his support, in spite of the long hours demanded by this book, and to our small son, Jack, for making me laugh and see the joy of life.

Contents at a Glance

Contents

CHAPTER 1

Cisco Certifications, the Routing Exam, and This Book's Features

The Cisco Certified Network Professional (CCNP) and Cisco Certified Design Professional (CCDP) certifications on the Routing and Switching career track are becoming increasingly popular. These certifications have as their foundation the Cisco Certifed Network Associate (CCNA) certification and these profesional-level certifications form the second rung in the ladder to the coveted Cisco Certified Internetwork Expert (CCIE) certification. The Routing 2.0 exam (#640-503) is one of three exams that you must pass to become a CCNP or CCDP. This book will help you prepare for that exam. Professional-level certification opens doors to career opportunities and is a prerequisite for other Cisco certifications as well. Generally, passing the Routing 2.0 exam means that you have mastered the concepts and implementation skills necessary to build a complex IP network of Cisco routers.

NOTE You must pass the Routing 2.0 exam (among other exams) to acheive either the CCNP or the CCDP certification. The CCNP and CCDP certifications are often referred to as the *professional-level certifications* throughout this book wherever the information at hand applies to CCNP and CCDP. For more information on the differences between the two professional-level certifications and the latest on Cisco exams and certifications, begin at the Cisco Career Certification page (www.cisco.com/warp/public/10/wwtraining/certprog/index.html) at Cisco Connection Online (CCO).

The Routing exam is a computer-based exam, with multiple-choice, fill-in-the-blank, and list-in-order style questions. The exam can be taken at any Sylvan Prometric testing center (1-800-829-NETS, www.2test.com). The exam will take about 75 minutes and has approximately 60 questions. You should check with Sylvan Prometric for the exact length of the exam. (Be aware that when you register for the exam, you might be told to allow a certain amount of time to take the exam that is longer than the testing time indicated by the testing software when you begin. This is because Sylvan Prometrics wants you to allow for some time to get settled and take the tutorial on the testing engine.)

NOTE This book uses the terms *Routing exam* and *Routing 2.0 exam*. These terms are used synonomously and refer to the the the exam #640-503.

The Routing 2.0 exam is not an easy exam. This is to say that you cannot simply read one book and expect to pass it. In fact, the exam is surprisingly difficult; this is so that Cisco can be sure that everyone who passes the test thoroughly understands the subject matter on a conceptual level and is not just good at exams. More importantly, Cisco is very interested in making sure that passing proves that you have the skills to actually implement the features, not just talk about them. The exam is difficult in subject matter and also in format. You can expect multiple-choice questions—some with multiple answers. You can also expect questions requiring you to pick the correct answer from output screens and configurations.

Another difficult aspect of the exam format is that, to ensure that you know your stuff, the exam does *not* allow you to go back and change an answer. Those CCNP/CCDP candidates who are unsure about the question will be forced to guess rather than have an extra 15 minutes to think about it at the end of the exam. Those who really know most of the answers will be rewarded by Cisco's attempts to preserve the integrety of the CCNP/CCDP certification. The professional-level certification will mean to all that you are highly qualified at the subject at hand.

Although this is a difficult exam, most networking professionals can expect to pass if they meet the prerequisites and spend the proper amount of time on training, on-the-job experience, and study. Like most certification exams, you might not pass the first time. Taking the exam a second time, however, might be easier because you have an idea of what to expect.

There are many questions on the Routing 2.0 exam that you might already know through your professional background and experiences, if you meet the prerequisites. This book offers you the opportunity to solidify and build on that knowledge as you make your final preparations to take the Routing exam. The concepts and commands covered on the exam are not secrets locked in some vault—the information is available in many places and forms, including this book. So, although the exam is difficult, passing is certainly attainable with study.

Goals of This Book

The goals for this book became somewhat obvious to me after considering the exam itself, as well as Cisco's exam philosophy. The first goal came straight from Cisco, who asked that I write a book that not only helps you pass the exam, but that also ensures that you really understand the concepts and implementation details. The second goal of this book is that the content should be the most comprehensive coverage of Routing 2.0 exam-related topics available, without too much coverage of topics not on the exam. The third and ultimate goal is to get you from where you are today to the point that you can confidently pass the Routing 2.0 exam. Therefore, all this book's features, which are outlined in this chapter, are geared toward helping you discover the IP routing topics that are on the Routing exam, where you have a knowledge deficiency in these topics, and what you need to know to master these topics.

This Book's Intended Audience

Although the only prerequisite for CCNP certificaion is CCNA status, and the only prerequisite for CCDP certification is CCNA and CCDA status, Cisco does not expect you to be able to pass the professional-level exams (such as the Routing exam) without training and experience. This is why Cisco's recommended training for CCNP/CCDP involves an official Cisco course. For the routing knowledge required of a CCNP/CCDP, Cisco recommends a course called Building Cisco Scalable Networks (BSCN).

As stated on the Cisco web site, the BSCN course is targeted toward enterprise network engineers (including systems engineers [SEs], customers, and resellers) who are responsible for network administration and implementation. The targeted audience performs one or more of the following tasks:

- Install and configure network devices
- Design and implement large enterprise networks
- Add services/applications to an existing network, and determine what router configurations are required to support the new services/applications
- Improve traffic flow, reliability, redundancy, and performance through the network

---

NOTE   BSCN replaces the old Advanced Cisco Router Configuration (ACRC) course, much as the new Routing 2.0 exam (#640-503) replaces the old ACRC exam (#640-403).

This book is a final stage preparation tool. Therefore, this book will be most effective as a study resource after you have taken the BSCN course or have acquired an equivalent level of on-the-job experience and training. The following are the prerequisites for the BSCN course, and, for all practical purposes, should be considered prerequsites for using this book effectively:

- Working knowledge of the OSI reference model and the hierarchical model
- Understanding of internetworking fundamentals
- Ability to operate and configure a Cisco IOS device
- Working knowledge of the TCP/IP stack and how to configure a routed protocol such as IP
- Understanding of distance vector routing protocol operation and configuring Routing Information Protocol (RIP) and Interior Gateway Routing Protocol (IGRP)
- Ability to determine when to use static and default routes, and how to enable them on a Cisco router
- Ability to display and interpret a Cisco router routing table

- Ability to enable a WAN serial connection

- Ability to configure Frame Relay permanent virtual circuits (PVCs) on interfaces and subinterfaces

- Ability to configure an IP standard and extended access list

- Ability to verify router configurations with available tools such as **show** and **debug** commands

The ideal audience for this book is someone who has attended the Interconnecting Cisco Networking Devices (ICND) course (or the retired Introduction to Cisco Router Configuration [ICRC] course), has acheived CCNA status, and has attended the BSCN course, or who has an equivalent level of on-the-job training and experience with Cisco switches and routers.

Cisco highly recommends that you take courses to support each certification level, but it also recognizes that attending courses might not be an option for everyone. Therefore, if you find yourself struggling with CCNA-level knowledge as you work through this book, you might want to review a copy of the *Interconnecting Cisco Networking Devices* coursebook (ISBN 1-57870-111-2) from Cisco Press. Similarly, if you want course details at the CCNP/CCDP level about routing, review the *Building Scalable Cisco Networks* coursebook (ISBN 1-57870-228-3), also from Cisco Press.

Overview of Cisco Certifications

Cisco's main motivation behind the current certification program is to provide a means of measuring the skills of people working for Cisco resellers and certified partners. Cisco fulfills only a small portion of its orders via direct sale from Cisco; normally, a Cisco reseller is involved. Also, Cisco has not attempted to become the primary source for consulting and implementation services for network deployment using Cisco products, preferring instead to use partners as much as possible. With that business model, there is a great need to distinguish, ensure, and certify the skill levels of the partner company's employees.

The CCIE program was Cisco's first foray into certifications. Introduced in 1994, the CCIE was designed to be one of the most respected, difficult-to-achieve certifications. To certify, a written test (also given at Sylvan Prometric) must be passed, and then a two-day hands-on lab test is administered by Cisco. Cisco does not publish numbers on pass/fail rates for CCIE or the other certifications, but rumors have the failure rate on all lab test takers at over 50 percent, with failure rate for first-time lab takers at over 80 percent.

Certifying resellers and services partners, by using the number of employed CCIEs as the gauge, worked well originally, partly because Cisco had far fewer partners than today. Cisco uses the number of CCIEs on staff as part of the criteria in determining the level of partner status for the company, which in turn dictates the discount received by the reseller when buying from Cisco. (For more insight into reseller certification, go to CCO, at www.cisco.com.) This practice continues to be a good way for Cisco to judge the commitment to having people with proven Cisco skills on staff, which in turn improves customer satisfaction—and customer satisfaction is tied to every Cisco executive's goals.

The CCIE certification became inadequate for helping certify resellers and other partners because, among other factors, the number of partners increased disproportionately to the difficulty of the CCIE exam. For instance, there are around 4500 CCIEs worldwide and 2500 resellers (and not all the CCIEs work for resellers, of course). Furthermore, many resellers that do not perform services do not require the extreme expertise of a CCIE on staff, other than to get a better discount. What Cisco needed were certifications that were less rigorous than CCIE and that would allow Cisco more granularity in judging the skills on staff at a partner company. So, Cisco started an entire Cisco Career Certification program, of which CCNP and CCDP are a part.

Cisco developed Routing and Switching career tracks, WAN Switching career tracks, and several specialization career tracks. Thus far, the Routing and Switching career tracks, which begin with CCNA/CCDA certification, have proven to be the most popular and make up the heart of Cisco certification. The Routing exam required for CCNP/CCDP certification is part of the Routing and Switching career tracks.

Two categories of certifications exist—one to certify implementation skills and the other to certify design skills. Resellers working in a presale environment need more design skills, whereas services companies need more implementation skills. So, the CCNA and CCNP are implementation-oriented certifications, whereas CCDA and CCDP are design-oriented certifications.

Rather than requiring just one level of certification besides CCIE, Cisco created two additional levels—an associate level and a professional level. The associate level (CCNA/CCDA) is the most basic, and the professional level (CCNP/CCDP) is the intermediate level between CCNA and CCIE.

Several of the certifications require other certifications as a prerequisite. For instance, CCNP certification requires that you have CCNA certification. Also, CCDP requires both CCDA and CCNA certification. CCIE, however, does not require any other certification prior to the written and lab tests. CCIE certification is extremely difficult, however, and it is unlikely that someone could acheive that level of certification without a level of experience and training equalled in attaining and practicing associate- and professional-level certification.

Cisco certifications have taken on a much larger role and importance in the networking industry in recent years. From a career standpoint, Cisco certification can certainly be used to help you get a new job or a promotion. Or, you can have certification added to your performance evaluation plan and then justify a raise based on passing an exam. If you are looking for a new job, not only might passing an exam help you land the job, but it may actually help you make more money.

Exams Required for Certification

In 2000, Cisco initiated a major revamping of the career certification exams. Several new exams were unveiled, and the Routing exam was one of those. The Routing 2.0 exam replaced the old ACRC exam; this is why the exam is called Routing 2.0 sometimes, even though there was never a Routing 1.0 exam.

To certify for CCNP, you must pass multiple exams. This book deals with the Routing 2.0 exam—Sylvan Promteric exam #640-503. The qualifying exams, the CCNA and the CCDA, require only a single exam. The exams generally match the same topics that are covered in one of the official Cisco courses, but in most cases—and certainly on the Routing 2.0 exam—more topics are covered on the exam than are in the course. Table 1-1 outlines the exams and the courses with which they are most closely matched.

Table 1-1   *Exams and Courses by Certification Level*

Certification	Exam Number	Name	Course Most Closely Matching Exam Requirements
CCNA	#640-507	CCNA exam	Interconnecting Cisco Network Devices (ICND)
CCDA	#640-441	DCN (or CCDA) exam	Designing Cisco Networks (DCN)
CCNP	#640-503	Routing exam	Building Scalable Cisco Networks (BSCN)
	#640-504	Switching exam	Building Cisco Multilayer Switched Networks (BCMSN)
	#640-505	Remote Access exam	Building Cisco Remote Access Networks (BCRAN)
	#640-509*	Foundation exam	BSCN, BCMSN, and BCRAN
	#640-506	Support exam	Cisco Internetwork Troubleshooting (CIT)
CCDP	#640-503	Routing exam	BSCN
	#640-504	Switching exam	BCMSN
	#640-505	Remote Access exam	BCRAN
	#640-509*	Foundation exam	BSCN, BCMSN, and BCRAN
	#640-025	CID exam	Cisco Internetwork Design (CID)

* Exam #640-509 meets the same requirements as passing these three exams: #640-503, #640-504, and #640-505.

Therefore, you can substitute exam #640-509 for those three exams, but you can expect a longer exam that covers the material in the other three exams.

Be cautioned that, although the exam coverage and course coverage are similar, there are no guarantees that if you know absolutely everything in the course, you will pass the test. Cisco is moving more toward the certifications being tied to technology, not to specific courses; note that the exam names do not match the course names as they previously did. As you can see, a Cisco Press Exam Certification Guide will help prepare you for the certification exam beyond how the courses can, with the added guidance of stressing the most important exam items and coverage of other topics not taught in the prerequisite courses. Cisco also maintains the right to change the exam content at will to ensure that the exam is current and fair.

What's on the Routing 2.0 Exam

Every one of us would like to know exactly what is on the Routing 2.0 exam, as well as the other Cisco certification exams. Well, to be honest, exactly what is on the exam is a very closely guarded secret. Only those who write the questions for Cisco and who have access to the entire question database truly know what is entirely on the exam.

The Routing 2.0 exam content that is made known by Cisco to the public is general. You can find a list of Cisco exams and the general outline that accompanies each exam at www.cisco.com/warp/public/10/wwtraining/certprog/testing/exam_list.htm.

You will have to download the outline for each exam. The following section contains excerpts from the Routing exam outline downloaded file.

Cisco Routing Exam Outline File Excerpts From CCO

Given your experience, this outline and guide will help you with the best methods of preparation for the Cisco Career Certifications exam.

The BSCN course is the recommended method of preparation for the Routing exam.

The topic areas listed in this outline are general guidelines for the type of content that is likely to appear on the exam. However, please be advised that other relevant or related topic areas may also appear.

The Routing (640-503) exam will contain a combination of the following topics:

1 Routing principles:

- List the key information routers need to route data.

- Describe classful and classless routing protocols.

- Compare distance vector and link-state routing protocol operation.

- Describe the use of the fields in a routing table.

- Given a preconfigured laboratory network, discover the topology, analyze the routing table, and test connectivity using accepted troubleshooting techniques.

2 Extending IP addresses:

- Given an IP address range, use variable-length subnet masks (VLSMs) to extend the use of the IP addresses.

- Given a network plan that includes IP addressing, explain whether route summarization is possible.

- Configure an IP helper address to manage broadcasts.

3 Configuring Open Shortest Path First (OSPF) in a single area:

- Explain why OSPF is better than RIP in a large internetwork.

- Explain how OSPF discovers, chooses, and maintains routes.

- Explain how OSPF operates in a single-area nonbroadcast multiaccess (NBMA) environment.

- Configure OSPF for proper operation in a single area.

- Verify OSPF operation in a single area.

- Given an addressing scheme and other laboratory parameters, configure a single-area OSPF environment, and verify proper operation (within described guidelines) of your routers.

- Given an addressing scheme and other laboratory parameters, configure single-area OSPF in an NBMA environment, and verify proper operation (within described guidelines) of your routers.

4 Interconnecting multiple OSPF areas:

- Describe the issues with interconnecting multiple areas, and tell how OSPF addresses each.

- Explain the differences between the possible types of areas, routers, and LSAs.

- Explain how OSPF supports the use of VLSM.

- Explain how OSPF supports the use of route summarization in multiple areas.

- Explain how OSPF operates in a multiple-area NBMA environment.

- Configure a multiarea OSPF network.

- Verify OSPF operation in multiple areas.

- Given an addressing scheme and other laboratory parameters, configure a multiple-area OSPF environment, and verify proper operation (within described guidelines) of your routers.

5 Configuring Enhanced IGRP (EIGRP):

- Describe EIGRP features and operation.

- Explain how EIGRP discovers, chooses, and maintains routes.

- Explain how EIGRP supports the use of VLSM.

- Explain how EIGRP operates in an NBMA environment.

- Explain how EIGRP supports the use of route summarization.

- Describe how EIGRP supports large networks.

- Configure EIGRP.

- Verify EIGRP operation.

- Given a set of network requirements, configure an EIGRP environment, and verify proper operation (within described guidelines) of your routers.

- Given a set of network requirements, configure EIGRP in an NBMA environment, and verify proper operation (within described guidelines) of your routers.

6 Configuring Basic Border Gateway Protocol (BGP):

- Describe BGP features and operation.

- Describe how to connect to another autonomous system using an alternative to BGP, static routes.

- Explain how BGP policy-based routing functions within an autonomous system.

- Explain how BGP peering functions.

- Describe BGP communities and peer groups.

- Describe and configure external and internal BGP.

- Describe BGP synchronization.

- Given a set of network requirements, configure a BGP environment, and verify proper operation (within described guidelines) of your routers.

7 Implementing BGP in scalable networks:

- Describe the scalability problems associated with internal BGP.

- Explain and configure BGP route reflectors.

- Describe and configure policy control in BGP using prefix lists.

- Describe methods to connect to multiple ISPs using BGP.

- Explain the use of redistribution between BGP and Interior Gateway Protocols (IGPs).

- Given a set of network requirements, configure a multihomed BGP environment, and verify proper operation (within described guidelines) of your routers.

8 Optimizing routing update operation:

- Select and configure the different ways to control routing update traffic.

- Configure route redistribution in a network that does not have redundant paths between dissimilar routing processes.

- Configure route redistribution in a network that has redundant paths between dissimilar routing processes.

- Resolve path selection problems that result in a redistributed network.

- Verify route redistribution.

- Configure policy-based routing using route maps.

- Given a set of network requirements, configure redistribution between different routing domains, and verify proper operation (within described guidelines) of your routers.

- Given a set of network requirements, configure policy-based routing within your pod, and verify proper operation (within described guidelines) of your routers.

9 Implementing scalability features in your internetwork:

- Given a set of network requirements, configure many of the features discussed in the course, and verify proper operation (within described guidelines) of your routers.

Author's Note About Exam Content

As Cisco's authorized external publishing company, Cisco Press is the only publisher that is partnered with Cisco. Cisco has shared other information with Cisco Press, part of which includes some details that are expected to be posted on Cisco's web site at a later date. At press time, Cisco had not finalized what other details about the exam will be posted on its web site, so I cannot list any of those details here. Fortunately, what does get posted by Cisco will be easily available to you! I encourage you to check Cisco's web site for the latest information on the exam.

Some points I would like to make about the exam as it relates to this book are as follows:

- If we at Cisco Press believe that a topic is definitely on the exam, it is covered in Chapters 2 through 10.

- For topics that we at Cisco Press believe have only a remote (but still possible) chance of being in Cisco's Routing 2.0 exam question database, the topic is covered briefly in the body of the book, but it is clearly stated that it is not part of the exam study. These marginal topics are placed in the body of the book so that the topics are in context.

- If we at Cisco Press believe that a topic is simply not in the Cisco Routing 2.0 exam question database, then it is not covered in this book. The only exception would be topics that must be explained to make a topic that is on the exam more understandable. Again, this is indicated within the book.

Topics in This Book

The list that follows outlines the topics that will be the focus of the exam. The topics are listed corresponding to the chapters in which they are covered.

- Chapter 2, "Managing Scalable Network Growth"
  - The key requirements of a network
  - The problem of network congestion
  - The symptoms of network congestion
  - Methods of controlling network traffic
  - Access lists, how to restrict vty access, and uses of access lists
  - Alternatives to access lists
- Chapter 3, "IP Addressing"
  - Prefix routing
  - The use of VLSM and its application
  - The use, application, and configuration of summarization
  - Key points in the design of an IP network
  - How to connect to the outside world and use NAT and private addresses
- Chapter 4, "IP Routing Principles"
  - The requirements of the routing process
  - The routing table
  - The differences between a classful and classless routing protocol
  - The difference between distance vector and link-state routing protocol
  - How routing tables are maintained
  - Path selection
- Chapter 5, "Using OSPF in a Single Area"
  - How a link-state routing protocol (such as OSPF) discovers, chooses, and maintains links

— How OSPF operates in a single NBMA area WAN

— How to configure OSPF in a single area

— How to verify the operation of and troubleshoot an OSPF network

- Chapter 6, "Using OSPF Across Multiple Areas"

    — The issues with interconnecting multiple OSPF areas

    — The differences between the possible types of areas, routers, and LSAs

    — How OSPF operates across multiple areas using NBMA

    — How OSPF supports the use of VLSM and summarization

    — The Cisco commands for implementing OSPF for multiple areas

- Chapter 7, "Using EIGRP in Enterprise Networks"

    — The features and operation of EIGRP

    — How EIGRP discovers, chooses, and maintains routes

    — How EIGRP supports the use of VLSM and summarization

    — How EIGRP functions in an NBMA environment

    — How EIGRP supports large networks

    — How to configure EIGRP, both in an enterprise network and in an NBMA network

    — How to verify an EIGRP configuration

- Chapter 8, "Connecting to Other Autonomous Systems—The Basics of BGP-4"

    — The features and operation of BGP

    — BGP terminology

    — Design issues with BGP

    — BGP communities, peer groups, and the peering function

    — The configuration of internal and external BGP

    — How to verify the BGP configuration

- Chapter 9, "Implementing and Tuning BGP for Use in Large Networks"

    — Scaling internal BGP

    — Configuring route reflectors

    — Determining policy control using prefix lists

— Connecting to multiple ISPs

— Redistributing between interior routing protocols and BGP

— Configuring and verifying the BGP configuration

- Chapter 10, "Controlling Routing Updates Across the Network"

— Selecting and configuring different ways to control routing updates

— Configuring route redistribution in networks with and without redundant paths between dissimilar routing processes

— Resolving problems occuring in a redistributed network

— Configuring policy-based route maps

— Verifying and troubleshooting redistribution and policy-based routing

- Chapter 11, "Scenarios for Final Preparation"

— Chapter 11 contains two scenarios that test you on various topics covered throughout the book instead of concentrating on a particular technology. This challenges your understanding at a profound level and places the topics in context.

How to Use This Book to Pass the Exam

One way to use this book is to start at the beginning and read it cover to cover. While that would certainly help you prepare, most people do not have that much time to spare, particularly if they already have mastered some of the topics in the book. However, if you want to read the entire book and answer all the CD-ROM questions, then that is a great way to prepare!

For the rest of you, you might want to consider different strategies for how best to use this book, depending on what training and experience you already have. With its prechapter analysis quizzes and chapter-ending summary sections and questions, as well as its traditional foundation sections, this book is designed to help you get the most out of the time you take to study.

The core material for the Routing 2.0 exam is covered in Chapters 2 through 10. At the beginning of each chapter, you are instructed on how to make best use of your time reading that chapter, assuming that you are not going to read every detail. The instructions on how to use each chapter is outlined in a figure in each chapter. That figure is repeated here as Figure 1-1.

Figure 1-1   *How to Use Chapters 2 Through 10*

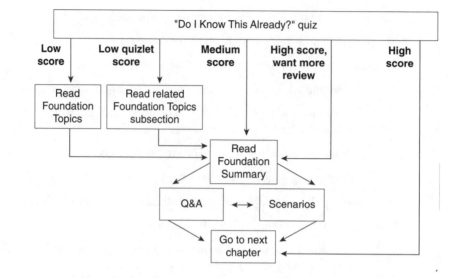

If you skip to the Foundation Summary, Q&A, and scenarios sections and have
trouble with the material there, you should go back to the Foundation Topics section.

Each of these chapters begins with a quiz, which is broken into subdivisions called quizlets. If
you get a high score, you might simply review the "Foundation Summary" section at the end of
the chapter. If you score well on one quizlet but low on another, you are directed to the section
of the chapter corresponding to the quizlet on which your score was low. If you score less than
50 percent on the overall quiz, it is recommended that you read the whole chapter. Of course,
these are simply guidelines—if you score well but want more review on that topic, read away!

After completing the core chapters (2 through 10), several options for your next study activity
exist. Because Chapter 11 is the next chapter in succession, the detailed directions on what you
can do are in the beginning of Chapter 11. However, here is a brief list of the study options
provided by this book, beyond the core chapters:

- Chapter 11 includes scenarios and questions to test your overall comprehension of several
  exam topics.

- All prechapter quiz and chapter-ending questions, with answers, are in Appendix A,
  "Answers to Quiz Questions." These conveniently located questions can be read and
  reviewed quickly, with explanations.

- The CD-ROM contains practice exam questions that you can use to take an overall sample
  exam or to test yourself on specific topics.

- Each core chapter has a "Foundation Summary" section near the end that contains concise tables and information for final review.

- Where appropriate, each chapter has a glossary for the terms introduced in that chapter. The chapter glossaries and Appendix C, "Glossary," are also good study aids.

When you are preparing for the Routing 2.0 exam, the guidelines at the beginning of each chapter should be adequate no matter what your level of knowledge is. However, if you would like some additional guidance, the remainder of this section gives a few additional strategies for study, based on how you have prepared before buying this book. So, find the section that most closely matches your background in the next few pages, and read about some additional ideas to help you prepare.

There are basically five different categories of students:

- Those who have taken the BSCN course

- Those who have taken the ACRC course

- Those who have attended the Cisco Networking Academies

- Those who will not be taking any classes and have not had much experience

- Those who will not be taking any classes but have some experience

I've Taken BSCN—Now What?

Well, first let me say that you've taken the best path to prepare yourself! However, let me temper that with the fact that if you retain more than 50 percent of what you heard in class, then you are an extraordinary person! That said, in my opinion, you need to follow these strategies:

- **Strategy 1**—Use this book exactly as described in the opening pages of Chapters 2 through 10. Each of the core chapters begins with a quiz that helps you assess what you need to study. It then directs you to the appropriate sections in the chapter rather than requiring you to read the entirety of each chapter.

- **Strategy 2**—Use the directions at the beginning of Chapter 11 to direct your final study before the exam. Chapter 11 is designed to review many concepts; in addition, it outlines a good process for study in the days leading up to your exam.

By using these strategies, you will fill in your gaps in knowledge and will be confident taking your Routing 2.0 exam.

I've Taken the Old ACRC Course—Now What?

It is true that the current version of the exam is a closer match to the BSCN class. However, if you were to compare the BSCN and ACRC courses, you would find there is much more in common than is different. In fact, more than half of the ACRC topics are retained in the BSCN course. Of course, if you retain more than 50 percent of what you heard in class, then you are an extraordinary person, so you probably still need to fill in some holes in your knowledge base. For you, the following strategies will be most helpful:

- **Strategy 1**—Begin with a review of Chapters 8 through 10. These chapters consist of almost completely new material of the Routing exam and should be studied in depth. Do not skip the configuration sections—they are very important.

- **Strategy 2**—Use this book exactly as described in the opening pages of Chapters 2 through 10. Each of the core chapters begins with a quiz that helps you assess what you need to study. It then directs you to the appropriate sections in the chapter rather than requiring you to read the entirety of each chapter. In fact, you probably should even use Chapters 8 through 10 this way, in spite of having read them already, because that will validate what you have learned.

- **Strategy 3**—Make it a point to read the sections of the book that cover topics not found in the ACRC course. Other than almost the entirety of Chapters 8 through 10 of this book, the subjects that you will want to make sure to read are as follows:

  — Chapter 3—Routing table analysis

  — Chapter 4—Hierarchical routing

  — Chapter 5—OSPF in an NBMA network, and OSPF operation

  — Chapter 6—OSPF across multiple areas

  — Chapter 7—Details of the EIGRP operation, particularly across an NBMA network, and design considerations in building a scalable network

- **Strategy 4**—Use the directions at the beginning of Chapter 11 to direct your final study before the exam. Chapter 11 is designed to review many concepts; in addition, it outlines a good process for study in the days leading up to your exam.

Therefore, compared to those who have taken BSCN, you should not require a lot of additional study time. The ACRC course did a great job of explaining the basics, and this book will help you fill in the gaps to confidently prepare to pass the exam!

I've Taken the Cisco Networking Academy Courses—Now What?

First, I'll start by congratulating you on having the foresight to get into the Cisco Networking Academy program—we need more people that can make this stuff work! For those of you who are did not take the Cisco Networking Academy track and are wondering what it is, visit www.cisco.com/warp/public/779/edu/academy/ for more information. Thankfully, the Networking Academy curriculum does a great job of preparing you with the skills and knowledge that you need to pass the Routing exam. Unfortunately, your study was probably spread over several semesters, and possibly over a couple years. So, the details that you do not use frequently may have been forgotten! On to the strategies for success on CCNP/CCDP—and, in particular, the Routing exam:

- **Strategy 1**—Pull out your Networking Academy curriculum and notes, and reread them. Exciting, huh? Nevertheless, most people's memory is exercised better by seeing familiar material, and even more so when that person wrote it down himself. If you have ever taken a test and pictured in your mind where the answer was on your page of notes, then you can recall the information easily.

- **Strategy 2**—Use this book exactly as described in the opening pages of Chapters 2 through 10. Each of the core chapters begins with a quiz that helps you assess what you need to study. It then directs you to the appropriate sections in the chapter rather than requiring you to read the entirety of each chapter.

- **Strategy 3**—Make it a point to read the sections that cover some of the theory and conceptual sections, and some of the standards. The biggest reason for that is that the Networking Academy is more oriented toward building skills, not theoretical knowledge. The subjects that I suggest are as follows:

  — Chapter 2—From the beginning of the "Foundation Topics" section up to the beginning of the routing table analysis section

  — Chapter 3—The section on VLSM and router summarization

  — The sections on operations in all the other chapters

- **Strategy 4**—Use the directions at the beginning of Chapter 11 to direct your final study before the exam. Chapter 11 is designed to review many concepts; in addition, it outlines a good process for study in the days leading up to your exam.

This book is designed to help you sift through the topics and choose the areas for study that you need to focus on in a timely fashion. Congratulations on your Networking Academy work and CCNA/CCDA certification—now add the CCNP or CCDP certification to take away any doubt in the minds of prospective employers that you know Cisco products and technology.

I'm New to Internetworking with Cisco, and I Will Not Be Taking the BSCN Course—Now What?

You can take and pass the Routing 2.0 exam without taking any courses. Cisco wants you to take the recommended courses for all the exams, though. Cisco's motivation is not to make more money, because the company does not actually deliver the training. Instead, Cisco's motivation is that it truly believes that the more people understand Cisco products, ultimately the happier the customers will be, and the more products Cisco will sell. In addition, Cisco believes that its official training is the best way to teach people about its products, so Cisco wants you to take the classes.

If you are not taking the course, there is no reason to worry! However, truthfully, you will need more than just this book to prepare. Cisco Press publishes the *Building Scalable Cisco Networks* coursebook (ISBN 1-57870-228-3), which is a book version of the BSCN course. The figures are exactly like those in the course, and the text comes from the course material and is even expanded and reorganized to work well in book format. Therefore, if you can't take the course, your best substitute is the *Building Scalable Cisco Networks* coursebook. This book will build on the BSCN material and help you assess what further study you need to pass the Routing exam. Here are my strategy suggestions for your case:

- **Strategy 1**—Read the *Building Scalable Cisco Networks* coursebook. Although Routing 2.0 is not entirely a course-based test, the BSCN course is listed as the recommended course for the Routing exam.

- **Strategy 2**—After reading BSCN, use this book exactly as described in the opening pages of Chapters 2 through 10. Each of the core chapters begins with a quiz that helps you assess what you need to study. It then directs you to the appropriate sections in the chapter rather than requiring you to read the entirety of each chapter.

- **Strategy 3**—Use the directions at the beginning of Chapter 11 to direct your final study before the exam. Chapter 11 is designed to review many concepts; in addition, it outlines a good process for study in the days leading up to your exam.

I've Learned a Lot About CCNP Topics Through Experience, But I Will Not Be Taking the BSCN Course—Now What?

If you feel like you know a fair amount about professional-level routing topics already (at a level that makes taking the BSCN course not very worthwhile), but you are worried about the few topics that you simply just have not worked with, then this strategy is for you. This book is designed to help you figure out what IP routing topics you need some help with, and then help you learn about them. Here is the simple strategy for you:

- **Strategy 1**—Use this book exactly as described in the opening pages of Chapters 2 through 10. Each of the core chapters begins with a quiz that helps you assess what you need to study. It then directs you to the appropriate sections in the chapter rather than requiring you to read the entirety of each chapter.

- **Strategy 2**—Use the directions at the beginning of Chapter 11 to direct your final study before the exam. Chapter 11 is designed to review many concepts; in addition, it outlines a good process for study in the days leading up to your exam.

You will be able to fill in the gaps in your knowledge this way, and not risk being bored in the BSCN class when it covers the topics that you already know!

The Features of This Book

After this brief introductory chapter, there are 10 chapters and three appendixes in this book. Each core chapter starts with a "Do I Know This Already?" quiz that allows you to decide how much time you need to devote to studying the subject at hand. Next, the "Foundation Topics" (the core material of the chapter) are presented. This section is the bulk of each chapter. At the end of each chapter, you will find a "Foundation Summary" section that is a collection of tables and quick-reference material that can be used as the last-minute review notes. Also contained in the "Foundation Summary" section of each chapter is a Chapter Glossary, which defines important terms used in the chapter. Reviewing the Chapter Glossary along with the rest of the "Foundation Summary" makes for excellent late-stage exam preparation. Each core chapter also has a "Q&A" section of review questions that test you on the chapter's contents. Finally, each core chapter contains a "Scenarios" section that tests you further on the material at hand.

The appendixes contain materials for your reference. Appendix A contains the answers to each chapter's "Do I Know This Already?" and "Q&A" quizzes. The answers to the "Scenarios" questions can be found at the end of each chapter.

This book is also accompanied by a CD-ROM that offers multiple-choice questions out of the entire book's content. Each question in the CD-ROM refers you to the chapter and section it is drawn from. The CD-ROM also contains a file called "Job Aids and Supplements." This material is taken from the BSCN course itself and provides further reference material on the following topics:

- IP addresses and subnetting

- Addressing review

- IP access lists

- Configuration and output examples of the following:

    — OSPF

    — EIGRP

    — BGP-4

    — Route optimization

Command Syntax Conventions

The conventions used to present command syntax in this book are the same conventions used in the *Cisco IOS Command Reference*, as follows:

- **Boldface** indicates commands and keywords that are entered literally as shown. In examples (not syntax), boldface indicates user input (for example, a **show** command).

- *Italics* indicates arguments for which you supply values.

- Square brackets ([and]) indicate optional elements.

- Braces ({ and }) contain a choice of required keywords.

- Vertical bars (I) separate alternative, mutually exclusive elements.

- Braces and vertical bars within square brackets—for example, [x {y I z}]—indicate a required choice within an optional element. You do not need to enter what is in the brackets, but if you do, you have some required choices in the braces.

References and Suggested Reading

The following is a list of suggested further reading, if you need additional information:

- *Routing in the Internet*, by Christian Huitema (Prentice Hall)

- *Internet Routing Architectures*, Second Edition, by Bassam Halabi (Cisco Press)

- RFC 1771, "BGP-4 Defined"

- RFC 1930, "Autonomous System Number Allocation"

- RFCs 1771–4, 1863, 1930, 1965, 1966, 1997, 1998, 2042, 2283, 2385, 2439

Strategies for The Exam Day

Here is a reminder of some simple things you can do to help you for the day of the exam.

On the day before the exam:

- Call Sylvan Prometrics to confirm your seat and the time and place of the exam center. Also check the confirmation number that was allocated for your exam.

- Ensure that you have directions for the center and the location of the nearest parking garage.

- Have a relaxing evening; do not be tempted to heavily review because this will simply emotionally exhaust you and prevent a good night's sleep. If you cannot resist some studying, simply read through the question and answer section at the end of the book.

On the exam day:

- Eat a nutritious meal before you leave. Rumbling stomachs are distracting, and it is proven that your brain functions better when fueled.

- Leave plenty of time to get to the testing center, park, and have a few moments to relax before the exam. Allow at least half an hour for traffic jams and the like.

- The testing center will provide pen and paper. You are not allowed any thing in the exam room, except a refreshment and the pen and paper provided. Leave all those heavy books at home.

- Wear loose, comfortable clothing.

During the exam:

- Work out the timing. If the exam still has 61 questions and you allowed 75 minutes to complete, that means you have approximately 1.25 minutes per question. This is very important. Because you cannot return to questions after you have passed them, you must try to allocate an equal amount of time to each question. It is counterproductive to miss questions or to guess unless you really have no idea of the answer. The exam tells you how many questions are left to answer and how much time is left.

- If you do not know the answer to a question, then try answering the question by a process of elimination. As Sherlock Holmes said, "When you have eliminated the impossible, whatever remains, however improbable, must be the truth."

- Use the paper provided to work out the logic of some questions.

- Try to stay calm. Remember that the exam can be taken multiple times, so even if you are struggling, you can use the exam to your advantage by remembering what topics are causing you trouble.

Conclusion

The CCNP certification has great value in the networking environment. It proves your competence and dedication. It is required for several certifications, and it is a further huge step in distinguishing yourself as someone who has proven knowledge of Cisco products and technology instead of just claiming that you know it.

The *CCNP Routing Exam Certification Guide* is designed to help you attain CCNP certification. It is a CCNP-certification book from the only Cisco-authorized publisher. We at Cisco Press believe that this book will help you achieve CCNP certification—but the real work is up to you! We hope you enjoy your time well spent with this book. Good luck.

This chapter covers the following foundation topics that you will need to master to successfully learn the details in this exam guide:

- Describe the key requirements of a network.

- Explain the problem of network congestion.

- Identify the symptoms of network congestion.

- Identify methods of controlling network traffic.

- IP access lists, distribute lists, prioritization, restricting vty access, and alternatives to access lists (such as null interface, IP helper address, and design).

CHAPTER 2

Managing Scalable Network Growth

This chapter sets the foundation for the rest of the topics covered in this book. Although these topics may not necessarily reflect questions on the exam, they lend a context for the course and provide a review of subjects dealt with in the Interconnecting Cisco Network Devices (ICND) course. The subsequent chapters assume your comprehension of the subjects dealt with in this chapter.

How to Best Use This Chapter

By taking the following steps, you can make better use of your study time:

- Keep your notes and the answers for all your work with this book in one place, for easy reference.

- When you take a quiz, write down your answers. Studies show that retention significantly increases by writing down facts and concepts, even if you never look at the information again.

- If the opportunity presents itself, practice the commands and configurations in a lab environment.

- Use the diagram in Figure 2-1 to guide you to the next step.

Figure 2-1   *How to Use This Chapter*

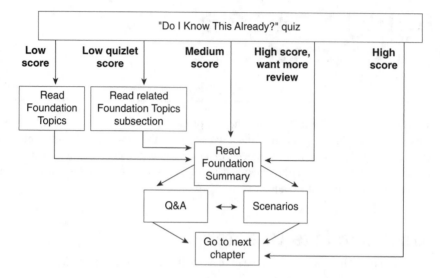

If you skip to the Foundation Summary, Q&A, and scenarios sections and have trouble with the material there, you should go back to the Foundation Topics section.

"Do I Know This Already?" Quiz

The purpose of the "Do I Know This Already?" quiz is to help you decide what parts of this chapter to use. If you already intend to read the entire chapter, you do not necessarily need to answer these questions now.

This 16-question quiz helps you determine how to spend your limited study time. The quiz is sectioned into four smaller four-question "quizlets," which correspond to the four topics in the chapter. Figure 2-1 outlines suggestions on how to spend your time in this chapter. Use Table 2-1 to record your scores.

Table 2-1   *Score Sheet for Quiz and Quizlets*

Quizlet Number	Topic	Questions	Score
1	Network congestion	1 to 4	
2	Cisco's hierarchical design	5 to 8	
3	IP access lists	9 to 12	
4	Reducing network traffic	13 to 16	
All questions		1 to 16	

1 List two symptoms of network congestion.

_____

_____

_____

2 If a switch has redundant links to another switch, what action would be taken if the Spanning-Tree Protocol fails to see a bridge protocol data unit (BPDU) in time (within the MaxAge Timer value)?

_____

_____

_____

3 How could the dropping of packets cause an increase of traffic on the network?

_____

_____

_____

4 How might network congestion cause a loss of services?

_____

_____

_____

5 In Cisco's hierarchical design, what is the function of the core layer?

_____

_____

_____

6 In Cisco's hierarchical design, where is the access layer located?

_____

_____

_____

7 In the hierarchical design suggested by Cisco, at which layer are access lists not recommended?

_____

_____

_____

8 What is the function of the distribution layer?

_____

_____

_____

9 If an access list is configured as an inbound list, will the packet be sent to the routing process?

_____

_____

_____

10 State three uses of access lists.

_____

_____

_____

11 In an IP standard access list, what is the default wildcard mask?

_____

_____

_____

12 If a packet does not match any of the criteria in an access list, what action will be taken?

_____

_____

_____

13 Why does the null interface not report an ICMP message stating that the packet is undeliverable?

_____

_____

_____

14 How would you restrict Telnet connectivity to the router that you were configuring?

_____

_____

_____

15 Which of the queuing techniques offered by the Cisco IOS are manually configured?

_____

_____

_____

16 Explain **ip helper address**. What is its function?

_____

_____

_____

The answers to this quiz are found in Appendix A, "Answers to Quiz Questions." The suggested choices for your next step are as follows:

- **2 or less on any quizlet**—Review the appropriate sections of the "Foundation Topics" portion of this chapter, based on Table 2-1. Then move on to the "Foundation Summary" section, the "Q&A" section, and the scenarios at the end of the chapter.

- **8 or less overall score**—Read the entire chapter. This includes the "Foundation Topics" and "Foundation Summary" sections, the "Q&A" section, and the scenarios at the end of the chapter.

- **9 to 12 overall score**—Begin with the "Foundation Summary" section, and then go to the "Q&A" section and the scenarios at the end of the chapter. If you have trouble with a particular area in the exercises, read the appropriate section in "Foundation Topics."

- **13 or more overall score**—If you want more review on these topics, skip to the "Foundation Summary" section, and then go to the "Q&A" section and the scenarios at the end of the chapter. Otherwise, move to the next chapter.

Foundation Topics

Introduction to Corporate Networks— Growth, Scalability, and Congestion

NOTE	Each chapter begins with a case study. The case study provides context for the topics dealt with in the chapter. The case study may be referred to throughout the chapter in an effort to further explain the technology, and the case study will also sometimes be revisited in the "Scenarios" section at the end of the chapter.
	Use the case study to focus your attention. In this way, you will learn the details more easily as you solve the problem presented at the beginning of the chapter. The concrete framework that the case studies provide should help you retain the theories throughout each chapter.

The company Pedopodgy, which is a private college, realized the need to network the central administrative offices five years ago. The initial network comprised of 45 PCs, 5 print *servers*, and 1 file server. It was a NetWare network, running IP. The administration at each of the five campuses was added two years later. Last year, the company provided Internet access for each student, with Internet connectivity accessed through corporate headquarters.

The network has grown considerably in the last five years. This growth has been in both *end nodes* and complexity. In end nodes alone, the network has grown from 45 PCs, with the 5 print servers and 1 file server, to more than 500 PCs connecting to 30 print servers and 20 file servers.

Everyone is complaining. The network is unreliable, unresponsive, and difficult to use, and there have been several security break-ins. The main problem is that the network has exceeded its original design, and the infrastructure of the network can no longer handle the volume of traffic generated. The IT department is being besieged by angry users.

This type of story is very familiar. Every network consultant has heard a variation of it a thousand times, and you can hear versions in conversations on the bus, the train, or the ferry.

This chapter addresses the problems seen in this case study. It identifies the key requirements of a network and illustrates how a structured design can simplify and help in the management of the network. This chapter also explains how excessive traffic on the network can thwart user needs and shows some of the ways that network traffic can be alleviated.

In designing a network, it is important to identify the key requirements of the network. Although any network will have the same core requirements, the business needs of a specific organization can elevate a particular network requirement above another.

As seen in the case study, a network that is inadequate to the needs of its users does not only frustrate the user base, but it also affects the organization's capability to function.

Key Requirements of a Network

When designing a network, you first must define and assess customer requirements and then put together a plan to meet these requirements. Therefore, an understanding of the business structure and current data flow within the existing environment is crucial to prioritizing the requirements of the network. The relative importance of each of the following broad key requirement categories is determined by the needs of the organization in question. For example, a small, growing catering company may place more importance on efficiency, adaptability, and accessibility than a large financial institution that demands reliability, responsiveness, and security. The college cited in the case study would require the network to be secure as well as reliable and responsive.

The sections that follow describe the key requirements of a network:

- Reliability

- Responsiveness

- Efficiency

- Adaptability/serviceability

- Accessibility/security

- Factors that increase network traffic

Reliability

For a hospital or bank, the network must be available 24 hours a day, seven days a week. In the first instance, lives are at stake. If network access cannot be granted to the blood bank, it may not be possible to give a life-saving transfusion. For a bank exchanging money throughout international markets across every time zone, a network fault can be extremely expensive. In such a situation, network downtime can cost millions of dollars per fraction of an hour. The capability to isolate and limit any problems that occur, therefore, is as important as solving the problem quickly.

Responsiveness

Excessive latency within a network appears to the end user as a lack of responsiveness. Frustration sets in and often leads the user to reboot or to repeat keystrokes. This response is the same one that might cause you to raise your voice to someone who does not answer your question; you assume that the person hasn't heard the question. In the network environment, however, repeating keystrokes generates more network traffic, which increases congestion and delays. Avoiding this is essential for network health. To do so, build in mechanisms to alleviate congestion and to prioritize certain protocols that are more sensitive to delay.

Efficiency

Designing a network that restricts traffic to allow only the necessary information to be carried across it proves extremely helpful in preventing congestion. The inefficiency in allowing network and service updates to travel to areas of your network that have no need for the information can seriously limit the available bandwidth left for data. For example, allowing users in Brussels, Belgium, to see printers in Palo Alto, California, is not very helpful and may saturate the 56-kbps serial link.

Adaptability/Serviceability

It is difficult to anticipate every change that your company may make in terms of mergers and organizational structure. Therefore, building an adaptable network protects capital investment. It also increases the reliability of the network. Because network administrators are not issued crystal balls, it is essential that attention be given to the interoperability of both products and applications when designing the network. Thus, when the company makes a business change, network changes may be needed. Imagine that Pedopodgy has recently acquired a marketing manager, who has bought five Macintoshes for his department, running graphic production software. The infrastructure of the network need to be considered in terms of not only the additional bandwidth requirements, but also the capability to share files. In short, the nature of the client/server interaction on the rest of the network should be determined.

Serviceability is related to adaptability, but it is more focused toward being able to make changes to production systems without disrupting normal operations (for example, hot redundancy and dual power supplies).

Accessibility/Security

Security is a popular topic and a major consideration, particularly as more companies connect to the Internet and thereby increase the chance of hackers, idly wandering into the network. Weighing the needs of users to access the network, particularly when remote access is required, against the need to secure company secrets is a difficult balance that requires careful consideration at the executive level. It is important to consider security as part of the initial design because it is very difficult to address this issue as an afterthought. In the case of the Pedopodgy case study, the security of student grades as well as tests that may be stored electronically is important.

Although this book identifies the main requirements of a network, only a few of these are examined in depth in the CCNP/CCDP Routing exam. One of the areas addressed in the exam is that of network congestion and the methods to alleviate it in an IP network.

Factors That Increase Network Traffic

It cannot be denied that company networks are growing at a dramatic rate. When designing a network, the challenge is to create a system that will grow with the company and be capable of dealing with increased demand. Obviously, the size, nature, and maturity of the business will affect the demand for increased network resources.

Networking is still young and has only very recently extended to the home and small business. Therefore, it is a safe assumption that networks and the demand for network traffic will continue to grow for some time. As seen in the case study at the beginning of the chapter, this can cause problems.

In addition to the increase in the number of users, applications have become more complex, evolving into highly graphic and often interactive packages.

If the design and implementation of the original network has been well managed, network growth increases dramatically within the first year. Networks must therefore adapt to change to allow growth. As an analogy, instead of constantly buying new clothes for the sprouting child, we can just let down hems and lengthen sleeves. Companies cannot afford either the capital investment or the hours involved in accommodating a network that must be redesigned frequently. The consequence of having a network incapable of scaling is that as it grows it becomes constricted, just like the child squeezed into a coat that is too small. The result within your company would be *network congestion*.

Identifying the Problems Created by Network Congestion

Network congestion results when too many packets are competing for limited bandwidth. The result is similar to that of heavy road traffic: collisions, delays, and user frustration.

Traffic Analysis and Network Design

The problems caused by network congestion are easily identified. By using network-monitoring tools, such as Cisco's TrafficDirector or a standard protocol analyzer, it is possible to ascertain the traffic volume either on an entire network or on individual segments. An understanding of the traffic volumes within the network can also be gained by issuing commands at the Cisco router. Commands such as **show interface**, **show buffers**, and **show queuing** can give a feel for the traffic levels within the network, without purchasing extra products. It is important to understand the context of the traffic flow within your network so that you can appropriately accommodate the requirements of the users and their applications, designing and building a network that will scale.

The traffic on the network typically follows the organization's business flow, responding not only to peaks and valleys in business cycles, but also to the direction of the traffic flow as well. Necessarily, the communication between the accounting department and the marketing department within the organization will reflect the network traffic. The appropriate placement of network resources, such as servers, can be considered after the organizational flow of data has been identified. The network and the placement of the servers dictate the traffic flow throughout the company. Poor design inevitably leads to congestion.

Problems Created by Network Congestion

The next sections cover the following problems created by network congestion:

- Excessive traffic
- Dropped packets
- Retransmission of packets
- Incomplete routing tables
- Incomplete server lists
- The Spanning-Tree Protocol breaks
- Runaway congestion

Excessive Traffic

If the traffic volume outgrows the network, the result is congestion. When this occurs on a single segment, the capacity of the medium overrun—resulting in the dropping of packets—and the medium can react adversely to excessive traffic.

Physical Problems of Ethernet

Ethernet illustrates this well. Ethernet has strict rules about accessing the medium, so, a physical problem—such as extraneous noise or just too many trying to access too little—results in excessive traffic, causing collisions. A collision requires all transmitting devices to stop sending data and to wait a random amount of time before attempting to send the original packet. Only the nodes involved in the collision are required to wait during the backoff period. Other nodes must wait until the end of the jam signal and the interframe gap (9.6 ms for Ethernet, 0.96 ms for Fast Ethernet, and 0.096 ms for Gigabit Ethernet). If after 16 attempts the device fails to transmit, it gives up and reports the error to the calling process. If for this or any other reason the device fails to transmit and drops the packet from its buffer, the application typically retransmits the original packet. This may result in increased congestion that grows exponentially, which is often referred to as *runaway congestion*.

Dropped Packets

One of the effects of congestion is that not all the packets can get through the network. Essentially, the queues and buffers in the intermediate forwarding devices (for example, routers) overflow and must drop packets, causing an OSI higher-layer process on either end device (for example, workstation) to time out. Typically, the transport or application layers have the responsibility to ensure the arrival of every piece of data.

Maintaining the integrity of the transmission requires the communication to be *connection-oriented*, giving the end devices the mechanisms to perform error detection and correction (for example, the TCP layer of TCP/IP) through windowing, sequencing, and acknowledgments.

Retransmission of Packets

If packets are dropped, the layer responsible for the integrity of the transmission will retransmit the lost packets. If the session or application layer does not receive the packets that were resent in time, the result will be either incomplete information or timeouts.

Incomplete Routing Tables

The application may be unaware that it did not receive all the data; this missing data may just appear as an error or may have more subtle and insidious effects. For example, if the routing table of an intermediate forwarding device such as a router is incomplete, it may make inaccurate forwarding decisions, resulting in loss of connectivity or even the dreaded *routing loop* (see Figure 2-2).

Using the case study earlier in this chapter, if the WAN connection between the campus site and the corporate headquarters becomes congested, packets may be dropped, possibly resulting in the receipt of partial routing updates. In Figure 2-2, for example, if Router X hears a full update, the routing table will know subnetworks 10, 20, and 30. Imagine that Router Y does not receive a full update from Router X. It knows only about subnetworks 20 and 30. When Workstation A tries to connect to Server B at the corporate offices, it has a problem. Router X can direct the traffic to Router Y. In turn, Router Y can forward traffic to Server B.

However, when Server B responds, Router Y has no way to forward back to Router X because it has no entry for remote subnetwork 10. In a more complex environment, routing loops often occur because of poor network design.

Figure 2-2 *Incomplete Routing Tables Cause Loss of Connectivity*

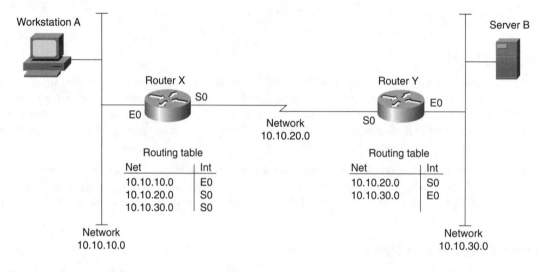

Incomplete Server Lists

Congestion results in the random loss of packets. Under extreme circumstances, packet loss may result in incomplete routing tables and server lists. Entries may ghost in and out of these tables. Users may find that their favorite service is sometimes unavailable. The intermittent nature of this type of network problem makes it difficult to troubleshoot.

The Spanning-Tree Protocol Breaks

The Spanning-Tree Protocol is maintained in each Layer 2 device, a *switch* or a *bridge*, allowing the device to ensure that it has only one path back to the root bridge. Any redundant paths will be blocked, as long as the Layer 2 device continues to see the primary path. The health of this primary path is ensured by the receipt of spanning-tree updates (called bridge protocol data units, or BPDUs). As soon as the Layer 2 device fails to see the updates, panic sets in and the device removes the block on the redundant path, falsely believing it to be the only path available. The block on the redundant path is removed after several updates have been missed, after the MaxAge timer has been exceeded. This ensures some stability in the network. However, if this problem occurs, in a short time, spanning-tree loops and broadcast storms will cause the network to seize up and die.

This is one of the reasons that the industry moved toward a routed network solution. However, organizations are beginning to reintroduce Spanning-Tree Protocol into their switched environments without any problems. This is a result of the vast improvements in the hardware, the increased bandwidth, and the use of VLANs to reduce the size of the broadcast domain, and, in a Cisco implementation, the spanning-tree domain. Another factor that positively affects the stability of large flat networks is the increasing use of multicast addresses. Multicast addresses are read only by devices belonging to the multicast address and are forwarded only to segments that contain such devices. Refer to the Cisco Design Guides, on the Cisco Connection Online (CCO) web page, for more information on these topics.

Runaway Congestion

When packets are dropped, requiring retransmission, the congestion will inevitably increase. In some instances, this may increase the traffic exponentially; this is often called runaway congestion. In relatively unsophisticated protocols, such as Spanning-Tree Protocol, it is almost unavoidable, although others may have methods of tracking the delays in the network and throttling back on transmission. Both TCP and AppleTalk's DDP use flow control to prevent runaway congestion. Therefore, it is important to understand the nature of the traffic on your network when designing scalable networks.

Symptoms of Congestion

The symptoms of congestion are intermittent, and the following problems may be due not to congestion but to some underlying problem within the network. This is another reason why problems that result from congestion are so difficult to diagnose.

The following example shows why congestion problems are difficult to identify. If the link is running near bandwidth capacity and the connected devices are overwhelmed, any additional traffic will cause problems. Because the packets are randomly dropped, it is difficult to track where the problems have occurred. Therefore, the network will have equally random failures. The symptoms of network congestion are consequently difficult to troubleshoot because some protocols are more sensitive than others and will time out after very short delays are experienced. However, the network administrator who knows his network well will soon identify these recurring problems. The following are three symptoms of network congestion:

- Applications time out.

- Clients cannot connect to network resources.

- Network death results.

NOTE   Packets are randomly dropped only if there is not quality of service (QoS) configured within the network.

Applications Time Out

The session layer of the OSI model is responsible for maintaining the communication flow between the two end devices. This includes assigning resources to incoming requests to connect to an application. To allocate resources adequately, idle timers disconnect sessions after a set time, releasing those resources for other requests. Note that although the OSI model assigns these duties to the session layer, many protocol stacks include the upper layers of the stack in the application. TCP/IP is such a protocol.

Clients Cannot Connect to Network Resources

The client/server environment is one in which applications take advantage of networks. Servers provide services to many clients that access them across the network. Both data and application software may be stored centrally on a server that allows many clients to share them. If all users depend on the client/server interaction, this can create excessive traffic across the network.

In a client/server environment, the available resources are communicated throughout the network. The dynamic nature of the resource tables (offering services, servers, or networks) gives an up-to-date and accurate picture of the network. NetWare, AppleTalk, Vines, and Windows NT all work on this principle. If these tables are inaccurate as a result of the loss of packets in your network, errors will be introduced because decisions were made with incorrect information. Some network systems are moving more toward a peer-to-peer system in which the end user requests a service identified not by the network, but by the administrator.

Network Death Results

The most common problems arising from network congestion are intermittent connectivity and excessive delays—users must wait a long time for screens to refresh, users are disconnected from applications, print jobs fail, and errors result when trying to write files to remote servers. If the response of the applications is to retransmit, congestion could reach a point of no recovery. Likewise, if routing or spanning-tree loops are introduced as a result of packet loss, the excessive looping traffic could bring your network down.

Creating a Network That Meets the Key Requirements

Although is important to know how to reduce network congestion when it occurs, it is crucial to build a network that can grow with the user needs, thus preventing a network that reels from crisis to crisis. Designing the network so that it can scale, therefore, is crucial. Cisco provides a hierarchical design that should simplify network management and also allow the network to grow. This growth may be a physical growth as well as a capacity growth.

Cisco's Hierarchical Design

To achieve these networks requirements that have been described—and to keep local traffic local, preventing network congestion—Cisco suggests a network design structure that allows for growth. The key to the design is that it is hierarchical. There is a division of functionality between the layers of the hierarchy, allowing only certain traffic —based on clear criteria—to be forwarded through to the upper levels. A filtering operation restricts unnecessary traffic from traversing the network. Thus, the network is more adaptable, scalable, and more reliable. Clear guidelines and rules govern how to design networks according to these principles. These guidelines and rules are covered in the Cisco design class as well as design guides provided by Cisco on its web page. The following section explains how the hierarchical network design proposed by Cisco reduces congestion.

Why Scaling Reduces Congestion

If the network is designed hierarchically, with each layer acting as a filter to the layer beneath it, the network can grow effectively. In this way, local traffic is kept local, and only data and information about global resources needs to travel outside the immediate domain.

Understanding that the layers are filtering layers begs the question of how many layers are required in your network. The answer is, it depends on the type of applications and network architecture, to name but a few criteria.

How Hierarchical Is Hierarchical?

Cisco's design methodology is based on simplicity and filtering. Cisco suggests that the largest networks currently require no more than three layers of filtering.

Because a hierarchical layer in the network topology is a control point for traffic flow, a hierarchical layer is the same as a routing layer. Thus, a layer of hierarchy is created with the placement of a router or, more recently, a Layer 3 switching device.

The number of hierarchical layers that you need to implement in your network reflects the amount of traffic control required. To determine how many layers are required, you must identify the function that each layer will have within your network.

The Functions of Each Layer

Each hierarchical layer in the network design is responsible for preventing unnecessary traffic from being forwarded to the higher layers (and then being discarded at a higher point in the network or by the receiving stations). The goal is to allow only relevant traffic to traverse the network and thereby reduce the load on the network. If this goal is met, the network can scale more effectively. The three layers of a hierarchy are as follows:

- The access layer

- The distribution layer
- The core layer

The Access Layer

In accordance with its name, the access layer is where the end devices connect to the network—where they gain access to the company network. The Layer 3 devices (such as routers) that guard the entry and exit to this layer are responsible for ensuring that all local server traffic does not leak out to the wider network. QoS classification is performed here along with other technologies that define the traffic that is to traverse the network. Service Advertisement Protocol (SAP) filters for NetWare and AppleTalk's GetZoneLists are implemented here, in reference to the design consideration of client/server connectivity.

The Distribution Layer

The distribution layer is responsible for determining access across the campus backbone by filtering out unnecessary resource updates and by selectively granting specific access to users and departments. Access lists are used not just as traffic filters, but as the first level of rudimentary security.

Access to the Internet is implemented here, requiring a more sophisticated security or firewall system.

The Core Layer

The responsibility of the core layer is to connect the entire enterprise. At the pinnacle of the network, reliability is of the utmost importance. A break in the network at this level would result in the incapability of large sections of the organization to communicate. To ensure continuous connectivity, the core layer should be designed to be highly redundant, and, as much as possible, all latency should be removed. Because latency is created when decisions are required, decisions relating to complex routing decisions, such as filters, should not be implemented at this layer. They should be implemented at the access or distribution layers, leaving the core layer with the simple duty of relaying the data as fast as possible to the remote site. In some implementations, QoS is implemented at this layer to ensure a higher priority to certain packets to prevent them from being lost during high congestion periods.

General Design Rules for Each Layer

A clear understanding of the traffic patterns within the organization—who is connecting to whom and when—helps to ensure the appropriate placement of client and servers, and eases the implementation of filtering at each layer. The filtering that is imposed by the router creates the network hierarchy illustrated in Figure 2-3. Without hierarchy, networks have less capacity to scale because the traffic must traverse every path to find its destination, and manageability becomes an issue.

It is important for each layer to communicate only with the layer above or below it. Any connectivity or meshing within a layer impedes the hierarchical design.

Organizations often design their networks with duplicate paths. This is to build network resilience so that the routing algorithm can immediately use the alternative path if the primary line fails. If this is the design strategy of your company, care should be taken to ensure that the hierarchical topology is still honored.

Figure 2-3 shows an illustration of the appropriate design and traffic flow.

Figure 2-3   *Redundant Connections Between Layers*

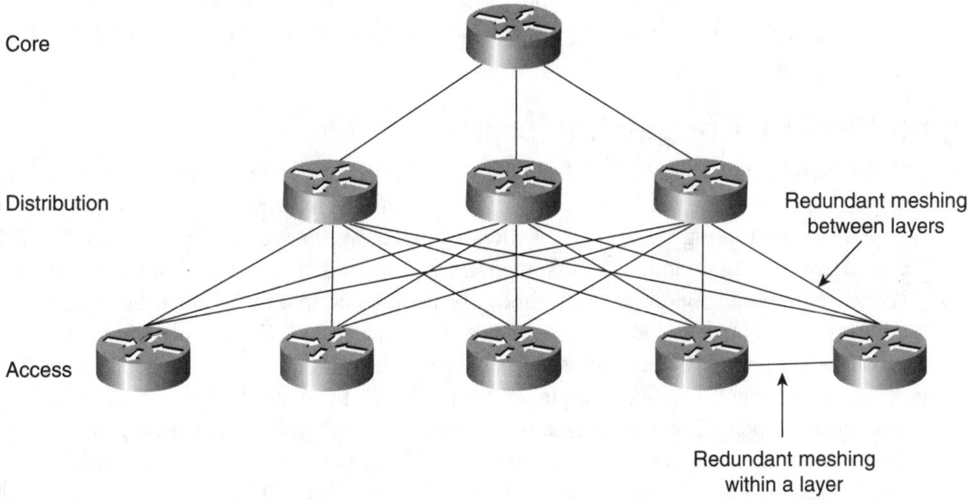

Core

Distribution

Redundant meshing between layers

Access

Redundant meshing within a layer

WARNING   Unless you have a profound knowledge of the current network and the placement of the servers, it is impossible to design a new network with the proper hierarchy.

IP Access Lists: Alleviating Congestion with Cisco Routers

Cisco router features enable you to control traffic, primarily through access lists. Access lists give you "what if" control of the network. They are crucial to the sophisticated programming of a Cisco router and allow for great subtlety in the control of traffic.

Given that the router operates at Layer 3, the control that is offered is extensive. The router can also act at higher layers of the OSI model. This proves useful when identifying particular traffic and protocol types for prioritization across slower WAN links.

Cisco Proprietary Solutions

With the assumption that connections are between Cisco routers, Cisco has optimized many network operations. This sometimes requires a proprietary solution. While defying some of the standards to streamline network traffic, Cisco has been conscientious by providing both the standard solution and a proprietary Cisco solution. To ensure the capability to integrate Cisco equipment into all networks, Cisco offers sophisticated methods of translation between the standard and the proprietary Cisco solution. The clearest example of this is the use of redistribution between Cisco's routing protocol, Enhanced Interior Gateway Routing Protocol (EIGRP), and any other routing protocol such as Open Shortest Path First (OSPF).

Managing Network Congestion for IP

IP is generally considered a well-behaved protocol because its communication is typically peer-to-peer, removing the necessity for excessive broadcasts throughout the network. The only broadcasts are routing updates and Address Resolution Protocol (ARP) requests. These characteristics can no longer be assumed, however, as client/server technologies start to offer IP as a communication protocol. It should be understood that the application demands determine the nature of the traffic on the network. Therefore, if the application relies on broadcasts to locate its server, the protocol used to communicate that broadcast is of little concern. The routed protocols AppleTalk and IPX, and the nonrouted protocol NetBIOS are the obvious examples of protocols used by client/server applications. These protocols were designed for LAN networks and tend to be very chatty in the communication between the client and the server. Recently these network protocols have utilized TCP/IP as the transport method, but the client/server communication is still based on a broadcast technology that defies the peer-to-peer architecture of TCP/IP and renders it chatty.

It would be misleading to suggest that improvements in network utilization have not been made by these protocols, which were originally designed for small LAN environments instead of the enterprise solutions for which they are now being sold. Nevertheless, it is important to emphasize the need to do careful analysis of the network traffic flow and to understand the communication requirements between the client and the server.

The Implementation of IP Access Lists

Access lists can be used to either restrict or police traffic entering or leaving a specified interface. They are also used to implement "what if" logic on a Cisco router. This gives you the only real mechanism of programming the Cisco router. The access lists used for IP in this way enable you to apply great subtlety in the router's configuration. This chapter reviews how to configure access lists and discusses their use in an IP network. The *Interconnecting Cisco Network Devices* coursebook and the *Cisco CCNA Exam #640-507 Certification Guide*, both from Cisco Press, deal with these subjects in more depth.

IP Access List Overview

Access lists are linked lists with a top-down logic, ending in an implicit **deny any** command, which will deny everything. Top-down logic means that the process will read from the top of the access list and stop as soon as it meets the first entry in the list that matches the packet's characteristics. Therefore, it is crucial that careful attention be given to their creation. Writing down the purpose of the proposed access list before attempting to program the system also proves helpful.

Access lists block traffic traversing the router. Remember that traffic generated by the router is not blocked by an access list.

Standard IP Access Lists

The following is syntax for a standard **access-list** command and an **ip access-group** command:

```
access-list access-list-number {permit | deny}{source [source-wildcard | any]}
ip access-group access-list-number {in | out}
```

Note that the *access-list-number* value must be within the range of 1 to 99 to create a standard access list.

Standard access lists are implemented at Layer 3. In general, both the source and destination addresses are identified as criteria in the logic of the list. IP access lists work slightly differently, however; they use the source address only.

The placement of the access list is crucial because it may determine the effectiveness of the control imposed. Because the decision to forward can be made on the source address only, the access list is placed as close to the destination as possible (to allow connectivity to intermediary devices).

For example, in Figure 2-4, the intention of the access list is to prevent the library terminals access to the administrative LAN in the college Pedopodgy. The reasoning in placing the access list so close to the source is to increase security and reduce traffic. In fact, all traffic from network 10.10.10.0 is denied access to the rest of the network, so Figure 2-4 shows incorrect access list placement.

Figure 2-4 *The Placement of a Standard Access List—Incorrect Placement*

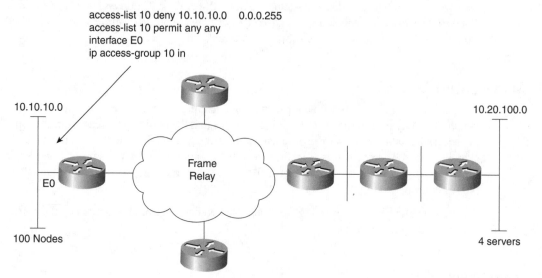

```
access-list 10 deny 10.10.10.0    0.0.0.255
access-list 10 permit any any
interface E0
ip access-group 10 in
```

In Figure 2-5, however, placing the access list as close to the destination as possible allows traffic from the source to freely roam the entire network, except for a barrier preventing student traffic from accessing the forbidden area. Figure 2-5 shows correct access list placement.

You can place an access list on either an inbound or an outbound interface. If this option is not configured, the default is for the access list to be placed on the outbound interface. The access list will examine traffic flowing only in the direction stated. In this way, traffic subject to an inbound access list will be examined before it is sent to the routing process.

To ensure that all paths to the remote location have been covered, access lists should be implemented with careful reference to the topology map of the network.

Extended IP Access Lists

Although the same rules apply for all access lists, extended access lists allow for a far greater level of control because decisions are made at higher levels of the OSI model.

The following is syntax of an extended **access-list** command:

```
access-list access-list-number {deny | permit} protocol
source source-wildcard destination destination-wildcard
ip access-group access-list-number {in | out}
```

The *access-list-number* value must be between 100 and 199 to create an extended access list.

Figure 2-5   *The Placement of a Standard Access List—Correct Placement*

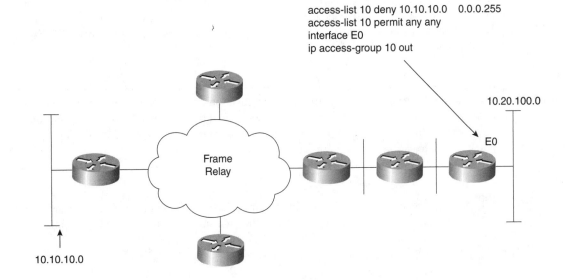

Table 2-2 explains the previous syntax.

Table 2-2   *Extended **access-list** Command Explanation*

Command	Description
access-list *access-list-number*	Gives the number of an access list. This is a decimal number from 100 to 199.
{**deny** | **permit**}	Denies or permits access if the conditions are matched.
source source-wildcard	Gives the source address and the wildcard mask.
destination destination-wildcard	Gives the destination address and the wildcard mask.
[**precedence** *precedence*]	(Optional) Packets can be filtered by precedence level, as specified by a number from 0 to 7, or by name, as listed on the CCO web page in the section "Usage Guidelines."
[**tos** *tos*]	(Optional) Packets can be filtered by type of service level, as specified by a number from 0 to 15, or by name as, listed on the CCO web page in the section "Usage Guidelines."
[**established**]	(Optional) For the TCP protocol only: Indicates an established connection. A match occurs if the TCP datagram has the ACK or RST bits set. The nonmatching case is that of the initial TCP datagram to form a connection.
[**log**]	(Optional) Gets access list logging messages, including violations.

In recent versions of the IOS, many additional options have been given to the creation of the access lists. These include the use of named access lists, as well as the capability to set timeouts on the access lists. This is outside the scope of this exam and, therefore, also the exam guide. For further details, refer to the Cisco CCO web pages for the "Managing the System" chapter in the *Configuration Fundamentals Configuration Guide*.

WARNING	When using extended access lists to prevent application connection, it is easy to become confused. TCP and UDP are the common protocols and these include both an optional source port and an optional destination port. A common mistake is to specify **stop telnet** using a source port of 23 instead of a destination port of 23.

When using extended access lists, it is important to consider the sequence of conditions within the list. Because top-down logic is employed, the ordering of the list may alter the entire purpose of the list.

Guidelines for Writing Access Lists

You should adhere to the following guidelines when writing an access list:

- Write out the purpose to be achieved by the access list in clear, simple language.

- Determine the placement of the access list in reference to a topology map of the network.

- Write out the access list, ensuring that the following is considered:

1 The most frequent instance of traffic is placed first in the list, if possible, to reduce CPU processing.

2 Specific access is stated before group access is defined.

3 Group access is stated before world access is defined.

4 There is an implicit **deny any** at the end of the list.

5 The implicit **deny** statement in the access list means that there must be at least one **permit** statement, or the access list will deny everything.

6 If no wildcard mask has been defined in a standard access list, the mask of 0.0.0.0 is assumed. This mask would match every bit in the address. If the address was that of a subnet rather than an end station, no match would be found, and the router would move on to the next criteria line. If that line is the ending **deny any**, problems may occur.

7 The access list will not take effect until it has been applied to the interface. The access list will default to an outgoing access list if a direction is not specified.

WARNING   Changes have been made to the way access lists function in terms of the **deny any** at the end of the access list. To avoid confusion, therefore, it is a good policy to read the documentation for your IOS version. To be safe, assume that everything will be denied by an implicit **deny any** at the end of the list because this will foster good practices.

- Test the access list with a utility such as ping. It is important to first ensure that the utility is permitted in the ACL. However, in more complex scenarios, ping may not suffice, and alternative methods should be used. Two common ways of doing this are to either use Telnet and modify the ports used, or, if possible, to obtain some type of port scanner and use only the specific ports allowed (as well as testing some that are not allowed).

- Use the **show** commands to verify the placement of the access list.

- If the access list needs to be modified, the list will have to be removed from the interface, deleted, and re-created as additional criteria is appended to the bottom of the list.

NOTE   However, named access lists behave slightly differently. These are not in the scope of the course and should be researched well before they are implemented on a live network.

- It is useful to save the access list to a Trivial File Transfer Protocol (TFTP) server and just edit it offline.

WARNING   Note that in some older versions of the IOS, deleting the access list at the global level without removing it from the interface may cause the interface to restrict all traffic through the interface in the direction that it was applied. This is because, although the access list is still applied to the interface, it has no content; therefore, the implicit **deny any** takes effect. Standard system management calls for making changes to the specific before moving back to the general—that is, removing the access group from a specific interface before deleting the global access list.

Verifying Filter Configuration

Whenever a network is configured, that configuration must be tested, and the changes must be documented. Called maintaining the *baseline*, this enables you to maintain a clear knowledge of the network functionality.

The commands to verify the filter configuration for either IP or IPX filters are most easily accomplished through the **show** commands:

```
show access list
show ip interface
```

Figure 2-6 illustrates the process logic used for access lists.

Figure 2-6 *Processing of an IP Access List—Incoming and Outgoing Packets*

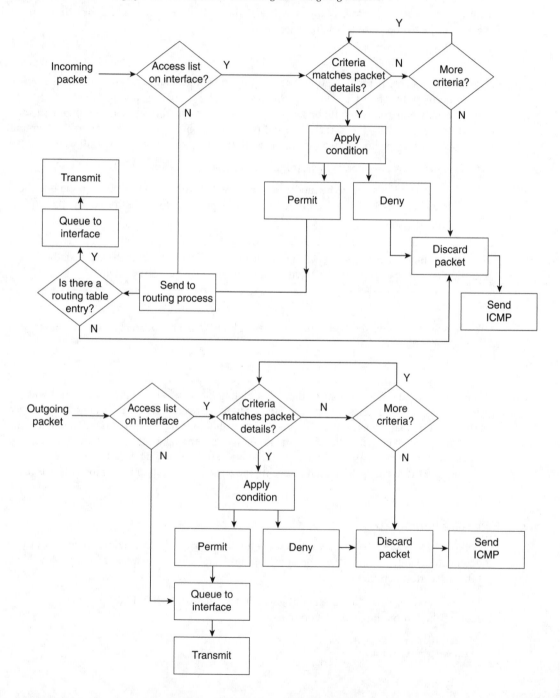

Access lists are extremely powerful when you are configuring the router to tune the data flow through the device. Because access lists take both CPU and memory, however, you must consider alternatives. The following section discusses these alternatives.

NOTE   Depending on the type of access list, the version of IOS, and the hardware configuration, some access lists are processed more quickly than others. This is because some access lists can be cached. For more information, refer to the configuration guides on the Cisco web page.

Uses of IP Access Lists

Because access lists can be used so subtly in system programming, they are used in many ways to solve many problems. IP access lists are used mainly to manage traffic.

Essentially, an access list is a list that uses a simple logic to decide whether to forward traffic. As such, access lists are sometimes used as a security system. Certain issues arise when using access lists for security purposes. The next section covers these in more detail.

Security Using Access Lists

Cisco recommends using alternative methods to access lists for security. Although access lists are complex to conceive and write, they are easy to spoof and break through. The 11.3 IOS has implemented full security features, and these sophisticated features should be utilized in preference to access lists. The Cisco Secure Integrated Software (IOS Firewall Feature Set) also is now available.

Some simple security tasks are well suited to access lists, however. Although access lists do not constitute complex security, they will deter the idle user exploring the company network.

The best way to use access lists for security is as the first hurdle in the system, to alleviate processing on the main firewall. Whether the processing on the firewall device is better designed for dealing with the whole security burden, or whether this task should be balanced between devices should be the topic of a capacity-planning project.

Controlling Terminal Access

Access lists filter traffic traversing the router; they do not prevent traffic generated by the router. To control Telnet traffic in which the router is the end station, an access list can be placed on the virtual terminal line (vty).

Five terminal sessions are available: vty 0 through vty 4. Because anticipating which session will be assigned to which terminal is difficult, control is generally placed uniformly on all virtual terminals. Although this is the default configuration, some platforms have different limitations on the number of vty interfaces that can be created.

Configuration

The syntax for virtual terminal line commands is as follows:

```
line {vty-number | vty-range}
access-class access-list-number {in | out}
```

Standard access lists are used for inbound access because the destination is known. The **access-class** command is the same as the **access-group** command but is used for terminal access. It could be applied as either an inbound or an outbound list. The access list used has the same structure as the standard access lists; even the range used in the command is the same, 1 through 99.

The following example of the configuration commands allow incoming Telnet access to the router only from hosts on network 131.99.55.0:

```
access-list 12 permit 131.99.55.0 0.0.0.255
line vty 0 4
access-class 12 in
```

When applied as an inbound **access-class** command to the vty, an access list restricts users from connecting to the router from the specified source addresses.

When applied as an outbound **access-class** command to the vty, an access list restricts users who have connected to the router and then attempt to connect to another system from that router. This is because the access list is still using the source address.

Other methods of restricting access are slightly more brutal. It is possible to issue the following command, for example:

```
no line vty 0 4
```

This command removes all terminal access.

It is also possible to issue the following commands:

```
line vty 0 4
login
no password
```

This requires a password. Because a password has not been established, however, it is impossible to correctly input a password. The result is no access. In the previous examples, the console is used to configure and manage the router. This can also be done with the Telnet application and is often none by mistake. Although this is a common error, it is occasionally used as a rudimentary security mechanism.

Traffic Control Through Routing Updates

Traffic on the network must be managed. Traffic management is most easily accomplished at Layer 3 of the OSI model. You must be careful, however, because limiting traffic also limits connectivity. Therefore, careful design and documentation is required.

Routing updates convey information about the available networks. In most routing protocols, these updates are sent out periodically to ensure that every router's perception of the network is accurate and current.

Distribute Lists

Access lists applied to routing protocols restrict the information sent out in the update and are called *distribute lists*. They work by omitting certain networks based on the criteria in the access list. The result is that remote routers unaware of these networks are not capable of delivering traffic to them. Networks hidden in this way are typically research-and-development sites, test labs, secure areas, or just unwanted networks. This is also a way to reduce overhead traffic in the network.

Why Use Distribute Lists?

These access lists are also used to prevent routing loops in networks that have redistribution between outing protocols.

When connecting two separate domains, the connection point of the domains or the entry point to the Internet is an area through which only limited information needs to be sent. Otherwise, routing tables become unmanageably large and consume large amounts of bandwidth.

Other Solutions to Traffic Control

It is popular to tune the update timers between routers, trading currency of the information for optimization of the bandwidth. All routers running the same routing protocol expect to hear these updates with the same frequency that they send out their own. If any of the parameters defining how the routing protocol works are changed, these alterations should be applied consistently throughout the network; otherwise, routers will time out and the routing tables will become unsynchronized.

WARNING   Tuning network timers of any type is an extremely advanced task and should be only done under very special circumstances and with the aid of the Cisco Telephone Support team.

Across WAN networks, it may be advantageous to turn off routing updates completely and to manually or statically define the best path to be taken by the router. Note also that sophisticated routing protocols such as EIGRP or OSPF send out only incremental updates; be aware, however, that these are correspondingly more complex to design and implement, although, ironically, the configuration is very simple.

Another method of reducing routing updates is to implement the technology *snapshot routing* available on Cisco routers and designed for use across WAN links. This allows the routing tables to be frozen and updated either at defined times, such as every two days or whenever the dialup line is raised. For more information on this topic, refer to the Cisco web page.

To optimize the traffic flow throughout a network, you must carefully design and configure the IP network. In a client/server environment, control of the network overhead is even more important. The following section discusses some concerns and strategies.

Prioritization

Access lists are not used just to determine which packets will be forwarded to a destination. On a slow network connection where bandwidth is at a premium, access lists are used to determine the order in which traffic is scheduled to leave the interface. Unfortunately, some of the packets may time out. Therefore, it is important to carefully plan the prioritization based on your understanding of the network. It is important to ensure that the most sensitive traffic (that is, traffic most likely to time out), such as IBM's Systems Network Architecture (SNA), is handled first.

Types of Prioritization

Many types of prioritization are available. Referred to as *queuing techniques*, they are implemented at the interface level and are applied to the interface queue. The weighted fair queuing technique is turned on by default and may not be tuned by the router administrator. These include the following:

The weighted fair queuing method is available in the later versions of the IOS. It is turned on automatically—in some instances, by the Cisco IOS—replacing the first-in, first-out (FIFO) queuing mechanism as the default. The queuing process analyzes the traffic patterns on the link, based on the size of the packets and the nature of the traffic, to distinguish interactive traffic from file transfers. The queue then transmits traffic based on its conclusions.

Queuing techniques that are manually configured with access lists are as follows:

- **Priority queuing**—This is a method of dividing the outgoing interface into four virtual queues. Importance or priority ranks these queues, so traffic is queued based on its importance and will be sent out of the interface accordingly. This method ensures that sensitive traffic, such as SNA traffic, on a slow or congested link is processed first.

- **Custom queuing**—The interface is divided into many subqueues. Each queue has a threshold stating the number of bytes that may be sent before the next queue must be processed. In this way, it is possible to determine the percentage of bandwidth that each protocol is given.

- **Class-based weighted fair queuing (CBWFQ)**—This queuing method extends the standard WFQ functionality to provide support for user-defined traffic classes. For CBWFQ, you define traffic classes based on match criteria, including protocols, access control lists (ACLs), and input interfaces. Packets satisfying the match criteria for a class constitute the traffic for that class. A queue is reserved for each class, and traffic belonging to a class is directed to that class's queue.

- **Low-latency queuing (LLQ)**—This feature brings strict priority queuing to CBWFQ. Configured by the **priority** command, strict priority queuing gives delay-sensitive data, such as voice, preferential treatment over other traffic. With this feature, delay-sensitive data is sent first (before packets in other queues are treated).

Reducing Network Traffic: Alternatives to Access Lists

Because of the resources required to process them, access lists are not always the most suitable solution. The null interface is a good example of when a technology can be used imaginatively to produce a low-resource solution.

Null Interface

The *null interface* is a virtual interface that exists only in the imagination of the router. Traffic may be sent to it, but it disappears because the interface has no physical layer. A virtual interface does not physically exist. Administrators have been extremely creative and have used the interface as an alternative to access lists. Access lists require CPU processing to determine which packets to forward. The null interface just routes the traffic to nowhere.

Configuration of Null Interfaces

The null interface command syntax is as follows:

```
ip route address mask null0
```

For example:

```
ip route 10.0.0.0 255.0.0.0 null0
```

Figure 2-7 clearly shows how you might implement a null interface in an organization. The example shows how it can be used to filter the private network from the Internet.

Internet Example

If the router receives traffic to be forwarded to network 10.0.0.0, it will be dropped through null0 into a black hole. Because this is a private address to be used solely within an organization, never to stray onto the Internet, this is a command that may well be configured on routers within the Internet.

Figure 2-7   *The Use of the Null Interface in the Internet*

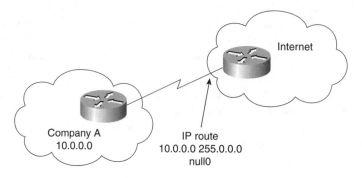

Within the organization, there is often a use for the null interface command. Figure 2-8 and the following text explain their use.

Intranet Example

Configuring the static route to null0 on an internal company router would prevent connectivity to the defined network because all traffic to that destination would be forwarded to a nonexistent interface. In Figure 2-8, Workstation A would not be capable of connecting to Server C, the development server used by the Research and Development department. The result is that the Research and Development department would be capable of seeing the rest of the organization. Indeed, the rest of the world can see the Research and Development department in a routing table. Any attempt to direct traffic to the network will be unsuccessful, however. The first router that sees the traffic will statically route it to the null interface, which metaphorically is a black hole. No error messages will be sent to the transmitting node because the traffic was successfully routed—although, unfortunately, to a black hole. This is considered beneficial for several reasons, one of which is additional security.

WARNING   Because the static route is entered into the routing table, it is important to remember that all the rules of static routing apply. If the router hears of the destination route via another source, it is ignored in favor of the static route that has a lower administrative distance (which gives it a higher priority).

Figure 2-8   *The Use of the Null Interface Within an Organization*

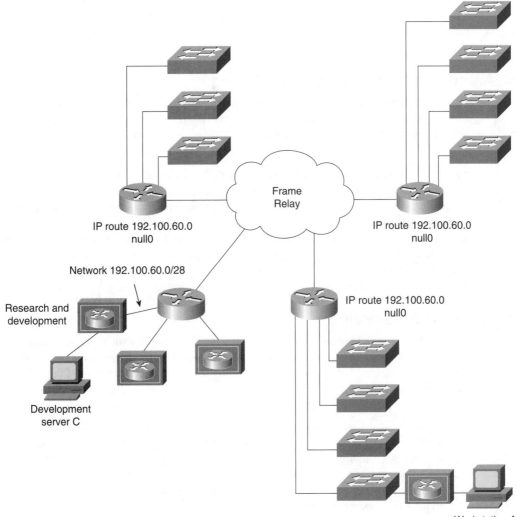

CPU Considerations and Additional Methods for Controlling Network Traffic

Access lists require CPU processing from the router. The more complex or the longer the access list, the greater the amount of CPU processing is required. In earlier versions of the Cisco IOS, pre-10.3, complex access lists prevented the caching of routing decisions, such as fast, autonomous, and silicon switching. These functions are now supported, particularly if *NetFlow* features are turned on. In this context, switching refers to traffic forwarding, a Cisco solution that was implemented in the earliest of Cisco's products and that has been consistently enhanced.

Fast, Autonomous, and Silicon Switching

These switching techniques were created to improve the capability of the router to forward traffic—at speed. The router caches the routing decisions it has made, which means that subsequent packets from the same source to the same destination do not have to be sent to the routing process, but instead can perform simple and speedy lookup.

After the routing process has made a routing decision, it sends the packet to the appropriate outbound interface. Meanwhile, the router holds a copy of the address details of the outbound frame in memory, along with a pointer to the appropriate outbound interface. This means that incoming traffic can be examined as it comes into the router. The router looks in the cache or memory to see whether a routing decision has already been made for that set of source and destination addresses. If an entry exists, the frame can be switched directly to the outbound interface, and the routing process is bypassed.

Cisco Express Forwarding

This is a very high-end solution and is available on 7500 routers with Versatile Interface Processors (VIPs) and the 8510. It is extremely fast and is used for high volumes of traffic. On some Cisco platforms, the Cisco processor automatically turns on this feature if the appropriate hardware and software are available.

NOTE   A real performance gain can be realized with the reduction of CPU cycles needed when NetFlow or fast switching are used. In fact, the risk of losing packets or buffer overflow is reduced because the router is working a lot faster. The different names for the available switching methods refer to where the cache is stored. For more information on this subject, refer to the Cisco documentation set.

If the router is not caching any of the routing decisions but is instead processing every packet with process switching, there may be negative implications on the router's CPU and memory utilization.

Placement of Client/Server

The location of the servers in relation to the clients dramatically affects the traffic patterns within the network.

The current philosophy is to create server farms so that the servers can be centrally administered. If the client finds the server via broadcasts, however, a serious problem will arise if there is a router between the broadcasts: Because routers are a natural broadcast firewall, they treat broadcasts as an unknown address and discard them. In such a scenario, the client sending a broadcast to locate a server will fail in the endeavor.

The careful design with centralized server farms on different networks will not work because the broadcasts sent between the clients and the server to establish connections are discarded by the intervening router. The clients will have no connectivity with their servers. The solution is to configure a helper address on the router.

Even carefully designed centralized server farms on different networks will not work because the intervening router discards broadcasts sent between the clients and the server. The clients will have no connectivity with their servers. The solution is to configure a helper address on the router. This is described in the section, "IP Helper Address."

Design Principles of a Client/Server Network

To design an effective network, it is essential to understand the data flow within a network. Where to place the server relative to the clients should be decided only after considering the following factors:

- The frequency of connection to the server

- The duration of the connection to the server

- The volume of traffic sent across the link to and from the server at a specific moment of the day

- The daily quantified average

Analyzing the traffic patterns over time to create a baseline of the network documents how the network functions today and allows the correct determination of server/client placement. Using standard systems analysis methodology, the status of the network must then be set against the future needs of the organization (to ensure the appropriate design of the network). Understand that the design of the network will directly influence the traffic patterns experienced within the network.

IP Helper Address

The *IP helper address* removes the broadcast destination address of a UDP packet received on an identified interface and replaces it with a specific destination address. The router has been programmed to say, "If a broadcast comes in on this interface, forward it to this destination address," where the destination address is that of the server.

A helper address is configured on the incoming interface. The destination address may be either an individual server or a subnet address. Multiple helper addresses can be identified, and all broadcasts received on the interface will be forwarded to each destination. This is a good way to create backup servers on different segments.

Configuration of IP Helper Address

The syntax for the **ip helper-address** command is as follows:

```
ip helper-address address
```

The IP helper address forwards broadcasts for the following UDP ports:

- TFTP (69)
- DNS (53)
- Time (37)
- NetBIOS name server (137)
- NetBIOS datagram service (138)
- BOOTP server (67)
- BOOTP client (68)
- TACAS (49)

In addition to the helper address, the IP forward protocol instructs the router to forward broadcasts. By stating the port number, particular types of broadcast may be identified. This is very useful when used in conjunction with the helper address because it identifies those broadcasts to be readdressed to specified destinations. It is possible to either add to the list of broadcasts that will be forwarded with the helper address or remove certain traffic types. You can tailor the **ip helper-address** command so that only necessary traffic is forwarded, which not only optimizes bandwidth but also prevents the servers from being overloaded. (Server overload can result in servers overflowing their buffers; this causes them to slow down or hang.) The syntax for the **ip forward-protocol** command is as follows:

```
ip forward-protocol {UDP [port] |nd | sdns}
```

Enhanced Interior Gateway Routing Protocol

EIGRP was designed to make efficient use of the available network bandwidth. The routing protocol can be used for IP as well as AppleTalk and IPX. The advantage of EIGRP is that it is incremental, sending updates only when a change in the network is experienced.

EIGRP is particularly efficient in sending network and server information for such client/server products as NetWare for IPX and AppleTalk because it automatically redistributes routing updates into the local protocol updates. EIGRP is proprietary to Cisco and is understood only by other Cisco devices. A powerful use of this technology would be to have EIGRP as the routing protocol between the routers across the WAN and the client/server traffic on the local segments.

It is advisable to use the latest versions of the Cisco IOS when implementing this technology and to ensure that all the devices are running the same version of the protocol. This subject is dealt with in more detail in Chapter 7, "Using EIGRP in Enterprise Networks."

WARNING   If possible, all routers should run the same version of IOS because this may make troubleshooting easier.

Tunneling into IP

Tunneling one protocol into another is the process by which a protocol at a specific layer of the OSI model is wrapped into another protocol of the same layer or one higher in the stack. An example of this would be IPX, which is a Layer 3 protocol being wrapped inside IP, another Layer 3 protocol. Other examples include AppleTalk inside IP, and NetBIOS or source-route bridging encapsulated in IP—this is an example of a Layer 2 protocol being wrapped inside a Layer 3 protocol.

Figure 2-9 illustrates the steps of the IPX protocol being encapsulated and transported through an IP tunnel:

Step 1   Data from the application layer is passed down the OSI model to the network layer.

Step 2   At the network layer, the data is encapsulated in an IPX packet.

Step 3   At the network layer, the IPX packet is encapsulated into an IP packet.

Step 4   The IP packet is then inserted into the frame format at the data link layer for the media in which the frame will be sent out.

Why would anyone want to configure anything quite so torturous? Such a configuration certainly will not reduce or control the traffic propagated onto the network. Conversely, it will increase the traffic load because the original data will now have the additional header.

On the end routers, which are responsible for adding this extra header, there are obviously increased CPU requirements.

Figure 2-9   *Tunneling IPX Within IP*

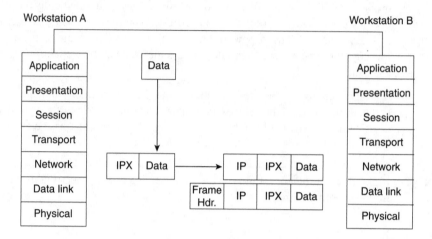

The reasons for this configuration are not justified in the name of network optimization. However, tunneling does make sense to ease the management of the entire network.

The administrator of the core no longer has to understand or worry about the vagaries of the disparate protocols. The client/server traffic should be kept locally to the user LAN networks, with traffic to remote networks connected via IP. Now the administrator can focus on the one protocol: IP.

Although the use of IP enables the administrator to utilize all the available optimization tools for IP, it should be understood that the nature of the traffic would still be inherently that of the originating protocol. A NetBIOS application generating a broadcast will be transformed into an IPX broadcast and tunneled in the IP protocol. It is delivered to the tunnel destination and stripped of the IP header, and the IPX broadcast is dealt with as normal. Some of the reasons for tunneling IPX through IP include the following:

- The traffic can utilize the advantages of IP and its sophisticated routing algorithms.

- The two ends of the tunnel appear as a single point-to-point link, although in reality they are separated by many routers.

- The network administrator for the backbone network to which the two LANs connect needs to understand only IP.

- The addressing scheme is simplified.

- Simple routing protocols may have a limited hop count, which is extended by the tunnel, which advertises the path across the tunnel as one hop.

Some things to consider when creating an IP tunnel for IPX include the following:

- The delay, or latency, created in tunneling the IPX traffic into IP may cause some applications to time out.

- Because the tunnel is viewed as a point-to-point link, separate tunnels are required for multiple links. Many tunnels on a physical interface can cause some memory problems on the interface.

- Care must be taken in redistributing routing protocols because the tunnel is often seen as a preferred path. This is because the route is advertised as a single hop. It may involve a much less favorable path, however. The tunnel may advertise the path as two hops—one hop through the tunnel and one hop to the destination. However, the 1 hop actually represents 10 hops across mixed media. The other path, which is rejected because it advertised three hops, is really only three hops away.

Configuration of Tunneling into IP

The following syntax shows the configuration for the **tunnel interface** command:

```
interface tunnel interface-number
```

The following shows syntax for the configuration of the tunnel associated with the tunnel interface.

```
tunnel source interface-number | ip-address
tunnel destination hostname | ip-address
```

Table 2-3 explains the previous syntax.

Table 2-3   *Tunneling Configuration Explanation*

Command	Description
interface tunnel	Creates the virtual interface
interface-number	Identifies the interface number to be created
tunnel source	Identifies the source of the tunnel
*interface-number	ip-address*	Specifies the port, connector, or interface card number/IP address to use as the source address for packets in the tunnel.
tunnel destination	Identifies the destination of the tunnel
*hostname	ip-address*	Gives the IP address of the host destination expressed in decimal in four-part, dotted notation

The following example shows the use of the tunnel commands:

```
Router(config)#interface tunnel0
Router(config-if))#tunnel source ethernet0
Router(config-if)#tunnel destination 131.108.164.19
```

Conclusion

IP is the dominant protocol within the industry. Many companies have moved to an IP-based network, forbidding any other protocol on the wire, to manage the network more efficiently. Dealing with one protocol has its obvious benefits. Because IP is the chosen protocol of the industry, a lot of effort has been placed into enhancing the utilities and support provided.

This chapter has reviewed the means of scaling this IP network, allowing it to grow with an organization's needs. Many design features, as well as Cisco features, allow the streamlining of the network. The following were considered:

- Network congestion, both its causes and symptoms
- How Cisco's hierarchical design can scale your network
- IP access lists to limit traffic and control network overhead
- Alternatives to access lists for reducing network traffic, particularly in a client/server environment

You have seen that an understanding of the network structure and the needs of the users and applications will make it possible to manage traffic flow within that network. Therefore, network administrators must know the network and its idiosyncrasies.

It is important to remember that a structural topology map of the physical and logical layout of the network is necessary to allow the design and appropriate implementation of the features described in this chapter.

Foundation Summary

The "Foundation Summary" Section is a collection of quick reference information that provides a convenient review of many key concepts in this chapter. For those of you who already feel comfortable with the topics in this chapter, this summary will help you recall a few details. For those of you who just read this chapter, this review should help solidify some key facts. For any of you doing your final preparations before the exam, these tables and figures will be a convenient way to review the day before the exam.

Tables 2-4 through 2-7 summarize the main points of the chapter. Because much of this chapter is a review of CCNA-level material, some of the points are not directly related to the exam objectives. Points that are directly associated with the Routing exam are marked with an "*." The intention is that the tables be used to remind you of the key points of the most important subjects that are covered in this chapter; refer to the body of the chapter for detail on points marked with an "*." The additional information is of use to the advanced student, who will see the chapter subjects in a wider context.

Table 2-4 identifies the reasons for congestion within a network and the solution that Cisco proposes. The subsequent tables deal with access lists, including their configuration and application.

Table 2-4   *Network Congestion: Causes and Cisco Solutions*

Causes of Network Congestion	Cisco Solutions
Excessive application traffic	* Use priority queuing across slow serial links.
	* Ensure appropriate server location in network design.
	Use compression across slow serial links.
	Use traffic shaping for Frame Relay with BECN.
	Use serial backup commands for dual point-to-point links.
	Adjust application and other timers so that they do not time out and retransmit.
	Increase the bandwidth using EtherChannel.
	Use load balancing, policy routing for IP .
Broadcast traffic due to large network	* Filter unnecessary networks from routing updates.
	Use snapshot routing across dialup lines.
	Manually configure static routes.
	Use a sophisticated routing protocol with incremental updates (for example EIGRP, OSPF).
	Split large networks into smaller subnets.
	Use address summarization.

continues

Table 2-4   *Network Congestion: Causes and Cisco Solutions (Continued)*

Causes of Network Congestion	Cisco Solutions
Broadcast traffic due to large client/server network	* Filter unnecessary servers/services/zones from service updates.
	Use a sophisticated routing protocol (for example, EIGRP).

Table 2-5   *Access List Features*

Access List Feature	Purpose
Decision to forward based on: Layer 3 source address only (standard access list) Layer 3 and above (extended access list)	* Determine packet movement through network or "what if?" programming.
Capability to filter on port numbers, packet size, and Layer 3 addresses	* Give a high level of granularity.
Named access lists (IOS v 11.2)	Provide ease of management.
Keywords for ports and wildcards	Provide ease of management.
Capability to apply access list as inbound or outbound	* Use flexibility in design considerations.
Capability to prevent ICMP messages from being generated when a packet is denied access	Provide increased security by making spoofing more difficult.
Use of the established parameter to allow outgoing TCP applications but to restrict incoming attempts	Allow users to Telnet into the Internet while preventing access to anyone trying to initiate a connection from the outside.
Capability to filter in TCP/IP by precedence	Speed up the propagation of traffic by sorting traffic by the precedence bits in the IP header. QoS is determined so that certain traffic types can be manipulated through the network by this means.
Lock and key	Allow users normally blocked to gain temporary access after the user is authenticated.
Reflexive access list	Provide dynamic filtering at the IP session layer.

Table 2-6   *Applications for Access Lists*

Type of Access List	Purpose
Standard	* Handles packet movement through the network or "what if?" programming
Virtual terminal access	* Restricts access to and from the vty line interfaces on the router
Distribute lists	Filters networks from the routing updates
Service filtering (for example, IPX SAP, GNS or AppleTalk ZIP, or GetZoneList filters)	Filters services from the server updates or from the replies to client requests
Queuing (for example, priority or custom queuing)	* Prioritizes traffic leaving an interface
Dial-on-demand routing (DDR)	Determines traffic that is defined as important enough to dial the remote the site

Table 2-7   *Points to Remember When Configuring Access Lists*

Point to Remember	Consideration
The access list is processed as a top-down link list. The list will be tested for a match. When the first match is found, the **deny** or **permit** will be applied, and the process will be terminated.	* Place the most specific criteria first. If more than one criteria is specific, place the most frequent match first.
There is an implicit **deny any** at the end of every list.	* There must be at least one permit statement. If reverse logic is used in the design of the access list (for example, deny these addresses but permit all other traffic), there must be a **permit any** at the end of the access list.
The wildcard uses zeros to indicate bits of the address to match, and uses ones for those to ignore.	This is the reverse of the use of the subnet mask and is easily confused. Where a subnet mask would use 213.99.32.0 with a mask of 255.255.224.0, a wildcard mask would use 0.0.31.255.
Additional criteria statements are added to the bottom of the access list.	Because there is no editing, and because placement of the criteria is important, it is advisable to save the access list configuration to a TFTP server where it can be edited with ease.
The access list is not active until applied to the interface.	* The access list will not work.

Chapter Glossary

This glossary provides an official Cisco definition for key words and terms introduced in this chapter. I have supplied my own definition for terms that the Cisco glossary does not contain. The words listed here are identified in the text by italics. A complete glossary, including all the chapter terms and additional terms, can be found in Appendix C, "Glossary."

connection-orientated—Software on two end nodes guarantees the transmission of network traffic because a circuit setup is established before sending any data. It requires the use of sequencing, windowing, and acknowledgements.

distribute list—An access list that is used to filter networks out of routing updates.

end node—A device that is connected to the network.

NetFlow—A Cisco solution that enhances the speed of transmission by caching routing decisions.

network congestion—A condition in which excessive traffic on the network is the cause of delays and packet loss.

routing loop—Occurs when routers have misinformation about the network and, instead of sending traffic to the destination, pass the packets between themselves in the belief that the other router knows the path.

runaway congestion—A condition in which the results of network congestion cause the network to generate more traffic and compound the problem.

server—A node or software program that provides services to clients.

Q&A

The following questions test your understanding of the topics covered in this chapter. The final questions in this section repeat the opening "Do I Know This Already?" questions. These are repeated to enable you to test your progress. After you have answered the questions, find the answers in Appendix A. If you get an answer wrong, review the answer and ensure that you understand the reason for your mistake. If you are confused by the answer, refer to the appropriate text in the chapter to review the concepts.

1 State two reasons to use an IP tunnel.

_____

_____

_____

2 State instances when access lists may be used for something other than filtering traffic.

_____

_____

_____

3 In configuring an IP tunnel, how many IP tunnels may be created with the same source and destination address?

_____

_____

_____

4 Associate the appropriate IOS feature to solve the network congestion problem experienced on the network in the following table.

_____

_____

_____

Network Congestion Problem	IOS Solution
Clients cannot connect to the centralized servers	Routing access list
Cisco environment in a large network with a large number of WAN connections	Prioritization on the interface
Large routing tables using RIP for IP	Reduction of the size of the broadcast domain by adding a router
Spanning tree is failing	IP helper address
SNA sessions are failing	EIGRP

5 Which command would prevent the router from forwarding data to a remote network without generating an ICMP message?

_____

_____

_____

6 Identify two commands that might be used to verify the configuration of an IP access list configuration.

_____

_____

_____

7 What UDP ports will the IP helper address forward automatically?

_____

_____

_____

8 If the number of workstations increases on a physical segment, the user may experience delays. Give two reasons why this might occur.

_____

_____

_____

9 State three considerations when deciding where to place extended IP access lists.

_____

_____

_____

10 What is the function of the access layer?

_____

_____

_____

11 What is the access list number range for IP extended access lists?

_____

_____

_____

12 What is priority queuing?

_____

_____

_____

13 List two symptoms of network congestion.

_____

_____

_____

14 If a switch has redundant links to another switch, what action would be taken if the Spanning-Tree Protocol fails to see a BPDU in time (within the MaxAge Timer value)?

_____

_____

_____

15 How could the dropping of packets cause an increase of traffic on the network?

_____

_____

_____

16 How might network congestion cause a loss of services?

_____

_____

_____

17 In Cisco's hierarchical design, what is the function of the core layer?

_____

_____

_____

18 In Cisco's hierarchical design, where is the access layer located?

_____

_____

_____

19 In the hierarchical design suggested by Cisco, at which layer are access lists not recommended?

_____

_____

_____

20 What is the function of the distribution layer?

_____

_____

_____

21 If an access list is configured as an inbound list, will the packet be sent to the routing process?

_____

_____

_____

22 State three uses of access lists.

_____

_____

_____

23 In an IP standard access list, what is the default wildcard mask?

_____

_____

_____

24 If a packet does not match any of the criteria in an access list, what action will be taken?

_____

_____

_____

25 Why does the null interface not report an ICMP message stating that the packet is undeliverable?

_____

_____

_____

26 How would you restrict Telnet connectivity to the router that you were configuring?

_____

_____

_____

27 Which of the queuing techniques offered by the Cisco IOS are manually configured?

_____

_____

_____

28 Explain **ip helper address**. What is its function?

_____

_____

_____

Scenarios

The following scenarios and questions are designed to draw together the content of the chapter and to exercise your understanding of the concepts. There is not necessarily a right answer. The thought process and practice in manipulating the concepts is the goal of this section. The answers to the scenario questions are found at the end of this chapter.

Scenario 2-1

The company Pedopodgy, which is a private college, realized the need to network the central administrative offices five years ago. The initial network comprised of 45 PCs, 5 print *servers*, and 1 file server. The company had a NetWare network, running IP. The administration at each of the five campuses was added two years later. Last year, Pedopodgy provided Internet access for each student, with Internet connectivity accessed through corporate headquarters.

As can be seen, the network has grown considerably in the last five years, in both *end nodes* and complexity. In end nodes alone, the network has grown from 45 PCs, with the 5 print servers and 1 file server, to more than 500 PCs connecting to 30 print servers and 20 file servers.

Everyone is complaining. The network is unreliable and unresponsive, it is difficult to use, and there have been several security break-ins. The main problem is that the network has exceeded its original design, and the infrastructure of the network can no longer handle the volume of traffic generated. The IT department is being besieged by angry users.

Figure 2-10 shows the network diagram for Scenario 2-1.

1 Give recommendations for the administrator to implement when trying to solve the problem of network delay.

2 Users on the network no longer have connectivity to the e-mail server. Upon investigation, you notice that the access list commands have been changed. What are the commands to remedy the situation?

```
Router(config-fi)#access list 110 permit 10.10.10.10 255.255.255.255 eq smtp
```

3 Noticing that someone has been changing the configuration of the routers, you decide to implement some first-line security. State some of the solutions that you might consider.

Figure 2-10   *Network Diagram for Scenario 2-1*

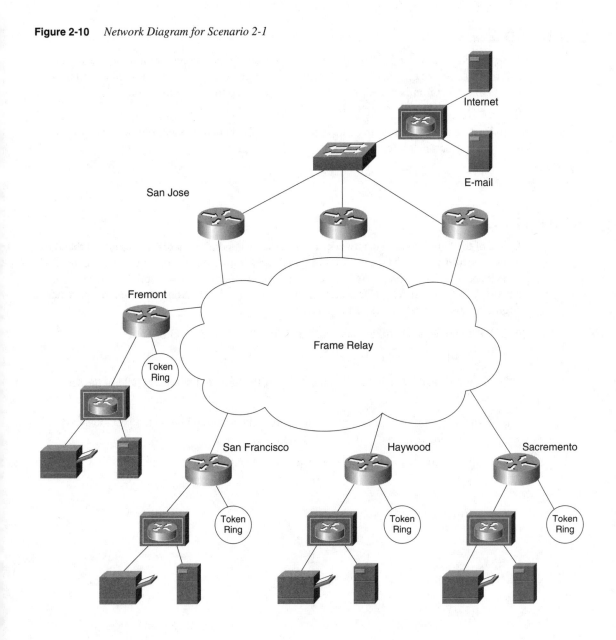

Scenario 2-2

Your company has recently created a lab for you to test TCP/IP configurations and explore new solutions. Although the lab needs to be connected to the entire network, it is important that access to this environment be limited. Although you need to be able to connect from anywhere in the lab to the network, no one else should have this access.

1   Write the access list(s) to achieve this, and apply them to the appropriate interface(s) of the appropriate routers(s).

2   Draw a diagram to support your configuration.

Scenario 2-3

In one of the buildings of the network campus, the local administrators have decided that they want to centrally administer the building servers. Each floor of the building is a separate IPX and IP network. The server farm is located in the network in the basement. The server farm consists of a DHCP server, a DNS server, and an IPX file server. None of the clients have been configured with the addresses of the servers.

The IP network address for the basement is 10.10.10.0. 255.255.255.0

1   Draw a diagram of the network.

2   What command would allow connectivity of the users to the servers held in the server farm?

3   Write the configuration commands to achieve the requirements stated previously. Make sure that this is reflected on your diagram.

4   Which commands would you use to verify the configuration?

Scenario Answers

The answers are in **bold**. The answers provided in this section are not necessarily the only possible answers to the questions. The questions are designed to test your knowledge and to give practical exercise in certain key areas. This section is intended to test and exercise skills and concepts detailed in the body of this chapter.

If your answer is different, ask yourself whether it follows the tenants explained in the answers provided. Your answer is correct not if it matches the solution provided in the book, but rather if it has included the principles of design laid out in the chapter.

In this way, the testing provided in these scenarios is deeper: It examines not only your knowledge, but also your understanding and ability to apply that knowledge to problems.

If you do not get the correct answer, refer back to the text and review the subject tested. Be certain to also review your notes on the question to ensure that you understand the principles of the subject.

Scenario 2-1 Answers

1 Give recommendations for the administrator to implement when trying to solve the problem of network delay.

The administrator could implement the following recommendations to ascertain that delays were being experienced on the network. Also listed here are some possible solutions to the problems.

— Use a protocol analyzer to verify that there is network congestion.

— Write an IP extended access list to prevent users from connecting to any server other than their local server, the e-mail server, or the gateway server.

2 Users on the network no longer have connectivity to the e-mail server. Upon investigation, you notice that the access list commands have been changed. What are the commands to remedy the situation?

```
Router(config-fi)#access list 110 permit 10.10.10.10 255.255.255.255 eq smtp
```

The problem with the access list is that it has had the source and destination transposed. The access list should read as follows:

```
Router(config-if)#access list 110 permit 10.10.10.10 255.255.255.255 eq smtp
```

3 Noticing that someone has been changing the configuration of the routers, you decide to implement some first-line security. State some of the solutions that you might consider.

The following are some suggestions of first-line security that could be implemented:

— Ensure that the routers are held in a physically secure environment.

— Write a standard access list to be applied on the vty line interfaces.

— Change the passwords on the routers.

— Turn on logging and accounting at the router.

Scenario 2-2 Answers

1 Write the access list(s) to achieve this, and apply them to the appropriate interface(s) of the appropriate routers(s).

To permit access from anywhere in the lab for only the administrator, you must apply extended access lists to the fddi 0 interface of Router Y. The access lists would be applied in both the inbound and outbound directions. A diagram has also been included to show the configuration in a simpler environment. The administrator may well be working from home and dialing in to the network. In this case, the configuration would be the same, but S0 is the interface that has the access lists applied. If the link were a dialup link, there would be additional configuration determining which traffic would raise the line.

Example 2-1 shows the commands required to achieve this:

Example 2-1 *Scenario 2-2 Configuration*

```
Router Y
Router(config)#
access-list 102 permit ip 10.0.0.0  0.255.255.255  0.0.0.0 255.255.255.255
Router(config)#
access-list 103 permit tcp 0.0.0.0  255.255.255.255  10.0.0.0 0.255.255.255
established
Router(config)#inter FDDI 0
Router(config-if)# ip access-group 102 in
Router(config-if)# ip access-group 103 out
```

2 Draw a diagram to support your configuration.

Figure 2-11 shows where the access lists described in Example 2-1 would be applied.

Figure 2-11   *Answer to Scenario 2-2, Applying Access Lists*

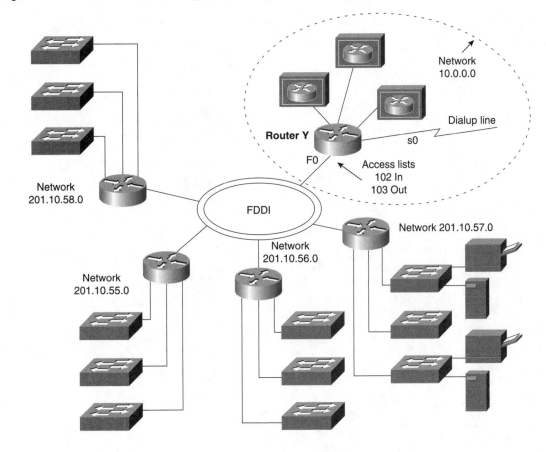

Scenario 2-3 Answers

1   Draw a diagram of the network.

   Figure 2-12 shows a diagram of the network.

Figure 2-12 *Answer to Scenario 2-3*

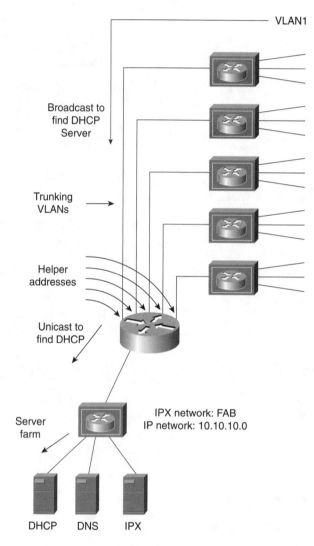

2 Write the configuration commands to achieve the requirements stated previously. Make sure that this is reflected on your diagram.

The following commands allow the IP clients to connect to the remote servers:

```
Router(config-if)# ip helper-address 10.10.10.255
```

The IPX clients will need no additional configuration because they will find their servers using the normal method of GNS requests and SAP updates.

3 Which commands would you use to verify the configuration?

The commands that you can use to verify the configuration of the helper addresses are as follows:

— show startup-config

— show running-config

— show ip interface

— show ipx interface

This chapter covers the following topics that you will need to master to pass the CCNP/CCDP Routing exam:

- Definition of a Layer 3 address

- IP subnet masks

- The problems in IP networks

- Solutions to the IP addressing limitations, including the explanation of prefix routing

- The use of VLSM and its application

- The use, application, and configuration of summarization

- Key points in the design of an IP network

- How to optimize address space

- How to connect to the outside world using Network Address Translation (NAT) and private addresses

- The Cisco features NAT and IP subnet 0

IP Addressing

This chapter is fundamental to the rest of the topics discussed within this book and will directly reflect questions on the exam. If you do not thoroughly understand the contents of this chapter, it is safe to say that it will be impossible to pass the exam. The entire Routing exam is based on IP addressing. For this reason, IP addressing is reviewed thoroughly in this book. Some of this chapter will review subjects dealt with in the Interconnecting Network Devices (ICND) course. The subsequent chapters will assume your comprehension of the subjects within this chapter.

How to Best Use This Chapter

By taking the following steps, you can make better use of your study time:

- Keep your notes and the answers for all your work with this book in one place, for easy reference.

- When you take a quiz, write down your answers. Studies show that retention significantly increases by writing down facts and concepts, even if you never look at the information again.

- Use the diagram in Figure 3-1 to guide you to the next step.

Figure 3-1 *How to Use This Chapter*

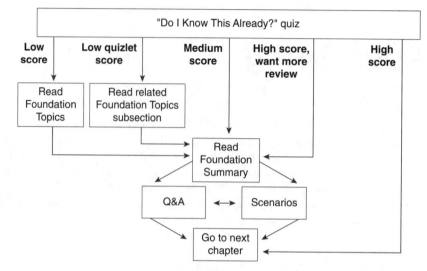

If you skip to the Foundation Summary, Q&A, and scenarios sections and have trouble with the material there, you should go back to the Foundation Topics section.

"Do I Know This Already?" Quiz

The purpose of the "Do I Know This Already?" quiz is to help you decide what parts of this chapter to use. If you already intend to read the entire chapter, you do not necessarily need to answer these questions now.

This 16-question quiz helps you determine how to spend your limited study time. The quiz is sectioned into four smaller four-question "quizlets," which correspond to four major topics in the chapter. Figure 3-1 outlines suggestions on how to spend your time in this chapter. Use Table 3-1 to record your scores.

Table 3-1 *Score Sheet for Quiz and Quizlets*

Quizlet number	Topic	Questions	Score
1	IP subnetting	1 to 4	
2	VLSM and prefix routing	5 to 8	
3	Summarization	9 to 12	
4	Private addressing and NAT	13 to 16	
All questions		1 to 16	

1 If given a Class C address with the requirement to accommodate 14 subnets and 10 hosts on each subnet, what subnet mask would you use?

_____

_____

_____

2 List the range of hosts available on the 136.122.10.192/28 subnet.

_____

_____

_____

3 Convert the subnet address 56.98.5.0/24 to binary notation, and state the class to which it belongs.

_____

_____

_____

4 Write out the decimal notation of the following subnet mask presented in this binary notation:

11111111.11111111.11111111.11111000

_____

_____

_____

5 What does VLSM stand for?

_____

_____

_____

6 The Class B network address of 133.222.0.0 has been given a mask of 255.255.255.0. The subnets, 133.222.8.0, 133.222.9.0, 133.222.10.0, 133.222.11.0, 133.222.12.0, 133.222.13.0, and 133.222.14.0 need to be summarized using VLSM. Give the subnet and new mask to achieve this summarization.

_____

_____

_____

7 Is 201.111.16.0/20 a valid subnet mask?

_____

_____

_____

8 Which routing protocols support VLSM?

_____

_____

_____

9 Briefly define _route summarization_.

_____

_____

_____

10 What sort of design scheme does route summarization require?

_____

_____

_____

11 In route summarization, where is the subnet mask moved?

_____

_____

_____

12 How does summarization allow for smaller routing tables?

_____

_____

_____

13 Identify two private addresses defined in RFC 1918.

_____

_____

_____

14 What is a discontiguous network?

_____

_____

_____

15 What does *CIDR* stand for?

_____

_____

_____

16 Which RFC is responsible for first describing the use of subnet masking?

_____

_____

_____

The answers to this quiz are found in Appendix A, "Answers to Quiz Questions." The suggested choices for your next step are as follows:

- **2 or less on any quizlet**—Review the appropriate sections of the "Foundation Topics" portion of this chapter, based on Table 3-1. Then move on to the "Foundation Summary" section, the "Q&A" section, and the "Scenarios" at the end of the chapter.

- **8 or less overall score**—Read the entire chapter. This includes the "Foundation Topics" and "Foundation Summary" sections, the "Q&A" section, and the "Scenarios" at the end of the chapter.

- **9 to 12 overall score**—Begin with the "Foundation Summary" section, and then go to the "Q&A" section and the "Scenarios" at the end of the chapter. If you have trouble with these exercises, read the appropriate sections in "Foundation Topics."

- **13 or more overall score**—If you want more review on these topics, skip to the "Foundation Summary" section, and then go to the "Q&A" section and the "Scenarios" at the end of the chapter. Otherwise, move to the next chapter.

Foundation Topics

Introduction: What Is a Layer 3 Address and How Does It Affect My Life?

The following case study illustrates some of the common issues that companies deal with as they grow. The company is often so focused on surviving infancy that it overlooks the internal technology requirements. This case study shows the problems seen when the network outgrows its addressing scheme.

Case Study

A small startup company, Mental Merge, has grown in the last year. No longer three recent college graduates, working out of a parent's guestroom, the founders now have their own premises and 100 employees.

The company has a flat, switched network providing print and file services using NT over IP. The owners have been simply adding devices as needed, without much heed to the future requirements of the company. Having run out of IP addresses once, and with an increase in delays, they realize that it is time to build an infrastructure with a well thought-out design and addressing scheme.

Networks, like children, grow. Often when you least suspect, you wake up and find them bigger, more complex, and thus more challenging. For many companies, although the network provides the tools by which the company does business, it is an irritating distraction from the business in hand. This was the case for Mental Merge. The owners were intelligent enough to string wire between PCs and read enough of the manual to install the client/server software. However, realizing that the company needs their full attention, they have just hired a network administrator.

Because Mental Merge is a small company, the owners hope to be bought out, so they intend to design an addressing scheme that will allow them to easily integrate into a larger network. Eventually, the network will be a routed one, and the addressing scheme certainly will reflect this intention.

This chapter considers many of the tasks that the new administrator must handle in readdressing the network with a design that enables future growth.

The Need for Layer 3 Addressing

A quick review of addressing at Layer 3 should remind you of the importance of the ability to overcome the need for broadcasts, which are the bane of a switched environment. This is a particular problem in a client/server environment, as Mental Merge is beginning to realize.

A Definition of a Layer 3 Address

A Layer 3 address allows network traffic to be directed to a specific destination. The whole purpose of any address is to find a specific destination, whether the address of a restaurant or the company e-mail server. To be directed, every address is hierarchical; just as a restaurant is in a city, on a street, at a street number, the e-mail server is on a network at a host number.

Network Structures and Data Flow

For data to be sent to its destination directly, the underlying physical structure, or wiring, should support the logical structure, or the Layer 3 addressing. It also seems reasonable that this structure should reflect the organizational data flow. It would make sense for servers to be accessible to departments that share information and for the physical wiring and logical addressing to support this sharing of resources. Therefore, the servers may be physically adjacent and on the same IP subnet. The reason that both the physical and the logical structure of the network should support the organizational data flow is that, without this structure, application data can wander throughout your network inefficiently, clogging up available bandwidth.

This chapter reviews some of the fundamental concepts of IP addressing. After mastering its subtleties, you will then be able to consider the network management power that results from careful design of the IP addressing scheme.

The Network and How It Is Addressed

Layer 3 provides the capability to logically address the network. The question is, what is a network? It is given many meanings, from describing a corporation's international computer system to describing a single piece of wire. It has been complicated further with the recent capability to override the traditional physical limitations of address allocation. The use of switched environments and *VLANs*, as well as the use of dynamic addressing with *DHCP*, has provided new challenges to the design rules of address allocation.

A Confusion of Network Terminology

To appreciate fully the power and purpose of the Layer 3 address, it is important to understand the meaning of the term *network* (as defined by Layer 3).

A network address has two parts: the network and the host portions. The host portion of the address identifies the individual device within a group. The network portion identifies a group of individual devices.

Unfortunately, the term *network* is used loosely; although it is often defined, the term is seldom understood. In addition, the term *network* appears in several different contexts, compounding the confusion created for the user.

It is increasingly important to have an accurate definition of a network because new technology—such as VLANs and *Layer 3 switching*—have blurred the distinctions between the different layers of the OSI model.

Network Terms Explained

The following list outlines the various uses of the term *network*:

- The piece of wire or physical medium to which a group of devices are connected. This is more accurately defined as a segment.

- A Layer 3 network.

- The local-area network (LAN).

- The corporate or organizational network.

For our purposes, the term *network* refers to the Layer 3 network.

A Definition of a Layer 3 Network

The network portion of a Layer 3 address is a border chosen by an administrator to group end devices. This group is given an identifier or label, which is the network number.

Network Characteristics

A Layer 3 network address has the following characteristics:

- It defines a group of end devices or hosts.

- The address is hierarchical, which allows decisions to be made on groups of devices.

- The devices running the Layer 3 protocol do not forward broadcasts.

- The group of identified devices is given a label to identify the group. This is the network number.

- The group address combined with their unique membership number for that group identifies the end device. This is the host address.

- Although the identifier for the end device may not be unique to the organization, it will be unique to the group or network.

- If the addressing is carefully planned and the addressing scheme allows, groups may be grouped together (cities into states, states into countries, countries into continents, for example). IP subnets are collected into a single address, or addresses are collected into an autonomous system number.

An Analogy for Understanding the Concept of a Network

Similar administrative lines are drawn between one city and another, between one state and another, and even between countries. These lines, or borders, serve the same purpose as the network portion of a Layer 3 address—that is, they allow rules to be placed on a group of end systems (in the geographic analogy, humans).

Traffic can now be specifically directed. Routing tables serve as maps and road signs.

It is very important to remember to carefully plan the placement of these boundaries to ensure the geographic proximity of the end devices or hosts. After they're defined, boundaries seldom change. This is not to say that they *cannot* change, however. To remain with the analogy a moment longer, remember that, historically, boundaries between cities, states, and counties are redefined. With the emergence of VLANs in recent years, this is increasingly true of networks.

NOTE   In the previous analogy, access lists are the equivalent of immigration officers. Access lists are placed strategically in the hierarchical design, where one is challenged at the country level only and not at the local city level. And although *flooding* (excessive broadcasts) might occur at a local level (to continue the geographic analogy, think local-election brochures), these broadcasts can now be contained to ensure that buffers (mailboxes) do not overflow with unnecessary information from farther afield.

An IP Address

TCP/IP is unique in that the network portion of the address has not been allocated a fixed address space. The number of bits that the network portion may use depends on the number of networks that need to be identified. Although a governing body allocates an original address, the network portion of the address can be extended. To identify how many of the address bits have been extended into the network portion of the address, a subnet mask is used.

Why IP?

Where do the unique addresses come from? These addresses, known by various names, are assigned by a governing body that the Internet community has placed in charge of such address allocation. These organizations can then take this address and subdivide it to identify efficiently each network and host within their specific environment.

IP Network Terminology

Unfortunately, the terminology is vague, and the address provided by the Internet community may be referred to by any of the following terms:

- NIC address

- Class address

- Supernet address

- Internet address

- Network address

- Major address

- And others yet unheard

NOTE   For the purposes of this book, the term *Internet address* is used to refer to the unique address of an end device or host.

The next question is why IP is the dominant Layer 3 protocol and why the Internet is so powerful. I shall avoid deep philosophical, sociological, economical, or even political discussions because these will not show up as questions on the exam. It can safely be concluded that the power of the Internet emanates from the fact that every end device can have a *unique address* within the global network. (Therefore, my PC in San Francisco can find my brother's PC in Tokyo). The power of the Internet comes from its public domain characteristics, with everyone readily accessing the same technology.

Network and Host Addressing

A TCP/IP address has great flexibility in the ratio of networks to hosts that can be addressed. This flexibility is possible because the address space is 32 bits long, and the boundary between the network and the host can be placed almost anywhere within these 32 bits.

This is the area that makes many people cross-eyed. In fact, however, this is very easy to implement because it is simply a matter of counting—counting in binary, but counting nonetheless. In addition, many charts can help ease the pain of binary-to-decimal translation.

The Internet Mask

The Internet community originally identified three classes of organization. Companies or organizations were deemed to fall into one of three sizes or classes: small organizations into Class C, medium organizations into Class B, and large organizations into Class A. Actually, five classes of addresses are used in the Internet. The other two classes represent multicast (Class D) and experimental addresses (Class E). Routing protocols and videoconferencing increasingly use Class D addresses.

A router identifies the class of address by looking at the first few bits of the 32-bit address. When looking at the address in a decimal format, the number in the first octet reveals the class of address. This is known as the first octet rule.

Table 3-2 shows how the classes are broken up.

Table 3-2   *The Classes of Addresses*

Class of Address	First Octet	Number of Hosts That Address Could Represent on One Network
Class A address	001 to 126	Could represent 16.77 million hosts on one network
Class B address	128 to 191	Could represent 65,000 hosts on one network
Class C address	192 to 223	Could represent 254 hosts on one network
Class D address	224 to 239	Not relevant
Class E address	240 to 254	Not relevant

The Internet Authoritative Bodies

The Internet community defines an organization with a unique binary pattern or *Internet address*. The group within the Internet community responsible for allocating unique Internet addresses has changed over the years. Originally, a government-funded body, known as the *Internet Assigned Numbers Authority (IANA)*, assigned numbers and was until recently commercially administered by Networks Solutions of Herndon, Virginia. On November 25, 1998, the Internet Corporation for Assigned Names and Numbers (ICANN) was officially recognized. This global nonprofit corporations, currently managed by the U.S. government, was created to perform administrative functions for the Internet. By September 2000, ICANN will have gradually taken over responsibility for coordinating the assignment of protocol parameters, the management of the domain name and root server systems, and the allocation of IP address space.

The growth of the Internet has led to regional organizations for the allocation of IP addresses, and under ICANN, the IANA continues to distribute addresses to the regional Internet registries.

The most recent list of these follows.

Regional registries:

- Asia-Pacific Network Information Center (APNIC), www.apnic.net

- American Registry for Internet Numbers (ARIN), www.arin.net

- Reseau IP Europeens (RIPE), www.ripe.net

Domain registration:

- InterNIC, www.internic.net

When it has possession of the Internet address, an organization is responsible for determining where to place the boundary between network and host and is responsible for addressing the network. This is a complex task, which is an exercise in network design.

After the placement of the boundary between network and host is decided, this boundary is conveyed to Layer 3 devices in the network via the subnet mask.

An Example of Bit Allocation in a Network Address

If 10 bits are allocated to the network portion of the address, 22 bits are left to the host portion of the address. In binary, 10 bits can be used to represent 1024 distinct entities (each being assigned a unique bit pattern or address). The 22 bits left to identify hosts can be used to represent four million hosts (actually, 4,194,304) *on each network.*

The total number of devices that can be addressed is calculated by multiplying the number of hosts' addresses available on each network by the number of networks that can be addressed, as follows:

$$4,194,304 \times 1,024 = 4,294,967,296$$

However, the administrator does not have the whole 32 bits to use. The Internet community, which manages the addresses to ensure their uniqueness, allocates a unique bit pattern to each organization that requests a connection to the Internet. This bit pattern is then used to uniquely identify the organization within the Internet.

The Subnet Mask

The subnet mask is used to extract the network portion of the address. The network address is needed by the Layer 3 devices to make routing decisions, as explained in Chapter 4, "IP Routing Principles." Remember that in IP, the boundary between the network and the hosts is not rigid.

Where to Place the Network Boundary

The number of networks required relative to the number of hosts per network determines the placement of the network boundary. This determination defines the respective number of bits allocated to both the network and the host portion of the address. This information must be conveyed to the Layer 3 devices (routers), which make decisions based on their tables that state where the network boundary lies. The *subnet mask* is the method of conveying the network boundary to end systems and network devices.

The Logical AND

When an address is assigned to an interface, it is configured with the subnet mask. Although represented in a *dotted decimal* form, the router converts the address and mask into binary and performs a logical AND operation to find the network portion of the address. This is a very simple math problem.

To perform a *logical AND*, the IP address is written out in binary, with the subnet or Internet mask written beneath it in binary. Each binary digit of the address is then ANDed with the corresponding binary digit of the mask.

The AND Operation Rules

The rules of the AND operation are as follows:

- Positive and positive is positive.

- Negative and anything is negative.

This means that the following is true:

- 1 AND 1 is 1.

- 1 AND 0 is 0.

- 0 AND 1 is 0.

- 0 AND 0 is 0.

ANDing Example

Figure 3-2 illustrates the ANDing logic.

Figure 3-2   *AND Logic and the Subnetwork*

IP address	144.100.16.8	
IP subnet mask	255.255.255.0	
IP address in binary	10010000.01100100.00010000.	00001000
IP subnet mask in binary	11111111.11111111.11111111.	00000000

The result of the logical AND   10010000.01100100.00010000. | 00000000

Layer 3 can now make a decision on how to route the network number that has been revealed. The result is the removal of the host portion of the address, and the subnet address is left intact. Therefore, the host 144.100.16.8 is a member of the subnet 144.100.16.0, which is the result of the logical AND converted to decimal.

With this information, the router can now perform a search on the routing table to see whether it can route to the remote network. Therefore, the correct mask is essential to ensure that traffic can be directed through the overall network.

<table>
<tr><td>NOTE</td><td>Again, the terms used to describe the mask are numerous and often vague. This book uses the term subnet mask when referring to the mask used within an organization, and it uses Internet mask or prefix mask when referring to the address allocated by ARIN.</td></tr>
</table>

When determining the subnet mask, certain rules must be followed. RFC 950 outlines these rules.

Familiar Rules in IP Subnetting

Because originally the routing protocols could not send the mask with the routing update, the first set of rules about applying IP addresses were different than they are now. For the most part, these rules still hold true. With the advent of new technology, however, it is now possible to surmount some of the previous limitations set out in RFC 950.

The earlier (and perhaps familiar) rules included the following:

- The network bits do not need to be contiguous, although they are advised to be contiguous.

- The network bits must not be all zeros or ones.

- The decision on the number of bits allocated to the network is made once per NIC number.

Reasons for the Familiar Rules

Because the original routing protocols did not send the subnet mask with the routing update, each router that received a subnet entry had to make some assumptions. The router assumed that the mask in use for the received subnet was the same as the one configured on its system.

If the subnet received in the routing update was of a different NIC address (it was not configured on one of the router's interfaces), the router resolved the network address to the class address. The class of network was determined by the *first octet rule*.

New technology means that routing protocols can now send the subnet mask with the routing update. Therefore, the earlier rules regarding network classes do not necessarily apply.

The Newer Subnet Rules

Because the newer routing protocols can send the mask with the routing update, it is possible to have greater flexibility in the IP addressing design of your network. In particular, it is no longer necessary to adhere to the rule that the subnet mask may be created only once per NIC number. This is because the mask is held with the subnet in the routing table, which allows the distinction between the broadcast address and the subnet address that has been defined. This requires variable-length subnet masks (VLSM).

Likewise, it is no longer necessary for either the NIC or the individual organization to conform to the rules of classful routing.

Classful routing occurs when the Layer 3 device observes the NIC class address boundaries of A, B, C, D, and E. It does this by using the first octet rule. This rule uses the first few bits of the address to identify the class of address.

This is shown in Table 3-3.

Table 3-3   *The First Octet Rule*

Bit Pattern	Class of Address	First Octet Range
0	A	0 to 127
10	B	128 to 191
110	C	191 to 223
1110	D	224 to 239
1111	E	240 to 255

A classful routing protocol does not transmit any information about the prefix length. It uses the first octet rule to determine the class address, and this is why the protocol cannot support VLSM. Therefore, if the protocol is not connected to a NIC number, it does not have a subnet mask, and it summarizes the address at the NIC boundary by using the first octet rule. Examples of classful routing protocols are Routing Information Protocol (RIP) and Interior Gateway Routing Protocol (IGRP).

This restriction also prevented the summarization of class addresses within the Internet. However, if the routing protocol supports classless routing, there is no reason why NIC addresses cannot be summarized in the same way as subnets. As long as the address is allocated with a prefix mask to identify the network portion of the address, the NIC can hand out an address without regard for the bit boundary at Class A, B, or C.

The address must be allocated with a prefix mask to identify the network portion of the address. RFC 1812 restricts the flexibility of the addressing slightly, however, by requiring contiguous bits be used in the mask.

It is also possible to overcome some of the rules regarding the allocation of network and host bits, which is explained later in the chapter.

IP Addressing Summary

Remember these following important points regarding IP addressing:

- The IP address is 32 bits long.

- The network/host boundary can be anywhere in the 32 bits.

- The Internet allocates a unique bit pattern. These bits are the first bits on the far left and are not available for the administrator to use for networks because they identify your organization to the Internet.

- The Internet authority ARIN (in the United States) will provide the left portion of the address to the organization to use for addressing within a network. These bits are zeroed.

- The network mask is the identification of the bits allocated to the network, defined on all participating routers.

Prefix Routing/CIDR

Prefix routing, commonly known as classless interdomain routing (CIDR), is possible because of the newer routing protocols sending the subnet mask with the routing updates.

A Definition of Prefix Routing/CIDR

Prefix routing is just the means by which the Internet identifies the portion of the 32-bit TCP/IP address that uniquely identifies the organization. In effect, this means that the Internet can allocate a group of class networks, which are represented by a single address. This allows for prefix routing and summarization within the routing tables of the Internet. Prefix masks represent a group of TCP/IP network addresses using the method of address or subnet masks.

This aggregation of Internet addresses defies the old structure of Class A, B, C addressing, or classful addressing. The aggregation of Internet addresses, therefore, is classless and deals with connectivity between organizations through the Internet, referred to as *interdomain routing*. This technology is called *classless interdomain routing (CIDR)*. Table 3-4 shows the RFCs that outline the use of CIDR in an IP network.

Table 3-4　　*RFCs on CIDR*

RFC Number	Description
1517	Applicability statement for the implementation of CIDR
1518	An architecture for IP address allocation with CIDR
1519	CIDR: an address assignment and aggregation strategy
1520	Exchanging routing information across provider boundaries in a CIDR environment

Problems with IP Addressing and the Internet

The Internet community found that small companies that wanted to connect to the Internet with 50 hosts needed a Class C address, although a Class C designation wasted 204 addresses.

Conversely, if an organization has more than 255 hosts but fewer than 65,000 hosts, the Internet must either waste a large number of addresses by allocating a Class B address or provide multiple Class C addresses. RFC 1466 discusses the low percentage of allocated addresses in use.

The Class A, B, C address structure just does not have enough granularity for today's Internet. Because the Internet has grown in popularity, this has become a pressing problem. In addition, the number of entries in the routing tables of the Internet was reaching capacity, although only a small percentage of the addresses allocated were being utilized. The Internet started to reclaim unused addresses, but this was obviously a short-term solution. The implementation of CIDR with prefix routing is solving both problems.

CIDR as a Solution

An organization requiring multiple Class C addresses is allocated consecutive Class C addresses but issues only one address for the Internet routing entry (representing the multiple addresses). This is achieved by pulling the network mask to the left.

The shorter the prefix, the more generally the network is defined; the longer the prefix, the more specific the identification is. Table 3-5 visually demonstrates the use of the prefix. The Internet IP addressing group ARIN, at www.arin.net, typically gives blocks of consecutive addresses to an Internet service provider (ISP) to allocate addresses to organizations that want to connect to the Internet. This reduces the routing tables even further, by placing some of the address management responsibilities on the ISP.

Table 3-5   *Table to Illustrate the Use of Prefix Masks*

Prefix	Mask	New Address Space
/27	255.255.255.224	12 percent of Class C
		30 hosts
/26	255.255.255.192	24 percent of Class C
		62 hosts
/25	255.255.255.128	50 percent of Class C
		126 hosts
/23	255.255.254.0	2 Class Cs
		510 hosts

continues

Table 3-5 *Table to Illustrate the Use of Prefix Masks (Continued)*

Prefix	Mask	New Address Space
/22	255.255.252.0	4 Class Cs
		1022 hosts
/21	255.255.248.0	8 Class Cs
		2046 hosts
/20	255.255.240.0	16 Class Cs
		4094 hosts

Summary of CIDR

In summary, CIDR solves the following problems:

- Address exhaustion—the Internet was just running out of addresses.

- The network resources required to manage huge routing tables were becoming untenable.

WARNING Connecting to an ISP requires some consideration because the addresses used in your organization were provided by the ISP. If you change your ISP, that address space will have to be relinquished back to the ISP. This requires readdressing of the network or some software application to translate the addresses. The Network Address Translation (NAT) product offered by Cisco is one such application, though there are many different solutions on the market.

An Example of the Use of CIDR

It is easy to see how this works when the address and the mask are written in binary, as the router processes them. The Internet community has allocated a group of Class C addresses, although they are presented as a single network. Table 3-6 shows an example of an IP address in both decimal and binary format.

Table 3-6 *An IP Address and Mask Shown in Binary*

Description	Octet 1	Octet 2	Octet 3	Octet 4
NIC address in decimal	200	100	48	0
NIC address in binary	11001000	01100100	00110000	00000000
Prefix as a subnet mask in decimal	255	255	248	0
Prefix as a subnet mask in binary	11111111	11111111	11111000	00000000

If it were a standard Class C address, the mask would be 255.255.255.0. By making the mask 255.255.248.0, the last three bits of the third octet essentially give the organization eight Class C networks.

An Example of CIDR in Use in the Case Study

Imagine that the company discussed in the case study at the beginning of the chapter, Mental Merge, has applied for a Class B address from the Internet authorities. To everyone's surprise, Mental Merge has been awarded seven Class C networks. The company owners are delighted because they were expecting only one Class C address.

Figure 3-3 shows the addresses awarded to Mental Merge, the use of CIDR addresses, and how prefix routing works at the binary level.

Figure 3-3   *Prefix Routing and the Use of CIDR*

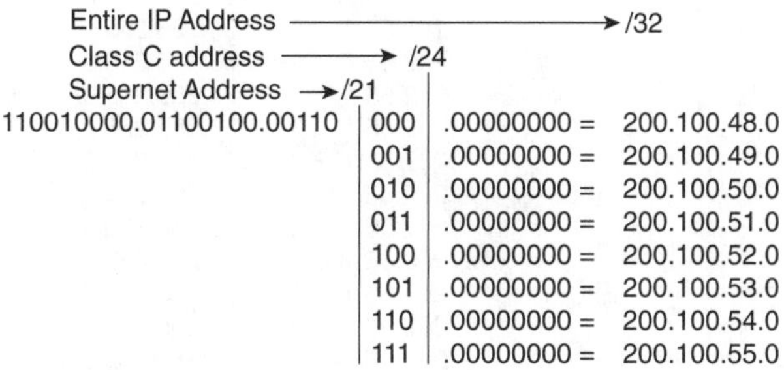

```
Entire IP Address ─────────────────────► /32
Class C address ──────────► /24
Supernet Address ──►/21
110010000.01100100.00110 │ 000 │ .00000000 =   200.100.48.0
                         │ 001 │ .00000000 =   200.100.49.0
                         │ 010 │ .00000000 =   200.100.50.0
                         │ 011 │ .00000000 =   200.100.51.0
                         │ 100 │ .00000000 =   200.100.52.0
                         │ 101 │ .00000000 =   200.100.53.0
                         │ 110 │ .00000000 =   200.100.54.0
                         │ 111 │ .00000000 =   200.100.55.0
```

Although eight Class C addresses are provided to the organization, they are identified to the Internet as one address: 200.100.48.0, with a prefix mask of /21, which is the subnet mask of 255.255.248.0.

The organization does not have to use the addresses as Class C addresses. In accordance with the original rules, the organization may use the right-most zeroed bits however they deem appropriate.

Advantages of Prefix Routing/CIDR

CIDR offers several advantages, including the reduction of the size of the routing table.

Prefix routing is used to reduce the size of Internet routing tables. As explained in the preceding example, the Internet gave away the equivalent of eight Class C networks, but just one network entry appeared in the Internet's routing table. In an environment that has more than 54,000 entries in the routing table—at the time of this writing, the size of the routing table in many ISPs has peaked at 54,000 entries—this is a significant reduction in the size of the routing table (which is expressed in terms of CPU utilization, memory, and bandwidth congestion).

In addition to the advantages of the original rules of TCP/IP addressing and subnet design, there is the flexibility granted to the Internet with prefix routing. The Internet no longer needs to abide by the rules of Classes A, B, and C. As shown, with some thought, many NIC networks may be presented as one network, thus reducing the network overhead. It could be said that the Internet has summarized many networks into one network. Figure 3-4 shows the effect of using prefix routing.

Figure 3-4   *Summarization of NIC Networks Using Prefix Routing*

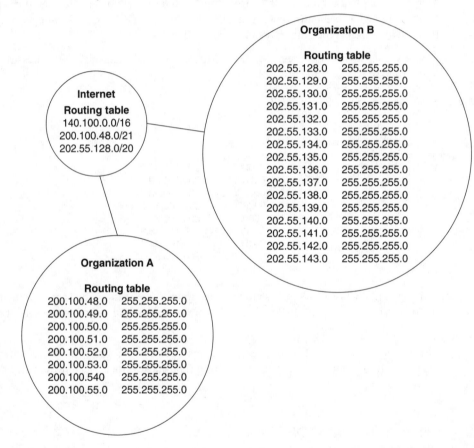

Prefix routing/CIDR or summarization achieves the same benefits in terms of the following:

* Reduction in the size of the routing table means

* Less overhead in terms of network traffic, CPU, and memory

* Greater flexibility in addressing the networks

An organization can use summarization for the same reason as the Internet uses it with prefix routing: to reduce network overhead. The length of the prefix in this case depends on the number of bits needed rather than the Class A, B, and C structure.

NOTE   The bit pattern provided by the Internet cannot be altered. The bits to the right of the unique address given by the Internet are at the disposal of the organization.

To utilize the power of summarization within an organization, a sophisticated routing protocol that sends the mask with the routing updates is required. The capability to move the network/host boundary is called VLSM.

Variable-Length Subnet Masks

Variable-length subnet mask (VLSM) is used within an organization instead of CIDR, which is used within the Internet. VLSMs enable you to allocate required host bits on a granular basis.

Because organizations are rarely uniform in the distribution of hosts, it is much more efficient to provide only those hosts bits to address the number of hosts on a particular network.

An Example of VLSM

Consider that Mental Merge has been given a Class B address. The company has grown and now has some satellite offices that connect via point-to-point serial lines. The remote offices have eight workstations, three printers, and a router connecting them to the outside world. The main site has a building with ten floors, and each floor has approximately 25 workstations and four printers. A server farm in the basement has three servers and two routers. In this scenario, it is impossible to create a mask that serves all these environments. If you use an older routing protocol, you will waste a considerable amount of the available address space.

VLSM requires a routing protocol that supports the sending of the subnet mask.

Routing Protocols That Support VLSM

The following routing protocols support VLSM:

- RIPv2
- OSPF
- IS-IS
- EIGRP
- BGP-4

NOTE   Static routes could be said to use VLSM. They are often used to redistribute between routing protocols sharing a NIC number when one routing protocol supports VLSM and the other does not. In these instances, the static route will define one summarized route for the non-VLSM routing protocol. This technique is also used when redistributing into BGP-4.

The following routing protocols do *not* support VLSM:

- RIPv1
- IGRP
- EGP

Rules for VLSM

The rules for variably subnetting an IP address are remarkably straightforward. The key is to remember that a hierarchical design in the addressing scheme is the goal. The physical network design also must reflect this logical hierarchy (as discussed in Chapter 2, "Managing Scalable Network Growth"). After the physical design is mapped, the logical structure can be placed on top of it.

The following rules apply when subnetting:

- A subnet can be used to address hosts, or it can be used for further subnetting.
- Within the allocation of subsequent subnets, the rule of not using all zeros or ones does not apply.
- The routing protocol must carry the subnet mask in its updates.
- Multiple IP addresses intended to be summarized must have the same high-order bits.
- Routing decisions are made on the entire address, and the router goes from more specific to more general when making routing decisions.

The Advantages of Using VLSM

The two main reasons for using VLSM are as follows:

- To make efficient use of the available addressing
- To enforce a good hierarchical design, allowing summarization and documentation

Figure 3-5 illustrates the use of VLSM for summarization and documentation.

Figure 3-5   *VLSM Used to Support the Hierarchical Design*

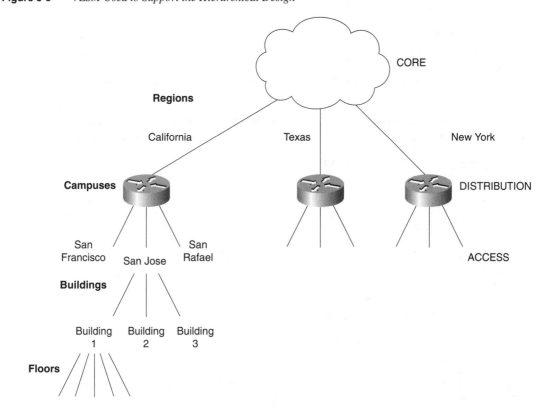

Case Study: Addressing the Network

For a complicated example, use a Class B address and create an addressing scheme for Mental Merge.

If the Internet assigns the address 140.100.0.0, how might you address the network shown in the diagram?

The first task is to determine the number of regions, campuses, buildings, floors, and hosts on each floor. You also need to consider any anticipated growth or change in the network.

For this example, the network is comprised of the following:

- Four regions exist, but the company has plans to expand into other areas. Any expansion will probably not exceed eight states (adequate to cover the country).

- Within each region/state, there are no more than three campuses.

- Within each campus, there are no more than four buildings. This number might increase, however.

- No building has more than three floors.

- No floor has more than 30 hosts.

With this topology and growth detailed, it is possible to start allocating bits of the network address.

Taking the address 140.100.0.0 and writing out the last 16 bits, you can easily assign them to the different addressing tasks at hand. Figure 3-6 covers assigning IP addressing bits for VLSM.

Figure 3-6   *Assigning IP Addressing Bits for VLSM*

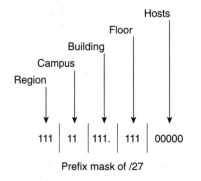

Consideration must be given to the subnetting rules (RFC 950, "Internet Standard Subnetting Procedure," and RFC 1878, "Variable-Length Subnet Table For IPv4") that state that there must not be all zeros or all ones in the following:

- The NIC portion of the address

- The subnet portion of the address

- The host portion of the address

The algorithm for calculating the number of networks or hosts available is $2^n - 2$ (where *n* is the number of bits).

This rule has become complicated recently regarding the subnet portion of the address. The number of subnets is still calculated by the 2n formula, where *n* is the number of bits by which the subnet mask was extended. However, it is possible to use the all-zero address for the subnet. This makes the formula 2n – 1.

WARNING	Although Cisco provides the utility of **subnet zero**, this command should be used only with full understanding of the network devices and the knowledge that there is no device that uses the zero broadcast. Even today, some systems, such as Sun Solaris 4.x, have problems using subnet zero even with OSPF.

The command to enable the use of the zero subnet became the default configuration in version 12.0 of the Cisco IOS.

Although the 2n – 2 rule is still true for the NIC portion of the address, it is not of concern. This is because the NIC portion of the address is out of your control because it was defined by the Internet.

However, attention must still be given to the host portion of the address. The host portion of the address must conform to the subnet rule as defined; otherwise, it is not possible for the router to distinguish between hosts and broadcast addresses. The host cannot use an IP address of all zeros in the subnet address or all ones in the subnet broadcast address. The all-zeros address is used to show the subnet delimiter.

Bit Allocation, the Subnet Rule, and VLSM

In truth, the subnet does have to conform to the rule as described. With VLSM, however, it is often forgotten that the entire subnet area is considered one subnet. Therefore, the rule must be obeyed once, not on each instance of variable subnetting.

In the preceding example, you would choose to obey the rule either in the bits allocated to the region, campus, or building, but not in each hierarchical layer. It would make most sense to adhere to the rule using the least-significant bits. In this case, three bits have been allocated to the access layer, enabling you to identify eight floors. You have no more than three floors to address in any building, however. Obeying the rule on this layer makes sense because you reduce the floors that may be addressed to six, which is still twice as many as required.

Allocating VLSM Addresses

Applying the addressing scheme designed in the preceding example is very simple after the design has been worked out.

Taking the region of California as the example to address, you will now address the entire region.

Figure 3-7 shows the bit allocation that was determined.

Figure 3-7   *Bit Allocation*

Region:
   California: 001
Campus:
   San Francisco: 01
   San Jose: 10
   San Rafael: 11
Buildings:
   Building 1: 001
   Building 2: 010
   Building 3: 011
   Building 4: 100
Floor:
   Floor 1: 001
   Floor 2: 010
   Floor 3: 011
   Floor 4: 100
   Floor 5: 101
Hosts:
   1-30

NOTE   Remember that you will conform to the rule of reserving the broadcast addresses in the access layer of the network.

NOTE   The buildings have the same bit pattern for each campus. Remember, however, that this bit pattern is unique within the whole address space because the pattern for the campus is unique and the address must be seen in its entirety.

The third host, on the fourth floor of the second building in San Jose, California, will be given the address shown in Figure 3-8.

The address in Figure 3-8 is represented as 140.100.50.131 in dotted decimal, with a mask of 255.255.255.224.

Worked this way, from the physical topology up, it is very straightforward. Many people are given the address 140.100.50.131 and work backward, which is very confusing. To avoid confusion, it is extremely helpful to document the addressing scheme within the organization's network (to make management of the network easier and to help maintain the administrator's sanity).

Figure 3-8   *Example of How to Apply VLSM*

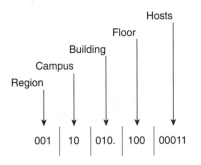

TIP   This use of VLSM shows clearly that when allocating addresses in IP, it is necessary to reduce the address to binary and to disregard the octet boundary. Reducing the address to binary and disregarding the octet boundary creates just a continuous set of bits to be applied as appropriate to address the network.

Summarization

Having assigned IP addressing based on a hierarchical design, you can now consider the full weight of the advantages. The primary advantage is the reduction in network traffic and the size of the routing table.

Summarization allows the representation of a series of networks in a single summary address.

The reasons that the Internet implemented CIDR are equally pertinent in a single organization. VLSM and CIDR use the same principles, with VLSM just being an extension of CIDR at the organizational level.

At the top of the hierarchical design, the subnets in the routing table are more generalized. The subnet masks are shorter because they have aggregated the subnets lower in the network hierarchy. These summarized networks are often referred to as *supernets*, particularly when seen in the Internet as an aggregation of class addresses. They are also known as *aggregated routes*. Figure 3-9 shows the physical network design for the case study discussed earlier. Figure 3-10 shows the allocation of addresses using VLSM to support summarization for this network design.

Figure 3-9 *The Application of Summarized Routes on a Hierarchically Designed Network*

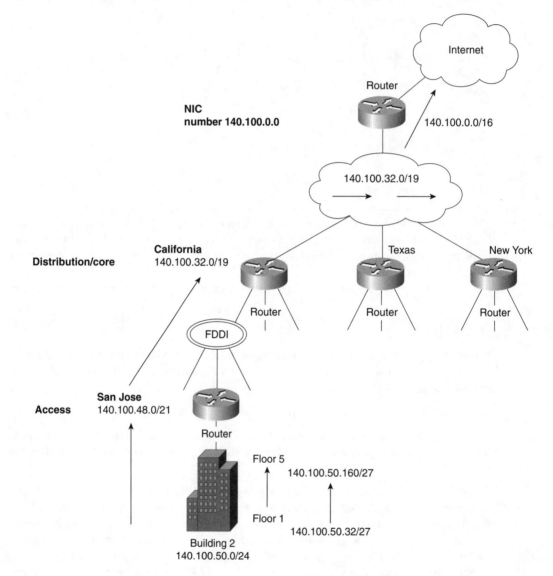

Figure 3-10   *The Binary Calculation of the Hierarchical Addressing for the Organization*

NIC number
140.100.0.0

Region 000   140.100.0.0/19
       001   140.100.32.0/19
       010   140.100.84.0/19
       011   140.100.96.0/19
       100   140.100.126/19
       101   140.100.160.0/19
       110   140.100.182.0/19
       111   140.100.224.0/19

Campus
001/00   140.100.32.0/21
    01   140.100.40.0/21
    10   140.100.48.0/21
    11   140.100.66.0/21

Building
001/10/000   140.100.48.0/24
       001   140.100.49.0/24
       010   140.100.50.0/24
       011   140.100.51.0/24
       100   140.100.52.0/24
       101   140.100.53.0/24
       110   140.100.54.0/24
       111   140.100.55.0/24

Floor
001/10/010./000   140.100.50.32/24
          001   140.100.50.64/24
          010   140.100.50.96/24
          011   140.100.50.128/24
          100   140.100.50.160/24
          101   140.100.50.192/24
          110

Hosts
001/10/010/100/00000   140.100.50.128
            00001   140.100.50.129
            00010   140.100.50.130
            00011   140.100.50.131
            00100   140.100.50.132
            00101   140.100.50.133
            00110   140.100.50.134
            00111   140.100.50.135
            01000   140.100.50.136
            01001   140.100.50.137
            01010   140.100.50.138
            01011   140.100.50.139
            01100   140.100.50.140
            01101   140.100.50.141
            01110   140.100.50.142
            01111   140.100.50.143
            10000   140.100.50.144
            10001   140.100.50.145
            10010   140.100.50.146
            10011   140.100.50.147
            10100   140.100.50.148
            10101   140.100.50.149
            10110   140.100.50.150
            10111   140.100.50.151
            11000   140.100.50.152
            11001   140.100.50.153
            11010   140.100.50.154
            11011   140.100.50.155
            11100   140.100.50.156
            11101   140.100.50.157

The Advantages of Summarization

The capability to summarize multiple subnets within a few subnets has the advantages discussed in the next few sections.

Reducing the Size of the Routing Table

In reducing the size of the routing table, the updates are smaller, demanding less bandwidth from the network. A smaller routing table also requires less memory in the router or CPU in the routing process itself because the lookup is quicker and more efficient.

Simplification

The recalculation of the network is also simplified by maintaining small routing tables.

Hiding Network Changes

If the routing table contains a summary of the networks beneath it, any changes in the network at these levels are not seen. This is both a good thing and a bad thing. If the network in the earlier example—140.100.50.128/27, the subnet on the fourth floor of the second building in San Jose, California—were to go down, the router at the core would be oblivious to the LAN problem. This is beneficial because there are no additional updates or recalculation.

The disadvantage is that any traffic destined for that subnet is sent on the assumption that it exists. To be more accurate, the core router sees the inbound IP packet destined for 140.100.50.131 and, instead of applying the /27 mask, uses the mask that it has configured. It employs the /19 mask that sees the subnet 140.100.32.0/19, although in reality the destination subnet is 140.100.50.128/27. If the subnet 140.100.50.128 is no longer available, all traffic is still forwarded to the subnet until it reaches a router that holds the same mask as the IP packet and therefore is aware that it is no longer available. An ICMP message that the network is unreachable is generated to the transmitting host. The host may stop transmitting after hearing that the network is down.

Although unnecessary traffic will traverse the network for a while, it is a minor inconvenience compared to the routing update demands on the network and the CPU utilization on the routers in large networks.

Network Growth

Summarization allows networks to grow because the network overhead can scale.

Other Solutions to Address Exhaustion

The use of the Cisco feature IP unnumbered is useful on the point-to-point serial lines because it saves the use of a subnet.

Cisco's use of secondary addressing is useful because it provides two subnets to a physical interface—and, therefore, more available host bits. This does not save address space, but it is a solution for routing protocols that do not support VLSM. Unfortunately, there are some compatibility issues with other TCP/IP stacks—for example, not all OSPF routing protocols will see the second subnet.

Configuring Summarization

In the newer routing protocols, summarization must be manually configured; this manual configuration lends greatly to its subtlety and strength. Each routing protocol deals with summarization in a slightly different way, and how summarization works or is configured depends on the routing protocol used. This is discussed in detail in Chapter 4.

NOTE   Although Border Gateway Protocol (BGP) and Enhanced IGRP (EIGRP) perform automatic summarization, the summarization is done at the NIC boundary, using the first octet rule. This is the same as with older routing protocols such as RIP.

Automatic Summarization

All routing protocols employ some level of summarization. The older protocols, such as RIP and IGRP, automatically summarize at the NIC or natural class boundary. They have no choice because the subnet mask is not sent in the routing updates. When a routing update is received, the router looks to see whether it has an interface in the same class network. If it has one, it applies the mask configured on the interface to the incoming routing update. With no interface configured in the same NIC network, there is insufficient information and the routing protocol uses the natural mask for the routing update. The first few bits in the address are used to determine to which class of address it belongs, and then the appropriate mask is applied. This is known as the first octet rule.

Manual Summarization

Both EIGRP and Open Shortest Path First (OSPF) are more sophisticated: They send the subnet mask along with the routing update. This feature allows the use of VLSM and summarization. When the routing update is received, it assigns the mask to the particular subnet. When the routing process performs a lookup, it searches the entire database and acts on the longest match, which is important because it allows the following:

- The granularity of the hierarchical design
- Summarization
- Discontiguous networks

Discontiguous Networks

A *discontiguous network* refers to a network in which a different NIC number separates two instances of the same NIC number. This can happen either through intentional design or through a break in the network topology. If the network is not using a routing protocol that supports VLSM, this creates a problem because the router does know where to send the traffic. Without a subnet mask, it resolves the address down to the NIC number, which appears as if there is a duplicate address. The same NIC number appears twice, but in different locations. In most cases, the router will load balance between the two paths if they are of equal cost. The symptoms that the network will see are those of intermittent connectivity.

Figure 3-11 shows an instance of a discontiguous network.

Figure 3-11 *Discontiguous Networks*

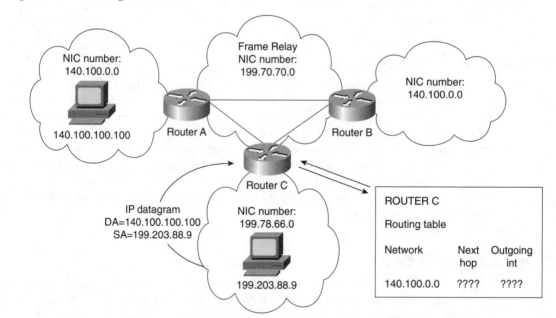

Considerations for Summarization with Discontiguous Networks

If there are discontiguous networks in the organization, it is important that summarization is turned off or not configured. Summarization may not provide enough information to the routing table on the other side of the intervening NIC number to be capable of appropriately routing to the destination subnets. This is especially true of EIGRP, which automatically summarizes at the NIC boundary, which would be disastrous in this situation.

In OSPF and EIGRP, manual configuration is required for any sophistication in the network design. It is not always possible to achieve summarization because this depends entirely on the addressing scheme that has been deployed. However, because EIGRP can perform summarization at the interface level, it is possible to select interfaces that do not feed discontiguous networks for summarization. This capability to summarize selectively is very powerful.

The key to whether summarization is configurable is determined by whether there are common high-order bits in the addresses.

Case Study

In the case study used earlier, the design immediately allows for summarization, as shown in the now familiar layout in Figure 3-8.

In this design, every campus within the same region will share the same high-order bits (those to the left). In California, every campus, building, floor, and host will share the bits 001. In this manner, every building in the San Jose campus will share the high-order bits of 00110. Therefore, it is very simple to configure summarization.

This is not necessarily the case if the addressing structure is already in place. Some analysis of the addressing scheme is required to decide whether summarization can be configured.

Alternatives to Summarization

If summarization is deemed impossible, you have the following two options:

- Not to summarize and understand the scaling limitations that have now been set on the network.

- To readdress the network. This task is not to be underestimated, although the advantages may well make it worthwhile.

VLSM also enables you to allocate the required bits for addressing a particular network.

Optimizing the IP Address Space

Particularly in the use of WANs, where there is a predominance of point-to-point connections, allocating an entire subnet is very wasteful. VLSM allows refinement of the address space to exactly that which is needed and no more.

As demonstrated, dealing with the use of VLSM to support the hierarchical design requires the consideration of the entire network topology. When using VLSM to optimize the IP address space, the network addressing can become extremely confused if it is not clearly managed and documented.

In the preceding example, no consideration was given to the connections between the regions, campuses, and buildings—all of which could be point-to-point lines.

Now it is important to consider the last part of the network addressing, which will illustrate the use of VLSM for IP address optimization.

Assigning IP VLSM Subnets for WAN Connections

One common approach is to allocate a subnet that has not been assigned to hosts, and to variably subnet it for use with connectivity between rather than within areas.

In this case study, it is sensible to take a subnet from the bits allocated to the buildings. Because there are enough bits allocated to address eight buildings, you have twice as many subnets as required. Even with the possibility of growth, one subnet would not be missed. Because the building bits come after the bits assigned to the campus, a choice must be made as to which campus will be selected for the honor of contributing a subnet of WAN addressing. This is an arbitrary decision that needs to be documented. If necessary, a building subnet can be commandeered from each campus.

If possible, the subnet used should have nothing to do with any of the existing subnets. That is, there is a consistency in numbering that identifies the WAN links, so in a troubleshooting environment, you can immediately see that a WAN link is causing the trouble and will not confuse the subnet (VLSM) with an existing segment.

In this example, if you use the bit pattern 000 as the network address for the building section; in addition for the campus and the region, the third octet would result in a 0. The network address for all interconnectivity would be 140.100.0. . .. The last octet would be available for further subnetting with VLSM.

The subnet chosen for the WAN connections will be subnetted further using 30 bits of subnetting. This allows for only two connections and is therefore a very efficient mask for point-to-point links.

Remember that the rule for not using all zeros or all ones is based on the entire subnet, not on the octet boundary. Figure 3-12 shows assigning IP VLSM subnets for WAN connections.

Figure 3-12 *Assigning IP VLSM Subnets for WAN Connections*

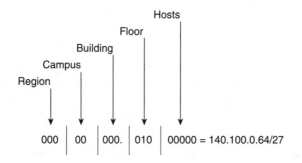

The following is an example of how the addressing might be broken down.

Between the buildings in California:

- 140.100.0.64/27.

- A 27-bit mask allows for 30 end-system addresses. This is in the expectation that the buildings are connected via FDDI or Fast Ethernet.

- The range of hosts is 140.100.0.65 to 140.100.0.94.

- The broadcast address is 140.100.0.95.

Between the buildings and the campuses in California:

- 140.100.0.32/30

- 140.100.0.20/30

- 140.100.0.24/30

- 140.100.0.28/30

This allows for point-to-point addresses using Frame Relay.

Between the campuses and the regions:

- 140.100.0.48/30

- 140.100.0.4/30

- 140.100.0.12/30

This allows for point-to-point addresses, which may also be using Frame Relay.

Between the regions:

- 140.100.0.96/30

- 140.100.0.16/30

- 140.100.0.8/30

This allows for point-to-point addresses, which may also be using Frame Relay or dedicated serial leased lines.

WARNING   In the instance of a subnet being used to address WAN connections, it may not be possible to summarize these networks.

The rules and conditions for creating a valid and appropriate IP addressing scheme for the network are complicated. Among other things, the addressing scheme must allow for growth, to scale over time. What works today may not be flexible for next year's business requirements. You cannot build a network that will accommodate every change and addition to its environment. With careful design, however, it may be possible to anticipate some of these changes and to ensure a network with enough flexibility to survive the changes.

Designing IP Networks

The topics that make up the rest of this chapter are not in the Building Scalable Cisco Networks (BSCN) course, upon which the Routing exam is partially based. Therefore, these topics might not be on the exam, but they have been included in this chapter because they place the topic of IP addressing into a wider context. These subjects should be studied not with the intention of answering questions on the exam, but rather as information that extends the subject matter. There will be no questions in the end of the chapter quiz, nor references to this material in the scenarios.

This is important both for understanding the subject. It is also crucial for use within the context of the Cisco certification.

Much of the design principles for an IP network have been dealt with in a practical manner in the preceding section. This section, therefore, examines the design criteria from a high-level perspective.

Certain questions should be asked before applying IP addresses to end devices:

- How many subnets exist currently on your network?

- How many hosts exist on each network?

- If the number of hosts varies on each subnet, how many hosts are there on the largest subnet and the smallest subnet? If there is an average number, this is also of interest.

- Where are these subnets in relation to the topology map of the network?

- In the next 3 to 12 months, how many more hosts will exist on each network?

- In the next 3 to 12 months, how many more networks will exist?

- How many subnets are available?

- If the network is short of address space, what must be done to make some available?

- Do you have a client/server environment?

- If so, where are the local servers located? On the same segment as the clients? On another segment and subnet?

- How much traffic is sent to the local servers?

- What is the nature of the traffic: high in volume, large packet size, sensitive to delay, bursty?

- Is access required from other subnets?

- If DHCP is used, where are the servers located?

- Are there any global resources that need to be accessed by everyone?

- If there are global resources on this subnet, is access required from other subnets?

- Do any security issues need to be considered?

- Are the clients mobile? Do they move around the campuses and require access from any location?

- Does the company require Internet access?

- If Internet access is required, for whom? Does this include e-mail, web browsing, remote access, or a web page for customers?

- Does your company have a NIC address from the Internet? If not, is it proposing to apply for one, or will it be connecting via an ISP?

- Is TCP/IP the only protocol on the network? If not, what are the other protocols, and is there any intention to tunnel these protocols through the WAN or core of the network using TCP/IP?

Not all of these questions may be pertinent to any particular organization. If this checklist is answered, however, the administrator or network design engineer will have a great deal of information with which to design the network. Although the questionnaire spans slightly more than the limited requirements for assigning IP addresses, the answers to these questions are crucial for the design of an IP network and in determining the traffic flow within the organization.

These questions should be considered against the topology map of the network. Without the support of the physical hierarchical design, it will not be possible to summarize the network traffic.

After the capacity of the network is understood, it is possible to design the addressing scheme. This will follow the same principles shown in the section "Allocating VLSM Addresses," earlier in this chapter.

Certain guidelines or key points should be used in the VLSM design of the network. The following section identifies these guidelines.

Keys Points to Remember When Designing an IP Network

The following list of items should be addressed when preparing the IP addressing plan for your network:

- Identifying how many hosts and subnets will be required in the future requires communication with other departments in terms of the growth of personnel as well as the budget for network growth. Without the standard-issue crystal ball, a wider view must be taken at a high level to answer these questions, with the answers coming from a range of sources, including the senior management and executive team of the organization.

- The design of the IP network must take into consideration the network equipment and whether consideration should be given to different vendor equipment. Interoperability may well be an issue, particularly with some of the features offered by each product.

- For route aggregation (summarization) to occur, the address assignments must have topological significance.

- When using VLSM, the routing protocol must send the extended prefix (subnet mask) with the routing update.

- When using VLSM, the routing protocol must do a routing table lookup based on the longest match.

- Make certain that enough bits have been allowed for at each level of the hierarchical design to address all devices at that layer. Also be sure that growth of the network at each level has been anticipated. What address space is to be used (Class A, B, C, private, registered), and will it scale with the organization?

TIP   Cisco offers many enhancements in its IOS. Most of these enhancements are interoperable. If they are not, they provide solutions for connecting to industry standards (which, of course, are fully supported by Cisco). Check with the Cisco web page (www.cisco.com) to review the latest features and any connectivity issues.

In many cases, not enough consideration is given to IP address design with regard to the routing process, making a decision based on the longest address match. This is essential to the design of a VLSM network.

Consider a network as described in the preceding section, "Assigning IP VLSM Subnets for WAN Connections," using the Class B NIC address 140.100.0.0.

The routing table has the following among its entries:

- 140.100.0.0/16
- 140.100.1.0/20
- 140.100.1.192/26

A packet comes into the router destined for the end host 140.100.1.209. The router will forward to the network 140.100.1.192 because the bit pattern matches the longest bit mask provided. The other routes are also valid, however, so the router has made a policy decision that it will always take the longest match.

This decision is based on the design assumption that has been made by the router that the longest match is directly connected to the router or that the network is out of the identified interface. If the end host 140.100.1.209 actually resides on network 140.100.1.208/29, this network must be accessible through the interface that has learned of the subnet 140.100.1.192. Summarization will have been configured because 140.100.1.192 is an aggregate of various networks, including the network 140.100.1.208.

If the network 140.100.1.208 resides out of the interface that has learned about 140.100.1.0, then no traffic will ever reach this subnet 140.100.1.208 because it will always forward based on the longest match in the routing table. The only solution is to turn off summarization and to list every subnet with the corresponding mask. If summarization is turned off, the subnet 140.100.1.208 will not be summarized into the network 140.100.1.0. It will consequently be the longest match in the routing table, and traffic will be sent to the destination network 140.100.1.208. Figure 3-13 shows an example of route summarization.

Up to this point, this discussion has dealt with organizations that are designing an IP network for the first time. In reality, this is rarely the case unless a decision has been made to readdress the entire network.

Often the network has been up and running for some years. If this is the case, the usual task is to use some of the newer technologies now available to reduce and manage network traffic so that the network can grow without pain.

The simplest solution is to implement a more sophisticated routing protocol. Ideally a routing protocol that supports VLSM will be chosen and summarization will be enabled. However, it may not be possible to use the summarization feature. As explained earlier, this capability is determined in part by how well the addressing scheme mirrors and is supported by the physical topology.

Figure 3-13   *Route Summarization and VLSM*

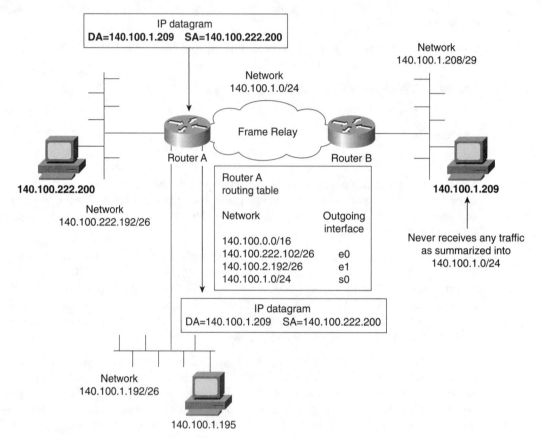

The following guidelines can be used to determine whether summarization may be configured within a particular network:

- Does the network addressing reflect the physical topology of the network?

- Is the physical and logical topology of the network hierarchical?

- Given the network addressing scheme, do the addresses to be summarized share the same high-order bits?

- If the subnet addresses are clearly set on a single binary border, this suggests a prefix mask of /21 or 255.255.248.0. Because the subnets are multiples of 8, they may be summarized by a higher subnet value that is divisible by 8, such as 140.100.64.0. The following subnets provide an example:

  — 140.100.72.0

— 140.100.80.0

— 140.100.88.0

— 140.100.96.0

— 140.100.104.0

— 140.100.112.0

- The nature of the traffic flow within the network should reflect the hierarchical logical and physical design.

- The routing protocol used must support VLSM.

Any design of a network requires very careful analysis of the current network and a clear understanding of the organization's plans. Unfortunately, it is not always possible to determine the nature or flow of data through a network. Intranets and internal web pages have made the nature of the traffic within an organization far more unpredictable.

The increased tendency for organizations to need flexibility or mobility in addressing can make the IP design very challenging. The design would need to include Dynamic Host Configuration Protocol (DHCP) and *Domain Name System (DNS)* servers to maximize the flexibility of the network.

It is also important to fully understand the nature of the traffic in the network, particularly if it is a client/server environment (in which the design must allow for servers to communicate with each other and with their clients).

It may not be possible to use the existing addressing of the organization. If this is the case, the decision must be made to readdress the network. The decision may be made either because the network cannot scale because of the limitations of the NIC number that has been acquired from the Internet, or because the original design did not allow for the current environment or growth.

If the addressing scheme is inadequate in size, you have several options. The first is to apply to the Internet for another address or to use private addressing.

Private Addresses on the Internet

Private addressing (along with VLSM, IP version 6 with an address field of 128 bits, and CIDR adressing and prefix routing) is one of the solutions the Internet community began to implement when it became apparent that there was a severe limitation to the number of IP addresses available on the Internet.

Private addressing was defined by RFC 1597 and was revised in RFC 1918. It was designed as an addressing method for an organization that has no intention of ever connecting to the Internet. If Internet connectivity were not required, there would be no requirement for a globally unique address from the Internet. The individual organization could address its network without any reference to the Internet, using one of the address ranges provided.

The advantage to the Internet was that none of the routers within the Internet would recognize any of the addresses designated as private addresses. Therefore, if (in error) an organization that had deployed private addressing as outlined in RFC 1918 connected to the Internet, all its traffic would be dropped. The routers of ISPs are configured to filter all network routing updates from networks using private addressing. Previously, organizations had been "inventing" addresses—which were, in fact, valid addresses that had already been allocated to another organization. There are many amusing and horrifying stories of organizations connecting to the Internet and creating duplicate addresses within the Internet. A small company inadvertently masquerading as a large state university can cause much consternation.

Table 3-7 outlines the IP address ranges reserved for private addressing, as specified in RFC 1918.

Table 3-7 *Private Address Ranges*

Address Range	Prefix Mask	Number of Classful Addresses Provided
10.0.0.0 to 10.255.255.2555	/8	1 Class A
172.16.0.0 to 172.31.255.255	/12	16 Class Bs
192.168.0.0 to 192.168.255.255	/16	256 Class Cs

The use of private addressing has now become widespread among companies connecting to the Internet. It has become the means by which an organization does not have to apply to the Internet for an address. As such, it has dramatically slowed, if not prevented, the exhaustion of IP addresses.

Because these addresses have no global significance, an organization cannot just connect to the Internet, but it must first go through a gateway that can form a translation to a valid, globally significant address. This is called a *NAT gateway.*

Configuring private addressing is no more complicated than using a globally significant address that has been obtained from the Internet and is "owned" by the organization. In many ways, it is easier because there are no longer any restrictions on the subnet allocation, particularly if you choose the Class A address 10.0.0.0.

The reasons for addressing your organization's network using private addressing include the following:

- Shortage of addressing within the organization.

- Security. Because the network must go through a translation gateway, it will not be visible to the outside world.

- Internet service provider change. If the network is connecting to the Internet through an Internet service provider, the addresses allocated are just on loan or are leased to your organization. If the organization decides to change its ISP, the entire network will have to be readdressed. If the addresses provided define just the external connectivity, not the internal subnets, however, readdressing is limited and highly simplified.

The use of private addressing has been implemented by many organizations and might be said to have had a dramatic impact on the design of IP networks and the shortage of globally significant IP addresses. As ever, you should bear some things in mind when designing an IP network address plan using private addressing, including the following:

- If connections to the Internet are to be made, hosts wanting to communicate externally will need some form of address translation performed.

- Because private addresses have no global meaning, routing information about private networks will not be propagated on interenterprise links, and packets with private source or destination addresses should not be forwarded across such links. Routers in networks not using private address space, especially those of ISPs, are expected to be configured to reject (filter out) routing information about private networks.

- Remember that in the future, you may be connecting, merging, or in some way incorporating with another company that has also used the same private addressing range.

- Security and IP encryption do not always allow NAT.

If private addressing is deployed in your network and you are connecting to the Internet, you will be using some form of NAT. The following section explains this technology.

Connecting to the Outside World

When connecting to the outside world, some filtering and address translation may be necessary. Unless an address has been obtained from the Internet or from an ISP, it is necessary to perform address translation. The RFC that defines NAT is RFC 1631.

NAT is the method of translating an address on one network into a different address for another network. It is used when a packet is traversing from one network to another and when the source address on the transmitting network is not legal or valid on the destination network, such as when the destination corresponds to a private address. The NAT software process must be run on a Layer 3 device or router (which is logical, because it deals with the translation of Layer 3 addresses). It is often implemented on a device that operates at higher layers of the OSI model because of their strategic placement in the organization. NAT is often used on a firewall system, for example, which is a security device that guards the entrance into the organization from the outside world. The position of the firewall makes it an excellent choice for NAT because most translations are required for traffic exiting an organization that has used private addressing as defined in RFC 1918.

NAT had a controversial childhood, particularly when it was used for translating addresses that did not use RFC 1918 guidelines for private addressing—perhaps the organization used an address that had just been imaginatively created by a network administrator. This practice occurred when there was no glimmer of a possibility that the organization would ever connect to the Internet. This certainty of never connecting is unrealistic, even for small companies, in an era when individual homes have connectivity to the Internet.

Therefore, NAT is useful in the following circumstances:

- To connect organizations that used address space issued to other organizations to the Internet

- To connect organizations that have used private address space defined in RFC 1918 and that want to connect to the Internet

- To connect together two organizations that have used the same private address, in line with RFC 1918

- When the organization wants to hide its addresses and is using NAT as part of firewall capabilities or is using additional security features

NOTE NAT is designed for use between an organization and the outside world, as shown in Figure 3-14. Although it may be used to solve addressing problems within an organization, this should be seen as a temporary fix. In such situations, NAT is seen as a transitory solution to keep the network functional while it is designed and readdressed appropriately.

Cisco supports the use of NAT on the majority of its platforms, as well as on its firewall product, the PIX box. Various levels of support are offered, depending on the platform and the IOS that has been purchased. NAT support is beginning to be bundled into the standard product offering. It started to be widely offered from IOS version 11.2 with the purchase of the "plus" software, and full NAT functionality became available in the Base IOS form version 12.0. NAT is currently at version 3.0. The following section lists the main features that Cisco offers.

TIP If you are considering implementing NAT instead of studying it for academic/exam purposes, contact Cisco via its web page. It is advisable to always contact the vendor of a product before purchase to fully appreciate the latest offerings and pricing. Because this industry is so dynamic, it is wise to verify the latest data.

Figure 3-14   *Connecting to the Outside World Using NAT*

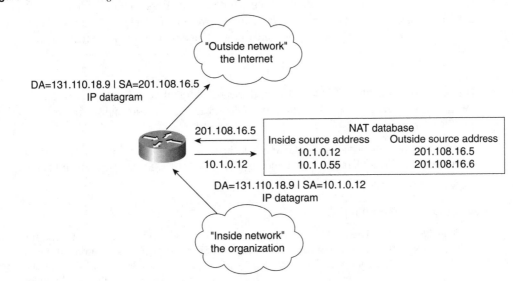

The Main Features of NAT

The main features of NAT, as supported by Cisco, include the following:

- **Static addressing**—This one-to-one translation is manually configured.

- **Dynamic source address translation**—Here, a pool of addresses is defined. These addresses are used as the product of the translation. They must be a contiguous block of addresses.

- **Port address translation (PAT)**—Different local addresses (within the organization) are translated into one address that is globally significant for use on the Internet. The additional identifier of a TCP or UDP port unravels the multiple addresses that have been mapped to single addresses. The uniqueness of the different local addresses is ensured by the use of the port number mapped to the single address.

- **Destination address rotary translation**—This is used for traffic entering the organization from the outside. The destination address is matched against an access list, and the destination address is replaced by an address from the rotary pool. This is used only for TCP traffic, unless other translations are in effect.

TIP   Many other features are supported by Cisco. Therefore, if you intend to implement this technology, take a look at Cisco's web page to discover the full range of options and features of the latest IOS version; Cisco is constantly upgrading and improving the feature set.

The basic operation of NAT is very straightforward, although the phraseology is rather confusing. The list of address definitions in Table 3-8 and the accompanying Figure 3-15 clarify the different terms.

To translate one network address into another, the process must differentiate between the functionality of the addresses being translated. Table 3-8 lists the categories of functions.

Table 3-8   *Categories of Functions*

Address	Definition
Inside global	The addresses that connect your organization indirectly to the Internet. Typically, these are the addresses provided by the ISP. These addresses are propagated outside the organization. They are globally unique and are the addresses used by the outside world to connect to inside the organization. Simply explained, they are the addresses that define how the *inside* addresses are seen *globally* by the outside.
Inside local	The addresses that allow every end device in the organization to communicate. Although these addresses are unique within the organization, they are probably not globally unique. They may well be private addresses that conform to RFC 1918. They are the *inside* addresses as seen *locally* within the organization.
Outside global	These are the Internet addresses (all the addresses outside the domain of the organization). They are the *outside* addresses as they appear to the *global* Internet.
Outside local	These addresses are external to the organization. This is the destination address used by a host inside the organization connecting to the outside world. This will be the destination address of the packet propagated by the internal host. This is how the *outside* world is seen *locally* from inside the organization.

Figure 3-15 illustrates the terms of Table 3-8.

Figure 3-15 *Use of the NAT Terms*

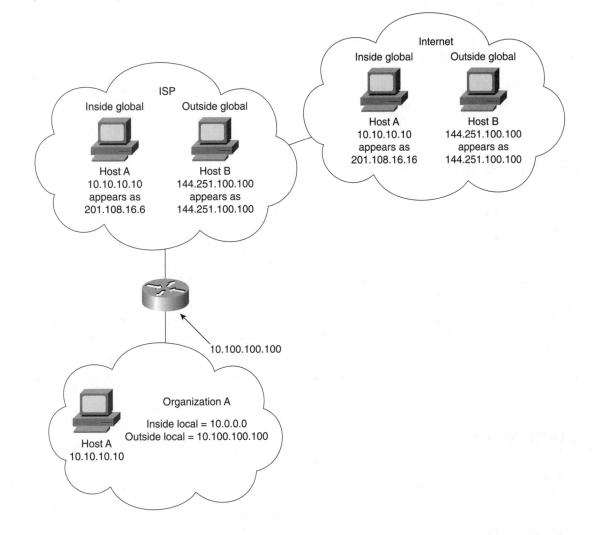

Conclusion

This chapter described various ways to conserve IP address space, as well as how to conserve memory and CPU in the network devices and bandwidth within the network itself. Despite the dramatic increase in low-cost bandwidth and computing power, these considerations are crucial to the health and well-being of your network.

Various technologies such as VLSM, summarization, private addressing, and NAT have been introduced and explained. Although these tools are useful, they are potentially deadly to your network if not administered with care and according to a well-conceived and network design.

Foundation Summary

The "Foundation Summary" is a collection of quick reference information that provides a convenient review of many key concepts in this chapter. For those of you who already feel comfortable with the topics in this chapter, this summary will help you recall a few details. For those of you who just read this chapter, this review should help solidify some key facts. For any of you doing your final preparations before the exam, these tables and figures will be a convenient way to review the day before the exam.

IP Addressing Summary

Remember these following important points regarding IP addressing:

- The IP address is 32 bits long.

- The network/host boundary can be anywhere in the 32 bits.

- The Internet allocates a unique bit pattern. These bits are the first bits on the far left and are not available for the administrator to use for networks because they identify your organization to the Internet.

- The Internet authority ARIN (in the United States) will provide the left portion of the address to the organization to use for addressing within their network. These bits are zeroed.

- The network mask is the identification of the bits allocated to the network, defined on all participating routers.

Summary of CIDR

In summary, CIDR solves the following problems:

- Address exhaustion was solved; the Internet was just running out of addresses.

- The network resources required to manage huge routing tables were becoming untenable.

Table 3-9 and Table 3-10 include further quick reference CIDR material.

Table 3-9   *RFCs on CIDR*

RFC Number	Description
1517	Applicability statement for the implementation of CIDR
1518	An architecture for IP address allocation with CIDR
1519	CIDR: an address assignment and aggregation strategy
1520	Method for exchanging routing information across provider boundaries in a CIDR environment

Table 3-10   *Table to Illustrate the Use of Prefix Masks*

Prefix	Mask	New Address Space
/27	255.255.255.224	12 percent of Class C 30 hosts
/26	255.255.255.192	24 percent of Class C 62 hosts
/25	255.255.255.128	50 percent of Class C 126 hosts
/23	255.255.254.0	2 Class Cs 510 hosts
/22	255.255.252.0	4 Class Cs 1022 hosts
/21	255.255.248.0	8 Class Cs 2046 hosts
/20	255.255.240.0	16 Class Cs 4094 hosts

An Example of the Use of CIDR

It is easy to see CIDR works when the address and the mask are written in binary, as the router processes them. In this example, the Internet community has allocated a group of Class C addresses, although they are presented as a single network. Table 3-11 shows an example of an IP address in both decimal and binary format.

Table 3-11   *An IP Address and Mask Shown in Binary*

Description	Octet 1	Octet 2	Octet 3	Octet 4
NIC address in decimal	200	100	48	0
NIC address in binary	11001000	01100100	00110000	00000000
Prefix as a subnet mask in decimal	255	255	248	0
Prefix as a subnet mask in binary	11111111	11111111	11111000	00000000

If it were a standard Class C address, the mask would be 255.255.255.0. By making the mask 255.255.248.0, the last three bits of the third octet are essentially giving the organization eight Class C networks.

Rules for VLSM

The rules for variably subnetting an IP address, are remarkably straightforward. The key is to remember that a hierarchical design in the addressing scheme is the goal. The physical network design also must reflect this logical hierarchy (as discussed in Chapter 2). After the physical design is mapped, the logical structure can be placed on top of it.

The following main rules apply when subnetting:

- A subnet can be used to address hosts, or it can be used for further subnetting.
- Within the allocation of subsequent subnets, the rule of not using all zeros or ones does not apply.
- The routing protocol must carry the subnet mask in its updates.
- Multiple IP addresses intended to be summarized must have the same high-order bits.
- Routing decisions are made on the entire address, preferring the longest bit pattern available.

The two main reasons for using VLSM are as follows:

- To make efficient use of the available addressing
- To enforce a good hierarchical design, allowing summarization and documentation

Advantages of Summarization

The advantages of summarization are as follows:

- To reduce the size of the routing table
- To reduce network overhead
- To make communication of routing updates more efficient
- To reduce CPU and memory utilization
- To simplify management
- To maximize the use of IP addresses
- To isolate topographical changes from other areas

Table 3-12 outlines the IP address ranges reserved for private addressing, as specified in RFC 1918.

Table 3-12   *Private Address Ranges*

Address Range	Prefix Mask	Number of Classful Addresses Provided
10.0.0.0 to 10.255.255.2555	/8	1 Class A
172.16.0.0 to 172.31.255.255	/12	16 Class Bs
192.168.0.0 to 192.168.255.255	/16	256 Class Cs

Chapter Glossary

This glossary provides an official Cisco definition for key words and terms introduced in this chapter. I have supplied my own definition for terms that the Cisco glossary does not contain. The words listed here are identified in the text by italics. A complete glossary, including all the chapter terms and additional terms, can be found in Appendix C, "Glossary."

aggregated route—The consolidation of advertised addresses in a routing table. Summarizing routes reduces the number of routes in the routing table, the routing update traffic, and overall router overhead. This is also called *route summarization.*

classful routing protocols—Routing protocols that do not transmit any information about the prefix length. Examples are RIP and IGRP.

classless interdomain routing (CIDR)—This is the means by which the Internet assigns blocks of addresses, typically Class C addresses, and summarizes them by using the prefix mask.

classless routing protocols—Routing protocols that include the prefix length with routing updates; routers running classless routing protocols do not have to determine the prefix themselves. Classless routing protocols support VLSM.

Domain Name System (DNS)—System used in the Internet for translating names of network nodes into addresses.

dot address—Refers to the common notation for IP addresses in the form n.n.n.n, where each number *n* represents, in decimal, 1 byte of the 4-byte IP address. This is also called dotted notation or four-part dotted notation.

dotted decimal notation—Syntactic representation for a 32-bit integer that consists of four 8-bit numbers written in base 10 with periods (dots) separating them. It is used to represent IP addresses in the Internet, as in 192.67.67.20. This is also called dotted quad notation.

Dynamic Host Configuration Protocol (DHCP)—Provides a mechanism for allocating IP addresses dynamically so that addresses can be reused when hosts no longer need them.

first octet rule—The mechanism by which the Layer 3 device identifies the class of IP address. If the protocol is a classful address, it is the only means available to determine the network portion of an address to which it is not directly connected.

flooding—A traffic-passing technique used by switches and bridges in which traffic received on an interface is sent out all the interfaces of that device, except the interface on which the information was originally received.

internet—Short for *internetwork*. Not to be confused with the Internet. *See also internetwork.*

Internet Assigned Numbers Authority (IANA)—Responsible for address allocation in the Internet.

internetwork—A collection of networks interconnected by routers and other devices that functions (generally) as a single network. It is sometimes called an internet, which is not to be confused with the Internet.

Layer 3 switching—Used in the context of VLANs, the mechanism by which a switch will route between VLANs. It also refers to routers, when the routing decision has been made and the result has been cached. The subsequent lookup involves switching (for example, fast switching), but on a Layer 3 decision.

logical AND—The mechanism by which a subnet is derived from an IP host address. The router maps the subnet mask, in binary, onto the host address, in binary. The result of the logical AND is the subnet address.

Network Address Translation (NAT)—Mechanism for reducing the need for globally unique IP addresses. NAT allows an organization with addresses that are not globally unique to connect to the Internet by translating those addresses into globally routable address space. Also known as *Network Address Translator*.

prefix mask—The prefix mask identifies the number of bits in the subnet mask. It is written in the /xx format after the address. It is used in supernetting and router aggregation.

private addressing—Private addressing is the means by which an organization can address its network without using a registered address from the Internet. This saves considerable address space in the Internet and eases restrictions within the organization.

routing table—A table stored in a router or some other internetworking device that keeps track of routes to particular network destinations and metrics associated with those routes.

subnet mask—A 32-bit number that is associated with an IP address; each bit in the subnet mask indicates how to interpret the corresponding bit in the IP address. In binary, a subnet mask bit of 1 indicates that the corresponding bit in the IP address is a network or subnet bit; a subnet mask bit of 0 indicates that the corresponding bit in the IP address is a host bit. The subnet mask then indicates how many bits have been borrowed from the host field for the subnet field. It sometimes is referred to simply as *mask*.

supernet—A summarization of class addresses given out by the Internet community. For example a group of Class C addresses 200.100.16.0 through 200.100.31.0 could be summarized into the address 200.100.16.0 with a mask of 255.255.224.0 (/19).

variable-length subnet mask (VLSM)—The capability to specify a different subnet mask for the same network number on different subnets. VLSM can help optimize available address space. Some protocols do not allow the use of VLSM. *See also classless routing protocols.*

virtual LAN—A logical grouping of devices, identified on switch ports instead of a physical segment attached to a router. This means that the devices associated with the logical network do not have to be geographically local to one another.

Q&A

The following questions test your understanding of the topics covered in this chapter. The final questions in this section repeat the opening "Do I Know This Already?" questions. These are repeated to enable you to test your progress. After you have answered the questions, find the answers in Appendix A. If you get an answer wrong, review the answer and ensure that you understand the reason for your mistake. If you are confused by the answer, refer to the appropriate text in the chapter to review the concepts.

1 Identify one criterion to help determine a subnet mask for classful addressing when designing a network-addressing scheme.

_____

_____

_____

2 Which command is used to forward broadcast traffic across a router to a particular destination?

_____

_____

_____

3 With a classless address of 204.1.64.0/20, what is the range of classful addresses that are included in the address? Write your answer in dotted decimal and the third octet in binary notation.

_____

_____

_____

4 What is a discontiguous network?

_____

_____

_____

5 For VLSM to be available as a design option in the network, what characteristic must the routing protocol possess?

_____

_____

_____

6 If summarization is to be implemented in the network, name one design criterion for the addressing scheme that must be in place?

_____

_____

_____

7 What networks are provided in RFC 1918, and what prefix mask accompanies each network?

_____

_____

_____

8 If the host portion of a subnet has been used to identify end devices, can that subnet be used again for VLSM?

_____

_____

_____

9 Describe the purpose of the **ip forward-protocol** command.

_____

_____

_____

10 Which command is used on point-to-point lines to conserve IP address space?

_____

_____

_____

11 Give one example of when route summarization would not be a good solution.

_____

_____

_____

12 Give one reason for implementing router summarization.

_____

_____

_____

13 Given an address of 133.44.0.0 and a prefix mask of /25, how many networks can be addressed, and how many hosts can exist on each network? Write the first and last possible subnets in binary and decimal notation.

_____

_____

_____

14 What class of address is 131.188.0.0, and how many hosts can be addressed if no subnetting is used?

_____

_____

_____

15 If given a Class C address with the requirement to accommodate 14 subnets and 10 hosts on each subnet, what subnet mask would you use?

_____

_____

_____

16 List the range of hosts available on the 136.122.10.192/28 subnet.

_____

_____

_____

17 Convert the subnet address 56.98.5.0/24 to binary notation, and state the class to which it belongs.

_____

_____

_____

18 Write out the decimal notation of the following subnet mask presented in the binary notation of 11111111.11111111.11111111.11111000.

_____

_____

_____

19 What does *VLSM* stand for?

_____

_____

_____

20 The Class B network address of 133.222.0.0 has been given a mask of 255.255.255.0. The subnets 133.222.8.0, 133.222.9.0, 133.222.10.0, 133.222.11.0, 133.222.12.0, 133.222.13.0, and 133.222.14.0 need to be summarized using VLSM. Give the subnet and new mask to achieve this summarization.

_____

_____

_____

21 Is 201.111.16.0/20 a valid subnet mask?

_____

_____

_____

22 Which routing protocols support VLSM?

_____

_____

_____

23 Briefly define *route summarization*.

_____

_____

_____

24 What sort of design scheme does route summarization require?

_____

_____

_____

25 In route summarization, where is the subnet mask moved?

_____

_____

_____

26 How does summarization allow for smaller routing tables?

_____

_____

_____

27 Identify two private addresses defined in RFC 1918.

_____

_____

_____

28 What is a discontiguous network?

_____

_____

_____

29 What does *CIDR* stand for?

_____

_____

_____

30 Which RFC is responsible for first describing the use of subnet masking?

_____

_____

_____

Scenarios

The following scenarios and questions are designed to draw together the content of the chapter and exercise your understanding of the concepts. There is not necessarily a right answer. The thought process and practice in manipulating the concepts is the goal of this section. The answers to the scenario questions are found at the end of this chapter.

Scenario 3-1

This scenario concentrates on correcting an addressing scheme in our original case study of Mental Merge. A network administrator devised the addressing scheme before there was any intention of connecting the company to the Internet and before the company had regional offices. Addresses were subsequently allocated without any policy or administrative control. This has led to problems in the current organization, which now needs to summarize its addresses. Using the addressing scheme in Figure 3-16, answer the following questions.

1 There are serious problems with the addressing scheme in Figure 3-16. If the network had this addressing scheme, would summarization be possible?

2 Design an alternative addressing scheme using VLSM that would summarize to the regional level.

3 Write out the addressing scheme in both binary and dotted decimal notation.

4 Could these addressing requirements be achieved with a Class C address?

5 If the answer to the preceding question is yes, write out the dotted decimal and binary notation to support it. If the answer is no, how many Class C addresses would be required? (Again, write out the dotted decimal and binary notation to support your argument.)

Figure 3-16   *An Addressing Scheme for Scenario 3-1*

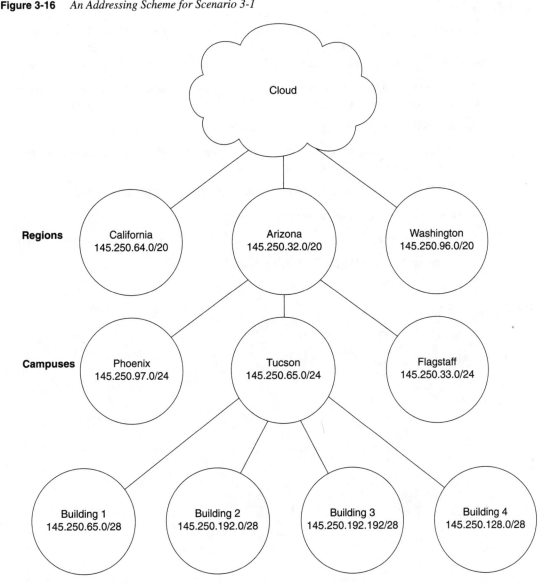

Scenario 3-2

A network has a remarkably even distribution of campuses, buildings, and hosts. The company has four campuses, each campus has four buildings, each building has five floors, and each floor has approximately 100 hosts. Each building also has a basement where the building servers are held.

There are eight locations distributed globally. Each location replicates this physical design. The locations are connected via dedicated leased T1 lines. Each T1 constitutes a subnet.

1 Draw the topology map for one of the locations.

2 Using the private network 10.0.0.0, design an addressing scheme that can be summarized. Apply the binary notation for the bit allocation to your diagram.

3 List the range of hosts on one of the subnets allocated to a floor in a building.

4 Indicate how summarization would work within the location.

5 Allocate a subnet to be used for VLSM to address the WAN links between the locations.

6 Is it possible to summarize the WAN subnets?

Scenario 3-3

Study Figure 3-17, and answer the questions that follow.

Figure 3-17   *Topology Map for Scenario 3-3*

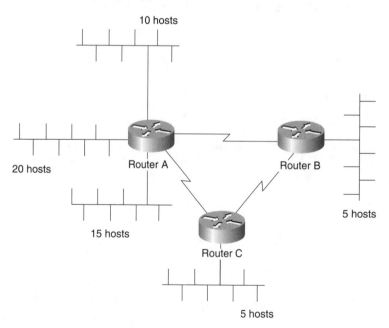

1 To address this network, what class of address would you apply to the Internet?

2 Could you use VLSM? Give reasons for your answer.

3 If you could use VLSM, write out the masks that you would deploy in binary notation.

4 Could summarization be implemented?

Scenario Answers

The answers are in **bold**. The answers provided in this section are not necessarily the only possible answers to the questions. The questions are designed to test your knowledge and to give practical exercise in certain key areas. This section is intended to test and exercise skills and concepts detailed in the body of this chapter.

If your answer is different, ask yourself whether it follows the tenets explained in the answers provided. Your answer is correct not if it matches the solution provided in the book, but rather if it has included the principles of design laid out in the chapter.

In this way, the testing provided in these scenarios is deeper: It examines not only your knowledge, but also your understanding and capability to apply that knowledge to problems.

If you do not get the correct answer, refer back to the text and review the subject tested. Be certain to also review your notes on the question to ensure that you understand the principles of the subject.

Scenario 3-1 Answers

1   There are serious problems with the addressing scheme in Figure 3-16. If the network had this addressing scheme, would summarization be possible?

Summarization is not possible, for the following reasons:

— The buildings do not share the same high-order bits as the campus.

— The campuses do not share the same high-order bits as the region.

— Depending on the physical design, the California campus and Building 1 could be seen as duplicate addresses.

2   Design an alternative addressing scheme using VLSM that would summarize to the regional level.

See Table 3-13.

3   Write out the addressing scheme in both binary and dotted decimal notation.

See Table 3-13.

Table 3-13 shows an alternative solution using the same address as before and the same bit allocation. If you have changed the bit allocation, ensure that there are enough bits for each level of the network. The requirements have not been stated, so you will have to state them for yourself or use the limited information that is provided. The question identifies three states, and you can assume three campuses in each state. Each campus has four buildings.

Table 3-13   *Alternative Addressing Scheme*

Entire Address in Decimal	Third and Fourth Octets in Binary	Prefix	Subnets	Hosts
145.250.16.0	00010000.00000000	/20	14	4094
145.250.32.0	00100000.00000000	/20	14	4094
145.250.48.0	00110000.00000000	/20	14	4094
145.250.17.0	00010001.00000000	/24	254	254
145.250.18.0	00010010.00000000	/24	254	254
145.250.19.0	00010011.00000000	/24	254	254
145.250.19.16	00010011.00010000	/28	4094	14
145.250.19.32	00010011.00100000	/28	4094	14
145.250.19.48	00010011.00110000	/28	4094	14
145.250.19.64	00010011.01000000	/28	4094	14

4 Could these addressing requirements be achieved with a Class C address?

It would not be possible to address this network, using a hierarchical design, with one Class C address. Given the minimum requirements shown in the question of three states, three campuses, and four buildings at each campus, 7 bits would be required. A Class C address allows only 8 bits in total, leaving 1 bit for host allocation. The rule of not using all zeros or all ones applies to the host portion of the address, so 1 bit would not enable you to address any hosts.

5 If the answer to the preceding question is yes, write out the dotted decimal and binary notation to support it. If the answer is no, how many Class C addresses would be required (again write out the dotted decimal and binary notation to support your argument).

It is interesting that although the first guess is that two is better than one, two Class C addresses do not really improve the situation. The need to address 12 buildings requires 4 bits, which would allow only 14 hosts in each building. The network could be addressed with two Class C addresses if 14 hosts in each building are all that is required. There is very little growth allowance in this scheme, making it inadvisable.

The most efficient addressing scheme with Class C addresses would be to use 40 Class C addresses. Consider, for example, the addressing scheme using Class C addresses.

A Class C address would be allocated to each building. This would allow 255 hosts in each building and subnetting to the floor, if necessary. The other three Class C addresses would be used with VLSM to identify the regions and campuses. Table 3-14 shows the addressing scheme for the one Class C address to address one region, three campuses, and four buildings.

Each region or state will now advertise five networks—the four Class C addresses for the buildings and the shared network for the state. One Class C network can be used for the state if the connections are point to point. Because there are 15 connections— four buildings per region, and three regions—this means 12 connections to the buildings, plus 3 connections to the state. A Class C address would easily accommodate this, even with redundant connections built into the design.

The reason that 40 Class C networks are needed is because the analysis of the state must be extrapolated to the entire organization. The organization covers three states, each with three regions, and each region has four buildings. Although the addressing described previously is correct, it would need to be extended to the other regions. This is calculated as follows:

The number of buildings requiring Class C networks in three states, each with three regions, and each region in turn with four buildings is $3 \times 3 \times 4 = 36$. Add to the three states requiring Class C networks the additional network required for the core cloud that connects the states, and you have $36 + 3 + 1 = 40$. In total, therefore, 40 Class C networks will be required.

Other than for academic interest in torturous addressing, this scenario would be an excellent candidate for a private Class B address.

Table 3-14   *The Class C Used to Identify the Network Above the Buildings for That Region*

Entire Address in Decimal	Fourth Octet in Binary	Prefix Mask
Region: Arizona		
210.10.32.0		
Campuses		
210.10.32.32	001 00000	/27
210.10.32.64	010 00000	/27
210.10.32.96	011 00000	/27
Buildings		
Tucson		
210.10.32.36	001001 00	/30
210.10.32.40	001010 00	/30

Table 3-14   *The Class C Used to Identify the Network Above the Buildings for That Region (Continued)*

Entire Address in Decimal	Fourth Octet in Binary	Prefix Mask
210.10.32.44	001011 00	/30
210.10.32.48	001100 00	/30
Flagstaff		
210.10.32.68	010001 00	/30
210.10.32.72	010010 00	/30
210.10.32.76	010011 00	/30
210.10.32.80	010100 00	/30
Phoenix		
210.10.32.100	011001 00	/30
210.10.32.104	011010 00	/30
210.10.32.108	011011 00	/30
210.10.32.112	011100 00	/30

Table 3-15 shows how to address the departments or floors within each building. For this discussion, use 210.10.64.0 as the example Class C address. Four bits taken in the fourth octet allows 14 networks, either distributed between the floors or between departments, with 14 hosts on each subnet.

Table 3-15   *How to Address a Building Using a Class C Network Address*

Entire Address in Decimal	Fourth Octet in Binary	Prefix Mask
210.10.64.16	0001 0000	/28
210.10.64.32	0010 0000	/28
210.10.64.48	0011 0000	/28
210.10.64.64	0100 0000	/28
210.10.64.80	0101 0000	/28
210.10.64.96	0110 0000	/28
210.10.64.112	0111 0000	/28
210.10.64.128	1000 0000	/28
210.10.64.144	1001 0000	/28
210.10.64.160	1010 0000	/28

continues

Table 3-15   *How to Address a Building Using a Class C Network Address (Continued)*

Entire Address in Decimal	Fourth Octet in Binary	Prefix Mask
210.10.64.176	1011 0000	/28
210.10.64.192	1100 0000	/28
210.10.64.208	1101 0000	/28
210.10.64.224	1110 0000	/28

Scenario 3-2 Answers

Using the private network 10.0.0.0, designing a summarized addressing scheme is straightforward.

When the last three octets are written in binary notation, it is easy to determine the bit allocation needed to fulfill the requirements.

Location	Campus	Building	Floor	Hosts
0000	**0000**	**.0000**	**0000**	**.00000000**

This design provides 16 locations, 16 campuses, and 16 buildings. To conform to the rule that excludes the use of all zeros and all ones in a subnet range, you would allocate 14 subnets per building. This would allow 254 hosts per floor or building subnet. Therefore, there is a lot of flexibility in this design for future growth. Draw the topology map for one of the locations.

  1 Draw the topology map for one of the locations.

    See Figure 3-18.

  2 Using the private network 10.0.0.0, design an addressing scheme that can be summarized. Apply the binary notation for the bit allocation to your diagram.

    See Figure 3-18.

Figure 3-18   *Topology Map of One of the Locations*

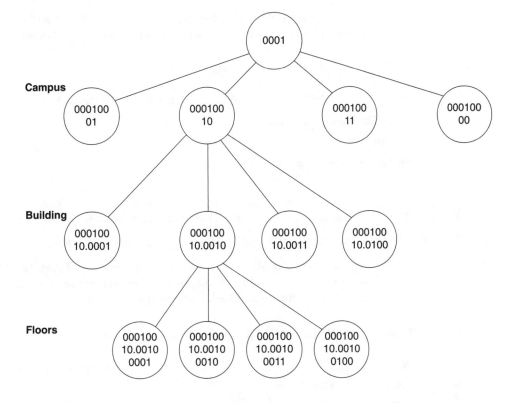

3 List the range of hosts on one of the subnets allocated to a floor in a building.

If one of the floors is given the subnet

Location	Campus	Building	Floor	Hosts
0000	0000	.0000	0000.	.00000000

Subnet in binary notation:

00001010.00010010.00100010.00000000

Subnet in decimal notation:

10.18.34.0

Range of hosts on that subnet:

10.18.34.1 to 10.18.34.254

4 Indicate how summarization would work within the location.

Summarization would work within a location because every device and subnet would share the same 4 high-order bits. The following example clearly demonstrates this:

Location	Campus	Building	Floor	Hosts
0000	0000	.0000	0000.	.00000000

Subnet in binary notation:

00001010.00010010.00100010.00000000

Subnet in decimal notation:

10.18.34.0

The summarized address advertised out of the location router would be 10.16.0.0/12.

5 Allocate a subnet to be used for VLSM to address the WAN links between the locations.

Many spare subnets are available in the addressing scheme designed. To address the WAN links, it would be sensible to select one of the subnets allocated to the floors and to reassign it to be further subnetted. For example:

Location	Campus	Building	Floor	Hosts
0000	0000	.0000	0000.	.00000000

Subnet in binary notation:

1000 0000 .1000   1000 .00000000

Subnet in decimal notation:

10.128.128.0/30

This allows 60 subnets, with each subnet allowing two hosts (ideal for point-to-point lines). The use of 128.128 in the second and third octets eases network management by readily identifying the serial connections.

6 Is it possible to summarize the WAN subnets?

It would not be easy to summarize these WAN subnets because they have a longer bit pattern than the other subnets beneath them. If summarization is possible, they could be summarized down to 10.128.128.0. It is equally sensible to use any easily recognizable address for WAN links (for example, 10.100.100.0).

Scenario 3-3 Answers

1 To address this network, what class of address would you apply to the Internet?

The network could be addressed using a Class C address.

2 Could you use VLSM? Give reasons for your answer.

VLSM can be used as long as a routing protocol is used to support the propagation of the subnet mask. It would be useful to have VLSM for the WAN links, but not essential.

3 If you could use VLSM, write out the masks that you would deploy in binary notation.

The bit allocation could be as follows:

Remote Subnet Locations	Hosts
000	**00000**

This would allow for six remote subnet locations, with 30 hosts on each subnet. The assumption was that the company was more likely to expand each existing location than to increase the number of remote sites. If the reverse were true, the mask would no longer be appropriate, and a single Class C may no longer be sufficient.

Because there are only three remote sites, with five networks to address and three WAN point-to-point links, and because there are six available subnets, one of the subnets could be further subnetted. This subnet would be used to address the WAN links. Another alternative is to use ip unnumbered on the serial links.

Remote Subnet Locations	Hosts
000	**00000**
110	**00000—Taken for WAN links**
New mask:	
110000	**00**

This would allow 14 WAN links to be identified.

NOTE   It is possible to address more links with the use of subnet zero.

---

4 Could summarization be implemented?

In this size of a network, summarization is not a concern and would not be possible; also, there is no hierarchy in the physical design.

It should be noted that this design does not allow for much network growth, and the organization may want to consider using a private Class B network.

This chapter covers the following topics that you will need to master to pass the CCNP/CCDP Routing exam:

- Explaining the routing process.

- Determining the requirements of the routing process.

- Analyzing the routing table.

- Describing the differences between a classful and classless routing protocol.

- Comparing the difference between a distance vector and link-state routing protocol, including an explanation of how routing tables are maintained, path selection, administrative distance, metrics, and convergence.

- Reviewing Cisco features that include **show ip route** and **clear ip route**.

CHAPTER 4

IP Routing Principles

The topics in this chapter are the basis of the BSCN course that feeds the Routing exam. The very name of the exam—the Routing exam—suggests that there are more than likely some questions on this very topic. In this chapter, the concepts of routing with IP and the mechanics of the process are dealt with generically as a foundation for the subsequent chapters, which deal with the individual routing protocols. The topics will directly reflect questions on the Routing exam. If you do not understand the contents of this chapter, it will be impossible for you to pass the exam. Some of this chapter reviews subjects dealt with in the ICND course. The subsequent chapters assume the comprehension of the subjects covered in this chapter.

How to Best Use This Chapter

By taking the following steps, you can make better use of your study time:

- Keep your notes and the answers for all your work with this book in one place, for easy reference.

- When you take a quiz, write down your answers. Studies show that retention significantly increases by writing down facts and concepts, even if you never look at the information again.

- Use the diagram in Figure 4-1 to guide you to the next step.

Figure 4-1 *How to Use This Chapter*

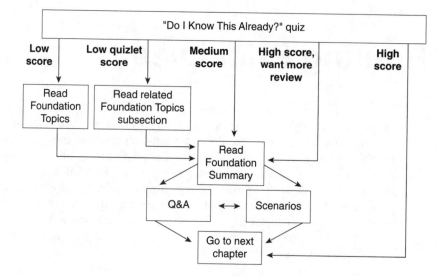

If you skip to the Foundation Summary, Q&A, and scenarios sections and have trouble with the material there, you should go back to the Foundation Topics section.

"Do I Know This Already?" Quiz

The purpose of the "Do I Know This Already?" quiz is to help you decide what parts of this chapter to use. If you already intend to read the entire chapter, you do not necessarily need to answer these questions now.

This 16-question quiz helps you determine how to spend your limited study time. The quiz is sectioned into four smaller four-question "quizlets," which correspond to four major topics in the chapter. Figure 4-1 outlines suggestions on how to spend your time in this chapter. Use Table 4-1 to record your scores.

Table 4-1 *Score Sheet for Quiz and Quizlets*

Quizlet Number	Topic	Questions	Score
1	The routing process	1 to 4	
2	Classful and classless routing protocols	5 to 8	
3	Distance vector and link-state routing protocols	9 to 12	
4	The routing table	13 to 16	
All questions	All	1 to 16	

1 Cisco distinguishes between the routing and the switching function—what is the difference?

_____

_____

_____

2 State the two ways that an outgoing interface is selected as the preferred path.

_____

_____

_____

3 What is administrative distance?

_____

_____

_____

4 If IGRP has three paths to a remote network in which each path has an equal metric, what will happen?

_____

_____

_____

5 Name the interior IP routing protocols that send the mask with the routing update.

_____

_____

_____

6 Name the interior routing protocol that sends a routing update on a Cisco router every 30 seconds by default.

_____

_____

_____

7 Does VLSM require a classful or classless routing protocol, and why?

_____

_____

_____

8 State one of the characteristics of a classful routing protocol.

_____

_____

_____

9 A distance vector routing protocol uses the mechanism of poison reverse—what is this?

_____

_____

_____

10 Name two distance vector routing protocols.

_____

_____

_____

11 Name two link-state IP routing protocols.

_____

_____

_____

12 Describe the mechanism of split horizon.

_____

_____

_____

13 What is the command syntax to empty the Cisco routing table of all its routes?

_____

_____

_____

14 What does 0.0.0.0 signify in an IP routing table?

_____

_____

_____

15 What is the command to show whether a specific network, such as 141.131.6.16, is present in the routing table?

_____

_____

_____

16 What is the next logical hop in the routing table?

_____

_____

_____

The answers to this quiz are found in Appendix A, "Answers to Quiz Questions." The suggested choices for your next step are as follows:

- **2 or less on any quizlet**—Review the appropriate sections of the "Foundation Topics" portion of this chapter, based on Table 4-1. Then move on to the "Foundation Summary" section, the "Q&A" section, and the "Scenarios" at the end of the chapter.

- **8 or less overall score**—Read the entire chapter. This includes the "Foundation Topics" and "Foundation Summary" sections, the "Q&A" section, and the "Scenarios" at the end of the chapter.

- **9 to 12 overall score**—Begin with the "Foundation Summary" section, and then go to the "Q&A" section and the "Scenarios" at the end of the chapter. If you have trouble with these exercises, read the appropriate sections in "Foundation Topics."

- **13 or more overall score**—If you want more review on these topics, skip to the "Foundation Summary" section, and then go to the "Q&A" section and the "Scenarios" at the end of the chapter. Otherwise, move to the next chapter.

Foundation Topics

Introduction: What Is a Routing Protocol?

The following case study illustrates some of the common concerns that a small company faces as it introduces routing into a switched/bridged network. This is a major transition and requires careful analysis to make the correct decisions regarding the choice of routing protocol as well as its implementation. This case study illustrates some of these issues with the Mental Merge company.

Case Study

A small startup company, Mental Merge, the company seen in the last chapter, still has a flat network. It has deployed several switches and an addressing scheme that divides the network into logical networks. The company has deployed virtual LANs (VLANs) in some areas, but it is not routing between them. On the end stations that need to communicate with servers on another network, Mental Merge has a problem, and these clients are in the ridiculous situation of having to physically connect from a system connected to the appropriate network. Those systems that are on different logical networks, but in the same VLAN the end systems have, overcome the routing problem by making themselves their own default gateway.

Despite the implementation of VLANs, the traffic is increasing, and congestion is beginning to cause delays.

It is time to purchase routers, to install them, and to turn on routing.

It is important for Mental Merge to understand the routing process to install the routers in the right place and to ensure that the network addressing is correct. The company also needs to choose a routing protocol for IP.

This chapter deals with these subjects and considers the network for Mental Merge in the "Scenarios" section.

What Is a Routing Protocol?

This section covers the definition, purpose, and operation of a routing protocol. It also covers the difference between a routing and routed protocol. It is necessary to understand the meaning of a protocol to understand exactly what a routing protocol is trying to achieve.

The Definition of a Routing Protocol

In simple terms, a protocol is an agreed set of rules that determine how something will operate.

A routing protocol is a set of rules that describes how Layer 3 routing devices will send updates between each other about the available networks. If more than one path to the remote network exists, the protocol also determines how the best path or route is selected.

The Purpose of a Routing Protocol

A routing protocol is the mechanism used to update the Layer 3 routing devices. When they all have the same accurate understanding of the network, they can route the data across the best path.

How the Routing Protocol Works

Participating routers advertise the routes that they know about to their neighbors in routing updates. Routes learned from routing updates are held in the routing table.

Routing and Routed

It is important to distinguish between the datagram and the routing protocol used to determine the path of the datagram.

The distinction is between the *routed* and the *routing* protocol.

The routed protocol is the Layer 3 protocol used to transfer data from one end device to another across the network. The routed protocol is the Layer 3 datagram that carries the application data as well as the upper-layer information.

The routing protocol is the protocol used to send updates between the routers about the networks that exist in the organization, thereby allowing the routing process to determine the path of the datagram across the network.

Table 4-2 provides a list of routed protocols and their corresponding interior routing protocols.

Table 4-2   *Routing and Routed Protocols*

Routed Protocol	Corresponding Interior Routing Protocol[1]
AppleTalk	RTMP, AURP, EIGRP
IPX	RIP, NLSP, EIGRP
Vines	RTP
DECnet IV	DECnet
IP	RIPv1, RIPv2, OSPF, IS-IS, IGRP, EIGRP

[1]IGRP and EIGRP are Cisco Systems proprietary routing protocols.

The router will reference the routing table and make a decision about forwarding data packets to the end destination identified in the destination address of the datagram/packet.

Table 4-3 shows the fields that are present in a typical routing table.

Table 4-3   *The Routing Table*

Network	Outgoing Interface	Metric	Next Logical Hop
140.100.100.0 /24	E0	6	131.108.13.15
140.100.110.0 /24	E0	7	131.108.13.15
140.100.120.0 /24	E0	8	131.108.13.15
140.100.130.0 /24	E0	8	131.108.13.15
166.99.0.0 /16	E1	10	131.108.14.11
166.90.0.0 /16	E1	11	131.108.14.11
145.0.88.0 /24	S0	3	131.108.10.9

It is useful to look at each field in the routing table to determine the functionality of the table to the routing process. The next sections cover the following fields of the routing table:

- The Network field
- The Outgoing Interface field
- The Metric field
- The Next Logical Hop field

The Network Field

The Network field contains the networks that the router knows exist in the organization. These entries either were entered manually as *static routes* or *default routes*, or were learned via a routing protocol as *dynamic routes*.

The Purpose of the Network Field

When a datagram comes into the router, the routing process attempts to forward it to the remote network, where it is hoped that it will find the destination host. To achieve this, it must know that the remote network exists. It determines this by looking in the routing table for the remote network.

How the Network Field Is Used

Typically, only the network portion of the address is stored in the table. Using the hierarchical strength of the addressing keeps the routing table small and the lookup short. The routing process makes a decision based on the longest match. This ensures that if VLSM has been deployed, the most specific network is chosen. Cisco IOS code mandates that the longest match can be a /32 or 255.255.255.255 mask. This is a match based on the full host address and is used in specific situations such as an OSPF environment. It is not encouraged as a common configuration because the size of the routing table grows rapidly.

The routes in the table are held in an order that speeds up the lookup process, ensuring that the routing decision is streamlined.

Later in the chapter, in the section "How the Routing Table Is Kept Current and Correct," you will see how the networks are placed in the table and how path selection to a remote network is chosen.

The Outgoing Interface Field

The Outgoing Interface is the interface on the router to which the routing process sends the datagram. This is the first step of its journey, the exit point of the router.

The Purpose of the Outgoing Interface Field

It is necessary for the routing process to know which interface queue to use to send the outbound datagram. It also informs the administrator of the interface through which the network was heard in the routing update—or, more accurately, the interface through which the chosen network was heard.

In summary, the outgoing interface field in the routing table indicates the following:

- Which interface to send the datagram to
- Which interface the routing update came through

The Metric Field

The metric is a value that is assigned to each path based on the criteria specified in the routing protocol. The Metric field is used to determine which path to use if there are multiple paths to the remote network. The metric used depends on the routing protocol.

This value is used to choose between different paths to the same destination network, to select the best path. If the values are the same, either the router selects the path that it heard first, or it uses both paths, sending the datagrams across each route.

It is the responsibility of the end device to reassemble the datagrams before sending them to the application.

Table 4-4 shows the metrics used by the different routing protocols.

Table 4-4   *Routing Protocol Metrics*

Routing Protocol	Metric
RIPv1	Hop count.
IGRP	Bandwidth, delay, load, reliability, MTU.
EIGRP	Bandwidth, delay, load, reliability, MTU.
OSPF	Cost. (The Cisco default states that the cost of an interface is inversely proportional to the bandwidth of that interface. A higher bandwidth indicates a lower cost.)
IS-IS	Cost.

NOTE   By default, on a Cisco router, if multiple equal cost paths exist in IP, up to six paths are used in a round-robin manner to load balance the traffic across the network.

The Next Logical Hop Field

The next logical hop is the destination address of the next forwarding router. The address of the next logical hop will be on the same subnet as the outgoing interface.

The Purpose of the Next Logical Hop Field

The purpose of identifying the next logical hop is so that the router can create the Layer 2 frame with the destination address. The reason that the logical address is stored instead of the MAC address of the next hop is to ensure that the information is accurate. The MAC address may change because of changes in the hardware; however, such changes do not affect the logical address. Also, the router is dealing at Layer 3 and just examines the source address of the routing update to determine the next hop. The simplicity of this action reduces the need for extra computation and memory.

TIP   It is useful for troubleshooting to remember that the next logical hop address is the address of the router directly connected to the forwarding router. Therefore, the address of the next logical hop shares the same subnet as the determining router.

The following section gives an example of a routing table. In the exam, you may be asked to interpret the output of the **show IP route** command, and it is necessary, therefore, to be able to extrapolate information from this table. The following section does this.

The show ip route Command

Router# **show ip route**

This command is used to show the IP routing table on the router. It details the network as known to the router and its sources for the information (such as the routing protocols). This command is excellent for troubleshooting configuration errors and understanding how the network is communicating about its routes.

To see a particular network in the routing table, issue this command:

Router# **show ip route** *network number*

Example 4-1 shows the output of this command. Table 4-5 explains how to read this information.

Example 4-1 show ip route *Output*

```
SanJose#show ip route
Codes: C - connected, S - static, I - IGRP, R - RIP, M - mobile, B - BGP
       D - EIGRP, EX - EIGRP external, O - OSPF, IA - OSPF inter area
       N1 - OSPF NSSA external type 1, N2 - OSPF NSSA external type 2
       E1 - OSPF external type 1, E2 - OSPF external type 2, E - EGP
       i - IS-IS, L1 - IS-IS level-1, L2 - IS-IS level-2, * - candidate default
       U - per-user static route, o - ODR
       T - traffic engineered route

Gateway of last resort is not set

     140.100.0.0/28 is subnetted, 3 subnets
C       140.100.17.192 is directly connected, FastEthernet3/0
C       140.100.17.128 is directly connected, FastEthernet1/0
C       140.100.32.0 is directly connected, Fddi2/0


Bldg_1#show ip route
Codes: C - connected, S - static, I - IGRP, R - RIP, M - mobile, B - BGP
       D - EIGRP, EX - EIGRP external, O - OSPF, IA - OSPF inter area
       N1 - OSPF NSSA external type 1, N2 - OSPF NSSA external type 2
       E1 - OSPF external type 1, E2 - OSPF external type 2, E - EGP
       i - IS-IS, L1 - IS-IS level-1, L2 - IS-IS level-2, * - candidate default
       U - per-user static route, o - ODR

Gateway of last resort is not set

     140.100.0.0/28 is subnetted, 3 subnets
O       140.100.17.192 [110/20] via 140.100.17.129, 00:07:44, Ethernet0
C       140.100.17.128 is directly connected, Ethernet0
O       140.100.32.0 [110/11] via 140.100.17.129, 00:07:44, Ethernet0
```

Table 4-5 explains the meaning of the important fields.

Table 4-5 *Explanation of the* **show IP route** *Command That Was Performed on Router Building 1*

Field	Explanation
O	Indicates the protocol that derived the route. Possible values include the following: **I**—IGRP-derived **R**—RIP-derived **O**—OSPF-derived **C**—Connected **S**—Static **E**—EGP-derived **B**—BGP-derived **i**—IS-IS-derived
140.100.17.192	Indicates the address of the remote network.
[110/20]	The first number in the brackets is the administrative distance of the information source; the second number is the metric for the route.
via 140.100.17.129	Specifies the address of the next router to the remote network.
00:07:44	Specifies the last time that the route was updated in hours:minutes:seconds.
Ethernet0	Specifies the interface through which the specified network can be reached.

These commands are useful to verify that the configuration has worked and that the OSPF network is functioning correctly. In a single-area environment, the full complexity of OSPF is not engaged. The full strength and complexity of OSPF come to the fore in the design and configuration of a multiarea network.

How the Routing Table Is Kept Current and Correct

The capability to send traffic from one end of the network to the other depends on how accurate and current the routing table in every router is within the network. Although all routing protocols have this written into their mission statements, the more recent routing protocols are more efficient, so their networks scale more easily. For example, RIP will send out the entire routing table every 30 seconds, while OSPF updates contain only the change and are sent only when that change occurs. Although OSPF sends the entire table every 30 minutes after the last update, this is far less demanding of network resources than the older protocol, RIP.

The accuracy of the table will be affected by how quickly it responds to changes in the network. These changes include the following:

- Learning new networks

- Learning a better path to an existing network

- Learning that a network is no longer available

- Learning an alternative route to a network

How each of these changes is achieved depends on the routing protocol.

Emptying the contents of the routing table and thus force the router to learn the information about the network is very useful in troubleshooting a network.

This command empties all the routes from the table:

```
Router# clear ip route *
```

This command removes the specific network from the table:

```
Router# clear ip route network
```

Switching Versus Routing

Cisco makes a distinction between the routing function and the switching function of a router. The difference is simple: Two jobs within a router need to be done to move a datagram from an incoming interface to the outgoing interface.

The Routing Function

The *routing function* is responsible for learning the logical topology of the network and then making decisions based on that knowledge. The decisions determine whether the incoming datagram can be routed and, if so, how.

The decisions include these:

- Is the protocol stack configured on the router?

- Is there an entry for the remote network in the routing table?

- Is there a default network configured?

- Is the network reachable?

- Which is the best path to that remote network?

- Are there equal-cost multiple paths?

- To which outgoing interface(s) should the datagram(s) be queued?

The Switching Function

The *switching function* is concerned with moving data across the router. It is responsible for forwarding the datagram. Switching takes over after the routing decisions have been made. Although the router has lookups to make, the few decisions that need to be made are performed in hardware. Therefore, this function is very fast.

The switching function does the following:

- Checks the incoming frame for validity

- Checks whether the frame is addressed (at Layer 2) to the router

- Checks whether the frame is within the scope of the framing criteria (too big or too small)

- Checks whether the frame passes CRC

- Strips the Layer 2 header and trailer from the frame, and checks the destination address against the cache entries

- Creates the appropriate frame header and trailer (if there is an entry in cache for the destination address), and forwards the frame to the outbound interface queue

---

TIP

Please note that the preceding section refers to the internals of the IOS, which is extremely complex. It has been described at the level required by the Routing exam. If live networks are to be designed and configured, it would be wise to understand in more depth some of the issues concerning caching and the placement of access lists. This information is readily available on the Cisco web page.

Functionality is broken into two components to ensure that the process is as fast as possible. After the routing decisions are made, the Cisco router caches the result, allowing subsequent datagrams to be switched.

The Routing/Switching Relationship in a Cisco Router

A packet transiting the router is accepted into the router if the frame header (of the frame in which the packet resides) contains the Layer 2 address of one of the router's interfaces. If properly addressed, after the framing is checked, the frame and its content (the packet) are buffered, pending further processing. The buffering occurs in main memory or some other specialized memory location.

If the source and destination Layer 3 address of the datagram have not been seen by this router before, the datagram will be process switched (routed). This involves the following actions:

1 When a datagram is to be forwarded, a process initiates a lookup in this routing table and a decision about how the datagram should be forwarded.

2 The packet is then encapsulated.

3 If fast switching is enabled, the packet is then examined again, and an entry is put into a route cache. The entry in this cache consists of the following:

— An IP prefix

— The output interface

— The link-layer header to be used in forwarding the packet

On subsequent packets, if the IP destination matches a prefix found in the route cache, the packet is forwarded using this information. The routing function is not disturbed, nor are the CPU cycles required to feed this monster expended.

The type of route cache used depends on the hardware used. The caches available are called *fast switching*, *autonomous switching*, *silicon switching*, and *Cisco Express Forwarding (CEF)*. If CEF switching is used, then the story changes again. With CEF switching, each card runs its own copy of the express forwarding and has its own copy of a *forwarding information base (FIB)*. In the event of a routing change, this new entry is forwarded by the CPU to each separate line card.

Types of Routing Protocols

Although the switching and routing functions within the router are set, there are many differences to be seen among the different routing protocols.

The routing protocols are essentially applications on the router. Their purpose is to ensure the correct and timely exchange of information about the network between the routers so that the routers can successfully perform the routing and switching functions described previously.

IP routing protocols can be divided into several distinct groups. The first is the difference between protocols that send the mask in the updates and the older protocols that do not. These are labeled classless and classful protocols, respectively.

Classful and Classless Routing Protocols

Classful routing protocols do not carry the subnet or routing mask in the update. The older distance vector protocols tend to be classful. This incapability to carry the subnetting information leads to design constraints in the IP network.

Classful Routing

Classful IP routing protocols include RIPv1 and IGRP. The characteristics of a classful routing protocol are listed here:

- Summarization occurs at the network boundary.

- Routes exchanged between foreign networks are summarized to the NIC number network boundary.

- Within the same network (NIC number), subnet routes are exchanged by routers, without the mask.

- The subnet mask is assumed to be consistent for a NIC number used within a network, so all router interfaces must share the subnet mask for interfaces in the same NIC network.

- The utilization of address space may be inefficient.

- VLSM is not possible within the network.

Classless Routing

Classless routing protocols were designed to overcome the constraints listed previously. The routing protocols that can do this are OSPF, EIGRP, RIPv2, IS-IS, and BGP.

The characteristics of a classless routing protocol are listed here:

- Router interfaces within the same network can have different subnet masks (VLSM).

- Some of the classless routing protocols, including BGP-4 and RIP v2, support the use of classless interdomain routing (CIDR).

- Some routes can be summarized within the major NIC number. This is done manually.

NOTE   BGP-4 and EIGRP summarizes at the network boundary automatically. Summarization within the NIC number boundary must be configured manually.

The distinctions of classless and classful are important between routing protocols. Another important distinction is based on the technology that they employ.

IP routing protocols use two main technologies: *link-state* and *distance vector* technologies. These are discussed next.

Distance Vector and Link-State Routing Protocols

Distance vector protocols are the earliest protocols, and they include RIPv1 and IGRP. These protocols are classful protocols, but RIPv2 and EIGRP are examples of classless routing protocols.

Distance vector protocols were designed for small networks. As the networks started to expand, enhancements were made to the distance vector protocols (RIPv2 and IGRP). At the same time, link-state protocols such as OSPF were introduced

Distance Vector Routing Protocols

Distance vector protocols send periodic updates. These updates are sent to directly connected neighbors. The update is periodic because it waits for the timer to expire before it sends an update. After receiving a neighbor's routing table, the router updates its table and sends the modified table in subsequent updates. This is the reason that distance vector routing protocols are said to be "routing by rumor."

The purpose of the protocol is to provide accurate, loop-free information to the routers. The update affects the entire routing table, excluding those networks that were learned through the interface through which the update is being sent. This is in accordance to the *split horizon rule*; this reduces network overhead and also prevents information from traveling in circles through the network, which can create *routing loops*.

To prevent routing loops, distance vector routing protocols employ the following techniques, which are described in more depth in the section on RIPv1:

- Split horizon
- Count to infinity
- Poison reverse
- Hold-down
- Triggered updates
- Aging of routes from the routing table

NOTE   Although EIGRP is defined by Cisco as an advanced distance vector routing protocol, it has adopted some of the link-state characteristics in favor of the distance vector solution. It does not use either count to infinity or hold-down timers.

The Distance Vector Routing Metrics

The metric used by distance vector protocols is often stated as being distance measured in the number of *hand-off points* or *hops* (routers) encountered on the way to the end device. Cisco defines IGRP and EIGRP as distance vector routing protocols. This muddies the original definition because IGRP and EIGRP use a composite and complex metric.

The path selection is made using the Bellman Ford algorithm based on the metric or value of each available path. RFC 1058 discusses this in depth in reference to RIPv1. EIGRP, however, uses a proprietary algorithm called *Diffusing Update Algorithm (DUAL)*.

TIP	If you are asked a question on distance vector metrics, it may be wise to use the original definition of hop count because IGRP and EIGRP are proprietary protocols. Cisco also uses the original definition in its documentation.

Link-State Routing Protocols

A *link-state routing protocol* is a sophisticated protocol dedicated to maintaining loop-free, accurate tables. It does not send the entire routing table via broadcasts every 30 seconds, as the original distance vector protocols (such as RIPv1) did, but it instead utilizes multicast addressing and incremental updates. Some routing protocols may be sent updates every 30 minutes (not 30 seconds) in addition to the incremental ones. Table 4-6 is a summary of IP routing protocols and the update timers.

Table 4-6   *A Summary of IP Routing Protocols and the Update Timers*

Protocol	Update Timer	Technology
RIPv1	Every 30 seconds, for entire routing table.	Distance vector.
OSPF	Incremental, with only the network change. However, 30 minutes after the last update was received, a compressed version of the table is propagated.	Link state.
EIGRP	Incremental updates, with network change only.	Advanced distance vector.
IGRP	Updates every 90 seconds, with incremental updates as needed.	Distance vector.
BGP-4	Incremental, with only the network change.	Path vector (an exterior routing protocol). The term refers to the list of autonomous system numbers that are carried in the BGP-4 updates, and the vector indicates the direction to send the traffic to find the path to a remote network.
IS-IS	Incremental, with only the network change. However, approximately 15 minutes after the last update was received, a compressed version of the table is propagated.	Link state.

The Meaning of Link State

As with a distance vector router, information is exchanged only with its directly connected neighbor. Unlike distance vector protocols, the information concerns only the local links (not the routes) connected to the router, and these links are propagated, unchanged, to every other router in the network. Therefore, every router has the same image of the network, created from the original updates from every other router in the network.

The purpose of link-state routers is to reduce the network overhead of the routing updates that are both current and thus accurate, allowing it to scale to large networks.

Sending an update about links is more efficient than sending data about routes because one link may effect many routes. Sending the links allows the routers to compute the routes that may be affected. The resources used are router CPU rather than network bandwidth.

Learning About the Network

A link-state routing protocol develops a relationship with an adjacent router, one that is on the same physical network. The two also must have the same subnet mask and have the same hello timers. The routing protocol develops and maintains the relationship by sending a simple message across the medium. When another router replies, it is identified as a *neighbor* for the routing process. This neighbor relationship is maintained as long as the simple message (Hello protocol) is received. Because the neighbor relationship is continuous, information can be exchanged between the routing processes quickly and efficiently. Therefore, changes in the network are realized very quickly.

Link-state routing protocols are used in larger networks because the method that they use to update the routing tables requires fewer network resources.

Learning About a Change in the Network

A router knows very quickly whether the neighbor, which may also be the next logical hop, is dead because the router no longer receives Hello protocol messages.

The routing process sends out a message immediately when it identifies a problem, without waiting for the update timer to expire. This is known as an *incremental update*. The update contains only the relevant information. The router also remains silent if there is no change in the network.

The incremental update improves *convergence* time and also reduces the amount of information that needs to be sent across the network. The network overhead on the physical media is eased, and the potential throughput of the network is improved.

Updating Local Network Tables

A link-state protocol holds a topology map of the network and can easily update the map and routing table database, via the incremental updates. In OSPF, these are called link-state advertisements (LSAs). After an update is received and forwarded, the router will compute a new topology map and, from this, a new path. It uses the Dijkstra algorithm to achieve this new understanding of the network.

Path Selection

The metric that is used is stated as cost, although many vendors supply a default that may be overridden manually. This is true of Cisco's implementation of OSPF, which uses bandwidth and delay as its default.

Examples of link-state routing protocols for IP are OSPF and IS-IS.

Another distinction that needs to be made between routing protocols is the difference between interior and exterior protocols. Interior protocols are those that update routers within an organization. Exterior protocols are those that update routers that connect different organizations to each other or to the Internet.

Interior and Exterior Routing Protocols

Routing protocols that operate within an organization are referred to as *interior routing protocols* (for example, RIPv1, IGRP, EIGRP, OSPF, and IS-IS).

Interior Routing Protocols

The boundaries of the organization are defined as the *autonomous system*. The unique number assigned to the autonomous system then identifies the organization. The autonomous system number may be viewed as another layer of hierarchy in the IP addressing scheme because the number can represent a collection of NIC numbers.

Exterior Routing Protocols

Routing protocols that exchange routing information between organizations are known as *exterior routing protocols*. Exterior routing protocols are highly complex. The complexity arises from the need to determine policies between different organizations. Border Gateway Protocol Version 4 (BGP-4) is an example of an exterior gateway protocol.

NOTE	This next section deals briefly with an older distance vector routing protocol, RIP; an improved distance vector routing protocol, IGRP; and a link-state routing protocol, OSPF. RIPv1 and IGRP are discussed here because they are not dealt with in the subsequent chapters. Although OSPF is dealt with in greater detail in the following chapters, it lends an interesting contrast to the two distance vector protocols.

RIP Version 1

Routing Information Protocol version 1 (RIPv1) is a simple routing protocol and, as such, works well in a small environment. As a distance vector routing protocol, it sends updates every 30 seconds. These updates comprise the entire routing table.

RIPv1 will support the following:

- **Count to infinity**—A router advertising networks heard from a neighboring router back to the same neighboring router could create a loop. In repeating networks to the router that informed the routing table, when a network goes down, each router may believe that there is an existing path through its neighbor. This problem is limited because each router increments the hop count before it sends out the update. When the hop count reaches 16, the network is rejected as unreachable because the diameter of a RIPv1 network cannot be greater than 15. This is called *counting to infinity*, where infinity equals 16. Although the liability is controlled, it will still slow convergence of the network.

- **Split horizon**—This is a mechanism to prevent loops and, thereby, the necessity of count to infinity. The routing process will not send networks learned through an interface in an update out that interface. It will not repeat information to the router that told of the networks.

- **Split horizon with poison reverse**—Split horizon on its own may not prevent loops. Poison reverse includes all the networks that have been learned from the neighbor, but it sets the metric to infinity (16). By changing the metric value to 16, the networks are reported to be unreachable. It acknowledges the network but denies a valid path. Although this increases network overhead by increasing the update size, it can prevent loops.

- **Holddown**—After deciding that a network in the routing table is no longer valid, the routing process waits for three routing updates (by default) before it believes a routing update with a less-favorable metric. Again, this is to prevent routing loops from generating false information throughout the network.

- **Triggered updates**—As soon as a routing process changes a metric for a network in its routing table, it sends an update. This informs the other routers immediately. If there is a problem in the network, all the affected routers go into holddown immediately instead of waiting for the periodic timer. This increases convergence and helps prevent loops.

- **Load balancing**—If the routing process sees multiple paths of equal cost to a remote network, it distributes the routed (datagram) traffic evenly among the paths. It will allocate datagrams to the different paths on a round-robin basis.

WARNING Because the metric used is hop count, one path may become saturated. A 56-kbps line and a 100-Mbps Fast Ethernet line may both offer paths of equal hop count; dividing the user traffic between them, but, may not optimize the bandwidth of the network.

Cisco has implemented all the preceding options, which are defined in RFC 1058.

RIPv1 is useful in small networks and is distributed with *Berkeley Standard Distribution* (BSD), which makes it widely available. It may not be suitable for large environments, however, because the protocol was never designed with the expectation of being used in huge organizations.

As the network grows, problems will be seen with applications timing out and congestion occurring on the network as the routers fail to adapt quickly to changes. When there has been a change in the network, the time that it takes for every router to register that change is known as the convergence time. The longer this timer takes, the greater the likelihood of problems on the network. Therefore, it is necessary either to contain the growth of the network or to use a routing protocol that scales to a larger size. OSPF is designed to scale and has the added advantage of being defined by the Internet Engineering Task Force (IETF), making it an industry standard in the public domain.

IGRP

IGRP is a distance vector routing protocol created by Cisco Systems in the mid-1980s. It is a distance vector routing protocol, but because it is proprietary, it has the advantage of being capable of improving many of the elements seen in RIPv1, including incremental updates, fewer network resources to maintain the routing protocol, a more complex and efficient metric, and no limitation in diameter of the network because of hop count.

Although IGRP can streamline its operation because it does not have to be all things to all people, it can be implemented only on Cisco routers. It is very efficient at sharing its information with other routing protocols, using redistribution.

NOTE It is unlikely that there will be direct questions on either RIPv1 or IGRP. There will be questions on the distance vector and link-state protocols. RIPv1 and IGRP are discussed here only as illustrations of distance vector protocols.

IGRP has the following characteristics of a distance vector routing protocol:

- Periodic updates
- Broadcasting updates
- Full routing table updates
- Count to infinity
- Split horizon
- Triggered updates with route poisoning
- Load balancing on equal paths (up to four, by default)
- Bellman Ford routing algorithm

It differs from RIPv1 in the following ways:

- The metric is a composite calculated from bandwidth, delay, loading, reliability, and MTU. In fact, although MTU was originally designed as part of the metric, it is tracked but not used in the calculation. It is possible to configure the use of all the calculated elements of the metric. If these are not configured, the system will use bandwidth and delay by default.
- The hop count is 100, configurable to 255 (although this is not used as a metric, but to age out datagrams).
- The update timer is set by default to 90 seconds (three times that of RIPv1).
- Unequal load sharing occurs on multiple paths.
- A more efficient packet structure is used.
- Autonomous systems (AS) are used to allow multiple processes within a routing domain, which allows the network to scale.

OSPF

NOTE   OSPF is dealt with in great depth in the following chapter. It is considered here so that general comparisons may be made between the array of different IP routing protocols and the technologies underlying them. Unfortunately, this means that there may be some level of repetition between the chapters. Subheadings have been carefully worded so that the reader can read relevant information in context while avoiding repetition.

OSPF is an improvement on RIPv1 for large networks because of the following reasons:

- It utilizes bandwidth more efficiently, sending incremental updates.

- The updates are not broadcast as in RIPv1 but are directed to multicast addresses 224.0.0.5 and 224.0.0.6.

- It propagates changes in the network more quickly, with incremental updates and neighbor relationships.

- It is not limited in size by a maximum hop count of 15.

- It allows for variation in network size throughout the organization, using VLSM.

- It has security options defined in the MD5 specification.

- The metric may be defined manually, allowing for greater sophistication in the path determination.

- It is more responsive to network changes, is flexible in network addressing and design, and scales to a larger size.

The following sections discuss these key points in detail.

Key Attributes of OSPF

OSPF is designed to offer the greatest flexibility for every situation. As an open standard, it is required to offer interoperability in conjunction with this flexibility, while allowing the network to grow. These requirements make OSPF a highly complex routing protocol.

To understand this complexity, it is useful to identify the main characteristics of OSPF. These key attributes of OSPF include the following:

- Maintaining a connection-oriented relationship with other routers on the same physical segment. These are known as *adjacent neighbors*. This is a TCP connection maintained by keepalives.

- Sending the minimum amount of information in an incremental update when there has been a change in the network. This allows for fast network convergence.

- Adding another level of hierarchy to the IP address, by designing networks into *areas*.

- Using VLSM and summarization.

- Assigning specific functionality to different routers to streamline the process of communication change in the network.

- Operating within an organization as an interior routing protocol.

Path Selection Between Routing Protocols

Clearly there are many IP routing protocols from which to choose. It is better if a single routing protocol can be chosen because this gives a consistency that relates directly to the strength of the network. It complicates the network to have more than a single routing protocol attempting to perform the same job. The routing table, in particular, sometimes deals with confusion in how to select one path to place into the routing table.

When more than one routing protocol is running on the router, the routing process must make a decision to have one entry per network in the routing table. The choice cannot be based on the metric because metrics differ between protocols. Instead, another method, called administrative distance, was devised to solve the problem.

NOTE   When it is necessary to have more than one routing protocol within an organization, *redistribution* is configured. However, the router that is responsible for redistribution will have more than one routing protocol informing the routing table.

Administrative Distance

The administrative distance will select one path to enter the routing table from several paths offered by multiple routing protocols.

In Figure 4-2, for example, both RIP and EIGRP have paths to the network 140.100.6.0. RIP is offering a metric of 2 hops, and EIGRP is tendering a metric of 768. Without redistribution, no conversion or choice is possible because there is no similar criteria for distinguishing the two paths. Therefore, the metric is ignored, and the administrative distance is used to make the selection.

In Figure 4-2, despite the speed of Frame Relay being set at 56 kbps as opposed to the 100 Mbps of FDDI, Router D would select the Frame Relay path based on administrative distance. In this case, manually configuring the administrative distance on Router D would be advisable.

Administrative distance is a rather arbitrary set of values placed on the different sources of routing information. The defaults can be changed, but care should be taken when subverting the natural path selection, and any manual configuration must be done with careful reference to the network design of the organization and its traffic flow.

Administrative distance reflects the preferred choice. The defaults are listed in Table 4-7.

Figure 4-2   *Path Selection Using Administrative Distance*

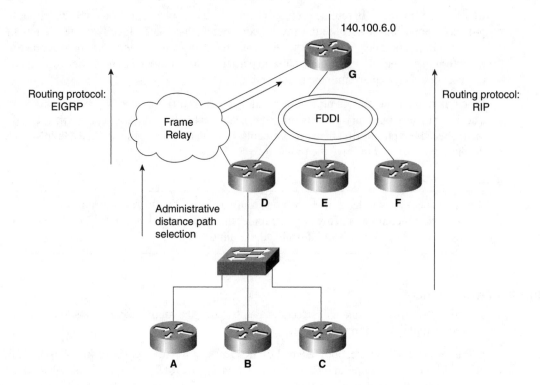

Table 4-7   *Default Administrative Distance*

Routing Source	Administrative Distance
Connected interface or static route that identifies the outgoing interface rather than the next logical hop	0
Static route	1
EIGRP summary route	5
External BGP	20
EIGRP	90
IGRP	100
OSPF	110
RIP	120
External EIGRP	170
Internal BGP	200
An unknown network	255 or infinity

The administrative distance can be manually configured. The reason for manually configuring the administrative distance for a protocol such as EIGRP is that it may have a less desirable path compared to one offered by another protocol such as RIP, which has a higher default AD.

Because the administrative distance is looked at with total disregard of the metrics, however, the EIGRP path will be selected. The other reason is that a directly connected network, which has precedence, is being used as a backup link for redundancy because the directly connected network is not used on a daily basis. Backup links for redundancy are often implemented on serial connections where the network charges are based on usage. This design is called a *floating static route.*

Convergence

Convergence occurs when all the routers in the routing domain agree on the routes that are available. Convergence time is the time that it takes for every router's routing table to synchronize after there has been a change in the network topology.

It is important to ensure that the time taken is as short as possible because while the routers disagree on the available networks, they cannot route data correctly or efficiently.

Each routing protocol has chosen a different method of updating the routing table. This affects convergence time. Some new concepts are introduced in the following comparison in protocol convergence methods. This is simply to show the relative merits of each approach. The concepts are explained in depth in the chapters that concentrate on the specific protocols. The terms shown in italics are defined in the glossary at the end of this chapter, as well as in the final glossary at the end of the book.

RIPv1 Convergence

The steps for RIPv1 convergence are as follows:

Step 1	When the local router sees a connected route disappear, it sends a *flash update* and removes the route entry from its table. This is called a *triggered update* with *poison reverse.*
Step 2	The receiving routers send flash updates and put the affected route in *holddown.*
Step 3	The originating router queries its neighbor for alternative routes. If the neighbor has an alternative route, it is sent; otherwise, the *poisoned route* is sent.
Step 4	The originating router installs the best alternative route that it hears because it has purged the original routes.
Step 5	Routers that are in holddown ignore the alternative route.

Step 6   When the other routers emerge from holddown, they will accept the alternative route.

Step 7   Convergence takes the time for detection, plus holddown, plus the number of routing updates (equal to the hop-count diameter of the network). This could take a long time.

IGRP Convergence

The steps for IGRP convergence are as follows:

Step 1   When the local router sees a connected route disappear, it sends a flash update and removes the route entry from its table. This is called a triggered update with poison reverse.

Step 2   The receiving routers send flash updates and put the affected route in holddown.

Step 3   The originating router queries its neighbor for alternative routes. If the neighbor has an alternative route, it is sent; otherwise, the poisoned route is sent.

Step 4   The originating router installs the best alternative route that it hears because it has purged the original routes. It sends a new flash update. This is either the routing table, with or without the network available, stating the higher metric.

Step 5   Routers that are in holddown ignore the alternative route.

Step 6   When the routers come out of holddown, they accept the alternative route.

When the other routers emerge from holddown, they will accept the alternative route.

Step 7   Convergence takes the time for detection, plus holddown, plus the number of routing updates (equal to the hop-count diameter of the network). Because the update timer is 90 seconds, this could take a very long time.

EIGRP Convergence

The steps for EIGRP convergence are as follows:

Step 1   When the local router sees a connected route disappear, it checks the *topology table* for a feasible successor.

Step 2   If no *feasible successor* exists, it moves into active state.

Step 3   The originating router queries its neighbor for alternative routes, the receiving router acknowledges.

Step 4   If an alternative exists, it is sent.

Step 5   If the router receives an acceptable successor, it adds the route to the table.

Step 6   A flash update of the path with the higher metric is sent out.

Step 7   Updates are acknowledged.

Convergence is very quick because it is the detection time, plus query, reply, and update time. If there is a feasible successor, then convergence is almost instantaneous.

OSPF Convergence

The steps for OSPF convergence are as follows:

Step 1   When a router detects a link failure, an LSA is sent to its neighbors. If the router is on a multiaccess link, then the update is sent to the DR and BDR, not to all neighbors.

Step 2   The path is removed from the originating router's tables.

Step 3   On receipt of the LSA, all routers update the topology table and flood the LSA out its interfaces.

Step 4   The *Dijkstra algorithm* is run to rebuild the routing table.

Convergence is detection time, plus LSA flooding, plus 5 seconds before computing the topology table. This comes to a few seconds. If convergence is deemed to be the topology table being updated, this could take longer.

Conclusion

This chapter reviewed IP routing protocols. It has shown how to untangle the various categories of routing protocols, how to analyze the IP routing table, and how to understand how routing decisions are made.

This information is crucial to the Routing exam because it is essentially an exam on IP routing. This chapter is a foundation to the other chapters, which deal in depth with particular technologies.

Foundation Summary

The "Foundation Summary" is a collection of quick reference information that provides a convenient review of many key concepts in this chapter. For those of you who already feel comfortable with the topics in this chapter, this summary will help you recall a few details. For those of you who just read this chapter, this review should help solidify some key facts. For any of you doing your final preparations before the exam, these tables and figures will be a convenient way to review the day before the exam.

Table 4-8 shows the metrics used by the IP routing protocols.

Table 4-8   *Routing Protocol Metrics*

Routing Protocol	Metric
RIPv1	Hop count.
IGRP	Bandwidth, delay, load, reliability, MTU.
EIGRP	Bandwidth, delay, load, reliability, MTU.
OSPF	Cost. (The Cisco default states that the cost of an interface is inversely proportional to the bandwidth of that interface. A higher bandwidth indicates a lower cost.)
IS-IS	Cost.

Table 4-9 explains how to read the information in the routing table, as explained in the **show ip route** command.

Table 4-9   *Explanation of the **show ip route** Command*

Code	Protocol That Derived the Route
I	IGRP.
D	EIGRP.
EX	External EIGRP.
R	RIP.
C	Connected.
S	Static.
E	EGP.
B	BGP.
I	IS-IS.
L1	IS-IS level 1.
L2	IS-IS level 2.

Table 4-9   *Explanation of the* **show ip route** *Command (Continued)*

Code	Protocol That Derived the Route
M	Mobile.
U	Per-user static route.
O	ODR.
T	Traffic-engineered route.
O	OSPF networks from within the same area as the router. These are networks learned from router and network LSAs.
IA	OSPF interarea. This is sent out by the ABRs and is created from the summary link LSA (type 3 and type 4). These routes will not be seen on a router within a totally stubby area because it will not receive LSAs external to the area.
N1	OSPF NSSA external type 1.
N2	OSPF NSSA external type 2.
E1	OSPF external type 1. These routes are generated by the ASBR and show routes that are external to the autonomous system. The cost of this external route is the summarization of the external cost, plus the cost of the path to the ASBR. These routes will not be seen in a stub or totally stubby area.
E2	OSPF external type 2. These routes do not take into account the cost of the path to the ASBR. They consider only the external cost.

Table 4-10 summarizes the major differences between distance vector routing protocols and link-state routing protocols.

Table 4-10   *Distance Vector Routing Protocols Versus Link-State Routing Protocols*

Distance Vector	Link-State
Sends its entire routing table at periodic intervals out of all interfaces (typically, this is based in seconds). It will also send triggered updates to reflect changes in the network.	Sends incremental updates when a change is detected. OSPF will send summary information every 30 minutes, regardless of whether incremental updates have been sent in that time.
Typically involves updates sent using a broadcast address to everyone on the link.	Typically involves updates sent to those routers participating in the routing protocol domain, via a multicast address.
Uses a metric based on how distant the remote network is to the router. (IGRP does not conform to this as a proprietary solution.)	Is capable of using a complex metric, referred to by OSPF as cost.
Has knowledge of the network based on information learned from its neighbors.	Has knowledge of the network based on information learned from every router in the area.

continues

Table 4-10 *Distance Vector Routing Protocols Versus Link-State Routing Protocols (Continued)*

Distance Vector	Link-State
Includes a routing table that is a database viewed from the perspective of each router.	Has a topological database that is the same for every router in the area. The routing table that is built from this database is unique to each router.
Uses Bellman Ford algorithm for calculating the best path.	Uses the Dijkstra algorithm.
Does not consume many router resources, but is heavy in the use of network resources.	Uses many router resources, but is relatively low in its demand for network resources.
Maintains one domain in which all the routes are known.	Has a hierarchical design of areas that allow for summarization and growth.
Is not restricted by addressing scheme.	For effective use, the addressing scheme should reflect the hierarchical design of the network.
Involves slower convergence because information of changes must come from the entire network (but indirectly). Each routing table on every intervening router must be updated before the changes reach the remote end of the network.	Involves quicker convergence because the update is flooded immediately throughout the network.

Table 4-11 summarizes the differences between RIPv1 and OSPF. Because RIPv1 is a distance vector routing protocol and OSPF is a link-state routing protocol, you will find it helpful to keep in mind the information in Table 4-10.

Table 4-11 *RIPv1 Versus OSPF*

RIPv1	OSPF
Is a simple protocol to design, configure, and maintain.	Is a complex protocol to design and, in some instances, to configure and maintain.
Does not require a hierarchical addressing scheme.	If full benefits of the protocol are to be harnessed, should use a hierarchical IP addressing scheme.
Does not pass the subnet mask in the routing update, and therefore is not capable of classless routing or VLSM.	Carries the mask in the update, and therefore can implement VLSM, summarization, and classless routing.
Is limited to a 15-hop diameter network.	Is unlimited in the diameter of the network, although it is suggested that an area not exceed more that 50 networks.
Does not acknowledge routing updates; just repeats them periodically (every 30 seconds).	Acknowledges updates.
Has a routing table that is sent out of every interface every 30 seconds (by default).	Involves updates sent as required (when changes are seen) and every 30 minutes after no change has been seen.

Table 4-11   *RIPv1 Versus OSPF (Continued)*

RIPv1	OSPF
Can transmit information about the network in two messages: the routing update and the triggered update.	Has protocols for discovering neighbors and forming adjacencies, as well as protocols for sending updates through the network. These protocols alone add up to nine message types.
Uses hop count as a metric, the number of routers to process the data.	Uses cost as a metric. Cost is not stated in the RFCs, but it has the capacity to be a complex calculation, as seen in Cisco's implementation.

Table 4-12 summarizes default administrative distances.

Table 4-12   *Default Administrative Distance*

Routing Source	Administrative Distance
Connected interface or static route that identifies the outgoing interface rather than the next logical hop	0
Static route	1
EIGRP summary route	5
External BGP	20
EIGRP	90
IGRP	100
OSPF	110
RIP	120
External EIGRP	170
Internal BGP	200
An unknown network	255 or infinity

Chapter Glossary

This glossary provides an official Cisco definition for key words and terms introduced in this chapter. I have supplied my own definition for terms that the Cisco glossary does not contain. The words listed here are identified in the text by italics. A complete glossary, including all the chapter terms and additional terms, can be found in Appendix C, "Glossary."

adjacent neighbors—A neighbor is a router that is directly connected to another router. They must also have same mask and hello parameters. An adjacent router is a router that has exchanged routing information with its neighbor.

area—A logical set of network segments and their attached devices. Areas are usually connected to other areas via routers, making up a single autonomous system. See also *AS*. Used in DECnet, IS-IS, and OSPF.

autonomous switching—Feature on Cisco routers that provides faster packet processing by allowing the ciscoBus to switch packets independently without interrupting the system processor.

autonomous system—A collection of networks under a common administration sharing a common routing strategy. Autonomous systems may be subdivided into areas.

Berkeley Standard Distribution (BSD)—Term used to describe any of a variety of UNIX-type operating systems based on the UC Berkeley BSD operating system.

Cisco Express Forwarding (CEF)—Advanced, Layer 3 IP switching technology. CEF optimizes network performance and scalability for networks with large and dynamic traffic patterns, such as the Internet, on networks characterized by intensive web-based applications or interactive sessions.

classful routing protocol—A protocol that does not carry the subnet mask. A distance vector routing protocol that will not allow VLSM or route summarization.

classless routing protocol—A routing protocol that carries the subnet mask in the routing update. This allows the implementation of VLSM and summarization.

convergence—Speed and capability of a group of internetworking devices running a specific routing protocol to agree on the topology of an internetwork after a change in that topology.

count to infinity—Problem that can occur in routing algorithms that are slow to converge, in which routers continuously increment the hop count to particular networks. Typically, some arbitrary hop count limit is imposed to prevent this problem.

default routes—A route that should be used if the destination network is not present in the routing table.

Diffusing Update Algorithm (DUAL)—A convergence algorithm used in Enhanced IGRP that provides loop-free operation at every instant throughout a route computation. This allows routers involved in a topology change to synchronize at the same time, while not involving routers that are unaffected by the change.

Dijkstra algorithm—Routing algorithm that iterates on length of path to determine a shortest-path spanning tree. Commonly used in link-state routing algorithms. Sometimes called *shortest path first algorithm*.

distance vector routing protocol—Class of routing algorithms that iterate on the number of hops in a route to find a shortest-path spanning tree. Distance vector routing algorithms call for each router to send its entire routing table in each update, but only to its neighbors. Distance vector routing algorithms can be prone to routing loops but are computationally simpler than link-state routing algorithms. These routing protocols also use the Bellman-Ford routing algorithm.

dynamic routes—Automatic rerouting of traffic based on sensing and analyzing current actual network conditions, not including cases of routing decisions taken on predefined information.

exterior routing—A routing protocol used to exchange information between autonomous systems or organizations, used to connect organizations into the Internet. BGP and EGP are examples of exterior routing protocols.

fast switching—A cache in the Cisco router that contains routing decisions. After the routing decision for a packet has been made, it can be cached in any one of a variety of caches. This means that the forwarding of traffic through the router is greatly enhanced.

feasible successor—A term used by EIGRP to describe a next-hop router that has a path to the remote network that EIGRP considers a viable route.

flash update—A routing update sent asynchronously in response to a change in the network topology. If there is a change in the metric, the update is sent immediately without waiting for the update timer to expire. Sometimes known as triggered updates.

floating static route—A route that has been manually configured. Manually configured routes will be chosen as the routing path first. A floating static route is a route that, although manually configured, has been identified as a route to choose only if the dynamically learned routes fail. These routes need to have a higher administrative distance than the routing protocol that you are using.

flooding—A traffic-passing technique used by switches and bridges in which traffic received on an interface is sent out to all the interfaces of that device, except the interface on which the information was originally received.

incremental update—A routing update that is sent only when there is a change in the topology, not periodically when a timer expires.

interior routing protocol—A routing protocol used to route information between routers within an autonomous system or organization.

link-state advertisement (LSA)—Broadcast packet used by link-state protocols that contains information about neighbors and path costs. LSAs are used by the receiving routers to maintain their routing tables.

link-state routing algorithm—A routing algorithm in which each router broadcasts or multicasts information regarding the cost of reaching each of its neighbors to all nodes in the internetwork. Compare with *distance vector routing protocol.*

neighbor—In OSPF or EIGRP, two routers that have interfaces to a common network.

poison reverse—Routing updates that specifically indicate that a network or subnet is unreachable, rather than implying that a network is unreachable by not including it in updates.

redistribution—Allowing routing information discovered through one routing protocol to be distributed in the update messages of another routing protocol. This is sometimes called route redistribution.

routed protocol—Protocol that can be routed by a router. A router must be capable of interpreting the logical internetwork as specified by that routed protocol. Examples of routed protocols include AppleTalk, DECnet, and IP.

routing function—Process of finding a path to a destination host. Routing is very complex in large networks because of the many potential intermediate destinations that a packet might traverse before reaching its destination host.

routing loop—A loop in which the routing information is fed back to the originating router as if from another router. This often happens when redistribution is configured. It can lead to confusion in the network because when the originating router loses the route, it may well believe that there is an alternative path.

routing protocol—Protocol that accomplishes routing through the implementation of a specific routing algorithm. Examples of routing protocols include IGRP, OSPF, and RIP.

routing table—Table stored in a router or some other internetworking device that keeps track of routes to particular network destinations and, in some cases, metrics associated with those routes.

silicon switching—Switching based on the Silicon Switch Engine (SSE), which allows the processing of packets independent of the Silicon Switch Processor (SSP) system processor. Silicon switching provides high-speed, dedicated packet switching.

split horizon rules—Routing technique in which information about routes is prevented from exiting the router interface through which that information was received. Split-horizon updates are useful in preventing routing loops.

static route—A route that is explicitly configured and entered into the routing table.

switching function—Forwarding packets from an inbound interface to an outbound interface.

topology table—Used by EIGRP and OSPF, the table that records all the routes in the network before determining which will be entered into the routing table.

triggered update—See *flash update*.

Q&A

The following questions test your understanding of the topics covered in this chapter. The final questions in this section repeat of the opening "Do I Know This Already?" questions. These are repeated to enable you to test your progress. After you have answered the questions, find the answers in Appendix A. If you get an answer wrong, review the answer and ensure that you understand the reason for your mistake. If you are confused by the answer, refer to the appropriate text in the chapter to review the concepts.

1 Name one routing protocol that sends periodic updates.

2 What is an incremental update, and how often is it sent out?

3 What is the routing algorithm used in OSPF?

4 State one method by which a link-state routing protocol attempts to reduce the network overhead.

5 Distance vector routing protocols naturally summarize at which boundary?

6 Which routing protocol technology uses the Bellman Ford algorithm?

_____

_____

_____

7 Give three reasons why RIPv1 has problems with working in a large network.

_____

_____

_____

8 What is the Dijkstra algorithm used for?

_____

_____

_____

9 What is the destination address of the distance vector periodic update?

_____

_____

_____

10 State one major difference between a classful and classless routing protocol.

_____

_____

_____

11 In the routing table, a field indicates the source of the routing information. If the field showed the letter C, what would this mean?

_____

_____

_____

12 In the routing table, how is the next logical hop indicated?

_____

_____

_____

13 Cisco distinguishes between the routing and the switching function—what is the difference?

_____

_____

_____

14 State the two ways that an outgoing interface is selected as the preferred path.

_____

_____

_____

15 What is administrative distance?

_____

_____

_____

16 If IGRP has three paths to a remote network in which each path has an equal metric, what will happen?

_____

_____

_____

17 Name the interior IP routing protocols that send the mask with the routing update.

_____

_____

_____

18 Name the interior routing protocol that sends a routing update on a Cisco router every 30 seconds by default.

_____

_____

_____

19 Does VLSM require a classful or classless routing protocol, and why?

_____

_____

_____

20 State one of the characteristics of a classful routing protocol.

_____

_____

_____

21 A distance vector routing protocol uses the mechanism of poison reverse—what is this?

_____

_____

_____

22 Name two distance vector routing protocols.

_____

_____

_____

23 Name two link-state IP routing protocols.

_____

_____

_____

24 Describe the mechanism of split horizon.

_____

_____

_____

25 What is the command syntax to empty the Cisco routing table of all its routes?

_____

_____

_____

26 What does 0.0.0.0 signify in an IP routing table?

_____

_____

_____

27 What is the command to show whether a specific network, such as 141.131.6.16, is present in the routing table?

_____

_____

_____

28 What is the next logical hop in the routing table?

_____

_____

_____

Scenarios

The following scenarios and questions are designed to draw together the content of the chapter and to exercise your understanding of the concepts. There is not necessarily a right answer. The thought process and practice in manipulating the concepts is the goal of this section. The answers to the scenario questions are found at the end of this chapter.

Scenario 4-1

Mental Merge, our poor congested company, with many ideas but no bandwidth with which to develop or communicate them, is badly in need of a routed solution. Taking the scenario solution provided for the addressing scheme, outlined in the previous chapter, it is now necessary to implement routing.

Using the network in Figure 4-3, answer the following questions.

1 Using the addressing skills developed in Chapter 3, "IP Addressing," and in reference to Figure 4-3, state where the routers should be placed.

2 The administrator has decided that a link-state routing protocol is the best solution for this network design. Justify his choice, explaining which characteristics of the link-state routing protocol would benefit this network.

3 The administrator must create an implementation plan for his team. List the IP routing protocol requirements for every router that may be used as a checklist for the installation staff.

4 The links between the various sites are leased lines with a backup link using a dialup line. Should the administrator be aware of any considerations?

Figure 4-3   *The Mental Merge Company Network for Scenario 4-1*

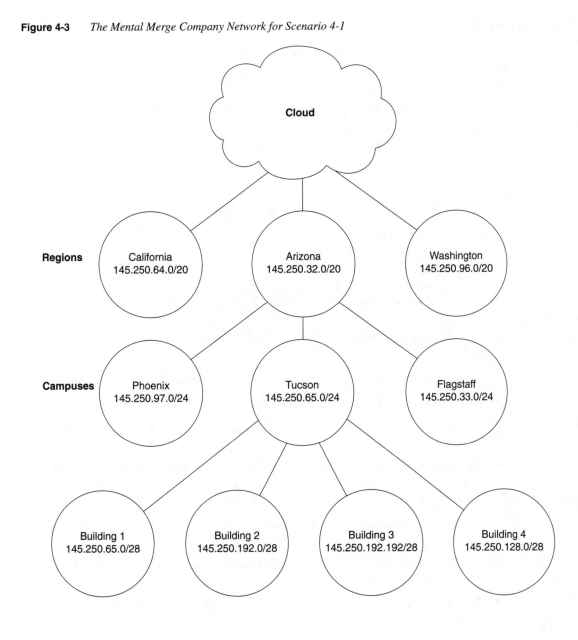

Scenario 4-2

Scenario 4-2 provides you with the data produced with the Cisco router IOS command **show ip route**. A legend defining the fields of the sample output is also provided to assist in answering the questions for Scenario 4-2.

Example 4-2 contains sample output from the **show ip route** command.

Example 4-2   **show ip route** *Command Output*

```
Codes: I - IGRP derived, R - RIP derived, H - Hello derived, O - OSPF derived
       C - connected, S - static, E - EGP derived, B - BGP derived
       * - candidate default route, IA - OSPF inter area route
       E1 - OSPF external type 1 route, E2 - OSPF external type 2 route

Gateway of last resort is 131.119.254.240 to network 129.140.0.0

O E2 150.150.0.0  [160/5]    via 131.119.254.6,   0:01:00, Ethernet2
E       192.67.131.0 [200/128] via 131.119.254.244, 0:02:22, Ethernet2
O E2 192.68.132.0 [160/5]    via 131.119.254.6,   0:00:59, Ethernet2
O E2 130.130.0.0  [160/5]    via 131.119.254.6,   0:00:59, Ethernet2
E       128.128.0.0  [200/128] via 131.119.254.244, 0:02:22, Ethernet2
E       129.129.0.0  [200/129] via 131.119.254.240, 0:02:22, Ethernet2
E       192.65.129.0 [200/128] via 131.119.254.244, 0:02:22, Ethernet2
E       131.131.0.0  [200/128] via 131.119.254.244, 0:02:22, Ethernet2
E       192.75.139.0 [200/129] via 131.119.254.240, 0:02:23, Ethernet2
```

The following information defines the fields reported in the **show ip route** command:

- The first column lists the protocol that derived the route.

- The second column may list certain protocol-specific information as defined in the display header.

- The third column lists the address of the remote network. The first number in the brackets is the administrative distance of the information source; the second number is the metric for the route.

- The fourth column specifies the address of the router that can build a route to the specified remote network.

- The fifth column specifies the last time that the route was updated, in hours:minutes:seconds.

- The final column specifies the interface through which the specified network can be reached.

Answer the following questions by using the output from the preceding **show ip route** command.

1 What routing protocol derived the route 130.130.0.0?

2 What router interface IP address is used to reach IP network 192.67.131.0?

3 When was the last time that the route 192.65.129.0 was updated?

4 Through which router interface can the IP network 128.128.0.0 be reached?

Scenario Answers

The answers are in **bold**. The answers provided in this section are not necessarily the only possible answers to the questions. The questions are designed to test your knowledge and to give practical exercise in certain key areas. This section is intended to test and exercise skills and concepts detailed in the body of this chapter.

If your answer is different, ask yourself whether it follows the tenets explained in the answers provided. Your answer is correct not if it matches the solution provided in the book, but rather if it has included the principles of design laid out in the chapter.

In this way, the testing provided in these scenarios is deeper: It examines not only your knowledge, but also your understanding and ability to apply that knowledge to problems.

If you do not get the correct answer, refer back to the text and review the subject tested. Be certain to also review your notes on the question to ensure that you understand the principles of the subject.

Scenario 4-1 Answers

1 Using the addressing skills developed in Chapter 3, and in reference to Figure 4-3, state where the routers should be placed.

   The routers should be placed in each location, with the option of adding routers within each building if the network grows considerably.

2 The administrator has decided that a link-state routing protocol is the best solution for this network design. Justify his choice, explaining which characteristics of the link-state routing protocol would benefit this network.

   A link-state routing protocol would be a good choice because of the large number of WAN interfaces. A distance vector routing protocol would increase congestion across these low-bandwidth links. The capability to use VLSM and to summarize these points would be an added advantage.

3 The administrator must create an implementation plan for his team. List the IP routing protocol requirements for every router that may be used as a checklist for the installation staff.

   Each person implementing the routing protocol on the router would have to ensure the following:

   • **That the appropriate interfaces had IP addresses that were on the same subnet as the other devices on the segment.**

- **That the routing protocol was configured correctly with the correct network addresses.**

- **That the routing table reflected the logical topology map of the network and that all the remote networks were present.**

- **If there were multiple paths available of equal cost, that the routing protocol was load sharing between the paths. This would mean all the paths were present in the routing table.**

4   The links between the various sites are leased lines with a backup link using a dialup line. Should the administrator be aware of any considerations?

The leased lines to the remote sites could be configured to be the primary link; as such, no traffic would traverse the dialup links. However, routing updates would be propagated out the dialup links so that the routing table would be aware of the potential path. To prevent this (and, thus, the dialup line being raised), the path could be manually entered into the routing table. However, this would render it the preferred path. Configuring the dialup paths as floating static routes would ensure that they were used only if the primary line failed, without having to generate network traffic across the link to maintain the routing table.

Scenario 4-2 Answers

1   What routing protocol derived the route 130.130.0.0?

OSPF.

2   What router interface IP address is used to reach IP network 192.67.131.0?

131.119.254.244. The fourth column of the sample output specifies the address of the router that can build a route to the specified remote network.

3   When was the last time that the route 192.65.129.0 was updated?

0:02:22. The fifth column of the sample output specifies the last time the route was updated, in hours:minutes:seconds.

4   Through which router interface can the IP network 128.128.0.0 be reached?

Ethernet2. The last column in the sample output specifies the interface through which the specified network can be reached.

This chapter covers the following topics that you will need to master to pass the CCNP/CCDP Routing exam:

- How a link-state routing protocol (in this case, OSPF) discovers, chooses, and maintains routes.

- How OSPF operates in a single nonbroadcast multiaccess (NBMA) area (such as a WAN).

- How to configure OSPF in a single area.

- How to verify the operation of and troubleshoot an OSPF network.

- The Cisco defaults in OSPF, the Cisco commands for implementing OSPF in a single area, and Cisco commands for reviewing the configuration.

CHAPTER 5

Using OSPF in a Single Area

The topics in this chapter detail the routing protocol OSPF. This chapter assumes knowledge of the previous chapter, which dealt conceptually with routing protocols and, in particular, link-state routing protocols. This chapter covers the essence of OSPF. It introduces OSPF by considering the protocol in its simplest form, within a single area. Both the basic operations of the protocol and its configuration are explained in this chapter. The following chapter builds on this understanding and explains how OSPF works within a large multiarea network. Each of these chapters is broken into two sections. The first part of the chapter deals theoretically with how the protocol works. The second part of the chapter covers how to implement and manage an OSPF network.

The topics in this chapter directly reflect questions on the exam. OSPF is the industry-standard interior routing protocol designed for use in large networks. Therefore, it is an obligatory subject in an exam on IP routing protocols. The BSCN course devotes 13 percent of its material to using OSPF in a single area, and you can expect approximately seven questions on the exam to be directly related to this subject. The following chapter assumes your comprehension of the subjects covered within this chapter.

How to Best Use This Chapter

By taking the following steps, you can make better use of your study time:

- Keep your notes and the answers for all your work with this book in one place, for easy reference.

- When you take a quiz, write down your answers. Studies show that retention significantly increases by writing down facts and concepts, even if you never look at the information again.

- Use the diagram in Figure 5-1 to guide you to the next step.

Figure 5-1 *How to Use This Chapter*

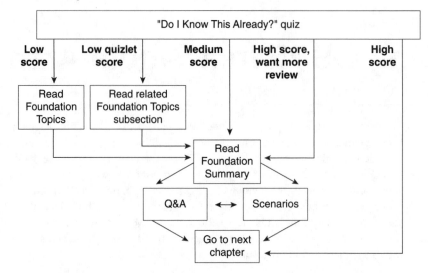

If you skip to the Foundation Summary, Q&A, and scenarios sections and have trouble with the material there, you should go back to the Foundation Topics section.

"Do I Know This Already?" Quiz

The purpose of the "Do I Know This Already?" quiz is to help you decide what parts of this chapter to use. If you already intend to read the entire chapter, you do not necessarily need to answer these questions now.

This 16-question quiz helps you determine how to spend your limited study time. The quiz is sectioned into four smaller four-question "quizlets," which correspond to four major topics in the chapter. Figure 5-1 outlines suggestions on how to spend your time in this chapter. Use Table 5-1 to record your scores.

Table 5-1   *Score Sheet for Quiz and Quizlets*

Quizlet Number	Topic	Questions	Score
1	How OSPF discovers, chooses, and maintains routes	1 to 4	
2	How OSPF operates in a single NBMA area	5 to 8	
3	How to configure OSPF in a single area	9 to 12	
4	How to verify OSPF operation in a single area	13 to 16	
All questions	All	1 to 16	

1 How often, by default, does OSPF send out hello packets on a broadcast multiaccess link?

_____

_____

_____

2 What is a neighbor in OSPF?

_____

_____

_____

3 What is an adjacency in OSPF?

_____

_____

_____

4 If the network is stable and sees no changes, how often will it send LSAs? Why are these updates sent out periodically?

_____

_____

_____

5 If a router has an OSPF priority set to 0, what does this indicate?

_____

_____

_____

6 What does *NBMA* stand for?

_____

_____

_____

7 RFC 2328 describes the operation of OSPF in two modes across an NBMA cloud. What are they?

_____

_____

_____

8 The Cisco solution point-to-point mode does not require the configuration of DR and BDR. Explain briefly why.

_____

_____

_____

9 The address 192.100.56.10 has been allocated to an interface on the router. This interface alone is to be included in the OSPF process. State the command that would start the process on this interface.

_____

_____

_____

10 What command would identify the designated router for your LAN?

_____

_____

_____

11 The metric used by OSPF is cost. How would you change the default setting on an interface?

_____

_____

_____

12 If the command **ip ospf network non-broadcast** is used, what additional statement is necessary?

_____

_____

_____

13 What command shows which router on a LAN is the BDR?

_____

_____

_____

14 Explain briefly what **show ip ospf database** will reveal.

_____

_____

_____

15 What command is used to show the state of adjacencies?

_____

_____

_____

16 It is possible to have more than one OSPF process on a router. Which command would achieve this?

_____

_____

_____

The answers to this quiz are found in Appendix A, "Answers to Quiz Questions." The suggested choices for your next step are as follows:

- **2 or less on any quizlet**—Review the appropriate sections of the "Foundation Topics" portion of this chapter, based on Table 5-1. Then move on to the "Foundation Summary" section, the "Q&A" section, and the "Scenarios" at the end of the chapter.

- **8 or less overall score**—Read the entire chapter. This includes the "Foundation Topics" and "Foundation Summary" sections, the "Q&A" section, and the "Scenarios" at the end of the chapter.

- **9 to 12 overall score**—Begin with the "Foundation Summary" section, and then go to the "Q&A" section and the "Scenarios" at the end of the chapter. If you have trouble with these exercises, read the appropriate sections in "Foundation Topics."

- **13 or more overall score**—If you want more review on these topics, skip to the "Foundation Summary" section, and then go to the "Q&A" section and the "Scenarios" at the end of the chapter. Otherwise, move to the next chapter.

Foundation Topics

Introduction: What Is OSPF?

OSPF stands for Open Shortest Path First, an open standard link-state routing protocol. This routing protocol was built by a committee, which is why it is an open standard. The word *open* means that anyone can read the rules or standard and write an application. The routing protocol as such belongs to no one, but to everyone.

OSPF's purpose as a routing protocol is to convey routing information to every router within the organizational network. The technology that has been selected is link-state technology, which was designed to be very efficient in the way it propagates updates, allowing the network to grow.

The following case study describes a small company that has been bought, along with other companies, by a large conglomerate. The need to change the routing protocol to inform the newly expanded network is urgent.

Case Study

The company Jackanory.com has been writing very successful multimedia applications for the last five years. The company is based in Los Angeles, although its clientele are located throughout the United States. Jackanory.com specializes in educational software tailored to a large company's specific training needs—for example, teaching the retail sales teams of a multinational car manufacturer how to sell cars. Internally, the company needs high-bandwidth pipes that cannot be clogged with network overhead. Until recently, there was little external communication, except for the occasional connection to a customer for maintenance.

However, the company was recently bought by a British company that merged them with a small company emerging in San Francisco. Consequently, the company has grown enormously in size and looks to be growing fast and furiously in the exciting new world of digital imaging.

RIPv1 is no longer adequate. Although it works well for the range of vendors within the network, it cannot cope with the WAN or the new size of the network. It has been decreed that OSPF is the routing protocol of choice.

The network administrators need to understand the mechanics of the routing protocol to design and implement it into the network. They also need to know how to interrogate the network to monitor, troubleshoot, and fix the network.

The first stage of implementation is to install OSPF on the original network in Los Angeles. The next stage will introduce the other locations after Los Angeles is installed and stable. These locations will be configured as separate areas, which is described in the following chapter.

OSPF Terminology

OSPF is an open standard link-state routing protocol for IP. As such, it has clear documentation that is freely available, allowing it to be offered by every vendor. This means that it can be used to connect various technologies and vendor solutions.

OSPF is a sophisticated protocol, but it is in essence quite straightforward. Rather like a Russian novel of the nineteenth century, when you know the different names of the protagonists and how they interrelate, the rest is simple.

Table 5-2 explains briefly the terminology used by OSPF that will be used in the next two chapters.

Table 5-2   *OSPF Terms*

Term	Description
adjacency	Formed when two neighboring routers have exchanged information and have the same topology table. The databases are synchronized, and they both see the same networks.
area	A group of routers that share the same area ID. Each router in the area has the same topology table. Each router in the area is an internal router. The area is defined on an interface basis in the configuration of OSPF.
autonomous system	Routers that share the same routing protocol within the organization.
backup designated router (BDR)	The backup to the designated router, in case the DR fails. The BDR performs none of the DR functions while the DR is operating correctly.
cost	The metric for OSPF. It is not defined in the standard with a value. Cisco use the default of the inverse of bandwidth so that the higher the speed of the link, the lower the cost—and, therefore, the more attractive the path. This default can be overridden by a manual configuration. This should be done only if you have a full knowledge of the network.
database descriptor	Referred to as DBDs or database descriptor packets (DDPs). These are packets exchanged between neighbors during the exchange state. The DDPs contain LSAs, which describe the links of every router in the neighbor's topology table.
designated router (DR)	Router responsible for making adjacencies with all neighbors on a multiaccess network, such as Ethernet or FDDI. The DR represents the multiaccess network, in that it ensures that every router on the link has the same topology database.
exchange state	Method by which two neighboring routers discover the map of the network. When these routers become adjacent, they must first exchange DDPs to ensure that they have the same topology table.

Table 5-2   *OSPF Terms (Continued)*

Term	Description
exstart	State in which the neighboring routers determine the sequence number of the DDPs and establish the master/slave relationship.
init	State in which a hello packet has been sent from the router, which is waiting for a reply to establish two-way communication.
internal router	A router that has all its interfaces in the same area.
link-state advertisement (LSA)	A packet describing a router's links and the state of those links. There are different types of LSAs to describe the different types of links. These are discussed in the following section.
link-state database	Otherwise known as the topology map. It has a map of every router, its links, and the state of the links. It also has a map of every network and every path to each network.
link-state request (LSR)	When the router receives a DDP complete with LSA, it compares the LSA against the topological database. If either the LSA entry is not present or the entry is older than the DDP, it will request further information.
link-state update (LSU)	Update sent in response to the LSR. It is the LSA that was requested.
neighbor	A router on the same link with whom routing information is exchanged.
neighbor table	A table built from the hello received from the neighbor. The hello carries a list of the neighbors.
priority	A Cisco tool by which the designated router can be manually elected—or, conversely, prevented from taking part in the DR/BDR election.
SPF tree	A tree of the topological network. It can be drawn after the SPF algorithm has been run. The algorithm prunes the database of alternative paths and creates a loop-free shortest path to all networks. The router is at the root of the network, which is perceived from its perspective.
topology table	The same as a link-state database. The table contains every link in the wider network.

OSPF has many features, and each one is dealt with here in turn, starting with the simplest design of a single area. After the main concepts have been identified, the chapter shows how to configure OSPF within a single area and how to verify that configuration. Chapter 6, "Using OSPF Across Multiple Areas," considers building large networks with OSPF using multiple areas. It then covers the detailed configuration of the OSPF protocol.

OSPF Neighbors

A neighbor in OSPF is a router that shares the same network link. This is the same physical segment. A router running OSPF discovers its neighbors by sending and receiving a simple protocol called the *hello protocol*.

A router configured for OSPF sends out a small hello packet periodically (10 seconds is the default on broadcast multiaccess media). It has a source address of the router and a multicast destination address set to AllSPFRouters (224.0.0.5). All routers running OSPF (or the SPF algorithm) listen to the protocol and send their own hello packets periodically.

How the Hello protocol works and how OSPF neighbors build their databases depend upon the media. OSPF identifies five distinct network types or topologies.

OSPF Network Topologies

How an OSPF protocol communicates to a network depends on the physical medium being used. OSPF identifies the different technologies as follows:

- **Broadcast multiaccess**—This is any LAN network such as Ethernet, Token Ring, or FDDI. In this environment, OSPF sends out multicast traffic. A designated router and backup designated router will be elected. Figure 5-2 illustrates a broadcast multiaccess network and the designated and backup designated routers.

Figure 5-2   *A Broadcast Multiaccess Network*

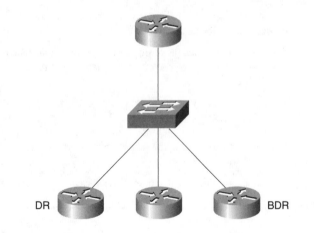

- **Point-to-point**—This technology is used where there is one other system directly connected to the transmitting or receiving router. A typical example of this is a serial line. OSPF has no need of a designated or backup designated router in this scenario. Network traffic uses the multicast address for OSPF AllSPFRouters, 224.0.0.5. Figure 5-3 illustrates a point to point network.

Figure 5-3 *Point-to-Point Network*

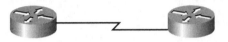

- **Point-to-multipoint**—This is a single interface that connects to many destinations. The underlying network treats the network as a series of point-to-point circuits. It replicates LSA packets for each circuit. The addressing of network traffic is multicast. There is no DR or BDR election. This technology uses one IP subnet.

  Physically, some point-to-multipoint networks cannot support multicast or broadcast traffic. In these cases, special configuration is required. The configuration and considerations of an NBMA network are considered later in this chapter. Figure 5-4 illustrates a point-to-multipoint network.

Figure 5-4 *Point-to-Multipoint Network*

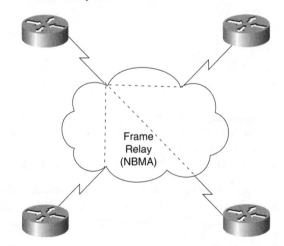

- **Nonbroadcast multiaccess (NBMA)**—This physically resembles a point-to-point line, but in fact, many destinations are possible. WAN clouds, including X.25 and Frame Relay, are examples of this technology. NBMA uses a fully meshed or partially meshed network. OSPF sees it as a broadcast network, and it will be represented by one IP subnet.

This technology requires manual configuration of the neighbors and the DR and BDR selection. The configuration options have increased with the different versions of Cisco IOS.

DR and BDR routers are elected, and the DR will generate an LSA for the network. The DR and BDR must be directly connected to their neighbors. All network traffic sent between neighbors will be replicated for each physical circuit using unicast addresses because multicast and broadcast addresses are not understood. Figure 5-5 illustrates an NBMA network.

Figure 5-5 *A Nonbroadcast Multiaccess (NBMA) Network*

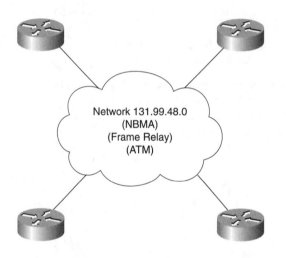

Network 131.99.48.0
(NBMA)
(Frame Relay)
(ATM)

- **Virtual links**—This is a virtual connection to a remote area that does not have any connections to the backbone (Area 0). Although OSPF treats this link as a direct, single-hop connection to the backbone area, it is a virtual connection that tunnels through the network. The OSPF network traffic is sent in unicast datagrams across these links.

The WAN topologies will be discussed in detail later in the chapter, in the section, "Configuring OSPF over an NBMA Topology." Suffice it to say that the method by which the routers in an OSPF network find one another and exchange information depends on the physical characteristics of the network.

The Hello Packet

Although the routers running OSPF transmit a small packet called the hello packet to establish neighbor relations, it serves other functions. The various fields in the hello packet have specific responsibilities. These are shown in the Table 5-3.

Table 5-3   *The Hello Packet*

Field	Characteristics	Function
Router ID	This is a 32-bit number. The highest IP address on the router is used as the ID. If a loopback address is configured, this will be used, even if it is not the highest address.	This field identifies the router within the autonomous system.
Hello/Dead Intervals	Dead Intervals=40 Hello=10 sec This field is used on broadcast, multiaccess networks.	Hello maintains the presence of the router in its neighbor's databases. It works like a keepalive. The dead interval is how long the router waits before it determines that a neighbor is unavailable.
Neighbors	The router ID of a neighbor is entered in the neighbor table when a two-way (bidirectional) communication is established within the RouterDeadInterval. The communication is established when the router sees itself listed as a neighbor in the hello packet generated by another router on the same physical segment.	A neighbor is another router with whom updates will be exchanged to synchronize databases.
Area ID	This is the area ID of the originating router's interface.	The hello packet must come from a router within the same area to be valid.
Router Priority	This is the priority of the source router interface. The higher the priority, the higher the likelihood of the router being selected as a DR or BDR.	This field is used to manually select the DR and BDR.
DR IP Address	This is the address of the existing DR.	This field is used to allow the router to create unicast traffic to the DR router.
BDR IP Address	This is the address of the existing BDR.	This field is used to allow the router to create unicast traffic to the BDR router.
Authentication Password	This specifies the authentication type and information. If set, the password must match the password stated on the router.	This field is used as security.
Stub Area Flag	This field is set if the area is a stub area. All routers in the area must have this flag set.	This field identifies which type of LSAs will be transmitted and accepted.

Adjacent OSPF Neighbors

After neighbors have been established by means of the Hello protocol, they exchange routing information. When their topology databases are the same or synchronized, the neighbors are *fully adjacent*. The Hello protocol continues to transmit by default every 10 seconds. The transmitting router and its networks reside in the topology database for as long as the other routers receive the Hello protocol.

Advantages of Having Neighbors

There are obvious advantages to creating neighbor relationships. These advantages include the following:

- There is another mechanism for determining that a router has gone down (obvious because its neighbor no longer sends Hello packets).

- Streamlined communication results because after the topological databases are synchronized, incremental updates will be sent to the neighbors as soon as a change is perceived, as well as every 30 minutes.

- Adjacencies created between neighbors control the distribution of the routing protocol packets.

The use of adjacencies and a neighbor relationship result in a much faster convergence of the network than can be achieved by RIPv1. This is because RIPv1 must wait for incremental updates and holddown timers to expire on each router before the update is sent out. Convergence on a RIPv1 network can take many minutes, and the real problem is the confusion created by the different routing tables held on different routers during this time. This problem can result in routing loops and black holes in the network.

The Designated Router

The designated router is a router on broadcast multiaccess media that is responsible for maintaining the topology table for the segment.

If routers are connected to a broadcast segment, one router on the segment is assigned the duty of maintaining adjacencies with all the routers on the segment. This router is known as the *designated router* and is elected by the use of the Hello protocol. The hello packet carries the information that determines the DR and the BDR. The election is determined by either the highest IP address or this command:

```
ip ospf priority number
```

All other routers need only peer with the designated router, which informs them of any changes on the segment.

Backup Designated Routers

The previous paragraph is only a half truth because there has been a lot of effort put into ensuring that the network does not fail. It is a little nerve-racking for the network administrator to have the responsibility of the segment fall to one router. This poses the frightening situation of a single point of failure, a term that raises the blood pressure of any of those in charge of the network. Redundancy has been built into the network with the backup designated router. Just like an understudy, the backup designated router knows all the words—in this case, the links for the segment. All routers actually have an adjacency not only with the designated router, but also with the backup designated router, which in turn has an adjacency with the designated router. If the designated router fails, the backup designated router immediately becomes the designated router.

Why Have Designated Routers?

Designated routers are created on multiaccess links because if there are many routers on the same segment, the intermesh of neighbor relationships becomes complex. On an FDDI ring, which forms the campus or building backbone, each router must form an adjacency with every other router on the segment. Although the Hello protocol is not networking-intensive, maintaining the relationships require additional CPU cycles. Also, there is a sharp increase in the number of LSAs generated.

Electing the Designated and Backup Designated Routers

The network administrator can manually elect the designated and backup designated routers, or they can be dynamically selected using the Hello protocol.

Dynamic Election

When selected dynamically, the designated router is elected arbitrarily. The selection is made on the basis of the highest router ID or IP address. It is wise to be aware that the highest IP address is the numerically highest number, not the class ranking of the addresses. Therefore, a remote, small router with a Class C address may end up as a designated router. This may not be the optimal choice.

If you are manually determining which routers are to be the designated and backup designated routers, it is easier to design your network to the optimum.

After the designated and backup designated routers have been elected, all routers on the broadcast medium will communicate directly with the designated routers. They will use the multicast address to all designated routers. The backup router will listen but will not respond; remember, it is the understudy waiting in the wings. The designated router will send out multicast messages if it receives any information pertinent to the connected routers for which it is responsible.

Manual Configuration of the Designated Router

To manually determine which router will be the designated router, it is necessary to set the priority of the router. A router interface can have a priority of 0 to 255. The value of 0 means that the router cannot be a designated router or backup designated router; otherwise, the higher the priority, the more favorable the chances are of winning the election.

If there is more than one router on the segment with the same priority level, the election process picks the router with the highest router ID.

Which Router Should Be Chosen as the Designated Router?

In Figure 5-6, the 2500 router for Building A, which is connected to the San Francisco campus via a hub, would be a reasonable choice as the designated router. Although it is small, size is not as important as fault tolerance in this situation.

Figure 5-6   *The Designated Router*

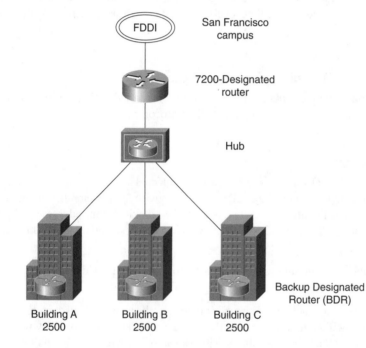

Because there are not many other routers on the segment, the number of LSAs and adjacencies that this router would have to record is small.

The larger 7200 Cisco router, which connects the building routers to the campus backbone, acts as the centralized router; therefore, the 7200 Cisco router makes sense as the router in charge of the connectivity for the FDDI segment. It would be a mistake to make the 7200 the designated router for both networks because this would increase the demand for resources and also would centralize all the responsibility on one router.

The Election of the Designated Router

The following is the process used to elect the designated and backup designated routers:

- All the neighbors who have a priority greater than 0 are listed.

- The neighbor with the highest priority is elected as the BDR.

- If there is no DR, the BDR is promoted as DR.

- From the remaining routers, the router with the highest priority is elected as the BDR.

- If there is a tie, the highest router IDs are used.

How OSPF Builds Its Routing Table

After a neighbor is discovered in OSPF, an adjacency is formed. It is important to understand how the neighbor adjacency is formed and, in this context, to understand the other messages that the routers receive.

Routing tables are built in two different ways. The next sections examine these in more detail.

A Router Joins the Network

The first way to build a routing table is for a new router to be added to the network and then for it to build a routing table by listening to the established routers with complete routing tables. Remember that every router within an area will have the same database and will know of every network within the area. The routing table built from this database is unique to the router because the decisions depend on the individual router's position within the area, relative to the remote destination network.

A Change in the Network

A change in the network topology also necessitates information to be propagated through the network. For example, the rest of the network notices that a new router has joined their ranks.

A particular router that notices a change floods the area with the update so that all routers can alter their routing tables to reflect the most current and accurate information.

Different techniques are used for these different routing table requirements. Essentially, the difference between the two techniques is simple:

- If a new router connects to a network, it will find a neighbor using the Hello protocol and will *exchange* routing information.

- If a change occurs in an existing network, the router that sees the change will *flood* the area with the new routing information.

NOTE   Both of these events must occur as stated because, although the new router must learn the network topology, its addition is a change to the rest of the network.

These two requirements for updating the routing table use different technologies and OSPF protocols. These technologies and protocols are often confused, so it is worth a moment to distinguish them. Understanding the distinction makes the OSPF operation much clearer.

Building the Routing Table on a New OSPF Router

Five packets are used to build the routing table for the first time:

- **Hello protocol**—Is used to find neighbors and to determine the designated and backup designated router. The continued propagation of the Hello protocol maintains the transmitting router in the topology database of those that hear the message.

- **Database descriptor**—Is used to send summary information to neighbors to synchronize topology databases.

- **Link-state request**—Works as a request for more detailed information, which is sent when the router receives a database descriptor that contains new information.

- **Link-state update**—Works as the link-state advertisement (LSA) packet issued in response to the request for database information in the link-state request packet. The different types of LSA are described in Chapter 6, in the section "The Link-State Advertisements."

- **Link-state acknowledgement**—Acknowledges the link-state update.

Consider the case of when a router joins the OSPF network for the first time. In Figure 5-7, the 2500 router in Building A at the San Francisco campus has just been connected.

The next sections detail what happens when a router joins a network.

Finding Neighbors with the Exchange Process

When it is connected to the network and has been configured to run OSPF, the new router must learn the network from the systems that are up and running. The method shown here, however, is the same as for a stable network.

This process is shown in the stages that the systems go through while exchanging information. It is possible to see what stage an interface running OSPF is in with the command **show ip ospf neighbor** as well as the command **debug ip ospf adjacency.** Care should be taken with the **debug** command because it can be CPU-intensive.

Figure 5-7   *Joining an OSPF Network*

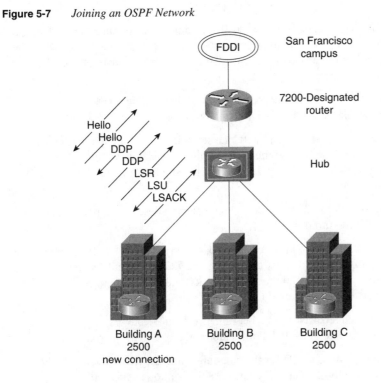

The different stages or states that the router goes through while creating a neighbor relationship are shown in the following list:

- **The down state**—The new router is in a *down state*. The 2500 router transmits its own hello packets to introduce itself to the segment and to find any other OSPF-configured routers. This is sent out as a hello to the multicast address 224.0.0.5 (AllSPFRouters). It sets the DR and BDR in the hello to be 0.0.0.0.

- **The init state**—The new router waits for a reply. Typically this is four times the length of the hello timer. The router is in the *init state*. Within the wait time, the new router hears a hello from another router and learns the DR and the BDR. If there is no DR or BDR stated in the incoming hello, an election takes place. However, in accordance with the description of the Hello protocol, the designated router has been elected: It is the 7200 router, which connects the campus to the campus backbone.

   Upon hearing the Hello protocol from the 2500, a router on the segment adds the router ID of the 2500 and replies as a multicast (224.0.0.5) with its own ID and a list of any other neighbors.

- **The two-way state**—The new router sees its own router ID in the list of neighbors, and a neighbor relationship is established. The new router changes its status to the *two-way state*.

Discovering Routes

The 2500 and the designated router have now established a neighbor relationship and need to ensure that the 2500 has all the relevant information about the network. The 7200 must update and synchronize the topology database of the 2500. This is achieved by using the exchange protocol with the database description packets.

The different stages or states that the router goes through while exchanging routing information with a neighbor are shown in the following list:

- **The exstart state**—One of the routers will take seniority, becoming the master router. This is the *exstart state*. The two neighbors determine a master/slave relationship based on highest IP interface address. This designation is not significant; it just determines who starts the communication.

- **The exchange state**—Both routers will send out database description packets, changing the state to the *exchange state*.

  In this example, the 2500 has no knowledge and can inform the 7200 only of the networks or links to which it is directly connected. The 7200 sends out a series of database description packets containing the networks held in the topology database. These networks are referred to as *links*.

  Most of these have been received from other routers (via link-state advertisements). The source of the link information is referred to by the router ID.

  Each link will have an interface ID for the outgoing interface, a link ID, and a metric to state the value of the path. The database description packet will not contain all the necessary information—just a summary (enough for the receiving router to determine whether more information is required or whether it already contains that entry in its database).

When the router has received the DDPs from the neighboring router, it compares the received network information with that in its topology table. In the case of a new router, such as the 2500, all the DDPs are new. The different stages or states that the router goes through gathering routing information form a neighbor are shown in the following list:

- **The loading state**—If the receiving router, the 2500, requires more information, it will request that particular link in more detail using the link-state request packet (LSR).

  The LSR will prompt the master router to send the link-state update packet (LSU).
  Figure 5-8 illustrates this as well. This is the same as a link-state advertisement (LSA) used to flood the network with routing information. While the 2500 is awaiting the LSUs from its neighbor, it is in the *loading state*.

- **The full state**—When these LSRs are received and the databases are updated and synchronized, the neighbors are *fully adjacent*.

This exchange is illustrated in the Figure 5-8.

Figure 5-8   *The Stages of Updating the Routers About the Network*

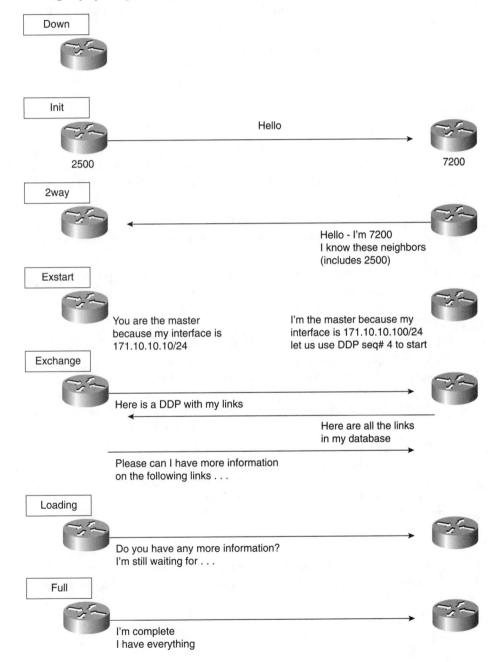

Down

Init

Hello

2500   7200

2way

Hello - I'm 7200
I know these neighbors
(includes 2500)

Exstart

You are the master   I'm the master because my
because my interface is   interface is 171.10.10.100/24
171.10.10.10/24   let us use DDP seq# 4 to start

Exchange

Here is a DDP with my links

Here are all the links
in my database

Please can I have more information
on the following links . . .

Loading

Do you have any more information?
I'm still waiting for . . .

Full

I'm complete
I have everything

The process described in the previous section takes you through the process of learning about the network. The first stage is to learn the neighbors at the other end of the link that directly attaches. This information is stored in the neighbor table.

The second stage is to learn from the neighbors the links throughout the network. This information described previously updates the topology database, sometimes referred to as the link-state database.

The Topology Database

The topology database is the router's view of the network within the area. It includes every OSPF router within the area and all the connected networks. This database is indeed a routing table, but a routing table for which no path decisions have been made; it is at present a topology database.

The topology database is updated by the LSAs. Each router within the area has exactly the same topology database. All routers must have the same vision of the network; otherwise, confusion, routing loops, and loss of connectivity will result.

The synchronization of the topology maps is ensured by the intricate use of sequence numbers in the LSA headers.

How the Topology Table Updates the Routing Table

From the topology map, a routing database is constructed. This database will be unique to each router, which creates a routing database by running the *shortest path first* (SPF) algorithm called the *Dijkstra algorithm*. Each router uses this algorithm to determine the best path to each network and creates an *SPF tree* on which it places itself at the top or root. If there are equal metrics for a remote network, OSPF includes all the paths and load balances the routed data traffic among them.

Occasionally a link may flap, go up and down. This is more usual on a serial line. If this happens, it could cause many LSAs to be generated in updating the network. To prevent this from happening, OSPF introduced timers. These timers forced OSPF to wait before recalculating SPF. These timers are configurable.

NOTE   Although RFC 2328 does not state the number of multiple, equal-cost paths that can be used at the same time, Cisco has defined a maximum of six paths that can be used simultaneously for load balancing.

A Change in the Network, Maintaining the Topological Database and the Routing Table

Now turn back to the 2500 router in Building A of the San Francisco campus in Figure 5-6. The router is now happily a member of the OSPF network. Now follow the process of hearing an update to the network in the form of an LSA.

As soon as a router realizes that there has been a change in the network topology, the router is responsible for informing the rest of the routers in the area. Typically, it will identify a change in the state of one of its links for one of the following reasons:

- The router loses the physical or data link layer connectivity on a connected network. It will propagate an LSU and send it to the DR on a multiaccess network or the adjacent router in a point-to-point network. From there, it is flooded to the network.

- The router fails to hear either an OSPF Hello protocol or a data link Hello protocol. It will propagate an LSU and send it to the DR on a multiaccess network or the adjacent router in a point-to-point network. From there, it is flooded to the network.

- It receives an LSA update from an adjacent neighbor, informing it of the change in the network topology. The LSU is acknowledged and flooded out the other OSPF interfaces.

In any of these instances, the router will generate an LSA and flood it to all its neighbors.

This discussion now turns to the process initiated when a router receives such an update. For this purpose, return to the 2500 connected to its designated router, the 7200.

Learning a New Route

When the 2500 receives a network LSA update from the designated router, it goes through the following logical steps:

1 The router takes the first entry from the update—the first network with information about the state of its link.

2 The router verifies the type of LSA is one that can be accepted by this router.

3 Having ascertained that it is a valid LSA that it can receive, the router issues a lookup to its topological database.

4 If the LSA entry is *not* in the topological database, it is flooded immediately out all the OSPF interfaces, except for the receiving interface.

5 If the LSA entry is in the topological database, further questions are required.

6 The router determines whether the new LSA has a more recent (higher) sequence number?

7 If the sequence numbers are the same, the router calculates the checksum for the LSAs and uses the LSA with the higher checksum.

8   If the checksum numbers are the same, the router checks the MaxAge field to ascertain which is the more recent update.

9   Having found that the latest LSU is the one that was received, the router determines whether it has arrived outside the wait period, before another computation is allowed (minsLSarrival).

10   If the new LSA entry passes these tests, it is flooded out all the OSPF interfaces, except for the receiving interface.

11   The current copy replaces the old LSA entry. If there was no entry, the current copy is just placed in the database.

12   The received LSA is acknowledged.

13   If the LSA entry was in the database, but the LSA that has just been received has an older sequence number, the process will ask whether the information in the database is the same.

14   If the information is the same and the new LSA has an older sequence number, the process just discards the packet. It may be old news, but there is no inconsistency in the database.

15   If the information is different and the newly received LSA has an older sequence number, however, the receiving router discards the LSA update. It issues its own LSA out the receiving interface to the source address of the out-of-date LSA. The logic is that the sending router either has bad or old information and must be updated because its topological database is obviously not synchronized with the rest of the area.

   This ensures that any packets that get out of sequence will be verified before action is taken. It also attempts to rectify a problem that it sees—that of multiple routers offering different paths because their topological databases are completely confused.

16   After the initial flood, things calm down, and updates are sent only when there are changes in the area or when the 30-minute timer goes off. This timer ensures that the databases stay synchronized.

This shows some of the internal complexity of OSPF. As you can see, the internals are extremely detailed. Therefore, the design of any OSPF network should be very carefully thought out. The configuration of the routing protocol, on the other hand, is incredibly straightforward.

Figure 5-9 shows a logical flowchart of how the OSPF topological database is updated.

As you have seen, different types of LSA are propagated through the network. Figure 5-10 illustrates graphically the flooding of an LSA through the network.

Figure 5-9   *Updating the Topological Database*

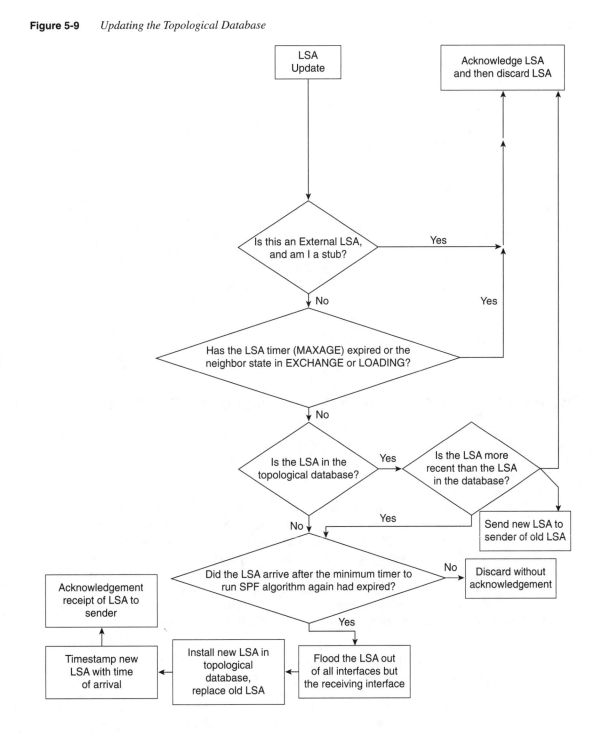

Figure 5-10 *Flooding LSAs Throughout the Area*

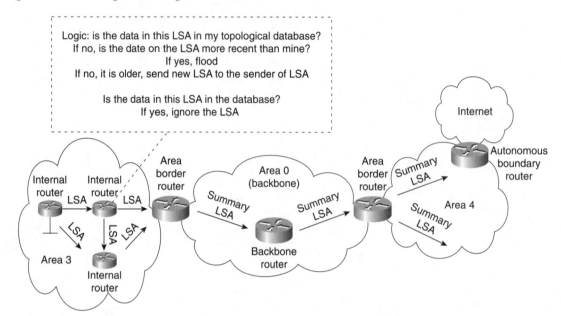

Choosing the Shortest Path First and Building the Routing Table

As with any routing protocol, OSPF examines all the available paths to every network that it knows about. It selects the shortest, most direct path to that destination.

The Metric

As with all routing protocols, this decision will be based on the metric used by the routing protocol. RIP uses hop count, which shows how many routers must be passed through to get to the destination. When CPU and memory were very expensive, the latency of traveling through the router had much higher implications on network performance. OSPF has few of those constraints and so chooses the metric of *cost.* Cost is not defined, however; it depends on the implementation of the protocol. The metric may be programmed to be either complex or simple. Cisco's implementation of a dynamic and default cost uses a predefined value based on the bandwidth of the router interface. The network administrator can manually override this default.

The cost is applied to the outgoing interface. The routing process will select the lowest accumulated cost of the interfaces to the remote network.

NOTE   If the network is manually configured, all routers connected to a particular network should agree on cost. Also, if manually configured, the cost should be thought through very carefully.

Information Needed in the Routing Table

Having determined the shortest path or multiple equal-cost paths, the routing process will need to supply additional information. To forward the data down the chosen path, the next logical hop, link, and outgoing interface must be ascertained. The routing table, or *forwarding database*, as it is sometimes called, requires this information.

The operation of OSPF across wide-area networks (WANs) is slightly different. The next section considers OSPF used over these different technologies.

OSPF Across Nonbroadcast Multiaccess Networks

A nonbroadcast multiaccess (NBMA) network has certain characteristics. The main ones are identified in the name of the technology: It is a network that cannot carry broadcast traffic but that has multiple destinations. Examples of NBMA networks include Frame Relay, X.25, and ATM. The Routing exam concentrates on the use of OSPF across Frame Relay.

The crux of the problem is how OSPF operates using multicast traffic to exchange network information and to create adjacencies to synchronize databases across this WAN cloud without using the multicast addresses.

The solution to the problem varies, depending on the technology involved and the network design. The modes available fall into two technologies, within which there are additional options. The two technologies are point-to-point and NBMA.

The NBMA technology is then subdivided into two categories, under which different configuration options are available. These two categories are the RFC-compliant solution and the Cisco-offered solution:

- **RFC-compliant**—The RFC-compliant category offers a standard's solution, which is independent of the vendor platform. The configuration options are these:
  - NBMA
  - Point-to-multipoint
- **Cisco-specific**—These configuration options are proprietary to Cisco and include these:
  - Point-to-multipoint nonbroadcast
  - Broadcast
  - Point-to-point

The option selected depends on the network topology that is in use. The OSPF technology is separate from the physical configuration, and the choice of implementation is based on the design topology.

The Frame Relay topologies include these:

- **Full mesh**—Every router is connected to every other router. This solution provides redundancy, and it may allow load sharing. This is the most expensive solution.

- **Partial mesh**—Some routers are connected directly; others are accessed through another router.

- **Star, or hub and spoke**—One router acts as the connection to every other router. This is the least expensive solution because it requires the fewest number of permanent virtual circuits (PVCs). Here a single interface is used to connect to multiple destinations.

Which Topology to Choose?

Some of the considerations in choosing the OSPF topology depend on its method of updating the network and its effect on network overhead. These considerations are mentioned in RFC 1586, which suggests that the different virtual circuits have different functions:

- **A point-to-point circuit**—Although no DR or BDR is required, each circuit will have an adjacency, which will create many more adjacencies on the network and will increase the need for network resources.

- **An NBMA environment**—This may require a DR and a BDR, unless the underlying technology is viewed as point-to point. This is economical for most routers, requiring only two adjacencies, except for the DR and BDR. However, it may require more administration in terms of configuration.

Subinterfaces

On a Cisco router, it is possible to configure a physical interface to be many logical interfaces. This is extremely useful in a WAN environment and truly means that the logical topology is independent of the physical configuration. These subinterfaces can be configured to be point-to-point or point-to-multipoint. One of the main determining factors is the number of subnets to be used. A point-to-point interface requires its own subnet to identify it.

Life is very simple in OSPF if the point-to-point option is selected because the routers at each end create adjacencies. This does require more network overhead and restricts some communication—in particular, the capability to indirectly connect through a hub router.

In a point-to-point network, the concept of a broadcast is not relevant because the communication is directly to another router. In a point-to-multipoint network, although OSPF simulates a broadcast, multicast environment, the network traffic is replicated and sent to each neighbor.

Table 5-4 indicates the characteristics and options for each case.

Table 5-4   *OSPF over NBMA*

	Point-point Nonbroadcast	Point-to-point	Broadcast	NBMA	Point-to Multipoint
Addressing	Unicast	Multicast	Multicast	Unicast	Multicast
DR/BDR	No	No	Yes	Manual Yes	No
Manual Configuration of Neighbors	Yes	No	No	Yes	No
Hello	30 seconds Dead=120	10 seconds Dead=40	10 seconds Dead=40	30seconds Dead=120	30seconds Dead=120
RFC/Cisco	Cisco	Cisco	Cisco	RFC 2328	RFC 2328
Network Supported	Star Partial mesh	Star Partial mesh, using subinterfaces	Full mesh	Full mesh	Star Partial mesh (seen as point-to-point)
Replicates Packets	Yes	Yes	Yes	Yes	Yes
Number of Subnets	1	Many (1 per circuit)	1	1	1

This can be very confusing because it is not clear which type of network corresponds to a particular physical configuration. The following list clarifies this:

- For serial interfaces with HDLC encapsulation, the default network type is point-to-point. Timers: hello 10, dead 40.

- For serial interfaces with Frame Relay encapsulation, the default network type is nonbroadcast. Timers: hello 30, dead 120.

- For serial interfaces with Frame Relay encapsulation and using point-to-point subinterfaces, the default network type is point-to point. Timers: hello 10, dead 40.

- For serial interfaces with Frame Relay encapsulation and using point-to-multipoint subinterfaces, the default network type is nonbroadcast. Timers: hello 30, dead 120.

Now that you understand the mechanism of the OSPF routing protocol, it is useful to understand how to configure the protocol on a Cisco router.

WARNING   If OSPF is used in an environment across different vendor equipment, it should be researched and tested to ensure interoperability.

Configuring OSPF in a Single Area

When configuring any device, it is important to establish why you are configuring the system and what you are trying to achieve.

This section examines the configuration of a Cisco router for OSPF within a single area. The commands are few and extremely simple; the implications are somewhat more difficult.

This section covers the following:

- Configuration of OSPF
  - Required configuration
  - Optional configuration
- Commands
  - What each configuration command achieves
  - How the configuration command achieves its goal

An example of a working configuration that uses the commands discussed in this section illustrates the use of those commands in context. A corresponding figure illustrates the configuration.

Required Commands for Configuring OSPF on an Internal Router

The router to be configured is the 2500, an internal router within a single area. The router needs to understand how to participate in the OSPF network. Therefore, it requires the following:

- **The OSPF process**—The routing protocol needs to be started on the router.

- **Participating router interfaces**—The router may not want to have all its interfaces send or receive OSPF routing updates. A classic example is a dialup line to a remote office. If there were only one subnet at the remote office, it would be more efficient to use default and static route commands because any updates would dial the line.

- **Identification of the area**—The router will define which area it is in on a per-interface basis.

- **A router ID**—This allows the router to be identified by the other routers in the network. The ID of the router advertising a link is used to determine the next logical hop, for example, if that link is used in the path selection to a remote network.

The following two commands are required for configuring OSPF on a single internal router:

- OSPF **process** command
- OSPF **network** command

Enabling The OSPF Routing Protocol

By default (unless the *SETUP script* is used), there is no IP routing protocol running on the Cisco router. This is not true of other protocols, however; for example, if an IPX network address is configured on an interface, the IPX RIP process will be automatically started.

To configure OSPF as the routing protocol, use the following command:

```
router ospf process number
```

Here, *process number* is a number local to the router. It is possible to have more than one process running on a router, although this is an unusual and expensive configuration in terms of router resources. The process number does not have to be the same on every router in the area or the autonomous system. In the interest of sanity, however, many administrators make it the same number.

NOTE   A common error in configuration is to confuse the process ID with the router ID or the area ID. These are not related in any way. The process ID is simply a mechanism to allow more than one process to be configured on a router. The router ID is the mechanism by which a router is identified within the OSPF domain, and the area ID is a mechanism of grouping routers that share full knowledge of OSPF-derived routes within the OSPF domain.

The OSPF network Command

Although OSPF has been turned on, it has no information on how to operate. The networks that are to participate in the OSPF updates, and the area that they reside in, must be defined. If the following information is not specified, the process will have nothing to do and will die:

```
network network number wildcard mask area area number
```

This command deserves a moment's explanation because it is the cause of many errors in configuration.

The **network** command in OSPF plays a similar role to that of the **network** command in RIP or IGRP. The difference is the level of granularity afforded to the administrator. In RIP and IGRP, the **network** command is defined at the class level. In OSPF, it is possible to identify the specific address of an interface.

What the network Command Will Do

After the **network** command has been entered, OSPF identifies which interfaces are participating in OSPF by comparing the interface IP address with the address given in the **network** command, filtered through the wildcard mask. The wildcard mask states how much of the address to pay attention to. It could just look at the class of address, such as everything in network 10.0.0.0, for example. At the other extreme, it can be more specific and identify an interface address. All interfaces that match the given network number will reside in the area specified in the **network** command.

WARNING   Take great care in the wildcard mask. Remember that it follows the same format as the wildcard mask in an access list. It is extremely easy to make errors in the configuration, and those errors may be difficult to find.

After identifying the interfaces on the router that are participating in the OSPF domain, the following happens:

- Updates will be received on the interface.

- Updates will be sent out of the interfaces.

- The interface will be placed in the defined area.

- If appropriate, the Hello protocol will be propagated. Depending on the interface type, a default hello and dead interval are defined (see Table 5-4).

This **network** command has many of the same characteristics as an access list. The wildcard mask has the same format and enables you to group interfaces into an area. It follows the same top-down logic of a link list that you saw before in configuring access lists in Chapter 2, "Managing Scalable Network Growth."

NOTE   If there are stub networks connected to a router, it is useful to issue the command **redistribute connected subnets**. This command is issued as part of the router process configuration, and it includes the connected subnets in OSPF advertisements without actually running OSPF on them. This is very useful for real OSPF configurations, particularly those that involve WAN pay-per-packet, low-bandwidth links.

Configuration Examples

The following examples show how one command can cover all router interfaces and also how each individual interface can be specified.

Given a router with six interfaces, three with addresses in the 10.0.0.0 class and three with addresses in the 172.16.0.0 class, the following would configure all interfaces to participate in OSPF Area 0:

```
network 0.0.0.0 255.255.255.255 area 0
```

The following would have only the interfaces addressed from 10.0.0.0 participating in OSPF Area 0:

```
network 10.0.0.0 0.255.255.255 area 0
```

The next example shows only two specific interfaces participating in OSPF Area 0:

```
network 10.12.0.1 0.0.0.0 area 0
network 172.16.15.1 0.0.0.0 area 0
```

As with an access list, the top-down logic should be thought through carefully. The most specific criteria must be defined before the general.

Why Is the network Command So Complex?

It is reasonable to ask why OSPF is so much more complex than either IGRP or RIP in this instance. The answer is that the level of precision available in the OSPF **network** command provides the capability to place different interfaces into different areas on the same router. The need for this complexity is not obvious in this example because an internal router is being configured within a single area.

The flexibility in defining which interfaces reside in which area is considered in Chapter 6, in the section "Configuration Commands for a Multiarea OSPF Network."

Options for Configuring OSPF on an Internal Router

The following are not necessary to make OSPF function properly within an area. However, they may be useful in your network design:

- The loopback interface
- The **cost** command
- The **priority** command

These are discussed in greater detail in the next sections.

The Loopback Interface and the Router ID

The router needs an ID to participate in the OSPF domain. The router ID is used to identify the source of LSA updates as shown in the OSPF database. This ID takes the form of an IP address. This address can either be defined by the administrator or left to the whim of the router. Most people define the ID so that it is easier to track events in the network, for internal documentation, and for other system-administration purposes.

The Default Router ID Selection

If no ID is stated, the router will take the highest IP address configured on the router. Although it is unlikely that this addresses will change, it is possible. From an administrative viewpoint, such a change would introduce an unnecessary level of chaos into the network.

Manual Configuration of Router ID

There is no command to define the OSPF router ID, but the Cisco rule states that the router ID will be taken from the address of the *loopback interface*. If no loopback interface is defined, it uses the highest IP address configured on the router.

The loopback interface is a virtual interface that does not exist physically. This characteristic makes it very powerful: If it does not exist, it can never go down. Therefore, the OSPF network is not vulnerable to hardware interface problems.

Having created a loopback interface, it needs an IP address. Many organizations choose a different addressing scheme for the loopbacks to distinguish them easily when troubleshooting. It is important to remember that each interface requires a separate subnet. The use of a private address from RFC 1918 may be wise in terms of both addressing issues and administrative documentation.

The following shows how to configure a loopback interface:

```
interface loopback interface number
ip address ip address subnet-mask
```

NOTE	When designing a network, consider whether to include the loopback interface address in the **network** commands. There are both advantages and disadvantages to this, and they should be researched in any network design. If the organization is running out of valid addresses, it may be advisable to use the loopback address only as a router ID and not insert it into the routing table. The disadvantage of this configuration is that it cannot be pinged for testing. This is known as a bogus RID. The preferred configuration would be to have an address in the routing table. These addresses can actually have a 32-bit mask.

Changing the Default Metric Using the cost Command

Another command that may be useful is the **cost** command. This command manually overrides the default cost that the router assigns to the interface. The default cost is calculated based on the speed of the outgoing interface.

The **cost** command syntax is as follows:

```
ip ospf cost cost
```

A lower cost increases the likelihood that the interface will be selected as the best or shortest path. The range of values configurable for the cost of a link is 1 to 65535.

In general, the path cost in Cisco routers is calculated using the formula $10^8/$ bandwidth. Table 5-5 shows examples of default costs.

Table 5-5   *Default Costs in OSPF*

Link Type	Default Cost
56-kbps serial link	1785
T1 (1.544-Mbps serial link)	64
Ethernet	10
16-Mbps Token Ring	6

NOTE   Serial lines have many different speeds. The default bandwidth is 1.544 Mbps. If the line is a slower speed, use the **bandwidth** command to specify the real link speed. The cost of the link will then change to correspond to the bandwidth that you configured.

It is now possible to control how OSPF calculates default metrics for the interface. Use the **ospf auto-cost reference-bandwidth** router global configuration command to change the numerator of the above OSPF cost formula:

```
ospf auto-cost reference-bandwidth reference-bandwidth
```

Here, *reference-bandwidth* is in megabytes per second. The range is 1 to 4294967; the default is 100.

This means that a cost of 1 = 100 Mbps, and a cost of 10 = 100/10 = 10 Mbps. If you're moving to gigabit, then you would want 1000 Mbps = 1 Gbps.

Any change using this command should be done on all routers in the AS so that they all use the same formula to calculate cost. The value set by the **ip ospf cost** command overrides the cost resulting from the **auto-cost reference-bandwidth** command.

In the Cisco IOS documentation, the **auto-cost** command is documented as **ospf auto-cost**. However, **auto-cost** is the actual command in the Cisco IOS.

cost Command Design Considerations

Considerations in using the **cost** command include the following:

- Never change defaults unless you can explain why the change is necessary. Reasons for using the **cost** option in OSPF include the following:

    — You want to maintain interoperability among different vendors running OSPF.

— There is a design reason to choose a different path than the one selected by the Cisco default metric.

— You want to allow greater granularity in the application of the cost metric.

- If the default is to be overridden by the manual configuration, it is important that it is done with due consideration to the physical and logical topology map of the network. Any change to the metric may change the traffic patterns in the network.

Determining the Designated Router Using the priority Command

The last command to consider is the **priority** command. This command is used to determine the designated and backup designated routers on a multiaccess link. Remember that the Hello protocol is the mechanism by which the designated routers are elected. To be "up for election," the priority must be a positive integer between 1 and 255. If the priority is 0, the router cannot participate in the election. The higher the priority, the greater the likelihood of being elected. If no priority is set, all Cisco routers have a default priority of 1, and the router ID is used as a tiebreaker. In effect, this means that the router ID is the determining factor.

priority Command Design Considerations

Reasons for changing the router priority include the following:

- The router has greater CPU and memory than the others do on the LAN.

- The router is the most reliable router on the segment.

- All the other routers on the LAN connect to stub networks. They all form the access layer of the network.

- There are point-to-multipoint connections in an NBMA cloud, and the hub router needs to be configured as the centralized resource, requiring it to be the designated router.

- The router is an ABR, and you don't want it to consume more resources as a designated router.

Seeing how these commands work in context makes their use and functionality much more apparent.

A Working Configuration of OSPF on a Single Router

Example 5-1 is a working configuration tested for verification. It should be used in conjunction with Figure 5-11.

Example 5-1 *Configuring OSPF*

```
SanJose(config)#router ospf 100
SanJose(config-router)#network 140.100.0.0 0.0.255.255 area 3
SanJose(config-router)#interface FastEthernet1/0
SanJose(config-if)#ip address 140.100.17.129 255.255.255.240
SanJose(config-if)#ip ospf priority 100
SanJose(config-if)#full-duplex
SanJose(config-if)#no shutdown
SanJose(config-if)#interface FastEthernet3/0
SanJose(config-if)#ip address 140.100.17.193 255.255.255.240
SanJose(config-if)#ip ospf cost 10
SanJose(config-if)#full-duplex
SanJose(config-if)#no shutdown
SanJose(config-if)#interface Fddi2/0
SanJose(config-if)#ip address 140.100.32.10 255.255.255.240
SanJose(config-if)#no ip directed-broadcast
SanJose(config-if)#no keepalive
SanJose(config-if)#no shutdown
```

Figure 5-11 *Diagram for the Configuring OSPF Example*

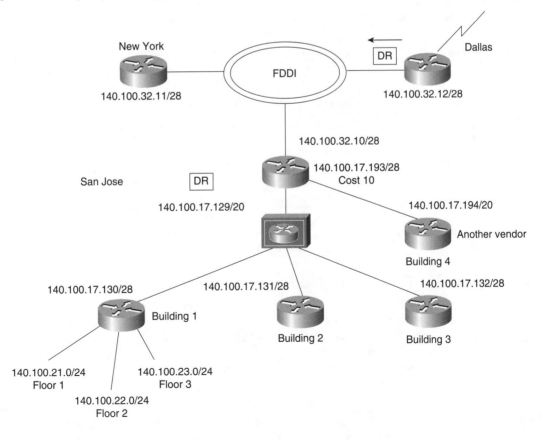

Configuring OSPF over an NBMA Topology

The design considerations of running OSPF over an NBMA topology are outside the scope of this book, but it is important to research this area because it speaks to the configuration choices that will be made. However, one of the common choices on a partially meshed network illustrates the kind of decisions that need to be made.

If the network is partially meshed, then the choice to use only point-to-point subnets can waste addresses. If a point-to-multipoint configuration is chosen, the network uses one subnet, and there is no DR/BDR negotiation. This has the advantage of saving addresses but behaving as if it is a series of point-to-point links.

When the decision is made as to which technology is to be implemented, the configuration is straightforward. The choice is defined on the interface as a **network** command. The **network** command syntax is as follows:

```
ip ospf network {broadcast | non-broadcast | {point-to-multipoint [non-broadcast]}}
```

Table 5-6 explains the command.

Table 5-6   *The **ip ospf network** Command*

Option	Description
nonbroadcast	Sets the network mode to nonbroadcast multiaccess (NBMA mode). This is the default mode for serial interfaces with Frame Relay encapsulation and point-to-multipoint subinterfaces.
point-to-multipoint	Sets the network mode to point-to-multipoint
point-to-multipoint nonbroadcast	(Optional) Sets the network mode to point-to-multipoint nonbroadcast.
broadcast	Sets the network mode to broadcast.
point-to-point	Sets the network mode to point-to-point. This is the default mode for point-to-point subinterfaces.

For the default encapsulations and hello timers, refer to Table 5-4.

Configuring OSPF in NBMA Mode

In NBMA mode, the design considerations are imperative because the selection of the DR and BDR need to have physical connectivity to all routers in the NBMA cloud. Remember that this is a nonbroadcast environment, so the DR and BDR must be configured with a static list of the other routers attached to the cloud so that they can become neighbors and create adjacencies. This is achieved with the use of the **neighbor** command.

NOTE   Other technologies have superceded the need to manually configure the neighbors.

The syntax of the command is as follows:

```
neighbor ip-address [priority number ] [poll-interval sec] [cost number]
```

The **neighbor** command is used to configure OSPF routers interconnecting to nonbroadcast networks. The different options used with the **neighbor** command are explained in Table 5-7.

Table 5-7 *The OSPF* **neighbor** *Command*

neighbor Command	Description
ip-address	Interface IP address of the neighbor.
priority number	(Optional) An 8-bit number indicating the likelihood of this router being elected as the BDR or the DR. The default is 0. This keyword does not apply to point-to-multipoint mode interfaces because no BDR or DR is selected.
poll-interval *sec*	(Optional) Unsigned integer value reflecting the poll interval. RFC 1247 recommends that this value be much larger than the hello interval. The default is 120 seconds (2 minutes). This keyword does not apply to point-to-multipoint mode interfaces.
	If a neighboring router has become inactive (hello packets have not been seen for the router dead interval period), it may still be necessary to send hello packets to the dead neighbor. These hello packets will be sent at a reduced rate called the poll interval.
cost *number*	(Optional) Value that assigns a cost or metric. It takes the form of an integer from 1 to 65535. Neighbors with no specific cost configured will assume the cost of the interface, based on the bandwidth or the **ip ospf cost** command. On point-to-multipoint mode interfaces, this is the only keyword and argument that make sense. This keyword does not apply to NBMA mode networks.

Example 5-2 shows how the command is used.

Example 5-2 *The OSPF* **neighbor** *Command*

```
ROUTER(config)#interface Serial0
ROUTER(config-if)#ip address 131.144.10.100 255.255.255.0
ROUTER(config-if)#encapsulation frame-relay
ROUTER(config-if)#ip ospf network non-broadcast
ROUTER(config)#router ospf 1
ROUTER(config-router)#network 131.144.10.100 0.0.0.255 area 0
ROUTER(config-router)#neighbor 131.144.10.2
ROUTER(config-router)#neighbor 131.144.10.3
ROUTER(config-router)#neighbor 131.144.10.5
```

NOTE   NBMA mode is used by default, so there is no need for the **ip ospf network non-broadcast** command. However, **neighbor** statements are necessary.

Configuring OSPF in Point-to-Multipoint Mode

An OSPF point-to-multipoint interface is seen as one or more numbered point-to-point interfaces. The cloud is configured as one subnet. A host route will be added for each router involved in the OSPF cloud.

NOTE   The **point-to-multipoint** non-broadcast command option is a new feature related to point-to-multipoint networks with Cisco IOS Release 11.3a. You can find more information on the subject by searching at www.cisco.com with the keywords OSPF point-to-multipoint network with separate costs per neighbor.

Design Points for the Point-to-Multipoint Mode

By default, the network is considered to be a series of point-to-point interfaces. There is no need to specify neighbors because the neighbors will see each other and simply become adjacent, with no need for the election of a DR or a BDR. However, you can specify neighbors with the **neighbor** command, in which case you should specify a cost to each neighbor. You are not required to have a fully meshed topology, which reduces the number of PVCs needed and the number of neighbor entries in the neighbor table.

It is possible to change default with the command **ip ospf network non-broadcast.** The point-to-multipoint network is then considered a nonbroadcast network, and the mode is a Cisco extension. The **neighbor** command is required to identify neighbors in a nonbroadcast network. Assigning a cost to a neighbor is optional.

Example 5-3 shows the necessary configuration for OSPF in point-to-multipoint mode (point-to-multipoint broadcast mode, compliant with the RFC, because the keyword **non-broadcast** is not specified). There is no need to configure neighbors, although this can be done if desired.

Example 5-3   *Configuring Point-to-Multipoint Networks*

```
ROUTER(config)#interface Serial0
ROUTER(config-if)#ip address 10.1.1.1 255.255.255.0
ROUTER(config-if)#encapsulation frame-relay
ROUTER(config-if)#ip ospf network point-to-multipoint
ROUTER(config)#router ospf 1
ROUTER(config-router)#network 10.1.1.0 0.0.0.255 area 0
```

Configuring OSPF in Broadcast Mode

The use of the broadcast mode is to avoid the use of the **neighbor** command and all the attendant configurations. This broadcast mode works best with a fully meshed network. Example 5-4 shows a typical configuration of OSPF in broadcast mode.

Example 5-4   *Configuring a Broadcast Network*

```
ROUTER(config)#interface Serial0
ROUTER(config-if)#ip address 10.1.1.1 255.255.255.0
ROUTER(config-if)#encapsulation frame-relay
ROUTER(config-if)#ip ospf network broadcast
ROUTER(config)#router ospf 1
ROUTER(config-router)#network 10.1.1.0 0.0.0.255 area 0
```

Configuring OSPF in Point-to-Point Mode on a Frame Relay Subinterface

In this mode, the adjacency created between the routers is automatic because each subinterface behaves as a physical point-to-point network. Therefore, the communication is direct and automatic.

The following steps explain how to configure OSPF point-to-point mode on subinterfaces:

Step 1   At the interface level, create a subinterface.

Step 2   It is recommended that you remove any network layer address assigned to the physical interface using the **no IP address** command. The Layer 3 address should be assigned to the subinterface.

Step 3   Configure Frame Relay encapsulation.

Step 4   Configure the subinterfaces as discussed earlier in this chapter.

Step 5   Configure the Layer 3 and Layer 2 (DLCI) addresses on the subinterface.

Step 6   Point-to-point mode is the default OSPF mode for point-to-point subinterfaces, so no further configuration is required.

Example 5-5 shows the necessary configuration required for a point-to-point Frame Relay subinterface.

Example 5-5   *Configuring a Point-to-Point Frame Relay Subinterface.*

```
ROUTER(config)#interface Serial0
ROUTER(config-if)#no ip address
ROUTER(config-if)#encapsulation frame-relay
ROUTER(config)#interface Serial0.1 point-to-point
ROUTER(config-subif)#ip address 10.1.1.1 255.255.255.0
ROUTER(config-subif)#frame-relay interface-dlci 51
ROUTER(config)#interface Serial0.2 point-to-point
ROUTER(config-subif)#ip address 10.1.2.1 255.255.255.0
ROUTER(config-subif)#frame-relay interface-dlci 52
ROUTER(config)#router ospf 1
ROUTER(config-router)#network 10.1.0.0 0.0.255.255 area 0
```

The shading in the previous example shows the configuration required to create a subinterface.

Of course, it is imperative to check any configuration on a network device because any errors could potentially bring down the entire network. To verify the configuration, there is a wealth of Cisco commands. They are covered in the following section.

Checking the Configuration of OSPF on a Single Router

The following set of commands is invaluable in both configuration and maintenance of a live network. These commands are particularly useful in troubleshooting the network. As such, these commands are a necessary set of tools for use on a daily basis, for the CCNP/CCDP Routing exam as well as the CCIE lab exam:

- **show ip ospf**—Shows the OSPF process and its details—for example, how many times the router has recalculated its routing table.

- **show ip ospf database**—Shows the contents of the topological database.

- **show ip ospf interface**—Gives information on how OSPF has been configured on each interface. Typing errors are easily seen with this command.

- **show ip ospf neighbor**—Displays all the information about the relationship that the router has with its neighbors—for example, the status of communication and whether it is initializing or transferring DDP packets.

- **show ip protocols**—Enables you to view the IP configuration on the router. This command is useful because it shows not only the interfaces, but the configuration of the IP routing protocols as well.

- **show ip route**—Shows detailed information on the networks that the router is aware of and the preferred paths to those networks. Also gives the next logical hop as the next step in the path (this command is covered in detail in Chapter 4, "IP Routing Principles").

Understanding the output of these commands is important. This is not just because the output may constitute questions on the exam, but because the capability to analyze what is happening on the network demands a thorough understanding of the concepts explained in this chapter. An understanding of the concepts in this chapter is required in interpreting the output of a **show** command.

The OSPF **show** commands are highly detailed and give a comprehensive understanding of the state of the network.

The show ip ospf Command

`show ip ospf` *process-id*

Example 5-6 shows the output of this command. Table 5-8 explains how to read this information.

Example 5-6 show ip ospf *Output*

```
SanJose#show ip ospf
 Routing Process "ospf 100" with ID 140.100.32.10
 Supports only single TOS(TOS0) routes
 SPF schedule delay 5 secs, Hold time between two SPFs 10 secs
 Minimum LSA interval 5 secs. Minimum LSA arrival 1 secs
 Number of external LSA 0. Checksum Sum 0x0
 Number of DCbitless external LSA 0
 Number of DoNotAge external LSA 0
 Number of areas in this router is 1. 1 normal 0 stub 0 nssa
    Area 3
    Number of interfaces in this area is 3
    Area has no authentication
    SPF algorithm executed 10 times
    Area ranges are
    Link State Update Interval is 00:30:00 and due in 00:18:54
    Link State Age Interval is 00:20:00 and due in 00:08:53
    Number of DCbitless LSA 2
    Number of indication LSA 0
    Number of DoNotAge LSA 0
```

Table 5-8 *Explanation of the* **show ip ospf** *Command Output*

Field	Explanation
SPF schedule delay	Specifies how long to wait to start the SPF calculation after receiving an LSA update.
Hold time between two SPFs	Specifies the minimum amount of time between SPF calculations.
Number of DCbitless external LSA	Is used with OSPF demand circuits. (Refer to CCO for greater detail on this subject.)
Number of DoNotAge external LSA	Is used with OSPF demand circuits, such as ISDN.
Routing Process "ospf 100" with ID 140.100.32.10	Shows the local process ID for OSPF and the router ID that it will advertise.
Supports only single ToS (TOS0) routes	OSPF is capable of carrying information about the type of service (ToS) that the IP datagram has requested. This is supported by Cisco in accordance to the RFCs but is not implemented. Therefore, ToS has the value of 0.

continues

Table 5-8 *Explanation of the* **show ip ospf** *Command Output (Continued)*

Field	Explanation
It is an internal router	Species the types of router that OSPF defines, including internal, Area Border, and autonomous system boundary router.
Summary Link update interval is 0:00:00 and the update is due in 0:00:00	An Area Border Router would transmit this link-state advertisement (LSA) into another area. Summarization occurs at the area border. As an internal router, this router is not capable of issuing this update.
External Link update interval is 0:00:00 and the update due in 0:00:00	An autonomous system boundary router would transmit this LSA into another routing protocol using redistribution. The update is external to the domain or AS. As an internal router, this router is not capable of issuing this update.
Area 3 Number of interfaces in this area is 3 Area has no authentication SPF algorithm executed 10 times Area ranges are	Specifies the number of areas of which this router is a member. As an internal router, it is configured for a single area and is a member of one area. At a glance, it is possible to see how many of the router's interfaces are in an area and whether the router is using MD5 security. It is very useful to see the number of times that the SPF algorithm has been executed, because this is an indication of the network stability. The area ranges show any summarization that has been configured.
Link State Update Interval is 00:30:00 and due in 00:18:54	The default update timer for the LSA update timer is 30 minutes. This is used to ensure the integrity of the topological databases. This field shows when the next update is and that the default has not been changed. These update timers should be the same throughout the area.
Link State Age Interval is 00:20:00 and due in 00:08:53	This specifies the MAX-AGED update deletion interval and shows when the database will next be purged of out-of-date routes.

The show ip ospf database Command

```
show ip ospf database
```

This command displays the contents of the router's topological database and the different LSAs that have populated the database. In this example, because the router used is an internal router, the LSAs displayed will be the router and network updates. This command has many parameters that enable the user to examine very specific information. This section considers the general command.

Example 5-7 shows the output of this command. Table 5-9 explains the meaning of the important fields.

Example 5-7   show ip ospf database *Output*

```
SanJose#show ip ospf database

        OSPF Router with ID (140.100.32.10) (Process ID 100)


          Router Link States (Area 3)

Link ID          ADV Router       Age         Seq#       Checksum Link count
140.100.17.131   140.100.17.131   471         0x80000008 0xA469   1
140.100.17.132   140.100.17.132   215         0x80000007 0xA467   1
140.100.17.194   140.100.17.194   1489        0x8000000B 0xFF16   1
140.100.23.1     140.100.23.1     505         0x80000006 0x56B3   1
140.100.32.10    140.100.32.10    512         0x8000000C 0x46BA   3
140.100.32.11    140.100.32.11    150         0x80000006 0x6A73   1
140.100.32.12    140.100.32.12    1135        0x80000002 0x8E30   1

          Net Link States (Area 3)

Link ID          ADV Router       Age         Seq#       Checksum
140.100.17.130   140.100.23.1     220         0x80000007 0x3B42
140.100.17.194   140.100.17.194   1490        0x80000002 0x15C9
140.100.32.11    140.100.32.11    150         0x80000004 0x379E
```

Table 5-9   *Explanation of the* show ip ospf database *Command*

Field	Explanation
OSPF Router with ID (140.100.32.10) (Process ID 100)	The router ID and the process ID of the router being viewed.
Displaying Router Link States (Area 3)	The router LSAs, showing the links connecting the router to neighbors discovered via the Hello protocol.
Link ID	The link ID, which is the same as the OSPF router ID.
ADV Router	The OSPF router ID of the advertising router. Note that the ID is the same as the link ID when describing the router LSAs. This is because the router is advertising these links in its router LSA to the area.
Age	The age is the length of time since the last update. It is shown in seconds.
Seq #	The sequence number, used to ensure that the LSA is truly an update that is more recent than anything currently in the topological database.
Checksum	The checksum on the entire LSA update. Ensures the integrity of the update.

continues

Table 5-9 *Explanation of the* **show ip ospf database** *Command (Continued)*

Field	Explanation
Link Count	The number of links that the router has configured for OSPF. Note that this field is shown only for the router LSA update.
Displaying Net Link States (Area 3)	Information taken from the network LSAs that have been received by the router.
Displaying Summary Net Link States (Area 3)	Information taken from the summary LSAs, which are passed between the Area Border Routers. As an internal router in a single area, this section of the display would be blank.

The show ip ospf interface Command

```
show ip ospf interface [type-number]
```

This command is used to show how OSPF has been configured on an interface level, as well as how it is working at the interface. This level of detail is excellent for troubleshooting configuration errors.

Example 5-8 shows the output of this command. Table 5-10 explains how to read this information.

Example 5-8 **show ip ospf interface** *[type-number] Output*

```
SanJose#show ip ospf interface fastethernet1/0
FastEthernet1/0 is up, line protocol is up
  Internet Address 140.100.17.129/28, Area 3
  Process ID 100, Router ID 140.100.32.10, Network Type BROADCAST, Cost: 1
  Transmit Delay is 1 sec, State DR, Priority 100
  Designated Router (ID) 140.100.32.10, Interface address 140.100.17.129
  Backup Designated router (ID) 140.100.23.1, Interface address 140.100.17.130
  Timer intervals configured, Hello 10, Dead 40, Wait 40, Retransmit 5
    Hello due in 00:00:06
  Neighbor Count is 3, Adjacent neighbor count is 2
    Adjacent with neighbor 140.100.17.132
    Adjacent with neighbor 140.100.17.131
    Adjacent with neighbor 140.100.23.1  (Backup Designated Router)
  Suppress hello for 0 neighbor(s)
```

Table 5-10   *Explanation of the* **show ip ospf interface** *Command*

Field	Explanation
FastEthernet1/0 is up, line protocol is up	This should be seen as two statements. The first half of the sentence indicates that the physical line is operational. This meaning differs with the type of interface; for Ethernet, it indicates the presence of the transceiver. The second portion of the sentence indicates that the data link layer is working.
Internet Address 140.100.17.129/28, Area 3	The IP address and mask configured on the interface.
Area 3	The OSPF area for which the interface is configured.
Process ID 100, Router ID 140.100.32.10	The autonomous system number, which is in fact the OSPF process ID. The router ID that will be advertised in the LSA updates.
Network Type BROADCAST	The type of network that the interface is connected to, which indicates how neighbors are found and adjacencies are formed.
Cost: 1	The metric cost of the link, which, although not stated, was probably dynamically chosen using the Cisco defaults.
Transmit Delay is 1 sec	The anticipated time taken to send an update to the neighbor. The default is 1 second.
State DR	The state of the link in reference to establishing adjacencies. This field is extremely useful in troubleshooting. Here are the states in order: **DOWN**—Heard from no one. **ATTEMPT**—Sent a hello on an NBMA, but haven't heard back. **INIT**—Heard a hello, but have not achieved neighbor status. **TWO-WAY**—Established full neighbor relationship; saw itself in the neighbor's hello table. **EXSTART**—Starting up the link for exchanging DDPs. **EXCHANGE**—Sending DDPs to other router. **LOADING**—Building the database and LSAs from the DDPs. **FULL**—Established adjacency. **DR**—Is the designated router for this LAN.

continues

Table 5-10 *Explanation of the* **show ip ospf interface** *Command (Continued)*

Field	Explanation
Priority 100	The priority is sent in the Hello protocol and is used to determine the election of the designated router and the backup designated router. The value of 1 means that the router is prepared to be elected. If every other router has the priority of 1, the highest router ID will select the routers.
Designated Router (ID) 140.100.32.10, Interface address 140.100.17.129	The address of the elected designated router. Note that the ID and the interface ID differ. This is a useful field for troubleshooting misconfiguration.
Backup Designated router (ID) 140.100.23.1, Interface address 140.100.17.130	The address of the backup designated router. Note that both the ID and the interface are given, and they differ.
Timer intervals configured, Hello 10, Dead 40, Wait 40, Retransmit 5	It is possible to change these timers and sometimes necessary if connecting to another vendor's equipment that has different defaults. These timers should be consistent throughout the area. The defaults are as follows: Hello: 10 Dead: 40 Wait: 40 Retransmit: 5
Hello due in 00:00:06	When the next hello packet is due to be sent out of the interface.
Neighbor Count is 3, Adjacent neighbor count is 2	The number of routers that have neighbor relationships. Note that the number of routers with which adjacency is established is less than the number of neighbors. This is because there is a designated router and a backup designated router, whose responsibility it is to maintain the adjacencies with all routers on the LAN.
Adjacent with neighbor 140.100.23.1 (Backup Designated Router)	The router ID of the adjacent router, which is the backup designated router in this case.

The show ip ospf neighbor Command

```
show ip ospf neighbor [type number] [neighbor-id] [detail]
```

This command is used to show OSPF neighbors. All the neighbors known to the router may be viewed, or the command can be made more granular and the neighbors can be shown on a per-interface basis. One neighbor also may be picked out for scrutiny. This level of detail is excellent for troubleshooting configuration errors.

Example 5-9 shows the output of this command. Table 5-11 explains how to read this information.

Example 5-9 show ip ospf neighbor *Output*

```
SanJose#show ip ospf neighbor

Neighbor ID      Pri   State          Dead Time   Address         Interface
140.100.17.132   1     FULL/DROTHER   00:00:36    140.100.17.132  FastEthernet1/0
140.100.17.131   1     FULL/DROTHER   00:00:37    140.100.17.131  FastEthernet1/0
140.100.23.1     1     FULL/BDR       00:00:38    140.100.17.130  FastEthernet1/0
140.100.32.12    1     FULL/DROTHER   00:00:35    140.100.32.12   Fddi2/0
140.100.32.11    1     FULL/DR        00:00:32    140.100.32.11   Fddi2/0
140.100.17.194   1     FULL/DR        00:00:31    140.100.17.194  FastEthernet3/0
```

To be more specific, in what is viewed, it is possible to look at the neighbors that have been discovered on a particular interface, as seen in Example 5-10.

Example 5-10 *The Neighbors That Have Been Discovered on a Particular Interface*

```
SanJose#show ip ospf neighbor fddi 2/0

Neighbor ID      Pri   State          Dead Time   Address         Interface
140.100.32.12    1     FULL/DROTHER   00:00:36    140.100.32.12   Fddi2/0
140.100.32.11    1     FULL/DR        00:00:32    140.100.32.11   Fddi2/0
```

To see all the neighbors in as much detail as possible, however, use the command displayed in Example 5-11.

Example 5-11 *Using the* show ip ospf neighbor detail *Command*

```
SanJose#show ip ospf neighbor detail
Neighbor 140.100.17.132, interface address 140.100.17.132
    In the area 3 via interface FastEthernet1/0
    Neighbor priority is 1, State is FULL, 6 state changes
    DR is 140.100.17.129 BDR is 140.100.17.130
    Options 2
    Dead timer due in 00:00:35
Neighbor 140.100.17.131, interface address 140.100.17.131
    In the area 3 via interface FastEthernet1/0
    Neighbor priority is 1, State is FULL, 6 state changes
    DR is 140.100.17.129 BDR is 140.100.17.130
    Options 2
    Dead timer due in 00:00:34
```

continues

Example 5-11 *Using the* **show ip ospf neighbor detail** *Command (Continued)*

```
Neighbor 140.100.23.1, interface address 140.100.17.130
  In the area 3 via interface FastEthernet1/0
  Neighbor priority is 1, State is FULL, 6 state changes
  DR is 140.100.17.129 BDR is 140.100.17.130
  Options 2
  Dead timer due in 00:00:36
Neighbor 140.100.32.12, interface address 140.100.32.12
  In the area 3 via interface Fddi2/0
  Neighbor priority is 1, State is FULL, 6 state changes
  DR is 140.100.32.11 BDR is 140.100.32.10
  Options 2
  Dead timer due in 00:00:32
Neighbor 140.100.32.11, interface address 140.100.32.11
  In the area 3 via interface Fddi2/0
  Neighbor priority is 1, State is FULL, 6 state changes
  DR is 140.100.32.11 BDR is 140.100.32.10
  Options 2
  Dead timer due in 00:00:38
Neighbor 140.100.17.194, interface address 140.100.17.194
  In the area 3 via interface FastEthernet3/0
  Neighbor priority is 1, State is FULL, 9 state changes
  DR is 140.100.17.194 BDR is 140.100.17.193
  Options 2
  Dead timer due in 00:00:38
```

Table 5-11 explains the meanings of the important fields from Examples 5-9 through 5-11.

Table 5-11　*Explanation of the* **show ip ospf neighbor** *Command*

Field	Explanation
ID	This is the router ID.
Pri	This is the priority sent out with the Hello protocol to elect the designated router and the backup designated router.
State	This shows the state, not of the link but whether the interface was elected. **DR**—Designated router. **BDR**—Backup designated router. **DROTHER**—The router was not chosen as the DR or the BDR. If the priority on the interface had been set to zero, the state would always be DROTHER because the router could not be elected as a DR or a BDR.
Dead Time	The dead time is how long the router will wait without hearing the periodic hello from its neighbor before it is declared dead. This timer should be consistent on the network; otherwise, there will be problems.

Table 5-11   *Explanation of the* **show ip ospf neighbor** *Command (Continued)*

Field	Explanation
Address	This is the interface address of the neighbor. Note that the router ID is not the same as the interface address. If the loopback address or the highest IP address on the router has been used, the address probably will differ.
Interface	This is the outgoing interface of the router, upon which the neighbor routers were heard.
Options	The option available is one of design. It identifies whether the area the neighbors inhabit is a stub area. The next section discusses this in detail.

The show ip protocols Command

`show ip protocols`

This command is used to show the configuration IP routing protocols on the router. It details how the protocols were configured and how they interact with one another. It also indicates when the next updates will occur. This command is excellent for troubleshooting configuration errors and understanding how the network is communicating about its routes.

Example 5-12 shows the output of this command. Table 5-12 explains how to read this information.

Example 5-12 *The* **show ip protocols** *Command Output*

```
SanJose#show ip protocols
Routing Protocol is "ospf 100"
  Sending updates every 0 seconds
  Invalid after 0 seconds, hold down 0, flushed after 0
  Outgoing update filter list for all interfaces is not set
  Incoming update filter list for all interfaces is not set
  Redistributing: ospf 100
  Routing for Networks:
    140.100.0.0
  Routing Information Sources:
    Gateway         Distance      Last Update
    140.100.17.131       110      00:50:23
    140.100.17.132       110      00:50:23
    140.100.17.194       110      00:07:39
    140.100.23.1         110      00:50:23
    140.100.32.11        110      00:07:39
    140.100.32.12        110      00:07:39
  Distance: (default is 110)
```

Table 5-12   *Explanation of the* **show ip protocols** *Command*

Field	Explanation
Routing Protocol is "ospf 100"	This routing protocol is configured on the router. If there is more than one routing protocol configured, the details of each are listed in turn.
Sending updates every 0 seconds	The frequency of the routing update is shown. It is not relevant for a link-state routing protocol that sends updates of changes as required (incremental updates).
Invalid after 0 seconds	This field is relevant for distant vector protocols. It indicates the period of time that a route is considered valid, from the time of the last update. If an update on the status of the route has not been received in this defined value, the route is marked unreachable.
hold down 0	Hold-down timers are used only in distance vector protocols. If a distance vector protocol suspects that a route in its table is bad, it will mark it down but will not accept another path with a less-favorable metric until the hold-down timer has expired. This is to avoid loops in the network. If a link-state protocol hears an update, it acts on the information.
flushed after 0	The 0 value indicates that this is a field used by distance vector routing protocols. After marking a route as invalid, it will flush it from the routing table after this timer has expired.
Outgoing update filter list for all interfaces is not set	Access lists may be set on an interface to filter networks from the routing update. This should be used carefully because it affects connectivity.
Incoming update filter list for all interfaces is not set	The access list can filter either outgoing or incoming updates.
Redistributing: ospf 100	If the routing protocol is sharing information with another routing protocol configured on the router, the information is listed here. This is a very important field because redistribution is complex and, therefore, easily misconfigured. If no redistribution is configured, the protocol is seen to be sharing information with itself.
Routing for Networks: 140.100.0.0	This reflects the use of the network commands when the protocol was configured. OSPF allows granularity in the use of the command. The entries here could be as specific as the interface addresses.
Routing Information Sources	This is a major heading for the gateway fields, which are the addresses of the routers sending updates to this router. They will become the next logical hop in the routing table.

Table 5-12   *Explanation of the* **show ip protocols** *Command (Continued)*

Field	Explanation
Gateway	This field is a subset of the Routing Information Sources field just discussed. It is the address of the router providing updates.
Distance	The administrative distance is the value given to the source of the update. Whereas the metric indicates which path to choose if there is more than one available, the administrative distance indicates which source (routing protocol) to choose if there is more than one providing a path to a remote network. The administrative distance takes precedence over the routing metric.
Last Update	This is the time since the last update was received from that source.
Distance: (default is 110)	The administrative distance may be changed for the entire routing protocol (the example here is OSPF), which would be listed here, or it can be changed per source, as seen earlier in the listing of each individual source (gateway).

The show ip route Command

```
show ip route
```

This command is used to show the IP routing table on the router. It details how the network is known to the router and its sources for the information. This command is excellent for troubleshooting configuration errors and understanding how the network is communicating about its routes. It is given detailed consideration in Chapter 4.

The commands covered in this section are useful to verify that the configuration has worked and that the OSPF network is functioning correctly. In a single-area environment, the full complexity of OSPF is not engaged. The full strength and complexity of OSPF come to the forefront in the design and configuration of a multiarea network.

Conclusion

You may conclude that OSPF is definitely more complex than RIP. To harness the power that this complexity offers, it is important to spend time in the analysis and design of the network. In many cases, the addressing scheme must be redesigned to support the hierarchical structure that OSPF requires.

OSPF is not a routing protocol to be taken lightly. However, the configuration commands are very simple. The work is in the addressing scheme and the design of the network, which requires old-fashioned analysis and design skills.

Foundation Summary

The "Foundation Summary" is a collection of quick reference information that provides a convenient review of many key concepts in this chapter. For those of you who already feel comfortable with the topics in this chapter, this summary will help you recall a few details. For those of you who just read this chapter, this review should help solidify some key facts. For any of you doing your final preparations before the exam, these tables and figures will be a convenient way to review the day before the exam.

Table 5-13 *OSPF Terms*

Term	Description
adjacency	Formed when two neighboring routers have exchanged information and have the same topology table. The databases are synchronized and see the same networks.
area	A group of routers that share the same area ID. Each router in the area has the same topology table. Each router in the area is an internal router. The area is defined on an interface basis in the configuration of OSPF.
autonomous system	Routers that share the same routing protocol within the organization.
backup designated router (BDR)	The backup to the designated router, in case the DR fails. The BDR performs none of the DR functions while the DR is operating correctly.
cost	The metric for OSPF. It is not defined in the standard with a value. Cisco uses the default of the inverse of bandwidth, so the higher the speed of the link, the lower the cost—and, therefore, the more attractive the path. This default can be overridden by a manual configuration. This should be done only if you have a full knowledge of the network.
database descriptor	Referred to as DBDs or Database Descriptor Packets (DDPs). These are packets exchanged between neighbors during the Exchange state. The DDPs contain LSAs, which describe the links of every router in the neighbor's topology table.
designated router (DR)	Router responsible for making adjacencies with all neighbors on a multiaccess network, such as Ethernet or FDDI. The DR represents the multiaccess network, in that it ensures that every router on the link has the same topology database.

Table 5-13   *OSPF Terms (Continued)*

Term	Description
exchange state	Method by which two neighboring routers discover the map of the network. When these routers become adjacent, they must first exchange DDPs to ensure that they have the same topology table.
exstart	State in which the neighboring routers determine the sequence number of the DDPs and establish the master/slave relationship.
init	State in which a hello packet has been sent from the router, which is waiting for a reply to establish two-way communication.
internal router	A router that has all its interfaces in the same area.
link-state advertisement (LSA)	A packet describing a router's links and the state of those links. There are different types of LSAs to describe the different types of links.
link-state database	Otherwise known as the topology map. It has a map of every router, its links, and the state of the links. It also has a map of every network and every path to each network.
link-state request (LSR)	When the router receives a DDP complete with LSA, it compares the LSA against the topological database. If the LSA entry is not present or the entry is older than the DDP, the router requests further information.
link-state update (LSU)	Update sent in response to the LSR. It is the LSA that was requested.
neighbor	A router on the same link with whom routing information is exchanged.
neighbor table	A table built from the hello received from the neighbor. The hello carries a list of the neighbors.
priority	A Cisco tool by which the designated router can be manually elected—or, conversely, prevented from taking part in the DR/BDR election.
SPF tree	A tree of the topological network. It can be drawn after the SPF algorithm has been run. The algorithm prunes the database of alternative paths and creates a loop-free shortest path to all networks. The router is at the root of the network, which is perceived from its perspective.
topology table	The same as a link-state database. The table contains every link in the wider network.

Table 5-14 *The Hello Packet*

Field	Characteristics	Function
Router ID	This is a 32-bit number. The highest IP address on the router is used as the ID. If a loopback address is configured, this will be used, even if it is not the highest address.	This field identifies the router within the autonomous system.
Hello/Dead Intervals	Dead Intervals=40 Hello=10 sec This field is used on broadcast, multiaccess networks.	Hello maintains the presence of the router in its neighbor's databases. It works like a keepalive. The dead interval is how long the router waits before it determines that a neighbor is unavailable.
Neighbors	The router ID of a neighbor is entered in the neighbor table when a two-way (bidirectional) communication is established within the RouterDeadInterval. The communication is established when the router sees itself listed as a neighbor in the hello packet generated by another router on the same physical segment.	A neighbor is another router with whom updates will be exchanged to synchronize databases.
Area ID	This is the area ID of the originating router's interface.	The hello packet must come from a router within the same area to be valid.
Router Priority	This is the priority of the source router interface. The higher the priority, the higher the likelihood of the router being selected as a DR or BDR.	This field is used to manually select the DR and the BDR.
DR IP address	This is the address of the existing DR.	This field is used to allow the router to create unicast traffic to the DR router.
BDR IP Address	This is the address of the existing BDR.	This field is used to allow the router to create unicast traffic to the BDR router.
Authentication Password	This is the authentication type and information. If this field is set, the password must match the password stated on the router.	This field is used as security.
Stub Area Flag	This field is set if the area is a stub area. All routers in the area must have this flag set.	This field identifies which type of LSAs will be transmitted and accepted.

Routing Table

Five packets are used to build the routing table for the first time:

- **Hello protocol**—Is used to find neighbors and to determine the designated and backup designated router. The continued propagation of the Hello protocol maintains the transmitting router in the topology database of those that hear the message.

- **Database descriptor**—Is used to send summary information to neighbors to synchronize topology databases.

- **Link-state request**—Works as a request for more detailed information, which is sent when the router receives a database descriptor that contains new information.

- **Link-state update**—Works as the LSA packet issued in response to the request for database information in the link-state request packet. The different types of LSAs are described in Chapter 6, in the section "The Link-State Advertisements."

- **Link-state acknowledgement**—Acknowledges the link-state update.

Learning a New Route

When the 2500 router receives a network LSA update from the designated router, it goes through the following logical steps:

1 The router takes the first entry from the update—the first network with information about the state of its link.

2 The router verifies that the type of LSA is one that can be accepted by this router.

3 Having ascertained that it is a valid LSA that it can receive, the router issues a lookup to its topological database.

4 If the LSA entry is *not* in the topological database, it will be flooded immediately out all the OSPF interfaces, except for the receiving interface.

5 If the LSA entry is in the topological database, further questions are required.

6 The router determines whether the new LSA has a more recent (higher) sequence number.

7 If the sequence numbers are the same, the router calculates the checksum for the LSAs and uses the LSA with the higher checksum.

8 If the checksum numbers are the same, the router checks the MaxAge field to ascertain which is the more recent update.

9 Having found the latest LSU is the one that was received, the router determines whether it has arrived outside the wait period, before another computation is allowed (minsLSarrival).

10 If the new LSA entry passes these tests, it is flooded out all the OSPF interfaces, except for the receiving interface.

11 The current copy replaces the old LSA entry. If there was no entry, the current copy is just placed in the database.

12 The received LSA is acknowledged.

13 If the LSA entry was in the database, but the LSA that has just been received has an older sequence number, the process asks whether the information in the database is the same.

14 If the information is the same and the new LSA has an older sequence number, the process just discards the packet. It may be old news, but there is no inconsistency in the database.

15 If the information is different and the newly received LSA has an older sequence number, however, the receiving router discards the LSA update. It issues its own LSA out of the receiving interface to the source address of the out-of-date LSA. The logic is that the sending router either has bad or old information or must be updated because its topological database is obviously not synchronized with the rest of the area.

This ensures that any packets that get out of sequence will be verified before action is taken. It also attempts to rectify a problem that it sees—that of multiple routers offering different paths because their topological databases are completely confused.

16 After the initial flood, things calm down, and updates are sent only when there are changes in the area or when the 30-minute timer goes off. This timer ensures that the databases stay synchronized.

Table 5-15 *OSPF over NBMA*

	Point-to-Point Nonbroadcast	Point-to-point	Broadcast	NBMA	Point-to-Multipoint
Addressing	Unicast	Multicast	Multicast	Unicast	Multicast
DR/BDR	No	No	Yes	Manual Yes	No
Manual Configuration of Neighbors	Yes	No	No	Yes	No
Hello	30 seconds Dead=120	10 seconds Dead=40	10 seconds Dead=40	30 seconds Dead=120	30 seconds Dead=120
RFC/Cisco	Cisco	Cisco	Cisco	RFC 2328	RFC 2328

Table 5-15   *OSPF over NBMA (Continued)*

	Point-to-Point Nonbroadcast	Point-to-point	Broadcast	NBMA	Point-to-Multipoint
Network Supported	Star Partial mesh	Star Partial mesh, using subinterfaces	Full mesh	Full mesh	Star Partial mesh (seen as point-to-point)
Replicates Packets	Yes	Yes	Yes	Yes	Yes
Number of Subnets	1	Many (1 per circuit)	1	1	1

Command Summaries

The following is a list of the commands explained in this chapter. This list is not intended to teach the use of the commands, but to remind the reader of the options available.

The commands in Table 5-16 are configuration commands.

Table 5-16   *OSPF Configuration Command Summary*

Command	Description
router ospf *process number*	Turns on the OSPF process and identifies it with a process ID.
network *network number wildcard mask* **area** *area number*	Identifies which networks—and, thus, interfaces—belong to which area.
interface loopback *interface number*	Creates the loopback interface that may now be used to create the router ID.
ip ospf cost *cost*	Sets the cost or metric for the outgoing interface.
auto-cost reference-bandwidth *reference-bandwidth*	Allows the administrator to change the formula used to calculate the metric.
ip ospf priority *number.*	Helps determine which router on a multiaccess network will be elected as the DR.
ip ospf network *network option address mask*	Identifies the type of network to the OSPF process, which will determine how the adjacencies are created.
neighbor *ip-address* [**priority** *number*] [**poll-interval** *sec*] [**cost** *number*]	States the neighbor, its address, and its capability to become the DR. This command also allows the configuration of cost and the timers on the interface.

The following commands are all executive commands to show the OSPF status and operation:

- **show ip ospf**—Shows the OSPF process and its details—for example, how many times the router has recalculated its routing table.

- **show ospf database**—Shows the contents of the topological database.

- **show ip ospf interface**—Gives information on how OSPF has been configured on each interface. Typing errors are easily seen with this command.

- **show ip ospf neighbor**—Displays all the information about the relationship that the router has with its neighbors—for example, the status of communication and whether it is initializing or transferring DDP packets.

- **show ip protocols**—Enables you to view the IP configuration on the router. It is useful because it shows not only the interfaces, but the configuration of the IP routing protocols as well.

- **show ip route**—Shows detailed information on the networks that the router is aware of and the preferred paths to those networks, as well as the next logical hop as the next step in the path (this command is covered in detail in Chapter 4).

Chapter Glossary

This glossary provides an official Cisco definition for key words and terms introduced in this chapter. I have supplied my own definition for terms that the Cisco glossary does not contain. The words listed here are identified in the text by italics. A complete glossary, including all the chapter terms and additional terms, can be found in Appendix C, "Glossary."

Dijkstra algorithm—A complex algorithm used by routers running link-state routing protocols to find the shortest path to the destination.

flood—A term that refers to network information. When it is flooded, it is sent to every network device in the domain.

fully adjacent—When the routing tables of the two neighbors are fully synchronized, with exactly the same view of the network.

loading state—State in which, if the receiving router requires more information during the process in which two routers are creating an adjacency, it will request that particular link in more detail using the link-state request packet (LSR). The LSR will prompt the master router to send the link-state update packet (LSU). This is the same as a link-state advertisement (LSA) used to flood the network with routing information. While the receiving router is awaiting the LSUs from its neighbor, it is in the loading state.

loopback interface—A virtual interface that does not exist physically. This characteristic makes it very powerful: If it does not exist, it can never go down.

setup script—A question-and-answer dialogue that is offered by the Cisco router. If the router is booted without an existing configuration, it will ask you if you want to enter the setup script to create a basic configuration.

shortest path first (SPF)—The same as the Dijkstra algorithm, which is the algorithm used to find the shortest path.

two-way state—State during the process in which two routers are creating an adjacency. The new router sees its own router ID in the list of neighbors, and a neighbor relationship is established. This is the stage before routing information is exchanged.

Q&A

The following questions test your understanding of the topics covered in this chapter. The final questions in this section repeat of the opening "Do I Know This Already?" questions. These are repeated to enable you to test your progress. After you have answered the questions, find the answers in Appendix A. If you get an answer wrong, review the answer and ensure that you understand the reason for your mistake. If you are confused by the answer, refer to the appropriate text in the chapter to review the concepts.

1 What information is held in the topology table?

2 What command is used to manually determine which router on a LAN will become the DR?

3 What details are used to determine the metric of a route in OSPF by default on a Cisco router?

4 It is possible to have more than one OSPF process on a router—how would this be achieved?

5 Which RFC identifies the use of OSPF over an NBMA cloud?

6 State the different types of packets used to build a routing table for the first time.

_____

_____

_____

7 In creating an adjacency, what is the exstart state?

_____

_____

_____

8 Explain the command **ip ospf network non-broadcast**.

_____

_____

_____

9 In which of the NBMA configuration choices is it necessary to manually state the neighbors? Why is this necessary?

_____

_____

_____

10 In a Frame Relay environment, which is fully meshed, which OSPF configurations might be chosen? Give reasons for your choice.

_____

_____

_____

11 How often by default does OSPF send out hello packets on a broadcast multiaccess link?

_____

_____

_____

12 What is a neighbor in OSPF?

_____

_____

_____

13 What is an adjacency in OSPF?

_____

_____

_____

14 If the network is stable and sees no changes, how often will it send LSAs? Why are these updates sent out periodically?

_____

_____

_____

15 If a router has an OSPF priority set to 0, what does this indicate?

_____

_____

_____

16 What does *NBMA* stand for?

_____

_____

_____

17 RFC 2328 describes the operation of OSPF in two modes across an NBMA cloud. What are they?

_____

_____

_____

18 The Cisco solution point-to-point mode does not require the configuration of DR and BDR. Explain briefly why.

_____

_____

_____

19 The address 192.100.56.10 has been allocated to an interface on the router. This interface alone is to be included in the OSPF process. State the command that would start the process on this interface.

_____

_____

_____

20 What command would identify the designated router for your LAN?

_____

_____

21 The metric used by OSPF is cost. How would you change the default setting on an interface?

_____

_____

_____

22 If the command **ip ospf network non-broadcast** is used, what additional statement is necessary?

_____

_____

_____

23 What command shows which router on a LAN is the BDR?

_____

_____

_____

24 Explain briefly what **show ip ospf database** will reveal.

_____

_____

_____

25 What command is used to show the state of adjacencies?

_____

_____

_____

26 It is possible to have more than one OSPF process on a router. Which command would achieve this?

_____

_____

_____

Scenarios

The following scenarios and questions are designed to draw together the content of the chapter and to exercise your understanding of the concepts. There is not necessarily a right answer. The thought process and practice in manipulating the concepts is the goal of this section. The answers to the scenario questions are found at the end of this chapter.

Scenario 5-1

The company Jackanory.com is still charged with configuring the LA site for OSPF. Figure 5-12 is a network diagram for this site. It is necessary to first understand the design requirements for the entire network. As the figure shows, Jackanory.com intends to use Frame Relay to connect the different sites. The company also has decided to use the private address of 10.0.0.0. The Los Angeles site is to be allocated 10.1.0.0 255.255.0.0, which can be subdivided. Referring to Figure 5-12, answer the following questions.

Figure 5-12 *Network Diagram for Scenario 5-1*

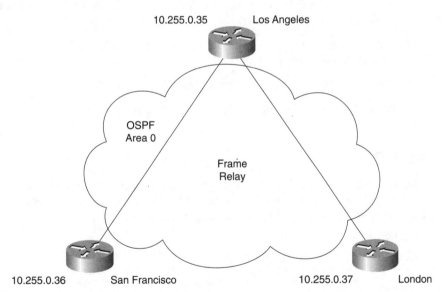

1 Design the addressing scheme for the site so that summarization can be implemented at a later stage.

2 Determine the configuration that will be implemented across the Frame Relay cloud.

3 State the configuration commands required to implement OSPF on the routers. Note that all the routers are to be in Area 0.

Scenario 5-2

In Figure 5-13, all routers share a common multiaccess segment. Because of the exchange of Hello packets, one router is elected the DR and another is elected the BDR. Use Figure 5-13 to answer the following questions.

Figure 5-13 *Network Diagram for Scenario 5-2*

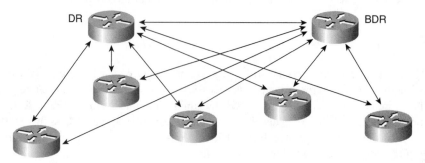

1 Which parameter determines the router that will be selected as the DR in an OSPF network?

2 Could a router with a priority value of zero assume the role of a DR or a BDR in the OSPF network shown in Figure 5-13?

3 How is the OSPF router ID determined on a Cisco router?

4 What is the role of the DR and BDR in the OSPF network shown in Figure 5-13?

Scenario 5-3

This scenario draws on some OSPF multiarea knowledge. This information is discussed in the following chapter. It is included in this chapter to show a more in-depth scenario. Using the configuration in Example 5-13, answer the questions that follow.

Example 5-13 *Configuration for Scenario 5-3*

```
Router(config)# router ospf 55
Router(config-router)#network 140.100.160.10  0.0.0.0 area 0
Router(config-router)#network 140.100.192.10  0.0.63.255 area 2
Router(config-router)#network 140.100.0.0  0.0.255.255 area 3
Router(config-router)#area 0 range 140.100.160.0 255.255.224.0
Router(config-router)#area 2 range 140.100.192.0 255.255.224.0
Router(config-router)#area 3 range 140.100.16.0 255.255.248.0
Router(config-router)#area 2 stub
Router(config-router)#area 3 stub no summary
Router(config-router)#area 3 default-cost 5
Router(config)#interface loopback 0
```

Example 5-13 *Configuration for Scenario 5-3 (Continued)*

```
Router(config-if)#ip address 140.100.200.200 255.255.255.255
Router(config)#interface ethernet 0
Router(config-if)#ip address 140.100.9.129 255.255.255.0
Router(config-if)#ip ospf priority 64
Router(config-if)#no shut
Router(config)#interface ethernet 1
Router(config-if)#ip address 140.100.12.193 255.255.255.0
Router(config-if)#ip ospf cost 5
Router(config-if)#no shut
Router(config)#interface fddi 0
Router(config-if)#ip address 140.100.160.10 255.255.255.0
Router(config-if)#no shut
Router(config)#interface ethernet 2
Router(config-if)#ip address 140.100.216.193 255.255.255.0
Router(config-if)#no shut
Router(config)#interface ethernet 3
Router(config-if)#ip address 140.100.208.10 255.255.255.0
Router(config-if)#no shut
```

1 Explain the summarization used in this configuration.

2 It is not clear from this configuration why cost has been manually configured. Give possible reasons for the use of cost in this configuration.

3 This router is the designated router for one of the LANs—identify which one. Give reasons why it may have been configured to ensure that it was the designated router. Why are the other LANs not chosen as the designated router?

4 What is the router ID for this system, and has it been configured correctly?

5 If you issued the command **show ip route**, to how many networks is the router directly connected?

Scenario Answers

The answers are in **bold**. The answers provided in this section are not necessarily the only possible answers to the questions. The questions are designed to test your knowledge and to give practical exercise in certain key areas. This section is intended to test and exercise skills and concepts detailed in the body of this chapter.

If your answer is different, ask yourself whether it follows the tenets explained in the answers provided. Your answer is correct not if it matches the solution provided in the book, but rather if it has included the principles of design laid out in the chapter.

In this way, the testing provided in these scenarios is deeper: It examines not only your knowledge, but also your understanding and ability to apply that knowledge to problems.

If you do not get the correct answer, refer back to the text and review the subject tested. Be certain to also review your notes on the question to ensure that you understand the principles of the subject.

Scenario 5-1 Answers

1 Design the addressing scheme for the site so that summarization can be implemented at a later stage.

An addressing scheme for the Los Angeles site could be as shown in Figure 5-14.

2 Determine the configuration that will be implemented across the Frame Relay cloud.

The Frame Relay configuration is a hub-and-spoke topology. Because Los Angeles is the central hub of the company, it is logical that it is also the network hub.

The configuration in Frame Relay would therefore be a point-to-multipoint one. This avoids the DR/BDR election process because it treats all the PVC links as a collection of point-to-point links, therefore removing the need for the DR/BDR. This is a good solution if the three different companies have a multivendor environment because it conforms to the RFC standards.

Figure 5-14   *Scenario 5-1 Answer*

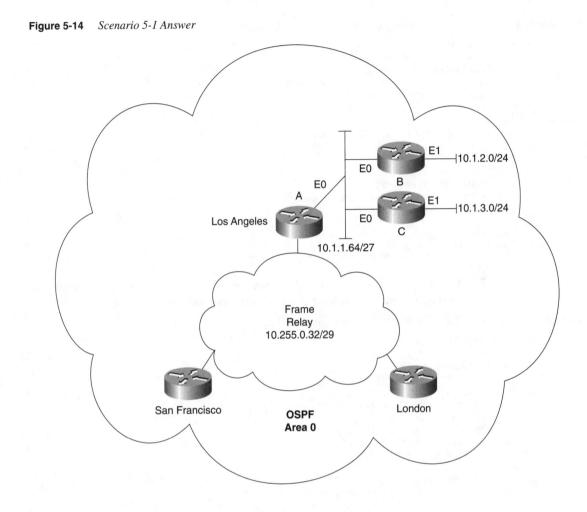

Example 5-14 shows a configuration that could be implemented.

Example 5-14 *Scenario 5-1 Configuration Question #2 Answer*

```
Los Angeles
interface serial 0
encapsulation frame-relay
ip address 10.255.0.35 255.255.255.248
ip ospf network point-to-multipoint

router ospf 100
network 10.0.0.0 0.255.255.255 area 0
```

continues

Example 5-14 *Scenario 5-1 Configuration Question #2 Answer (Continued)*

```
San Francisco
interface serial 0
encapsulation frame-relay
ip address 10.255.0.36 255.255.255.248
ip ospf network point-to-multipoint

router ospf 100
network 10.0.0.0 0.255.255.255 area 0

London
interface serial 0
encapsulation frame-relay
ip address 10.255.0.37 255.255.255.248
ip ospf network point-to-multipoint

router ospf 100
network 10.0.0.0 0.255.255.255 area 0
```

If individual point-to-point networks are chosen, then a separate PVC and IP subnet will be required for the configuration. This is illustrated in Example 5-15.

Example 5-15 *Scenario 5-1 Configuration Question #2 Answer*

```
Los Angeles
interface serial 0
no IP address
encapsulation frame-relay
interface serial0.1 point-to-point
ip address 10.255.0.35 255.255.255.252
frame-relay interface-dlci 21
interface serial0.1 point-to-point
ip address 10.255.0.49 255.255.255.252
frame-relay interface-dlci 28

router ospf 100
network 10.0.0.0 0.255.255.255 area 0

San Francisco
interface serial 0
no IP address
encapsulation frame-relay
interface serial0.1 point-to-point
ip address 10.255.0.36 255.255.255.252
frame-relay interface-dlci 44

router ospf 100
network 10.0.0.0 0.255.255.255 area 0

London
interface serial 0
no IP address
```

Example 5-15 *Scenario 5-1 Configuration Question #2 Answer (Continued)*

```
encapsulation frame-relay
interface serial0.1 point-to-point
ip address 10.255.0.50 255.255.255.252
frame-relay interface-dlci 66

router ospf 100
network 10.0.0.0 0.255.255.255 area 0
```

Note that the Frame Relay cloud is a continuation of Area 0. This is a logical first step; it is advisable to change this configuration when OSPF is being run throughout the organization. When the other sites are up and running OSPF, Los Angeles site could become another area. This would allow the summarization of routes across the Frame Relay cloud, which would reduce the traffic, cost, and possibility for congestion.

3 State the configuration commands required to implement OSPF on the routers. Note that all the routers are to be in Area 0.

The configuration on the Los Angeles routers, not including the Frame Relay configuration, is shown in Example 5-16.

Example 5-16 *Scenario 5-1 Configuration Question #3 Answer*

```
Router A:
router ospf 100
network 10.0.0.0 area 0

interface ethernet 0
ip address 10.1.1.65 255.255.255.224
ip ospf priority 10

Router B:
router ospf 100
network 10.0.0.0 area 0

interface ethernet 0
ip address 10.1.1.66 255.255.255.224

interface ethernet 1
ip address 10.1.2.1 255.255.255.0

Router C
router ospf 100
network 10.0.0.0 area 0

interface ethernet 0
ip address 10.1.1.67 255.255.255.224

interface ethernet 1
ip address 10.1.3.0 255.255.255.0
```

Note that Router A has been given a priority of 10, ensuring that it becomes the DR. Although this is not essential, it is a clear configuration and is advisable because this router is a larger system and very reliable. For the same reasons, it is also considered good system management to define the priority for the BDR.

Scenario 5-2 Answers

1   Which parameter determines the router that will be selected as the DR in an OSPF network?

The router with the highest OSPF priority on a segment will become the DR for that segment. The default for the interface OSPF priority is 1. If multiple routers have the same priority, the router with the highest RID will be selected as the DR.

2   Could a router with a priority value of zero assume the role of a DR or BDR in the OSPF network shown in Figure 5-13?

No. A priority value of zero indicates an interface is not to be elected as a DR or BDR. The state of the interface with priority zero will be DROTHER.

3   How is the OSPF router ID determined on a Cisco router?

The OSPF router ID is the highest IP address on the box, or the highest loopback address, if one exists.

4   What is the role of the DR and the BDR in the OSPF network shown in Figure 5-13?

Instead of each router exchanging updates with every other router on the segment, every router will exchange the information with the DR and the BDR. The DR and the BDR will relay the information to everybody else. In mathematical terms, this cuts the information exchange from $O(n \times n)$ to $O(n)$, where n is the number of routers on a multiaccess segment.

Scenario 5-3 Answers

1   Explain the summarization used in this configuration.

The summarization used in Scenario 5-3 will be broken out by area and is demonstrated in Table 5-17.

Table 5-17 *Allocation of Addresses*

Area	Subnet/Prefix	Range	Reasons
0	140.100.160.0/19	The range of addresses in Area 0 is 140.100.160.0 to 140.100.191.254.	With the use in the third octet of the address bit pattern 10100000-10111110, there is a great deal of possible expansion, even though this is unlikely to be used in the transit Area 0.
2	140.100.192.0/19	The range of addresses in Area 2 is 140.100.192.0 to 140.100.223.254.	This is a stub area, which suggests that there are non-Cisco routers within the area; otherwise, the area would probably be a totally stubby area. By using the address bit pattern of 11000000-11011110, further use of VLSM is allowed.
3	140.100.16.0/20	The range of addresses in Area 3 is 140.100.16.0 to 140.100.31.254.	The address bit pattern used is 00010000-00011110. This is a smaller environment that will have less capability to grow, but it can still use VLSM effectively within the LAN environment.

2 It is not clear from this configuration why cost has been manually configured. Give possible reasons for the use of cost in this configuration.

The command cost manually dictates the metric for the link. It is commonly used for interoperability among vendors, or it is used to force the path taken. This suggests that there are duplicate paths.

3 This router is the designated router for one of the LANs—identify which one. Give reasons why it may have been configured to ensure that it was the designated router. Why are the other LANs not chosen as the designated router?

The router is the designated router for the e0 link. Because it is an ABR router, it is probably serving many routers within each area. If any of those routers share a link with the ABR, it makes sense that the ABR should be the designated router.

This may not be the case in Area 0, where this router may be updating a router within Area 0 that is connected to an ASBR. The key is the position of the router relative to the others on the multiaccess link, in terms of the network hierarchy.

4   What is the router ID for this system, and has it been configured correctly?

The router ID for this router is 140.100.200.200. This is taken from the loopback interface that was configured. It is configured correctly because OSPF supports host routing, and the 255.255.255.255 mask is in fact used in a loopback configuration to save address space.

5   If you issued the command **show ip route**, to how many networks is the router directly connected?

It is directly connected to five interfaces—and, therefore, five networks—and one host. The host is the loopback interface with a 32-bit mask.

This chapter covers the following topics that you will need to master to pass the CCNP/CCDP Routing exam:

- The issues with interconnecting multiple areas.

- The differences between the possible types of areas, routers, and LSAs.

- How OSPF operates across multiple areas using NBMA.

- How OSPF supports the use of VLSM and summarization.

- The Cisco defaults in OSPF, the Cisco commands for implementing OSPF for multiple areas, and Cisco commands for reviewing the configuration.

Using OSPF Across Multiple Areas

The topics in this chapter detail the routing protocol OSPF across multiple areas. This chapter assumes your knowledge of the previous chapter, which dealt with OSPF concepts and its configuration in a single area. This chapter builds on this understanding and explains

---

how OSPF works within a large multiarea network. Each of these chapters covers two major sections. The first deals theoretically with how the protocol works. The second covers how to implement and manage an OSPF network. This chapter introduces OSPF areas and explains the operation of the protocol across those areas. Both the network communication that the protocol uses and its configuration are explained in this chapter.

The topics in this chapter will directly reflect questions on the exam. OSPF is the industry-standard interior routing protocol designed for use in large networks. Therefore, it is an obligatory subject in an exam on IP routing protocols. Nine percent of the BSCN course material is devoted to interconnecting multiple OSPF areas, and you can expect approximately four to five questions on the Routing exam to be directly related to this subject.

How to Best Use This Chapter

By taking the following steps, you can make better use of your study time:

- Keep your notes and the answers for all your work with this book in one place, for easy reference.

- When you take a quiz, write down your answers. Studies show that retention significantly increases by writing down facts and concepts, even if you never look at the information again.

- Use the diagram in Figure 6-1 to guide you to the next step.

Figure 6-1 *How to Use This Chapter*

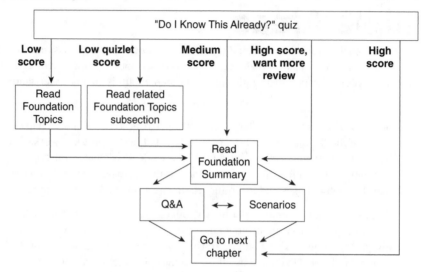

If you skip to the Foundation Summary, Q&A, and scenarios sections and have trouble with the material there, you should go back to the Foundation Topics section.

"Do I Know This Already?" Quiz

The purpose of the "Do I Know This Already?" quiz is to help you decide what parts of this chapter to use. If you already intend to read the entire chapter, you do not necessarily need to answer these questions now.

This 16-question quiz helps you determine how to spend your limited study time. The quiz is sectioned into four smaller four-question "quizlets," which correspond to four major topics in the chapter. Figure 6-1 outlines suggestions on how to spend your time in this chapter. Use Table 6-1 to record your scores.

Table 6-1   *Score Sheet for Quiz and Quizlets*

Quizlet Number	Topic	Questions	Score
1	Issues with connecting multiple areas and NBMA	1 to 4	
2	Differences between routers, areas, and LSAs	5 to 8	
3	Summarization and VLSM	9 to 12	
4	Configuring and verifying OSPF across multiple areas	13 to 16	
All questions	All	1 to 16	

1 A virtual link in OSPF is used to solve what problem?

_____

_____

_____

2 State one disadvantage for making an NBMA Frame Relay cloud Area 0.

_____

_____

3 State one advantage in making the centralized routers and network resources dwell in Area 0 while the Frame Relay cloud and the stub remote LANs reside in satellite stub areas.

_____

_____

_____

4 How does creating the number of areas in OSPF reduce the number of SPF calculations?

_____

_____

_____

5   How does a stub area differ from the backbone area?

_____

_____

_____

6   How does a totally stubby area differ from a stub area?

_____

_____

_____

7   State the different LSA types.

_____

_____

_____

8   Where does the backbone router reside, and what is its function?

_____

_____

_____

9   Are there any considerations for OSPF configured with VLSM sending routing updates into RIPv1?

_____

_____

_____

10   There are two types of summarization. What are they?

_____

_____

_____

11 Can the following subnets with a mask of 255.255.255.0 be summarized? If so, state the subnet and mask that can be used.

19.44.16.0	19.44.24.0
19.44.17.0	19.44.25.0
19.44.18.0	19.44.26.0
19.44.19.0	19.44.27.0
19.44.20.0	19.44.28.0
19.44.21.0	19.44.29.0
19.44.22.0	19.44.30.0
19.44.23.0	19.44.31.0

_____

_____

_____

12 Why can interarea summarization be configured only on ABRs?

_____

_____

_____

13 What command would be used to create a totally stubby area?

_____

_____

_____

14 What is a virtual link, and what command would be used to create it?

_____

_____

_____

15 Where would you issue the command to summarize IP subnets? State the command that would be used.

_____

_____

_____

16 How would you summarize external routes before injecting them into the OSPF domain?

_____

_____

_____

The answers to this quiz are found in Appendix A, "Answers to Quiz Questions." The suggested choices for your next step are as follows:

- **2 or less on any quizlet**—Review the appropriate sections of the "Foundation Topics" portion of this chapter, based on Table 6-1. Then move on to the "Foundation Summary" section, the "Q&A" section, and the "Scenarios" at the end of the chapter.

- **8 or less overall score**—Read the entire chapter. This includes the "Foundation Topics" and "Foundation Summary" sections, the "Q&A" section, and the "Scenarios" at the end of the chapter.

- **9 to 12 overall score**—Begin with the "Foundation Summary" section, and then go to the "Q&A" section and the "Scenarios" at the end of the chapter. If you have trouble with these exercises, read the appropriate sections in "Foundation Topics."

- **13 or more overall score**—If you want more review on these topics, skip to the "Foundation Summary" section, and then go to the "Q&A" section and the "Scenarios" at the end of the chapter. Otherwise, move to the next chapter.

Foundation Topics

The following section examines the implications of using OSPF in a larger network.

OSPF in a Multiple Area Network

The first consideration must be why multiple areas are needed. There is a lot of noise about multiple areas in OSPF, and indeed it is one of the main distinguishing features between the distance vector protocols and the link-state OSPF.

Case Study

Returning to the company Jackanory.com, you will recall that in the previous chapter, Jackanory.com was acquired along with some other companies. The company is still operating intact but must communicate with the other companies and with the holding company that purchased it. Most of the communication occurs with the parent company, although there is occasional work done on a project basis with the other companies. The parent company needs to be capable of communicating with all the small companies that it holds.

The infrastructure within the companies is to stay the same, but a Frame Relay network has been created to connect the sites. OSPF has been implemented internally at Jackanory.com, and it is working well. Now it is necessary to implement OSPF at the other sites and to have a complete understanding of all the networks available.

The network administrators have been charged with making this happen. There is more to be done than simply typing in the appropriate commands, of course. The administrators need to understand and decide on several things. These include whether summarization is possible and desired for the Frame Relay design, what design is appropriate for the OSPF areas, and whether any of the areas should be stub, totally stubby, or not so stubby areas. To make these decisions, the administrators must understand the OSPF operation over multiple areas. This chapter addresses these subjects and then, in the final section, shows the configuration options and requirements.

Why Multiple Areas?

An area is a logical grouping of routers that are running OSPF with identical topological databases. It is a subdivision of the greater OSPF domain. The creation of multiple areas solves the problem of a large network outgrowing its capacity to communicate the details of the network to the routing devices charged with maintaining control and connectivity throughout the network.

The division of the AS into areas allows routers in each area to maintain their own topological databases. This limits the size of the topological databases, and summary and external links ensure connectivity between areas and networks outside the AS.

How to Determine Area Boundaries

Although there is an obvious need for the multiple areas, the practical question of how this is implemented arises. There are two approaches. The first approach is to grow a single area until it becomes unmanageable. The second approach is to design the network with multiple areas, which are very small, in the expectation that the networks will grow to fit comfortably into their areas.

Both approaches are valid. The first approach requires less initial work and configuration. Great care should be put into the design of the network, however, because this may cause problems in the future, particularly in addressing.

In practice, many companies convert their networks into OSPF from a distance vector routing protocol when they realize that they have outgrown the existing routing protocol. This allows the planned implementation of the second approach.

Now consider the implications of implementing the first approach to OSPF—that of configuring one area and adding others as needed. By looking at the issues, you can learn many things beyond just how to create multiple areas.

Problems with OSPF in a Single Area

To understand the true benefits of multiple areas, consider why someone might decide to create multiple areas from one area.

The following symptoms that you will observe on the network provide a clue that a single area is becoming overpowered:

- The frequency of the SPF algorithm being run will increase. The larger the network, the greater the probability of a network change and, thus, a recalculation of the entire area. Each recalculation will also take longer.

- The routing table will become extremely large. The routing table is *not* sent out wholesale as in a distance vector routing protocol; however, the greater the size of the table, the longer each lookup becomes. The memory requirements on the router also increase.

- The topological database will increase in size and will eventually become unmanageable for the same reasons. The topology table is exchanged between adjacent routers at least every 30 minutes.

- As the various databases increase in size and the calculations become increasingly frequent, the CPU utilization will increase as the available memory decreases. This will make the network response time very sluggish (not because of congestion on the line, but because of congestion within the router itself). It can also cause congestion on the link.

TIP   To check the CPU utilization on the router, use the **show cpu process** command. To check the memory utilization, issue the **show memory** command.

OSPF Areas

Now that you understand why the size of the areas should be controlled, it is important to consider the design issues for the different areas, including the technology that underpins them and their communication (both within and between the areas).

OSPF Within an Area

One of the main strengths of OSPF is its capability to scale and to support large networks. It achieves this by creating areas from groups of subnets. The area is seen internally almost as if it is a small organization or entity on its own. It communicates with the other areas, exchanging routing information; this exchange is kept to a minimum, however, allowing only that which is required for connectivity. All computation is kept within the area.

In this way, a router is not overwhelmed by the entirety of the organization's network. This is crucial because the nature of a link-state routing protocol is more CPU- and memory-intensive.

Router Types

Given the hierarchical nature of the OSPF network, you will see routers operating within an area, routers connecting areas, and routers connecting the organization or autonomous system to the outside world. Each of these routers will have a different set of responsibilities, depending on their position and functionality within the OSPF hierarchical design.

The following list identifies the different OSPF routers:

- **Internal router**—Within an area, the functionality of the router is straightforward. It is responsible for maintaining a current and accurate database of every subnet within the area. It is also responsible for forwarding data to other networks by the shortest path. Flooding of routing updates is confined to the area. All interfaces on this router are within the same area.

- **Backbone router**—The design rules for OSPF require that all the areas be connected through a single area, known as the *backbone area* or *Area 0*. Area 0 is also known as Area 0.0.0.0 on other routers. A router within this area is referred to as a *backbone router*. It may also be an internal router or an Area Border Router.

- **Area Border Router (ABR)**—This router is responsible for connecting two or more areas. It holds a full topological database for each area to which it is connected and sends LSA updates between the areas. These LSA updates are summary updates of the subnets within an area. It is at the area border that summarization should be configured for OSPF because this is where the LSAs make use of the reduced routing updates to minimize the routing overhead on both the network and the routers.

- **Autonomous System Boundary Router (ASBR)**—To connect to the outside world or to any other routing protocol, you need to leave the OSPF domain. OSPF is an *interior routing protocol* or *Interior Gateway Protocol* (IGP); *gateway* is an older term for a router. The router configured for this duty is the ASBR. If there is any redistribution between other protocols to OSPF on a router, it will be an ASBR. Although you can place this router anywhere in the OSPF hierarchical design, it should reside in the backbone area. Because any traffic leaving the OSPF domain will also likely leave the router's area, it makes sense to place the ASBR in a central location that all traffic leaving its area must traverse.

Figure 6-2 shows how the different router types are interrelated.

Figure 6-2　*Router Definitions for OSPF*

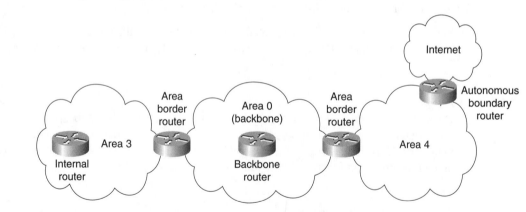

Figure 6-3 shows the connectivity and functionality of the different areas.

The routers will send out routing updates and other network information through LSAs. The function or type of router will determine the LSAs that are sent.

Figure 6-3   *The Different Types of OSPF Areas and LSA Propagation*

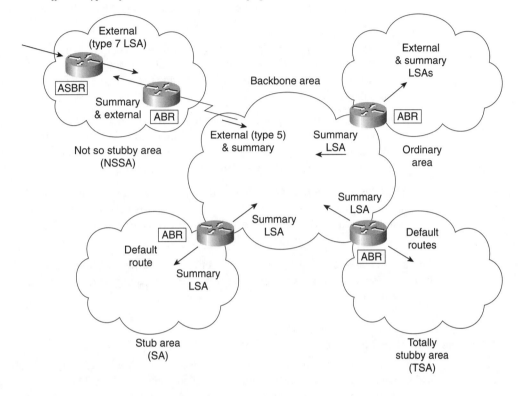

The Link-State Advertisements

Five commonly used types of link-state advertisements (LSAs) exist. The standard lists 11 types of LSA, although currently not all of these are in use. Six LSAs are listed here; this discussion focuses only on those advertisements sent between routers in the same area and on the same segment.

The five link-state advertisements are as follows:

The router link—This LSA is generated for each area to which the router belongs. This LSA gives the link states to all other routers within an area. This LSA is flooded into an area. This is identified as a Type 1 LSA.

The network link—This LSA is sent out by the designated router and lists all the routers on the segment for which it is the designated router and has a neighbor relationship. The LSA is flooded to the whole area. This is identified as a Type 2 LSA.

The network summary link—This LSA is sent between areas and summarizes the IP networks from one area to another. It is generated by an ABR. This is identified as a Type 3 LSA.

The AS external ASBR summary link—This LSA is sent to a router that connects to the outside world (ASBR). It is sent from the Area Border Router to the Autonomous System Boundary Router. The LSA contains the metric cost from the ABR to the ASBR. This is identified as a Type 4 LSA.

The external link—This LSA is originated by AS boundary routers and is flooded throughout the AS. Each external advertisement describes a route to a destination in another autonomous system. Default routes for the AS can also be described by AS external advertisements. This is identified as a Type 5 LSA.

The NSSA External LSA—Identified as Type 7, these LSAs are created by the ASBR residing in a not so stubby area (NSSA). This LSA is very similar to an autonomous system external LSA, except that this LSA is contained within the NSSA area and is not propagated into other areas.

Figure 6-4 clearly shows the relationships between the different LSAs. This section discusses the router and network LSAs. The LSAs concerned with communication outside an area are considered later.

The ABRs and ASBR Propagation of LSAs

When a router is configured as an ABR, it generates summary LSAs and floods them into the backbone area. Routes generated within an area are Type 1 or Type 2, and these are injected as Type 3 summaries into the backbone. These summaries are then injected by the other ABRs into their own areas, unless they are configured as totally stubby areas. Any Type 3 or Type 4 LSA received from the backbone will be forwarded into the area by the ABR.

The backbone will also forward external routes both ways unless the ABR is a stub router, in which case they are blocked.

If a summary is received from within the area, it cannot be forwarded, and summaries received from the backbone cannot be further summarized.

NOTE   The different types of areas mentioned in this section are described in the later section "The Different Types of Areas."

Figure 6-4   *The Propagation of LSAs*

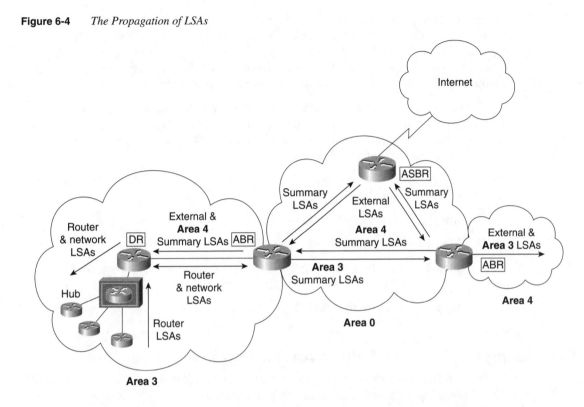

It is necessary for certain conditions to be met before any LSAs can be flooded out of all interfaces:

- The LSA was not received through the interface.

- The interface is in a state of exchange or full adjacency.

- The interface is not connected to a stub area (no LSA Type 5 will be flooded).

- The interface is not connected to a totally stubby area (no Type 3,4, or 5 will be propagated).

OSPF Path Selection Between Areas

The OSPF routing table that exists on a router depends on the following factors:

- The position that the router has in the area and the status of the network

- The type of area that the router is located in

- Whether there are multiple areas in the domain

- Whether there are communications outside the autonomous system

Remember the sequence of events. The router receives LSAs. It builds the topological database. Then it runs the Dijkstra algorithm, from which the shortest path first is chosen and entered into the routing table. The routing table is therefore the conclusion of the decision-making process. It holds information on how that decision was made by including the metric for each link. This enables the network administrator to view the operation of the network.

Different LSAs hold different weighting in the decision-making process. It is preferable to take an internal route (within the area) to a remote network rather than to traverse multiple areas just to arrive at the same place. Not only does multiple-area traveling create unnecessary traffic, but it also can create a loop within the network.

The routing table reflects the network topology information and indicates where the remote network sits in relation to the local router.

The router will process the LSAs in this order:

> **Step 1**   The internal LSA (Type 1 and 2).
>
> **Step 2**   The LSAs of the AS (Type 3 and 4). If there is a route to the chosen network within the area (Type 1 or 2), this path will be kept.
>
> **Step 3**   The external LSAs (Type 5).

Calculating the Cost of a Path to Another Area

There are paths to networks in other areas, and then there are paths to networks in another AS. The costs of these paths are calculated slightly differently.

The Path to Another Area

This is calculated as the smallest cost to the ABR, added to the smallest cost to the backbone. Thus, if there were two paths from the ABR into the backbone, the shortest (lowest-cost) path would be added to the cost of the path to the ABR.

The Path to Another AS

External routes are routes passed between a router within the OSPF domain and a router in another autonomous system or routing domain. The routes discovered by OSPF in this way can have the cost of the path calculated in one of two ways:

- **E1**—The cost of the path to the ASBR is added to the external cost to the next-hop router outside the AS.

- **E2**—The cost of the path to the ASBR is all that is considered in the calculation. This is the default configuration. This is used when there is only one router advertising the route and no selection is required. If both an E1 and an E2 path are offered to the remote network, the E1 path will be used.

At the side of the routing table is a column indicating the source of the routing information. Typically, this is the routing protocol. In the instance of OSPF, however, it includes the LSA type that provided the path.

Table 6-2 shows the codes used in the routing table.

Table 6-2   *OSPF Routing Table Codes and Associated LSAs*

LSA Type	Routing Table Entry	Description
1 Router Link	O	This is generated by the router, listing all the links to which it is connected, their status, and their cost. It is propagated within the area.
2 Network Link	O	This is generated by the designated router on a multiaccess LAN to the area.
3 or 4 Summary Link (between areas)	IA	LSA Type 3 includes the networks or subnets within an area that may have been summarized and that are sent into the backbone and between ABRs. LSA Type 4 is information set to the ASBR from the ABR. These routes are not sent into totally stubby areas.
5 Summary Link/External Link (between autonomous systems)	E1 OR E2	The routes in this LSA are external to the autonomous system. They can be configured to have one of two values. E1 will include the internal cost to the ASBR to the external cost reported by the ASBR. E2 does not compute the internal cost—it just reports the external cost to the remote destination.

TIP   The exam focuses on the LSA Types 1 through 5.

The Different Types of Areas

The only obligatory area is Area 0, also known as the backbone area or Area 0.0.0.0. In addition to the backbone area, which connects the other areas, OSPF networks use several other types of areas. The following are the different types of areas:

- **An ordinary or standard area**—This area, described earlier, connects to the backbone. The area is seen as an entity unto itself. Every router knows about every network in the area, and each router has the same topological database. However, the routing tables will be unique from the perspective of the router and its position within the area.

- **A stub area**—This is an area that will not accept external summary routes. The LSAs blocked are Types 4 (summary link LSAs that are generated by the ABRs) and 5. The consequence is that the only way that a router within the area can see outside the autonomous system is via the configuration of a default route. Every router within the area can see every network within the area and the networks (summarized or not) within other areas. It is typically used in a hub-and-spoke network design.

- **A totally stubby area**—This area does not accept summary LSAs from the other areas or the external summary LSAs from outside the autonomous system. The LSAs blocked are Types 3, 4, and 5. The only way out of the area is via a configured default route. A default route is indicated as via 0.0.0.0. This type of area is particularly useful for remote sites that have few networks and limited connectivity with the rest of the network. This is a proprietary solution offered only by Cisco. Cisco recommends this solution if you have a totally Cisco shop because it keeps the topological databases and routing tables as small as possible.

- **A not so stubby area (NSSA)**—This area is used primarily to connect to ISPs, or when redistribution is required. In most respects, it is the same as the stub area. External routes are not propagated into or out of the area. It does not allow Type 4 or Type 5 LSAs. This seems contradictory to the opening sentence of this paragraph, which stated that this type of area was used to connect to an ISP or for redistribution, both of which are external routes to OSPF. It *is* contradictory, and this area designed for the exception. Possible examples are an area with a few stub networks but with a connection to a router that runs only RIP, or an area with its own connection to an Internet resource needed only by a certain division.

To create an area that is seen as a stub area but that can receive external routes that it will not propagate into the backbone area, and thus the rest of the OSPF domain, involves creating a NSSA. Another LSA, Type 7, is created for the NSSA. This LSA may be originated and communicated throughout the area, but it will *not* be propagated into other areas, including Area 0. If the information is to be propagated into throughout the AS, it is translated into an LSA Type 5 at the NSSA ABR.

It is not always possible to design the network and determine where redistribution is to occur. RFC 1587 deals with this subject.

- **The backbone area**—This area is often referred to as Area 0, and it connects all the other areas. It can propagate all the LSAs except for LSA Type 7, which would have been translated into LSA Type 5 by the ABR.

Some restrictions govern creating a stub or totally stubby area. These restrictions are in place because no external routes are allowed in these areas:

- No external routes are allowed.

- No virtual links are allowed.

- No redistribution is allowed.

- No ASBR routers are allowed.

- The area is not the backbone area.

- All the routers are configured to be stub routers.

Now that you understand many components of OSPF, it is important to focus on some of the design implications of creating multiple areas. This focus will reinforce the concepts detailed in the chapter.

Design Considerations in Multiple Area OSPF

The major design consideration in OSPF is how to divide the areas. This is of interest because it impacts the addressing scheme for IP within the network.

An OSPF network works best with a hierarchical design, in which the movement of data from one area to another comprises only a subset of the traffic within the area itself.

It is important to remember that with all the interarea traffic disseminated by the backbone, any reduction of overhead through a solid hierarchical design and summarization is beneficial. The lower the number of summary LSAs that need to be forwarded into the backbone area, the greater the benefit to the entire network. This will allow the network to grow more easily because the network overhead is at a minimum.

With this in mind, summarization is the natural consequence. As shown in Chapter 3, "IP Addressing," summarization is not something that can be imposed on a network. It must be part of the initial network design. The addressing scheme must be devised to support the use of summarization.

WARNING   Although it is possible to have more than three areas (per router) in OSPF, the Cisco Technical Assistance Center (TAC) recommends that a greater number of areas be created only after careful consideration. The results of having more areas will vary depending on the router (memory and CPU), as well as network topology and how many LSAs are generated. It is recommended that you not exceed 50 routers in an OSPF area, but again, this is a guideline and not a strict rule. Remember that OSPF is very CPU-intensive in its maintenance of the databases and in the flooding of LSAs, as well as when it calculates the routing table, a process based on LSAs.

Therefore, it is not strictly the number of routers or areas that is important, but the number of routes and the stability of the network. These issues must be considered because the number of LSAs in your network is proportional to the amount of router resources required.

With this understanding, the general rules stated by Cisco for OSPF design are that the following numbers should not be exceeded:

- Routers per area: 50

- Neighbors per router: 60

- Areas per router: 3

- A router may not be a DR or BDR for more than 1 LAN

Summarization

Two types of summarization exist:

- **Interarea summarization**—This is performed at the ABR and creates Type 3 and 4 LSAs.

- **External summarization**—This is performed at the ASBR and creates Type 5 LSAs.

Both have the same fundamental requirement of contiguous addressing.

OSPF is stringent in its demand for a solid hierarchical design—so much so that it has devised some commands to deal with situations that break its rules of structure.

The Virtual Link

The main dictate in OSPF is that the multiple areas must all connect directly to the backbone area. The connection to the backbone area is via an ABR, which is resident in both areas and holds a full topological database for each area.

OSPF has provided for the unhappy occasion that this rule cannot be followed. The solution is called a *virtual link*. If the new area cannot connect directly to the backbone area, a router is configured to connect to an area that does have direct connectivity.

The configuration commands create a tunnel to the ABR in the intermediary area. From the viewpoint of OSPF, it has a direct connection.

The reasons such a situation may occur are listed here:

- There is no physical connection to Area 0. This may be because the organization has recently merged with another or because of a network failure.

- There are two Area 0s because of a network merger. These Area 0s are connected by another area (for example, Area 5).

- The area is critical to the company, and an extra link has been configured for redundancy.

Although this is an extremely powerful command, it is not recommended as part of the design strategy for your network; instead, it is a temporary solution to a connectivity problem. It is necessary to ensure that the following is observed in creating a virtual link:

- Both routers must share a common area.

- One of the routers must be connected to Area 0.

Figure 6-5 illustrates the use of a virtual link to provide a router in Area 10 connectivity to the backbone in Area 0.

Figure 6-5   *Virtual Links in a Multiple-Area OSPF Network*

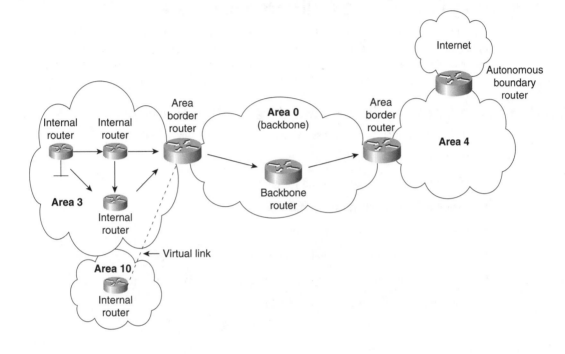

OSPF over an NBMA Network

Another design consideration is the design of the NBMA network as part of the OSPF domain. There are two main ways to approach the inclusion of an NBMA network:

- The NBMA network can be created as Area 0. The reasoning is that if the NBMA is used to connect all remote sites, all traffic will have to traverse this network. If the remote sites are made satellite areas, then all traffic will have to traverse the NBMA, so it makes sense to make it the backbone area. This works well in a full-mesh environment, although it will result in a large number of LSAs being flooded into the WAN and puts extra demands on the routers connecting to the NBMA network.

- In a hub-and-spoke NBMA network, it makes sense to assign the hub network as Area 0 with the other remote sites and the NBMA network as other areas. This is a good design if the satellite areas are stub areas because it means that the routing information—and, thus, network overhead—is kept to a minimum over the NBMA cloud. Depending on the design, the rest of the network may constitute one other area or multiple areas. This will depend on the size and growth expectations of the OSPF domain.

After the design of the network is in place, it is time to configure the routers. The configuration of a basic OSPF network is demonstrated in Chapter 5, "Using OSPF in a Single Area".

Configuring OSPF on a Multiarea Network

Some of these commands were dealt with in Chapter 5, in the section "Configuring OSPF in a Single Area." Commands that have been covered already are reviewed briefly here, and the additional parameters for configuration in a multiarea environment are explained in detail.

Configuration Commands for a Multiarea OSPF Network

The following commands are necessary to configure a multiarea OSPF network:

- The OSPF **network** command

- The OSPF **area range** command for an ABR

- The OSPF **summarization** command for an ASBR

- The OSPF command for a stub area

- The OSPF command for a totally stubby area

- The OSPF command for the cost of a default route propagated into the area

- The command for configuring a virtual link

The network Command

The first command to consider is one that was dealt with in Chapter 5. The **network** command was explained in terms of identifying the interfaces that participated in the OSPF routing process. The command will now be used to identify not only the interfaces that are sending and receiving OSPF updates, but also the area in which they reside. This configuration is used on an ABR.

The following is the syntax for the OSPF **network** command:

```
network network number wildcard mask area area number
```

NOTE   The area requested in the preceding syntax is the area in which the interface or interfaces configured with the network address reside.

Care must be taken now in the use of the wildcard mask. In a single-area configuration, all the interfaces are in the same area. The network commands just identify the network numbers in use. Therefore, they may be configured to the Internet number, as they are in IGRP and RIP. The only reason to be more specific would be to exclude some interfaces from the OSPF domain.

Figure 6-6 illustrates the example configuration that follows.

Figure 6-6   *The **network** Command*

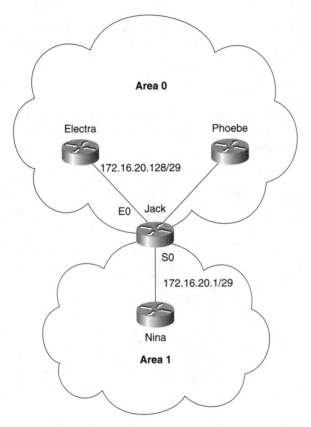

Example 6-1 shows two interfaces, each with a subnet of the same major network where the interfaces are placed into different areas. The network number has been subnetted into the last octet so that you can truly see the power and granularity of the wildcard mask at work.

Example 6-1   *The **network** Command*

```
network 172.16.20.128 0.0.0.7 area 0
network 172.16.20.8 0.0.0.7 area 1
```

The need now to identify areas on an interface basis brings into use the other part of the command. Although the command itself is very simple, it adds complexity to the use of the mask. It is to be remembered that the **network** command follows the rule of a linked list. The order of the statements is important: The most specific should be stated first because the OSPF process will act on the first match that is found.

The OSPF area range Command for an ABR

The **area range** command is configured on an ABR because it dictates the networks that will be advertised out of the area.

Use the **area** router configuration command with the **range** keyword to consolidate and summarize routes at an area boundary. Use the **no** form of this command to disable this function for the specified area:

```
area area-id range address mask
no area area-id range address mask
```

In the preceding syntax, *area-id* is the identifier (ID) of the area about which routes are to be summarized. It can be specified as either a decimal value or an IP address. Here, *address* is the IP address, and *mask* is the IP mask.

Figure 6-7 illustrates the example configuration that follows.

Figure 6-7   *The OSPF **area range** Command for an ABR*

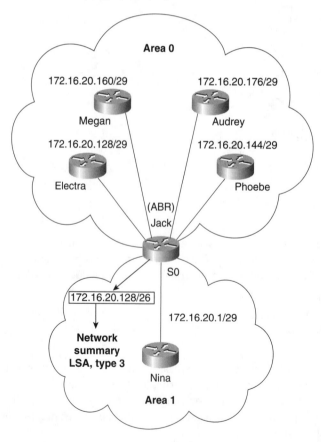

Example 6-2 shows the configuration required to summarize the following five individual subnets (which can address six hosts each) into one subnet. This summarized subnet may then be propagated across the OSPF network, saving both bandwidth and CPU:

- 172.16.20.128 /29

- 172.16.20.144 /29

- 172.16.20.160 /29

- 172.16.20.176 /29

These subnets are summarized into one subnet:

- 172.16.20.128 /26

This one subnet will then be propagated into Area 1.

Example 6-2   *The OSPF* **area range** *Command for an ABR*

```
Router Jack
router ospf 100
network 172.16.20.128 0.0.0.7 area 0
network 172.16.20.8 0.0.0.7 area 1
area 0 range 172.16.20.128 255.255.255.192
```

NOTE   The area ID requested is the area that the subnets originated from. It is not the destination area. The summarization update populates the topological databases of the routers in the destination area. These routers will need to know the source area for the summarized subnet to know where to send the data traffic.

The OSPF summarization Command for an ASBR

The **summarization** command is used on the ASBR to summarize the networks to be advertised to the outside world.

The syntax for the OSPF **summarization** command for an ASBR is as follows:

    summary-address *address mask* [**not advertise**][**tag** *tag*]

The syntax for the OSPF **summarization** command for an ASBR is as follows:

    summary-address *address mask*

In the preceding syntax, *address* is the summary address designated for a range of addresses, and *mask* is the IP subnet mask used for the summary route.

The design and implementation of the addressing scheme are crucial to the success of the OSPF network and cannot be stressed too strongly. Refer to Chapter 3 for details on IP addressing and summarization.

Figure 6-8 illustrates the example configuration that follows.

Figure 6-8   *The OSPF* **summarization** *Command for an ASBR*

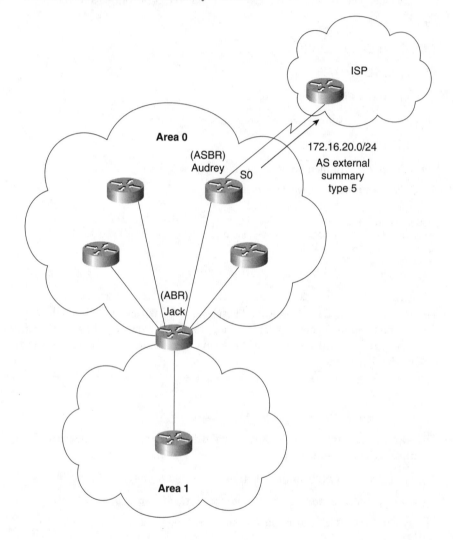

Example 6-3 shows the summarization of the network address 172.16.20.0, which will be propagated into the ISP's autonomous system.

Example 6-3 *The OSPF* **summarization** *Command for an ASBR*

```
Router Audrey
router ospf 100
network 172.16.20.176 0.0.0.7 area 0
summary-address 172.16.20.0 255.255.255.0
```

The OSPF Command for a Stub Area

After designing the addressing scheme for the network, it should be clear which areas, if any, are suitable candidates for configuration as a stub, totally stubby, or not so stubby areas.

NOTE   In this age of jargon and complex language, it is refreshing that the industry sense of humor allows such descriptive yet slightly ludicrous terms to have official status.

The syntax for the OSPF router command for a stub area is as follows:

area *area-id* **stub**

Figure 6-9 illustrates the example configuration that follows.

Figure 6-9   *The Configuration of a Stub Area*

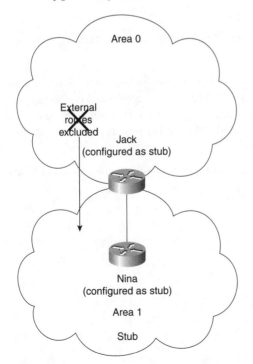

Example 6-4 shows the creation of a stub area. Note that both the ABR and the internal router share this configuration.

Example 6-4   *The Configuration of a Stub Area*

```
Router Nina
ospf 100
network 0.0.0.0 255.255.255.255 area 1
area 1 stub
Router Jack
router ospf 100
network 172.16.20.128 0.0.0.7 area 0
network 172.16.20.8 0.0.0.7 area 1
area 0 range 172.16.20.128 255.255.255.192
area 1 stub
```

NOTE   All OSPF routers inside a stub area must be configured as stub routers. This is because whenever an area is configured as a stub, all interfaces that belong to that area will start exchanging hello packets with a flag that indicates that the interface is a stub. Actually, this is just a bit in the hello packet (E bit) that gets set to 0. All routers that have a common segment must agree on that flag. If they don't, they will not become neighbors, and routing will not take effect.

The OSPF Command for a Totally Stubby Area

The syntax for the OSPF command for a totally stubby area is as follows:

```
area area-id stub no-summary
```

This addition of the **no-summary** parameter informs the ABR not to send summary updates from other areas into the area. This command needs to be configured only on the ABR because it is the only router with this responsibility. This command is configurable only on a Cisco router because it is a proprietary command. All the other routers are configured as stub-area internal routers.

Figure 6-10 illustrates the example configuration of a totally stubby area that follows.

Figure 6-10   *The Configuration of a Totally Stubby Area*

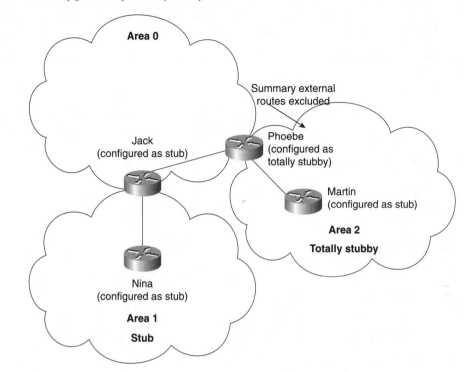

Example 6-5 shows the configuration of a totally stubby area.

Example 6-5   *The Configuration of a Totally Stubby Area*

```
Router Phoebe
ospf 100
network 172.16.20.144 0.0.0.7 area 0
network 172.16.20.16 0.0.0.7 area 2
area 2 stub no-summary
area 0 range 172.16.20.128 255.255.255.192
Router Martin
router ospf 100
network 0.0.0.0 255.255.255.255 area 2
area 2 stub
```

As a totally stubby area, no summary or external routes are propagated by the ABR into the area. To reach networks and hosts outside their area, a workstation must send to a default route, which the ABR advertises into the area.

The OSPF Command for the Cost of a Default Route Propagated into the Area

To define the cost to the default route, the following command is used. If the cost is not specified, the path will be calculated as the internal area cost plus 1.

The syntax for the OSPF command for the cost of a default route propagated into the area is as follows:

> **area** *area-id* **default-cost** *cost*

The ABR attached to the stub area automatically advertises a default route with a destination of 0.0.0.0 into the stub area. Figure 6-11 illustrates the example configuration that follows.

Figure 6-11   *The OSPF Command for the Default Route Propagated into the Area*

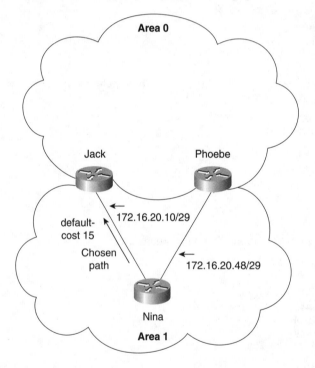

Example 6-6 shows how the default cost can be set in the configuration. Setting a cost on the default route is useful when the stub area has more than one ABR: It allows the ABR used to exit the area to be determined.

Example 6-6   *The OSPF Command for the Default Route Propagated into the Area*

```
Router Nina
ospf 100
network 0.0.0.0 255.255.255.255 area 1
area 1 stub
Router Jack
router ospf 100
network 172.16.20.128 0.0.0.7 area 0
network 172.16.20.8 0.0.0.7 area 1
area 0 range 172.16.20.128 255.255.255.192
area 1 stub
area 1 default-cost 15
Router Phoebe
ospf 100
network 172.16.20.144 0.0.0.7 area 0
network 172.16.20.16 0.0.0.7 area 2
network 172.16.20.48.0 0.0.0.7 area 1
area 2 stub no-summary
area 1 stub
area 1 default-cost 30
area 0 range 172.16.20.128 255.255.255.192
```

NOTE   This command needs to be configured only on the ABR because it is the only router with this responsibility. However, Example 6-6 has shown the configuration on both routers to illustrate the choice. The second ABR, Phoebe, will only be used if Jack fails. If there were no configuration on Jack, it would still be used by all internal routers as the ABR because the default cost is 1.

Configuring a Virtual Link

When it is not possible to connect an area to Area 0 directly, a solution is to create an IP tunnel called a virtual link. This is remarkably easy to configure. As with many things in OSPF, of course, this ease of configuration belies the complexity of the technology being used. Many things can go wrong. The most common problem is in the address of the other end of the virtual link. The command is given between ABRs, at least one of which must be in Area 0. The command, issued at both ABRs, states the transit area and the router ID of the remote destination ABR. This creates essentially a tunnel through the transit area, which, although it may involve many routers to forward the traffic, appears to the remote ABRs as next hops.

NOTE   The virtual link command is potentially included in the Routing exam and, for that reason, is worth mentioning. In practice, virtual links are a design nightmare and are best avoided. They are useful when mending a network on a temporary basis while awaiting a moment's peace to rectify the design of the network.

The syntax to configure a virtual link is as follows:

```
area area-id virtual-link router-id
```

Here, *area-id* is the ID assigned to the transit area for the virtual link. There is no format.

In addition, *router id* is the router ID of the virtual link neighbor.

Seeing how these commands work in context makes their use and functionality much more apparent.

Figure 6-12 illustrates the example configuration that follows.

Example 6-7 shows the setting of the loopback interfaces that provide the router ID. It then shows the configuration of the virtual link through the network.

Example 6-7 *Configuring a Virtual Link*

```
Router Jack
interface loopback 0
ip address 10.10.10.33 255.255.255.0
router ospf 100
network 172.16.20.128 0.0.0.7 area 0
network 172.16.20.8 0.0.0.7 area 1
area 0 range 172.16.20.128 255.255.255.192
area 1 stub
area 1 default-cost 15
area 5 virtual-link 10.10.10.30
Router Darius
loopback interface 0
ip address 10.10.10.30 255.255.255.0
ospf 100
network  172.16.20.32 0.0.0.7 area 5
network 172.16.20.64 0.0.0.7 area 1
area 5 virtual-link 10.10.10.33
```

Figure 6-12 *Configuring a Virtual Link*

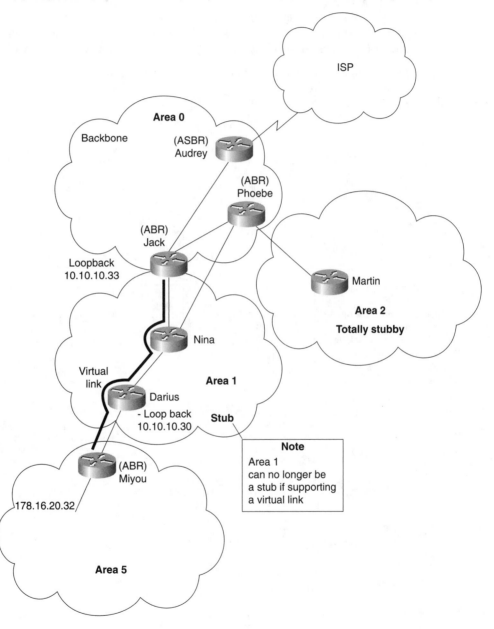

A Working Configuration of OSPF on a Multiarea Network

Example 6-8 is a working configuration tested for verification. It includes many of the commands explained earlier in this chapter. This is so that you see an entire working configuration rather than the relevant segment for configuring a particular networking nuance.

The configuration should be used in conjunction with Figure 6-13.

Figure 6-13 *Diagram of the Example 6-8 Network*

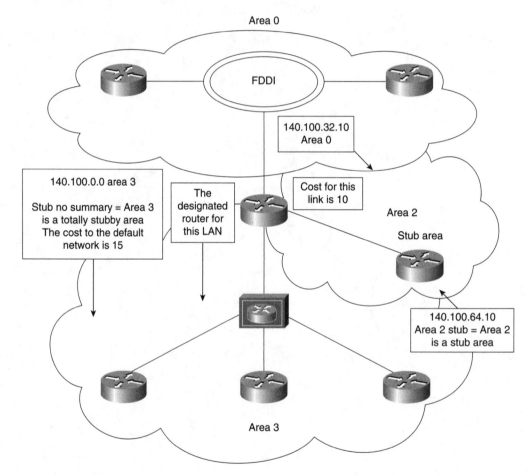

Example 6-8   *Configuring OSPF in a Multiarea Network*

```
Router(config)#router ospf 100
Router(config-router)#network 140.100.17.128 0.0.0.15 area 3
Router(config-router)#network 140.100.17.192 0.0.0.15 area 2
Router(config-router)#network 140.100.32.0 0.0.0.255 area 0
Router(config-router)#area 2 stub
Router(config-router)#area 3 stub no-summary
Router(config-router)#area 3 default-cost 15
!
Router(config-router)#interface FastEthernet0
Router(config-if)#ip address 140.100.17.129 255.255.255.240
Router(config-if)#no ip directed-broadcast
Router(config-if)#ip ospf priority 100
!
Router(config-if)#interface FastEthernet1
Router(config-if)#ip address 140.100.17.193 255.255.255.240
Router(config-if)#no ip directed-broadcast
Router(config-if)#ip ospf cost 10
!
Router(config-if)#interface Fddi0
Router(config-if)#ip address 140.100.32.10 255.255.255.240
Router(config-if)#no ip directed-broadcast
Router(config-if)#no keepalive

Router(config-if)#exit
```

Of course, it is imperative to check any configuration on a network device because any errors could potentially bring down the entire network. To verify the configuration, a wealth of Cisco commands are available. They are covered in the following section.

Checking the Configuration of OSPF on a Multiarea Network

The **show** commands shown here are in addition to the commands described in Chapter 5, in the section, "Checking the Configuration of OSPF on a Single Router." The single router commands are also extremely useful in a multiarea configuration. They are all invaluable in both the configuration and maintenance of a live network. They are particularly useful in troubleshooting the network. The following are the additional commands that you can use in conjunction with single router commands when verifying OSPF operation on a multiarea network:

- The **show ip ospf border-routers** command
- The **show ip ospf virtual-links** command

The capability to analyze the output of a **show** command demonstrates more than rote learning; it also demonstrates an understanding of the concepts that make up the foundations of OSPF design and configuration.

The commands explained in this book constitute a small subset of the commands available in OSPF. Because the OSPF command set is very comprehensive, the capability to monitor the network and thereby maintain and troubleshoot it requires advanced OSPF knowledge.

The show ip ospf border-routers Command

```
show ip ospf border-routers
```

This command shows the OSPF ABRs and ASBRs for which the internal router has entries in its routing table. This command is excellent for troubleshooting configuration errors and understanding how the network is communicating about its routes.

Example 6-9 shows the output of this command.

Example 6-9   show ip ospf border-routers *Output*

```
Router# show ip ospf border-routers
OSPF Process 100 internal Routing Table
Destination     Next Hop        Cost    Type    Rte Type    Area        SPF No
160.89.97.53    144.144.1.53    10      ABR     INTRA       0.0.0.3         3
160.89.103.51   160.89.96.51    10      ABR     INTRA       0.0.0.3         3
160.89.103.52   160.89.96.51    20      ASBR    INTER       0.0.0.3         3
160.89.103.52   144.144.1.53    22      ASBR    INTER       0.0.0.3         3
```

Table 6-3 explains the meaning of the important fields in the output of the **show ip ospf border-routers** command.

Table 6-3   *Explanation of the* **show ip ospf border-routers** *Command Output*

Field	Explanation
OSPF Process 100 Internal Routing Table	This is the OSPF routing process ID for the router.
Destination	This is the router ID of the destination router, whether an ABR or an ASBR.
Next Hop	If the ABR or ASBR is not directly connected, this is the address of the next logical hop in the chosen path to the ABR or ASBR.
Cost	This is the metric or cost of taking this path to the destination.
Type	This states whether the destination router is an ABR or ASBR or both.

Table 6-3   *Explanation of the* **show ip ospf border-routers** *Command Output (Continued)*

Field	Explanation
Rte Type	The is the type of this route; it is either an intra-area or interarea route.
Area	This is the area ID of the area that this route is learned from.
SPF No	This is the SPF calculation number that installed this route into the routing table.

The **show ip ospf border-routers** command is useful to verify that the configuration has worked and that the OSPF network is functioning correctly. In a multiarea network, **show ip ospf border-routers** command can immediately indicate why users cannot connect outside their area.

It is helpful to extract this information from what could be a long routing table, within which this information is scattered.

The show ip ospf virtual-links Command

This command shows the configured virtual links that are in existence.

```
show ip ospf virtual-links
```

Another command to use in conjunction with this is **show ip ospf neighbors**.

Example 6-10 shows the output of the **show ip ospf virtual-links** command.

Example 6-10 show ip ospf virtual-links *Output*

```
Router# show ip ospf virtual-links
Virtual Link to router 140.100.32.10 is up
Transit area 0.0.0.1, via interface Ethernet0, Cost of using 10
Transmit Delay is 1 sec, State DROTHER
Timer intervals configured, Hello 10, Dead 40, Wait 40, Retransmit 5
Hello due in 0:00:08
Adjacency State FULL
```

Table 6-4 explains the meaning of the important fields in the output of the **show ip ospf virtual-links** command.

Table 6-4 *Explanation of the* **show ip ospf virtual-links** *Command*

Field	Explanation
Virtual Link to router 140.100.32.10 is up	This shows the router ID of the other end of the virtual link, which is seen as a neighbor.
Transit area 0.0.0.1	This is the area through which the virtual link is tunneled.
via interface Ethernet0	This is the outgoing interface on the router that connects the virtual link to Area 0.
Cost of using 10	This is the cost of reaching the OSPF neighbor through the virtual link.
Transmit Delay is 1 sec	This is the delay of the link, how long it will take to transit an LSA. This value must be less than the retransmit timer setting.
State DROTHER	This gives the state of the OSPF neighbor.
Hello 10	This gives the timed update interval for the Hello protocol, in seconds. This is the default.
Dead 40	This tells how long the router will wait without hearing a hello from the neighbor before it declares the neighbor dead. The default is 40 seconds.
Retransmit 5	The retransmit interval is the time in seconds that the router will wait without hearing an acknowledgment for the LSA that it has sent to its neighbor. The default is 5 seconds.
Hello due in 0:00:08	This shows when the next Hello is expected from the neighbor.
Adjacency State FULL	This specifies the state of the neighbor adjacency. The two routers have fully synchronized their topological databases.

Conclusion

OSPF has the advantage of being an industry standard, ensuring international interoperability as long as everyone conforms to the standard. It is a very stable protocol, having been available for many years. At the heart of OSPF is the concept of areas that allow summarization and the capability to contain the breadth of LSA flooding and thus knowledge of the network and SPF computation. This capability to impose a hierarchy upon a network was revolutionary at the time that OSPF was conceptualized. OSPF is still a hot contender to EIGRP because it is the only viable option of providing the open forum with scalable growth for the network. As can be seen by this chapter, although many solutions may be implemented, the health of the network still depends on well-conceived designs based on a careful analysis of the network.

Foundation Summary

The "Foundation Summary" is a collection of quick reference information that provides a convenient review of many key concepts in this chapter. For those of you who already feel comfortable with the topics in this chapter, this summary will help you recall a few details. For those of you who just read this chapter, this review should help solidify some key facts. For any of you doing your final preparations before the exam, these tables and figures will be a convenient way to review the day before the exam.

OSPF Routers

The following list identifies the different OSPF routers:

- **Internal router**—Within an area, the functionality of the router is straightforward. It is responsible for maintaining a current and accurate database of every subnet within the area. It is also responsible for forwarding data to other networks by the shortest path. Flooding of routing updates is confined to the area.

- **Backbone router**—The design rules for OSPF require that all the areas be connected through a single area known as the *backbone area* or *Area 0.* A router within this area is referred to as a *backbone router*. It may also be an internal router or an Area Border Router.

- **Area Border Router (ABR)**—This router is responsible for connecting two or more areas. It holds a full topological database for each area to which it is connected and sends LSA updates between the areas. These LSA updates are summary updates of the subnets within an area. It is at the area border that summarization should be configured for OSPF because this is where the LSAs make use of the reduced routing updates to minimize the routing overhead on both the network and the routers.

- **Autonomous System Boundary Router (ASBR)**—To connect to the outside world, or to any other routing protocol, you need to leave the OSPF domain. OSPF is an *interior routing protocol* or *Interior Gateway Protocol* (IGP); *gateway* is an older term for a router. The router configured for this duty is the ASBR. Although you can place this router anywhere in the OSPF hierarchical design, it should reside in the backbone area. Because any traffic leaving the OSPF domain will likely also leave the router's area, it makes sense to place the ASBR in a central location that all traffic leaving its area must traverse.

Link-State Advertisements

The five link-state advertisements are as follows:

- **The router link**—This LSA states all the links to the router sending out the LSA. The list is of all the neighbors attached to the router. The LSA is flooded to the area.

- **The network link**—This LSA is sent out by the designated router and lists all the routers on the segment for which it is the designated router and has a neighbor relationship. The LSA is flooded to the whole area.

- **The network summary link**—This LSA is sent between areas and summarizes the IP networks from one area to another. It is generated by an ABR.

- **The AS external (ASBR) summary link**—This LSA is sent to a router that connects to the outside world (ASBR). It is sent from the ABR to the ASBR. The LSA contains the metric cost from the ABR to the ASBR.

- **The external link**—This LSA is originated by AS boundary routers and flooded throughout the AS. Each external advertisement describes a route to a destination in another autonomous system. Default routes for the AS can also be described by AS external advertisements.

Routing Table Codes

Table 6-5 shows the codes used in the routing table.

Table 6-5   *OSPF Routing Table Codes And Associated LSAs*

LSA Type	Routing Table Entry	Description
1 Router Link	O	This is generated by the router, listing all the links to which it is connected, their status, their and cost. It is propagated within the area.
2 Network Link	O	This is generated by the designated router on a multiaccess LAN to the area.
3 or 4 Summary Link (between areas)	IA	LSA Type 3 includes the networks or subnets within an area that may have been summarized and that are sent into the backbone and between ABRs. LSA Type 4 is information set to the ASBR from the ABR. These routes are not sent into totally stubby areas.

Table 6-5   *OSPF Routing Table Codes And Associated LSAs (Continued)*

LSA Type	Routing Table Entry	Description
5 Summary Link/External Link (between autonomous systems)	E1 OR E2	The routes in this LSA are external to the autonomous system. They can be configured to have one of two values. E1 will include the internal cost to the ASBR to the external cost reported by the ASBR. E2 does not compute the internal cost—it just reports the external cost to the remote destination.

Command Summaries

This section contains a list of the commands explained in this chapter. This list is not intended to teach the use of the commands, but to remind you of the options available.

Table 6-6   *OSPF Command Summary*

Command	Description
network *network number wildcard mask* **area** *area id*	This command identifies the interfaces that are running OSPF and places them in the appropriate area.
summary-address *address mask* [**not-advertise**][**tag** *tag*]	This command consolidates routes into a summary route before injecting them into the external world. Remember that the mask is the subnet, not the wildcard mask. The options to not advertise will suppress routes that match the mask. The **tag** option is for use with redistribution.
area *area-id* **range** *address mask*	This command is used to summarize the routes at the ABR before injecting them into another area.
no area *area-id* **range** *address mask*	This command disables the configured summarization at the ABR.
area *area-id* **stub**	This command turns the area into a stub area. This command must be configured by every router in the area.
area *area-id* **stub no-summary**	This command turns a router into a totally stubby area.
area *area-id* **default-cost** *cost*	This configures the cost for the default summary route used for a stub or totally stub area. The default is 1.
area *area-id* **virtual-link** *router-id*	This command creates a virtual link.
show ip ospf border-routers	This command lists the ABR routers in the AS.
ip ospf virtual-links	This command shows the virtual links and the current parameters.

Q&A

The following questions test your understanding of the topics covered in this chapter. The final questions in this section repeat the opening "Do I Know This Already?" questions. These are repeated to enable you to test your progress. After you have answered the questions, find the answers in Appendix A. If you get an answer wrong, review the answer and ensure that you understand the reason for your mistake. If you are confused by the answer, refer to the appropriate text in the chapter to review the concepts.

1 In a totally stubby area, which routes are not propagated into the area?

_____

_____

_____

2 Where would you see whether a learned network was within the same area as the router you were looking at?

_____

_____

_____

3 An Area Border Router must be resident in which area?

_____

_____

_____

4 What does *ABR* stand for, and what LSAs will it forward?

_____

_____

_____

5 State two advantages in creating areas in OSPF.

_____

_____

_____

6 What is an external route, and on which type of router will this route be introduced?

_____

_____

_____

7 Which command in OSPF shows the network LSA information?

_____

_____

_____

8 Why is the use of VLSM important in the design of OSPF?

_____

_____

_____

9 Given the networks 144.12.8.0 and 144.12.12.0, both with the mask of 255.255.255.0, is it possible to summarize these into one subnet? If so, state the new subnet and mask.

_____

_____

_____

10 What is a discontiguous network?

_____

_____

_____

11 A virtual link in OSPF is used to solve what problem?

_____

_____

_____

12 State one disadvantage for making an NBMA Frame Relay cloud Area 0.

_____

_____

_____

13 State one advantage in making the centralized routers and network resources dwell in Area 0 while the Frame Relay cloud and the stub remote LANs reside in satellite stub areas.

_____

_____

_____

14 How does creating the number of areas in OSPF reduce the number of SPF calculations?

_____

_____

_____

15 How does a stub area differ from the backbone area?

_____

_____

_____

16 How does a totally stubby area differ from a stub area?

_____

_____

_____

17 State the different LSA types.

_____

_____

_____

18 Where does the backbone router reside, and what is its function?

_____

_____

_____

19 Are there any considerations for OSPF configured with VLSM sending routing updates into RIPv1?

_____

_____

_____

20 There are two types of summarization. What are they?

_____

_____

_____

21 Can the following subnets with a mask of 255.255.255.0 be summarized? If so, state the subnet and mask that can be used.

19.44.16.0	19.44.24.0
19.44.17.0	19.44.25.0
19.44.18.0	19.44.26.0
19.44.19.0	19.44.27.0
19.44.20.0	19.44.28.0
19.44.21.0	19.44.29.0
19.44.22.0	19.44.30.0
19.44.23.0	19.44.31.0

_____

_____

_____

22 Why can interarea summarization be configured only on ABRs?

_____

_____

_____

23 What command would be used to create a totally stubby area?

_____

_____

_____

24 What is a virtual link, and what command would be used to create it?

_____

_____

_____

25 Where would you issue the command to summarize IP subnets? State the command that would be used.

_____

_____

_____

26 How would you summarize external routes before injecting them into the OSPF domain?

_____

_____

_____

Scenarios

The following scenarios and questions are designed to draw together the content of the chapter and to exercise your understanding of the concepts. There is not necessarily a right answer. The thought process and practice in manipulating the concepts is the goal of this section. The answers to the scenario questions are found at the end of this chapter.

Scenario 6-1

Refer to Figure 6-14, and design the addressing scheme for the network. After this is designed, write the configuration for the central router.

Ensure that you include the following:

1 Address the network using the private network 10.0.0.0. Design the addressing scheme so that it allows for the summarization of addresses between areas. Show the summarization that you allocate, and explain your reasons for your choices.

Area 0 is using a prefix of 28 bits within the area.

Area 2 is using a prefix of 22 bits within the area.

Area 3 is using a prefix of 24 bits within the area.

Area 4 is using a prefix of 30 bits for the serial connections. It is using a 28-bit prefix for the connections to the Ethernet routers. Do not include the subnets attached to the LANs in Area 4.

2 Issue the commands for the main router Figure 6-14 to configure the following:

— The router ID

— The network commands to place the appropriate interfaces into the correct areas

— The configuration of the totally stubby area (Area 4)

— The configuration of the stub (Area 4)

— Summarization between areas

— The election of the central router as designated router, where appropriate

Figure 6-14 *The Diagram for Configuration Scenario 6-1*

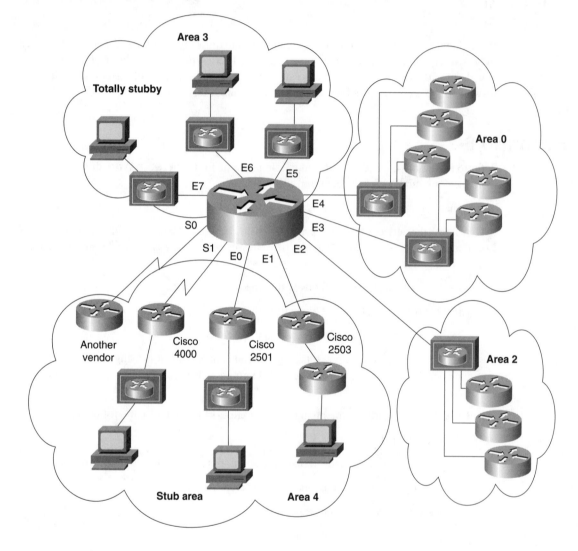

Scenario 6-2

Using Figure 6-15, answer the questions that follow.

Figure 6-15   *The Diagram for Configuration Scenario 6-2*

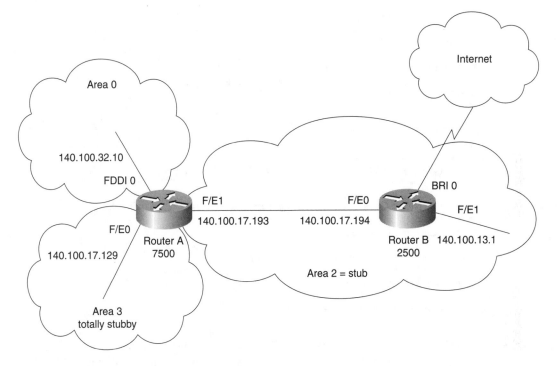

The users in the network are complaining about the slowness of the network, particularly when trying to access the Internet. Examine the configuration in Example 6-11 in conjunction with Figure 6-15, and give reasons for any slowness or lack of connectivity that you can see on the network. Provide current configuration commands to correct any errors that you find.

Example 6-11 *Configuring OSPF Example for Scenario 6-2*

```
ROUTER A
Router(config)#router ospf 100
Router(config-router)#network 140.100.17.128 0.0.0.15 area 3
Router(config-router)#network 140.100.17.192 0.0.0.15 area 2
Router(config-router)#network 140.100.32.0 0.0.0.0 area 0
Router(config-router)#area 2 stub
Router(config-router)#area 3 stub no-summary
Router(config-router)#area 3 default-cost 15
```

continues

Example 6-11 *Configuring OSPF Example for Scenario 6-2 (Continued)*

```
!
Router(config-router)#interface FastEthernet0
Router(config-if)#ip address 140.100.17.129 255.255.255.240
Router(config-if)#no ip directed-broadcast
!
Router(config-if)#interface FastEthernet1
Router(config-if)#ip address 140.100.17.193 255.255.255.240
Router(config-if)#no ip directed-broadcast
!
Router(config-if)#interface Fddi0
Router(config-if)#ip address 140.100.32.10 255.255.255.240
Router(config-if)#no ip directed-broadcast
Router(config-if)#no keepalive

Router(config-if)#exit
ROUTER B
Router(config)#router ospf 100
Router(config-router)# network 140.100.0.0 0.0.0.15 area 2
!
Router(config-router)#interface FastEthernet0
Router(config-if)#ip address 140.100.17.194 255.255.255.240
Router(config-if)#no ip directed-broadcast
Router(config-if)#ip ospf priority 100
!
Router(config-if)#interface FastEthernet1
Router(config-if)#ip address 140.100.13.1 255.255.255.240
Router(config-if)#no ip directed-broadcast
!
Router(config-if)#exit
```

1 There are problems with router B. There is inconsistency in the routing table, and the system is extremely slow. What commands would be used to identify the problem? In examining the diagram and configuration, what problems can you see?

2 Router A is having problems connecting to Area 0, which is causing problems in other areas because this router is used to connect to Area 0. What commands would be used to identify the problem? In examining the diagram and configuration, what problems can you see?

3 Issue the commands that would be used to correct the configuration problems that you see in the example configuration for routers A and B.

4 When you issue the **show ip ospf** interface command, you notice that there is a discrepancy in the timers on the link between routers A and B. The transmit timer on Router A is set to 5, and the retransmit timer is set to 1. What problems would this cause? What command would be used to change the timers, and what are the default settings?

5 There is an ISDN link into the Internet from Router B. The network manager has suggested that this link is the cause of some performance problems on the router. You have noticed that the interface is included in the OSPF **network** command. What might be the cause of the problem, and how could it be fixed?

Scenario 6-3

1 Explain the purpose of the virtual link in Figure 6-16.

Figure 6-16 *Network Diagram #1 for Scenario 6-3*

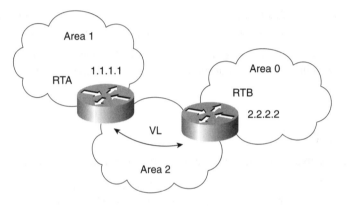

2 Is the configuration of the OSPF network shown in Figure 6-17 a valid configuration?

Figure 6-17 *Network Diagram #2 for Scenario 6-17*

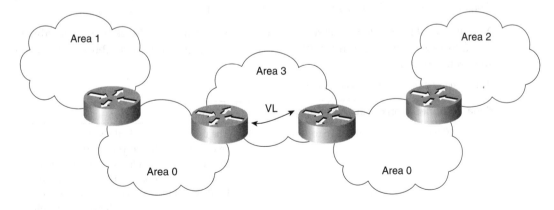

3 Why would a company implement this design?

Example 6-12 *Sample Configuration of Scenario 6-1 (Continued)*

```
Router(config)# interface e0
Router(config-if)# ip address 10.4.0.33 255.255.255.240
Router(config)# interface e1
Router(config-if)# ip address 10.4.0.17 255.255.255.240
Router(config)# interface e2
Router(config-if)# ip address 10.2.4.1 255.255.252.0
!Election of Designated Router
Router(config-if)# ip ospf priority 64
Router(config)# interface e3
Router(config-if)# ip address 10.0.0.193 255.255.255.240
!Ensures Router not elected as Designated Router
Router(config-if)# ip ospf priority 0
Router(config)# interface e4
Router(config-if)# ip address 10.0.0.129 255.255.255.240
!Ensures Router not elected as Designated Router
Router(config-if)# ip ospf priority 0
Router(config)# interface e5
Router(config-if)# ip address 10.3.3.1 255.255.255.0
Router(config)# interface e6
Router(config-if)# ip address 10.3.2.1 255.255.255.0
Router(config)# interface e7
Router(config-if)# ip address 10.3.1.1 255.255.255.0
Router(config)# interface s0
Router(config-if)# ip address 10.4.0.9 255.255.255.252
Router(config)# interface s1
Router(config-if)# ip address 10.4.0.5 255.255.255.252
!Router ID set by configuring the Router ID
Router(config)# interface loopback 0
Router(config-if)# ip address 10.100.100.101 255.255.255.255
```

Scenario 6-2 Answers

1 There are problems with Router B. There is inconsistency in the routing table, and the system is extremely slow. What commands would be used to identify the problem? In examining the diagram and configuration, what problems can you see?

Router B has been configured to be the designated router for the LAN, which means that it is dealing with all the traffic on the LAN associated with the management of OSPF. Given that the system is a 2500, it is a poor choice for a designated router. A better choice would be Router A, which is a larger system that connects directly to Area 0, making it is a better choice from the standpoint of the network design. If Router B were a larger system than a 2500, there could be an argument for making it the designated router to elevate Router A, which would otherwise be functioning as the ABR as well as the designated router.

The router has not been configured as a stub, so the communication between Router A and Router B will be confused, preventing any communication between the two routers.

2 Router A is having problems connecting to Area 0, which is causing problems in other areas because this router is used to connect to Area 0. What commands would be used to identify the problem? In examining the diagram and configuration, what problems can you see?

Router A is configured incorrectly. The command that would show the problem would be either show ip route, show ip protocols, or show ip ospf database. The lack of LSA traffic would indicate a configuration problem. When examining the configuration, you would see that the mask on the configuration of the network command for Area 0 is wrong. Therefore, there will be no communication of OSPF LSAs between the areas.

3 Issue the commands that would be used to correct the configuration problems that you see in the example configuration for routers A and B.

The commands that would solve these problems are as follows:

On Router A:

```
router ospf 100
network 140.100.32.0 0.0.0.15 area 0
interface fastethernet 1
no ip ospf cost 10
ip ospf priority 100
```

On Router B:

```
router ospf 200
network 140.100.13.0 0.0.0.15 area 2
area 2 stub
interface FastEthernet0
no ip ospf priority 100
```

4 When you issue the **show ip ospf** interface command, you notice that there is a discrepancy in the timers on the link between routers A and B. The transmit timer on Router A is set to 5, and the retransmit timer is set to 1. What problems would this cause? What command would be used to change the timers, and what are the default settings?

The default setting for the transmit timer is set to 1 second, and the retransmit timer is set to 5 seconds. The transmit timer determines the estimated number of seconds that it takes to send a LSA to a neighbor. The retransmit timer states the number of seconds to wait for an acknowledgment before retransmitting an LSA.

If the transmit timer is not smaller than the retransmit timer, the interface retransmits in the belief that the other side did not receive the LSA. This leads to excess traffic, confusion in the topology database, and the possibility of flapping links. To correct the settings, issue the following subinterface commands:

```
ip ospf retransmit-interval seconds
ip ospf transmit-delay seconds
```

5 There is an ISDN link into the Internet from Router B. The network manager has suggested that this link is the cause of some performance problems on the router. You have noticed that the interface is included in the OSPF **network** command. What might be the cause of the problem, and how could it be fixed?

If the ISDN interface is configured for dial-on-demand routing (DDR) and is also included in OSPF network commands, you may find that the link that the DDR process establishes will cause the routing updates to be propagated throughout the network, causing additional CPU utilization on the routers and flooding of packets throughout the network. The solution is to ensure that the interface is not included in the network command to the OSPF process. A more important problem is that Router B is in a stub area and will not track external routes. Router B cannot connect to the Internet as an ASBR because it will not propagate the Type 5 LSAs. The BRI interface cannot partake in the OSPF network. Therefore, the network will not be slow; it will be down.

Scenario 6-3 Answers

1 Explain the purpose of the virtual link in Figure 6-16.

In this example, Area 1 does not have a direct physical connection into Area 0. A virtual link must be configured between RTA and RTB. Area 2 is to be used as a transit area, and RTB is the entry point into Area 0. This way, RTA and Area 1 will have a logical connection to the backbone.

2 Is the configuration of the OSPF network shown in Figure 6-17 a valid configuration?

Yes, the configuration is a valid one.

3 Why would a company implement this design?

OSPF allows for linking discontinuous parts of the backbone using a virtual link. In some cases, different Area 0s need to be linked together. This can occur, for example, if a company is trying to merge two separate OSPF networks into one network with a common Area 0. In other instances, virtual links are added for redundancy in case some router failure causes the backbone to be split in two. Whatever the reason may be, a virtual link can be configured between separate ABRs that touch Area 0 from each side and that have a common area.

This chapter covers the following topics that you will need to master to pass the CCNP/ CCDP Routing exam:

- The features and operation of EIGRP.

- How EIGRP discovers chooses and maintains routes.

- How EIGRP supports the use of VLSM and summarization.

- How EIGRP functions in an NBMA environment.

- How EIGRP supports large networks.

- How to configure EIGRP, both in an enterprise network and in an NBMA network.

- How to verify an EIGRP configuration.

- Cisco defaults in EIGRP, the Cisco commands for implementing EIGRP, and the Cisco commands for reviewing the configuration of EIGRP.

CHAPTER 7

Using EIGRP in Enterprise Networks

This chapter covers in detail the Enhanced Interior Gateway Routing Protocol (EIGRP). Although EIGRP has the capability of supporting IP, AppleTalk, and IPX, the Routing exam will deal with only the mechanics of the IP routing protocol. This chapter expands on

---

the understanding of routing within large enterprise networks that is covered in the previous chapter on OSPF within a large multiarea network.

This chapter is also broken into two topics. The first part of the chapter deals theoretically with how EIGRP works. How to implement and manage an EIGRP network is described at the end of the chapter. The operation of EIGRP, some of the options available, and design considerations are explained in this chapter, particularly in reference to scaling EIGRP and its use over a nonbroadcast multiaccess (NBMA) WAN environment. Both the network communication that the protocol uses and its configuration are explained in this chapter.

The topics in this chapter directly reflect questions on the Routing exam. EIGRP is designed for use in large networks. As a proprietary routing protocol for Cisco, it is therefore an obligatory subject in a Cisco exam on IP routing protocols. The BSCN course devotes 15 percent of its material to configuring EIGRP, and you can expect approximately 10 questions on the Routing exam to be directly related to this subject.

How to Best Use This Chapter

By taking the following steps, you can make better use of your study time:

- Keep your notes and the answers for all your work with this book in one place, for easy reference.

- When you take a quiz, write down your answers. Studies show that retention significantly increases by writing down facts and concepts, even if you never look at the information again.

- Use the diagram in Figure 7-1 to guide you to the next step.

Figure 7-1 *How to Use This Chapter*

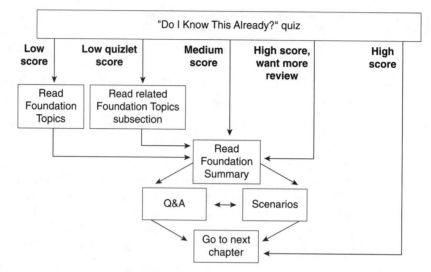

If you skip to the Foundation Summary, Q&A, and scenarios sections and have trouble with the material there, you should go back to the Foundation Topics section.

"Do I Know This Already?" Quiz

The purpose of the "Do I Know This Already?" quiz is to help you decide what parts of this chapter to use. If you already intend to read the entire chapter, you do not necessarily need to answer these questions now.

This 16-question quiz helps you determine how to spend your limited study time. The quiz is sectioned into four smaller four-question "quizlets," which correspond to four major topics in the chapter. Figure 7-1 outlines suggestions on how to spend your time in this chapter. Use Table 7-1 to record your scores.

Table 7-1   *Score Sheet for Quiz and Quizlets*

Quizlet Number	Topic	Questions	Score
1	Features and operation of EIGRP, including NBMA networks	1 to 4	
2	How EIGRP discovers, chooses, and maintains routes	5 to 8	
3	How EIGRP supports large networks, including VLSM, summarization, and design	9 to 12	
4	How to configure and verify EIGRP (including NBMA networks)	13 to 16	
All questions	All	1 to 16	

1 EIGRP may be used to send information about which three routing protocols?

_____

_____

_____

2 Which EIGRP packets are sent reliably?

_____

_____

_____

3 In what instances will EIGRP automatically redistribute?

_____

_____

_____

4 How long is the holdtime, by default?

_____

_____

_____

5 What is an EIGRP topology table, and what does it contain?

_____

_____

_____

6 What is the advertised distance in EIGRP, and how is it distinguished from the feasible distance?

_____

_____

_____

7 What EIGRP algorithm is run to create entries for the routing table?

_____

_____

_____

8 When does EIGRP place a network in active mode?

_____

_____

_____

9 By default, EIGRP summarizes at which boundary?

_____

_____

_____

10 What is Stuck in Active?

_____

_____

_____

11 What is the **variance** command used for?

_____

_____

_____

12 State two factors that influence EIGRP scalability.

_____

_____

_____

13 What command is used to display which routes are in passive or active mode?

_____

_____

_____

14 What command is used in EIGRP to perform manual summarization?

_____

_____

_____

15 For Frame Relay, when would you configure the physical interface (as opposed to a subinterface) with the **bandwidth** command?

_____

_____

_____

16 Which command is used to display all types of EIGRP packets that are both received and sent by a router?

_____

_____

_____

The answers to this quiz are found in Appendix A, "Answers to Quiz Questions." The suggested choices for your next step are as follows:

- **2 or less on any quizlet**—Review the appropriate sections of the "Foundation Topics" portion of this chapter, based on Table 7-1. Then move on to the "Foundation Summary" section, the "Q&A" section, and the "Scenarios" at the end of the chapter.

- **8 or less overall score**—Read the entire chapter. This includes the "Foundation Topics" and "Foundation Summary" sections, the "Q&A" section, and the "Scenarios" at the end of the chapter.

- **9 to 12 overall score**—Begin with the "Foundation Summary" section, and then go to the "Q&A" section and the "Scenarios" at the end of the chapter. If you have trouble with these exercises, read the appropriate sections in "Foundation Topics."

- **13 or more overall score**—If you want more review on these topics, skip to the "Foundation Summary" section, and then go to the "Q&A" section and the "Scenarios" at the end of the chapter. Otherwise, move to the next chapter.

Foundation Topics

Introduction: EIGRP in an Enterprise Network

EIGRP is an enhanced version of IGRP, hence the name. It uses the same distance vector technology. The changes were effected in the convergence properties and the operating efficiency of the protocol. It has some characteristics similar to those of a link-state routing protocol. Therefore, it is sometimes referred to as a hybrid routing protocol, although Cisco calls it an advanced distance vector protocol. It is an efficient, although proprietary, solution to networking large environments as it scales well. Its ability to scale is, like OSPF, dependent on the design of the network.

Case Study

The company Gargantuan, Inc., is a large multinational. It has its main offices in London, New York, San Francisco, and Tokyo. As a manufacturing company that produces cleaning products, it has plants in England, Mexico, and Japan. It has an extensive network that is running EIGRP. The network is used for local administrative purposes as well as coordinating the product movement from the manufacturing plant to the grocery store. There have been complaints during the past year about poor response times on the network. This has reached critical proportions because the problems are no longer simply irritations for the users, but they are now potentially devastating delays in shipping orders and transfers in electronic funds and manufacturing details.

A careful analysis of the network is required to identify the problem. A consultant has said that the entire organization needs to be readdressed and that configuration changes need to be made to the network. This involves an analysis of the network topology and data flow to appropriately design a new TCP/IP addressing scheme for the organization.

The CIO recently left, and there is very little documentation, so the network administrators have been charged with creating a network diagram and presenting some immediate solutions. This means that they have to thoroughly understand the operation of EIGRP in large environments. This chapter deals with the concepts of EIGRP and explains how it works within an enterprise. It considers design issues, particularly in reference to NBMA networks, and discusses the configuration and verification of the operation of the protocol.

EIGRP Defined

The focus of this chapter is on how EIGRP works so that those networks can be designed to maximize efficiency and truly scale the network.

The major concern in scaling an organizational network is controlling the network overhead that is sent, in particular over slow WAN links. The less information about the network, its services, and networks that need to be sent, the greater the capacity available for the data between clients and servers. Although sending less routing information relieves the network, it gives the routers less information with which to make decisions. Every designer of routing protocols and every network administrator must deal continually with this trade-off. As seen with summarization, static and default routes can lead to poor routing decisions and loss of connectivity.

OSPF was the first protocol to attempt to address these problems. Alternatives to OSPF that offer the capability to scale to the size of modern networks are few. Static routing is one possibility, but it demands so much from the network administrator that it would never scale. IGRP offers another alternative; as a proprietary distance vector protocol, IGRP has solved many of the problems. However, it does face some issues with regard to scaling because of the inherent nature of distance vector. Although still distance vector and proprietary, EIGRP addresses many of the problems related to scaling the network that IGRP never anticipated.

This chapter discusses EIGRP. As a proprietary routing protocol, EIGRP can solve many problems seen in standards-based protocols that have to please all of the devices all of the time.

Operation of EIGRP

EIGRP is a revised and improved version of IGRP. Its goal is to solve the scaling limitations that IGRP faces, using the distance vector technology from which it grew. EIGRP increases the potential growth of a network by reducing the convergence time. This is achieved by the following:

- The Diffusing Update Algorithm (DUAL)
- Loop-free networks
- Incremental updates
- Multicast addressing for updates
- Holding information about neighbors as opposed to the entire network

These features depend on proprietary technology, which centers on local computation. The DUAL algorithm diffuses this computation over multiple routers, with each router responsible for its own small calculation and making requests of neighboring routers when necessary. A full understanding of the concepts and operation of EIGRP will aid you in the design, implementation, and maintenance of EIGRP networks, and will definitely help you pass an exam on the subject.

The main concepts of EIGRP are as follows:

- Advanced distance vector
- Loop-free routing tables
- Support for different topologies

- Rapid convergence

- Reduced bandwidth use

- Use of a composite metric (bandwidth and delay as the default)

- Unequal load balancing

- Neighbor discovery

- DUAL

- Successors, the selection process for a feasible successor

- Passive and active routes

- Protocol independence at Layer 3, allowing support for IP, AppleTalk, and IPX

- Reliable sending of routing updates

- VLSM, which allows efficient addressing, discontiguous networks, and the use of classless networks

- Manual summarization

- Compatibility with IGRP

- Easy-to-configure nature

- Fewer design constraints than OSPF

How EIGRP Works

Cisco identifies four main components of EIGRP:

- Protocol-dependent modules

- Reliable Transport Protocol

- Neighbor discovery/recovery

- DUAL

These components are discussed in this section. However, to understand how EIGRP works, there must be some familiarity with the terminology. Table 7-2 defines the main concepts and gives a brief synopsis of each term.

Table 7-2 *Terminology for EIGRP for IP*

Term	Definition
Neighbor	A router running EIGRP that is directly connected.
Neighbor table	A list of every neighbor, including the IP address, the outgoing interface, the holdtime, SRTT, and uptime or how long since the neighbor was added to the table. This table is built from information on hellos received from adjacent routers (neighbors).
Route table	The routing table, or list of available networks and the best paths. A path is moved from the topology table to the routing table when a feasible successor is identified.
Topology table	A table that contains all the paths advertised by neighbors to all the known networks. This is a list of all the successors, feasible successors, the feasible distance, the advertised distance, and the outgoing interface. DUAL acts on the topology table to determine successors and feasible successors by which to build a routing table.
Hello	Used to find and maintain neighbors in the topology table. They are sent periodically and are sent reliably.
Update	An EIGRP packet containing change information about the network. It is sent reliably. It is sent only when there is a change in the network to affected routers: When a neighbor first comes up When a neighbor transitions from active to passive for a destination When there is a metric change for a destination
Query	Sent from the router when it loses a path to a network. If there is no alternate route (feasible successor), it will send out queries to neighbors inquiring whether they have a feasible successor. This makes the route state change to active. The queries are sent reliably.
Reply	A response to the query. If a router has no information to send in a reply, it will send queries to all its neighbors. A unicast is sent reliably.
ACK	A hello packet with no data that is an acknowledgment of packets sent reliably.
Holdtime	Sent in the hello packet. It determines how long the router waits for hellos from a neighbor before declaring it unavailable. This information is held in the neighbor table.

Table 7-2   *Terminology for EIGRP for IP (Continued)*

Term	Definition
Smooth Round Trip Time (SRTT)	The time that the router waits after sending a packet reliably to hear an acknowledgment. This is held in the neighbor table and is used to calculate the RTO.
Retransmission Timeout (RTO)	Timer calculated in reference to the SRTT. RTO determines how long the router waits for an ACK before retransmitting the packet.
Reliable Transport Protocol (RTP)	Requirement that the packets be delivered in sequence and guaranteed.
Diffusing Update Algorithm (DUAL)	An algorithm performed on the topology table to converge the network. It is based on a router detecting a network change within a finite time, with the change being sent reliably and in sequence. As the algorithm is calculated simultaneously, in order and within a finite time frame on all affected routers, it ensures a loop-free network.
Advertised distance (AD)	The cost of the path to the remote network from the neighbor (the metric from the next-hop router).
Feasible distance (FD)	The lowest-cost distance (metric) to a remote network.
Feasible condition (FC)	When a neighbor reports a path (AD) that is lower than the router's FD to a network. The neighbor's (next-hop router's) path has a lower metric than the router's path.
Feasible successor (FS)	The neighbor reporting the AD that is lower than the router's FD becomes the feasible successor. The next-hop router that meets the FC.
Successor	The next-hop router that passes the FC. It is chosen from the FSs as having the lowest metric to the remote network.
Stuck in Active (SIA)	When a router has sent out network packets and is waiting for ACKs from all its neighbors. The route is active until all the ACKs have been received, if they do not appear after a certain time, the router is Stuck in Active for the route.
Query scoping	Another term for SIA.
Active	Route state when a network change is seen, but on interrogation of the topology table, there is no FC. The router queries its neighbors for alternative routes.
Passive	An operational route is passive. If the path is lost, the router examines the topology table to find an FS. If there is an FS, it is placed in the routing table and the router does not query the others, which would send it into active mode.

Even if the computation of the network is local, the router must know about the entire network. The explanation of the routing protocol will be given through the viewpoint of one router. When the network communication between the routers running EIGRP is understood, the operation of EIGRP will become clear; the concepts and terms will be placed in context. This facilitates the memorization of the subject; rote learning is no longer necessary.

The Hello Protocol

The router sends out a small hello packet to dynamically learn of other routing devices that are in the same broadcast domain.

NOTE A broadcast domain identifies devices that are within the same Layer 2 domain. Although they may not be directly connected to the same physical cable, if they are in a switched environment, from a logical Layer 2 or Layer 3 perspective, they are on the same link. If a broadcast is sent out, all the devices within the broadcast domain will hear the message and expend resources determining whether it is addressed to them. A Layer 3 device is a broadcast firewall, in that a router does not forward broadcasts.

Becoming a Neighbor

The Hello protocol uses a multicast address of 224.0.0.10, and all routers periodically send hellos. On hearing hellos, the router creates a table of its neighbors. The continued receipt of these packets maintains the *neighbor table*. If a hello from a known neighbor is not heard within a predetermined amount of time, as stated in the *holdtime*, the router will decide that the neighbor is no longer operational and will take the appropriate action. The holdtime is set at the default of three times the Hello timer. Therefore, if the router misses three hellos, the neighbor is declared dead. The Hello timer on a LAN is set to 5 seconds; the holdtime, therefore, is 15 seconds. On a WAN link, the Hello timer is 60 seconds, and the holdtime correspondingly is 180 seconds.

To become a neighbor, the following conditions must be met:

- The router must hear a hello packet or an ACK from a neighbor.

- The AS number in the packet header must be the same as that of the receiving router.

- The neighbor's metric settings must be the same.

The Neighbor Table

Each Layer 3 protocol has its own neighbor table—which makes sense because the neighbor, topology, and routing tables would differ greatly. Although all the information could be held in one table, the different EIGRP processes would all have to access the same table, which would complicate and slow down the lookup.

The Contents of the Neighbor Table

The neighbor table includes the following information:

- The address of the neighbor.

- The interface through which the neighbor's hello was heard.

- The holdtime.

- The uptime, how long since the router first heard from the neighbor.

- The sequence number. The neighbor table tracks all the packets sent between the neighbors. It tracks both the last sequence number sent to the neighbor and the last sequence number received from the neighbor. Although the Hello protocol is a connectionless protocol, other protocols used by EIGRP are connection-oriented. The sequence number is in reference to these protocols.

- *Smooth Round Trip Time (SRTT)* is used to calculate the *retransmission timeout (RTO)*. This is the time in milliseconds that it takes a packet to be sent to a neighbor and a reply to be received.

- RTO, the retransmission timeout. This states how long the router will wait on a connection-oriented protocol without an acknowledgment before retransmitting the packet. If the original packet that was unacknowledged was multicast, the retransmitted packets will be unicast.

- The number of packets in a queue. This is a means by which administrators can monitor congestion on the network.

Packets from Neighbors That Build the Topology Table

After the router knows who its neighbors are, it is in a position to create a database of feasible successors. This view of the network is held in the topology table.

The *topology table* is created from *updates* received from the neighboring routers. The updates are exchanged between the neighbors.

Packets called *replies* will also update the topology table. Replies are sent in response to *queries* sent by the router, inquiring about suspect routes.

The queries and responses used by EIGRP for the DUAL algorithm are sent reliably as multicasts. If a router does not hear an acknowledgment within the allotted time, it retransmits the packet as a unicast. If there is no response after 16 attempts, the router marks the neighbor as dead. The window for the RTP is set as 1. The router must hear an acknowledgment from every router before it can send the next packet. The capability to send unicast retransmissions decreases the time that it takes to build the tables.

Figure 7-2 demonstrates building the neighbor table.

Figure 7-2 *Building the Neighbor Table*

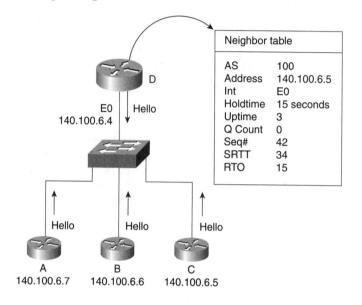

The Topology Table

The topology table in EIGRP manages the selection of routes to be added to the routing table.

The topology table has a record of all known network routes within the organization. The table is built from the update packets that are exchanged by the neighbors and by replies to queries sent by the router. When the router has an understanding of the network, it runs DUAL to determine the best path to the remote network. The result is entered into the routing table.

Maintaining the Topology Table

The topology table is updated because the router either gains or loses direct connectivity with a router or hears a change through the network communication of EIGRP.

The following three reasons may cause a topology table to be recalculated:

- The router hears a change when a new network is available because of one of the following reasons:

  — The topology table receives an update stating that there is a new remote network.

  — The interface sees carrier sense for the network that is configured for a Layer 3 protocol supported by EIGRP, and the routing process has been configured with the appropriate network command.

- The router will change the successor in the topology table and routing table in these circumstances:

  — The topology table receives a reply or a query from a neighbor.

  — There is local configuration of a directly connected interface to change the cost of the link.

- The router hears a change from a neighbor when a network has become unavailable because of one of the following reasons:

  — The topology table receives a query, reply, or update stating that the remote network is down.

  — The neighbor table does not receive a hello within the holdtime.

  — The network is directly connected and the router senses a loss of carrier.

Figure 7-3 illustrates the traffic flow seen when a router loses a direct connection.

Figure 7-3   *Maintaining the Topology Table—the Traffic Flow*

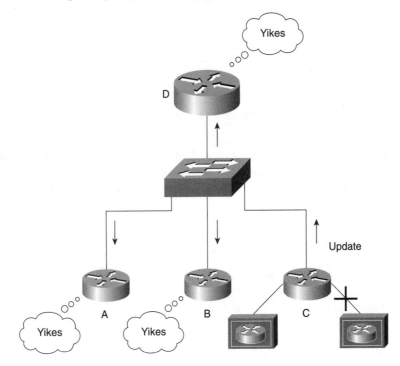

Just as the neighbor table tracks the receipt of the EIGRP packets, the topology table records the packets that have been sent by the router to the neighbors. It also identifies the status of the networks in the table. A healthy network is marked as *passive*; it will be labeled as *active* if the router is attempting to find an alternative path to the remote network that is believed to be down.

Because the routing table is built from the topology table, the topology table must have the information required by the routing table. This includes the next logical hop, or the address of the neighbor that sent the update with that network. The routing table will also calculate the metric to the remote network.

EIGRP Metrics

The metrics used in EIGRP are very similar to those of IGRP. The main difference is that the result of the calculation is held in a 32-bit field. This means that the decision can be much finer or detailed. The DUAL algorithm will use this metric to select the best path or paths to a destination. The computation is performed on paths held in the topology table to identify the best path to place into the routing table. There can be up to six paths held for one destination, and there can be three different types of paths. These three path types are described in Table 7-3.

Table 7-3   *EIGRP Routing Types*

Route Type	Description
Internal	Internal to the AS
Summary	Internal paths that have been summarized
External	External to the AS that have been redistributed into this EIGRP AS

The metric is the same composite metric used by IGRP, with the default being bandwidth and delay. Although it is possible to change the metric, this must be done only with great care and consideration to the network design. Any changes made must be effected on every router in the EIGRP AS.

The equation for the default metric used is this:

$$[(10000000 \div \text{smallest bandwidth kbps}) + \text{delay}] \times 256$$

Table 7-4 explains the metric values.

Table 7-4   *EIGRP Metric Values*

Metric Symbol	Metric Value	Description
K1	Bandwidth	Selects the smallest bandwidth media between the source and destination hosts. The equation used is $[10000000 \div \text{bandwidth kbps}] \times 256$.
K2	Loading	Is based on the statistics held at the outgoing interface and is recorded in bits per second.
K3	Delay	Is the delay calculated on the outgoing interface. The value used is the summarization of the delay on all the interfaces between the hosts.
K4	Reliability	Is based on the statistics held on the outgoing interface gained from keepalives, and is exponentially averaged over 5 minutes.
K5	MTU	Is the smallest MTU found configured on an interface on route. This value is included although it has not been used as part of the metric calculation.

The new terminology can be very confusing and is best understood in context. It is easier to remember a concept or term when the function is understood. Given the overall understanding of how EIGRP works, a consideration of the topology table and its components will help explain the detail of EIGRP operation.

The DUAL Finite-State Machine

DUAL is responsible for maintenance of the topology table and the creation of the routing table. The topology table records the metric as received from the advertising router, or the next logical hop. It then adds the cost of getting to that neighbor, the one that is advertising the route.

The cost to the destination network from the advertising router, plus the cost to that router, equals the metric to the destination network from the router.

The metric or cost from the neighbor advertising the route is known as the *advertised distance*. The metric or cost from the router is referred to as the *feasible distance*. If the AD is less than the FD, then the next-hop router is downstream and there is no loop. This is fundamental to EIGRP.

Figures 7-4 and 7-5 illustrate these distances. Note that the metric shown in these figures has been simplified for the purposes of this example.

When no alternative route is found in the routing table, the following actions are taken (using the network in Figure 7-5 as an example):

- In Figure 7-5, the topology table of Router A has a path (successor) of A to D to G to X.

- The FD is 20, and the AD from Neighbor D is 15.

- When Router D dies, Router A must find an alternative path to X.

- Neighbors B, C, E, and F have ADs of 27, 27, 20, and 21, respectively.

- Because all the neighbors have an AD that is the same or greater than the successor FD, none of these are acceptable as FSs.

- Router A must go into active mode and send queries to the neighbors.

- Both Routers E and F reply with an FS because both have an AD from G of 5. Remember the equation FD > AD; their FD is 20, and 20 > 5.

- This is acceptable. The topology and routing tables will be updated, DUAL will be calculated, and the network will be returned to passive mode.

- From this information received from Routers E and F in Figure 7-5, the router selects the path through E as the best route because it has the lower cost.

- The result is placed in the routing table as the valid neighboring router. EIGRP refers to this neighboring router as a *successor.*

- Router F will be stored as an FS in the topology table.

The details on how EIGRP computes successors are complex, but the concept is simple.

Choosing a Successor

To determine whether a path to a remote network is feasible, EIGRP considers the FC of the route. Essentially, each router holds a routing table that is a list of the available networks and the best or most efficient path to each of them. The term used to describe this is the *feasible distance of the successor*, otherwise known as the metric for the route. The router also holds the routing table of its neighbors, referred to as the AD. If the AD is within scope, this route may be identified as an alternative route, or an FS.

A neighbor can become an FS for a route only if its AD is less than the FD. This is DUAL's fundamental key to remaining loop-free; if a route contains a loop, the AD will be greater than the FD and therefore will fail the FC. By holding the routing tables of the neighbors, the amount of network overhead and computation is reduced. When a path to a remote network is lost, the router may well be capable of finding an alternative route with minimal fuss, computation, or network traffic. This gives the much-advertised benefit of very fast convergence.

The Topology Table Fields

The topology table includes the following information:

- Whether the route is passive or active.

- That an update has been sent to the neighbors.

- That a query packet has been sent to the neighbors. If this field is positive, at least one route will be marked as active.

- If a query packet has been sent, another field will track whether any replies have been received from the neighbors.

- That a reply packet has been sent in response to a query packet received from a neighbor.

- The remote networks.

- The prefix or mask for the remote network.

- The metric for the remote network, the FD.

- The metric for the remote network advertised by the next logical hop, the AD.

- The next logical hop.

- The outgoing interface to be used to reach the next logical hop.

- The successors, the path to the remote network stated in hops.

Adding a Network to the Topology Table

Imagine the router (Router A) that hears a new network. The administrator has plugged in another Ethernet cable to service a department that has moved into the building.

- As soon as Router A becomes aware of the new network, it starts to send Hello packets out the new interface. No one answers because this is an access router giving connectivity to the workstations and other end devices.

- There are no new entries in the neighbor table because no neighbors have responded to the Hello protocol. There is a new entry in the topology table, however, because this is a new network.

- EIGRP, sensing a change, is obliged to send an update to all its neighbors, informing them of the new network. The sent updates are tracked in the topology table and the neighbor table because the updates are connection-oriented and the acknowledgments from the neighbors must be received within a set time frame.

- Router A, having added the network to the topology table, adds the network to the routing table. The network will be marked as passive because it is operational.

- Router A's work is done. Router D's work has just begun. Router D is the backbone router in the basement of the building acting at the distribution layer. Its neighbors are routers on each floor and the routers in the other buildings.

- On hearing the update from Router A, Router D updates the sequence number in the neighbor table and adds the network to the topology table. It calculates the FD and the successor to place in the routing table. It is then in a position to send an update to all of its neighbors, except Router A. It is obeying the split horizon rule here.

In this manner, the new network is propagated to the affected routers. Figure 7-6 shows this propagation. The initial bit is set in the EIGRP header to indicate that the routes in the update represent a new neighbor relationship.

Figure 7-6   *EIGRP—Updating the Topology Table with a New Router*

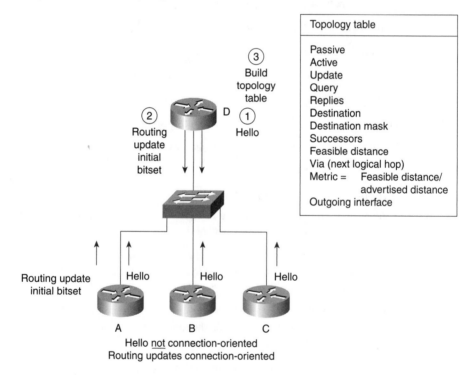

Removing a Path or Router from the Topology Table

This process is far more complex and gets to the crux of EIGRP. The following process uses Figure 7-6 and Figure 7-7 and focuses on Router D:

- If a network connected to Router A is disconnected, Router A updates its topology and routing table, and sends an update to its neighbors.

Figure 7-7   *EIGRP—Maintaining the Topology Table, Router D*

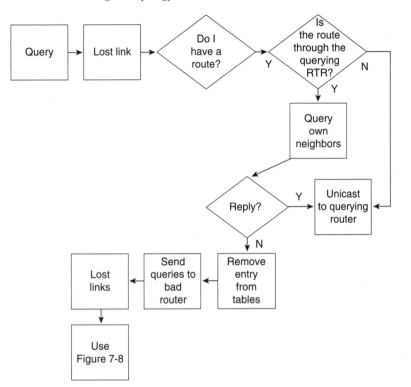

- When Router D receives the update, it updates the neighbor table and the topology table.

- As a router, it is programmed to find an alternative route to the remote network. It examines the topology table for alternatives. Because there was only one path to the remote network, no alternatives will be found.

- The router then sends out a query to the neighbors requesting that they look in their tables for paths to the remote network. The route is marked active in the topology table at this time.

- The query is tracked and, when all the replies are in, the neighbor and topology tables are updated.

- DUAL, which starts to compute as soon as a network change is registered, runs to determine the best path, which is placed in the routing table.

- Because no alternative route is available, the neighbors reply to the query stating that they have no path.

- Before they respond, they have queried their own neighbors; in this way, the search for an alternative path extends throughout the organization.

- When no router can supply a path to the network, all the routers remove the network from their routing and topology tables.

Life becomes more interesting when a neighbor does have an alternative route.

Figure 7-7 shows the actions taken when a router receives a query from another router asking for an alternative route to a destination. Note that if the queried router has no route to offer, it is still obliged to respond to the querying router.

Figure 7-8 illustrates the logic flow in a router that realizes a link has been lost, which may occur because a directly connected interface has lost a carrier signal or because the router has received an update or query.

Finding an Alternative Path to a Remote Network

When the path to a network is lost, EIGRP goes to a lot of trouble to find an alternative path. This process is one of the major benefits of EIGRP. The method it has chosen is very reliable and very fast. Figure 7-9 and the following list describe the process.

NOTE   Note that the metric shown in Figure 7-9 has been simplified for the purposes of this example.

Using Figure 7-9 as reference for the topology of the network, follow the sequence of events:

- Router D marks the routes that were reached by sending the traffic to Router G.

- It looks in the topology table, which has every network and path of the network, to determine whether there is an alternative route. It is looking for an FS.

- An FS is determined by a clear equation. The topology table has listed for every route or successor an AD and an FD. This comprises the metric by which the route was selected.

- Router D adds the alternative route to X via B, found in the topology table, without moving into active mode because the AD is still less than the original FD. The AD is 5; the original FD was 15. It needs to send updates to its neighbors because the distance has changed.

- If the router did not have an FS, it would have placed the route into an active state while it actively queried other routers for an alternative path.

- After interrogating the topology table, if a feasible route is found, the neighbor replies with the alternative path.

Figure 7-8 *Maintaining the Topology Table—Choosing a Feasible Successor*

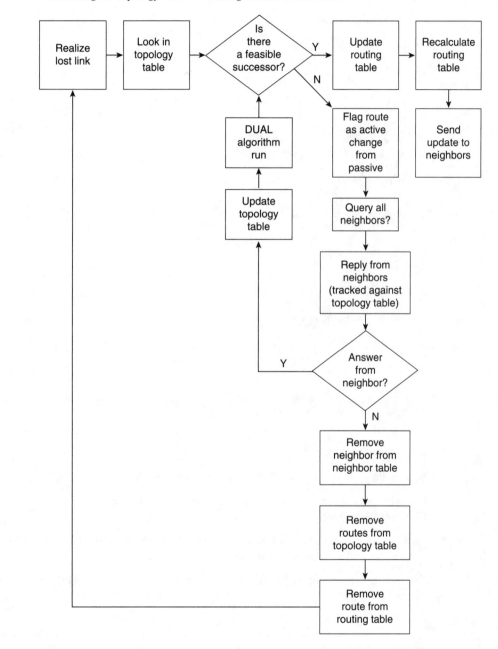

Figure 7-9   *Campus Topology Map Showing Alternative Path Selection*

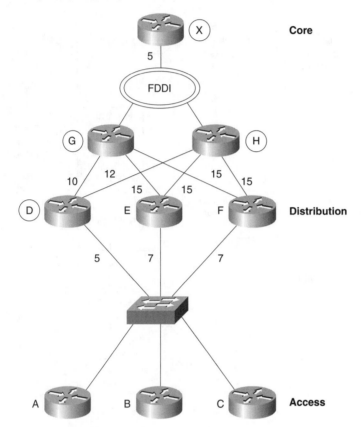

- This alternative path is then added to the topology table.

- Next, in the last steps of the DUAL algorithm, the routing table is updated.

- The network is placed back into a passive state as the router returns to sleep until the next change in the network.

- If a neighbor that has been queried has no alternative path or FS, it places the network into active mode and queries its neighbors.

- If no answer is heard, the messages are propagated until they hit a network or autonomous system boundary.

NOTE   Figures 7-4 and 7-5 illustrate the process described in the previous sections, "Updating the Routing Table in Passive Mode with DUAL," and "Updating the Routing Table in Active Mode with DUAL."

Figure 7-10 illustrates the boundary for the propagation of query packets.

Figure 7-10   *The Propagation of Query Packets*

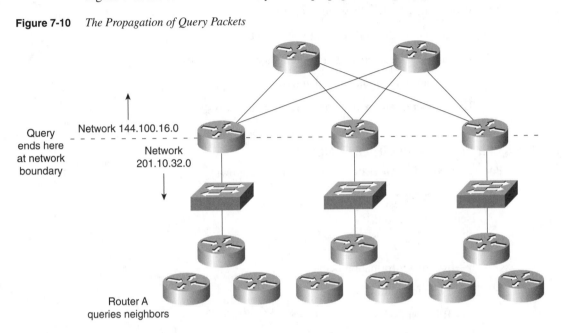

When the router sends a query packet, it is recorded in the topology table. This to ensure a timely reply. If the router does not hear a reply, the neighbor is removed from the neighbor table; all the networks held in the topology table for that neighbor are seen as suspect, and the networks are queried. Occasionally, because of slow links and burdened routers in a large network, problems can occur. In particular, a router may not receive a reply from all the queries that it sent out. This leads to the route being declared *Stuck in Active (SIA)*; the neighbor that failed to reply will be removed from the neighbor table, and DUAL will assume a reply giving an infinite metric.

As can be seen in the explanation for finding an FS, queries can be sent throughout the organization's network. This is the design key to ensuring that EIGRP scales.

Scaling EIGRP

EIGRP is designed to work in very large networks. However, as with OSPF, this is design-sensitive. Scaling a network—or, in other words, its capability to grow in size and complexity—are major concerns in today's organizations. New demands are constantly driving the networks into using applications that require more bandwidth and other resources from the network. Simply consider the need for every desktop and every user to be able to attach to centralized resources as well as the Internet. The need to understand the complications that arise from this need to grow networks is dealt with in detail in Chapter 2, "Managing Scalable Network Growth." Although it is not within the scope of the exam, it is the goal of much of its content.

Reasons for a Poorly Scaled EIGRP Network

The factors that can affect the scaling of EIGRP are these:

- The amount of information sent between neighbors

- The number of routers that are sent updates

- How far away the routers are that have to send updates

- The number of alternative paths to remote networks

Symptoms of a Poorly Scaled EIGRP Network

Poorly scaled EIGRP networks can result in the following:

- A route being SIA

- Network congestion

    — Delays

    — Routing information being lost

    — Flapping routes

    — Retransmission

- Router memory running low

- Router CPU overutilized

- Unreliable circuit or unidirectional link

Some of these symptoms are caused by other factors, such as poor design, with resources overwhelmed by the tasks assigned. Often many of these symptoms will be characterized by a route being flagged as SIA, as the router waits for a reply from a neighbor across a network that cannot handle the demands made upon it.

Careful design and placement of network devices can remedy many of the problems seen in a network.

Solutions to EIGRP Scaling Issues

The design of the network is very important to the ability to scale any network. The following solutions all revolve around a carefully thought-out network.

- Contiguous allocation of addresses, to allow summarization

- A hierarchical tiered network design, to allow summarization

- Summarization

- Sufficient network resources (both H/W and S/W) on network devices

- Sufficient bandwidth on WAN links
- Appropriate EIGRP configuration on WAN links (detailed later in this chapter)
- Filters
- Network monitoring

Design Issues Particular to EIGRP

It should be remembered that the queries must be limited to ensure that EIGRP can properly scale. If the queries are allowed to traverse the entire organization, then the problems and symptoms described will ravage your network.

Many believe that dividing the organization's network into different EIGRP autonomous systems is a good way of limiting the query range. This is true because EIGRP does not share updates with another AS. However, many organizations that created the autonomous systems to replicate OSPF areas naturally redistribute between them so that the entire organization can share routing information. At this point, the query is propagated into the new AS, and the problem continues. Summarization is the best way to limit the query range of EIGRP networks.

If redistribution is used, then it should be accompanied by route filters to ensure that feedback loops are not generated.

Certain topologies, although valid in most instances, pose problems for the EIGRP network. This is true in particular for the hub-and-spoke design often seen implemented between the remote sites and the regional offices. The popular dual-homed configuration, while providing redundancy, also allows the potential for routers to reflect queries back to one another. Summarization and filters make this network design work well while also allowing queries to be managed effectively.

The Routing Table

The routing table is built from the topology table after DUAL has been run. The topology table is the foundation of EIGRP: This is where all the routes are stored, even after DUAL has been run. It is in the routing table that the best paths are stored and accessed by the routing process.

Now that the tables have been built, the router can make routing decisions (a process explained in the preceding chapter).

Having built the appropriate tables, the technology holds one more secret: how to maintain the tables as current and accurate.

If you understand the principles of EIGRP functionality, configuring it is straightforward. The following section deals with the commands required to configure EIGRP. Before effective configuration can be achieved, the entire network should be analyzed from a design perspective, particularly with regard to summarization. Refer to Chapter 3, "IP Addressing," for a review of summarization.

Configuring EIGRP

The commands for EIGRP are consistent with the other IP routing protocols. Although IP routing is on automatically, the chosen routing protocol must be configured and the participating interfaces must be identified.

EIGRP allows for VLSM and, therefore, summarization because the mask is sent in the update packets. Although summarization is automatic, EIGRP summarizes at the NIC or major network boundary. To summarize within the NIC number, it must be manually configured. Unlike OSPF that can only summarize at the Area Border Router (ABR), EIGRP can summarize at any router.

WARNING   EIGRP is a new protocol and has evolved over the past few years. It is essential that, in a practical situation, the commands and configuration be researched for the IOS code level that is installed in your network.

This section covers the following:

- Required configuration commands of EIGRP
- Optional configuration commands of EIGRP
- What each configuration command achieves
- An example of how the configuration command achieves its goal

The Required Commands for Configuring EIGRP

The router needs to understand how to participate in the EIGRP network. Therefore, it requires the following:

- **The EIGRP process**—The routing protocol needs to be started on the router.

- **The EIGRP autonomous system number**—All routers sharing routing updates and participating in the larger network must be identified as part of the same autonomous system. A router will not accept an update from a router configured with a different AS number.

- **Participating router interfaces**—The router may not want to have all its interfaces to send or receive EIGRP routing updates. A classic example is a dialup line to a remote office. If there were only one subnet at the remote office, it would be more efficient to use default and static route commands because any updates would dial the line.

By default (unless the **SETUP** script is used), there is no IP routing protocol running on the Cisco router. This is not true of other protocols, however. If an IPX network address is configured on an interface, for example, the IPX RIP process will be automatically started.

To configure EIGRP as the routing protocol, the following command syntax is used:

```
router eigrp autonomous system number
```

Although EIGRP has been turned on, it has no information on how to operate. The connected networks that are to be sent in the EIGRP updates and the interfaces that participate in the EIGRP updates must be defined. If the EIGRP information is not specified, the process with insufficient configuration will never start.

WARNING   Most versions of the IOS do not offer an error message, and this can make troubleshooting more difficult. Refer to the section titled "Verifying the EIGRP Operation," later in this chapter, for more information.

The following command syntax shows the use of the **network** command prior to IOS 12.0(4)T:

```
network network number
```

The **network** command plays a similar role to that of the **network** command in RIP or IGRP. Unlike OSPF, in which it is possible to identify the specific address of an interface, the **network** command for EIGRP is stated at the class level. EIGRP does not have the design specification of areas and, therefore, has no need for granularity.

WARNING   A common error is to configure the **network** command with an inappropriate wildcard mask when you're confused as to which class of address is being used.

From Cisco IOS 12.0(4)T, there have been some significant changes to the **network** command. It is now possible to identify which interfaces are running EIGRP by stating a wildcard mask. This is similar to the use of the **network** command in OSPF. However, OSPF has the added parameter, which defines the area for the interface.

The new syntax is as follows:

```
network network-number [wildcard network-mask]
no network network-number [wildcard network-mask]
```

The following syntax illustrates the use of the **network** command (the router has two Ethernet interfaces):

```
interface  e1
ip address 155.16.1.1 255.255.255.0
!
interface e2
ip address 155.16.2.2 255.255.255.0
```

The following command indicates that EIGRP will run on interface e1 only:

```
router eigrp 100
network 155.16.1.1 0.0.0.0
```

In earlier versions, as soon the first part of the command was configured, the operating system corrected the address to the NIC or major network number, 155.16.0.0, which would include both e1 and e2:

```
network 155.16.1.1
```

After the network has been defined to EIGRP, it will identify the interfaces directly connected to the routers that share that network address.

Having identified the interfaces on the router that are participating in the EIGRP domain, the following will happen:

- Updates will be received on the interface.

- Updates will be sent out the interfaces.

- The network will be advertised out all EIGRP interfaces.

- If appropriate, the Hello protocol will be propagated.

The Optional Commands for Configuring EIGRP

These commands are used to tune the way EIGRP works within your network. They should be used in reference to the design of the network and its technical requirements.

This section considers the following optional EIGRP commands:

- no auto-summary

- variance

- ip summary address

- bandwidth

- bandwidth-percent

Summarization with EIGRP

This subject has been dealt with in depth in several other locations within this book. References are given to those sections in the interests of brevity. These should be referred to for revision purposes because summarization in EIGRP solves the same problems of scaling as seen in other networks.

For more information, refer to the sections, "Design Considerations in Multiple-Area OSPF," in Chapter 6, "Using OSPF Across Multiple Areas," and, "Summarization," in Chapter 3.

The difference in the configuration between EIGRP and OSPF is that the OSPF is summarized only at the area boundary. Because EIGRP does not use the concept of areas, it may be configured on any router in the network. Consideration in where to summarize is determined by the hierarchical structure of the network. If summarization is not configured, EIGRP will automatically summarize at the class boundary.

There are two commands for summarization with EIGRP. The first command is **no auto-summary**. This command is IOS-specific, and research should be done on your IOS code level before configuring your live network.

The command applies to the entire router. This is very important because if there are slow serial interfaces or congested links, they will transmit all the subnets known on the router. This may significantly increase the overhead for the link. The solution is to configure the **summary** command on all interfaces, which in turn demands careful deployment of addresses.

Manual summarization is configured at the interface level, as shown here:

```
interface S0
ip summary address eigrp autonomous-system-number address mask
```

Load Balancing in EIGRP

EIGRP automatically load-balances across links of equal cost. Whether the traffic is sent on a per-destination or round-robin basis depends on the internal switching within the router. It is possible to configure EIGRP to load-balance across unequal paths using the **variance** command. This command allows the administrator to identify by the use of the multiplier parameter the metric scope for including additional paths.

The command structure is shown here:

```
variance multiplier
```

The multiplier is a number that ranges from 1 to 128. The default is 1, which allows for equal-cost load balancing. If the number is higher, it will multiply the best cost or metric value for a path by the number stated as the multiplier. All paths to the same destination that have metrics within this new range are now included in load balancing. The amount of traffic sent over each link is proportional to the metric for the path.

For example, the route to network A has four paths to it from router F and the best path gave a metric value of 10. The available routes shown in Figure 7-11 reflect these paths:

F to E to A = 30
F to D to B = 15
F to C to B = 15
F to C to G = 10

Figure 7-11 *The **variance** Command*

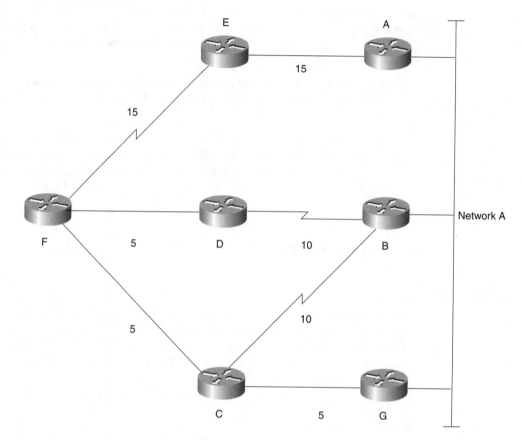

If the **variance** command was configured with a variance (multiplier) of 2; then the best metric is $10 \times 2 = 20$.

These paths would all load-balance traffic from Router F to Network A:

> F to D to B = 15
> F to C to B = 15
> F to C to G = 10

One and a half packets would be sent across the path F to C to G for every one packet sent across the other two available paths.

NOTE   The router cannot really send only one and a half packets and then switch the link, because the routers can't stop transmitting after they've started sending a packet. From a practical perspective, two packets are transmitted. This the same case for custom queuing.

NOTE	Only those paths that are in the topology table as FS are eligible to be included in the **variance** command. Also, appreciate that the example and figure shown are highly simplified for the purpose of explanation.

Bandwidth Control

A perennial concern of network administrators is the amount of bandwidth used for overhead traffic. Administrators want to minimize the amount of network control traffic sent through the network, to maximize the bandwidth available for user data. One of the major benefits of both EIGRP and OSPF is that they send as little network traffic as possible. This has the advantage of decreasing the convergence time of the network and ensuring that the network traffic that is sent arrives at the destination.

EIGRP Defaults in Bandwidth Utilization

EIGRP will not use more than 50 percent of the stated bandwidth on a link. The **bandwidth** command used on the interfaces of a Cisco router allows the default settings on links to be overridden. This is often necessary on serial links because the default bandwidth is 1.544 Mbps or a T1. If in reality the link is 56 kbps, it is easy to see how EIGRP could saturate the link. EIGRP will try to use 50 percent of a T1 link (772 kbps), far exceeding the real bandwidth of the line. This will mean not only the dropping of data packets due to congestion, but also the dropping of EIGRP packets. This will cause confusion in the network, not to mention miscalculated routes, retransmission, and user irritation as the network slows.

It is essential to configure all interfaces to reflect the true speed of the line.

NOTE	Other technologies on a Cisco router will use this value to make decisions. Therefore, ensure that the bandwidth stated is indeed the speed of the link. When you issue the **show interface** command, the configured bandwidth of the link will be shown along with a field identifying the load on the line. The load is the amount of traffic sent out of the interface, proportional to the bandwidth of the link, in which the bandwidth is the stated bandwidth and not the speed of the interface. If it is necessary to artificially lower the **bandwidth** command, this should be done in consideration of the other network applications. The bandwidth is a logical construct whose value can have wide-reaching implications on the functioning of your network. It does not affect the actual speed of the link.

EIGRP and the Use of the bandwidth Command in WANs

The developers of EIGRP have provided configurations to suit the three different WAN environments. The three WAN environments are as follows:

- Point-to-point

- NBMA, such as Frame Relay, X25, or ATM

- Multipoint

    — Point-to-point

    — NBMA hybrid (this is a combination of the point-to-point and multipoint designs)

When configuring the **bandwidth** command, it is important to consider the actual speed of the link. It is practical to configure this only on serial lines, where the speed of the link will vary considerably. However, do not confuse the speed of the interface or access line with the bandwidth or committed information rate (CIR) of the virtual circuit (VC).

Rules in Configuring Bandwidth over an NBMA Cloud

Cisco identifies three rules that should be followed when configuring EIGRP over an NBMA cloud:

- EIGRP traffic should not exceed the CIR capacity of the VC.

- EIGRP's aggregated traffic over all the VCs should not exceed the access line speed of the interface.

- The bandwidth allocated to EIGRP on each VC must be the same in both directions.

If these rules are understood and followed, EIGRP works well over the WAN. If care is not taken in the configuration of the WAN, EIGRP can swamp the network.

Configuring Bandwidth over a Multipoint Network

The configuration of the **bandwidth** command in an NBMA cloud depends on the design of the VCs. If the serial line has many VCs in a multipoint configuration, then EIGRP will evenly distribute its overhead between the VCs, without the use of subinterfaces. The **bandwidth** command should therefore reflect the access link speed into the Frame Relay cloud. If the serial interface is accessing an NBMA environment such as Frame Relay, the situation is straightforward. Your company may have five VCs from your router's serial interface. Each VC is 56 kbps. The access link will need a capacity of 5×56 kbps, or at least 2046 kbps. Remember, the aggregate configured bandwidth cannot exceed the access speed of the interface.

Configuring Bandwidth over a Hybrid Multipoint Network

If the multipoint network has differing speeds allocated to the VCs, a more complex solution is needed. There are two main approaches.

- To take the lowest CIR and to simply multiply this by the number of circuits. This is applied to the physical interface. The problem with this configuration is that the higher-bandwidth links will be underutilized for some things.

- If possible, it is much easier to configure and manage an environment that has used subinterfaces, where a VC is logically treated as if it were a separate interface or point-to point. The **bandwidth** command may be configured on each subinterface, which allows different speeds on each VC. In this second solution, subinterfaces are configured for the links with the differing CIRs. The links that have the same configured CIR are presented as a single subinterface with a bandwidth, which reflects the aggregate CIR of all the circuits.

  Cisco recommends this as the preferred solution.

The following syntax shows the structure of the **bandwidth** command:

```
interface S0
bandwidth speed of line
```

The Configuration of the Pure Point-to-Point Network

If there are many VCs, there may not be enough bandwidth at the access speed of the interface to support it. The subinterfaces should be configured with a bandwidth that is much lower than the real speed of the circuit. In this case, it is necessary to use the **bandwidth-percent** command to indicate to the EIGRP process that it can still function.

The Use of The bandwidth-percent Command

Another command specific to EIGRP is the **bandwidth-percent** command. It is easier and simpler to use the **bandwidth** command than the **bandwidth-percent** command.

The **bandwidth-percent** command interacts with the **bandwidth** command on the interface. The reason for using this command is primarily because in your network, the **bandwidth** command does not reflect the true speed of the link. The **bandwidth** command may have been altered to manipulate the routing metric and path selection of a routing protocol, such as IGRP or OSPF. It might be better to use other methods of controlling the routing metric and return the bandwidth to a true value. Otherwise, the **bandwidth-percent** command is available. It is possible to set a bandwidth percent that is larger than the stated bandwidth. This is in the understanding that although the bandwidth may be stated to be 56 kbps, the link is in fact 256 kbps. The following shows the structure of the **bandwidth-percent** command:

```
interface S0
ip bandwidth-percent eigrp autonomous-system-number percent
```

EIGRP can also be configured as a routing protocol for IPX and AppleTalk. The next section discusses this.

Configuring EIGRP for IPX

NOTE   This section is included to place EIGRP in context. *The exam will test only on topics pertaining to EIGRP using IP.* Therefore, this section should be read only for interest and should not be studied in depth in preparation for the Routing exam.

The configuration of IPX is very similar to IP. The difference is that IPX is a client/server-based protocol that was originally designed to operate in a LAN environment. Although Novell has improved its technology over the past few years to allow the networks to scale across the enterprise domain, IPX can still prove both a design and an implementation headache for the administrator. Typically, the amount of overhead generated in a client/server network is greater than that of a peer-to-peer network. This overhead becomes problematic when slower WAN links are used and bandwidth is at a premium. In this environment, EIGRP is a powerful tool.

EIGRP offers the following main features to an IPX enterprise network:

- Incremental updates for both RIP and SAP traffic
- Faster convergence of the network
- An increased diameter of the network, through the use of the metric and hop count
- A more complex and sophisticated routing metric
- Automatic redistribution of networks among IPX RIP, NLSP, and EIGRP

The operation of EIGRP for IPX is the same as that of IP, although the EIGRP metric uses both bandwidth and delay in calculating the best path.

EIGRP for IPX uses the same major components:

- Reliable transport mechanism for updates
- DUAL
- Neighbor discovery/recovery
- Protocol-dependent modules

It is important to remember that IPX is still designed as a proprietary LAN client/server protocol. EIGRP is also a proprietary protocol, and although there are some devices on the market that support EIGRP, it cannot be assumed that these include IPX systems. In the design of the network using EIGRP, IPX RIP/SAP or NLSP will be running. These protocols are found on the LAN in the traditional client/server domain.

In the design of IPX in an enterprise network, EIGRP is used between Cisco routers when bandwidth is a precious commodity. Therefore, EIGRP is configured in the WAN, where it is unlikely that there are any clients or servers requiring RIP/SAP updates.

When IPX is configured on a Cisco router, it is necessary to turn on IPX routing and to allocate network addresses to the appropriate interfaces. This allows the router to route IPX traffic through those interfaces and to send and receive RIP/SAP updates.

Configuring EIGRP for IPX requires some additional commands. An additional routing protocol must be identified along with the interfaces that it supports. These interfaces are then removed from the RIP/SAP update schedule.

Example 7-1 is a sample configuration of a network that has both RIP/SAP and EIGRP running.

Example 7-1 *Configuring EIGRP for IPX*

```
Router(config)# ipx routing
Router(config)# ipx router eigrp 100
Router(config-router)# network FADED
Router(config)# ipx router rip
Router(config-router)#no network FADED
Router(config)#interface E0
Router(config-if)#ipx network FAB
Router(config)#interface E1
Router(config-if)#ipx network CAB
Router(config)#interface E2
Router(config-if)#ipx network DAB
Router(config)#interface s0
Router(config-if)#ipx network FADED
```

NOTE

The autonomous system number used in the configuration of EIGRP for IPX must be the same on every router that wants to share routing updates. This is the same as the configuration for IP. The IPX autonomous system number is completely independent of the IP autonomous system number.

It is important to remember to remove the **network** command in IPX RIP routing configuration, as shown in the previous example. Otherwise, the system will continue sending IPX RIP updates in addition to IPX EIGRP updates, thus further affecting performance in the serial link.

Table 7-5 explains the meaning of the important fields in Example 7-2.

Table 7-5   *Explanation of the* **show ip eigrp neighbors** *Command Results*

Field	Explanation
process 100	The autonomous system number used to identify routers from whom to accept routing updates.
Address	IP address of the EIGRP neighbor.
Interface	Interface on which the router is receiving hello packets from the neighbor.
Holdtime	Length of time, in seconds, that the router will wait to hear from the neighbor before declaring it down. The default is 15 seconds.
Uptime	Time, measured in hours, minutes, and seconds, since the router first heard from this neighbor.
Q Count	Number of EIGRP packets (update, query, and reply) that the router has queued and is waiting to send.
Seq Num	The sequence number of the last packet that was received from the neighbor.
SRTT	Smooth Round Trip Time. The time is measured in milliseconds and is from the sending of the packet to the receipt of an acknowledgment from the neighbor.
RTO	Retransmission timeout, in milliseconds. This shows how long the router will wait before it retransmits the packet.

The show ip eigrp topology Command

This command shows the topology table. It allows for the analysis of DUAL. It will show whether the successor or the route is in an active or passive state. The syntax is as follows:

```
show ip eigrp topology [autonomous-system-number | [[ip-address] mask]]
```

Example 7-3 shows the output of this command.

Example 7-3   **show ip eigrp topology** *Output*

```
Router# show ip eigrp topology
IP-EIGRP Topology Table for process 100
Codes:P - Passive, A - Active, U - Update, Q - Query, R - Reply, r - Reply status
P 140.100.56.0 255.255.255.0, 2 successors, FD is 0
via 140.100.32.22 (46251776/46226176), Ethernet0
via 140.100.48.22 (46251776/46226176), Ethernet1
via 140.100.32.31 (46277376/46251776), Ethernet0
P 140.100.48.0 255.255.255.0, 1 successors, FD is 307200
via Connected, Ethernet1
via 140.100.48.22 (307200/281600), Ethernet1
140.100.32.22 (307200/281600), Ethernet0
via 140.100.32.31 (332800/307200), Ethernet0
```

Table 7-6 explains the meaning of the important fields in Example 7-3.

Table 7-6   *Explanation of the* **show ip eigrp topology** *Command Results*

Field	Explanation
P	Passive—The router has not received any EIGRP input from a neighbor, and the network is assumed to be stable.
A	Active—When a route or successor is down, the router attempts to find an alternative path. After local computation, the router realizes that it must query the neighbor to see whether it can find a feasible successor or path.
U	Update—A value in this field identifies that the router has sent an update packet to a neighbor.
Q	Query—A value in this field identifies that the router has sent a query packet to a neighbor.
R	Reply—A value here shows that the router has sent a reply to the neighbor.
r	This is used in conjunction with the query counter; the router has sent out a query and is awaiting a reply.
140.100.48.0	This is the destination IP network number.
255.255.255.0	This is the destination subnet mask.
Successors	These are the number of routes or the next logical hop. The number stated here is the same as the number of routes in the routing table.
FD	Feasible distance—This is the metric or cost to the destination from the router.
Replies	These are the number of replies that the router is still waiting for from this neighbor. This is relevant only when the route is in an active state.
State	This is the EIGRP state of the route. It can be the number 0, 1, 2, or 3. This is relevant when the destination is active.
Via	This is the address of the next logical hop, or the neighbor that told the router about this route. The first N of these entries are the current successors. The remaining entries on the list are feasible successors.
(46251776/46226176)	The first number is the EIGRP metric that represents the feasible distance, or the cost to the destination. The number after the slash is the EIGRP metric that the peer advertised, or the advertised distance.
Ethernet0	This is the interface through which the EIGRP packets were received and, therefore, the outgoing interface.

The show ip eigrp traffic Command

The command shows the EIGRP traffic received and generated by the router. The following is the command syntax:

```
show ip eigrp traffic [autonomous-system-number]
```

Example 7-4 shows the output of this command.

Example 7-4   **show ip eigrp traffic** *Output*

```
Router# show ip eigrp traffic
IP-EIGRP Traffic Statistics for process 100
Hellos sent/received: 218/205
Updates sent/received: 7/23
Queries sent/received: 2/0
Replies sent/received: 0/2
Acks sent/received: 21/14
```

Table 7-7 explains the meaning of the important fields in Example 7-4.

Table 7-7   *Explanation of the* **show ip eigrp traffic** *Command Output*

Field	Explanation
process 100	The autonomous system number, used to identify routers from whom to accept routing updates
Hellos sent/received	Number of hello packets sent and received by the router
Updates sent/received	Number of update packets sent and received by the router
Queries sent/received	Number of query packets sent and received by the router
Replies sent/received	Number of reply packets sent and received by the router
Acks sent/received	Number of acknowledgment packets sent and received by the router

NOTE   The **show ip route eigrp** command is also an extremely useful command. In fact, the **show ip route** command is one of the primary troubleshooting tools available to the network administrator, especially in conjunction with the **show ip protocols** command. This command shows the configuration of the routing protocols on the system and is an immediate way of spotting conflicts and misconfiguration. Both of these commands are dealt with extensively in Chapter 5, in the section, "Checking the Configuration of OSPF on a Single Router."

The ability to interpret these screens in conjunction with the physical and logical topology diagrams of your organization will ensure your understanding of the operation of EIGRP.

The debug Commands

An excellent although dangerous tool in troubleshooting and monitoring the network is the **debug** command. Care should be exercised in the use of this command because it can be very greedy in terms of the resources that it consumes. It should be used only for a specific option and a finite time.

The options available for monitoring EIGRP are covered in Table 7-8.

Table 7-8   **debug** *Command Options for EIGRP*

Command Option	Description
debug eigrp packet	Shows the packets sent and received by the router. The packet types to be monitored can be selected. Up to 11 types are available.
debug eigrp neighbors	Shows the hello packets sent and received by the router and the neighbors discovered by this process.
debug ip eigrp route	Is the default if the command **debug ip eigrp** is issued. Shows dynamic changes made to the routing table.
debug ip eigrp summary	Shows a summary of the EIGRP activity, including neighbors, distance, filtering, and redistribution.
show eigrp events	Shows the types of packets sent and received and statistics on routing decisions.

Conclusion

EIGRP is an IP routing protocol that attempts to solve many of the problems experienced by standards-based solutions. As a proprietary protocol, it has the freedom to create a very specific product that works well with the technology that the company produces. After a troubled childhood, EIGRP has proved itself an excellent solution for large corporations that need a routing protocol that will scale. With the use of redistribution, which will be dealt with in a future chapter, it can be integrated into a multivendor network. The functionality of using EIGRP as the routing protocol for desktop networks, such as AppleTalk or IPX, has diminished in importance as IP has risen in popularity as the protocol of choice.

Foundation Summary

The "Foundation Summary" is a collection of quick reference information that provides a convenient review of many key concepts in this chapter. For those of you who already feel comfortable with the topics in this chapter, this summary will help you recall a few details. For those of you who just read this chapter, this review should help solidify some key facts. For any of you doing your final preparations before the exam, these tables and figures will be a convenient way to review the day before the exam.

Table 7-9 summarizes the EIGRP packet types sent between neighbors.

Table 7-9   *Summary of Packet Types*

Packet Type	Address	Reliable	Unreliable	Purpose
Hello	Multicast		X	To find and maintain neighbors for the neighbor table. The packet has a 0 in the Acknowledgment field.
ACK	Unicast	X		A hello packet with no data. It has a positive number in the Acknowledgment field.
Update	Unicast and multicast (Reply to a single router is unicast, but a change in topology table is multicast.)	X		Route information sent to affected routers.
Query	Multicast	X		A part of the DUAL algorithm. Queries are sent out when a route in the topology table goes down and there is no FS.

NOTE   Any packet sent as a reliable multicast will be sent as a unicast if the neighbor does not acknowledge the packet. The packet will be retransmitted up to 16 times. This will speed up convergence and is an attempt to prevent the route being SIA. For this reason, some documentation will state that queries and hellos are sent both multicast and unicast. Because unicasts in this situation are used as a backup in case of failure, the answer in the exam would be multicast.

Table 7-10 summarizes the commands covered in this chapter.

Table 7-10   *Summary of Commands*

Command	Function
router eigrp *autonomous system number*	Starts the EIGRP processes on the router with the specified autonomous system number.
network *network number*	Shows the networks to be advertised.
no auto-summary	Given a hierarchical addressing design, disables the automatic summarization to the Internet NIC network address.
ip summary address eigrp *autonomous system number address mask*	Enables you to manually summarize the networks, having disabled automatic summarization.
bandwidth *speed of line*	Is issued at the interface level and is a logical construct to manually determine the real bandwidth. This command is used mainly on serial lines. Bandwidth will influence some routing decisions and dial-on-demand implementations.
ip bandwidth-percent eigrp *autonomous-system-number* [*percent*]	Enables you to change the bandwidth percentage. EIGRP by default will only take up to 50 percent of bandwidth.
variance *multiplier number*	Allows unequal paths to load-balance. Paths included in the equation will send a proportional amount of traffic across the unequal links.
ipx router eigrp *autonomous system number*	Configures EIGRP for IPX.
ipx sap-incremental eigrp *autonomous system number*	States to EIGRP that incremental updates should be used. By default, the process will send periodic updates out LAN interfaces and incremental updates through WAN interfaces. If an FDDI ring were used as a backbone, it would be advantageous to use incremental updates if all the devices on the ring were Cisco systems.
show ip eigrp neighbors	Displays information drawn from the neighbor table.
show ip eigrp topology	Displays information drawn from the topology table.
show ip eigrp traffic	Shows the EIGRP traffic passing through the router.

Chapter Glossary

This glossary provides an official Cisco definition for key words and terms introduced in this chapter. I have supplied my own definition for terms that the Cisco glossary does not contain. The words listed here are identified in the text by italics. A complete glossary, including all the chapter terms and additional terms, can be found in Appendix C, "Glossary."

ACK—A hello packet with no data that is an acknowledgment of packets sent reliably.

active—Route state in which when a network change is seen, but on interrogation of the topology table, there is no FC. The router queries its neighbors for alternative routes.

advertised distance (AD)—The cost of the path to the remote network from the neighbor (the metric from the next-hop router).

Diffusing Update Algorithm (DUAL)—An algorithm performed on the topology table to converge the network. It is based on a router detecting a network change within a finite time, with the change being sent reliably and in sequence. Because the algorithm is calculated simultaneously, in order and within a finite time frame on all effected routers, it ensures a loop-free network.

feasible condition (FC)—When a neighbor reports a path (AD) that is lower than the router's FD to a network, the neighbor's (next-hop router's) path has a lower metric than the router's path.

feasible distance (FD)—The lowest-cost distance (metric) to a remote network.

feasible successor (FS)—The neighbor reporting the AD that is lower than the router's FD becomes the feasible successor. This is the next-hop router that meets the FC.

hello—Used to find and maintain neighbors in the topology table. They are sent periodically and are sent reliably.

holdtime—Sent in the hello packet. It determines how long the router waits for hellos from a neighbor before declaring it unavailable. This information is held in the neighbor table.

neighbor—A router running EIGRP that is directly connected.

neighbor table—A list of every neighbor, including the IP address, the outgoing interface, the holdtime, the SRTT, and the uptime, or how long since the neighbor was added to the table. The table is built from information on hellos received from adjacent routers (neighbors).

passive—An operational route is passive. If the path is lost, the router examines the topology table to find an FS. If there is an FS, it is placed in the routing table, and the router does not query the others, which would send it into active mode.

query—Message sent from the router when it loses a path to a network. If there is no alternate route (feasible successor), the router will send out queries to neighbors inquiring whether they have a feasible successor. This makes the route state change to active. The queries are sent reliably.

query scoping—Another term for SIA.

Reliable Transport Protocol (RTP)—Requires that the packets be delivered in sequence and be guaranteed.

reply—A response to the query. If a router has no information to send in a reply, it will send queries to all its neighbors. A unicast is sent reliably.

Retransmission Timeout (RTO)—Timer that is calculated in reference to the SRTT. RTO determines how long the router waits for an ACK before retransmitting the packet.

route table—The routing table, or list of available networks and the best paths. A path is moved from the topology table to the routing table when a feasible successor is identified.

Smooth Round Trip Time (SRTT)—The time that the router waits after sending a packet reliably to hear an acknowledgment. This is held in the neighbor table and is used to calculate the RTO.

Stuck in Active (SIA)—State in which a router has sent out network packets and is waiting for ACKs from all its neighbors. The route is active until all the ACKs have been received. If they do not appear after a certain time, the router is Stuck in Active for the route.

successor—The next-hop router that passes the FC. It is chosen from the FSs as having the lowest metric to the remote network.

topology table—Table that contains all the paths advertised by neighbors to all the known networks. This is a list of all the successors, feasible successors, the feasible distance, the advertised distance, and the outgoing interface. DUAL acts on the topology table to determine successors and feasible successors by which to build a routing table.

update—An EIGRP packet containing change information about the network. It is sent reliably. It is sent only when there is a change in the network to affected routers:

- When a neighbor first comes up
- When a neighbor transitions from active to passive for a destination
- When there is a metric change for a destination

Q&A

The following questions test your understanding of the topics covered in this chapter. The final questions in this section repeat of the opening "Do I Know This Already?" questions. These are repeated to enable you to test your progress. After you have answered the questions, find the answers in Appendix A. If you get an answer wrong, review the answer and ensure that you understand the reason for your mistake. If you are confused by the answer, refer to the appropriate text in the chapter to review the concepts.

1 If a router does not have a feasible successor, what action will it take?

_____

_____

_____

2 When does EIGRP need to be manually redistributed into another EIGRP process?

_____

_____

_____

3 Which timers are tracked in the neighbor table?

_____

_____

_____

4 What is the difference between an update and a query?

_____

_____

_____

5 When does EIGRP recalculate the topology table?

_____

_____

_____

6 EIGRP has a default limit set on the amount of bandwidth that it can use for EIGRP packets. What is the default percentage limit?

_____

_____

_____

7 State two rules for designing a scalable EIGRP network.

_____

_____

_____

8 What is the preferred configuration for a hybrid multipoint NBMA network when one VC has a CIR of 56 kbps and the other five VCs each have a CIR of 256 kbps?

_____

_____

_____

9 With four Frame Relay circuits in a multipoint solution and a bandwidth configuration of 224, what is the allocation per circuit, and where would the **bandwidth** command be configured?

_____

_____

_____

10 Explain the purpose of the command **no auto-summary**.

_____

_____

_____

11 Explain the meaning of the command **ip bandwidth-percent eigrp 63 100.**

_____

_____

_____

12 EIGRP may be used to send information about which three routing protocols?

_____

_____

_____

13 Which EIGRP packets are sent reliably?

_____

_____

_____

14 In what instances will EIGRP automatically redistribute?

_____

_____

_____

15 How long is the holdtime, by default?

_____

_____

_____

16 What is an EIGRP topology table, and what does it contain?

_____

_____

_____

17 What is the advertised distance in EIGRP, and how is it distinguished from the feasible distance?

_____

_____

_____

18 What EIGRP algorithm is run to create entries for the routing table?

_____

_____

_____

19 When does EIGRP place a network in active mode?

_____

_____

_____

20 By default, EIGRP summarizes at which boundary?

_____

_____

_____

21 What is Stuck in Active?

_____

_____

_____

22 What is the **variance** command used for?

_____

_____

_____

23 State two factors that influence EIGRP scalability.

_____

_____

_____

24 What command is used to display which routes are in passive or active mode?

_____

_____

_____

25 What command is used in EIGRP to perform manual summarization?

_____

_____

_____

26 For Frame Relay, when would you configure the physical interface (as opposed to a subinterface) with the **bandwidth** command?

_____

_____

_____

27 Which command is used to display all types of EIGRP packets that are both received and sent by a router?

_____

_____

_____

Scenarios

The following scenarios and questions are designed to draw together the content of the chapter and to exercise your understanding of the concepts. There is not necessarily a right answer. The thought process and practice in manipulating the concepts are the goals of this section. The answers to the scenario questions are found at the end of this chapter. The information used in these scenarios was adapted from the Cisco web page, "Cisco Configuration Guidelines."

Scenario 7-1

The multinational company Gargantuan, Inc., from the introduction of this chapter, has had a consultant completely readdress the company. The company has used the private network 10.0.0.0 and has created a very hierarchical addressing structure. Refer to Figure 7-12 to see this addressing scheme.

Figure 7-12   *Diagram for Scenario 7-1*

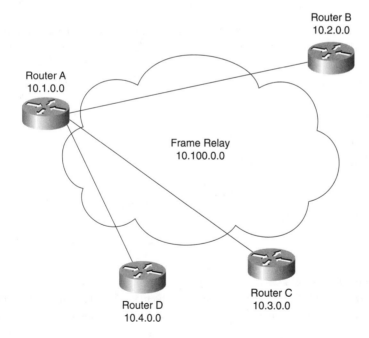

The addressing of the network was a major project, with all the necessary pitfalls that attend such a major exercise. The network is now stable, and it is time to solve the problems that are being experienced in timeouts and network crashes.

The consultant assured the company that the resolution to the delays was the addressing scheme, but although the network is easier to manage, there has been no change in the congestion on the network. In addition, EIGRP appears to be losing routes from its routing tables, which is adding to the problem.

The consultant was correct: The network needed to be readdressed to allow EIGRP to function effectively. Unfortunately, the company did not read the report carefully and missed the other part of the solution.

1   What needs to be done in addition to solve the problems caused by EIGRP? Give the configuration commands necessary to activate this solution on Router A.

   The WAN is a Frame Relay cloud, and Router A is the hub in the hub-and-spoke configuration. Each VC is 56 kbps.

2   Give the commands to configure Router A for EIGRP over this NBMA cloud.

3   Give the commands to configure Router B for EIGRP over this NBMA cloud.

Scenario 7-2

Given the configuration of EIGRP in Example 7-5, perform the tasks and answer the questions listed. The WAN has light user traffic and is a hub-and-spoke configuration, as shown in Figure 7-13.

Example 7-5   *Scenario 7-2 Configuration*

```
interface Serial 0
    encapsulation frame-relay

    interface Serial 0.1 point-to-point
    bandwidth 25
    ip bandwidth-percent eigrp 123 90

    interface Serial 0.2 point-to-point
    bandwidth 25
    ip bandwidth-percent eigrp 123 90

        . . .
```

The 256 kbps access line to the hub has 56 kbps access lines to each of 10 spoke sites. Each link has a Frame Relay CIR of 56 kbps. The access line to each router reflects the CIR. The access line to the hub router, Router A, is 256 kbps, but the CIR of the hub is the same as its access line.

From a Frame Relay perspective, it is said that a circuit is oversubscribed when the sum of CIRs of the remote circuits is higher than the CIR of the hub location. With 10 links, each with a CIR of 56 kbps, this circuit is clearly oversubscribed.

Figure 7-13   *Diagram for Scenario 7-2*

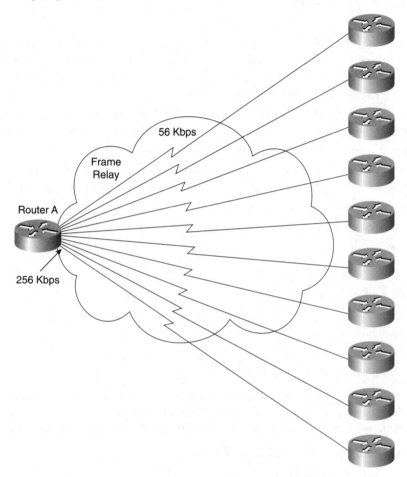

1   How much bandwidth has each circuit been allocated? Why was this value chosen by the administrator?

2   What bandwidth utilization is available to EIGRP? Why was this value chosen by the administrator?

3   If Router A died, what would the effect be on the network?

4   Is summarization possible only on the routers entering the WAN cloud, or is it possible on the networks not shown in the figure, but on the other side of the routers? Give reasons for your answers.

Scenario Answers

The answers are in **bold**. The answers provided in this section are not necessarily the only possible answers to the questions. The questions are designed to test your knowledge and to give practical exercise in certain key areas. This section is intended to test and exercise skills and concepts detailed in the body of this chapter.

If your answer is different, ask yourself whether it follows the tenets explained in the answers provided. Your answer is correct not if it matches the solution provided in the book, but rather if it has included the principles of design laid out in the chapter.

In this way, the testing provided in these scenarios is deeper: It examines not only your knowledge, but also your understanding and ability to apply that knowledge to problems.

If you do not get the correct answer, refer back to the text and review the subject tested. Be certain to also review your notes on the question to ensure that you understand the principles of the subject.

Scenario 7-1 Answers

1   What needs to be done in addition to solve the problems caused by EIGRP? Give the configuration commands necessary to activate this solution on Router A.

The WAN is a Frame Relay cloud, and Router A is the hub in the hub-and-spoke configuration. Each VC is 56 kbps.

The other solution that the consultant suggested was to perform summarization to limit the query range of the routers. This would prevent the routes in the topology table being SIA, which seriously affects the performance of the network.

The commands required are as follows:

```
router(config)# router eigrp 63
router(config)# no auto-summary
router(config)# network 10.0.0.0
router(config)# int s0
router(config-if)# ip summary-address 10.1.0.0 255.255.0.0
```

2   Give the commands to configure Router A for EIGRP over this NBMA cloud.

The configuration on Router A is as follows:

```
router(config)# serial 0
router(config-if)# frame relay encapsulation
router(config-if)# bandwidth 178
```

3 Give the commands to configure Router B for EIGRP over this NBMA cloud.

The configuration on Router B is as follows:

```
router(config)# serial 0
router(config-if)# frame relay encapsulation
router(config-if)# bandwidth 56
```

Scenario 7-2 Answers

1 How much bandwidth has each circuit been allocated? Why was this value chosen by the administrator?

Because a maximum of 256 kbps is available, you cannot allow any individual PVC to handle more than 25 kbps (256/10). Note that EIGRP will not use more than 22.5 kbps (90 percent of 25 kbps) on this interface, even though its capacity is 56 kbps. This configuration will not affect user data capacity, which will still be able to use the entire 56 kbps.

2 What bandwidth utilization is available to EIGRP? Why was this value chosen by the administrator?

Because this data rate is low, and because you don't expect very much user data traffic, you can allow EIGRP to use up to 90 percent of the bandwidth.

3 If Router A died, what would the effect be on the network?

If Router A died, there would be no communication between the routers in the WAN because Router A is the hub. Each site would function, but they all would be isolated from each other. The neighbor tables would fail to hear the hellos from the other routers connecting to the WAN and would time out all routes that they had heard from these routers. The topology table would be updated, and the routers would send updates to all their other neighbors.

4 Is summarization possible only on the routers entering the WAN cloud, or is it possible on the networks not shown in the figure, but on the other side of the routers? Give reasons for your answers.

Summarization is possible on all interfaces in EIGRP, as long as the addressing scheme allows for it to be implemented. This is one of the major advantages of EIGRP over OSPF. OSPF can summarize only at Area Boundary Routers (ABRs).

This chapter covers the following topics that you will need to master to pass the CCNP/CCDP Routing exam:

- The features and operation of BGP-4

- When not to use BGP-4 and the alternatives available

- How BGP-4 achieves policy-based routing within the autonomous system

- The BGP-4 peering functions

- The BGP-4 communities and peer groups

- How to configure internal BGP-4 and external BGP-4

- BGP-4 synchronization

- How to verify and troubleshoot the BGP-4 network

- Cisco commands for implementing BGP-4 and Cisco commands for reviewing the configuration.

CHAPTER 8

Connecting to Other Autonomous Systems—The Basics of BGP-4

This chapter details Border Gateway Protocol 4 (BGP-4). Although BGP-4 is covered briefly in the ACRC exam, it is given far greater attention in the CCNP/CCDP Routing exam. Even so, the exam barely scratches the surface of the detail available to the protocol. This chapter deals with the basic concepts and configuration commands of BGP-4 and leads into greater complexity in the next chapter. This chapter builds on the understanding of routing within large enterprise networks that was dealt with previously.

This chapter is broken into two major areas. The first area of the chapter deals theoretically with how BGP-4 works. Implementing and managing a BGP-4 network is described at the end of the chapter.

The topics in this chapter directly reflect questions on the exam. BGP-4 is a routing protocol designed for use in large networks. It is a mandatory topic in the exam. The BSCN course devotes 13 percent of its material to configuring basic Border Gateway Protocol, and you can expect approximately 10 questions on the exam to be directly related to this subject.

How to Best Use This Chapter

By taking the following steps, you can make better use of your study time:

- Keep your notes and the answers for all your work with this book in one place, for easy reference.

- When you take a quiz, write down your answers. Studies show that retention significantly increases by writing down facts and concepts, even if you never look at the information again.

- Use the diagram in Figure 8-1 to guide you to the next step.

Figure 8-1   *How to Use This Chapter*

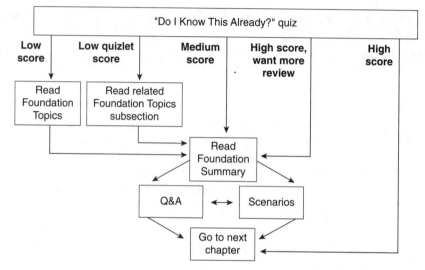

If you skip to the Foundation Summary, Q&A, and scenarios sections and have trouble with the material there, you should go back to the Foundation Topics section.

"Do I Know This Already?" Quiz

The purpose of the "Do I Know This Already?" quiz is to help you decide what parts of this chapter to use. If you already intend to read the entire chapter, you do not necessarily need to answer these questions now.

This 16-question quiz helps you determine how to spend your limited study time. The quiz is sectioned into four smaller four-question "quizlets," which correspond to four major topics in the chapter. Figure 8-1 outlines suggestions on how to spend your time in this chapter. Use Table 8-1 to record your scores.

Table 8-1   *Score Sheet for Quiz and Quizlets*

Quizlet Number	Topic	Questions	Score
1	Features and operation of BGP-4 (including alternatives)	1 to 4	
2	Policy-based routing within the autonomous system routing domain	5 to 8	
3	Communities and peer groups in BGP-4	9 to 12	
4	How to configure and verify BGP-4	13 to 16	
All questions	All	1 to 16	

1 What type of routing protocol is BGP-4 classified as, and what does this mean?

_____

_____

_____

2 What is a static route?

_____

_____

_____

3 What is the transport protocol for BGP-4?

_____

_____

_____

4 What is a default route?

_____

_____

_____

5 State two attributes of BGP-4.

_____

_____

_____

6 State four message types of BGP-4.

_____

_____

_____

7 What is policy-based routing?

_____

_____

_____

8 What do the letters MED represent? Give a brief explanation of what this does.

_____

_____

_____

9 What is a community in BGP-4?

_____

_____

_____

10 Give two reasons why peer groups are useful.

_____

_____

_____

11 Explain the term "third-party next hop."

_____

_____

_____

12 What is the difference between a peer and a neighbor?

_____

_____

_____

13 Explain briefly the synchronization rule.

_____

_____

_____

14 In BGP-4, describe the purpose of the **network** command.

_____

_____

_____

15 Explain the command **neighbor** {*ip-address* | *peer-group-name*} **next-hop-self**.

_____

_____

_____

16 Which command is used to show all BGP-4 connections?

_____

_____

_____

_____

_____

_____

The answers to this quiz are found in Appendix A, "Answers to Quiz Questions." The suggested choices for your next step are as follows:

- **2 or less on any quizlet**—Review the appropriate sections of the "Foundation Topics" portion of this chapter, based on Table 8-1. Then move on to the "Foundation Summary" section, the "Q&A" section, and the "Scenarios" at the end of the chapter.

- **8 or less overall score**—Read the entire chapter. This includes the "Foundation Topics" and "Foundation Summary" sections, the "Q&A" section, and the "Scenarios" at the end of the chapter.

- **9 to 12 overall score**—Begin with the "Foundation Summary" section, and then go to the "Q&A" section and the "Scenarios" at the end of the chapter. If you have trouble with these exercises, read the appropriate sections in "Foundation Topics."

- **13 or more overall score**—If you want more review on these topics, skip to the "Foundation Summary" section, and then go to the "Q&A" section and the "Scenarios" at the end of the chapter. Otherwise, move to the next chapter.

Foundation Topics

Introduction: BGP-4 and Communicating with other Autonomous Systems

The BSCN course deals with connectivity to the Internet via a service provider. One of the methods used to make this connection is the external routing protocol BGP-4.

The Routing 2.0 exam, recognizing that BGP-4 is increasingly important in larger environments to communicate with the Internet agent or service provider, covers a conceptual overview of BGP-4. A solid base to BGP-4 is given in addition to basic configuration commands. It is stressed however, that if your network is a simple one, using static and default routes may be configurations that are more appropriate.

Case Study

The large multinational company Humugos has offices in 250 countries. Each country operates as a separate company, conforming to the tax and legal laws of the country. It is still important that the parts of organization be capable of connecting to one another, but EIGRP is no longer feasible for a number of reasons. The main issue is the number of connections that each country has into the Internet. There is also some need to manipulate the traffic, particularly in terms of resource sharing between business units internationally.

Figure 8-2 illustrates the network topology of the case study, Humugos.

NOTE   Figure 8-2 has been simplified and does not contain the 250 autonomous systems as the case study suggests.

BGP-4 has been suggested as a solution for various reasons. First is the need for yet another level of hierarchy. Second, the multiple connections to the Internet need to be managed with a sophisticated routing protocol. The capability to determine the traffic path that will be taken by a variety of parameters is also very important. This adds another dimension to the simple metric, which proves inadequate to the task of determining subtle distinctions in path selection.

Figure 8-2   *Diagram of Case Study—Humugos*

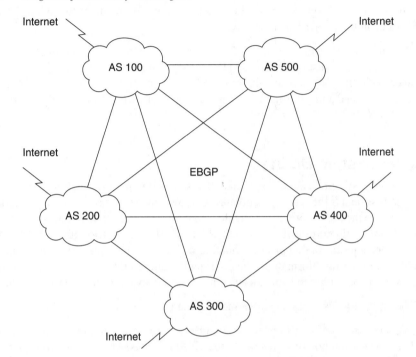

This chapter introduces the concepts behind BGP-4 that make it the ideal solution for Humugos to use both between countries and in its connections into the Internet.

BGP-4 Operation

BGP-4 is an extremely complex protocol used within the Internet and multinational organizations. Its main purpose is to connect very large networks that are mainly autonomous systems. Large companies may use BGP-4 as the glue between the countries; for example, a government may use it as the glue between the divisions of the administration, and the military might use it between the Army, the Navy, and the Air Force. Lists of RFCs that define it, along with other references, are given at the end of this chapter.

The routing update is the characteristic that makes it appropriate in these environments. The protocol is not interested in communicating a full knowledge of every subnet within the organization. It takes summarization to the extreme, communicating only that which is defined, as necessary. The routing update carries a list of autonomous system numbers and aggregated prefix addresses, as well as some policy routing information. The little information that it carries is extremely important, so great efforts are made to ensure the reliability of the transport carrying the updates and to ensure that the databases are synchronized. This is the pinnacle of hierarchical routing design. Because of this fact, the transport medium for BGP is TCP, which provides an additional layer of reliability.

The other distinctive characteristic of BGP-4 is the concept of *policy routing*. Unlike interior routing protocols that just communicate all that they know about the networks within the routing domain, BGP-4 can be configured to advocate one path above another. This is done in a more sophisticated and controlled manner than can the metric afforded to the interior routing protocols.

An Autonomous System Defined

An autonomous system is a routing domain that shares routing information. Typically, an autonomous system is the same as an organization. Within the context of internal security, every network within the organization is available, and information about the networks is transmitted via an interior routing protocol such as EIGRP, OSPF, RIP, or IGRP. Although there may be more than one interior routing protocol running within the autonomous system, the probability is that they are sharing information. This sharing is achieved through redistribution, and it allows every router within the domain awareness of every available network within the domain.

The Cisco glossary describes an autonomous system as follows:

A collection of networks under a common administration sharing a common routing strategy. An autonomous system is subdivided by areas. An autonomous system must be assigned a unique 16-bit number by IANA.

The reason for defining an autonomous system is to be able to determine the demarcation between organizations and the Internet. The capability of the Internet to identify an entire organization by the means of the unique 16-bit integer allows for great constriction of the amount of information that needs to be held in routing tables or transmitted in routing updates. This level of hierarchy is crucial to the successful operation and maintenance of the Internet.

BGP-4 is the routing protocol that is used between autonomous systems to carry this pared down information into and across the Internet. If the autonomous system is connecting directly into the Internet, then it is necessary to acquire a unique autonomous system number from the IANA. However, many organizations connect to the Internet via a service provider, who will have an autonomous system for connecting into the Internet, which includes all organizations connecting through them.

Many organizations are using BGP-4 without connecting directly to the Internet and are using private autonomous system numbers. This is done for reasons of scale and requires the same precautions as using private IP addresses.

Characteristics of BGP-4

The main characteristics of BGP-4 may be distilled into a few short points. The interaction of these components and their relative importance to the operation or design of a BGP-4 network is discussed in the rest of the chapter.

The key features of BGP-4 include these:

- It is a path vector protocol.

- Full routing updates are sent at the start of the session, trigger updates are sent subsequently.

- It creates and maintains connections between peers, using TCP port 179.

- The connection is maintained by periodic keepalives.

- The failure to see a keepalive, an update, or a notification is the means by which destination networks and paths to those destinations are tracked. Any change in the network results in a triggered update.

- The metric used in BGP-4 is intricate and is the source of its complexity and its strength. The metric, referred to as attributes, allows great granularity in path selection.

- The use of hierarchical addressing and the capability to manipulate traffic flow results in a network that is designed to grow.

- It has its own routing table, although it is capable of both sharing and inquiring of the interior IP routing table.

- It is possible to manipulate the traffic flow by using the complex metric called attributes, but policy-based routing is based on the hop-by-hop paradigm. This means that no router can send traffic on a route that the next-hop router would not choose for itself.

How BGP-4 works and an explanation of some of these characteristics are given in the following section.

Overview of the BGP-4 Operation

BGP-4 is connection-oriented. When a neighbor is seen, a TCP peering session is established and maintained. BGP-4 probes are sent out periodically to sustain the link and maintain the session. These probes, otherwise known as keepalives, are simply the 19 byte header used in the BGP updates.

Having established the session, the routing tables are exchanged and synchronized. The routers now send incremental updates only when changes occur. The update refers to a single path and the networks that may be reached via that path. Having corrected the routing table, the BGP-4 process propagates the change to all neighbors, with a few exceptions, based on an algorithm to ensure a loop-free network.

The establishment of a BGP-4 peer is shown in Figure 8-3.

The operation of BGP-4 is very straightforward. Indeed, all the complexity of the protocol is delivered in only a few different types of routing packets.

Message Types

Four different message types are used in BGP-4:

- **Open messages**—Used to establish connections with peers.

- **Keepalives**—Sent periodically between peers to maintain connections and verify paths held by the router sending the keepalive. These packets are sent unreliably. If the periodic timer is set to a value of 0, this equates to infinity, and no keepalives are sent.

- **Update messages**—Contain paths to destination networks and the path attributes. Routes that are no longer available or withdrawn routes are included in updates. There is one path per update, requiring many updates for many paths. The information contained in the update includes the path attributes such as origin, Autonomous System path, neighbor, and inter-Autonomous System metric.

- **Notification**—Used to inform the receiving router of errors.

BGP-4 comes in two flavors: internal and external BGP-4. The difference depends on the function of the routing protocol. The router will determine if the peer BGP-4 router is going to be an external BGP-4 peer or an internal BGP-4 peer by checking the autonomous system number in the open message that was sent.

Internal BGP-4 is used within an autonomous system. It conveys information to all BGP-4 routers within the domain and ensures that they have a consistent understanding of the networks available. Internal BGP-4 is used within an ISP or a large organization to coordinate the knowledge of that autonomous system. The routers are not required to be physical neighbors on the same medium, and they often sit on the edges of the network. Internal BGP-4 is used to convey BGP-4 information about other autonomous systems across a *transit autonomous system*. Another routing protocol, an interior routing protocol such as OSPF, is used to route the BGP-4 packets to their remote locations. To achieve this, internal BGP requires the destination BGP neighbor's IP address to be contained within the normal routing table kept by another routing protocol (static routing, OSPF, EIGRP, and so on). The integration of these different routing protocols can be challenging.

External BGP-4 complies with the common perception of an external routing protocol; it sends routing information between differing autonomous systems. Therefore, the border router between different autonomous systems is the external BGP router. Figure 8-4 shows the application of internal and external BGP-4.

Figure 8-3   *Establishing a BGP-4 Peer*

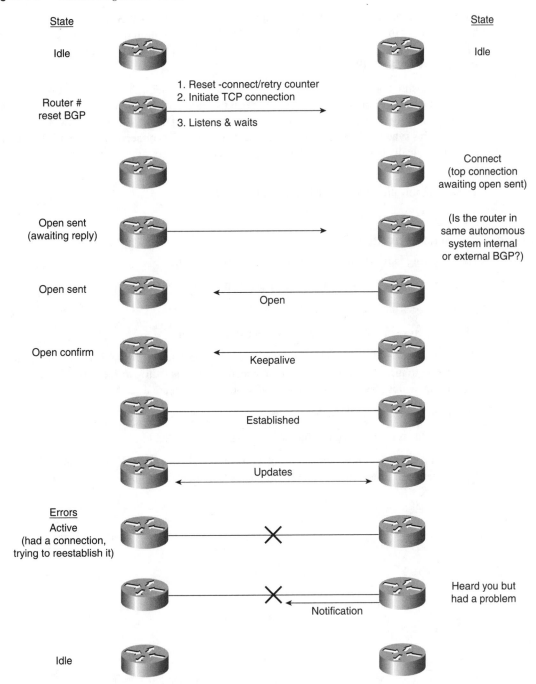

Synchronization

A simple rule states that before IBGP-4 can propagate a route into another autonomous system handing it over to EBGP-4, the route must be totally known within the autonomous system. That is to say that the Internal Gateway Protocol (IGP) or internal routing protocol must be synchronized with BGP-4.

This is to ensure that if traffic is sent into the autonomous system, the interior routing protocol can direct it to its destination. It makes sense that this rule is on by default and should be turned off only if all routers in the autonomous system are running BGP-4. Likewise, although it is not referred to as synchronization, this case also applies for IBGP connections. If the IBGP routers are not physically connected, the IGP needs to be capable of routing the updates to the BGP-4 peer.

The synchronization rule is illustrated in Figure 8-5.

Benefits of the Synchronization Rule

The following list gives reasons for the synchronization rule:

- It prevents traffic from being forwarded to unreachable destinations.
- It reduces unnecessary traffic.
- It ensures consistency within the autonomous system.

On some occasions it is useful to turn off synchronization. This is rare, and, as with any default, it is unwise to turn off this option without a detailed understanding of the network. The occasions when it may be useful to turn off synchronization are as follows:

- If all the routers in the autonomous system are running BGP-4.
- If all the routers inside the autonomous system are meshed.
- When the autonomous system is not a transit domain. A transit domain is an autonomous system that is used to carry BGP-4 updates from one autonomous system to another.

Figure 8-4   *Internal and External BGP-4*

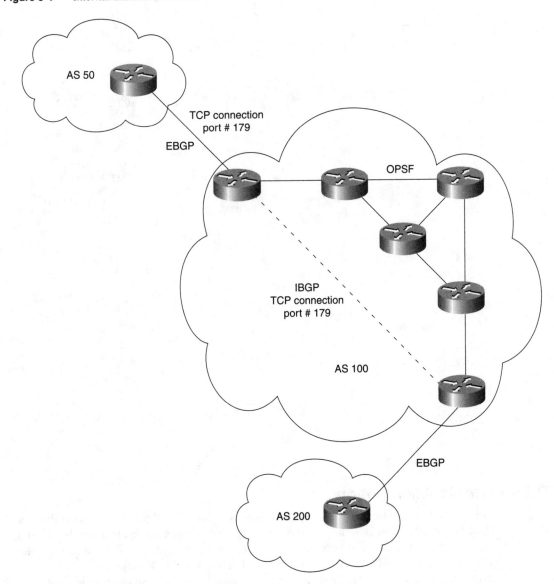

Figure 8-5 *Synchronization Rule and BGP-4*

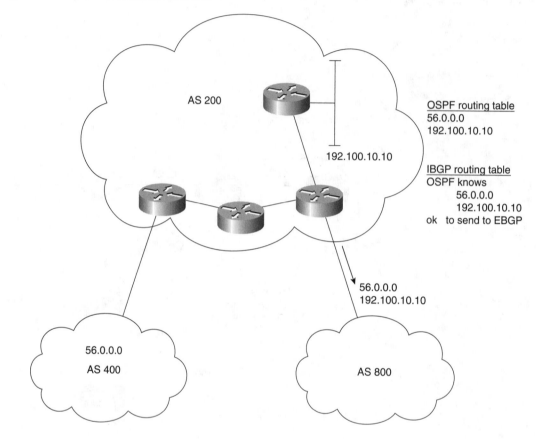

CIDR and Route Aggregation

As explained in Chapter 3, "IP Addressing," there is a shortage of IP addresses in the Internet. There is also a problem with the size of the routing tables, in terms of the memory, bandwidth, and CPU that they consume when updating the routing tables. Classless interdomain routing (CIDR) is one of the main solutions implemented in recent years. This is a method of consolidating addresses into a few summary addresses. Instead of a subnet having a subnet mask to identify the network portion of the address, it has a prefix mask, which is simply a number that indicates the number of bits that have been allocated to the network.

BGP-4 will propagate the prefix and the prefix mask together, allowing not only for the design of a truly hierarchical network, but also for the streamlining of the network resources. A router can pass on the aggregated routes, although it is capable of aggregating routes itself. Therefore, a router can send either aggregated routes, routes that have not been summarized, or a mixture of both.

The process of how BGP-4 aggregates routes in compliance to CIDR is shown in the Figure 8-6.

Several attributes are connected to the use of address aggregation in BGP-4. Table 8-2 covers some of these attributes.

Table 8-2   *Route Aggregation Attributes*

Attribute	Type of Attribute	Description of Attribute
Atomic aggregate	Well known, discretionary	This is the default attribute. The originator of the aggregate route is stated. It is useful because it shows that some information has been lost due to the aggregation of routes. It states to the receiving router in another autonomous system that the originator of the route aggregated the routes.
Aggregator	Optional, transitive	This attribute gives the router ID and the autonomous system of the router that performed the aggregation.
AS_Path	Well known, mandatory	This attribute can include a list of all the autonomous systems that the aggregated routes have passed through.

BGP-4 Policy-Based Routing

Policy-based routing gives the administrator the ability to define how traffic will be routed at the autonomous system level. This is a level of control above the dynamic routing protocol. Given that many variables in BGP-4 can influence dynamic routing (these are called variables), this is a very high level of control. This other dimension distinguishes BGP-4 from other routing protocols.

Policy-based routing is a form of static routing enforced by specialized access lists called route maps.

Rules of Policy Routing

Some rules are associated with Policy routing. The following rules seem repetitive, but, in fact, each point raises a subtly different nuance:

Figure 8-6 *BGP-4 and CIDR*

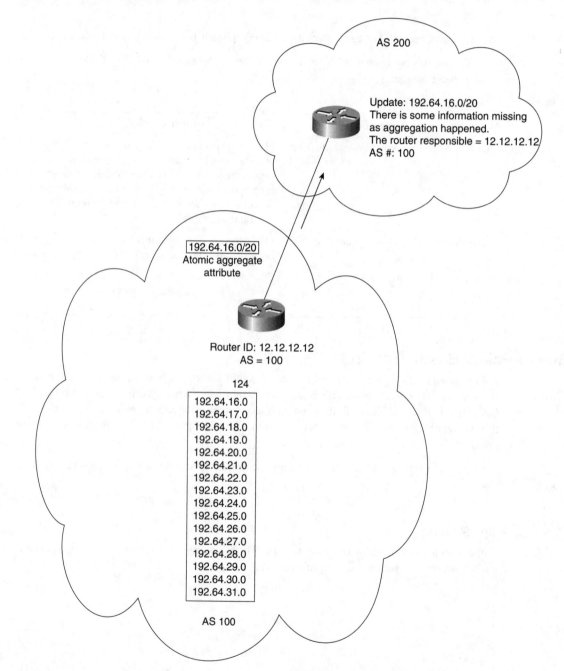

- Traffic can be directed on either the source address or both the source and destination addresses.

- Policy routing affects only the next hop in the path to the destination.

- Policy routing does not affect the destination of the packet. It affects the path used to get to the destination.

- Policy routing does not allow traffic sent into another autonomous system to take a different path from the one that would have been chosen by that autonomous system.

- It is possible to influence only how traffic will get to a neighboring autonomous system, not how it will be routed within that autonomous system.

- BGP-4 can implement any rule associated to the hop-by-hop paradigm. That is the capability to influence which router will be the next-hop router, potentially dictating this at every router and thus influencing the entire path of the traffic, hop by hop.

- As policy routing examines the source address, it is configured on the inbound interface.

Disadvantages of Policy Routing

Some things should be considered before arbitrarily deciding to implement policy routing:

- A backup path should be in place in case the defined next-hop router goes down. If there is no alternative defined, policy routing will default to dynamic routing decisions.

- Additional CPU is required to examine every source address to effect the defined policy.

- Extra configuration is required.

- The possibility exists that other traffic will be disrupted.

BGP-4's capability to choose the routing path via conditional programming was used for policy routing in other situations before it became an option in the Cisco IOS. BGP-4 was deployed in some situations to use the policy routing options; for example, it was used by the two early deployments of tag routing as the only means of programming policy routing. This is a powerful tool and can be used in many situations, such as forcing traffic entering your routing domain to pass through the firewall or in a situation in which there are multiple connections to the Internet, load balancing among those connections. Refer to Figure 8-7 for an example of how policy routing could be implemented.

In Router A in Figure 8-7, the traffic from 192.17.50.6 network is from the graphic design department. It is high-volume, sensitive traffic; therefore, you should send it on a path dedicated to such traffic—always direct it to Router C.

Figure 8-7 *Example of Policy Routing Using BGP-4*

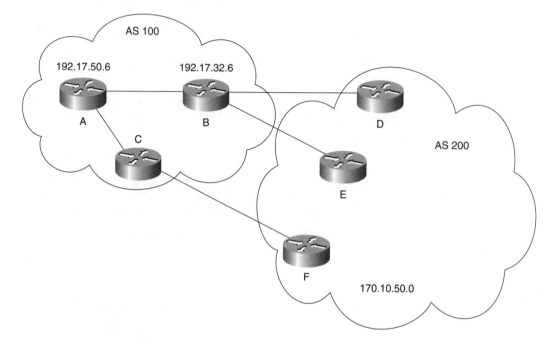

BGP-4 Attributes

Attributes in BGP-4 are used to determine the best path to be selected. In essence, they are the metric for BGP-4. However, they are more than a list of variables by which a route is selected. They also carry information that decisions are based on—hence the name attributes. The variables describe characteristics or attributes of the path to the destination. These characteristics can be used to distinguish the paths, and this allows a choice to be made among the paths.

Some of the information carried in the update messages is more important than others. Indeed, some of this information is crucial to the successful operation of BGP-4, so it must be carried through the network to every router running BGP-4.

Because the BGP-4 information in the updates varies in significance to the BGP-4 network, it has been categorized by importance. The attributes are divided into two types, well known and optional. The well-known attributes are those attributes that are mandatory, while the optional ones are just that—optional. Both of these are subdivided into two further categories, allowing considerable granularity. This is very simple when viewed in Table 8-3.

The attributes are appropriately carried in the updates that inform the routers of the routes.

Table 8-3   *The Four Categories of Attributes*

Category	Description
Well-known: Mandatory (required by all routers) Discretionary (required by all routers and recognized by all routers)	These attributes are required and are therefore recognized by all BGP-4 implementations. It is not required that these attributes be present in the update messages, but if they are present, all routers running BGP-4 will recognize and act on the information contained.
Optional: Transitive Nontransitive	The router may not recognize these attributes, but if this is the case, it marks the update as partial and sends the update, complete with attributes, to the next router. The attributes traverse the router unchanged, if they are not recognized. Nontransitive attributes are dropped if they fall onto a router that does not understand or recognize the attribute. These attributes will *not* be propagated to the BGP-4 peers. Unrecognized nontransitive optional attributes must be quietly ignored and not passed along to other BGP peers. New transitive optional attributes may be attached to the path by the originator or by any other AS in the path (see RFC 1771).

Although there are other Attributes, the following list includes the ones supported by Cisco. The attributes and a description of their characteristics are listed in Table 8-4 for quick reference and comparison.

Table 8-4   *The BGP-4 Attributes*

Attribute Name	Category	Code	Preference	Description
Origin	Well known, mandatory	1	Lowest origin code Where: IGP < EGP < Incomplete	This path attribute identifies the source of the routing update. The possible sources of routing information are as follows: • The path originates from within the autonomous system. It was created with the IBGP-4 network command. The route will be marked in the routing table with an "I. • If the source is an exterior routing protocol, it will be identified with an "e" in the routing table. • The route could have been redistributed into BGP-4, so there is incomplete information. The route is marked by "?."

continues

Table 8-4 *The BGP-4 Attributes (Continued)*

Attribute Name	Category	Code	Preference	Description
AS_Path	Well known, mandatory	2	Shortest path	This is a sequence of the autonomous systems that the packet has traversed.
Next hop	Well known, mandatory	3	Shortest path or IGP metric	The next hop attribute states the next hop on the path for the router to take. In EBGP-4, this will be the source address of the router that sent the update. In IBGP-4, for routes originated outside the AS, the address will still be the source address of the router that sent the update. The protocol states that the next hop advertised by EBGP-4 should be carried into IBGP-4. Therefore, it is important for the IGP to be aware of this network so that any router within the autonomous system can reach the next hop.
Multiple Exit Discriminator (MED)	Optional, nontransitive	4	Lowest value	This attribute informs routers outside the autonomous system which path to take into the autonomous system. It is known as the external metric of a route. Therefore, it is passed between the autonomous systems, but it will not be propagated into a third autonomous system.
Local preference	Well known, discretionary	5	Highest value	This attribute is used to tell routers within the autonomous system how to exit the autonomous system in the case of multiple paths. It is the opposite of the MED attribute. This value is passed solely between IBGP peers only.
Atomic aggregate	Well known, discretionary	6	Information not used in path selection	This attribute states that the routes have been aggregated and that some information has been lost.
Aggregator	Optional, transitive	7	Information not used in path selection	This attribute states the BGP-4 router ID and autonomous system number of the router that was responsible for aggregating the route.

Table 8-4   *The BGP-4 Attributes (Continued)*

Attribute Name	Category	Code	Preference	Description
Community	Optional, transitive	8	Information not used in path selection	This is the capability to tag certain routes that have something in common. They are thereby made members of the same club or community. This is often used in conjunction with another attribute that will affect route selection for the community. For example, the use of the local preference and community attributes would allow the network administrators and other privileged beings to use the high-speed link to the Internet, while others shared a fractional T1. Communities have no geographical or logical limits. BGP-4 can filter on incoming or outgoing routes for filtering, redistribution, or path selection.
Originator ID	Optional, nontransitive	9	Information not used in path selection	The route reflector (described in the following chapter) appends this attribute. It carries the router ID of the originating router in the local autonomous system. It is used to prevent loops.
Cluster list	Optional, nontransitive	10	Information not used in path selection	The cluster identifies the routers involved in the route reflection. The cluster list shows the reflection path that has been taken. This is used to prevent looping errors.
Weight	Cisco-defined		Highest value	This is proprietary to Cisco and is used in route selection. It is local to the router and, because it is not propagated to other routers, there is no problem with compatibility. When there are multiple paths, it selects a path to a destination with different next hops to the same destination. Note that the weight attribute has no code. Because it is a local attribute and is not propagated to other routers, no code is needed.

The Next-Hop Attribute and a Broadcast Multiaccess Network

It is worth mentioning a potential problem with one of the attributes, namely the Next Hop attribute. The method of ascribing a next hop is straightforward, particularly on a multiaccess network. The rule is that because on a multiaccess network, such as Ethernet, it would be unwise for the router to install its own address into the source address, if the route came from another router on the same network. If this happened, then the packets may well be sent to every router on the multiaccess network. This is obviously inefficient. The rule, therefore, is that the address of the router that originally sent the update onto the multiaccess network should remain as the source address.

The problem solved by this attribute is illustrated in the Figure 8-8.

Figure 8-8   *The Next-Hop Router in a Multiaccess Network*

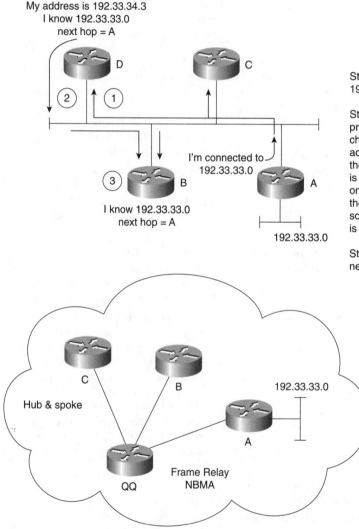

Step 1: Router A sends update about 192.33.33.0.

Step 2: Router D receives update and propagates on. However, if Router D changed the source address to its own address (as is usual in routing updates) there would be a confusion, because this is a multiaccess network and everyone on the network would declare themselves the next hop. To avoid this confusion, the source address of the originating update is not changed.

Step 3: Router B knows Router A is the next hop to network 192.33.33.0.

To avoid the problem in Figure 8-8 on multiaccess networks, the rule is this: Don't change the source address when sending an update back onto multiaccess. Thus, the next-hop address is always the source—in this case, this is Router A in the top network of Figure 8-8.

When this rule is applied to NBMA (as in the bottom network in Figure 8-8), problems arise because although Router B may correctly point to Router A, Router B cannot see Router A in this NBMA cloud. Extra configuration is needed.

The Next Hop Attribute and a Nonbroadcast Multiaccess Network

The problem arises in the NBMA network. As a multiaccess network, it plays by the same rules of maintaining the source address of the router that originated the route on the network. However, there is a potential problem because the other routers are not going to be communicating directly with the source router if the NBMA cloud has a hub-and-spoke configuration. If this is the case, the problem can be solved with a command that forces the router to advertise itself as the source.

Route Selection Process

As can be seen, BGP-4 has many options by which to select one route above another. If EIGRP is complicated in its selection of feasible routes, then BGP-4 is dramatic in its choice of criteria by which the selection is made. That is the key difference. It is not the maintenance of a loop-free network with a very low convergence time that is the goal for BGP-4, but rather the capability to manipulate the traffic flow through the network. That the network is loop-free is critical to the success of the protocol. This requirement is embedded into the architecture, but the key to the protocol is the capability to divert traffic into different directions based on criteria determined by the network architects.

The means by which the traffic flow is diverted is by the use of the attributes. This is different from policy routing, which is a sophisticated method of forcing traffic down a particular path in spite of the dynamic routing decisions. The use of attributes refers to the use of variables in the selection of the best path for the dynamic routing protocol BGP-4.

The flowchart in Figure 8-9 illustrates the logic of the selection process.

Figure 8-9 *Path Selection in BGP-4*

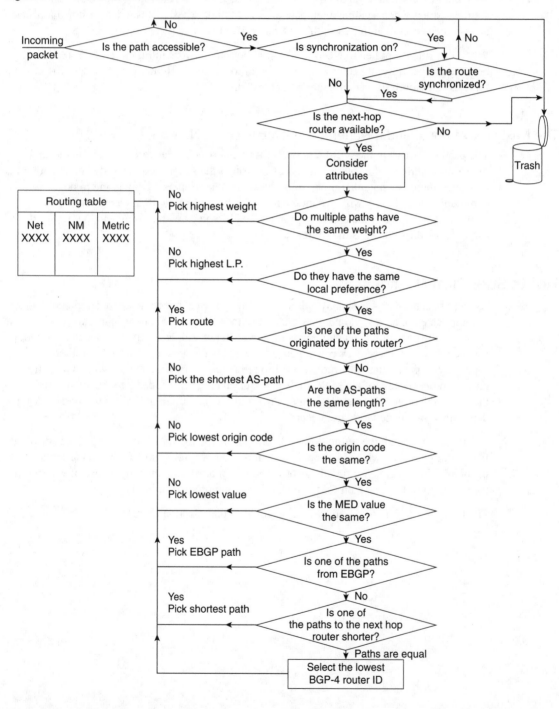

The following process further illustrates the logic of the selection process:

1 If the router has a valid route to the destination, use that route.

2 If there is more than one valid route to the destination, take the route with the highest weight (Cisco proprietary).

3 If the weights are the same, then select the route with the highest local preference.

4 If the routes have the same local preference, then prefer the route that originated on that router.

5 If there are no routes that originated on the router, then examine the AS_Path and select the shortest path.

6 If the AS_Path is the same, then examine and choose the lowest origin code.

7 If the origin codes are the same, then select the path with the lowest MED (the MED values must have been sent from the same neighboring autonomous system).

8 If the MED values are the same, then choose an external BGP-4 route above an internal BGP-4 route.

9 If there is no external route, then choose the shortest path to the next-hop router for IBGP-4.

10 If all else fails, then choose the router with the lowest BGP-4 router ID.

NOTE   The preceding is a simplification of the selection process. For more detailed information on how the routing decisions are made, refer to RFC 1771, "A Border Gateway Protocol 4 (BGP-4)."

This document, together with its companion document, RFC 1772, "Application of the Border Gateway Protocol in the Internet," defines an interautonomous system routing protocol for the Internet.

Basic Configuration Commands to Connect to Another Autonomous System

To connect to another autonomous system, it is necessary to configure the following:

- The start of the routing process
- The networks to be advertised
- The BGP-4 neighbor that the routing process will be synchronizing routing tables with over a TCP session

Starting the Routing Process

The command to configure the routing process is the same command as seen for the interior routing protocols. The syntax is as follows:

```
router bgp autonomous system number
```

Defining the Networks to Be Advertised

To define the network that is to be advertised for this autonomous system, the following command is used (each network requires a separate command):

```
network network-number mask network-mask
```

The **network** command determines the networks that are originated by this router. This is a different use of the command that you are accustomed to configuring with EIGRP, OSPF, and RIP. This command is not identifying the interfaces upon which to run BGP; instead, it is stating the networks that are to be advertised by BGP. The **network** command must include all the networks in the autonomous system to be advertised, not just those that are directly connected to the router. The mask portion is used because BGP-4 can handle subnetting and supernetting.

Identifying Neighbors and Defining Peer Groups

In internal BGP-4, the remote autonomous system number that is defined for the BGP-4 peer will be the same; in external BGP-4, these numbers will differ. The syntax is as follows:

```
neighbor ip-address | peer-group-name remote-as autonomous system number
```

The use of the *peer-group-name* allows the identification of this router as a member of a peer group.

A peer group is a group of neighbors that share the same update policy. This is the mechanism by which routers can be grouped to simplify configuration.

Forcing the Next-Hop Address

On a multiaccess network, the rule is that the source address of a packet is that of the router that originated the packet onto the network. This can cause problems on a NBMA network that appears to be a multiaccess network but that in reality may not have full connectivity to all the routers on the network. If the source address is the address of the initiating router, the other routers may not have a path to this next hop, and packets will be dropped. To overcome this problem, the next-hop address can be configured to be that of the transmitting router. The syntax of the command is as follows:

```
neighbor {ip-address | peer-group} next-hop-self
```

This issue is described earlier in this chapter, in the section "The Next-Hop Attribute and a Broadcast Multiaccess Network."

Disabling Synchronization

If a IBGP-4 network is fully meshed, it is possible and maybe desirable to turn off synchronization. The following command is used:

```
no synchronization
```

This allows routers to advertise routes into BGP-4 before the IGP has a copy of the route in its routing table.

Aggregating Routes

To summarize or aggregate routes within the BGP-4 domain, use the following command from the config-router mode:

```
aggregate-address ip address mask[summary-only] [as-set]
```

If the parameter **summary-only** is used, then the specific routes are suppressed and the summary route is the only one propagated. If the parameter **as-set** is used, then all the autonomous systems that have been traversed will be recorded in the update message. This is the default configuration.

Because it may be necessary to redistribute BGP-4 into the IGP, care must be taken to avoid routing loops and not to overwhelm the routing tables. The administrative distance of BGP-4 helps prevent this problem (see Figure 8-10).

Figure 8-10   *Administrative Distance and BGP-4*

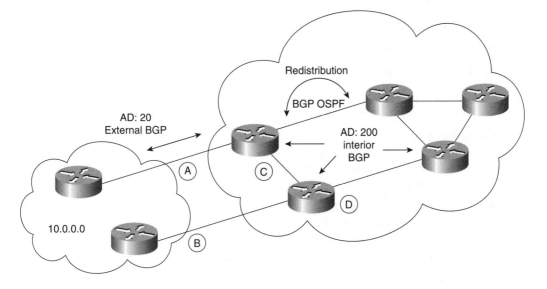

In Figure 8-10, because BGP-4 (internal) has an administrative distance of 200, it is effectively the last choice. Router C will always choose the direct path to 10.0.0.0 through Router A because it has an administrative distance of 20. The route through D and B to find network 10.0.0.0 will have an administrative distance of 110 or 200, depending on the configuration.

Managing and Verifying the BGP-4 Configuration

After configuration changes in BGP-4, it is necessary to reset the TCP session between neighbors. This can be forced with the following command:

```
clear ip bgp {* | address}[soft [in | out]]
```

This command disconnects the session between the neighbors and re-establishes it using the new configuration that has been entered. The soft option does not tear down the sessions, but it resends the updates. The **in** and **out** options allow the configuration of inbound or outbound soft updates. The default is for both.

NOTE   The **clear ip bgp** command is an executive command executed at the privileged level. It is not a configuration command.

The **show** commands for BGP-4 are comprehensive and give clear information about the BGP-4 sessions and routing options. These informative commands and their functions are as follows:

- **show ip bgp**—Displays the BGP routing table.

- **show ip bgp paths**—Displays the topology table.

- **show ip bgp summary**—Displays information about the TCP sessions.

- **show ip bgp neighbors**—Displays information about the TCP connections to neighbors. When the connection is established, the neighbors can exchange updates.

Another command that helps to troubleshoot any implementation and that should be considered in the BGP-4 configuration is the **debug** command. An entire book in the IOS documentation set is devoted to this command. For BGP-4, **debug** is a very useful command. It is shown here with all the possible options:

- **debug ip bgp [dampening | events | keepalives | updates]**—This command displays live information of events as they occur. The options available display events, routing updates as they are sent or received, keepalives to maintain the TCP session with the peer, and dampening information.

Given its complexity and role in internetworking, BGP-4 is very seldom used by private organizations. Despite the rush to connect to the expanding Internet resources, service providers have emerged to set up and manage the connection. This is advantageous to everyone. For a small fee, the organization or individual has a complex connection created and maintained; the Internet's burden is also eased because it is still dealing with large corporations and organizations rather than the millions of individual users.

For this reason, the information on troubleshooting BGP-4 is not broken into as much detail as has been done in previous chapters for other technologies.

When to Use BGP-4

Although the alternatives to BGP-4 are preferred for their simple connections to the Internet, on some occasions it is advantageous to use the power of this complex protocol. These reasons to use BGP-4 include the following:

- Your organization is connecting to multiple ISPs or autonomous systems and is actively using those links. Many organizations use this for redundancy purposes, justifying the additional cost by using all the links and reducing bottlenecks and congestion. In this case, policy routing decisions may need to be made on a link-by-link basis.

- The routing policy of the ISP and your company differ. The cost of the link depends on usage; time of day and other factors may need to be programmed into the BGP-4 configuration to make the best use of the connection by manipulating the traffic.

- The traffic in your organization needs to be distinguished from that of the ISP. They cannot logically appear as one autonomous system.

- Your organization is an ISP and, therefore, conforms to all of the previous criteria. The nature of your business requires the traffic from other autonomous systems to travel across your autonomous system, treating it as a transit domain.

When Not to Use BGP-4

It is a truism that a simple network is a network that is easier to manage and maintain, which is the main reason to avoid BGP-4 configuration in the network. Therefore, if your network has the following characteristics, use other methods, such as static and default routing, to achieve connectivity to the ISP or to another autonomous system network:

- The ISP and your organization have the same routing policy.

- Although your company has multiple links to the ISP, these links are redundant and there are no plans to activate more than one link to the Internet.

- There are limited network resources, such as memory and CPU, on the routers.

- The bandwidth between the autonomous system is low, and the additional routing overhead would detract from routing data.

- You lack confidence or expertise in BGP-4 and route filtering.

Alternative Methods of Connecting to an ISP

If BGP-4 is unnecessary in your network, consider the other possibilities, including the following:

- A default route into the ISP and a static route from the ISP into the organization.

- A routing protocol into the ISP, making the ISP part of your autonomous system. The ISP will be using redistribution within its domain, and it is advisable for the organization to use some form of security, in the form of access lists or a firewall.

Typically the ISP will give you a written sheet explaining the required configuration, or it will request access to your autonomous system boundary router to configure it itself. Either way, it is useful to be cognizant about the procedure.

There are too many variations to be considered in the configuration of an internal routing protocol to detail in this chapter. The main principles are dealt with in Chapter 10, "Controlling Routing Updates Across the Network."

The use of the default and static routes is worth pondering. This is a solution that has been used for years in connecting remote satellite networks, particularly those connected via a dialup link.

The solution is simple: The smaller network defines a default route, which is propagated throughout the domain. The default route points to the exit point of the network into the ISP. The larger network—in this case, the ISP—configures static routes to the organization. These routes are summarized in the master routing table to the Internet or NIC address of the IP address. The static routes must also be propagated throughout the ISP's network so that they can eventually be advertised into the Internet, connecting the smaller organization into the global internetwork. Figure 8-11 illustrates the use of default and static routes and shows how they would be propagated.

Figure 8-11 *Default and Static Route Configuration into the Internet*

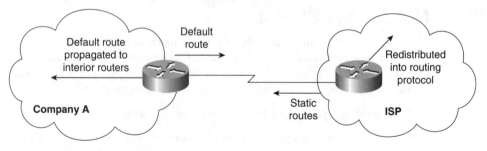

The command syntax to configure a static route is as follows:

```
ip route prefix mask {interface | ip-address} [distance]
```

It is possible to specify either the outgoing interface or the IP address of the next logical hop. If the outgoing interface is specified, the link is treated as if it is directly connected. The default administrative distance of a directly connected link is 0. If the IP address is configured, it is given the administrative distance of 1.

In either case, the administrative distance will ensure that this path will be chosen above all others. If this static route is a redundant link into the ISP and will not be used unless there is no alternative, it may be necessary to change the administrative distance.

To propagate the static routes throughout the domain, it is necessary to redistribute them in the appropriate routing protocol.

Conclusion

This chapter has dealt with a basic introduction to BGP-4. It showed the complexity of the design of large networks—particularly because they seldom start as large entities and instead evolve into such. As they evolve, the needs and requirements of the different divisions change, and the organizational structure often mutates or reforms. This leads to different technological requirements that must sustain the existing structure while allowing for the development of the new environment at the same time.

The design and configuration solutions are vast. This chapter has merely introduced some of the possible solutions and has pointed out the danger areas to avoid. For a true implementation on a live network, it cannot be stressed enough how important the analysis and design of the network is for an effective solution.

Foundation Summary

The "Foundation Summary" is a collection of quick reference information that provides a convenient review of many key concepts in this chapter. For those of you who already feel comfortable with the topics in this chapter, this summary will help you recall a few details. For those of you who just read this chapter, this review should help solidify some key facts. For any of you doing your final preparations before the exam, these tables and figures will be a convenient way to review the day before the exam.

The Key Features of BGP-4

- BGP-4 is an enhanced distance vector protocol.

- BGP-4 creates and maintains connections between peers, using TCP port 179.

- The connection is maintained by periodic keepalives.

- The failure to see a keepalive, an update, or a notification is the means by which destination networks and paths to those destinations are tracked. Any change in the network results in a triggered update.

- The metric used in BGP-4 is intricate and is the source of its complexity and its strength. The metric, referred to as attributes, allows great granularity in path selection.

- The use of hierarchical addressing and the capability to manipulate traffic flow results in a network that is designed to grow.

- BGP-4 has its own routing table, although it is capable of both sharing and inquiring of the interior IP routing table.

- It is possible to manipulate the traffic flow by using the complex metric called attributes, but policy-based routing is based on the hop-by-hop paradigm. This means that no router can send traffic on a route that the next-hop router would not choose for itself.

Tables 8-5 through 8-7 summarize the information that you will need to be familiar with to master the objectives of this chapter.

Table 8-5   *The Four Categories of Attributes*

Category	Description
Well Known: Mandatory (required by all routers)	These attributes are required and are therefore recognized by all BGP-4 implementations.
Discretionary (required by all routers and recognized by all routers)	It is not required that these attributes be present in the update messages, but if they are present, all routers running BGP-4 will recognize and act on the information contained.

Table 8-5   *The Four Categories of Attributes (Continued)*

Category	Description
Optional: Transitive Nontransitive	The router may not recognize these attributes, but if this is the case, it marks the update as partial and sends the update, complete with attributes, to the next router. The attributes traverse the router unchanged, if they are not recognized. Nontransitive attributes are dropped if they fall onto a router that does not understand or recognize the attribute. These attributes will *not* be propagated to the BGP-4 peers. Unrecognized nontransitive optional attributes must be quietly ignored and not passed along to other BGP peers. New transitive optional attributes may be attached to the path by the originator or by any other AS in the path (see RFC 1771).

The attributes are appropriately carried in the updates that inform the routers of the routes.

The attributes and their attributes are listed in Table 8-6 for quick reference and comparison.

Table 8-6   *The BGP-4 Attributes*

Attribute Name	Category	Code	Preference	Description
Origin	Well known, mandatory	1	Lowest origin code Where: IGP < EGP < Incomplete	This path attribute identifies the source of the routing update. The possible sources of routing information are as follows: • The path originates from within the autonomous system. It was created with the IBGP-4 network command. The route will be marked in the routing table with an "I." • If the source is an exterior routing protocol, it will be identified with an "e" in the routing table. • The route could have been redistributed into BGP-4; as such, there is incomplete information. The route is marked by "?."
AS_Path	Well known, mandatory	2	Shortest path	This is a Sequence of the autonomous systems that the packet has traversed.

continues

Table 8-6 *The BGP-4 Attributes (Continued)*

Attribute Name	Category	Code	Preference	Description
Next hop	Well known, Mandatory	3	Shortest path or IGP metric	The next hop attribute states the next hop on the path for the router to take. In EBGP-4, this will be the source address of the router that sent the update. In IBGP-4, for routes that originated outside the autonomous system, the address will still be the source address of the router that sent the update. The protocol states that the next hop advertised by EBGP-4 should be carried into the IBGP-4. Therefore, it is important that the IGP is aware of this network so that any router within the autonomous system can reach the next hop.
Multiple Exit Discriminator (MED)	Optional, nontransitive	4	Lowest value	This attribute informs routers outside the autonomous system which path to take into the autonomous system. It is known as the external metric of a route. Therefore, it is passed between the autonomous systems, but it will not be propagated into a third autonomous system.
Local preference	Well known, discretionary	5	Highest value	This attribute is used to tell routers within the autonomous system how to exit the autonomous system in the case of multiple paths. It is the opposite of the MED attribute. This value is passed solely between IBGP peers only.
Atomic aggregate	Well known, discretionary	6	Information not used in path selection	This attribute states that the routes have been aggregated and that some information has been lost.
Aggregator	Optional, transitive	7	Information not used in path selection	This attribute states the BGP-4 router ID and the autonomous system number of the router that was responsible for aggregating the route.

Table 8-6   *The BGP-4 Attributes (Continued)*

Attribute Name	Category	Code	Preference	Description
Community	Optional, transitive	8	Information not used in path selection	This is the capability to tag certain routes that have something in common. They are thereby made members of the same club or community. This is often used in conjunction with another attribute that will affect route selection for the community. For example, the use of the local preference and community attributes would allow the network administrators and other privileged beings to use the high-speed link to the Internet, while others shared a fractional T1. Communities have no geographical or logical limits. BGP-4 can filter on incoming or outgoing routes for filtering, redistribution, or path selection.
Originator ID	Optional, nontransitive	9	Information not used in path selection	The route reflector (described in the following chapter) appends this attribute. It carries the router ID of the originating router in the local autonomous system. It is used to prevent loops.
Cluster list	Optional, nontransitive	10	Information not used in path selection	The cluster identifies the routers involved in the route reflection. The cluster list shows the reflection path that has been taken. This is used to prevent looping errors.
Weight	Cisco-defined		Highest value	This is proprietary to Cisco and is used in route selection. It is local to the router and, because it is not propagated to other routers, there is no problem with compatibility. When there are multiple paths, it selects a path to a destination with different next hops to the same destination. Note that the weight attribute has no code. Because it is a local attribute and is not propagated to other routers, no code is needed.

Figure 8-12 shows the logic of the path selection used in BGP-4.

Figure 8-12   *Path Selection in BGP-4*

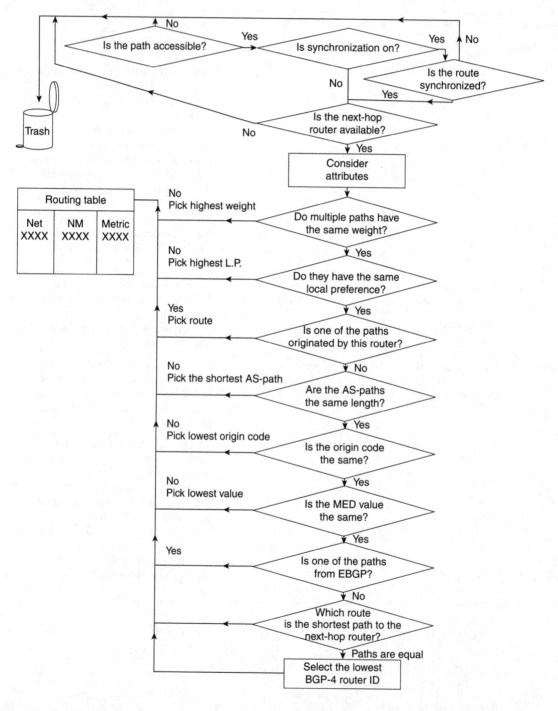

Use Figure 8-12 in association with the following list of the selection process steps.

1 If the router has a valid route to the destination, use that route.

2 If there is more than one valid route to the destination, take the route with the highest weight (Cisco proprietary).

3 If the weights are the same, then select the route with the highest local preference.

4 If the routes have the same local preference, then prefer the route that originated on that router.

5 If there are no routes that originated on the router, then examine the AS_Path and select the shortest path.

6 If the AS_Path is the same, then examine and choose the lowest origin code.

7 If the origin codes are the same, then select the path with the lowest MED (the MED values must have been sent from the same neighboring autonomous system).

8 If the MED values are the same, then choose an external BGP-4 route above an internal BGP-4 route.

9 If there is no external route, then choose the shortest path to the next-hop router for IBGP-4.

10 If all else fails, then choose the router with the lowest BGP-4 router ID.

Table 8-7 summarizes the commands covered in this chapter.

Table 8-7   *Summary of BGP-4 Commands*

Command	Function
router bgp *autonomous system number*	Starts the BGP routing process.
network *network-number* **mask** *network-mask*	Identifies the networks to be advertised by the process.
neighbor {*ip-address* | *peer-group-name*} **remote-as** *autonomous system number*	Identifies the neighbor with whom the router is synchronizing its routing table, and activates a TCP session with the neighbor.
neighbor {*ip-address* | *peer-group-name*} **next-hop-self**	To avoid the problem of selecting the next-hop router on a NBMA network inappropriately, is used to force the router to use its own IP address as the next hop when advertising to neighbors.
no synchronization	Turns off synchronization and the need for the IGP to know of a route before BGP-4 can advertise it. This is used when the IBGP-4 network is fully meshed.

continues

Table 8-7   *Summary of BGP-4 Commands (Continued)*

Command	Function
aggregate-address *ip-address mask* [**summary-only**] [**as-set**]	Used to create an aggregate address. The summary only advertises the summary, and the AS-set lists the autonomous system numbers that the more specific routes have traversed.
debug ip bgp [**dampening** | **events** | **keepalives** | **updates**]	It is possible to be very specific about the **debug** parameters.
clear ip bgp {***** | *address*} [**soft** [**in** | **out**]]	Resets the session between the neighbors and re-establishes it with the new configuration that has been entered. The soft option does not tear down the sessions, but it resends the updates. The **in** and **out** options allow the configuration of inbound or outbound soft updates. The default is for both.
show ip bgp [**summary** | **neighbors**]	Shows the BGP connections. A network can be specified to retrieve information on the lone network. The **summary** option will give the status of the BGP connections. The neighbor option gives both TCP and BGP connections.

Chapter Glossary

This glossary provides an official Cisco definition for key words and terms introduced in this chapter. I have supplied my own definition for terms that the Cisco glossary does not contain. The words listed here are identified in the text by italics. A complete glossary, including all the chapter terms and additional terms, can be found in Appendix C, "Glossary."

attribute—The metric used by BGP-4.

autonomous system (AS)—Definition for the organizational boundary. Within the terminology of the routing protocols, it defines all the routers within an administrative domain, where each router has full knowledge of the subnets within the domain. This becomes confused with the introduction of summarization within an autonomous system. If you are connecting directly to the Internet using BGP, the autonomous system number must be unique and obtained from the Internet addressing committees.

Exterior Gateway Protocol (EGP)—Protocol that runs between autonomous systems. There is a protocol with this name, which was the precursor to BGP.

external BGP—When BGP is used to connect different autonomous systems.

Interior Gateway Protocol (IGP)—In the past, the term *gateway* was used to define a router. This is a routing protocol that runs within an autonomous system.

internal BGP—When BGP is used to connect routers resident in the same autonomous system.

transit autonomous system—An autonomous system that is used to carry BGP-4 traffic across it to another autonomous system. None of the traffic is destined for any router within the autonomous system; it is simply being routed through it.

Q&A

The following questions test your understanding of the topics covered in this chapter. The final questions in this section repeat the opening "Do I Know This Already?" questions. These are repeated to enable you to test your progress. After you have answered the questions, find the answers in Appendix A. If you get an answer wrong, review the answer and ensure that you understand the reason for your mistake. If you are confused by the answer, refer to the appropriate text in the chapter to review the concepts.

1 If the weight attribute is used, is a higher or lower weight preferred?

2 When would you use external BGP-4 as opposed to internal BGP-4?

3 What is an alternative to using BGP-4 as the method of connection to the ISP?

4 State two reasons for the synchronization rule.

5 What does the command **clear ip bgp** * achieve, and why should it be used cautiously?

6 Give three reasons why you should not use BGP-4 to connect to the Internet.

_____

_____

_____

7 Explain the use of the command **neighbor 10.10.10.10 remote-as 250.**

_____

_____

_____

8 Explain briefly the purpose of the community attribute.

_____

_____

_____

9 In the route selection process, place the following in order of preference: origin code, highest weight, local preference, and MED. State the method of selection for the individual attributes themselves.

_____

_____

_____

10 What command is used to enable the BGP-4 process?

_____

_____

_____

11 Which command is used to show the BGP-4 connections between peers?

_____

_____

_____

12 What is a mandatory attribute?

_____

_____

_____

13 What type of routing protocol is BGP-4 classified as, and what does this mean?

_____

_____

_____

14 What is a static route?

_____

_____

_____

15 What is the transport protocol for BGP-4?

_____

_____

_____

16 What is a default route?

_____

_____

_____

17 State two attributes of BGP-4.

_____

_____

_____

18 State four message types of BGP-4.

_____

_____

_____

19 What is policy-based routing?

_____

_____

_____

20 What do the letters MED represent? Give a brief explanation of what this does.

_____

_____

_____

21 What is a community in BGP-4?

_____

_____

_____

22 Give two reasons why peer groups are useful.

_____

_____

_____

23 Explain the term "third-party next hop."

_____

_____

_____

24 What is the difference between a peer and a neighbor?

_____

_____

_____

25 Explain briefly the synchronization rule.

_____

_____

_____

26 In BGP-4, describe the purpose of the **network** command.

_____

_____

_____

27 Explain the command **neighbor** {*ip-address* | *peer-group-name*} **next-hop-self**.

_____

_____

_____

28 Which command is used to show all BGP-4 connections?

_____

_____

_____

Scenarios

The following scenarios and questions are designed to draw together the content of the chapter and to exercise your understanding of the concepts. There is not necessarily a right answer. The thought process and practice in manipulating the concepts are the goals of this section. The answers to the scenario questions are found at the end of this chapter.

Scenario 8-1

The company Humugos is still waiting for the consultant to configure the network. The requirement is to give each country its own autonomous system number. The countries will be connected via EBGP-4 and will be using leased lines. The autonomous system numbers are private because the connection to the Internet is dealt with by using an Internet service provider at each local site. For the first phase of the switchover, EIGRP is removed from the connections between the countries, and the BGP-4 configuration needs to be synchronized to ensure a smooth transition. The intention is that each country will have the same configuration to ease management and troubleshooting.

1   Using the diagram in Figure 8-13 as a reference, issue the commands that need to be configured at each country or autonomous system.

Figure 8-13   *Diagram for Scenario 8-1*

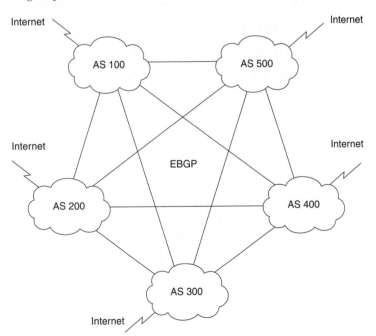

NOTE   Figure 8-13 has been simplified and does not contain the 250 autonomous systems as the case study suggests.

---

2 The BGP-4 network is a full-mesh network. Are there going to be any scaling problems ensuing from this?

3 What commands would indicate that there was a problem of scaling?

Scenario 8-2

A small company called Insolvent, Inc., has a main office in Chicago and satellite offices on the West Coast of the United States. The company has recently changed its routing protocol to OSPF.

Insolvent has a connection to the Internet from each site, over which it does all its business. The link is a fractional T1 at the satellite offices and a full T1 at the main office. The network administrator at the main office is responsible for the corporate network and is currently trying to recruit staff to manage the local networks. He was advised at a technical seminar that BGP-4 is what he needs to connect to the Internet. Figure 8-14 shows the network.

1 Given the description of the company, and with reference to Figure 8-14, do you agree that BGP-4 is a requirement for this network? Give reasons for your answer.

2 What alternatives are available?

3 Give the alternative configuration commands for the satellite site to connect to Internet.

4 What commands would show that the link is up and operational?

Figure 8-14   *Diagram for Scenario 8-2*

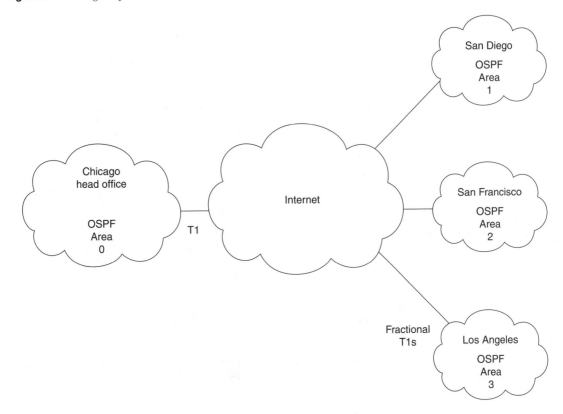

Scenario 8-3

Review the output in Example 8-1, and answer the following questions.

Example 8-1   *Scenario 8-3 Output*

```
FARADAY-gw#show ip bgp neighbor
BGP neighbor is 155.94.83.1,  remote AS 2914, external link
 Index 1, Offset 0, Mask 0x2
  BGP version 4, remote router ID 129.250.116.16
  BGP state = Established, table version = 457046, up for 1w5d
  Last read 00:00:20, hold time is 180, keepalive interval is 60 seconds
  Minimum time between advertisement runs is 30 seconds
  Received 890723 messages, 0 notifications, 0 in queue
  Sent 36999 messages, 0 notifications, 0 in queue
```

continues

Example 8-1 *Scenario 8-3 Output (Continued)*

```
            Inbound path policy configured
            Outbound path policy configured
            Outgoing update AS path filter list is 1
            Route map for incoming advertisements is limit-verioverdi
            Connections established 3; dropped 2
            Last reset 1w5d, due to : User reset request
            No. of prefix received 11031
           No. of prefix received 11031
   Connection state is ESTAB, I/O status: 1, unread input bytes: 0
   Local host: 155.94.83.2, Local port: 11036
   Foreign host: 155.94.83.1, Foreign port: 179
   Enqueued packets for retransmit: 0, input: 0  mis-ordered: 0 (0 bytes)
   Event Timers (current time is 0x845DFA38):
   Timer          Starts   Wakeups          Next
   Retrans        18473       11             0x0
   TimeWait           0        0             0x0
   AckHold        86009    50293             0x0
   SendWnd            0        0             0x0
   KeepAlive          0        0             0x0
   GiveUp             0        0             0x0
   PmtuAger           0        0             0x0
   DeadWait           0        0             0x0
   iss:  829352113  snduna:  829702916  sndnxt:  829702916    sndwnd:  16004
   irs:  625978143  rcvnxt:  652708970  rcvwnd:       16342  delrcvwnd:     42
   SRTT: 300 ms, RTTO: 607 ms, RTV: 3 ms, KRTT: 0 ms
   minRTT: 4 ms, maxRTT: 764 ms, ACK hold: 300 ms
   Flags: higher precedence, nagle
   Datagrams (max data segment is 536 bytes):
   Rcvd: 122915 (out of order: 0), with data: 105023, total data bytes: 26731112
   Sent: 109195 (retransmit: 11), with data: 18461, total data bytes: 350802
   !
   !
   BGP neighbor is 144.39.228.49,  remote AS 701, external link
    Index 2, Offset 0, Mask 0x4
     BGP version 4, remote router ID 144.39.3.104
     BGP state = Established, table version = 457055, up for 2w0d
     Last read 00:00:08, hold time is 180, keepalive interval is 60 seconds
     Minimum time between advertisement runs is 30 seconds
     Received 50265 messages, 0 notifications, 0 in queue
     Sent 37016 messages, 0 notifications, 0 in queue
     Inbound path policy configured
     Outbound path policy configured
     Outgoing update AS path filter list is 1
     Route map for incoming advertisements is limit-uunetmemenet
     Connections established 2; dropped 1
     Last reset 2w0d, due to : Peer closing down the session
     No. of prefix received 1635
   Connection state is ESTAB, I/O status: 1, unread input bytes: 0
   Local host: 144.39.228.50, Local port: 179
   Foreign host: 144.39.228.49, Foreign port: 11013
   Enqueued packets for retransmit: 0, input: 0  mis-ordered: 0 (0 bytes)
   Event Timers (current time is 0x845F16B8):
   Timer          Starts   Wakeups          Next
```

Example 8-1 *Scenario 8-3 Output (Continued)*

```
Retrans          20357         4          0x0
TimeWait             0         0          0x0
AckHold          29701     26058          0x0
SendWnd              0         0          0x0
KeepAlive            0         0          0x0
GiveUp               0         0          0x0
PmtuAger             0         0          0x0
DeadWait             0         0          0x0
iss: 3360945234  snduna: 3361331966  sndnxt: 3361331966   sndwnd:   15890
irs: 2976917809  rcvnxt: 2977685910  rcvwnd:       15072  delrcvwnd: 1312
SRTT: 306 ms, RTTO: 642 ms, RTV: 15 ms, KRTT: 0 ms
minRTT: 4 ms, maxRTT: 908 ms, ACK hold: 300 ms
Flags: passive open, nagle, gen tcbs
Datagrams (max data segment is 1460 bytes):
Rcvd: 48675 (out of order: 0), with data: 29705, total data bytes: 768119
Sent: 46955 (retransmit: 4), with data: 20353, total data bytes: 386750
```

1 How many sessions are active?

2 What is the state of the sessions, and what do the states mean?

Scenario Answers

The answers are in **bold**. The answers provided in this section are not necessarily the only possible answers to the questions. The questions are designed to test your knowledge and to give practical exercise in certain key areas. This section is intended to test and exercise skills and concepts detailed in the body of this chapter.

If your answer is different, ask yourself whether it follows the tenets explained in the answers provided. Your answer is correct not if it matches the solution provided in the book, but rather if it has included the principles of design laid out in the chapter.

In this way, the testing provided in these scenarios is deeper: It examines not only your knowledge, but also your understanding and ability to apply that knowledge to problems.

If you do not get the correct answer, refer back to the text and review the subject tested. Be certain to also review your notes on the question to ensure that you understand the principles of the subject.

Scenario 8-1 Answers

1 Using the diagram in Figure 8-13 as a reference, issue the commands that need to be configured at each country or autonomous system.

The commands configured at each country or autonomous system would be the same structurally, although the details, such as the IP addresses and the autonomous system numbers, would change.

Example 8-2 shows the configuration of the autonomous system 100, which is the San Francisco router. It has been assigned network 10.2.0.0.

Example 8-2 *Scenario 8-1 Configuration*

```
Router(config)#
router bgp 100
no auto-summary
neighbor 10.1.100.1 remote-as 1
neighbor 10.3.100.1 remote-as 3
neighbor 10.4.100.1 remote-as 4
neighbor 10.5.100.1 remote-as 5
neighbor 10.6.100.1 remote-as 6
neighbor 10.7.100.1 remote-as 7
neighbor 10.8.100.1 remote-as 8
neighbor 10.9.100.1 remote-as 9
neighbor 10.10.100.1 remote-as 10
  ¦
  ¦
  \/
neighbor 10.250.100.1 remote-as 250
network 10.2.0.0
```

The protocol has had the neighbors in each autonomous system defined with their next-hop IP address and the number of the autonomous system to which they are connecting. The no auto-summary command is used to ensure that the subnets of network 10.0.0.0 are advertised; otherwise, each subnet would need to be defined as a network command.

2   The BGP-4 network is a full-mesh network. Are there going to be any scaling problems ensuing from this?

There should not be a problem with this design because although there are an enormous number of TCP connections, the traffic is minimal, particularly if aggregation is configured. Also, BGP sends only triggered updates, so if the network is stable and route aggregation is configured, then bandwidth should not be a concern. However, considering the propagation delays, the BGP timers may need to be reviewed. Regarding CPU, a high-power router should be used for this purpose.

3   What commands would indicate that there was a problem of scaling?

The commands that should be used to determine whether there is a problem are as follows:

— show ip bgp neighbors

— show ip bgp sessions

— show ip bgp

— show processes cpu

Scenario 8-2 Answers

1   Given the description of the company, and with reference to Figure 8-14, do you agree that BGP-4 is a requirement for this network? Give reasons for your answer.

Because the company is small and has only a single connection per site into the Internet, it would be too complex to configure and maintain BGP-4 when there simply are not enough resources. The bandwidth is inadequate for the task, and the administrative expertise is already overstretched. It would be far better to configure a static/default route to the Internet and to redistribute this route into the IGP running within the autonomous system.

2   What alternatives are available?

The only real alternative is the one already mentioned, to configure a default route into the Internet from every location and to redistribute this default route into the IGP for the autonomous system.

3 Give the alternative configuration commands for the satellite site to connect to Internet.

Each site would have the same configuration structure, although the details may differ:

```
ip route 0.0.0.0 0.0.0.0
router ospf 100
network 207.111.9.0 0.0.0.255 area 0
default-information originate always
```

The first line configures the default route.

The second line turns on the OSPF process 100.

The third line identifies which interfaces are participating in OSPF and what area they are in.

The fourth line propagates the default route into the network, whether or not the advertising router has a path to the network.

4 What commands would show that the link is up and operational?

The commands to prove that the link is up and operational would be the show ip route command as well as the ping and traceroute commands. Refer to CCO or the ICND course or coursebook for more details on these commands.

Scenario 8-3 Answers

1 How many sessions are active?

There are two active sessions. In reading the large amount of information on the show ip bgp neighbor command, there is a line at the beginning of each session identifying the neighboring peer. The lines in this output screen are as follows:

```
BGP neighbor is 155.94.83.1,   remote AS 2914, external link
BGP neighbor is 144.39.228.49,   remote AS 701, external link
```

2 What is the state of the sessions, and what do the states mean?

```
BGP state = Established, table version = 457046, up for 1w5d
BGP state = Established, table version = 457055, up for 2w0d
```

Both the peers have established sessions. This means that they have a TCP session. They are now in a position to exchange routing tables and to synchronize their databases. The rest of the line indicates how many times the table has been updated and how long the session has been maintained. In this example, the first peer has had a session with the local router for one week and five days, while the second peer has been up for exactly two weeks. How many autonomous systems are there?

There are three autonomous systems in this configuration. The first peer belongs to autonomous system 2914, and the second belongs to 701. Because both of these neighbors belonging to their autonomous systems have an external BGP-4 session, there must be a third autonomous system, within which the local router resides.

```
BGP neighbor is 155.94.83.1,  remote AS 2914, external link
BGP neighbor is 144.39.228.49,  remote AS 701, external link
```

Table 8-8, taken from the documentation set for BGP commands on the CCO Web page, explains the fields in the show ip bgp neighbors command.

Table 8-8   **show ip bgp neighbors** *Field Descriptions*

Field	Description
BGP Neighbor	IP address of the BGP neighbor and its autonomous system number. If the neighbor is in the same autonomous system as the router, then the link between them is internal; otherwise, it is considered external.
BGP Version	BGP version being used to communicate with the remote router; the neighbor's router ID (an IP address) is also specified.
BGP State	Internal state of this BGP connection.
Table Version	Indication that the neighbor has been updated with this version of the primary BGP routing table.
Up For	Amount of time that the underlying TCP connection has been in existence.
Last Read	Time that BGP last read a message from this neighbor.
Holdtime	Maximum amount of time that can elapse between messages from the peer.
Keepalive Interval	Time period between sending keepalive packets, which help ensure that the TCP connection is up.
Received	Number of total BGP messages received from this peer, including keepalives.
Notifications	Number of error messages received from the peer.
Sent	Number of error messages that the router has sent to this peer.
Connections Established	Number of times that the router has established a TCP connection and that the two peers have agreed to speak BGP with each other.
Dropped	Number of times that a good connection has failed or been taken down.
Connection State	State of BGP peer.
Unread Input Bytes	Number of bytes of packets still to be processed.

continues

Table 8-8   **show ip bgp neighbors** *Field Descriptions (Continued)*

Field	Description
Local Host, Local Port	Peering address of local router, plus port.
Foreign Host, Foreign Port	Foreign host, foreign port.
Event Timers	Table that displays the number of starts and wakeups for each timer.
Iss	Initial send sequence number.
Snduna	Last send sequence number that the local host sent but has not received an acknowledgment for.
Sndnxt	Sequence number that the local host will send next.
Sndwnd	TCP window size of the remote host.
Irs	Initial receive sequence number.
rcvnxt	Last receive sequence number that the local host has acknowledged.
rcvwnd	Local host's TCP window size.
delrecvwnd	Delayed receive window. Data that the local host has read from the connection but that has not yet subtracted from the receive window that the host has advertised to the remote host. The value in this field gradually increases until it is larger than a full-sized packet, at which point it is applied to the rcvwnd field.
SRTT	A calculated, smoothed round-trip timeout.
RTTO	Round-trip timeout.
RTV	Variance of the round-trip time.
KRTT	New round-trip timeout (using the Karn algorithm). This field separately tracks the round-trip time of packets that have been retransmitted.
minRTT	Smallest recorded round-trip timeout (hard-wire value used for calculation).
maxRTT	Largest recorded round-trip timeout.
ACK hold	Time that the local host will delay an acknowledgment to piggyback data on it.
Flags	IP precedence of the BGP packets.
Datagrams: Rcvd	Number of update packets received from a neighbor.
With Data	Number of update packets received with data.
Total Data Bytes	Total bytes of data.

Table 8-8   **show ip bgp neighbors** *Field Descriptions (Continued)*

Field	Description
Sent	Number of update packets sent.
With Data	Number of update packets with data sent.
Total Data Bytes	Total number of data bytes.

This chapter covers the following topics that you will need to master to pass the CCNP/CCDP Routing exam:

- The scalability problems inherent in BGP-4.

- The concept and configuration of route reflectors.

- The concept and configuration of policy control using prefix lists.

- Methods of connecting to multiple autonomous systems.

- Redistribution between IGPs and EBGP.

- The Cisco commands for tuning BGP-4 and the Cisco commands for reviewing the configuration.

CHAPTER 9

Implementing and Tuning BGP for Use in Large Networks

The topics in this chapter concern the advanced configuration of BGP-4. You will need to apply your understanding of the basic concepts and configuration of BGP-4 that you gained in the last chapter because, in this chapter, the full complexity and sophistication of BGP-4 is explained. In this chapter, the true use of BGP-4 is explored—whether its use is to connect to an ISP or even to act as an ISP with several connected organizations. The chapter covers how BGP-4 can be configured to select a particular path and the design features and pitfalls of BGP. In this discussion of the advanced configuration of BGP-4, the explanation of the technology is coupled with configuration examples so that your conceptual understanding of BGP is reinforced by concrete implementation examples.

The topics in this chapter will directly reflect questions on the Routing exam. BGP-4 is a routing protocol designed for use in large networks. As a well-known attribute to the networking world, it is a mandatory topic in the Routing exam. The BSCN course devotes 11 percent of its material to implementing BGP in scalable networks. Because nearly a quarter of the BSCN course is devoted to BGP, as reflected in Chapter 8, "Connecting to Other Autonomous Systems—The Basics of BGP-4," and Chapter 9, "Implementing and Tuning BGP for Use in Large Networks," you should expect quite a few BGP questions on the test to reflect this concentration.

How to Best Use This Chapter

By taking the following steps, you can make better use of your study time:

- Keep your notes and the answers for all your work with this book in one place, for easy reference.

- When you take a quiz, write down your answers. Studies show that retention significantly increases by writing down facts and concepts, even if you never look at the information again.

- Use the diagram in Figure 9-1 to guide you to the next step.

Figure 9-1 *How to Use This Chapter*

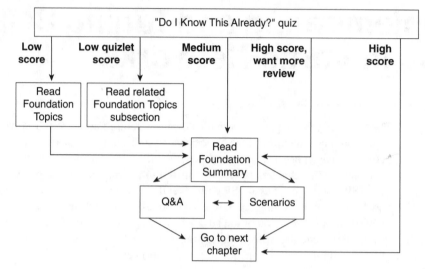

If you skip to the Foundation Summary, Q&A, and scenarios sections and have trouble with the material there, you should go back to the Foundation Topics section.

"Do I Know This Already?" Quiz

The purpose of the "Do I Know This Already?" quiz is to help you decide what parts of this chapter to use. If you already intend to read the entire chapter, you do not necessarily need to answer these questions now.

This 16-question quiz helps you determine how to spend your limited study time. The quiz is sectioned into four smaller four-question "quizlets," which correspond to the four major topics in the chapter. Figure 9-1 outlines suggestions on how to spend your time in this chapter. Use Table 9-1 to record your scores.

Table 9-1   *Score Sheet for Quiz and Quizlets*

Quizlet Number	Topic	Questions	Score
1	Scalability problems with IBGP-4	1 to 4	
2	Configuring route reflectors and policy control using prefix lists	5 to 8	
3	Methods of connecting to multiple ISPs using redistribution between an organization and the ISP	9 to 12	
4	How to configure and verify BGP-4	13 to 16	
All questions	All	1 to 16	

1 Why does IBGP-4 need to be fully meshed?

_____

_____

_____

2 How is a fully meshed network avoided in IBGP-4?

_____

_____

_____

3 What is the formula to determine the number of sessions needed in a fully meshed BGP-4 network?

_____

_____

_____

4 Why does a fully meshed network in IBGP-4 cause problems?

_____

_____

_____

5 State two benefits to using route reflectors.

_____

_____

_____

6 Can the next-hop-self option be used between EBGP-4 peers?

_____

_____

_____

7 Explain the difference between a cluster-ID and an originator-ID.

_____

_____

_____

8 State two advantages in using prefix lists over access lists.

_____

_____

_____

9 If the ISP has provided a default route, how will the router within the autonomous system select the exit path in a multihomed environment?

_____

_____

_____

10 What is a disadvantage of an autonomous system receiving full routing updates from all providers?

_____

_____

_____

11 What is the danger of redistributing BGP-4 into the IGP?

_____

_____

_____

12 What are the advantages of a fully meshed IBGP-4 network?

_____

_____

_____

13 In configuring a route reflector, how is the client configured?

_____

_____

_____

14 What command is used to display the route reflector clients?

_____

_____

_____

15 What commands are used to display the BGP-4 router ID that identifies the router that is sending the updates and peering with its neighbor?

_____

_____

_____

16 Which command is used to display the AS_Path?

_____

_____

_____

The answers to this quiz are found in Appendix A, "Answers to Quiz Questions." The suggested choices for your next step are as follows:

- **2 or less on any quizlet**—Review the appropriate sections of the "Foundation Topics" portion of this chapter, based on Table 9-1. Then move on to the "Foundation Summary" section, the "Q&A" section, and the "Scenarios" at the end of the chapter.

- **8 or less overall score**—Read the entire chapter. This includes the "Foundation Topics" and "Foundation Summary" sections, the "Q&A" section, and the "Scenarios" at the end of the chapter.

- **9 to 12 overall score**—Begin with the "Foundation Summary" section, and then go to the "Q&A" section and the "Scenarios" at the end of the chapter. If you have trouble with these exercises, read the appropriate sections in "Foundation Topics."

- **13 or more overall score**—If you want more review on these topics, skip to the "Foundation Summary" section, and then go to the "Q&A" section and the "Scenarios" at the end of the chapter. Otherwise, move to the next chapter.

Foundation Topics

Introduction—Communicating with Other Autonomous Systems with BGP-4

The BSCN course deals with connectivity to the Internet via a service provider. One of the methods used to make this connection is the external routing protocol BGP-4.

The Routing 2.0 exam, recognizing that BGP-4 is increasingly important in larger environments to communicate with the Internet agent or service provider, covers a conceptual overview of BGP-4. A solid understanding of BGP-4, as well as basic configuration commands, is expected on the Routing exam. However, you should know that if your network is a simple one, using static and default routes may be configurations that are more appropriate. This chapter builds on the basic BGP-4 concepts and commands that were outlined in the previous chapter and deals with the complexities of traffic management and path selection in large BGP-4 environments.

Case Study

As seen in the last chapter, the large multinational company Humugos has offices in 250 countries. Each country operates as a separate company, conforming to the tax and legal laws of the country. It is still important that each part of the organization must be capable of connecting to the others, but EIGRP is no longer feasible for a number of reasons. The main issue is the number of connections that each country has into the Internet. There is also some need to manipulate the traffic, particularly in terms of resource sharing between business units internationally.

The network topology of the case study Humugos is illustrated in Figure 9-2.

BGP-4 has been suggested as a solution for various reasons. First, the company needs yet another level of hierarchy. Second, the multiple connections to the Internet need to be managed with a sophisticated routing protocol. The capability to determine the traffic path that will be taken by a variety of parameters is also very important. This adds another dimension to the simple metric, which proves inadequate to the task of determining subtle distinctions in path selection.

The countries have now been configured to communicate using BGP-4 as the routing protocol between each country or autonomous system. This chapter deals with the design and configuration of the company's connections into the Internet.

Figure 9-2   *Diagram of BGP Case Study—Humugos*

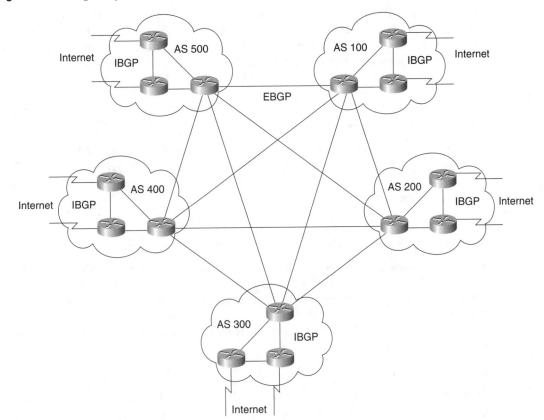

Designing and Configuring a Scalable BGP-4 Network

It is ironic that the opening section in a chapter dealing with the configuration of a sophisticated and large network using BGP-4 should have to discuss the problems that the protocol has with managing the routing information across a large network. After all, BGP-4 was designed for use in the Internet, the largest network of all. In reality, it comes down to design and the truism that most things used inappropriately can be transformed from a life-giver to an instrument of death. Consider the drug insulin, which keeps many diabetics healthy and alive but that has also featured as the murder weapon in some very famous trials.

Why Does BGP-4 Require a Fully Meshed Network?

The issue with BGP-4's capability ton, scale is confined to that of Internal BGP-4, where a fully meshed configuration is required to ensure full connectivity. Remember that to avoid routing loops, the protocol must follow the rule that no updates learned from Internal peers can be sent to other internal peers. This is similar to the IGP split horizon rule. An IBGP-4 router will propagate a route under the following conditions:

- If it is a route generated by the transmitting router

- If it is a connected route

Remember, if the router was learned via an update from a BGP-4 peer within the same autonomous system, it can propagate this route only to an EBGP-4 peer. For this reason, internal BGP-4 peers must all be connected to one another (fully meshed) to have a complete knowledge of the network.

Why Is a Fully Meshed Network a Problem?

The problem is that BGP-4 maintains up-to-date and accurate routing information by sending incremental updates across a TCP connection. The TCP connection is an excellent way of ensuring the accuracy of the information, but it is costly in network resources. The greater the number of connections, the greater the number of required resources. A simple equation demonstrates the problem, one that is also seen in the consideration of designing fully meshed Frame Relay networks.

The Equation for Determining the Number of IBGP-4 Sessions

The equation for determining the number of sessions required is as follows:

$$n \, (n-1) \, / \, 2$$

In plain English, that is the number of routers minus 1, multiplied by the number of routers, and then divided by 2. Thus, 10 routers would mean $10 \, (10-1) \, / \, 2 = 10 \times 9 \, / \, 2 = 45$ sessions.

This works well in environments that require a few connections, such as a company with multiple connections into the Internet. However, if the network is an ISP that is using BGP-4 throughout its network, some careful design should be put in place.

To be fair to TCP, it is not simply the maintenance of the connection that eats up resources, but the amount of updates that traverse those links. If every router is connected to every other router, a lot of the information that is being sent is duplicated. Figure 9-3 illustrates the redundancy.

Figure 9-3   *IBGP-4 and a Fully Meshed Network*

IBGP
before route reflectors

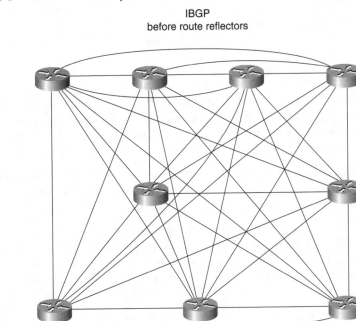

Route Reflectors: The Solution to a Fully Meshed IBGP-4 Network

A route reflector is a router that has been configured to forward routing updates to neighbors or peers within the same autonomous system. These IBGP-4 peers need to be identified in the configuration.

The route reflector defies the split horizon rule that states that the IBGP-4 router will not propagate a route that was learned from a peer within the same autonomous system (an IBGP-4 peer).

However, when a router has been configured as a route reflector, it forwards learned paths from IBGP-4 peers to other IBGP-4 peers. It forwards only to those routers that have been identified as route reflectors and to IBGP/EBGP neighbors clients. This means that a logical hub-and-spoke design can be implemented within an autonomous system between IBGP-4 peers, thus reducing the number of sessions required.

WARNING	The route reflector concept means that there is more overhead on the route reflector and, if configured incorrectly, can cause serious routing loops.

Designs That Avoid a Fully Meshed IBGP-4 Network

The problem presented by a fully meshed IBGP-4 network can be solved by design. If a hub-and-spoke network were developed, this would streamline the TCP connections. This is a good thing, but it does require some additional design and configuration. The solution is the implementation of *route reflectors* and the network design that they support.

The design can become quite complicated with multiple route reflectors that afford redundancy, which is always reassuring. Multiple levels of route reflector can even be configured, creating a hierarchical design.

Nonroute reflector routers are not affected by the change in design and routing update propagation. Indeed, they are blissfully unaware of any changes because they still receive the updates that they need. The updates are also unchanged because no changes are made to the attribute values. This makes migration to a network design incorporating route reflectors very straightforward.

The only design requirement is that the IBGP-4 route reflectors must be fully meshed to ensure the correct propagation of updates. This is illustrated in Figure 9-4.

The benefits of route reflectors include these:

- The capability to scale the network, given the other characteristics

- A strong hierarchical design

- A reduction of traffic on the network

- A reduction in the memory and CPU to maintain TCP sessions on the client IBGP-4 peers

- Faster convergence because synchronization is not needed

- Faster convergence and a simpler network because two routing protocols are implemented:

    — IBGP-4 for external routing information traversing the autonomous system

    — IGP for routes internal to the autonomous system

The solution provided by route reflectors is used in large IBGP-4 environments such as ISP networks, where a fully meshed IBGP-4 network could result in a large number of TCP sessions.

Figure 9-4   *Design of IBGP-4 Network Using Route Reflectors*

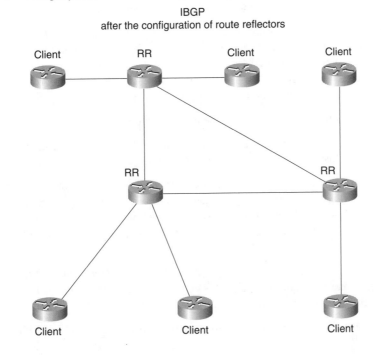

IBGP
after the configuration of route reflectors

How Route Reflectors Operate

This section contains a summary of some of the characteristics of route reflectors. These characteristics determine how route reflectors operate.

Characteristics of Route Reflectors

The following are the chief characteristics of route reflectors:

- A *route reflector* is a router that forwards updates to its clients. When a client sends an update to the route reflector, it is forwarded or reflected to the other clients.

- The route reflector is the only router that is configured or that has the remotest idea that it is anything other than a peer.

- A *client* is a router that receives updates from a route reflector.

- Both a route reflector and a client, therefore, form a unit that shares information. This unit is called a *cluster*.

- The autonomous system is divided into clusters, and the router reflector is identified and configured. There must be at least one route reflector per cluster.

- The route reflector and client require a full peer relationship because the route reflector forwards updates from other clients, but peering between the clients is not needed.

- In all probability, a route reflector is connected to peers for which it is not forwarding routes. From the route reflector's view, these neighbors or peers are *nonclients*. If an update from a client is received by the route reflector, the update is forwarded to other clients as well as nonclients (both IBGP-4 and EBGP-4 peers). The only router that does have the update forwarded to it is the originator of the route.

- Nonclients must be fully meshed with the route reflector.

- The route reflector connects to other route reflectors. These route reflectors need to be fully meshed. This is to ensure that the IBGP-4 routing tables are complete.

- When the route reflector forwards an update, the Originator-ID attribute is set. This is the BGP-4 router ID of the router that originated the path. The purpose of this attribute is not to award honors to the originating router, but so that if this router receives back the update, it will see its own ID and will ignore the packet. This prevents the possibility of routing loops.

- If there are multiple route reflectors in the cluster, to provide redundancy, then the originating router is identified by the Cluster-ID attribute. This serves the same purpose as the Originator-ID in preventing routing loops.

Figure 9-5 illustrates the relationship between route reflectors, clients, and other clusters.

The Rules by Which Route Reflectors Propagate Updates

The following are the rules by which route reflectors propagate updates:

- If a route reflector receives multiple paths to the same destination, it chooses the best path.

- Routes received from a client are reflected to clients and nonclients by the route reflector. This excludes the originator of the route.

- Routes received from a nonclient are reflected to clients only by the route reflector.

- Routes received from EBGP-4 are reflected to clients and nonclients by the route reflector.

The command for configuring a route reflector is very straightforward. It is explained in the following syntax:

```
neighbor ip-address route-reflector-client
```

To remove a router as a client, issue the following command:

```
no neighbor ip-address route-reflector-client
```

Note that if all clients are removed, the route reflector loses its status and becomes a standard IBGP-4 router. If this happens, then the IBGP-4 routers need to be fully meshed, or the BGP-4 updates must be redistributed into an IGP. Table 9-2 breaks down the syntax of the command to configure a route reflector and identify the clients.

Figure 9-5   *Clusters and Route Reflector Meshing*

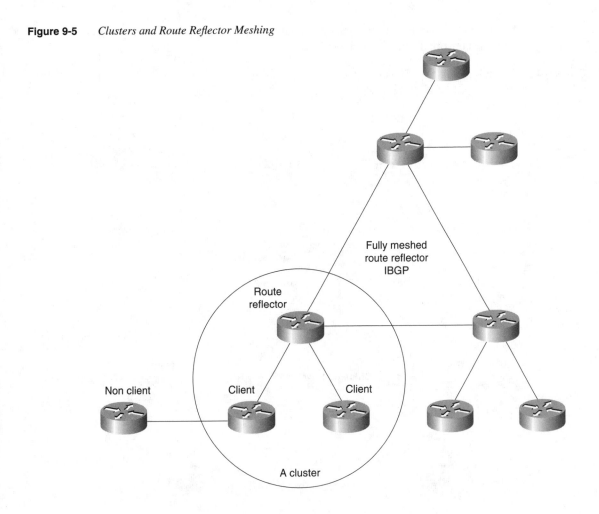

Table 9-2   *Explanation of the Route Reflector Configuration Command*

Syntax	Description
neighbor	Identifies that the rest of the command is directed at a BGP-4 peer.
ip address	Is the IP address of the neighboring router being identified as a client.
route-reflector-client	Points to the client of the route reflector. Note that the client is not configured and is unaware of its change of status. It does nothing but continue to send updates to the route reflector, which forwards them unchanged to other clients.

Example 9-1 illustrates the concepts explained in this section. Use this example in conjunction with the network displayed in Figure 9-6.

Figure 9-6 *Figure Supporting the Example 9-1*

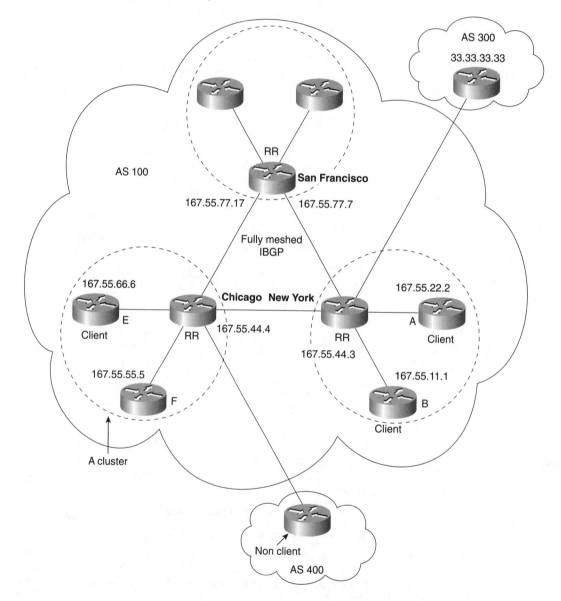

Example 9-1 *Configuration of a Route Reflector*

```
New York#
router bgp 100
! Create a connection to Router A, a client
neighbor 167.55.22.2 remote-as 100
!make Router A as seen in Figure 9-6 a route reflector client
neighbor 167.55.22.2 route-reflector-client
! connection to B
neighbor 167.55.11.1 remote-as 100
neighbor 167.55.11.1 route-reflector-client
! connection to San Francisco
neighbor 167.55.77.7 remote-as 100
! connection to Chicago
neighbor 167.55.44.4 remote-as 100
neighbor 33.33.33.33 remote-as 300
RTB#
router bgp 100
! connection to New York
neighbor 3.3.3.3 remote-as 100
Chicago#
router bgp 100
! connection to Router E
neighbor 167.55.66.6 remote-as 100
neighbor 167.55.66.6 route-reflector-client
! connection to Router F
neighbor 167.55.55.5 remote-as 100
neighbor 167.55.55.5 route-reflector-client
! connection to San Francisco
neighbor 167.55.77.7 remote-as 100
! connection to New York
neighbor 167.55.33.3 remote-as 100
```

After any BGP-4 configuration, it is necessary to reset the TCP session so that the changes can take effect. The command to do this is as follows:

```
clear ip bgp *
```

NOTE   This command is described in detail in Chapter 8, in the section "Managing and Verifying the BGP-4 Configuration."

It is also important to verify that everything is working. Example 9-2 demonstrates the command that verifies the configuration.

Example 9-2   *Example of the* **show ip bgp neighbors** *Command*

```
New York# show ip bgp neighbors 167.55.44.4
 BGP neighbor is 167.55.44.4,  remote AS 100, Internal link
 Index 1, Offset 0, Mask 0x2
  Inbound soft reconfiguration allowed
  BGP version 4, remote router ID 167.55.44.4
  BGP state = Established, table version = 27, up for 00:06:12
  Last read 00:00:12, hold time is 180, keepalive interval is 60 seconds
  Minimum time between advertisement runs is 30 seconds
  Received 19 messages, 0 notifications, 0 in queue
  Sent 17 messages, 0 notifications, 0 in queue
  Inbound path policy configured
  Route map for incoming advertisements is testing
  Connections established 2; dropped 1
 Connection state is ESTAB, I/O status: 1, unread input bytes: 0
 Local host: 167.55.44.3, Local port: 11002
 Foreign host: 167.55.44.4, Foreign port: 179

 Enqueued packets for retransmit: 0, input: 0, saved: 0
 Event Timers (current time is 0x530C294):
 Timer          Starts    Wakeups         Next
 Retrans          12        0             0x0
 TimeWait          0        0             0x0
 AckHold          12       10             0x0
 SendWnd           0        0             0x0
 KeepAlive         0        0             0x0
 GiveUp            0        0             0x0
 PmtuAger          0        0             0x0
 iss:  133981889  snduna:  133982166  sndnxt:  133982166    sndwnd:   16108
 irs: 3317025518  rcvnxt: 3317025810  rcvwnd:      16093  delrcvwnd:    291
 SRTT: 441 ms, RTTO: 2784 ms, RTV: 951 ms, KRTT: 0 ms
 minRTT: 0 ms, maxRTT: 300 ms, ACK hold: 300 ms
 Flags: higher precedence, nagle
 Datagrams (max data segment is 1460 bytes):
 Rcvd: 15 (out of order: 0), with data: 12, total data bytes: 291
 Sent: 23 (retransmit: 0), with data: 11, total data bytes: 276
```

Table 9-3 describes the fields shown in Example 9-2.

Table 9-3   *Explanation of the* **show ip bgp neighbors** *Command*

Field	Descriptions
BGP Neighbor	IP address and autonomous system of the BGP neighbor. If the autonomous system numbers are the same, then internal BGP-4 (IBGP-4) is running between the neighbors; otherwise, external BGP-4 (EBGP-4) is in use.
BGP Version	BGP version being used to communicate with the remote router. The neighbor's router ID (an IP address) is also specified.
BGP State	Internal state of this BGP connection.

Table 9-3   *Explanation of the* **show ip bgp neighbors** *Command (Continued)*

Field	Descriptions
Table Version	Indication that the neighbor has been updated with this version of the primary BGP routing table.
Up For	Amount of time that the underlying TCP connection has been in existence.
Last Read	Time that the BGP last read a message from this neighbor.
Holdtime	Maximum amount of time that can elapse between messages from the peer or neighbor.
Keepalive Interval	Time period between sending keepalive packets, which maintain the TCP connection.
Received	Number of total BGP messages received from this peer, including keepalives.
Sent	Total number of BGP messages that have been sent to this peer, including keepalives.
Notifications	Number of error messages that the router has sent to this peer.
Connections Established	Number of times that the router has established a TCP connection for BGP-4 between the two peers.
Dropped	Number of times that a valid TCP connection has failed or been taken down.
Connection State	State of BGP peer.
Unread Input Bytes	Number of bytes of packets still to be processed.
Local Host, Local Port	Peering address of local router, plus port.
Foreign Host, Foreign Port	Neighbor's peering address.
Event Timers	Table that displays the number of starts and wakeups for each timer.
Iss	Initial send sequence number.
Snduna	Last send sequence number that the local host sent but for which an acknowledgment is outstanding.
Sndnxt	Sequence number that the local host will send next.
Sndwnd	TCP window size of the remote host.
irs	Initial receive sequence number.
Rcvnxt	Last receive sequence number that the local host has acknowledged.
Rcvwnd	Local host's TCP window size.

continues

Table 9-3 *Explanation of the* **show ip bgp neighbors** *Command (Continued)*

Field	Descriptions
Delrecvwnd	Delayed receive window. Data that the local host has read from the connection but that has not yet been subtracted from the receive window that the host has advertised to the remote host. The value in this field gradually increases until it is larger than a full-sized packet, at which point it is applied to the rcvwnd field.
SRTT	A calculated smoothed round-trip timeout.
RTTO	Round-trip timeout.
RTV	Variance of the round-trip time.
KRTT	New round-trip timeout (using the Karn algorithm). This field separately tracks the round-trip time of packets that have been retransmitted.
minRTT	Smallest recorded round-trip timeout (hard-wire value used for calculation).
maxRTT	Largest recorded round-trip timeout.
ACK hold	Time that the local host will delay an acknowledgment to piggyback data on it.
Flags	IP precedence of the BGP packets.
Datagrams Rcvd	Number of update packets received from neighbor with data.
With Data Total Data Bytes	Total bytes of data.
Sent	Number of update packets sent.
With Data	Number of update packets with data sent.
Total data bytes	Total data bytes.

TIP   When implementing clusters and route reflectors, select the route reflector carefully in accordance with the physical topology of the network. Keep the design simple, placing one route reflector in a cluster. When the logical cluster design is in place, configure one cluster at a time and one route reflector at a time. After the route reflector in the cluster is configured, remove the BGP-4 configuration that has the BGP-4 sessions between the clients.

Controlling BGP-4 Traffic

BGP-4 updates can be controlled. It is often advantageous to limit the way that the BGP-4 routing updates are propagated, for the same reasons that any routing protocol is best limited to those updates that are required. This not only streamlines the traffic flow on the network, but it also simplifies the network and thus its maintenance. Designing how the routing information should be forwarded through the network forms a basic level of security and can reduce the possibility of routing loops.

Filtering is essentially traffic control. There are three main flavors of filtering on a Cisco router:

- **Access list**—This is used in BGP-4 for the creation of route maps, forming the "what if" logic of the route map. An access list is also used in BGP-4 to filter updates sent from a peer based on the autonomous system path. In addition, other technologies use access lists for standard filtering.

- **Prefix list/distribute list**—Distribute lists filter routing updates, particularly in redistribution. From Cisco IOS version 11.2, ISPs were given prefix lists, which are a more efficient form of filtering. Prefix lists filter based on the prefix of the address. This option was made a part of the general release IOS in version 12.0. Both prefix lists and distribute lists filter on network numbers, not autonomous system paths, for which access lists are used.

- **Route maps**—A route map is a sophisticated access list that defines criteria upon which a router acts when a match is found for the stated criteria. It is used in BGP-4 for setting the attributes that determine the basis for selecting the best path to a destination.

Prefix lists were introduced to BGP-4 because they are a very efficient form of filtering. Because they search on the prefix of the address as defined by the administrator, the lookup is very fast. This is particularly important in the potentially huge routing tables that can be generated in BGP-4 networks.

Another great advantage to prefix lists is the capability to edit them, particularly if they become large. Access lists cannot be dynamically edited unless they are ported to an application that allows them to be edited.

Ease of use is the main difference that the users experience. This is not only true with the editing features, but also with the improved interface, which affords greater flexibility.

How Prefix Lists Work

Before using a prefix list in a command, you must set up a prefix list. Each line in the prefix list is associated with a sequence number, similar to the number identifying a line of code in a computer program. The editing of the prefix list is achieved by referencing the line or sequence number. This is not available in access lists, which requires the rewriting of the entire list, unless you have the forethought to cut and paste the configuration file into a word processor. In planning the prefix list, it is advisable to assign sequence numbers to the entries in the prefix list in accordance with the rules by which prefix lists are processed.

How Prefix Lists Are Processed

Prefix lists work by matching the prefixes in the list to the prefixes of routes that are under scrutiny. The manner in which this is done is very similar to that of access lists. When there is a match, the route is used.

More specifically, whether a prefix is permitted or denied is based upon the following rules:

- If a route is permitted, the route is used.

- If a route is denied, the route is not used.

- If the prefix list is empty, all prefixes are permitted.

- At the bottom of every prefix list is an implicit **deny all**. Thus, if given prefix does not match any entries of a prefix list, it is denied.

- When multiple entries of a prefix list match a given prefix, the entry with the smallest sequence number is used.

- The router begins the search at the top of the prefix list, with the sequence number 1. When a match is made, the search stops. Processing time will be reduced if the most common matches or denies are near the top of the list. This will prevent having to process criteria that are seldom met every time a route is examined.

- Sequence numbers are generated by default. To configure the sequence numbers manually, use the **seq** *seq-value* argument of the **ip prefix-list** command.

- A sequence number does not need to be specified when removing a configuration entry.

How to Configure a BGP-4 Prefix List

Configuring a prefix list is very straightforward if attention is given to the processing rules.

Creating a Prefix List

The following command creates an entry in a prefix list and assigns a sequence number to the entry:

```
ip prefix-list list-name [seq seq-value ] {deny | permit}
network/len [ge ge-value] [le le-value]
```

To configure a router to use a prefix list as a filter in distributing routes, use the following command:

```
neighbor {ip address | peer-group} prefix-list prefix-list-name {in | out}
```

Prefix List Examples

An example of a simple prefix list follows:

```
ip prefix-list tryout permit 44.0.0.0/8
ip prefix-list tryout permit 130.0.0.0/8
```

The prefix list tryout will allow the networks 44.0.0.0 and the supernet 130.0.0.0 to pass.

Sometimes it is necessary to create a criteria range as opposed to an absolute. For example, you could change "all 2-year-old children are allowed into the playground," to "children between the ages of 2 and 4 allowed into the playground." This grants greater flexibility and thus accuracy to the searches. The way to do this in a prefix list is to use the **ge** and **le** parameters.

These optional keywords allow a range of the prefix length to be specified, as opposed to the *network/len*, which is the absolute. Therefore, 10.2.3.0/24 is an example of the *network/len*, which states the prefix to be matched and the length of the prefix. The equations are confusing until you sit and work them out. The following are some key points:

- **ge** is used if the prefix is greater than the value stated in the list.

- **le** is used if the prefix is less than the value stated in the list.

Simply put, the ge-value is the barrier for the lower limit, in that the number must be greater than the value stated in for the ge-value. Likewise, the le-value is the barrier for the upper limit, in that the number must be less than that stated in the le-value. So, children entering the playground must be older than 2 (ge-value of 2) and younger than 4 (le-value of 4). Therefore, the formula requires the following condition:

len < ge-value < or = le-value < or = 32

For example, to permit all prefixes between /8 and /24, you would use the following:

```
ip prefix-list tryone permit 0.0.0.0/0 ge 8 le 24
```

NOTE	An exact match is assumed when neither **ge** nor **le** is specified. The range is assumed to be from ge-value to 32 if only the **ge** attribute is specified, and from len to le-value if only the **le** attribute is specified.

Verifying the Prefix List Configuration

As always, it is important to check the configuration, especially if it involves the filtering of routes or routing updates. Table 9-4 lists the various **show** commands available for prefix lists.

To display information about a prefix list or prefix list entries, use the **show ip prefix-list** exec command:

```
show ip prefix-list [detail-summary] name [network/len] [seq seq-num]
[longer] [first-match]
```

Table 9-4 *Displaying Prefix Lists—Command Options*

Command	Description
show ip prefix-list [**detail** I **summary**]	Displays information about all prefix lists, including the hit count, which is the number of times that a match has been found for the criteria in the prefix list. This is very important in troubleshooting for capacity planning and security.
show ip prefix-list [**detail** I **summary**] *name*	Displays a table showing the entries in a prefix list identified by name.
show ip prefix-list *name* [*network/len*]	Displays the filtering associated with the node based on the absolute of the defined prefix.
show ip prefix-list *name* [**seq** *seq-num*]	Displays the prefix list entry with a given sequence number.
show ip prefix-list *name* [*network/len*] **longer**	Displays all entries of a prefix list that are more specific than the given network and length.
show ip prefix-list *name* [*network/len*] **first-match**	Displays the entry of a prefix list that matches the given prefix (network and length of prefix).

NOTE   The **show** commands always include the sequence numbers in their output.

Example 9-3 shows the output of the **show ip prefix-list** command with details about the prefix list tryout.

Example 9-3   *A Sample Output of the* **show IP prefix-list** *Command*

```
Router# show ip prefix-list detail tryout
ip prefix-list tryout:
Description: tryout-list
 count: 1, range entries: 0, sequences: 5 - 10, refcount: 3
 seq 5 permit 130.0.0.0/8 (hit count: 0, refcount: 1)
 seq 10 permit 44.0.0.0/8 (hit count: 0, refcount: 1)
```

Redundant Connections into the Internet—Multihoming

An enormous amount of traffic leaves an organization in search of the Internet. This is not only the use of e-mail as a means of communication, but also people doing research on the Internet tidal wave. The majority of it is valid work, not the ritualistic homage to music sites and radio shows.

As the use of the Internet expands as both an individual tool and a major mechanism of finance and commerce, it becomes increasingly necessary for the network administrator to provide constant access to the Internet, with load balancing and redundancy.

Multiple Connections into the Internet

To have more than one connection into the Internet is to be multihomed. The reason for complicating the network is clear: The need for Internet access nowadays is too great for the responsibility to fall onto the shoulders of one link. Multiple links not only provide redundancy, but they also allow for load balancing and thus present an improvement in performance.

The following are some concerns about connecting to more than one ISP:

- The providers may not each be propagating the same routes into or from the Internet. If the providers are sending subsets of the required routes, there could be a major problem with connectivity if the link to one of the providers fails.

- It is possible that if you are connected to two different providers, your autonomous system could become a transit autonomous system between the ISPs. This could happen if a router in the autonomous system of one provider sees a path to a destination via the other provider's autonomous system, and your autonomous system gives the best route to the autonomous system of the other provider.

Configuration at the ISP level is the solution to these concerns and is dealt with when setting up the service. Therefore, it is important that the need for multihoming is raised during the negotiations so that the Internet service provider is aware of the need for the additional configuration.

Receiving Routing Information from the Internet

When connecting into something as vast as the Internet, some planning and forethought is necessary. In particular, it is essential to decide what updates are to be sent to the outside world and how routers within the autonomous system are to know about the outside world and all that it offers.

There are three main approaches to the selection of routes from the Internet:

- Accept only default routes from all providers
- Accept partial routes as well as default routes from all providers
- Accept full routing updates from all providers

The decision process is clear: It is a balance of network resources against information.

Table 9-5 summarizes the different approaches to obtaining routing information from the Internet.

Table 9-5 *Receiving Routing Updates from Multiple ISPs*

Which Routes Are Accepted from the Internet	Memory	CPU	IGP Chooses Best Metric to Default Network?	BGP-4 Attribute Selects Best Path to External Network?	Can Exit Path be Tuned via BGP-4 Attributes?	AS Sends All Its Routes to ISPs?	ISP Chooses Entry Path to AS?
Default routes only from all ISPs	Low	Low	Yes	Go to nearest gateway that is advertising the route	No	Yes	Yes
Select routes and default routes from ISPs	Medium	Medium	Yes	Yes; normally the AS_Path is the attribute that selects the exit path into the Internet	Yes	Yes	Yes
Full routing tables from ISPs	High	High	Yes	Yes; normally the AS_Path is the attribute that selects the exit path into the Internet	Yes	Yes	Yes

Figure 9-7 illustrates the various options available in exchanging routing information with the Internet.

NOTE   The second solution of accepting partial routes from the ISP requires the filtering of the updates sent to the autonomous system, either by your autonomous system or by the ISP. If the responsibility falls to your organization, you will need to study the use of route maps and regular expressions. This is complex subject, which is explained in detail on CCO. As of press time for this book, the best information on this subject could be found at http://www.cisco.com/warp/public/459/27.html.

Figure 9-7   *Exchanging Routing Information with the Internet*

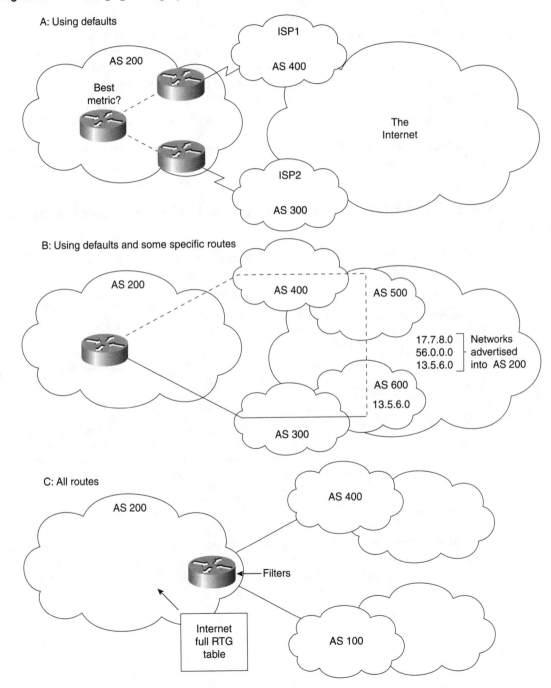

A: Using defaults

B: Using defaults and some specific routes

C: All routes

Determining the BGP-4 Path by Tuning the Attributes

So far, the chapter has covered the strength of BGP-4 as a protocol that allows the determination of the route that traffic takes through the network. This has been accompanied by an explanation of way that BGP-4 selects one path above the other. You have seen the advantages of connecting to more than one ISP and how path selection is achieved in this situation. All of this is important, but you have yet to learn how to configure BGP-4 to take a path to a destination based on different criteria.

This section covers how to manipulate the traffic flow through your network using BGP-4.

The attributes discussed in this section are local preference and weight, with the latter being a Cisco-proprietary solution.

Commands to Tune BGP-4—Using the Local Preference and Weight Attributes

To configure the weight attribute, use the following command:

```
neighbor {ip-address | peer-group-name} weight weight
```

Table 9-6 explains the meaning of the preceding syntax.

Table 9-6 *An Explanation of the Command to Configure the Weight Attribute*

Syntax	Description
neighbor	This identifies that the rest of the command is directed at a BGP-4 peer.
ip address	This is the IP address of the neighboring router.
peer-group-name	This identifies the BGP-4 peer group, if there is one.
weight *weight*	This is proprietary to Cisco and is used in route selection. It is local to the router and, because it is not propagated to other routers, there is no problem with compatibility. When there are multiple paths, it selects a path to a destination with different next hops to the same destination. This identifies the weight attribute, and a value is placed immediately afterward. The default is 32768, although the range extends from 0 to 65535.

The weight attribute selects the exit path out of the router when there are multiple paths to the same destination. The higher the weight value, the better the path. Figure 9-8 illustrates this, and Example 9-4 shows how the path through San Francisco is chosen.

Figure 9-8   *The Weight Attribute and Selecting a Path*

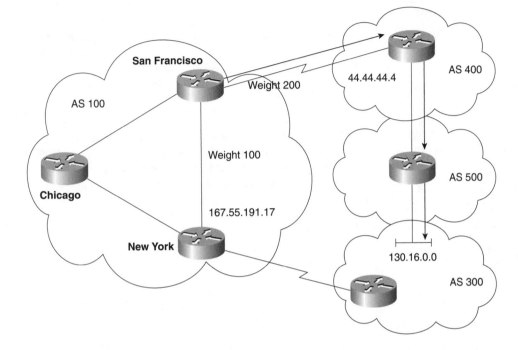

Example 9-4   *A Sample Configuration to Illustrate How to Tune the Weight Attribute*

```
SanFrancisco#
router bgp 100
neighbor 44.44.44.44 remote-as 400
neighbor 44.44.44.44 weight 200
! route to 130.16.0.0 from San Francisco will have 200 weight
neighbor 167.55.191.17 remote-as 100
neighbor 167.55.191.17 weight 100
! route to 130.16.0.0 from NewYork will have 100 weight
```

The local preference is equally easy to configure, and the syntax is as follows:

bgp default local-preference *value*

Table 9-7 explains the various parts of this command.

Table 9-7   *Configuring the Local Preference Attribute*

Syntax	Description
bgp default local-preference	This attribute is used to tell routers within the autonomous system how to exit the autonomous system in the case of multiple paths. It is the opposite of the MED attribute.
value	Local preference has a range from 0 to 4,294,967,295 (just over 4 billion).

Example 9-5 is based on Figure 9-9. The local preference set in the San Francisco router to 200 is propagated in the updates to all its peers. Likewise, the local preference of 140 set in the New York router is propagated to its peers. When Chicago has to decide on a path to the network 130.16.0.0, the local preference attribute dictates the New York router as the exit point from the autonomous system.

Figure 9-9   *Using Local Preference to Select a Path*

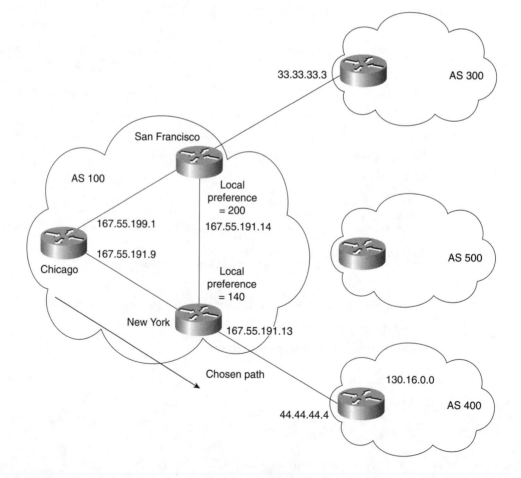

Example 9-5 *A Sample Configuration to Illustrate How to Tune the Local Preference Attribute*

```
SanFrancisco#
router bgp 100
neighbor 33.33.33.33 remote-as 300
neighbor 167.55.191.1 remote-as 100
bgp default local-preference 150

NewYork#
router bgp 100
neighbor 44.44.44.44 remote-as 400
neighbor 167.55.191.9 remote-as 100
bgp default local-preference 200

SanFrancisco#
router bgp 100
neighbor 44.44.44.44 remote-as 400
neighbor 44.44.44.44 weight 200
! route to 130.16.0.0 from SanFrancisco will have 200 weight
neighbor 167.55.191.17 remote-as 100
neighbor 167.55.191.17 weight 140
!route to 130.16.0.0 from NewYork will have 140 weight
```

These configurations are reflected in the **show** commands in Example 9-6.

Verifying the Configuration of Attributes

It is always important to be able to check your work, particularly when that work defines an entire organization's method of connecting into the Internet.

The **show ip bgp** command shows all the values of all the attributes and their status. Therefore, this is a good command to verify any configurations that change attributes to tune the system and effectively manage the traffic flow to and from the autonomous system.

Examples 9-6 through 9-8 show sample output from the **show ip bgp** command.

Example 9-6 is before the configuration in Example 9-5 has been run on the San Francisco router. The next hop is to 44.44.44.4, which is in autonomous system 100 because the traffic would be routed via New York.

Example 9-6 *The **show ip bgp** Command Example #1*

```
SanFrancisco#-gw#show ip bgp
BGP table version is 570031, local router ID is 167.55.191.14
Status codes: s suppressed, d damped, h history, * valid, > best, i - internal

Origin codes: i - IGP, e - EGP, ? - incomplete
```

continues

Example 9-6   *The* **show ip bgp** *Command Example #1 (Continued)*

```
      Network               Next Hop         Metric LocPrf Weight Path
 *> 9.2.0.0/16         44.44.44.4              0 100 i
 *> 15.4.126.0/24      44.44.44.4              0 100 i
 *> 15.96.91.0/24      44.44.44.4              0 100 i
 *> 130.16.2.0/23      44.44.44.4              0 100 i
 *> 130.16.7.0/24      44.44.44.4              0 100 i
 *> 130.16.8.0/24      44.44.44.4              0 100 i
 *> 130.16.14.0/24     44.44.44.4              0 100 i
 *> 130.16.123.0/24    44.44.44.4              0 100 i
 *> 130.16.124.0/23    44.44.44.4              0 100 i
 *> 130.16.176.0/20    44.44.44.4              0 100 i
 *> 130.16.32.0/23     44.44.44.4              0 100 i
 *> 130.16.35.0/24     44.44.44.4              0 100 i
 *> 130.16.36.0/23     44.44.44.4              0 100 i
 *> 130.16.0.0/18      44.44.44.4              0 100 i
 *> 130.16.24.0/21     44.44.44.4              0 100 i
 *> 130.16.0.0/18      44.44.44.4              0 100 i
 *> 130.16.0.0/24      44.44.44.4              0 100 i
 *> 130.16.0.0/19      44.44.44.4              0 100 i
```

Example 9-7 is after the configuration for New York has been run; the local preference is 200, and the weight is 140.

Example 9-7   *The* **show ip bgp** *Command Example #2*

```
NewYork#-gw#show ip bgp
BGP table version is 570035, local router ID is 167.55.191.13
Status codes: s suppressed, d damped, h history, * valid, > best, i - internal
Origin codes: i - IGP, e - EGP, ? - incomplete

      Network               Next Hop         Metric LocPrf Weight Path
 *> 31.2.0.0/16        44.44.44.4   200     140 400 i
 *> 55.4.126.0/24      44.44.44.4   200     140 400 i
 *> 55.96.91.0/24      44.44.44.4   200     140 400 i
 *> 130.16.2.0/23      44.44.44.4   200     140 400 i
 *> 130.16.7.0/24      44.44.44.4   200     140 400 i
 *> 130.16.8.0/24      44.44.44.4   200     140 400 i
 *> 130.16.14.0/24     44.44.44.4   200     140 400 i
 *> 130.16.123.0/24    44.44.44.4   200     140 400 i
 *> 130.16.124.0/23    44.44.44.4   200     140 400 i
 *> 130.16.176.0/20    44.44.44.4   200     140 400 i
 *> 130.16.32.0/23     44.44.44.4   200     140 400 i
 *> 130.16.35.0/24     44.44.44.4   200     140 400 i
 *> 130.16.36.0/23     44.44.44.4   200     140 400 i
 *> 130.16.0.0/18      44.44.44.4   200     140 400 i
 *> 130.16.24.0/21     44.44.44.4   200     140 400 i
 *> 130.16.0.0/18      44.44.44.4   200     140 400 i
 *> 130.16.0.0/24      44.44.44.4   200     140 400 i
 *> 130.16.0.0/19      44.44.44.4   200     140 400 i
```

Example 9-8 is after the San Francisco router has been configured; it is possible to see a change in the neighbor table. The local preference and weight have been altered.

Example 9-8 *The* **show ip bgp** *Command Example #3*

```
SanFrancisco#-gw#show ip bgp
BGP table version is 570139, local router ID is 199.172.136.21
Status codes: s suppressed, d damped, h history, * valid, > best, i - internal
Origin codes: i - IGP, e - EGP, ? - incomplete

     Network          Next Hop         Metric LocPrf Weight Path
*>  15.2.0.0/16       44.44.44.4    150    200 100 i
*>  31.4.126.0/24     44.44.44.4    150    200 100 i
*>  55.96.91.0/24     44.44.44.4    150    200 100 i
*>  130.16.2.0/23     44.44.44.4    150    200 100 i
*>  130.16.7.0/24     44.44.44.4    150    200 100 i
*>  130.16.8.0/24     44.44.44.4    150    200 100 i
*>  130.16.14.0/24    44.44.44.4    150    200 100 i
*>  130.16.123.0/24   44.44.44.4    150    200 100 i
*>  130.16.176.0/20   44.44.44.4    150    200 100 i
*>  130.16.32.0/23    44.44.44.4    150    200 100 i
*>  130.16.35.0/24    44.44.44.4    150    200 100 i
*>  130.16.36.0/23    44.44.44.4    150    200 100 i
*>  130.16.0.0/18     44.44.44.4    150    200 100 i
*>  130.16.24.0/21    44.44.44.4    150    200 100 i
*>  130.16.0.0/18     44.44.44.4    150    200 100 i
*>  130.16.0.0/24     44.44.44.4    150    200 100 i
*>  130.16.0.0/19     44.44.44.4    150    200 100 i
```

Table 9-8 describes significant fields shown in Examples 9-6 through 9-8.

Table 9-8 *Explanation of Output from the* **show ip bgp** *Command*

Field	Description
BGP Table Version	Internal version number of the table. This number is incremented whenever the table changes.
Local Router ID	The highest IP address of the router
Status Codes	Status of the table entry. The status is displayed at the beginning of each line in the table. It can be one of the following values: **s**—The table entry is suppressed. *****—The table entry is valid. **>**—The table entry is the best entry to use for that network. **i**—The table entry was learned via an internal BGP session.

continues

Table 9-8   *Explanation of Output from the* **show ip bgp** *Command (Continued)*

Field	Description
Origin	The origin of the entry. The origin code is placed at the end of each line in the table. It can be one of the following values: **i**—Entry originated from IGP and was advertised with a network router configuration command. **e**—Entry originated from EGP. **?**—Origin of the path is not clear. Usually, this is a router that is redistributed into BGP from an IGP.
Network	A destination IP address of a network.
Next Hop	IP address of the next logical device in the path to the destination. The forwarded packets are sent to this address. An entry of 0.0.0.0 indicates that the router has some non-BGP routes to this network.
Metric	If shown, this is the value of the metric between autonomous systems. This field is frequently not used.
LocPrf	Local preference values as set on the routers with interfaces to other autonomous systems. It defines how preferable that router is as a transit point out of the autonomous system. The default value is 100.
Weight	Weight of the route, determining which path the router will choose. It is proprietary to Cisco and is an attribute local to the router.
Path	Autonomous system paths to the destination network. There can be one entry in this field for each autonomous system in the path.

NOTE   These configurations are extremely simple. Although they work very well, it would be wise for you to understand route maps. Route maps are more complex but more efficient, and they offer greater flexibility with their greater level of sophistication.

Redistribution Between the IGP and BGP-4

Up until now, the discussion has been about BGP-4, its operation, and the configuration options available. However, for most, BGP-4 is the means by which information about the Internet is brought into the internal organizational routing domain. Disseminating this information throughout the autonomous system is the subject of this next section.

If the organization is not an ISP, there is a fair chance that the network is running an IGP within the autonomous system. The IP routing table generated by this protocol or protocols is distinct from the BGP-4 routing table, although as you have seen, they communicate freely. The use of synchronization is a case in point. However, populating these tables with routes from the other table needs to be manually configured.

Obviously, routes can be injected from the IGP into BGP-4, or from the BGP-4 into the IGP.

Advertising Routes from an IGP into BGP-4

First, consider the advertising routes into BGP-4. There are three ways of populating the BGP-4 table with IGP routes:

- **Using the network command**—This is used to advertise routes that are in the IP routing table.

- **Redistributing static routes**—These are routes that have been summarized to a supernet, such as a Class C address with a prefix mask of 16 bits. This requires statically routing to null 0. This fools the system by creating a route that has no exit point from the router because the route does not exist. The command places the route into the routing table without fear of it being used and creating a black hole. This is because lookups are based on the longest match, and the outgoing interface is null 0, which is nowhere.

    The problem is that if the route in the IGP routing table disappears, BGP-4 still advertises the route, causing traffic to journey into the autonomous system only to die. Therefore, Cisco suggests that you use the **aggregate-address** command for BGP-4 instead.

- **Redistributing dynamically learned routes from the IGP**—This configuration is not advised because there is a great reliance on the IGP table. It is imperative that external routes carried in IBGP-4 are filtered out; otherwise, routing loops are generated when BGP-4 routes are fed into IGP, only to be advertised back into BGP-4 further down the network.

Advertising Routes from a BGP-4 into an IGP

Redistributing the routes from the Internet into a small network is bizarre. What makes it so alarming is how large the Internet is and how enormous the routing tables are, even with the large amount of aggregation and filtering. There is still a lot of information to carry over.

Do ISPs Need to Redistribute Paths from BGP-4 into the IGP?

Because ISPs tend to run EBGP-4 and IBGP-4 extensively, they tend to run these exclusively for exterior routes, using an IGP only for internal routes. This requires no redistribution, which is easier for the routers and means the following:

- Redistribution is not necessary, and the resources are spared.

- The IGP routing table is spared.

- BGP-4 can converge faster because it does not have to wait for a hello.

The **synchronization** command does not apply in this type of network because IBGP-4 is running in a fully meshed environment. With either a fully meshed network or carefully designed route reflectors, the synchronization rule can be turned off.

Redistribution from BGP-4 into an IGP in an Organizational Network

If IBGP-4 is not fully meshed and the autonomous system is multihomed, then redistribution from BGP-4 into the IGP is needed. The IGP needs to carry the external routes across the autonomous system to the other BGP-4 router. Also, any device wanting to connect to the Internet needs to have either a default route or specific routes to direct traffic forward. Filtering must be configured; otherwise, the internal routing tables will become overwhelmed. This is illustrated in the Figure 9-10.

Figure 9-10   *Redistributing BGP-4 Routes into a Non-ISP Organization*

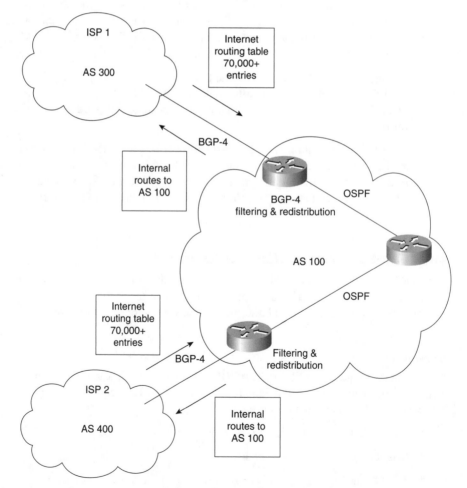

Conclusion

This chapter dealt with an advanced configuration of BGP-4. Building on the foundation of the previous chapter, it showed the complexity of the design of large networks. This chapter dealt with the need to scale the BGP-4 network and considered the need to filter and determine paths to be taken to specific destination networks.

More than any other routing protocol, BGP-4 allows the configuration of human decisions. Although it is called policy routing and path manipulation, it allows for more than the selection of a path based on network requirements; instead, it allows the intrusion of political and economic factors to be programmed into the network.

The design and configuration solutions are vast. This chapter has merely introduced some of the possible solutions and has pointed out the danger areas to avoid. For a true implementation on a live network, it cannot be stressed enough how important the analysis and design of the network is for an effective solution.

Foundation Summary

The "Foundation Summary" is a collection of quick reference information that provides a convenient review of many key concepts in this chapter. For those of you who already feel comfortable with the topics in this chapter, this summary will help you recall a few details. For those of you who just read this chapter, this review should help solidify some key facts. For any of you doing your final preparations before the exam, these tables and figures will be a convenient way to review the day before the exam.

Table 9-9   *Summary of Commands Used in this Chapter*

Command	Description
neighbor *ip-address* **route-reflector-client**	Configures the route reflector to view a specified neighbor as a client. It reflects all routes received from this router to other clients.
no neighbor *ip-address* **route-reflector-client**	Removes a neighbor as a client.
show ip bgp neighbors	Gives details about a specified neighbor.
ip prefix-list *list-name* [**seq** *seq-value*] **deny** | **permit** *network/len* [**ge** *ge-value*] [**le** *le-value*]	Creates a prefix list that is used to filter routes from updates based on the prefix length of the route.
neighbor *ip address* | *peer-group-name* **prefix-list** *prefix-list-name* **in** | **out**	Configures a router to use a prefix list as a filter in distributing routes.
show ip prefix-list detail *name*	Shows a prefix list by name. It shows what the list is filtering on and how many matches to the criteria have seen logged. This is known as the number of hits.
neighbor {*ip-address* | *peer-group-name*} **weight** *weight*	Sets the weight attribute to influence BGP-4 path selection. Weight is a Cisco-proprietary attribute. It is a local attribute, which is not propagated to other routers. It selects the best path if there are multiple exits from the router into the Internet.
bgp default local-preference *value*	Sets the local preference attribute. Again, this is used to influence the router's selection of the best path based on its selection process. This attribute is passed on the routing updates to other routers in the Internet.
show ip bgp	Shows a lot of details about the BGP-4 configuration on your network.

Route Reflectors

The benefits of route reflectors include the following:

- The capability to scale the network, given the other characteristics

- A strong hierarchical design

- A reduction of traffic on the network

- A reduction in the memory and CPU to maintain TCP sessions

- Faster convergence because synchronization is not needed

- Faster convergence and a simpler network because two routing protocols are implemented:

    — IBGP-4 for external routing information traversing the autonomous system

    — IGP for routes internal to the autonomous system

Characteristics of route reflectors are as follows:

- A route reflector is a router that forwards updates to its clients. When a client sends an update to the route reflector, it is forwarded or reflected to the other clients.

- The route reflector is the only router that is configured or that has the remotest idea that it is anything other than a peer.

- A client is a router that receives updates from a route reflector.

- Both a route reflector and a client, therefore, form a unit that shares information. This unit is called a cluster.

- The autonomous system is divided into clusters and is configured. There must be at least one route reflector per cluster; otherwise, the clients will not get the updates reflected to them.

- The route reflector and the client no longer require a full peer relationship because the route reflector forwards updates from other clients.

- In all probability, a route reflector is connected to peers for whom it is not forwarding routes. These are regular neighbors or peers but, from the route reflector's view, they are nonclients.

- Nonclients must be fully meshed with the route reflector.

- The route reflector connects to other route reflectors. These route reflectors need to be fully meshed because the old rule of not propagating routes that are not defined in the network command is now operational. This is to ensure that the IBGP-4 routing tables are complete.

- When the route reflector forwards an update, the Originator-ID attribute is set. This is the BGP-4 router ID of the router that originated the path. The purpose of this attribute is not to award honors to the originating router, but so that, if this router receives the update, it will see its own ID and will ignore the packet. This prevents the possibility of routing loops.

- If there are multiple route reflectors in the cluster, to provide redundancy, then the originating router is identified by the Cluster-ID attribute. This serves the same purpose as the Originator-ID in preventing routing loops.

The rules by which route reflectors propagate updates are as follows:

- If a route reflector receives multiple paths to the same destination, it chooses the best path.

- If the route is received from a client, then the route reflector reflects/forwards the update to clients and nonclients, except for the originator of the route.

- If the route is received from a nonclient, then the route reflector reflects the update only to clients.

- If the route is received from EBGP-4, then the route reflector reflects it to all nonclients as well as clients.

Prefix Lists

Whether a prefix is permitted or denied is based upon the following rules:

- If a route is permitted, the route is used.

- If a route is denied, the route is not used.

- If the prefix list is empty, all prefixes are permitted.

- At the bottom of every prefix list is an implicit **deny all**. Thus, if given prefix does not match any entries of a prefix list, it is denied.

- When multiple entries of a prefix list match a given prefix, the entry with the smallest sequence number is used.

- The router begins the search at the top of the prefix list, with the sequence number 1. When a match is made, the search stops. Processing time will be reduced if the most common matches or denies are near the top of the list. This will prevent having to process criteria that are seldom met every time a route is examined.

- Sequence numbers are generated by default. To configure the sequence numbers manually, use the **seq** *seq-value* argument of the **ip prefix-list** command.

- A sequence number does not need to be specified when removing a configuration entry.

Table 9-10   *Displaying Prefix Lists—Command Options*

Command	Description
**show ip prefix-list [detail	summary]**	Displays information about all prefix lists, including the hit count, which is the number of times that a match has been found for the criteria in the prefix list. This is very important in troubleshooting for capacity planning and security.
**show ip prefix-list [detail	summary]** *name*	Displays a table showing the entries in a prefix list identified by name.
show ip prefix-list *name* [*network/len*]	Displays the filtering associated with the node based on the absolute of the defined prefix.
show ip prefix-list *name* [**seq** *seq-num*]	Displays the prefix list entry with a given sequence number.
show ip prefix-list *name* [*network/len*] **longer**	Displays all entries of a prefix list that are more specific than the given network and length.
show ip prefix-list *name* [*network/len*] **first-match**	Displays the entry of a prefix list that matches the given prefix (network and length of prefix).

NOTE   The **show** commands always include the sequence numbers in their output.

Routing Updates from Multihomed Connections to the Internet

Table 9-11 summarizes the different approaches to obtaining routing information from the Internet.

Table 9-11   *Receiving Routing Updates from Multiple ISPs*

Which Routes Are Accepted from the Internet	Memory	CPU	IGP Chooses Best Metric to Default Network?	BGP-4 Attribute Selects Best Path to External Network?	Can Exit Path be Tuned via BGP-4 Attributes?	AS Sends All Its Routes to ISPs?	ISP Chooses Entry Path to AS?
Default routes only from all ISPs	Low	Low	Yes	Go to nearest gateway that is advertising the route	No	Yes	Yes

continues

Table 9-11   *Receiving Routing Updates from Multiple ISPs (Continued)*

Which Routes Are Accepted from the Internet	Memory	CPU	IGP Chooses Best Metric to Default Network?	BGP-4 Attribute Selects Best Path to External Network?	Can Exit Path be Tuned via BGP-4 Attributes?	AS Sends All Its Routes to ISPs?	ISP Chooses Entry Path to AS?
Select routes and default routes from ISPs	Medium	Medium	Yes	Yes; normally the AS_Path is the attribute that selects the exit path into the Internet	Yes	Yes	Yes
Full routing tables from ISPs	High	High	Yes	Yes; normally the AS_Path is the attribute that selects the exit path into the Internet	Yes	Yes	Yes

BGP-4 show Commands

Example 9-9 shows a list of all the **show** commands available to the BGP-4 administrator.

Example 9-9   *BGP-4 show Command Options*

```
FARADAY-gw#show ip bgp ?
  A.B.C.D          Network in the BGP routing table to display
  cidr-only        Display only routes with non-natural netmasks
  community        Display routes matching the communities
  community-list   Display routes matching the community-list
  dampened-paths   Display paths suppressed due to dampening
  filter-list      Display routes conforming to the filter-list
  flap-statistics  Display flap statistics of routes
  inconsistent-as  Display only routes with inconsistent origin ASs
  neighbors        Detailed information on TCP and BGP neighbor connections
  paths            Path information
  peer-group       Display information on peer-groups
  regexp           Display routes matching the AS path regular expression
  summary          Summary of BGP neighbor status
  <cr>
```

Chapter Glossary

This glossary provides an official Cisco definition for key words and terms introduced in this chapter. I have supplied my own definition for terms that the Cisco glossary does not contain. The words listed here are identified in the text by italics. A complete glossary, including all of the chapter terms and additional terms, can be found in Appendix C, "Glossary."

cluster-ID—The cluster-ID is another attribute used in configuring route reflectors. If the cluster has more than one route reflector, the cluster-ID is to recognize updates from other route reflectors within the cluster.

originator-ID—This is a BGP-4 attribute. It is an optional nontransitive attribute that is created by the route reflector. The attribute contains the router ID of the router that originated the route in the update. The purpose of this attribute is to prevent a routing loop. If the originating router receives its own update, it ignores it.

prefix list—These replace distribute lists for BGP-4. The prefix list is used to control how BGP-4 learns or advertises updates.

route reflector—This is the router that is configured to forward routes from other identified IBGP-4 clients. This removes the necessity for a fully meshed IBGP-4 network, which preserves network resources.

route reflector client—A client is a router that has a TCP session with its IBGP-4 peer. It forwards routes to the route reflector, which propagates these on to other routers. The client does not have peer connections with other clients.

route reflector cluster—A cluster is the group of route reflector and clients. There can be more than one route reflector in a cluster.

synchronization rule—This rule states that a router cannot forward a route to an EBGP-4 peer unless the route is in the IP routing table. This requires that the IGP and BGP-4 routing table are synchronized. This is to prevent BGP-4 from advertising routes that the autonomous system cannot direct to the destination.

Q&A

The following questions test your understanding of the topics covered in this chapter. The final questions in this section repeat the opening "Do I Know This already?" questions. These are repeated to enable you to test your progress. After you have answered the questions, find the answers in Appendix A. If you get an answer wrong, review the answer and ensure that you understand the reason for your mistake. If you are confused by the answer, refer to the appropriate text in the chapter to review the concepts.

1 If a route reflector hears an update from a nonclient, what action will be taken?

2 In version 11.0 of the Cisco IOS, what method would be used to restrict routing information from being received or propagated?

3 Explain the purpose and use of the command **show ip prefix-list** *name* [**seq** *seq-number*].

4 How and why would you redistribute static routes into BGP-4?

5 Give the command that would change the weight attribute for the path to the next hop 192.16.5.3.

6 Why do route reflectors have to be fully meshed with IBGP-4?

_____

_____

_____

7 Why is filtering often required when redistributing BGP-4 into an IGP?

_____

_____

_____

8 What are the advantages of multihoming?

_____

_____

_____

9 What are the two most common forms of multihoming?

_____

_____

_____

10 Which command will show the local preference and weight attribute values?

_____

_____

_____

11 Why does IBGP-4 need to be fully meshed?

_____

_____

_____

12 How is a fully meshed network avoided in IBGP-4?

_____

_____

_____

13 What is the formula to determine the number of sessions that are needed in a fully meshed BGP-4 network?

_____

_____

_____

14 Why does a fully meshed network in IBGP-4 cause problems?

_____

_____

_____

15 State two benefits to using route reflectors.

_____

_____

_____

16 Can the next-hop-self option be used between EBGP-4 peers?

_____

_____

_____

17 Explain the difference between a cluster-ID and an originator-ID.

_____

_____

_____

18 State two advantages in using prefix lists over access lists.

_____

_____

_____

19 If the ISP has provided a default route, how will the router within the autonomous system select the exit path in a multihomed environment?

_____

_____

_____

20 What is a disadvantage of an autonomous system receiving full routing updates from all providers?

_____

_____

_____

21 What is the danger of redistributing BGP-4 into the IGP?

_____

_____

_____

22 What are the advantages of a fully meshed IBGP-4 network?

_____

_____

_____

23 In configuring a route reflector, how is the client configured?

_____

_____

_____

24 What command is used to display the route reflector clients?

_____

_____

_____

25 What commands are used to display the BGP-4 router ID that identifies the router that is sending the updates and peering with its neighbor?

_____

_____

_____

26 Which command is used to display the AS_Path?

_____

_____

_____

Scenarios

The following scenarios and questions are designed to draw together the content of the chapter and to exercise your understanding of the concepts. There is not necessarily a right answer. The thought process and practice in manipulating the concepts are the goals of this section. The answers to the scenario questions are found at the end of this chapter.

Scenario 9-1

The company Humugos has successfully implemented IBGP-4 in each country, with EBGP connecting the autonomous systems. The company now wants to change the way it connects to the Internet. Currently, it has one connection into the Internet per autonomous system. Figure 9-11 provides the diagram for the network in this scenario.

Figure 9-11 *Diagram for Scenario 9-1*

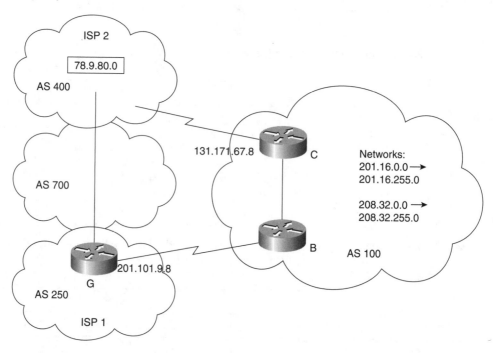

1 Give reasons to support Humugos's desire to have multiple connections to the Internet.

2 The company has been advised to redistribute static routes into the Internet BGP-4. It had intended to redistribute dynamic OSPF routes directly into the ISP provider. Explain why the ISP was not in favor of this configuration.

3 Using Figure 9-11, give the configuration commands that would redistribute the static routes, configured to supernets with an /16 prefix.

4 Using Figure 9-11, issue the configuration commands that would allow Router B connecting into the Internet to select the path to network 78.9.80.0 via Router G. Use the local preference attribute to select the path.

NOTE   This network scenario is oversimplified for learning purposes. Normally, it would be very difficult to obtain multiple autonomous system numbers from the Internet. Therefore, private autonomous system numbers would have to be used. That would make connections into the Internet complex.

Scenario 9-2

The ISP, Interconnect Corp., is a startup company that is configuring its network. The company has a well-resourced network and is in the process of configuring the IBGP within the autonomous system. Figure 9-12 provides the diagram for the network in this scenario.

Figure 9-12   *Diagram for Scenario 9-2*

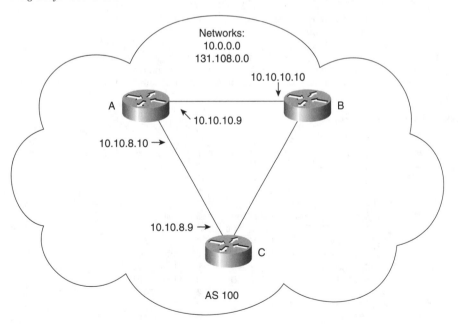

1   The original design required a fully meshed IBGP-4 network. This was calculated to mean 250 connections, which was deemed unacceptable because it would be too great of a drain on resources. Route reflectors are obviously the answer. Configure Router A to run BGP and as a route reflector to clients B and C.

2   Configure routers B and C to run BGP as clients to Router A.

3   Having configured the cluster, are any other tasks necessary?

4   The company has decided in its early stages to require organizations connecting into it to use default routes. How would these routes be disseminated without the organization's autonomous system, and how would an interior router running only an IGP determine which path out of the routing domain to take if it had more than one connection?

5   Given that the use of a default route by the client organization gives it the least configuration power to manage and manipulate its traffic flow, how would the network administrator justify this simple approach?

Scenario 9-3

Review output screens in Examples 9-10 and 9-11, and answer the questions that follow.

Example 9-10 *Scenario 9-3 Screen 1*

```
Router# show ip prefix-list detail tryout
ip prefix-list tryout:
Description: tryout-list
 count: 1, range entries: 0, sequences: 5 - 10, refcount: 3
 seq 5 permit 130.0.0.0/8 (hit count: 0, refcount: 1)
 seq 10 permit 44.0.0.0/8 (hit count: 28, refcount: 1)
```

Example 9-11 *Scenario 9-3 Screen 2*

```
FARADAY-gw# show ip bgp
BGP table version is 457017, local router ID is 200.172.136.21
Status codes: s suppressed, d damped, h history, * valid, > best, i - internal
Origin codes: i - IGP, e - EGP, ? - incomplete

    Network          Next Hop        Metric   LocPrf Weight Path
*> 7.2.0.0/16        144.39.228.49      0       100   701 i
*         144.39.128.7       0      100   99 17i
*> 17.4.126.0/24     144.39.228.49      0       100   701 i
*> 17.96.91.0/24     144.39.228.49      0       100   701 i
*> 33.48.2.0/23      144.39.228.49      0       100   701 i
*> 33.48.7.0/24      144.39.228.49      0       100   701 i
*> 33.48.8.0/24      144.39.228.49      0      100   701 i
*> 33.48.14.0/24     144.39.228.49      0       100   701 i
*> 33.48.123.0/24    144.39.228.49      0      100   701 i
```

Example 9-11 *Scenario 9-3 Screen 2 (Continued)*

```
*> 33.48.124.0/23    144.39.228.49     0   200   701 I
*         144.39.128.7  0  100      99 17 i
*> 33.48.176.0/20    144.39.228.49     0   100   701 i
*> 33.49.32.0/23     144.39.228.49     0   100   701 i
*> 33.49.35.0/24     144.39.228.49     0   100   701 i
*> 33.49.36.0/23     144.39.228.49     0   100   701 i
*> 33.96.0.0/18      144.39.228.49     0   100   701 i
*> 33.143.24.0/21    144.39.228.49     0   100   701 i
*> 33.154.0.0/18     144.39.228.49     0   100   701 i
*> 33.216.0.0/24     144.39.228.49     0   100   701 i
*> 33.216.0.0/19     144.39.228.49     0   150   701 i
```

1 Using screen 1, identify how many times the route 44.0.0.0/8 has been sent in outgoing updates from the router.

2 Which path will be chosen in screen 2 to get to 33.48.124.0, and why?

3 What is the most likely reason for the source of a route to be flagged as incomplete?

4 To send packets to network 7.2.0.0/16, the router will direct traffic to a next-hop router. The data frame at Layer 2 will be addressed to this next hop, which will route it on to the next router in the journey to its destination. What is the L3 address of the next logical hop, and why was it selected?

Scenario Answers

The answers are in **bold**. The answers provided in this section are not necessarily the only possible answers to the questions. The questions are designed to test your knowledge and to give practical exercise in certain key areas. This section is intended to test and exercise skills and concepts detailed in the body of this chapter.

If your answer is different, ask yourself whether it follows the tenets explained in the answers provided. Your answer is correct not if it matches the solution provided in the book, but rather if it has included the principles of design laid out in the chapter.

In this way, the testing provided in these scenarios is deeper: It examines not only your knowledge, but also your understanding and ability to apply that knowledge to problems.

If you do not get the correct answer, refer back to the text and review the subject tested. Be certain to also review your notes on the question to ensure that you understand the principles of the subject.

Scenario 9-1 Answers

1 Give reasons to support Humugos's desire to have multiple connections to the Internet.

   Multiple connections to the Internet would not only provide redundancy, but they could be configured to load-balance traffic into the Internet. If load balancing is not an option because the multiple connections are to different ISPs, traffic management could still be enforced by using each link for different purposes. Tuning the attributes and configuring prefix lists would do this very effectively.

2 The company has been advised to redistribute static routes into the Internet BGP-4. It had intended to redistribute dynamic OSPF routes directly into the ISP provider. Explain why the ISP was not in favor of this configuration.

   If the ISP accepted routes that had been dynamically redistributed into its autonomous system from OSPF, it could have a very unstable network. The problem is that every time there is a change anywhere that results in an update to be generated by OSPF, it will be redistributed in BGP-4, requiring BGP-4 to process this change and generate an update. The probability is also that no aggregation is configured, which leads to additional traffic and large routing tables. The last problem is that any problem experienced by OSPF propagates into BGP-4 and can cause black holes.

3 Using Figure 9-11, give the configuration commands that would redistribute the static routes, configured to supernets with an /16 prefix.

```
router bgp 100
redistribute static
ip route 201.16.0.0 0.0.255.255 null 0
ip route 208.32.0.0 0.0.255.255 null 0
```

This configuration is an incomplete BGP configuration, but it achieves the redistribution of the networks that have been aggregated into supernets. The static route command is the only way to get the aggregated route into the routing table; if aggregated routes were not being used, network commands would be preferable. Of course, it is necessary to have all the networks 201.16.0.0 to 201.16.255.0 and 208.32.0.0 to 208.32.255.0 allocated by IANA to your organization before stating ownership to them for the Internet. Always work with the ISP when configuring connections into its domain.

4 Using Figure 9-11, issue the configuration commands that would allow Router B connecting into the Internet to select the path to network 78.9.80.0 via Router G. Use the local preference attribute to select the path.

Given the design of the network, the path to network 78.9.80.0 has a longer AS_Path through Router G. To tune the local preference to select this path is to alter the selection that it would naturally have taken. The configuration commands are as follows:

```
Router B(config)#router bgp 100
network 167.55.0.0 mask 255.255.0.0
neighbor 131.171.67.8 remote-as 100
neighbor 201.101.9.8 remote-as 250
bgp default preference 250
```

Remember that the higher the preference, the more likely the selection.

Scenario 9-2 Answers

1 The original design required a fully meshed IBGP-4 network. This was calculated to mean 250 connections, which was deemed unacceptable because it would be too great of a drain on resources. Route reflectors are obviously the answer. Configure Router A to run BGP and as a route reflector to clients B and C.

```
router bgp 100
network 10.0.0.0
network 131.108.0.0
neighbor 10.10.10.10 remote-as 100
neighbor 10.10.10.10 route-reflector-client
neighbor 10.10.8.9 remote-as 100
neighbor 10.10.8.9 remote-as 100 route-reflector-client
```

2 Configure routers B and C to run BGP as clients to Router A.

Router B:

```
router bgp 100
network 10.0.0.0
neighbor 10.10.10.9 remote-as 100
```

Router C:

```
router bgp 100
network 10.0.0.0
neighbor 10.10.8.10 remote-as 100
```

3 Having configured the cluster, are any other tasks necessary?

Given that the route reflector is now forwarding the routes between B and C, the link between these routers is no longer necessary, and the BGP-4 link between them should be broken. This simply requires the removal of the neighbor statements that create the link on both routers B and C.

4 The company has decided in its early stages to require organizations connecting into them to use default routes. How would these routes be disseminated without the organization's autonomous system, and how would an interior router running only an IGP determine which path out of the routing domain to take if it had more than one connection?

The routers in the client organization do not need to run BGP-4. They simply need to configure a default route and propagate this into the routing domain, in accordance with the interior routing protocol that is being run.

If the autonomous system were multihomed into the Internet, there would be more than one default route propagated throughout the system. Any router within the autonomous system would determine the best path to the outside world by comparing the routing protocol metrics between the default routes. Thus, RIP would select the lowest hop count, EIGRP the lowest combination of bandwidth and delay, and OSPF the lowest cost.

5 Given that the use of a default route by the client organization gives its the least configuration power to manage and manipulate its traffic flow, how would the network administrator justify this simple approach?

The default route, while giving the least control over the connection to the Internet, is very robust in that it has no working parts to fail. Therefore, it requires very little CPU or memory. The lack of redistribution eliminates the possibility of routing loops, and no routing protocol running over the physical link to the Internet frees up bandwidth for data.

Scenario 9-3 Answers

1 Using screen 1, identify how many times the route 44.0.0.0/8 has been sent in outgoing updates from the router?

The prefix list tryout has 28 hits logged for the network 44.0.0.0/8. This means that 28 updates have been sent with the network 44.0.0.0 from the router to its neighbors.

2 Which path will be chosen in screen 2 to get to 33.48.124.0, and why?

The path using 144.39.228.49 as the next hop will be used even though it has the longer AS_Path. The local preference is set to 200. Because the local preference is looked at before the AS_Path, this path will be selected.

3 What is the most likely reason for the source of a route to be flagged as incomplete?

The route was probably redistributed into BGP-4, and it therefore cannot identify as much information as if it were received as a routing update with attributes attached.

4 To send packets to network 7.2.0.0/16, the router will direct traffic to a next-hop router. The data frame at Layer 2 will be addressed to this next hop, which will route it on to the next router in the journey to its destination. What is the L3 address of the next logical hop, and why was it selected?

The next logical hop for the route 7.2.0.0/16 is 144.39.228.49. This address was selected because it is the next hop in the best path to the destination. BGP-4 determined the best path based on AS_PATH. The alternate route has to journey through two autonomous systems to find the destination network, so this path has a more direct route. Because neither the weight attribute nor the local preference attribute has been tuned, the AS_Path is the determining attribute.

This chapter covers the following topics that you will need to master to pass the CCNP/CCDP Routing exam:

- Selecting and configuring the different ways to control route update traffic.

- Configuring route redistribution in a network that does not have redundant paths between dissimilar routing processes.

- Configuring route redistribution in a network that has redundant paths between dissimilar routing processes.

- Resolving path selection problems that result in a redistributed network.

- Verifying route redistribution.

- Configuring policy based routing using route maps.

- The Cisco commands for configuring passive interfaces, static routes, default routes, administrative distance, default metrics, redistribution, distribution lists, and routes maps. Cisco commands for reviewing and testing the configuration are also covered.

CHAPTER 10

Controlling Routing Updates Across the Network

The topics in this chapter deal with the traffic generated by the routing updates in terms of both the network resources that they use and the information contained within them. This covers two different but related areas. The network overhead involved in routing updates has already been dealt with in other chapters, and it keeps recurring as a theme because all network traffic directly influences the network's capability to scale or grow. The issue is very complex and deals with the design of the network and configuring around that design.

The information propagated through the network is complex when dealing with one routing protocol. When multiple protocols have to share information so that the larger network can see every route available within the routing domain, life can become very confused. At this point, the information flow must be controlled and managed very closely.

This chapter deals with these issues, focusing mainly on the configuration of redistribution and route filtering. This is founded in a conceptual explanation and a brief consideration of the design issues that may affect the configuration. The Routing exam will probably concentrate on the configuration commands because the other areas are very esoteric and are very dependent on the individual design of any given network.

The BSCN course devotes 16 percent of its material to redistribution and filtering, which is more than any other single subject is allocated. The majority of these BSCN pages are concerned with configuration, so it is fair to conclude that the exam may concentrate on this area.

One of the reasons that the course is concerned with redistribution is because the fundamentals of filtering comprise many of the calls to the telephone support group. In addition, the Routing exam is one of the steps to becoming a CCNP, a highly coveted title that tells the world that you have competency in the management of large networks. Many of these large networks have some level of redistribution, and nearly all contain route filtering in some form.

How to Best Use This Chapter

By taking the following steps, you can make better use of your study time:

- Keep your notes and the answers for all your work with this book in one place, for easy reference.

- When you take a quiz, write down your answers. Studies show that retention significantly increases by writing down facts and concepts, even if you never look at the information again.

- Use the diagram in Figure 10-1 to guide you to the next step.

Figure 10-1   *How to Use This Chapter*

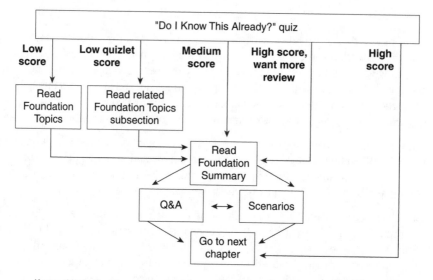

If you skip to the Foundation Summary, Q&A, and Scenarios sections and have trouble with the material there, you should go to the Foundation Topics section.

"Do I Know This Already?" Quiz

The purpose of the "Do I Know This Already?" quiz is to help you decide what parts of this chapter to use. If you already intend to read the entire chapter, you do not necessarily need to answer these questions now.

This 16-question quiz helps you determine how to spend your limited study time. The quiz is sectioned into four smaller four-question "quizlets," which correspond to four major topics in the chapter. Figure 10-1 outlines suggestions on how to spend your time in this chapter. Use Table 10-1 to record your scores.

Table 10-1   *Score Sheet for Quiz and Quizlets*

Quizlet Number	Topic	Questions	Score
1	What redistribution is and what various options are available	1 to 4	
2	Configuring redistribution in networks with both redundant and nonredundant paths	5 to 8	
3	Configuring and verifying redistribution	9 to 12	
4	Configuring and verifying policy-based routing using route maps	13 to 16	
All questions	All	1 to 16	

1 Give two reasons for using multiple routing protocols.

_____

_____

_____

2 How many IP routing tables are there?

_____

_____

_____

3 When implementing redistribution, state one possible problem that you might experience, and explain why it is a problem.

_____

_____

_____

4 Which has a lower administrative distance, IGRP or OSPF?

_____

_____

_____

5 What command is used to configure an outbound route filter?

_____

_____

_____

6 What is a passive interface?

_____

_____

_____

7 What is the purpose of administrative distance?

_____

_____

_____

8 What is the concern of redistributing into a redundant network?

_____

_____

_____

9 What is a default network?

_____

_____

_____

10 Why is it necessary to configure a default metric when redistributing between routing protocols?

_____

_____

_____

11 Which command is used to modify the administrative distance of a route?

_____

_____

_____

12 What is the difference in processing for an inbound and an outbound route filter?

_____

_____

_____

13 State two benefits of using policy-based routing.

_____

_____

_____

14 How are matching routes modified in a route map?

_____

_____

_____

15 Explain the command **set ip default-next-hop** [_ip-address...ip-address_].

_____

_____

_____

16 Which command displays route maps that are configured on interfaces?

_____

_____

_____

The answers to this quiz are found in Appendix A, "Answers to Quiz Questions." The suggested choices for your next step are as follows:

- **2 or less on any quizlet**—Review the appropriate sections of the "Foundation Topics" portion of this chapter, based on Table 10-1. Then move on to the "Foundation Summary" section, the "Q&A" section, and the "Scenarios" at the end of the chapter.

- **8 or less overall score**—Read the entire chapter. This includes the "Foundation Topics" and "Foundation Summary" sections, the "Q&A" section, and the "Scenarios" at the end of the chapter.

- **9 to 12 overall score**—Begin with the "Foundation Summary" section, and then go to the "Q&A" section and the "Scenarios" at the end of the chapter. If you have trouble with these exercises, read the appropriate sections in "Foundation Topics."

- **13 or more overall score**—If you want more review on these topics, skip to the "Foundation Summary" section, and then go to the "Q&A" section and the "Scenarios" at the end of the chapter. Otherwise, move to the next chapter.

Foundation Topics

The following section examines the implications of using redistribution.

Introduction: Controlling the Routing Updates Using Redistribution and Filtering

Redistribution is often necessary within a network, if only as a transitional implementation. Nonetheless, it should not be thought of as a quick and easy solution. Although route redistribution is often a lifesaver for your network, is fraught with complexity. Understanding the operation of the processes that you have implemented and how this influences your network is crucial. This chapter deals with the main topics dealing with the implementation of the network.

Case Study

Duddleduddle is a large hospital with several sites in the city. Although the sites connect to a centralized patient and administration database, the hospital has fought for local autonomy based on the specialization of the site and the fact that it is its own business unit. An IT group manages the central administration and oversees the other sites. The chief information officer (CIO) who ran this group and the overall network has left because of political wrangling. The new CIO, recently appointed, is attempting to sort out the mess.

This new CIO has the agreement of the other hospital sites that there should be one routing protocol, as opposed to the four that are currently running. In turn, he has agreed to implement filtering to improve the network performance, grant some basic security, and indulge some turf wars.

The first step to creating a single routing protocol network is to redistribute the protocols so that the network can see all the available routes. Unfortunately, the routing protocols are aware of multiple path destinations. Therefore, the implementation must be done not only with consideration to preventing routing loops, but also with optimal path selection. This chapter deals with these concerns; the solution for the Duddleduddle hospital is addressed in the "Scenarios" section.

Redistribution Between Routing Protocols

It is rare to find just one routing protocol running within an organization. If the organization is running more than one routing protocol, it is necessary to find some way of passing the networks learned by one routing protocol into another so that every workstation can reach every other workstation. This process is called *redistribution*.

Although the organization as a whole has one routing domain, each routing protocol considers the routing updates as propagated by another domain or autonomous system. The routing protocol views these redistributed updates as external. This distinction allows a different value to be placed on those routes during the path selection process.

Redistribution within an organization is illustrated in Figure 10-2.

Figure 10-2   *Autonomous Systems Within an Organization*

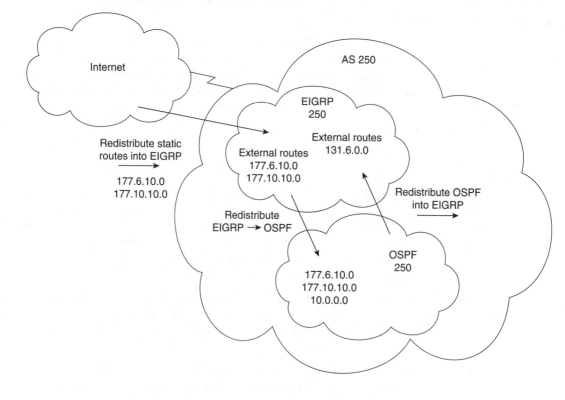

NOTE   The interior routing protocols within the organization see an autonomous system as containing one routing protocol. This is a defining characteristic of an autonomous system.

The exterior routing protocols see the organization as the autonomous system that connects to the Internet or a service provider.

Although the concept of redistribution is straightforward, the design and implementation are extremely tricky. It is well known that redistribution can result in "fun and games with routing loops." Although multiple routing protocols may be a necessity of life, it is critical that the implementation and maintenance be managed with a full, documented understanding of both the network and the traffic flows.

To manage the complexity of these networks and to reduce the possibility of routing loops, some level of restriction in the information sent across the various domains is often necessary.

Controlling Routing Updates

Various methods enable you to control the routing information sent between routers. These methods include the following:

- **Passive interfaces**—An interface that does not participate in the routing process. In RIP and IGRP, the process listens but will not send updates. In OSPF and EIGRP, the process neither listens nor sends updates because no neighbor relationship can form.

  The interfaces that participate in the interior routing process are controlled by the interface configuration. During configuration, the routing process is instructed via the **network** command on which interfaces to use. Because most protocols express the networks at the major boundary, interfaces that have no reason to send this protocol's updates propagate the data across the network. This is not only a waste of bandwidth, but in many cases, it can lead to confusion.

- **Default routes**—A route used if there is no entry in the routing table for the destination network. If the lookup finds no entry for the desired network and no default network is configured, the packet is dropped.

  If the routing process is denied the right to send updates, the downstream routers will have a limited understanding of the network. To resolve this, use default routes. Default routes reduce overhead, add simplicity, and can remove loops.

- **Static routes**—A route that is manually configured. It takes precedence over routes learned via a routing process because it has lower administrative distance.

  If no routing process is configured, static routes may be configured to populate the routing table. This is not practical in a large network because the table cannot learn of changes in the network topology dynamically. In small environments or for stub networks, however, this is an excellent solution.

- **The null interface**—An imaginary interface that is defined as the next logical hop in a static route. All traffic destined for the remote network is carefully routed into a black hole.

  This can be used in a similar way to the passive interface, but it allows for greater granularity in the denied routes.

It is also used to feed routes into another routing protocol. Its allows another mask to be set and is therefore useful when redistribution occurs between a routing protocol that uses VLSM and one that does not. In this way, it aggregates routes as shown in the previous chapter.

- **Distribution lists**—Access lists applied to the routing process, determining which networks will be accepted into the routing table or sent in updates.

When communicating to another routing process, it is important to control the information sent into the other process. This control is for security, overhead, and management reasons. Access lists afford the greatest control for determining the traffic flow in the network.

- **Route maps:** Complex access lists permitting conditional programming. If a packet or route matches the criteria defined in a **match** statement, then changes defined in the **set** command are performed on the packet or route in question.

NOTE   Each of these methods of controlling routing updates is considered in detail later in the chapter.

Figure 10-3 shows the use of the options for controlling routing updates in a large and complex network.

In Figure 10-3, Ethernet 0 has a distribute list that is denying the propagation of the network 140.100.32.0 out of E3, which is the network connected to E2. This may be because network 140.100.32.0 has some security reasons for not being seen by the networks connected to Router B. This network could be a test or an R&D project for the department connecting to Router B, and connectivity would confuse the situation.

S0 and S1 have static routes configured. In the case of S0, this is the connection into the Internet, and the static routes are configured by the ISP. This allows them to connect to the ISP without having to receive dynamic routing updates from the ISP. The routing tables from the ISP containing the Internet routing tables could be huge.

The organization has a default route set so that anyone wanting to flee the organization's network can send to the default route, thus keeping the routing tables small and the update traffic to a minimum.

On S1, the router's interface is configured with static routes so that the router at the other end does not need to run a routing protocol. The router at the other end has a default route configured, and the suggestion is that this is a stub network. This ensures that Router C has a simple configuration with few demands on the router.

Figure 10-3   *Controlling Routing Updates*

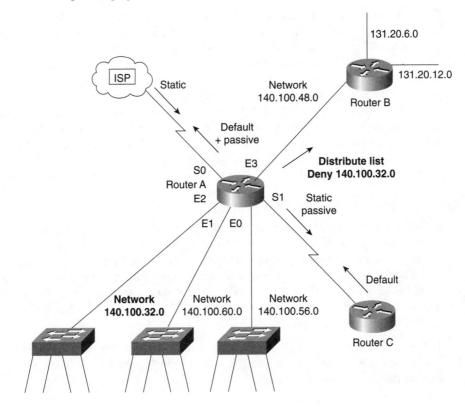

Reasons to Control Routing Updates

Controlling routing updates via redistribution and filtering is useful for many reasons. The reasons for controlling routing updates include these:

- To hide certain networks from the rest of the organization

- To control the network overhead or traffic on the wire

- For simple security reasons

WARNING   Design and control are critical in the configuration of a network that uses more than one routing protocol. This kind of network requires some level of communication between those protocols through redistribution, which can add to the complexity and can add confusion to the network.

The Main Features of Redistribution

Redistribution is used when a router is receiving information about remote networks from various sources. Although all the networks are entered into the routing table and routing decisions will be made on all the networks present in the table, a routing protocol propagates only those networks that it learned through its own process. When there is no sharing of network information between the routing processes, this is referred to as *ships in the night*, or *SIN*, routing. Redistribution can occur only between processes routing the same Layer 3 protocol. So, for example OSPF, RIP, IGRP, and EIGRP can redistribute routing updates between them because they all support the same TCP/IP stack and share the same routing table. How one redistributes between the routing protocols differs between protocols. However, there can be no network redistribution between AppleTalk and IPX.

Default Redistribution Between Routing Protocols

EIGRP is a routing protocol that carries updates for multiple protocols. The key to how this works is the separate routing tables held for each protocol, using the routing protocol as the mechanism for the forwarding of updates and path selection. EIGRP supports AppleTalk's RTMP, IPX's RIP and NLSP, as well as IP. Automatic redistribution is performed between RTMP and EIGRP, and IPX RIP and EIGRP. EIGRP must be manually redistributed into NLSP. There is also automatic redistribution between IGRP and EIGRP as long as they are members of the same autonomous system.

In Figure 10-4, the routing table for Router B has entries from RIP and OSPF. There are no entries for EIGRP because this is a single network directly connected to the router. You can see that the RIP updates sent out the interfaces do not include networks from OSPF. There are no entries for EIGRP.

Some routing protocols automatically exchange networks, although others require some level of configuration. Table 10-2 shows the subtleties of automatic redistribution.

Figure 10-4   *Routing Updates Without Using Redistribution*

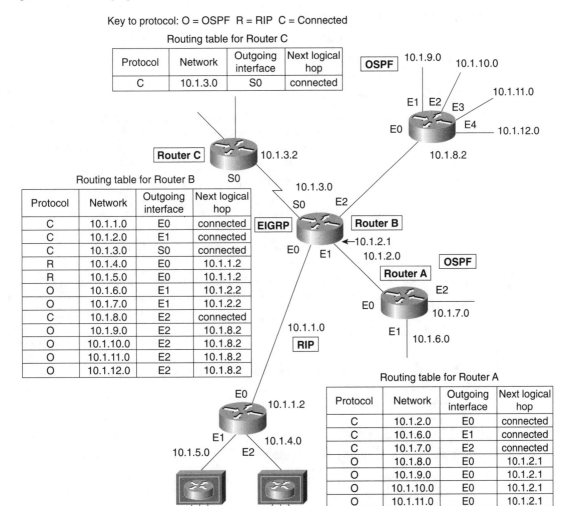

Key to protocol: O = OSPF R = RIP C = Connected

Routing table for Router C

Protocol	Network	Outgoing interface	Next logical hop
C	10.1.3.0	S0	connected

Routing table for Router B

Protocol	Network	Outgoing interface	Next logical hop
C	10.1.1.0	E0	connected
C	10.1.2.0	E1	connected
C	10.1.3.0	S0	connected
R	10.1.4.0	E0	10.1.1.2
R	10.1.5.0	E0	10.1.1.2
O	10.1.6.0	E1	10.1.2.2
O	10.1.7.0	E1	10.1.2.2
C	10.1.8.0	E2	connected
O	10.1.9.0	E2	10.1.8.2
O	10.1.10.0	E2	10.1.8.2
O	10.1.11.0	E2	10.1.8.2
O	10.1.12.0	E2	10.1.8.2

Routing table for Router A

Protocol	Network	Outgoing interface	Next logical hop
C	10.1.2.0	E0	connected
C	10.1.6.0	E1	connected
C	10.1.7.0	E2	connected
O	10.1.8.0	E0	10.1.2.1
O	10.1.9.0	E0	10.1.2.1
O	10.1.10.0	E0	10.1.2.1
O	10.1.11.0	E0	10.1.2.1
O	10.1.12.0	E0	10.1.2.1

Table 10-2   *Automatic Redistribution Between Routing Protocols*

Routing Protocol	Redistribution Policy
Static	Requires manual redistribution into other routing protocols.
Connected	Unless included in the **network** command for the routing process, requires manual redistribution.
RIP	Requires manual redistribution.
IGRP	Will automatically redistribute between IGRP and EIGRP if the autonomous system number is the same. Otherwise, processes with different IGRP autonomous system numbers, or IGRP and EIGRP processes with different autonomous system numbers require manual redistribution.
EIGRP	Will automatically redistribute between IGRP and EIGRP if the autonomous system number is the same. Otherwise, processes with different EIGRP autonomous system numbers, or IGRP and EIGRP processes with different autonomous system numbers require manual redistribution.
	EIGRP for AppleTalk will automatically redistribute between EIGRP and RTMP.
	EIGRP for IPX will automatically redistribute between EIGRP and IPX RIP/SAP; in later versions, NLSP can be manually redistributed.
OSPF	Requires manual redistribution between different OSPF process IDs and routing protocols.

Redistribution is therefore sometimes a necessary evil. It should be avoided if possible; sometimes this is not possible.

Why Use Multiple TCP/IP Protocols?

The main reasons for multiple protocols existing within an organization are as follows:

- The organization is transitioning from one routing protocol to another because the network has grown and there is a need for a more sophisticated protocol that will scale.

- Although a vendor solution is preferred, there is a mix of different vendors within the network, so the vendor solution is used in the areas available. This is particularly true in client/server networks.

- Historically, the organization was a series of small network domains that have recently been tied together to form one large enterprise network. The company may well have plans to transition to a single routing protocol in the future.

- Some departments might have host-based solutions that require differing protocols.

- The filtering policy is inadequate in other departments, and filtering routing traffic into your department or terminating the routing protocol at your doorstep may be necessary.

- Often after a merger or a takeover, when several companies become one, it takes planning, strategy, and careful analysis to determine the best overall design for the network.

- Politically, there are ideological differences among the different network administrators, which until now have not been resolved.

- In a very large environment, the various domains may have different requirements, making a single solution inefficient. A clear example is in the case of a large multinational corporation, where EIGRP is the protocol used at the access and distribution layer, but BGP is the protocol connecting the core.

If there are so many reasons why a network may have multiple routing processes for one Layer 3 protocol, why is it advisable to use one routing protocol, if possible?

The Reason for Using One Routing Protocol

The reason is simple for configuring one routing protocol:

The added complexity of having multiple routing processes can cause many problems within the network. These are typically very difficult to troubleshoot because the symptom often appears some distance from the configuration error.

Problems of Configuring Multiple Routing Protocols

The problems experienced as a result of multiple routing processes and their redistribution include the following:

- The wrong or a less efficient routing decision being made because of the difference in routing metrics. The choice of the less efficient route is referred to as choosing the *suboptimal path.*

- A routing loop occurring, in which the data traffic is sent in a circle without ever arriving at the destination. This is normally due to routing feedback, where routers send routing information received from one autonomous system back into that same autonomous system.

- The convergence time of the network increasing because of the different technologies involved. If the routing protocols converge at different rates, this may also cause problems. In some cases, this may result in timeouts and the temporary loss of networks.

Dealing with each of these problems in turn, the selection of the suboptimal path may occur because of the method used to make a routing decision.

Path Selection Within a Routing Protocol

The routing table contains a list of decisions.

When a routing process does a routing table lookup for a destination network, it finds the best path in accordance with the routing decision that was made earlier.

If the routing process knows of several paths to a remote network, it chooses the most efficient path based on its metric and routing algorithm, and places this into the routing table.

If there is more than one path with the same metric, the routing process may add up to six of these paths and then distribute the traffic equally between them. This is routing protocol-dependent.

It is also possible in IGRP and EIGRP to load-share over unequal cost paths by using the **variance** command. This is something to take into consideration when designing the network.

Routing Metrics

The routing metric is the value assigned to routes learned by a routing protocol. It is the means by which the routing protocol can choose among multiple routes to a destination. However, each routing protocol uses a different metric to make these decisions, as described in Chapter 3, "IP Addressing." If the different protocols now want to share information, there must be some form of translation of the metrics. This requires manual configuration in most cases—the exception being EIGRP for AppleTalk and RTMP, EIGRP for IPX, and RIP/SAP for NLSP. EIGRP and IGRP use the same metric algorithm and have no problem in automatic redistribution if the autonomous system number is the same. The configuration commands are dealt with in the section "Configuring Redistribution," later in this chapter.

Why Path Selection Populates the Routing Table

Path selection by a routing protocol is how a single routing protocol selects a single path to put into the routing table. This keeps processing to a minimum because the decisions are made before the packets arrive for routing. When the routing table is complete, the packets are just switched to the destination based on the decisions made earlier and stored in the routing table. Figure 10-5 shows the selection of one path using the value of the metric assigned to various routes.

In Figure 10-5, the route from A to E will see the EIGRP path as having three equal-cost routes:

A to B to E
A to C to E
A to D to E

Therefore, it load balances among these three paths. (Note that the metric shown has been simplified for the purposes of this example. EIGRP metrics will be larger numbers.)

Figure 10-5   *The Selection of a Path Using the Metric*

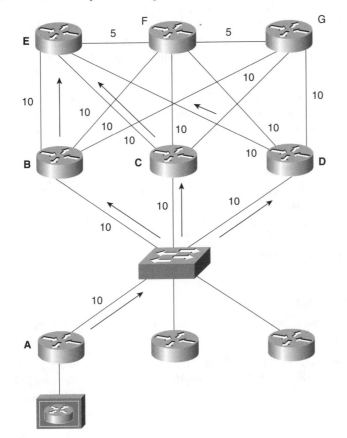

It is slightly more complicated when there is more than one routing protocol running on the same device.

After one packet has been routed to its destination, all other packets that originate from the same source and that are bound to the same destination do not need to be process-switched. When a packet is processed-switched, it means that it has gone through the complete routing process, including route table lookups. This is very expensive in terms of router memory and CPU. However, when the lookups and so on have been performed, all other packets from the same source to the same destination can simply be forwarded based on the decisions made for the first packet. This is true as long as the routing decision has been cached in memory. The decision can be stored in various locations, notably in the autonomous or fast switch caches. By default, most protocols have fast switching enabled.

This is a good thing, but there is one consideration to be aware of in a live network. If there are multiple equal-cost paths to a destination, you would expect the protocol to load-balance across the links. When fast switching is in force, the load-balancing feature is turned off. The reason for this is that the cache has one path cached, so the packets are load-balanced to the destination on a session basis. This is not a problem as long as you are aware of how the traffic flows across your network and the implication of this feature.

It is important also to check with Cisco CCO on the IOS version and hardware model that you are using because this behavior is version- and platform-specific.

Path Selection Between Routing Protocols

On occasions, more than one routing protocol is running on the router. If they have paths to the same remote destination network, the routing process must decide which path to enter into the routing table, to have one entry per network. Because the metrics differ between the protocols, selection based on the metric is ruled out as a solution. Instead, another method was devised to solve the problem, the *administrative distance*.

Administrative Distance

The administrative distance selects one path to enter into the routing table from several paths offered by multiple routing protocols.

In Figure 10-6, for example, both RIP and EIGRP have paths to the network 140.100.6.0. RIP is offering a metric of 2 hops, and EIGRP is tendering a metric of 768. Without redistribution, no conversion or choice is possible because there is no similar criteria for distinguishing the two paths. Therefore, the metric is ignored, and the administrative distance is used to make the selection.

In Figure 10-6, despite the speed of the Frame Relay being set at 56 kbps instead of the 100 Mbps of FDDI, Router D would select the Frame Relay path based on administrative distance. In this case, manually configuring the administrative distance on Router D would be advisable.

The administrative distance is a rather arbitrary set of values placed on the different sources of routing information. The defaults can be changed, but care should be taken when subverting the natural path selection, and any manual configuration must be done with careful reference to the network design of the organization and its traffic flow.

The administrative distance reflects the preferred choice. The defaults are listed in Table 10-3.

Figure 10-6   *Path Selection Using Administrative Distance*

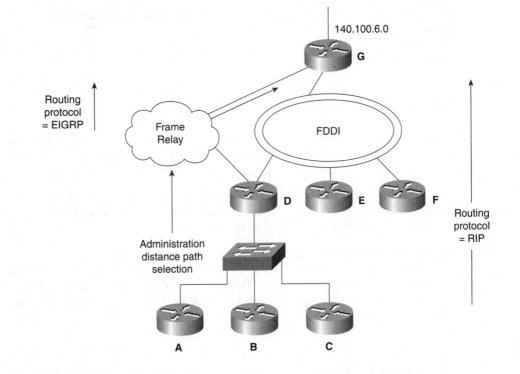

Table 10-3   *Default Administrative Distance*

Routing Source	Administrative Distance
Connected interface or static route that identifies the outgoing interface rather than the next logical hop	0
Static route	1
EIGRP summary route	5
External BGP	20
EIGRP	90
IGRP	100
OSPF	110
IS-IS	115
RIP v1, v2	120

continues

Table 10-3 *Default Administrative Distance (Continued)*

Routing Source	Administrative Distance
EGP	140
External EIGRP	170
Internal BGP	200
An unknown network	255 or infinity

The administrative distance can be manually configured. The reason for manually configuring the administrative distance for a protocol such as EIGRP is that it may have a less desirable path compared to one offered by another protocol such as RIP, which has a higher default AD.

The administrative distance is looked at with total disregard of the metrics. In Figure 10-6, this means that the EIGRP path will be selected even though it is the slower and more expensive link. However, the Enhanced IGRP path will be selected.

Another occasion when the administrative distance would select the suboptimal path is that of a directly connected network. A network that is directly connected to the router has precedence in terms of administrative distance. In this instance, however, it is being used as a backup link for redundancy because the directly connected network is not used on a daily basis. Backup links for redundancy are often implemented on serial connections in which the network charges are based on usage. This design is called a *floating static route*.

NOTE   Details on how to change the administrative distance are given in the section "Configuring Redistribution."

Avoiding Routing Loops When Redistributing

Routing loops occur when a routing protocol is fed its own networks—for example, networks that originated within that routing process, but that the routing protocol now learns from another routing protocol through redistribution. The routing protocol may now see a network that it owns as having a more favorable path although this will send the traffic in the opposite direction, into a different routing protocol domain. The confusion that can be caused is enormous, and it is very easy to create routing loops when redistributing, as shown in Figure 10-7.

Figure 10-7   *How Route Feedback Can Cause Routing Loops*

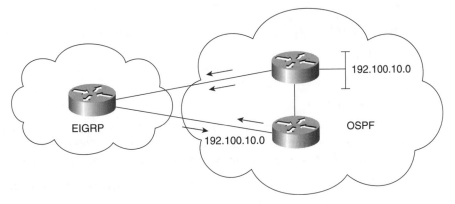

This is solved by the following:

- Changing the metric

- Changing the administrative distance

- Using default routes

- Using passive interfaces

- Using distribution lists

NOTE   These configurations are discussed in the section of the chapter titled "Configuring Redistribution."

Redistribution and Problems with Network Convergence

To maintain consistent and coherent routing among different routing protocols, you must consider the different technologies involved. A major concern is the computation of the routing table and how long it takes the network to converge. Although Enhanced IGRP is renowned for its speed in convergence, RIP has a poorer reputation in this regard. Sharing the network information across the two technologies may cause some problems.

The first problem is just that the network takes time to converge. At some point, this will create timeouts and possibly routing loops. Adjusting the timers may solve the problems, but any routing protocol configuration must be done with a sound knowledge of the entire network and of the routers that need to be configured. Timers typically require every router in the network to be configured to the same value.

Guidelines in Network Design to Avoid Routing Loops

The principles are summarized as follows:

- Have a sound knowledge and clear documentation of the following:

  — The network topology (physical and logical)

  — The routing protocol domains

  — The traffic flow

- Do not overlap routing protocols. It is much easier if the different protocols can be clearly delineated into separate domains, with routers acting in a similar function to Area Border Routers in OSPF. This is often referred to as the core and edge protocols.

  — Identify the boundary routers on which redistribution is to be configured.

  — Determine which protocol is the core and which protocol is the edge protocol.

  — Determine the direction of redistribution, into which routing protocol are the routers to be distributed.

- If distribution is needed, ensure that it is a one-way distribution, to avoid networks being fed back into the originating domain. Use default routes to facilitate the use of one-way distribution, if necessary.

- If two-way distribution cannot be avoided, the mechanisms described in this section, such as the following, can help you avoid problems:

  — Manually configuring the metric

  — Manually configuring the administrative distance

  — Using distribution access lists

The concepts of redistribution are detailed in the following examples with configuration scripts. This will reinforce the concepts and understanding of the technology.

Configuring Redistribution

Redistribution configuration is very specific to the routing protocol itself. Before any implementation is contemplated, reference should be made to the configuration guides from Cisco.

Generic Steps Required for Redistribution

All protocols require the following steps for redistribution:

- Configure redistribution.

- Define the default metric to be assigned to any networks that are distributed into the routing process.

The commands for redistribution are configured as subcommands to the routing process. The **redistribute** command identifies the routing protocol *from* which the updates are to be accepted. It identifies the source of the updates.

Redistribution Configuration Syntax

To configure redistribution between routing protocols, the following command syntax is used:

```
redistribute protocol [process-id] {level-1 | level-1-2 | level-2}
[metric metric-value] [metric-type type-value]
[match {internal | external 1 | external 2}] [tag tag-value]
[route-map map-tag] [weight weight] [subnets]
```

This command is explained in Table 10-4.

Table 10-4   *Command Description of Redistribution*

Command	Description
protocol	This is the routing protocol that is providing the routes. Remember, most commands with two parameters have the structure of from a value to a value, or from a source to a destination. Routes are being redistributed from this source protocol. It can be one of the following keywords: **connected, bgp, eigrp, egp, igrp, isis, iso-igrp, mobile, ospf, static,** or **rip**.
process-id	For BGP-4, EGP, EIGRP, or IGRP, this is an autonomous system number. For OSPF, this is an OSPF process ID. RIPv1 and RIPv2 do not use either a process ID or an autonomous system number.
level-1	For IS-IS, Level 1 routes are redistributed into other IP routing protocols independently.
level-1-2	For IS-IS, both Level 1 and Level 2 routes are redistributed into other IP routing protocols.
level-2	For IS-IS, Level 2 routes are redistributed into other IP routing protocols independently.
metric *metric-value*	This optional parameter is used to specify the metric used for the redistributed route. When redistributing into protocols other than OSPF, if this value is not specified and no value is specified using the **default-metric** router configuration command, routes may not be redistributed. Use a value consistent with the destination protocol; remember that you are influencing the path selection made by the routing process. Refer to the section "The Default or Seed Metric."

continues

Table 10-4 *Command Description of Redistribution (Continued)*

Command	Description
metric-type *type-value*	This is an optional OSPF parameter that specifies the external link type associated with the default route advertised into the OSPF routing domain. This value can be **1** for type 1 external routes, or **2** for type 2 external routes. The default is 2. Refer to Chapter 6, "Using OSPF Across Multiple Areas," for more detail on OSPF external route types.
match	This is an optional OSPF parameter that specifies the criteria by which OSPF routes are redistributed into other routing domains. It can be one of the following: **internal**: Redistribute routes that are internal to a specific autonomous system. **external 1**: Redistribute routes that are external to the autonomous system but that are imported into OSPF as a type 1 external route. **external 2**: Redistribute routes that are external to the autonomous system but that are imported into OSPF as a type 2 external route.
tag *tag-value*	(Optional) The tag-value is a 32-bit decimal value attached to each external route. It is not used by the OSPF protocol itself, but it may be used to communicate information between autonomous system boundary routers. If no value is specified, then the remote autonomous system number is used for routes from BGP and EGP; for other protocols, zero (0) is used.
route-map	(Optional) This instructs the redistribution process that a route map must be referenced to filter the routes imported from the source routing protocol to the current routing protocol. If it is not specified, all routes are redistributed because no filtering is performed. If this keyword is specified but no route map tags are listed, no routes will be imported. It is important, therefore, to pay attention to the configuration.
map-tag	This is the optional identifier of a configured route map to filter the routes imported from the source routing protocol to the current routing protocol. Route maps are covered later in this chapter.
weight *weight*	(Optional) This sets the attribute of network weight when redistributing into BGP. The weight determines the preferred path out of a router when there are multiple paths to a remote network. This is an integer between 0 and 65535.
subnets	(Optional) For redistributing routes into OSPF, this is the scope of redistribution for the specified protocol.

The command is very complex because it shows all the parameters for all the different protocols.

The Default or Seed Metric

A metric is calculated in terms of how far the network is from the router. Where there is only one protocol, this is straightforward. Another way of looking at the metric is that the router to which the network is connected issues a *seed metric*. This seed metric is added to as the path information is passed through the network in routing updates. However, a route that has been redistributed is not directly connected to the router, so no seed metric can be determined.

This is a problem because in accepting the new networks, the receiving process must know how to calculate the metric. Therefore, it is necessary to define the default metric to be assigned to the networks that are accepted from the other routing protocol. This is like manually configuring the seed metric.

This metric will be assigned to all the redistributed networks from that process and will be incremented from now on as the networks are propagated throughout the new routing domain.

Configuring the Default Metric

The default metric can be configured in several ways. The first is to include the metric in the **redistribute** command, as shown in the preceding command syntax and as illustrated in Example 10-1.

Example 10-1 *Including the Metric in the* **redistribute** *Command*

```
router eigrp 100
redistribute rip metric 10000 100 255 1 1500
network 140.100.0.0
passive interface e1
```

This configuration shows the following:

- The use of the **redistribute** command

- The routing process from which the routes are being accepted

- The metric parameter, allowing the configuration of the EIGRP to state the new metric that the old RIP networks will use while traversing the EIGRP network

Configuring the Default Metric for OSPF, RIP, EGP or BGP-4

Alternatively, it is possible to redistribute the routing protocol and then, with a separate command, to state the default metric. The advantage of this is it is a simpler configuration visually, which is helpful in troubleshooting. Also, if more than one protocol is being redistributed into the routing protocol, the default metric applies to all the protocols being redistributed.

To configure the default metric for OSPF, RIP, EGP, or BGP-4, use the following command syntax:

```
default-metric number
```

The **default-metric** command is used in Example 10-2.

Configuration for EIGRP or IGRP

To configure the default metric for IGRP or EIGRP, use the following command syntax:

```
default-metric bandwidth delay reliability loading mtu
```

Typically, you should take the values shown on one of the outgoing interfaces of the router being configured, by issuing this exec command:

```
show interface
```

The significance of the metric values is shown in Table 10-5.

Table 10-5 *The Parameters of the* **default metric** *Command*

Command Parameter	Description
bandwidth	The minimum bandwidth seen on route to the destination. It is presented in kilobits/per second (kbps).
delay	The delay experienced on the route and presented in microseconds.
reliability	The probability of a successful transmission given the history of this interface. The value is expressed in a number from 0 to 255, where 255 is indicates that the route is stable and available.
loading	A number range of 0 to 255, where 255 indicates that the line is 100 percent loaded.
mtu	The maximum packet size that can travel through the network.

The **default metric** command is used in Example 10-2 and is illustrated in Figure 10-8.

Example 10-2 shows the configuration of the default metric when redistributing between routing protocols.

Example 10-2 *Configuring the Default Metric*

```
router eigrp 100
redistribute rip
redistribute ospf 10
default-metric 10000 100 255 1 1500
network 140.100.0.0
passive interface e1
passive interface e2
```

Figure 10-8 *Configuring the Default Metric*

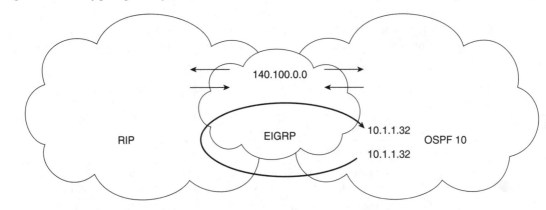

140.100.0.0

RIP

EIGRP

10.1.1.32

10.1.1.32

OSPF 10

Beware of route feedback causing poor network performance.

Explanation of Redistribution Example

In Example 10-2, networks from both RIP and OSPF are assigned the same seed metric on entrance to the EIGRP process. Although this design and configuration seems complex, it is fairly common. Imagine the situation in which OSPF and RIP have been running. The choice for OSPF was because of a need to conform to the standards for political reasons. These reasons disappeared with the CIO. The decision to transition the network to EIGRP has been made. The network designed for EIGRP will run in the core, with the edge routers running redistribution. RIP has been included in the design map to accommodate the UNIX systems running ROUTED.

The default metric used is the bandwidth, delay, reliability, load, and maximum transmission unit (mtu), which reflect the compound metric used by IGRP and Enhanced IGRP. As shown, RIP and OSPF would just supply a number for hop count and cost, respectively.

When to Configure the Administrative Distance

As shown, it is important to ensure that routes redistributed into another routing protocol are assigned an appropriate metric. However, it is equally important to consider the need to control the choice that the routing process makes when presented with multiple routes to the same destination from different routing protocols. The metric is not appropriate because the multiple routes are from different routing protocols that are not redistributing. Changing the administrative distance, discussed earlier allows the best path to be chosen.

Configuring the Administrative Distance

To ensure that the optimal path is chosen, it is sometimes necessary to change the administrative distance, to make it less favorable. The command structure is protocol-dependent, in that EIGRP requires a separate command. The following command syntax is used for EIGRP:

```
distance eigrp internal-distance external-distance
```

The distance command, as used to configure the EIGRP administrative distance, is explained in Table 10-6.

Table 10-6 *Configuring Administrative Distance for EIGRP*

Command	Description
internal-distance	Administrative distance for EIGRP internal routes. These are routes learned from another entity within the same autonomous system, such as IGRP.
external-distance	Administrative distance for EIGRP external routes. These are routes for which the best path is learned from a neighbor external to the autonomous system, such as EIGRP from another autonomous system or another TCP/IP routing protocol such as OSPF.

To configure the administrative distance for the other IP protocols, the following command syntax is used:

```
distance weight [address mask] [access-list-number | name] [ip]
```

The **distance** command to configure the administrative distance for other IP protocols is explained in Table 10-7.

Table 10-7 *Configuring Administrative Distance for Other IP Protocols*

Command	Description
weight	Administrative distance, an integer from 10 to 255, where 255 means that the route is unreachable. The values 0 to 9 are reserved for internal use.
address	Optional IP address. Allows filtering of networks according to the IP address of the router supplying the routing information.
mask	Optional wildcard mask for IP address. A bit set to 1 in the mask argument instructs the software to ignore the corresponding bit in the address value.
access-list-number | name	Optional number or name of standard access list to be applied to the incoming routing updates. Allows filtering of the networks being advertised.
ip	Optional. Specifies IP-derived routes for Intermediate System-to-Intermediate System (IS-IS).

The Passive Interface

The passive interface is the interface that listens but does not speak. It is used for routing protocols that send updates through every interface with an address that is included in the **network** command. If the routing protocol is not running on the next-hop router, it is a waste of time to send updates out of the interface.

The command reduces the spending of limited resources without compromising the integrity of the router. The router processes all routes received on an interface.

The command syntax to configure a passive interface is as follows:

```
passive-interface type number
```

where *type* and *number*, indicate the interface to be made passive.

Static Routes

Another method of controlling routes is to manually configure the entries into the routing table. The reasons for doing this include the following:

- This may be done to prevent the need for a routing protocol to run on the network, reducing the network overhead to nil, zero, and zilch. This is used in dialup lines (dial-on-demand routing).

- This also may be done if there are two autonomous systems that do not need to exchange the entire routing table, but simply a few routes.

- The other reason is to change the mask of the network. For example, as seen in BGP-4, you can statically define a supernet and redistribute the static route into the BGP-4 process. This is also done when redistributing from a routing protocol that understands VLSM to one that does not.

The following explains the syntax for configuring the static route:

```
ip route prefix mask address [distance] [tag tag] [permanent]
```

This defines the path by stating the next-hop router to which to send the traffic. This configuration can be used only if the network address for the next-hop router is in the routing table. If the static route needs to be advertised to other routers, it should be redistributed.

```
ip route prefix mask interface [distance] [tag tag] [permanent]
```

In some versions of the IOS, this route is automatically redistributed because it is viewed as a connected network, as long as the output interface is referred in the static route instead of an IP address.

Table 10-8 explains the options available in the static route command.

Table 10-8 *Explanation of the IP Route Options*

Command	Description
prefix	The route prefix for the destination.
mask	The prefix mask for the destination.
address	The IP address of the next-hop router that can be used to reach that network.
interface	The network interface to use to get to the destination network.
distance	Optional administrative distance to assign to this route. (Recall that administrative distance refers to how believable the routing protocol is.)
tag *tag*	Optional value that can be used as a match value in route maps.
permanent	Specification that the route will not be removed even if the interface associated with the route goes down.

NOTE Use static routes only with the outgoing interface configuration on point-to-point interfaces. Static routes configured on multipoint or multiaccess interfaces need a next-hop address. On point-to-point interfaces, the information is sent to the only other device on the network.

In Example 10-3 (and the corresponding Figure 10-9), the use of a static route as well as the **passive interface** command is illustrated. Additional configuration is included to place the commands in context; the commands relevant to this section are placed in bold.

Example 10-3 *The use of Static Routing and Passive Interfaces*

```
Router A
ipx routing 0200.aaaa.aaaa
username RouterB password Shhh
dialer-list 1 protocol ip permit
interface bri 0
encapsulation ppp
ip addr 10.1.2.1 255.255.255.0
ipx network 1012
ppp authentication chap
dialer map ip 10.1.2.2 broadcast name RouterB 1222555222201
dialer-group 1
interface ethernet 0
ip address 10.1.1.1 255.255.255.0
ipx network 1011
ip route 10.1.3.0 255.255.255.0 10.1.2.2
router igrp 1
network 10.0.0.0
passive interface s0
```

In this example, the link between routers A and B is raised when the Router A sees "interesting traffic" try to exit the serial interface. "Interesting traffic" is traffic that is permitted in a preconfigured access list. In this example, all IP traffic is considered interesting. This example is perfectly valid for occasional access, except for the few additional ISDN parameters that need to be added. Figure 10-9 illustrates the use of both static routes and passive interfaces.

Figure 10-9   *The Use of Static Routes Across a Dialup Link*

Note: No routing protocol is running.

In this example, you see that IGRP updates do not flow across the dialup line because the interface s0 has been configured as a passive interface. The same configuration has been applied to Router B so that no updates raise the WAN link.

Neither Router A nor Router B knows of the networks on the other side of the WAN, so static routes must be configured.

Default Routes

A default route is a route that is used when the routing table has no entry for the destination network in a packet that it is attempting to forward.

In larger networks, there may well be many static routes to be configured. Not only is this a chore for the administrator, but it also requires vigilance so that changes in the routing table can be reconfigured. It may be that turning on a routing protocol is advised, or, alternatively you can configure a specialized static route, called a static default route. To configure a default route, use the following syntax:

```
ip default-network network-number
```

This command will generate a default route to be sent in updates. It does not generate a default network on the router that was configured.

```
ip route 0.0.0.0 0.0.0.0 s0
```

This is more obviously a static default route and will generate a default route on the router configured.

NOTE   The different TCP/IP protocols treat these commands differently when redistributing them into the routing protocol. Reference the CCO documentation set for detailed explanations.

These default routes are propagated through the network dynamically or can be configured into the individual routers.

If a router has a directly connected interface onto the specified default network, the dynamic routing protocols running on that router will generate or source a default route. In the case of RIP, it will advertise the pseudonetwork 0.0.0.0. In the case of IGRP, the network itself is advertised and flagged as an exterior route.

IGRP and EIGRP's Gateway of Last Resort

When default information is being passed along through a dynamic routing protocol, no further configuration is required. In the case of RIP, there can be only one default route, network 0.0.0.0. However, in the case of IGRP, several networks can offer default routes, although only one is used.

If the router is not directly connected to the default network but does have a route to it, it is considered as a candidate default path. When there are multiple default routes in the routing table, the route candidates are examined. As you would expect, the best default path is selected based on administrative distance and metric. The gateway to the best default path then becomes the gateway of last resort for the router. This is displayed in the gateway of last resort display in this command:

```
show IP route
```

Occasions for Using a Default Route

The obvious example of a need for a default route is when connecting into the Internet or simply out of your organization's intranet. The outside world contains many networks in the routing tables of the systems that serve it. It is not necessary for your router to know of all the possibilities available; it must simply know that the door to the great outdoors will suffice.

Another occasion for configuring a default route would be for a stub network to connect to the larger network.

Both these examples are shown in Figure 10-10.

Figure 10-10 *The Use of Default and Static Routes*

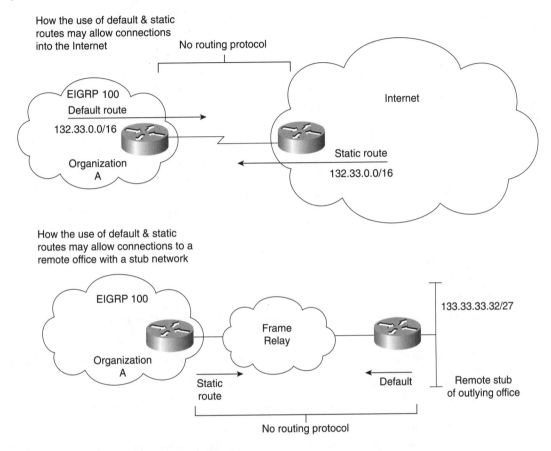

Controlling Routing Updates with Filtering

Despite all the mechanisms for controlling and reducing the routing updates on your network, it is sometimes necessary to wield greater and more flexible power. This comes in the form of access lists, which when applied to routing updates are referred to as *distribute lists*.

The logic used in the distribute lists is similar to that of an access list. It is summarized in the flowchart in Figure 10-11 and the process listed in the following text.

Figure 10-11 *Distribute List Logic on an Incoming Update*

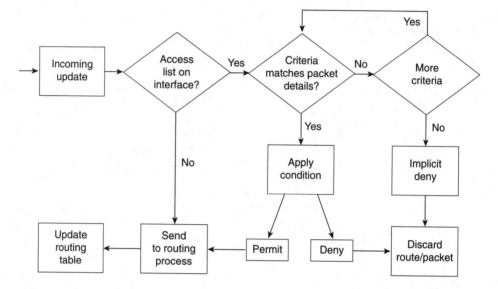

1 The router receives a routing update or is about to send a routing update about one or more networks.

2 The router looks at the appropriate interface involved with the action to check for filtering.

3 The router determines whether a filter is associated with the interface.

4 If a filter is present, the router examines the access list to see if there is a match on any of the networks in the routing update.

5 If there is no filter on the interface, the routing update is sent directly to the routing process as normal.

6 If there is a match, then the route entry is processed as configured.

7 If no match is found in the access list, the implicit **deny any** at the end of the access list will cause the update to be dropped.

Routing updates can be filtered for any routing protocol by defining an access list and applying it to a specific routing protocol.

When creating a routing filter or distribute list, the following steps should be taken:

• Write out in longhand what you are trying to achieve.

• Identify the network addresses to be filtered, and create an access list.

- Determine whether you are filtering routing updates coming into the router or updates to be propagated to other routers.

- Assign the access list using the **distribute-list** command.

Use the following command syntax to configure the distribute list to filter incoming updates:

```
distribute-list {access-list-number | name} in [type number]
```

Table 10-9 explains the options of this command.

Table 10-9   *Explanation of the* **distribute-list in** *Command Options*

Command	Description
access-list-number I name	Gives the standard access list number or name
in	Applies the access list to incoming routing updates
type number	Gives the optional interface type and number from which updates will be filtered

Use the following command syntax to configure the distribute list to filter outgoing updates:

```
distribute-list {access-list-number | name} out
[interface-name | routing-process |autonomous-system-number]
```

Table 10-10 explains the options of this command.

Table 10-10   *Explanation of the* **distribute-list out** *Command Options*

Command	Description
access-list-number I name	Gives the standard access list number or name
out	Applies the access list to outgoing routing updates
interface-name	Gives the optional interface name out which updates will be filtered
routing-process	Gives the optional name of the routing process, or the keyword **static** or **connected**, from which updates will be filtered
autonomous-system-number	Gives the optional autonomous system number of routing process

NOTE   It is not possible to filter OSPF outgoing updates at the interface.

Redistribution Examples

The following examples are case studies that pull together the concepts learned in this section on redistribution. Redistribution involves complex design and configuration considerations. Therefore, it is best to see the various problems and solutions illustrated in context.

This section presents three examples.

- Route redistribution without redundant paths between different routing protocols.

- Route redistribution with redundant paths between different routing protocols. The example also covers resolving the path selection problems that result into redistributed networks.

- The use of a default network in a redistributed environment.

Redistribution Example 1

Refer to Figure 10-12 for this example of route redistribution, without redundant paths, between different routing protocols.

Figure 10-12 *Simple Redistribution Between RIP and EIGRP*

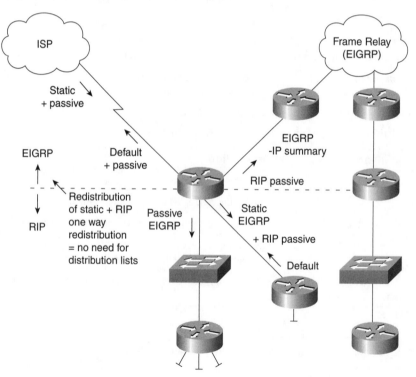

Figure 10-12 shows local offices connecting to the main office via Frame Relay. Each office has a point-to-point PVC to a router in the main office.

EIGRP is being run through the Frame Relay cloud to reduce the network overhead. The LANs are running IP for NT, and there is no need for a routing protocol to be run on the LAN segments.

RIP is being run at the main office. This is to allow the corporate servers to have an understanding of the network. The servers are UNIX systems running the ROUTED daemon. ROUTED listens only to RIP updates. Redistribution allows the servers to know about the EIGRP networks.

If the EIGRP networks need to know about each other, the RIP networks would need to be redistributed into the EIGRP environment. This is unlikely because the servers are centrally held at the main office, and there will be little lateral traffic flow. The configuration shown in Figure 10-12 is simple because there are no redundant links. The Frame Relay cloud uses point-to-point PVCs. In the future, the company may want to add redundancy by meshing the Frame Relay cloud and consolidating the three core routers into one large router. Currently the company has a simple and low-cost solution using existing equipment.

Redistribution Example 2

Refer to Figure 10-13 for this example, which covers route redistribution with redundant paths between different routing protocols and resolving path selection problems that result in redistributed networks.

In Figure 10-13, Router A is connected to networks 140.100.1.0 and 140.100.2.0 that are advertised via RIP to routers C and B.

The routing table of Router A will show the information presented in Table 10-11.

Table 10-11 *Router A Routing Table Information*

Routing Protocol	Network/Subnet	Next Logical Hop	Metric
Connected	140.100.1.0/24	Connected E0	0
Connected	140.100.2.0/24	Connected E1	0
Connected	140.100.3.0/24	Connected E2	0
RIP	10.10.10.8/30	140.100.3.2	1 hop
RIP	10.10.10.12/30	140.100.3.2	1 hop
RIP	10.10.10.16/30	140.100.3.2	1 hop
RIP	10.10.10.20/30	140.100.3.2	1 hop
RIP	10.10.10.24/30	140.100.3.2	1 hop
RIP	10.10.10.28/30	140.100.3.2	1 hop
RIP	10.10.10.32/30	140.100.3.2	1 hop
RIP	193.144.6.0/24	140.100.3.2	1 hop
RIP	193.144.7.0/24	140.100.3.2	1 hop
RIP	193.144.8.0/24	140.100.3.2	1 hop

Figure 10-13 *Choosing the Optimal Path, Through Administrative Distance and Distribution Lists, When Redistribution Is Using Redundant Paths*

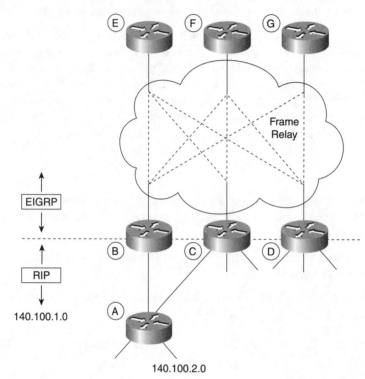

The routing table of Router B will show the information presented in Table 10-12.

Table 10-12 *Router B Routing Table Information*

Routing Protocol	Network/Subnet	Next Logical Hop	Metric
RIP	140.100.1.0/24	140.100.3.1	1 hop
RIP	140.100.2.0/24	140.100.3.1	1 hop
Connected	140.100.3.0/24	Connected E0	0
Connected	10.10.10.8/30	Connected S0	0
Connected	10.10.10.12/30	Connected S0	0
Connected	10.10.10.16/30	Connected S0	0
EIGRP	10.10.10.20/30	10.10.10.9	2221056
EIGRP	10.10.10.24/30	10.10.10.9	2221056
EIGRP	10.10.10.28/30	10.10.10.13	2221056

Table 10-12   *Router B Routing Table Information (Continued)*

Routing Protocol	Network/Subnet	Next Logical Hop	Metric
EIGRP	10.10.10.32/30	10.10.10.13	2221056
EIGRP	193.144.6.0/24	10.10.10.9	2221056
EIGRP	193.144.7.0/24	10.10.10.13	2221056
EIGRP	193.144.8.0/24	10.10.10.17	2221056

The routing table sees all the paths as unique, so it is clear which paths are accessible through RIP or EIGRP. Even after redistribution, the routing table will not change; the confusion occurs after the propagation of the EIGRP updates through the network.

The EIGRP updates will be sent to all the routers in the domain, and Routers E, F, and G will have no confusion. Depending on the timing of the updates and convergence, however, Router C may well become confused. The Routers E, F, and G will have sent information on how to get to the networks 140.100.1.0 and 140.100.2.0. Router C will also receive information from Router A. Sending the data traffic to A is obviously the optimum path, however; because EIGRP has a significantly better administrative distance, the EIGRP route will be placed in the routing table as having the best path. On the assumption that the Frame Relay PVCs all have the same bandwidth, the routing table will see all three paths and distribute the traffic evenly among them.

Example 10-4 shows how to configure Routers B, C, and D to change the administrative distance to favor RIP for the LANs within its domain. The networks 140.100.1.0 and 140.100.2.0 are given an administrative distance of 200 in accordance with the access list. This ensures that the RIP path will be favored if it is available.

Example 10-4 *Changing the Administrative Distance to Favor RIP*

```
router rip
network 140.100.0.0
passive interface S0.1
redistribute igrp 100 metric 3
router igrp 100
network 140.100.0.0
passive interface E0
default-metric 10000 100 255 1 1500
distance 200 0.0.0.0 255.255.255.255 3
access-list 3 permit 140.100.1.0
access-list 3 permit 140.100.2.0
```

The **distance** command sets the administrative distance for the IGRP 100 process. It changes the distance from 100 to 200, which now makes the routes that RIP offers more favorable because RIP has an administrative distance of 120. The use of 0.0.0.0 with a wildcard mask of 255.255.255.255 is just as a placeholder indicating that, although the command allows for a network to be specified so that the administrative distance can be applied selectively to that network, in this configuration no network has been selected. The command has been applied to all networks. You do want the administrative distance to be altered on two networks, however. This granularity cannot be stated in the **distance** command; therefore, an access list is used. In the example, the number *3* at the end of the command line points to the access list that carries that number as an identifier. The access list, by permitting networks 140.100.1.0 and 140.100.2.0, is identifying the networks to which the **distance** command is to be applied.

Redistribution Example 3

The use of the default network simplifies the configuration of a redistributed network by allowing the redistribution to be one-way. This significantly reduces the possibility of feedback of networks into the originating domain. The configuration for this example is inset within Figure 10-14 because the configuration of more than one router is shown.

Figure 10-14 *The Use of a Default Network in a Redistributed Network to Resolve Problems with Path Selection*

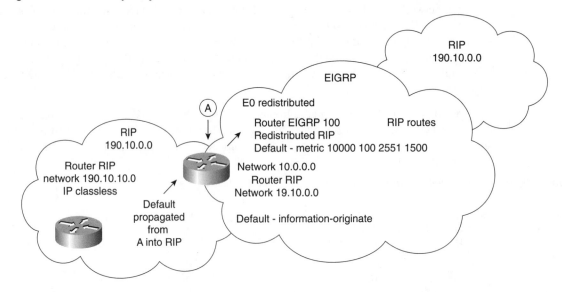

In this design, every router and, therefore, workstation within the RIP domain sees its own internal networks, but all other networks are accessed via the default route.

The router that straddles both the EIGRP and the RIP domain acts rather as an ABR in OSPF and is where the default route is configured. This is propagated throughout the RIP domain. The internal RIP-only routers must be configured to accept a default route with a destination network that they are not directly connected to; this is achieved with the **ip classless** command.

The redistribution on Router A can now be one-way. EIGRP needs to know all the networks in the RIP domain, but RIP, when configured with a default route, needs no understanding of the outside world. The RIP domain works in a similar fashion to a stub network in OSPF.

Policy-Based Routing Using Route Maps

Route maps are very similar to access lists. They both perform "if then" programming, in that they state criteria that is used to determine whether specific packets are to be permitted or denied.

The main difference is that the route map has the additional capability of adding a set criterion to the match criterion. In an access list, the match criterion is implicit; in a route map, it is a keyword. This means that if a packet is matched to the criterion given in the route map, some action can be taken to change the packet.

For example, an access list could state something similar to this logic: If the cupcake is lemon-flavored, keep it, but if it is has walnuts in it, throw it away.

Along the same lines, a route map could specify logic such as this: If it is a lemon-flavored cupcake, ice it with lemon butter frosting. If it has walnuts, then ice it with melted chocolate. If it has neither a lemon flavor nor walnuts, leave it alone. The route map is obviously more powerful because it can change the entity.

Now to make this simple example slightly more complex, to show the additional complexity of route maps, add a logical AND and a logical OR. For example, if it is a lemon-flavored cupcake AND it contains poppy seeds, ice it with lemon butter frosting. If it has walnuts OR it was baked today, then ice it with melted chocolate. If it has neither a lemon flavor nor walnuts, leave it alone.

The route map would look something like this:

```
route map cupcakes permit 10
match lemon flavored poppy seed
set add lemon butter frosting
route map cupcakes permit 15
match walnuts
match baked today
set melted chocolate frosting
route map cupcakes permit 20
```

For the mathematicians among you, this could be written as follows:

If {(a or b) match} then set c
Else
    If {(x and y) match} then set z
       Else
           Set nothing

Uses for Route Maps

Route maps can be used for the following purposes:

- To control redistribution
- To control and modify routing information
- To define policies in policy routing

Characteristics of Route Maps

A route map has certain characteristics:

- A route map has a list of criteria, stated with the **match** statement.

- A route map can change packets or routes that are matched by using the **set** statement.

- A collection of route map statements that have the same route map name are considered one route map.

- Within a route map, each route map statement is numbered with sequence numbers and, therefore, can be edited individually.

- The statements in a route map correspond to the lines of an access list. Specifying the match conditions in a route map is similar to specifying the source and destination addresses and masks in an access list.

- The statements in the route map are compared to the route to see if there is a match. The statements are examined in turn from the top, as in an access list.

- The first match found for a route is applied, and the route map will not examine further.

- The **match route map** configuration commands are used to define the conditions to be checked.

- The **set route map** configuration commands are used to define the actions to be followed if there is a match.

- The single **match** statement may contain multiple conditions. At least one condition in the **match** statement must be true. This is a logical OR.

- A route map statement may contain multiple **match** statements. All **match** statements in the route map statement must be considered true for the route map statement to be considered matched. This is a logical AND.

- The *sequence number* is also used to specify the order in which conditions are checked. Thus, if there are two statements in a route map named BESTEST, one with sequence 5 and the other with sequence 15, sequence 5 is checked first. If there is no match for the conditions in sequence 5, then sequence 15 will be checked.

- Like an access list, there is an implicit **deny any** at the end of a route map. The consequences of this **deny** depend on how the route map is being used. The specifics for policy-based routing are discussed later in this section.

The Route Map Command Syntax

The **route-map** command is shown here and is followed by the route map configuration commands **match** and **set**.

```
route-map map-tag [[permit | deny] | [sequence-number]]
```

Table 10-13 describes the syntax options available for the **route-map** command.

Table 10-13   *The **route-map** Command Options*

Command	Description
map-tag	This is the name of the route map. This name is used to reference the route map when using the **redistribute** router configuration command.
permit | **deny**	(Optional) If the match criteria are met for this route map and **permit** is specified, the route is redistributed as defined by the set actions.
	If the match criteria are not met and **permit** is specified, the next route map with the same map tag is tested.
	If a route passes none of the match criteria for the set of route maps sharing the same name, it is not redistributed by that set because it hits the implicit deny **any** at the end of the list.
	(Optional) If the match criteria are met for the route map and **deny** is specified, the route is not redistributed, and no further route maps sharing the same map tag name will be examined.
sequence-number	(Optional) The sequence number indicates the position that a new route map will have in the list of route map statements already configured with the same name.

Example 10-5 is very simple, but it clearly illustrates the functionality of the route map. Study the example in reference to Figure 10-15.

This route map examines all updates from RIP and redistributes those RIP routes with a hop count equal to 3 into OSPF. These routes will be redistributed into OSPF as external link-state advertisements with a metric cost of 6, a metric type of Type 1, and a tag equal to 1.

Figure 10-15 *Route Map to Distribute RIP into OSPF*

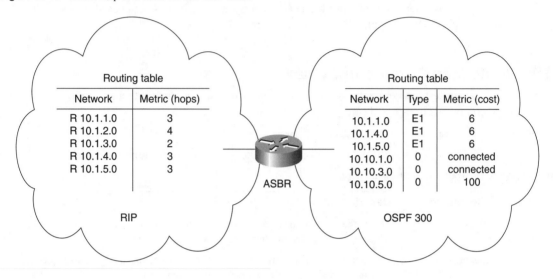

Example 10-5 *Route Map to Distribute RIP into OSPF*

```
router ospf 25
redistribute rip route-map rip-routes

route-map rip-routes permit
match metric 3
set metric 6
set metric-type type1
set tag 1
```

Policy-Based Routing Using Route Maps

Policy routing is a means of adding sophistication into the use of the static route. It just gives a greater granularity and scope to the criteria by which the next-hop router is decided.

While static routes forward packets based on the destination network address, a policy route forwards packets based on the source address. If access lists are used with the route map, then the parameters in an extended access list can be used to route traffic based on such criteria as the port numbers.

Characteristics of Policy Routing

The rules that define policy routing are as follows:

- Traffic can be directed on either the source address or both the source and destination addresses.

- Policy routing affects only the routing of the router on which it is configured in determining the next hop in the path to the destination.

- Policy routing does not affect the destination of the packet.

- Policy routing does not allow traffic sent into another autonomous system to take a different path from the one that would have been chosen by that autonomous system.

- It is possible only to influence how traffic will get to a neighboring router.

- As policy routing examines the source address, it is configured on the inbound interface.

Route maps were introduced in Cisco IOS Release 11.0, allowing policies that defined different paths for different packets based on defined criteria.

Policy-based routing also provides a mechanism to mark packets with different types of service (TOS). This feature can be used in conjunction with Cisco IOS queuing techniques so that certain kinds of traffic can receive preferential service.

The Benefits of Policy Based Routing

The benefits of implementing policy-based routing in networks include the following:

- **Source-based transit provider selection**—ISPs in particular use policy-based routing to make routing decisions based on the source address. This allows traffic belonging to different customers to be routed through different Internet connections, across the policy routers in accordance with whatever human policy needs to be adhered to.

- **Quality of service (QoS)**—By setting the precedence or TOS values in the IP packet headers in routers at the edge of the network, organizations can provide QoS. In this way, the traffic can be differentiated, and queuing mechanisms can be implemented to prioritize traffic based on the QoS in the core or backbone of the network. This improves network performance because the configuration is done only at the edge of the network.

- **Cost savings**—The bulk traffic generated by a specific activity can be diverted to use a higher-bandwidth, high-cost link for a short time. Meanwhile, interactive traffic is provided basic connectivity over a lower-bandwidth, low-cost link. For example, a dial-on-demand ISDN line might be raised in response to traffic to a finance server for file transfers selected by policy routing.

- **Load sharing**—This allows the implementation of policies to distribute traffic among multiple paths based on the traffic characteristics. This does not detract from the dynamic load-sharing capabilities offered by destination-based routing that the Cisco IOS software has always supported.

Disadvantages of Policy Routing

Some things should be considered before arbitrarily deciding to implement policy routing:

- A backup path should be in place in case the defined next-hop router goes down. If there is no alternative defined, policy routing will default to dynamic routing decisions.

- Additional CPU is required to examine every source address to effect the defined policy.

- Extra configuration is required.

- The possibility exists that other traffic will be disrupted.

Criteria by Which Policy-Based Routes Are Determined

Instead of routing by the destination address, policy-based routing allows network administrators to determine and implement routing policies to allow or deny paths based on the following:

- The identity of a particular end system

- The application being run

- The protocol in use

- The size of packets

How Policy-Based Routing Works Using Route Maps

The following list tells how policy-based routing works using route maps:

- Policy-based routing is applied to *incoming* packets. When a packet is received on an interface with policy-based routing enabled, it goes through this procedure.

- If there is a match and the action is to permit the route, then the route is policy-routed in accordance to the **set** command.

- If there is a match and the action is to deny the route, then the route is not policy-routed but is passed back to the forwarding engine.

- If there is no match and there is no configuration for what to do in this event, then the default is to deny the packet, which would return it to the routing process.

- To prevent packets that find no match from being returned to normal forwarding, specify a **set** statement to route the packets to interface null 0 as the last entry in the route map.

The decision process is shown in the logic flowcharts in Figures 10-16 and 10-17.

Figure 10-16   *Route Map Logic for Policy Routing #1*

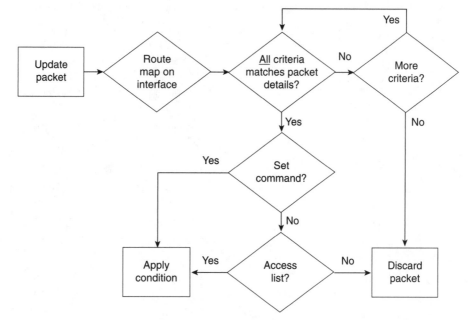

To understand this properly, you need to see exactly how route maps operate. The following section explains the process or logic by which route maps work. A section follows this on how to configure route maps that place things further in context.

The Route Map Statements

The following characterize the operation of route map statements:

- The route map statements used for policy-based routing can be marked as permit or deny.

- The route map will stop as soon as a match is made, just as an access list does.

- Only if the statement is marked as permit and the packet meets all of the match criteria will all the **set** commands are applied.

- IP standard or extended access lists can be used to establish policy-based routing.

    — A standard IP access list can be used to specify match criteria for the source address of a packet.

    — Extended access lists can be used to specify match criteria based on source and destination addresses, application, protocol type, TOS, and precedence.

Figure 10-17 *Route Map Logic for Policy Routing #2*

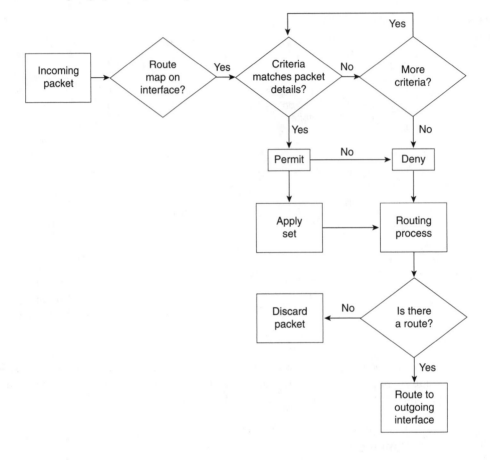

Configuring Route Maps for Policy Routing

The following commands are summarized here into groups: the **match** commands that can be configured for policy routing, and the **set** commands that can be applied if the packet matches the criteria stated.

The match Commands for Policy Routing with Route Maps

The following **match** commands are used to determine whether the packet is one that is to be policy-routed, as opposed to being sent on its merry way. If so, it is sent down a different path, typically one less traveled.

The **match** command is as follows:

```
match {actions}
```

The **match** commands used in policy routing are summarized in Table 10-14.

Table 10-14   **match** *Commands Used in Policy Routing*

Command	Description
match *ip address* [*access-list-number* | *name*] [*...access-list-number* | *name*]	This states the number or name of a standard or extended access list that will be used to examine incoming packets. The access list is used to match a packet with characteristics defined in it. If multiple access lists are specified, matching any one will result in a match.
match length *min max*	This command is used to define the criteria based on the Layer 3 length of the packet. The *min* parameter states the minimum inclusive length of the packet allowed for a match. The *max* parameter states the maximum inclusive length of the packet allowed for a match. In this way, interactive traffic that is time-sensitive, such as SNA traffic tunneled in IP, can be sent on a dedicated route.

The following **set** commands are used after the **match** criteria has been satisfied. Whereas the **match** parameter determines whether the packet will be policy-routed, the **set** parameter determines how the packet is to be policy-routed.

The **set** command is as follows:

```
set {actions}
```

The **set** commands used in policy routing are summarized in Table 10-15.

Table 10-15   **set** *Commands Used in Policy Routing*

Command	Description
set default interface *type number* [*...type number*]	If the routing table has no explicit route for the destination network of the packet, this set provides a list of default outbound interfaces. The packet being considered for policy routing is routed to the available outbound interface in the list of specified default interfaces.
set interface *type number* [*...type number*]	If there is a route for the destination network of the packet in the routing table, this set provides a list of outgoing interfaces through which to route the packets. If more than one interface is specified, then the first functional outgoing interface is used. This command has no effect and is ignored if the packet is a broadcast or is destined to an unknown address. This is because no explicit route for the destination of the packet was found in the routing table.

continues

Table 10-15 set *Commands Used in Policy Routing (Continued)*

Command	Description
set ip default next-hop *ip address* [*...ip address*]	If the routing table has no explicit route for the destination network of the packet, this set provides a list of default next-hop routers. The packet being considered for policy routing is routed to the available next hop in the list. This must be the address of an adjacent router.
set ip next hop *ip address* [*...ip address*]	If there is a route for the destination network of the packet in the routing table, this set provides a list of next-hop routers to which to forward the packet. If more than one next hop is specified, then the first available next-hop router is used. This must be the address of an adjacent router.
set ip precedence *precedence*	This is used to set the precedence bits in the Type of Service field of the IP header of the matched packet. This determines the IP precedence in the IP packets.
set ip tos *type-of-service*	This is used to set the IP TOS value in the Type of Service field of the IP header.

The **set** commands can be used in conjunction with each other.

NOTE   The **match** and **set** commands to configure a route map for redistribution are equally confusing. You will be delighted to hear that they are not covered in the course, and it is unlikely that they will appear on the exam.

Having configured the route map, it must be called into service. Until it is called, it has no power.

The command used to recruit the services of the router map to an incoming interface follows:

```
ip policy route-map map-tag
```

map-tag is the name of the route map to use for policy routing. This must match a map tag specified by a **route-map** command.

NOTE   Policy-based routing is configured on the incoming interface that receives the packets, not on the outgoing interface from which the packets are sent.

Example 10-6 shows a sample of this configuration.

Example 10-6 *Calling a Route Map into Service*

```
interface serial 0
ip policy route-map soupspoon
!
route-map soupspoon
match ip address 201.14.222.18
set ip next-hop 191.5.6.11
```

Configuration Notes

There are many things to be aware of in configuring a router that is directing the network traffic. These devices are responsible largely for the end users being able to accomplish their work and return home in the evening to loved ones. When configuring policy routing or route maps, pay very careful attention to the logic and rules by which they operate. Refer to the guidelines for writing access lists in Chapter 2, "Managing Scalable Network Growth."

The following are a couple warnings to illustrate the need to pay attention when configuring anything as powerful as a route map:

- When editing a route map statement with the **no** version of the existing command line, if you forget to type in the sequence number, you will delete the entire route map,

- When editing a route map statement to add a statement, if you forget to specify the sequence number, the default sequence number will be issued. This is the number 10 and will simply replace the command line with the sequence number 10.

Route Maps, Policy Routing, and Route Switching

Speed through the network is influenced by the capability of the devices on the network to process the traffic on the network. Cisco is continually striving to enhance features while at the same time reducing the resources and thus the time it takes to provide those features.

Cisco achieved this goal in 11.2F of the IOS. In this version of the IOS, IP policy routing is fast-switched. Previous versions process switch policy-routed traffic, allowing for an output of approximately 1000 to 10,000 packets per second. This resulted in application timeouts.

How to Ensure That Packets Are Switched at Speed (Fast)

To fast-switch policy-routed traffic, ensure the following:

- Fast switching of policy routing is disabled by default. It must be manually configured.

- Configure policy routing before you configure fast-switched policy routing.

- When policy routing is configured, turn on the fast switching with this interface command:

  ```
  ip route-cache policy
  ```

- Fast-switched policy routing supports all of the **match** commands and most of the **set** commands, except for the following restrictions:

  — The **set ip default** command is not supported.

  — The **set interface** command is supported only over point-to-point links, unless a route-cache entry exists using the same interface specified in the **set interface** command in the route map. In addition, when process switching, the routing table is consulted to determine a path to the destination. During fast switching, the software does not make this check because fast switching is a cache of the process switch lookup. Instead, if the packet matches, the software blindly forwards the packet to the specified interface. This is a similar situation to the one described in reference to load balancing earlier.

Verifying, Maintaining, and Troubleshooting the Redistribution Implementation

The main key to maintaining and troubleshooting the redistribution within your network is to have a clear understanding of the network topology from both a physical and a logical perspective. The traffic flows—the peaks and lows in the traffic volume—are also important in truly understanding the connectivity issues within the network. From this vantage point, it is possible to interpret the output presented by the various tools available.

Most of the appropriate commands in tracking redistribution problems are ones that have been examined earlier. They include the following:

- show ip protocol
- show ip route
- **show ip route** *routing protocol*
- show ip eigrp neighbors
- show ip ospf database

In addition to these commands, the use of the such as **trace** and **extended ping** are also very useful.

traceroute

trace or **traceroute** are invoked from the exec privileged level. This shows the routers that a packet has passed through to reach its destination.

The extended **traceroute** test is called by entering the command without any destination. This results in the utility asking a series of questions, allowing you to change the defaults.

Extended ping

To check host reachability and network connectivity, use the **ping** (IP packet Internet groper function) privileged exec command. The extended **ping** utility is called by entering the command without any destination. This results in the utility asking a series of questions, allowing you to change the defaults.

Using trace and Extended ping

I do not use **trace** to determine the path taken, but rather to identify where there is a problem in the network. Where the **trace** utility fails indicates a good starting point for troubleshooting a complex network.

trace is not very reliable in reflecting the routing path because path changes are not shown. The extended **ping** command, however, is very useful because it announces every interface that it traverses. The limitation is the maximum hops that it can report, which is nine.

It is also possible to specify a source address in the **trace** or **ping** commands (as long as it is an interface on the router). This can be useful for testing certain types of access lists, route maps, and so on.

These commands are generic to TCP/IP troubleshooting.

Specific Commands for Monitoring Policy-Routing Configurations

To monitor the policy-routing configuration, use the following exec commands described in Table 10-16.

Table 10-16   *Commands to Monitor Policy Routing*

Command	Description
show ip policy	Displays the route maps used for policy routing on the router's interfaces.
show route-map	Displays configured route maps.
debug ip policy	Displays IP policy-routing packet activity. This command helps you determine what policy routing is doing. It displays information about whether a packet matches the criteria and, if so, the resulting routing information for the packet.

NOTE	Because the **debug ip policy** command generates a significant amount of output, use it only when traffic on the IP network is low so that other activity on the system is not adversely affected. This is true of all **debug** commands.

Conclusion

Any limitation on the traffic flow in the network, particularly in terms of routing updates, will limit connectivity. Very careful analysis and design is therefore required.

Redistribution is an extremely powerful tool that allows the otherwise segmented portions of your organization to appear as one. To prevent the child's game of rumors from taking over and destroying your network, some level of control is required as soon as redistribution is introduced to the network.

Policy routes are even more powerful, particularly with the capability to change the path of traffic based on specific criteria. Although this subject is advanced and, as such, has the feel of a loaded gun, it is crucial to the successful management of any large network. It is important to understand these subjects to pass the exam ahead, but it is more important to understand them in the light of how they can support your network.

Foundation Summary

The "Foundation Summary" is a collection of quick reference information that provides a convenient review of many key concepts in this chapter. For those of you who already feel comfortable with the topics in this chapter, this summary will help you recall a few details. For those of you who just read this chapter, this review should help solidify some key facts. For any of you doing your final preparations before the exam, these tables and figures will be a convenient way to review the day before the exam.

Methods of Controlling Routing Updates

Various methods enable you to control the routing information sent between routers. These methods include the following:

- **Passive interfaces**—An interface that does not participate in the routing process. In RIP and IGRP, the process listens but will not send updates. In OSPF and EIGRP, the process neither listens nor sends updates because no neighbor relationship can form.

  The interfaces that participate in the interior routing process are controlled by the interface configuration. During configuration, the routing process is instructed via the **network** command on which interfaces to use. Because most protocols express the networks at the major boundary, interfaces that have no reason to send this protocol's updates propagate the data across the network. This is not only a waste of bandwidth, but in many cases, it also can lead to confusion.

- **Default routes**—A route used if there is no entry in the routing table for the destination network. If the lookup finds no entry for the desired network and no default network is configured, the packet is dropped.

  If the routing process is denied the right to send updates, the downstream routers will have a limited understanding of the network. To resolve this, use default routes. Default routes reduce overhead, add simplicity, and can remove loops.

- **Static routes**—A route that is manually configured. It takes precedence over routes learned via a routing process.

  If no routing process is configured, static routes may be configured to populate the routing table. This is not practical in a large network because the table cannot learn of changes in the network topology dynamically. In small environments or for stub networks, however, this is an excellent solution.

- **The null interface**—An imaginary interface that is defined as the next logical hop in a static route. All traffic destined for the remote network is carefully routed into a black hole.

This can be used in a similar way as the passive interface, but it allows for greater granularity in the denied routes.

It is also used to feed routes into another routing protocol. Its allows another mask to be set and, therefore, is useful when redistribution occurs between a routing protocol that uses VLSM and one that does not. In this way, it aggregates routes as shown in the previous chapter.

- **Distribution lists**—Access lists applied to the routing process, determining which networks will be accepted into the routing table or sent in updates.

When communicating to another routing process, it is important to control the information sent into the other process. This control is for security, overhead, and management reasons. Access lists afford the greatest control for determining the traffic flow in the network.

- **Route maps**—Complex access lists permitting conditional programming. If a packet or route matches the criteria defined in a **match** statement, then changes defined in the **set** command are performed on the packet or route in question.

Automatic Redistribution Between Routing Protocols

Table 10-17 *Automatic Redistribution Between Routing Protocols*

Routing Protocol	Redistribution Policy
Static	Requires manual redistribution into other routing protocols.
Connected	Unless included in the **network** command for the routing process, requires manual redistribution.
RIP	Requires manual redistribution.
IGRP	Will automatically redistribute between IGRP and EIGRP if the autonomous system number is the same. Otherwise, processes with different IGRP autonomous system numbers, or IGRP and EIGRP processes with different autonomous system numbers, require manual redistribution.
EIGRP	Will automatically redistribute between IGRP and EIGRP if the autonomous system number is the same. Otherwise, processes with different EIGRP autonomous system numbers, or IGRP and EIGRP processes with different autonomous system numbers, require manual redistribution.
	EIGRP for AppleTalk will automatically redistribute between EIGRP and RTMP.
	EIGRP for IPX will automatically redistribute between EIGRP and IPX RIP/SAP; in later versions, NLSP can be manually redistributed.
OSPF	Requires manual redistribution between different OSPF process IDs and routing protocols.

Default Administrative Distance

Table 10-18 *Default Administrative Distance*

Routing Source	Administrative Distance
Connected interface or static route that identifies the outgoing interface rather than the next logical hop	0
Static route	1
EIGRP summary route	5
External BGP	20
EIGRP	90
IGRP	100
OSPF	110
IS-IS	115
RIP v1, v2	120
EGP	140
External EIGRP	170
Internal BGP	200
An unknown network	255 or infinity

The Logic Used in Distribute Lists

Use the following list and Figure 10-18 to understand the logic used in a distribute list:

1 The router receives a routing update or is about to send a routing update about one or more networks.

2 The router looks at the appropriate interface involved with the action to check for filtering.

3 The router determines whether a filter is associated with the interface.

4 If a filter is present, the router examines the access list to see if there is a match on any of the networks in the routing update.

5 If there is no filter on the interface, the routing update is sent directly to the routing process, as normal.

6 If there is a match, then the route entry is processed as configured.

7 If no match is found in the access list, the implicit **deny any** at the end of the access list will cause the update to be dropped.

Figure 10-18 *Distribute List Logic on an Outgoing Update*

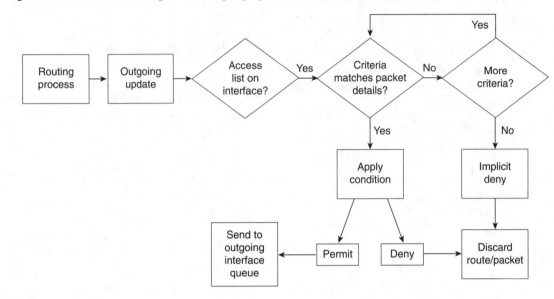

Chapter Glossary

This glossary provides an official Cisco definition for key words and terms introduced in this chapter. I have supplied my own definition for terms that the Cisco glossary does not contain. The words listed here are identified in the text by italics. A complete glossary, including all the chapter terms and additional terms, can be found in Appendix C, "Glossary."

administrative distance—A rating of the trustworthiness of a routing information source. The higher the value, the lower the trustworthiness rating. This is used when there are multiple routing protocol updating the IP routing table and when another method than metric is required to select the best route.

distribute list—An access list that is applied to the routing protocol. It is used to control routing updates by filtering out those updates that are not to be propagated. This is particularly useful in preventing routing loops in redistributed networks.

floating static route—A static route that has a higher administrative distance than a dynamically learned route so that it can be overridden by dynamically learned routing information. This is used to create a DDR backup to an existing link.

redistribution—The process of exchanging routing updates between different routing protocols. This can be done only between protocols that support the same protocol suite at Layer 3—for example, EIGRP and OSPF for TCP/IP. Redistribution cannot happen between Layer 3 protocols such as AppleTalk and IPX.

seed metric—The metric that is given to a route when it enters the routing protocol. Most routes start with a metric of 0 because they first become known to the routing protocol to which they are directly connected. However, if they are redistributed into the routing protocol, there is no starting point from which to increment the route metric. Therefore, the default metric is configured to provide a seed metric for the redistributed routes.

ships in the night (SIN)—Routing that advocates the use of a completely separate and distinct routing protocol for each network protocol so that the multiple routing protocols essentially exist independently.

suboptimal path—A path that is not the best path. Sometimes a less desirable path is chosen.

Q&A

The following questions test your understanding of the topics covered in this chapter. The final questions in this section repeat the opening "Do I Know This Already?" questions. These are repeated to enable you to test your progress. After you have answered the questions, find the answers in Appendix A. If you get an answer wrong, review the answer and ensure that you understand the reason for your mistake. If you are confused by the answer, refer to the appropriate text in the chapter to review the concepts.

1 State two of the methods that Cisco recommends for controlling routing traffic.

_____

_____

_____

2 What is the administrative distance for RIP?

_____

_____

_____

3 State two instances when you do not want routing information propagated.

_____

_____

_____

4 In what instances will Enhanced IGRP automatically redistribute?

_____

_____

_____

5 Which command is used to view the administrative distance on a route?

_____

_____

_____

6 When is redistribution required?

_____

_____

_____

7 Why does Cisco recommend that you not overlap routing protocols?

_____

_____

_____

8 Why would you want to prevent routing updates across an on-demand WAN link?

_____

_____

_____

9 What is the metric used for in a routing protocol?

_____

_____

_____

10 Explain the command **match** _ip-address_ {_access-list-number_ | _name_} [access-list _number_ | _name_].

_____

_____

_____

11 Explain the command **ip-route-cache policy.**

_____

_____

_____

12 Give two reasons for using multiple routing protocols.

_____

_____

_____

13 How many IP routing tables are there?

_____

_____

_____

14 When implementing redistribution, state one possible problem that you might experience, and explain why it is a problem.

_____

_____

_____

15 Which has a lower administrative distance, IGRP or OSPF?

_____

_____

_____

16 What command is used to configure an outbound route filter?

_____

_____

_____

17 What is a passive interface?

_____

_____

_____

18 What is the purpose of administrative distance?

_____

_____

_____

19 What is the concern of redistributing into a redundant network?

_____

_____

_____

20 What is a default network?

_____

_____

_____

21 Why is it necessary to configure a default metric when redistributing between routing protocols?

_____

_____

_____

22 Which command is used to modify the administrative distance of a route?

_____

_____

_____

23 What is the difference in processing for an inbound and an outbound route filter?

_____

_____

_____

24 State two benefits of using policy-based routing.

_____

_____

_____

25 How are matching routes modified in a route map?

_____

_____

_____

26 Explain the command **set ip default-next-hop** [*ip-address...ip-address*].

_____

_____

_____

27 Which command displays route maps that are configured on interfaces?

_____

_____

_____

Scenarios

The following scenarios and questions are designed to draw together the content of the chapter and to exercise your understanding of the concepts. There is not necessarily a right answer. The thought process and practice in manipulating the concepts are the goals of this section. The answers to the scenario questions are found at the end of this chapter.

Scenario 10-1

Reconsider the case study at the beginning of the chapter. Duddleduddle is a large hospital with several sites in the city. Although the sites connect to a centralized patient and administration database, the hospital has fought for local autonomy based on the specialization of the site and the fact that it is its own business unit. An IT group manages the central administration and oversees the other sites. The chief information officer (CIO) who ran this group and the overall network has left because of political wrangling. The new CIO, recently appointed, is attempting to sort out the mess.

This new CIO has the agreement of the other hospital sites that there should be one routing protocol, as opposed to the four that are currently running. In turn, he has agreed to implement filtering to improve the network performance, grant some basic security, and indulge some turf wars.

The first step to creating a single routing protocol network is to redistribute the protocols so that the network can see all the available routes. Unfortunately, the routing protocols are aware of multiple path destinations. Therefore, the implementation must be done with not only consideration to preventing routing loops, but also with optimal path selection.

Figure 10-19 shows the network topology for the hospital Duddleduddle.

Using the figure as reference, complete the following exercises.

1 Issue the configuration commands for the RIP network to be redistributed on Router A into EIGRP.

2 Ensure that the interfaces running EIGRP do not have RIP updates generated through them or that the RIP interfaces do not have EIGRP updates running through them.

3 The site running IGRP and the site running EIGRP are running different autonomous system numbers. How would you implement a transition to both sites running EIGRP using the same autonomous system number?

4 The OSPF redistribution into RIP has been implemented, but users are complaining about delays. State the first step that you would take to verify the configuration.

5 The CIO has been asked to submit a transition plan to the board of trustees that includes a reasoned explanation for the need for redistribution. What should it look like?

Figure 10-19 *Topology for the Scenario 10-1 Network*

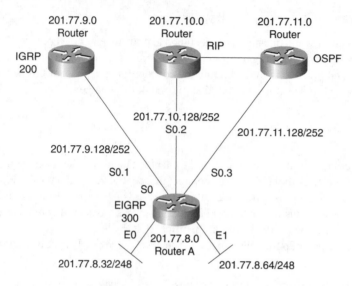

Scenario 10-2

The Hospital Duddleduddle still needs to implement a routing policy using route maps. This is to ensure the optimum use of bandwidth. The x-ray department requires an enormous amount of bandwidth when transferring MMR images to the centralized database.

Using Figure 10-20 and given the criteria within the questions, configure the route maps on Router B.

1 The hospital policy states that the FTP traffic from the x-ray department (201.77.11.0/24) should be forwarded to the Biggun Server at 201.77.12.79 and that it should be sent across the leased line, which is a T1 connection. What would the configuration look like?

2 The Telnet sessions and e-mail connections should be sent across the Frame Relay link. This traffic is from the same department (201.77.8.0.0/24) and is connecting to the same server. What would the configuration look like?

3 What commands would you use to verify that the policy routing is configured correctly and operating normally?

Figure 10-20 *Route Maps Example for Scenario 10-2*

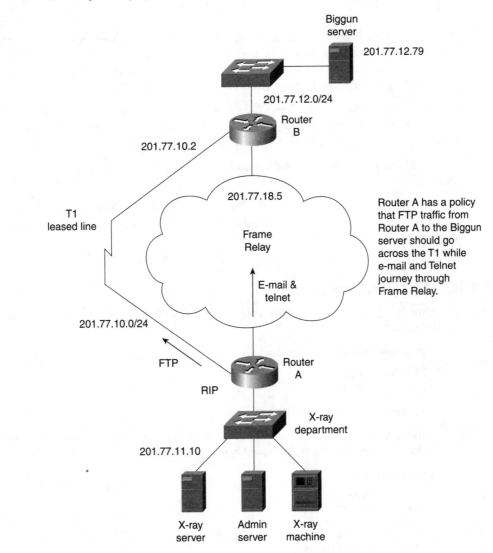

Scenario Answers

The answers are in **bold**. The answers provided in this section are not necessarily the only possible answers to the questions. The questions are designed to test your knowledge and to give practical exercise in certain key areas. This section is intended to test and exercise skills and concepts detailed in the body of this chapter.

If your answer is different, ask yourself whether it follows the tenets explained in the answers provided. Your answer is correct not if it matches the solution provided in the book, but rather if it has included the principles of design laid out in the chapter.

In this way, the testing provided in these scenarios is deeper: It examines not only your knowledge, but also your understanding and ability to apply that knowledge to problems.

If you do not get the correct answer, refer back to the text and review the subject tested. Be certain to also review your notes on the question to ensure that you understand the principles of the subject.

Scenario 10-1 Answers

1 Issue the configuration commands for the RIP network to be redistributed on Router A into EIGRP.

   The commands are as follows:

   ```
   router eigrp 300
   network 210.77.8.0
   redistribute rip
   default-metric 10000 100 255 1 1500
   ```

2 Ensure that the interfaces running EIGRP do not have RIP updates generated through them or that the RIP interfaces do not have EIGRP updates running through them.

   To ensure this:

   ```
   router eigrp 300
   network 210.77.8.0
   redistribute rip
   default-metric 10000 100 255 1 1500
   passive interface s0.2
   router rip
   network 201.77.10.0
   passive interface s0.1
   passive interface s0.3
   passive interface e0
   passive interface e1
   ```

3 The site running IGRP and the site running EIGRP are running different autonomous system numbers. How would you implement a transition to both sites running EIGRP using the same autonomous system number?

There are several ways to transition from different autonomous systems to one autonomous system so that IGRP and EIGRP automatically redistribute. The methods include the following:

- **Configuring redistribution at both sites and in a controlled manner, during down time switching all the routers in the IGRP site to the same autonomous system as that of EIGRP. Because the prevailing routing protocol is to be EIGRP, it makes sense that IGRP is the protocol to change the autonomous system number. When this is working, the same approach could be made to switch to EIGRP in the IGRP site.**

- **Another approach, and one favored by many, is to configure EIGRP with the same autonomous system number on all routers at the IGRP site. As part of the configuration, increase the administrative distance of EIGRP to be 200 so that none of the routes is acceptable to the routing process. Then during down time on the systems, cut over to the EIGRP process by changing its administrative distance back to the default of 90. This can be done by simply adding the word no in front of the existing command. The beauty of this plan is that everything can be put in place before the cutover; if problems are experienced, it is equally easy to reverse the command to return to the IGRP configuration.**

4 The OSPF redistribution into RIP has been implemented, but users are complaining about delays. State the first step that you would take to verify the configuration.

The first step is to issue the following commands:

- **show ip route—To ensure that each routing process sees the appropriate paths. A routing loop might be visible here.**

- **extended ping—To see the path that is taken to the remote locations. A routing loop could be detected.**

- **show ip protocols—To see how RIP and OSPF are being redistributed, what the default metrics are, and whether there any distribute lists are impeding the flow of updates.**

- **show ip ospf database—To ensure that all the routes are in place. Again, errors leading to a routing loop could be detected here.**

- **show ip ospf neighbor—To ensure that OSPF can still see the adjacent routers.**

5 The CIO has been asked to submit a transition plan to the board of trustees that includes a reasoned explanation for the need for redistribution. What should it look like?

It should include the following:

The transition would happen at the main site where the centralized records and databases are maintained. This is because this site must be the most stable because it servers the other sites.

The next step would be to review the addressing scheme to ensure that it was hierarchical and could support summarization and VLSM.

The redistribution between IGRP and EIGRP is the easiest to effect and should be performed in accordance to the answer in question 3.

Because the equipment for RIP and OSPF machines may not support EIGRP, a careful assessment should be done, and plans should be made to upgrade the equipment as necessary. However, the network administrator should be reminded that it is not necessary for hosts to run RIP. If hosts run RIP it can lead to a very unstable network. Therefore all hosts should be configured with a default gateway address.

For this last point alone, it is necessary to have redistribution configured in the network to ensure the full connectivity throughout the campuses.

When redistribution is in place, centralization of resources and maintenance of the data and network can be implemented, granting a full exchange of information throughout the hospital to harness the power of the information available.

Scenario 10-2 Answers

1 The hospital policy states that the FTP traffic from the x-ray department (201.77.11.0/24) should be forwarded to the Biggun Server at 201.77.12.79 and that it should be sent across the leased line, which is a T1 connection. What would the configuration look like?

The configuration would be as follows:

```
interface e0
ip address 201.77.11.1 255.255.255.0
ip policy route-map xray

access-list 101 permit tcp 201.77.11.0 0.0.0.255 eq ftp any
access-list 101 permit tcp 201.77.11.0 0.0.0.255 eq ftp-data any
route-map xray permit 10
match ip address 101
set ip next-hop 201.77.10.2
```

2   The Telnet sessions and e-mail connections should be sent across the Frame Relay link. This traffic is from the same department (201.77.8.0.0/24) and is connecting to the same server. What would the configuration look like?

The configuration would be as follows:

```
interface e0
ip address 201.77.11.1 255.255.255.0
ip policy route-map xray

access-list 101 permit tcp 201.77.11.0 0.0.0.255 eq ftp any
access-list 101 permit tcp 201.77.11.0 0.0.0.255 eq ftp-data any
access-list 106 permit tcp 201.77.11.0 0.0.0.255 eq smtp any

route-map xray permit 10
match ip address 101
set ip next-hop 201.77.10.2
route-map xray permit 20
match ip address 106
set ip next-hop 201.77.8.5
```

3   What commands would you use to verify that the policy routing is configured correctly and operating normally?

The commands that should be used to verify the policy-based routing are as follows:

- **show ip policy**

- **show route map** *name*

- **debug ip policy**

CHAPTER 11

Scenarios for Final Preparation

This chapter is designed to assist you in final preparation for the Routing exam by providing additional practice with the core topics of the exam. These exercises and tasks require a broad perspective, which means that you will need to draw on knowledge that you acquired in each of Chapters 2 through 10. This chapter also focuses on configuration and verification commands. These scenarios are designed with the following assumptions in mind:

- You might forget many details of a particular technology by the time you have completed your study of the other chapters. These scenarios cover the entire breadth of topics to remind you about many of these details.

- The scenarios not only cover the entire breadth of the course, but they also put the topics in context. This makes it easier to comprehend each subject because it is no longer presented in a vacuum.

- The ability to apply knowledge in different contexts proves an understanding that goes way beyond simple learning. The mind is exercised outside the scope of the individual facts that are presented, which makes those facts much easier to remember.

- This application of the technology is a good preparation not only for the Routing exam, but also for day-to-day administrative tasks.

- Your understanding of the concepts at this point in your study is complete; practice and repetition is useful so that you can answer quickly and confidently on the exam.

Further Study for Final Preparation

This chapter is not the only chapter that you should use when doing your final preparation for the Routing exam. Not all the subjects in the exam are covered in this chapter. Here is a brief list of the study options provided by this book, beyond the core chapters and this scenarios chapter:

- All prechapter quiz and chapter-ending questions, with answers, are in Appendix A, "Answers to Quiz Questions." These conveniently located questions can be read and reviewed quickly, with explanations.

- The CD-ROM contains practice exam questions that you can use to take an overall sample exam or test yourself on specific topics. The CD-ROM also contains an electronic version of the book as well as supplemental material.

- Each core chapter has a "Foundation Summary" section near the end that contains concise tables and information for final review.

- Where appropriate, each chapter has a glossary for the terms introduced in that chapter. The chapter glossaries and Appendix C, "Glossary," are also good study aids.

How to Best Use This Chapter

This chapter includes two types of scenarios. The chapter is divided into two sections:

- **Scenarios**—Standard questions based on a presented situation. These are Scenarios 11-1, 11-2, and 11-3. The answers to these scenarios follow the three scenarios.

- **Three-part scenarios**—More complicated scenarios that require planning, configuration, and verification. These are Scenarios 11-4 and 11-5. The solutions to the three-part scenarios are contained within each scenario.

The focus of these scenarios is easily forgotten items. The first such items are the **show** and **debug** commands. Their options are often ignored, mainly because you can get online help about the correct option easily when using the Cisco CLI. However, questions about the exact command options used to see a particular piece of information are scattered throughout the exam. Take care to review the output of the commands in these scenarios.

Another focus of this chapter is a review of command-line tricks and acronym trivia. Like it or not, part of the preparation involves memorization; hopefully, these reminders will help you answer a question or two on the exam.

Finally, this chapter contains more configurations for almost all options already covered in the book. If you can configure these options without online help, you should feel confident that you can choose the correct command from a list.

Scenarios

The following case studies and questions are designed to draw together the content of the chapters and to exercise your understanding of the concepts. There is not necessarily a right answer. The thought process and practice in manipulating the concepts are the goals of this section. The answers to these scenarios immediately follow Scenario 11-3.

Scenario 11-1

The last network administrator of your company left abruptly. You were recently hired to the position and cannot find any documentation on the network. Using a network-management tool, you now have a topology map of the network.

Refer to Figure 11-1 and answer the questions that follow.

1　Offer some reasons why the routing protocol EIGRP has recently been implemented in the network, and give the reasons for its deployment in that particular area of the network.

2　The ISP has decided that the company should set a default route into its domain. Write out the commands that would configure the default route.

3　Is the router connecting to the ISP the only router that needs configuration? If this is the case, explain the reasons for your decision. If other routers need configuration, write out the commands required, and explain why they are needed and where they would be applied.

4　The ISP router connecting into the company network will need static route(s) configured. Write out the commands to configure the router.

5　Will these routes need to be redistributed into the ISP domain? If the answer is yes, explain the reason for your decision, and then write out the configuration commands. If the answer is no, explain the reasons for your decision.

6　Are filters required in this design? If so, state why, describe the type of filters required, and tell how and where they would be applied.

7　It has been suggested that Enhanced IGRP should be configured using summarization. If this plan were to be implemented, on which routers would it be configured, and why?

Figure 11-1 *Diagram of Network for Scenario 11-1*

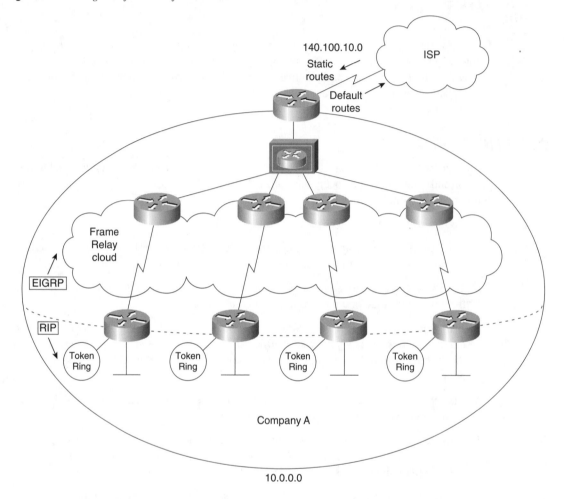

10.0.0.0

Scenario 11-2

The company has recently merged with another company that has OSPF as its routing protocol. It has been determined that this is going to be the company standard.

 1 Router A was chosen as the designated router on the LAN in the OSPF domain. Explain why this design choice was made, and give the command that would ensure its selection as the designated router.

 2 Redistribution is occurring between IGRP and OSPF on Router A; state the configuration commands that would be used for both IGRP and OSPF.

3 The new headquarters of the merged company is in the OSPF domain. Therefore, because the connection to the Internet is also in this domain, it has been decided that Router A will have a default route configured to point to the OSPF domain from the IGRP domain. It will be necessary to configure the **ip classless** command for the IGRP domain. Explain why the **ip classless** command is needed and what it achieves.

4 Explain the use of the **subnet** command in OSPF, and tell why it is required in redistribution.

5 Explain why it may be necessary to filter when redistributing, and tell what it achieves in this network.

Scenario 11-3

Your company has decided to change its routing protocol from RIP to Enhanced IGRP. The company is currently running both IPX and IP. With reference to Figure 11-2, devise a design for the new network.

Figure 11-2   *Diagram of Network for Scenario 11-3*

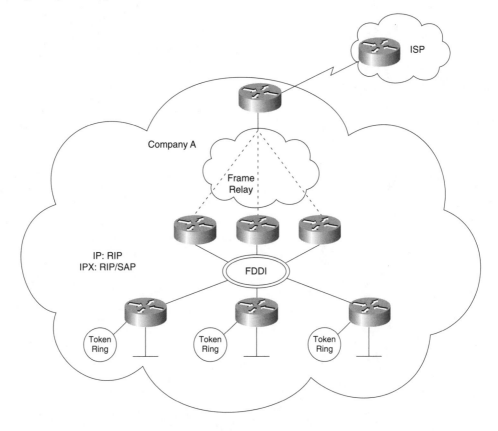

Ensure that you include the following:

1 Create a transition plan, showing how the final design will be implemented.

2 If the transition plan requires redistribution, indicate these points on the diagram and provide the configuration commands.

3 The company has also decided to connect to the Internet using Enhanced IGRP, which the ISP providing the Internet connectivity has agreed upon. Is any redistribution required? Give reasons for your answers.

4 Explain the neighbors that you see on the LAN segment and the path selection on Router B.

5 Create a diagram that shows the final network design, with configuration commands for Enhanced IGRP.

6 Write out the configuration commands for Router B.

Scenario Answers

The answers are in **bold**. The answers provided in this section are not necessarily the only possible answers to the questions. The questions are designed to test your knowledge and to give practical exercise in certain key areas. This section is intended to test and exercise skills and concepts detailed in the body of this chapter.

If your answer is different, ask yourself whether it follows the tenets explained in the answers provided. Your answer is correct not if it matches the solution provided in the book, but rather if it has included the principles of design laid out in the chapter.

In this way, the testing provided in these scenarios is deeper: It examines not only your knowledge, but also your understanding and ability to apply that knowledge to problems.

If you do not get the correct answer, refer back to the text and review the subject tested. Be certain to also review your notes on the question to ensure that you understand the principles of the subject.

Scenario 11-1 Answers

1 Offer some reasons why the routing protocol Enhanced IGRP has recently been implemented in the network, and give the reasons for its deployment in that particular area of the network.

   Enhanced IGRP is being run across the Frame Relay WAN in areas where there are no client or server workstations. The network routers are all Cisco devices, which understand Enhanced IGRP.

   Using Enhanced IGRP is far more efficient on a WAN because incremental updates can be sent across the limited bandwidth. In particular, if either AppleTalk or IPX is running at the access level, the routing updates can be sent in Enhanced IGRP, which gives far more control and flexibility because it is a new, more sophisticated, proprietary routing protocol.

2 The ISP has decided that the company should set a default route into its domain. Write out the commands that would configure the default route.

   The configuration commands to establish a default route from the company's network to the ISP domain are as follows:

   ```
   Router(config)# router eigrp 100
   Router(config-router)# network 10.0.0.0
   Router(config-router)# network 140.100.10.0
   Router(config)# ip default network 140.100.0.0
   ```

   The network command is also required for EIGRP to propagate the network in the updates.

3 Is the router connecting to the ISP the only router that needs configuration? If this is the case, explain the reasons for your decision. If other routers need configuration, write out the commands required, explain why they are needed, and tell where they would be applied.

The router connecting to the ISP is the only router that needs to be configured. The default route will be propagated to all the other EIGRP routers automatically. Although default routes redistributed into a RIP environment require that the ip classless command be configured, this is for routers that are downstream from the router that is dealing with the redistribution. Because the routers at the redistribution points will have routes redistributed into them by Enhanced IGRP, they will have no problem in the lookup.

4 The ISP router connecting into the company network will need static route(s) configured. Write out the commands to configure the router.

The configuration commands to establish static routes from the ISP domain into the company's network are as follows:

```
Router(config)# ip route 140.100.0.0 255.255.0.0    140.100.60.3
Router(config)# ip route 200.10.20.0 255.255.255.0 140.100.60.3
Router(config)# ip route 199.56.10.0 255.255.255.0 140.100.60.3
Router(config)# ip route 222.22.10.0 255.255.255.0 140.100.60.3
```

5 Will these routes need to be redistributed into the ISP domain? If the answer is yes, explain the reason for your decision, and then write out the configuration commands. If the answer is no, explain the reasons for your decision.

The static commands will need to be redistributed into the ISP domain. Static routes are not redistributed automatically. Static routes configured with the outgoing interface as opposed to the next-hop address are considered by the router to be directly connected.

The commands for redistribution of static routes are as follows:

```
Router(config)# Router EIGRP 100
Router(config)# redistribute static
Router(config)# default-metric 10000 100 255 1 1500
```

6 Are filters required in this design? If so, state why, describe the type of filters required, and tell how and where they would be applied

Because there are no redundant paths in the redistribution between protocols, no filters are required in the configuration of the routers. There will be no feedback between the protocols.

Because there is no routing protocol running between the company and the ISP, there is no requirement for filters here, either. If any filters were required, they would be for internal security and traffic control, and would be typically configured on the access routers entering the Frame Relay cloud. There could also be some distribution lists at the distribution layer to limit connectivity among the different regions.

7 It has been suggested that Enhanced IGRP should be configured using summarization. If this plan were to be implemented, on which routers would it be configured, and why?

Summarization would be configured at the access level to limit the number of updates that need to traverse the WAN.

Scenario 11-2 Answers

Figure 11-3 illustrates the answer for Scenario 11-2.

Figure 11-3   *Answer Diagram for Scenario 11-2*

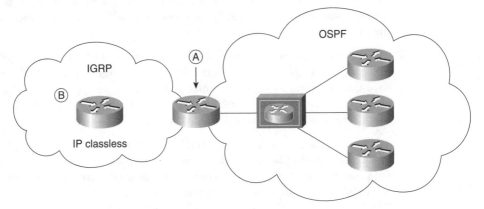

1 Router A was chosen as the designated router on the LAN in the OSPF domain. Explain why this design choice was made, and give the command that would ensure its selection as the designated router.

The router was selected by the administrator to be the designated router because it is an Autonomous System Boundary Router (ASBR). This makes it the most sensible choice. All traffic must pass through it to reach another domain. It is hopefully also a more powerful router because it must calculate redistribution and filtering and also handle the role of designated router. The command to ensure that this router is chosen as the designated router is as follows:

```
router ospf 100
interface e0
ip ospf priority 100
```

The designated router will have been selected manually by using this priority command or by configuring the router with the highest OSPF ID. This is achieved by allocating a loopback address.

2   Redistribution is occurring between IGRP and OSPF on Router A; state the configuration commands that would be used for both IGRP and OSPF.

The configuration commands for redistributing OSPF into IGRP and IGRP back into OSPF follow:

```
router igrp 100
passive int e0
network 201.100.10.0
redistribute ospf 100 metric 10000 100 255 1 1500

router ospf 100
passive interface e1
network 144.250.0.0 0.0.255.255 area 0
redistribute igrp 100 metric 30 metric-type 1 subnets
```

The use of the passive interface is unnecessary because the routing processes do not use the same Internet number. These commands will allow full connectivity between the two domains.

3   The new headquarters of the merged company is in the OSPF domain. Therefore, because the connection to the Internet is also in this domain, it has been decided that Router A will have a default route configured to point to the OSPF domain from the IGRP domain. It will be necessary to configure the **ip classless** command for the IGRP domain. Explain why the **ip classless** command is needed, and tell what it achieves.

The ip classless command is required in a classful routing protocol that is doing a lookup in a routing table that does not contain the route because redistribution has not propagated the route to this router. So, when a default route is redistributed into a classful routing domain, the downstream routers cannot see the network that they should forward to. This command solves that problem.

4   Explain the use of the **subnet** command in OSPF, and tell why it is required in redistribution.

The subnet command is used to propagate subnetworks into the OSPF domain instead of propagating the larger classful address obtained from the InterNIC.

5   Explain why it may be necessary to filter when redistributing, and tell what it achieves in this network.

The filter prevents feedback from OSPF into IGRP, and vice versa. This avoids routing loops.

Scenario 11-3 Answers

1 Create a transition plan, showing how the final design will be implemented.

Figure 11-4 shows the answer to this question.

Figure 11-4 *Answer Diagram for Scenario 11-3, Question 1*

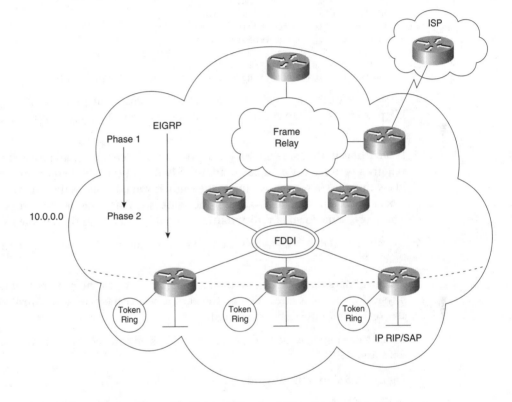

In Figure 11-4, the transition would start at the core and move down to the
distribution layer routers. The first move would be to place EIGRP in the Frame
Relay cloud to alleviate the network overhead. After this is operational, the second
phase would be to implement EIGRP in the FDDI ring because there are no end
stations on the ring that require IPX RIP/SAP.

2 If the transition plan requires redistribution, indicate these points on the diagram and
provide the configuration commands.

The configuration commands that provide for the redistribution between the different routing protocols are as follows:

```
Router(config)# router rip
Router(config-router)#network  10.0.0.0
Router(config-router)#passive int E0
Router(config-router)#redistribute eigrp 100
Router(config-router)# default-metric  3
Router(config)# router eigrp 100
Router(config-router)#network  10.0.0.0
Router(config-router)#passive int  E1
Router(config-router)#passive int  Token 0
Router(config-router)#redistribute rip
Router(config-router)# default-metric 10000 100 255 1 1500
```

3 The company has also decided to connect to the Internet using Enhanced IGRP, which the ISP providing the Internet connectivity has agreed upon. Is any redistribution required? Give reasons for your answers.

If the ISP is in the same autonomous system as the company, no redistribution is required between the company and the ISP. Within the ISP domain, however, it is likely that the router connecting to the company in question is the only router that is a part of the autonomous system of the company. This is for security reasons. Therefore, some form of redistribution probably will be required in the ISP domain.

4 Explain the neighbors that you see on the LAN segment and the path selection on Router B.

The neighbors that are seen on the LAN segment are all the routers that share the physical medium. Router B chose the path as a successor because it provided the shortest path to the networks stated.

5 Create a diagram that shows the final network design, with configuration commands for Enhanced IGRP.

Figure 11-5 shows the answer.

In Figure 11-5, ip summary-address may be configured where appropriate at the distribution layer (the routers entering the Frame Relay cloud).

Figure 11-5   *Answer Diagram to Scenario 11-3, Question 5*

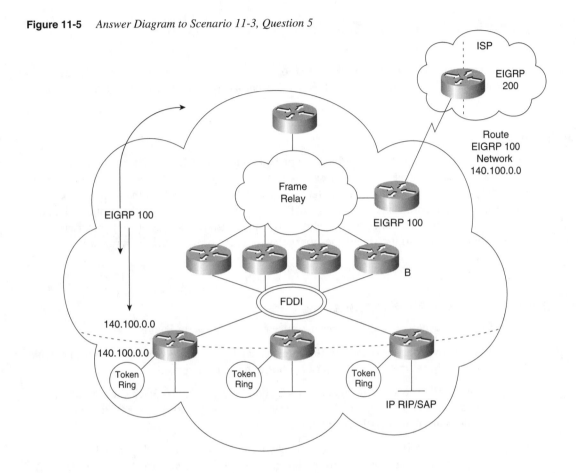

6 Write out the configuration commands for Router B.

The configuration commands for Router B are as follows:

```
Router(config)#router eigrp 100
Router(config-router)#network 140.100.0.0
Router(config-router)#no auto-summary
Router(config-router)#ip summary-address 140.100.64.0 255.255.240.0
```

Three-Part Scenarios

This section contains two three-part scenarios that require planning, configuration, and verification. The solutions to these three-part scenarios are contained within each scenario.

Scenario 11-4

Part A of Scenario 11-4 begins with some planning guidelines that include planning IP addresses, designing the VLSM addressing scheme, identifying the OSPF areas, and determining what type of areas they should be. After you complete Part A, Part B of the scenario asks you to configure the three routers to implement the planned design and a few other features. Finally, Part C asks you to examine router command output to discover details about the current operation. Part C also lists some questions related to the user interface and protocol specifications.

Scenario 11-4, Part A—Planning

Your job is to deploy a new network with three sites, as shown in Figure 11-6.

The OSPF network has a shortage of IP addresses. It has been decided to readdress the network using VLSM. For Part A of this scenario, perform the following tasks:

1   Plan the IP addressing, using the Class B address of 131.99.0.0. Each site consists of two buildings, with seven floors. Each floor has approximately 100 devices. The company plans to install an ISDN backup link between the buildings.

2   In the expectation of growth, the company has decided that each site should be an area. Currently each site has only two buildings, connected via a switch. One of the sites has a department running UNIX servers that are using RIP. The RIP networks are redistributed into the OSPF network.

Define the location of the areas.

Define the type and number of each area, stating your reasons for your choices.

3   The plan is for a backup ISDN link to be set up between the two buildings on each site. It has been designed as a floating static route.

Would this static route need to be redistributed into OSPF?

What other considerations are there?

Figure 11-6 *Scenario 11-4 Network Diagram*

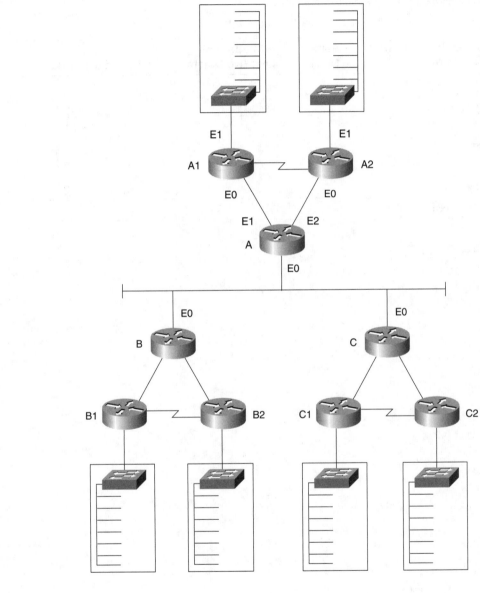

Table 11-1 and Table 11-2 are provided as a convenient place to record your IP subnets when performing the planning tasks for this scenario.

Table 11-1   *Scenario 11-4, Part A—IP Subnet Network Planning Chart*

Geographic Location of Subnet/Network	Subnet Number	Bit Pattern of Last Two Octets	Prefix	Subnet Mask
A				
Ethernet 0				
B				
Ethernet 0				
C				
Ethernet 0				
Serial between A1 and A2				
A1				
Ethernet 1				
VLANs				
Floor 1				
Floor 2				
Floor 3				
Floor 4				
Floor 5				
Floor 6				
Floor 7				
A2				
Ethernet 1				
VLANs				
Floor 1				
Floor 2				
Floor 3				
Floor 4				
Floor 5				
Floor 6				
Floor 7				

Table 11-1   *Scenario 11-4, Part A—IP Subnet Network Planning Chart (Continued)*

Geographic Location of Subnet/Network	Subnet Number	Bit Pattern of Last Two Octets	Prefix	Subnet Mask
Serial between B1 and B2				
B1				
Ethernet 1				
VLANs				
Floor 1				
Floor 2				
Floor 3				
Floor 4				
Floor 5				
Floor 6				
Floor 7				
B2				
Ethernet 1				
VLANs				
Floor 1				
Floor 2				
Floor 3				
Floor 4				
Floor 5				
Floor 6				
Floor 7				
Serial between C1 and C2				

continues

Table 11-1 *Scenario 11-4, Part A—IP Subnet Network Planning Chart (Continued)*

Geographic Location of Subnet/Network	Subnet Number	Bit Pattern of Last Two Octets	Prefix	Subnet Mask
C1				
Ethernet 1				
VLANs				
Floor 1				
Floor 2				
Floor 3				
Floor 4				
Floor 5				
Floor 6				
Floor 7				
C2				
Ethernet 1				
VLANs				
Floor 1				
Floor 2				
Floor 3				
Floor 4				
Floor 5				
Floor 6				
Floor 7				

Table 11-2 *Scenario 11-4, Part A—OSPF Area Planning Chart*

Router Location	Router Type	Reason
A		
B		
C		

Table 11-2   *Scenario 11-4, Part A—OSPF Area Planning Chart (Continued)*

Router Location	Router Type	Reason
A1		
A2		
B1		
B2		
C1		
C2		

Solutions to Scenario 11-4, Part A—Planning

Keeping the design as simple as possible—yet not too simple, so that it is still useful as the network evolves—is a good practice. In the suggested answers in Tables 11-3 and 11-4, a numbering scheme is presented. Remember, this is one of many solutions available. The reasoning behind this planning is to allow summarization at the Area Border Routers. The first few bits in the third octet indicate the summarization bits. Note that these bits reflect the area; 1 bit or 128 identifies area 1, while 3 bits or 224 identify area 3.

Table 11-3   *Scenario 11-4, Part A—IP Subnet Network Planning Chart Solution*

Geographic Location of Subnet/Network	Subnet Number	Bit Pattern of Last Two Octets	Prefix	Subnet Mask
A				
Ethernet 0	131.99.0.48	00000000 0011 0000	/28	255.255.255.240
Ethernet 1	131.99.136.128	10001000 1000 0000	/28	255.255.255.240
Ethernet 2	131.99.144.128	10010000 1000 0000	/28	255.255.255.240

continues

Table 11-3   *Scenario 11-4, Part A—IP Subnet Network Planning Chart Solution (Continued)*

Geographic Location of Subnet/Network	Subnet Number	Bit Pattern of Last Two Octets	Prefix	Subnet Mask
B				
Ethernet 0	131.99.0.48	**00000000 0011** 0000	/28	255.255.255.240
Ethernet 1	131.99.192.192	**11000000 1100** 0000	/28	255.255.255.240
Ethernet 2	131.99.216.192	**11011000 1100** 0000	/28	255.255.255.240
C				
Ethernet 0	131.99.0.48	**00000000 0011** 0000	/28	255.255.255.240
Ethernet 1	131.99.224.224	**11100000 1110** 0000	/28	255.255.255.240
Ethernet 2	131.99.232.224	**11101000 1110** 0000	/28	255.255.255.240
Serial between A1 and A2	131.99.128.128	**10000000 10**00 0000	/26	255.255.255.192
A1				
Ethernet 0	131.99.136.128	**10001000 1000** 0000	/28	255.255.255.240
Ethernet 1				
VLANs				
Floor 1	131.99.136.0	**10001000 0** 0000000	/25	255.255.255.128
Floor 2	131.99.137.0	**10001001 0** 0000000	/25	255.255.255.128
Floor 3	131.99.138.0	**10001010 0** 0000000	/25	255.255.255.128
Floor 4	131.99.139.0	**10001011 0** 0000000	/25	255.255.255.128
Floor 5	131.99.140.0	**10001100 0** 0000000	/25	255.255.255.128
Floor 6	131.99.141.0	**10001101 0** 0000000	/25	255.255.255.128
Floor 7	131.99.142.0	**10001110 0** 0000000	/25	255.255.255.128
A2				
Ethernet 0	131.99.144.128	**10010000 1000** 0000	/28	255.255.255.240
Ethernet 1				
VLANs				
Floor 1	131.99.144.0	**10010000 0** 0000000	/25	255.255.255.128
Floor 2	131.99.145.0	**10010001 0** 0000000	/25	255.255.255.128
Floor 3	131.99.146.0	**10010010 0** 0000000	/25	255.255.255.128
Floor 4	131.99.147.0	**10010011 0** 0000000	/25	255.255.255.128
Floor 5	131.99.148.0	**10010100 0** 0000000	/25	255.255.255.128
Floor 6	131.99.149.0	**10010101 0** 0000000	/25	255.255.255.128
Floor 7	131.99.150.0	**10010110 0** 0000000	/25	255.255.255.128

Table 11-3   *Scenario 11-4, Part A—IP Subnet Network Planning Chart Solution (Continued)*

Geographic Location of Subnet/Network	Subnet Number	Bit Pattern of Last Two Octets	Prefix	Subnet Mask
Serial between B1 and B2	131.99.192.128	**11000000 10** 000000	/26	255.255.255.192
B1				
Ethernet 0	131.99.192.192	**11000000 1100** 0000	/28	225.255.255.240
Ethernet 1				
VLANs				
Floor 1	131.99.200.0	**11001000 0** 0000000	/25	255.255.255.128
Floor 2	131.99.201.0	**11001001 0** 0000000	/25	255.255.255.128
Floor 3	131.99.202.0	**11001010 0** 0000000	/25	255.255.255.128
Floor 4	131.99.203.0	**11001011 0** 0000000	/25	255.255.255.128
Floor 5	131.99.204.0	**11001100 0** 0000000	/25	255.255.255.128
Floor 6	131.99.205.0	**11001101 0** 0000000	/25	255.255.255.128
Floor 7	131.99.206.0	**11001110 0** 0000000	/25	255.255.255.128
B2				
Ethernet 0	131.99.216.192	**11011000 1100** 0000	/28	225.255.255.240
Ethernet 1				
VLANs				
Floor 1	131.99.216.0	**11011000 0** 0000000	/25	255.255.255.128
Floor 2	131.99.217.0	**11011001 0** 0000000	/25	255.255.255.128
Floor 3	131.99.218.0	**11011010 0** 0000000	/25	255.255.255.128
Floor 4	131.99.219.0	**11011011 0** 0000000	/25	255.255.255.128
Floor 5	131.99.220.0	**11011100 0** 0000000	/25	255.255.255.128
Floor 6	131.99.221.0	**11011101 0** 0000000	/25	255.255.255.128
Floor 7	131.99.222.0	**11011110 0** 0000000	/25	255.255.255.128
Serial between C1 and C2	131.99.224.128	**11100000 10** 000000	/26	255.255.255.192

continues

Table 11-3 *Scenario 11-4, Part A—IP Subnet Network Planning Chart Solution (Continued)*

Geographic Location of Subnet/Network	Subnet Number	Bit Pattern of Last Two Octets	Prefix	Subnet Mask
C1				
Ethernet 0	131.99.224.224	**111**00000 1110 0000	/28	225.255.255.240
Ethernet 1				
VLANs				
Floor 1	131.99.224.0	**111**00000 0 0000000	/25	255.255.255.128
Floor 2	131.99.225.0	**111**00001 0 0000000	/25	255.255.255.128
Floor 3	131.99.226.0	**111**00010 0 0000000	/25	255.255.255.128
Floor 4	131.99.227.0	**111**00011 0 0000000	/25	255.255.255.128
Floor 5	131.99.228.0	**111**00100 0 0000000	/25	255.255.255.128
Floor 6	131.99.229.0	**111**00101 0 0000000	/25	255.255.255.128
Floor 7	131.99.230.0	**111**00110 0 0000000	/25	255.255.255.128
C2				
Ethernet 0	131.99.232.224	**111**01000 1110 0000	/28	255.255.255.240
Ethernet 1				
VLANs				
Floor 1	131.99.232.0	**111**01000 0 0000000	/25	255.255.255.128
Floor 2	131.99.233.0	**111**01001 0 0000000	/25	255.255.255.128
Floor 3	131.99.234.0	**111**01010 0 0000000	/25	255.255.255.128
Floor 4	131.99.235.0	**111**01011 0 0000000	/25	255.255.255.128
Floor 5	131.99.236.0	**111**01100 0 0000000	/25	255.255.255.128
Floor 6	131.99.237.0	**111**01101 0 0000000	/25	255.255.255.128
Floor 7	131.99.238.0	**111**01110 0 0000000	/25	255.255.255.128

Table 11-4 *Scenario 11-4, Part A—OSPF Area Planning Chart Solution*

Router Location	OSPF Router Type	Reason
A in Area 0 and Area 1	Backbone router and Area Border Router (ABR). The interface into Area 1 is configured as a stub area.	The router has an interface in both Area 0 and Area 1; it is at the core of the network. The interface into Area 1 will not send external routes into the area, but it may generate default route and summary routes.
B in Area 0 and Area 2	Backbone router and Area Border Router (ABR). The interface into Area 1 is configured as a stub area.	The router has an interface in both Area 0 and Area 1; it is at the core of the network. The interface into Area 2 will not send external routes into the area, but it may generate default route and summary routes.

Table 11-4   *Scenario 11-4, Part A—OSPF Area Planning Chart Solution (Continued)*

Router Location	OSPF Router Type	Reason
C in Area 0 and Area 3	Backbone router and Area Border Router (ABR). The interface into Area 1 is *not* configured as a stub area because the area has RIP redistributed into the area.	The router has an interface in both Area 0 and Area 1; it is at the core of the network. The interface into Area 3 will not send external routes into the area, but it will generate a default route. Because this area is the only area that has external routes, this is not an issue. However if the organization ever connects into the Internet, then additional configuration will be necessary to distinguish between the Internet and the RIP network.
A1	Internal router and stub area router into Area 1.	It is in Area 1 only using summarization, with no need for the RIP networks; it can therefore be configured as a stub area.
A2	Internal router and stub area router into Area 1.	It is in Area 1 only using summarization with no need for the RIP networks; it can therefore be configured as a stub area.
B1	Internal router and stub area router into Area 2.	It is in Area 2 only using summarization with no need for the RIP networks; it can therefore be configured as a stub area.
B2	Internal router and stub area router into Area 2.	It is in Area 2 only using summarization with no need for the RIP networks; it can therefore be configured as a stub area.
C1	Internal router to Area 3.	This router cannot be a stub area router because the area has RIP redistributed into it.
C2	An Autonomous System Border Router (ASBR)	Because the building that this router serves has UNIX servers running RIP, and because these networks need to be accessible to the organization, RIP needs to be redistributed into the OSPF domain. Redistributed routes are considered as external routes—thus the configuration of an ASBR.

Scenario 11-4, Part B—Configuration

The next step in your job is to deploy the network designed in Scenario 11-4, Part A. Use the solutions for Part A of Scenario 11-4 to direct you in configuring the addressing and summarization at the area border routers. For Scenario 11-4, Part B, perform the following tasks:

1 Configure basic OSPF for routers A, B, and C based on Scenario 11-4, Part A's design.

2 Configure summarization on routers A, B, and C.

3 Configure routers A and B to connect to stub areas.

Solutions to Scenario 11-4, Part B—Configuration

Example 11-1, Example 11-2, and Example 11-3 show the configurations for Scenario 11-4, Part B, given the criteria.

Example 11-1 *Scenario 11-4 Router A Configuration*

```
interface e0
ip address 131.99.0.49 255.255.255.240
! 4 bits allows 14 hosts
interface e1
ip address 131.99.136.129 255.255.255.128
! 7 bits allows  127 hosts
interface e2
ip address 131.99.144.129 255.255.255.128
! 7 bits allows  127 hosts
!!
router ospf 100
network 131.99.0.49 0.0.0.0 area 0
! The wildcard mask 0.0.0.0 places the interface E0 into area 0
network 0.0.0.0 255.255.255.255 area 1
! The wildcard mask 255.255.255.255 places all other interfaces into area 1
area 1 range 131.99.128.0 255.255.240.0
! All addresses from area 1 will be summarized into this one network
area 1 stub
! Area 1 is defined as a stub network that will not receive network information
! outside the autonomous system
```

Example 11-2 *Scenario 11-4 Router B Configuration*

```
interface e0
ip address 131.99.0.50 255.255.255.240
! 4 bits allows 14 hosts
interface e1
ip address 131.99.192.193 255.255.255.128
! 7 bits allows 127 hosts
interface e2
ip address 131.99.216.193 255.255.255.128
! 7 bits allows 127 hosts
!!
router ospf 100
network 131.99.0.50 0.0.0.0 area 0
network 0.0.0.0 255.255.255.255 area 2
area 2 range 131.99.192.0 255.255.240.0
area 2 stub
```

Example 11-3 *Scenario 11-4 Router C Configuration*

```
interface e0
ip address 131.99.0.51 255.255.255.240
! 4 bits allows 14 hosts
interface e1
ip address 131.99.224.225 255.255.255.128
! 7 bits allows 127 hosts)
interface e2
ip address 131.99.232.225 255.255.255.128
! 4 bits allows 14 hosts
!!
router ospf 100
network 131.99.0.51 0.0.0.0 area 0
network 0.0.0.0 255.255.255.255 area 3
area 3 range 131.99.224.0 255.255.240.0
```

Scenario 11-4 Part C—Verification and Questions

The Routing 2.0 exam tests your memory for information that can be found in the output of various **show** commands. Using the output from Examples 11-4 through 11-6, answer the questions that follow.

NOTE	In the network from which these commands were captured, several administrative settings not mentioned in the scenario were configured. For instance, the enable password was configured. Any **show running-config** commands in the examples in this chapter might have other unrelated configuration.

Example 11-4 *The* **show** *and* **debug** *Output Screens for Scenario 11-4, Router A*

```
routerA#
routerA#show version
Cisco Internetwork Operating System Software
IOS (tm) 3600 Software (C3620-JS56I-M), Version 12.0(7)T,  RELEASE SOFTWARE (fc2)
Copyright (c) 1986-1999 by cisco Systems, Inc.
Compiled Wed 08-Dec-99 11:16 by phanguye
Image text-base: 0x600088F0, data-base: 0x612B4000

ROM: System Bootstrap, Version 11.1(20)AA2, EARLY DEPLOYMENT RELEASE SOFTWARE
(fc1)

routerA uptime is 28 minutes
System returned to ROM by reload
System image file is "flash:c3620-js56i-mz.120-7.T.bin"
```

continues

Example 11-4 *The* **show** *and* **debug** *Output Screens for Scenario 11-4, Router A (Continued)*

```
cisco 3620 (R4700) processor (revision 0x81) with 59392K/6144K bytes of memory.
Processor board ID 19276534
R4700 CPU at 80Mhz, Implementation 33, Rev 1.0
Bridging software.
X.25 software, Version 3.0.0.
SuperLAT software (copyright 1990 by Meridian Technology Corp).
TN3270 Emulation software.
1 Ethernet/IEEE 802.3 interface(s)
1 Serial network interface(s)
1 ATM network interface(s)
DRAM configuration is 32 bits wide with parity disabled.
29K bytes of non-volatile configuration memory.
16384K bytes of processor board System flash (Read/Write)

Configuration register is 0x2102

routerA#show running-config
Building configuration...

Current configuration:
!
version 12.0
service timestamps debug datetime msec localtime show-timezone
service timestamps log datetime msec localtime show-timezone
service password-encryption
!
hostname routerA
!
enable password 7 1511021F0725
!
!
!
ip subnet-zero
!
cns event-service server
!
!
!
interface Ethernet1
 ip address 131.99.136.129 255.255.255.128
 no ip directed-broadcast
!
interface Ethernet2
 ip address 131.99.144.129 255.255.255.128
 no ip directed-broadcast
!
interface Ethernet0
 ip address 131.99.0.49 255.255.255.240
 no ip directed-broadcast
!
interface Serial0/0
 no ip address
 no ip directed-broadcast
```

Example 11-4 *The* **show** *and* **debug** *Output Screens for Scenario 11-4, Router A (Continued)*

```
         no ip mroute-cache
         shutdown
         no fair-queue
         !
         interface ATM1/0
         no ip address
         no ip directed-broadcast
         shutdown
         no atm ilmi-keepalive
         !
         router ospf 100
          area 1 stub
          area 1 range 131.99.128.0 255.255.240.0
          network 131.99.0.49 0.0.0.0 area 0
          network 0.0.0.0 255.255.255.255 area 1
         !
         ip classless
         no ip http server
         !
         !
         !
         line con 0
          transport input none
         line aux 0
         line vty 0 4
          password 7 045802150C2E
          login
         !
         end

         routerA#
         routerA#show interface
         Ethernet0 is up, line protocol is up
           Hardware is AmdP2, address is 0001.96ea.af61 (bia 0001.96ea.af61)
           Internet address is 131.99.0.49/28
           MTU 1500 bytes, BW 10000 Kbit, DLY 1000 usec,
              reliability 255/255, txload 1/255, rxload 1/255
           Encapsulation ARPA, loopback not set
           Keepalive set (10 sec)
           ARP type: ARPA, ARP Timeout 04:00:00
           Last input 00:00:05, output 00:00:05, output hang never
           Last clearing of "show interface" counters never
           Queueing strategy: fifo
         Output queue 0/40, 0 drops; input queue 0/75, 0 drops
           5 minute input rate 0 bits/sec, 0 packets/sec
           5 minute output rate 0 bits/sec, 0 packets/sec
              241 packets input, 22186 bytes, 0 no buffer
              Received 228 broadcasts, 0 runts, 0 giants, 0 throttles
              0 input errors, 0 CRC, 0 frame, 0 overrun, 0 ignored
              0 input packets with dribble condition detected
              266 packets output, 35619 bytes, 0 underruns
```

continues

Example 11-4 *The* **show** *and* **debug** *Output Screens for Scenario 11-4, Router A (Continued)*

```
        0 output errors, 0 collisions, 1 interface resets
        0 babbles, 0 late collision, 0 deferred
        0 lost carrier, 0 no carrier
        0 output buffer failures, 0 output buffers swapped out
Serial0/0 is administratively down, line protocol is down
    Hardware is QUICC Serial
    MTU 1500 bytes, BW 2048 Kbit, DLY 20000 usec,
        reliability 255/255, txload 1/255, rxload 1/255
    Encapsulation HDLC, loopback not set
    Keepalive set (10 sec)
    Last input never, output never, output hang never
    Last clearing of "show interface" counters 00:27:38
    Queueing strategy: fifo
Output queue 0/40, 0 drops; input queue 0/75, 0 drops
    5 minute input rate 0 bits/sec, 0 packets/sec
    5 minute output rate 0 bits/sec, 0 packets/sec
        0 packets input, 0 bytes, 0 no buffer
        Received 0 broadcasts, 0 runts, 0 giants, 0 throttles
        0 input errors, 0 CRC, 0 frame, 0 overrun, 0 ignored, 0 abort
        7 packets output, 930 bytes, 0 underruns
        0 output errors, 0 collisions, 1 interface resets
        0 output buffer failures, 0 output buffers swapped out
        0 carrier transitions
        DCD=down  DSR=down  DTR=down  RTS=down  CTS=down

ATM1/0 is administratively down, line protocol is down
    Hardware is RS8234 ATMOC3
    MTU 4470 bytes, sub MTU 4470, BW 155000 Kbit, DLY 80 usec,
        reliability 0/255, txload 1/255, rxload 1/255
    Encapsulation ATM, loopback not set
    Keepalive not supported
    Encapsulation(s): AAL5
    1024 maximum active VCs, 0 current VCCs
    VC idle disconnect time: 300 seconds
    Last input never, output never, output hang never
    Last clearing of "show interface" counters never
    Input queue: 0/75/0 (size/max/drops); Total output drops: 0
    Queueing strategy: Per VC Queueing
5 minute input rate 0 bits/sec, 0 packets/sec
    5 minute output rate 0 bits/sec, 0 packets/sec
        0 packets input, 0 bytes, 0 no buffer
        Received 0 broadcasts, 0 runts, 0 giants, 0 throttles
        0 input errors, 0 CRC, 0 frame, 0 overrun, 0 ignored, 0 abort
        0 packets output, 0 bytes, 0 underruns
        0 output errors, 0 collisions, 1 interface resets
        0 output buffer failures, 0 output buffers swapped out
Ethernet1 is up, line protocol is up
  Hardware is AmdP2, address is 0001.96ea.af61 (bia 0001.96ea.ae31)
  Internet address is 131.99.136.129/25
  MTU 1500 bytes, BW 10000 Kbit, DLY 1000 usec,
        reliability 255/255, txload 1/255, rxload 1/255
  Encapsulation ARPA, loopback not set
  Keepalive set (10 sec)
```

Example 11-4 *The* **show** *and* **debug** *Output Screens for Scenario 11-4, Router A (Continued)*

```
              ARP type: ARPA, ARP Timeout 04:00:00
              Last input 00:20:53, output never, output hang never
              Last clearing of "show interface" counters never
              Queueing strategy: fifo
          Output queue 0/0, 0 drops; input queue 0/75, 0 drops
              5 minute input rate 0 bits/sec, 0 packets/sec
              5 minute output rate 0 bits/sec, 0 packets/sec
                  0 packets input, 0 bytes, 0 no buffer
                  Received 0 broadcasts, 0 runts, 0 giants, 0 throttles
                  0 input errors, 0 CRC, 0 frame, 0 overrun, 0 ignored, 0 abort
                  3 packets output, 159 bytes, 0 underruns
                  0 output errors, 0 collisions, 0 interface resets
                  0 output buffer failures, 0 output buffers swapped out
          Ethernet2 is up, line protocol is up
          Hardware is AmdP2, address is 0001.96ea.af61 (bia 0001.96ea.aa21)
          Internet address is 131.99.144.129/25
          MTU 1500 bytes, BW 10000 Kbit, DLY 1000 usec,
              reliability 255/255, txload 1/255, rxload 1/255
              Encapsulation ARPA, loopback not set
              Keepalive set (10 sec)
              ARP type: ARPA, ARP Timeout 04:00:00
              Last input 00:20:54, output never, output hang never
              Last clearing of "show interface" counters never
              Queueing strategy: fifo
          Output queue 0/0, 0 drops; input queue 0/75, 0 drops
              5 minute input rate 0 bits/sec, 0 packets/sec
              5 minute output rate 0 bits/sec, 0 packets/sec
                  0 packets input, 0 bytes, 0 no buffer
                  Received 0 broadcasts, 0 runts, 0 giants, 0 throttles
                  0 input errors, 0 CRC, 0 frame, 0 overrun, 0 ignored, 0 abort
                  3 packets output, 159 bytes, 0 underruns
                  0 output errors, 0 collisions, 0 interface resets
                  0 output buffer failures, 0 output buffers swapped out
          routerA#
          routerA#show ip protocols
          Routing Protocol is "ospf 100"
            Sending updates every 0 seconds
            Invalid after 0 seconds, hold down 0, flushed after 0
            Outgoing update filter list for all interfaces is
            Incoming update filter list for all interfaces is
            Redistributing: ospf 100
            Routing for Networks:
              131.99.0.49/32
              0.0.0.0
            Routing Information Sources:
              Gateway         Distance      Last Update
              131.99.232.225       110      00:14:49
              131.99.216.193       110      00:14:49
            Distance: (default is 110)
```

continues

Example 11-4 *The* **show** *and* **debug** *Output Screens for Scenario 11-4, Router A (Continued)*

```
routerA# show ip route
Codes: C - connected, S - static, I - IGRP, R - RIP, M - mobile, B - BGP
       D - EIGRP, EX - EIGRP external, O - OSPF, IA - OSPF inter area
       N1 - OSPF NSSA external type 1, N2 - OSPF NSSA external type 2
       E1 - OSPF external type 1, E2 - OSPF external type 2, E - EGP
       i - IS-IS, L1 - IS-IS level-1, L2 - IS-IS level-2, ia - IS-IS inter area
       * - candidate default, U - per-user static route, o - ODR
       P - periodic downloaded static route

Gateway of last resort is not set

     131.99.0.0/16 is variably subnetted, 6 subnets, 4 masks
O IA    131.99.224.0/20 [110/11] via 131.99.0.51, 00:14:56, Ethernet0
O IA    131.99.192.0/20 [110/11] via 131.99.0.50, 00:14:56, Ethernet0
C       131.99.0.48/28 is directly connected, Ethernet0
C       131.99.136.128/25 is directly connected, Ethernet1
C       131.99.144.128/25 is directly connected, Ethernet2
O IA    131.99.216.193/32 [110/11] via 131.99.0.50, 00:14:56, Ethernet0
routerA#debug ip ospf events
OSPF events debugging is on
routerA#
*Mar  1 00:29:19.507 UTC: OSPF: Rcv hello from 131.99.216.193 area 0 from
 Ethernet0/0 131.99.0.50
*Mar  1 00:29:19.507 UTC: OSPF: End of hello processing
*Mar  1 00:29:20.383 UTC: OSPF: Rcv hello from 131.99.232.225 area 0 from
 Ethernet0/0 131.99.0.51
*Mar  1 00:29:20.383 UTC: OSPF: End of hello processing
*Mar  1 00:29:29.507 UTC: OSPF: Rcv hello from 131.99.216.193 area 0 from
 Ethernet0/0 131.99.0.50
*Mar  1 00:29:29.507 UTC: OSPF: End of hello processing
*Mar  1 00:29:30.383 UTC: OSPF: Rcv hello from 131.99.232.225 area 0 from
 Ethernet0/0 131.99.0.51
*Mar  1 00:29:30.383 UTC: OSPF: End of hello processing
*Mar  1 00:29:39.507 UTC: OSPF: Rcv hello from 131.99.216.193 area 0 from
 Ethernet0/0 131.99.0.50
*Mar  1 00:29:39.507 UTC: OSPF: End of hello processing
*Mar  1 00:29:40.383 UTC: OSPF: Rcv hello from 131.99.232.225 area 0 from
 Ethernet0/0 131.99.0.51
*Mar  1 00:29:40.383 UTC: OSPF: End of hello processing
routerA#undebug all
All possible debugging has been turned off
routerA#
routerA#debug ip routing
IP routing debugging is on
routerA#config t
Enter configuration commands, one per line.  End with CNTL/Z.
routerA(config)#interface lo0
routerA(config-if)#shut
routerA(config-if)#
*Mar  1 00:30:18.191 UTC: %LINK-3-UPDOWN: Interface Loopback0,
 changed state to up
*Mar  1 00:30:19.191 UTC: %LINEPROTO-5-UPDOWN: Line protocol on
 Interface Loopback0, changed state to up
```

Example 11-4 *The* **show** *and* **debug** *Output Screens for Scenario 11-4, Router A (Continued)*

```
*Mar  1 00:30:21.347 UTC: %LINK-5-CHANGED: Interface Loopback0,
 changed state to administratively down
*Mar  1 00:30:22.347 UTC: %LINEPROTO-5-UPDOWN: Line protocol on
 Interface Loopback0, changed state to down
routerA(config-if)#
routerA(config-if)#
routerA(config-if)#
routerA(config-if)#
routerA(config-if)#interface lo0
routerA(config-if)#no shut
routerA(config-if)#^Z
routerA#
*Mar  1 00:30:41.299 UTC: %SYS-5-CONFIG_I: Configured from console by console
*Mar  1 00:30:41.751 UTC: %LINK-3-UPDOWN: Interface Loopback0,
 changed state to up
*Mar  1 00:30:42.751 UTC: %LINEPROTO-5-UPDOWN: Line protocol on
 Interface Loopback0, changed state to up
routerA#
routerA#debug ip ospf packets
OSPF packet debugging is on
routerA#
*Mar  1 00:31:09.507 UTC: OSPF: rcv. v:2 t:1 l:52 rid:131.99.216.193
      aid:0.0.0.0 chk:189B aut:0 auk: from Ethernet0
*Mar  1 00:31:10.387 UTC: OSPF: rcv. v:2 t:1 l:52 rid:131.99.232.225
      aid:0.0.0.0 chk:189B aut:0 auk: from Ethernet0
*Mar  1 00:31:19.507 UTC: OSPF: rcv. v:2 t:1 l:52 rid:131.99.216.193
      aid:0.0.0.0 chk:189B aut:0 auk: from Ethernet0
*Mar  1 00:31:20.387 UTC: OSPF: rcv. v:2 t:1 l:52 rid:131.99.232.225
      aid:0.0.0.0 chk:189B aut:0 auk: from Ethernet0
*Mar  1 00:31:29.507 UTC: OSPF: rcv. v:2 t:1 l:52 rid:131.99.216.193
      aid:0.0.0.0 chk:189B aut:0 auk: from Ethernet0
*Mar  1 00:31:30.391 UTC: OSPF: rcv. v:2 t:1 l:52 rid:131.99.232.225
      aid:0.0.0.0 chk:189B aut:0 auk: from Ethernet0
routerA#undebug all
All possible debugging has been turned off

routerA#show ip interface brief
Interface              IP-Address      OK? Method Status     Protocol
Ethernet0              131.99.0.49     YES manual  up         up

Serial0/0              unassigned      YES unset  administratively down down

ATM1/0                 unassigned      YES unset  administratively down down

Loopback0              unassigned      YES manual up                    up

Ethernet1              131.99.136.129  YES manual up                    up

Ethernet2              131.99.144.129  YES manual up                    up
```

continues

Example 11-4 *The* **show** *and* **debug** *Output Screens for Scenario 11-4, Router A (Continued)*

```
routerA#
routerA#show ip ospf database

        OSPF Router with ID (131.99.144.129) (Process ID 100)


                Router Link States (Area 0)

Link ID         ADV Router      Age         Seq#        Checksum Link count
131.99.144.129  131.99.144.129  1071        0x80000004 0xEB16    1
131.99.216.193  131.99.216.193  1122        0x80000004 0xE00F    1
131.99.232.225  131.99.232.225  1122        0x80000004 0x296E    1

                Net Link States (Area 0)

Link ID         ADV Router      Age         Seq#        Checksum
131.99.0.51     131.99.232.225  1072        0x80000002 0x516B

                Summary Net Link States (Area 0)

Link ID         ADV Router      Age         Seq#        Checksum
131.99.128.0    131.99.144.129  1079        0x80000001 0xB436
131.99.144.129  131.99.144.129  1079        0x80000001 0x400A
131.99.192.0    131.99.216.193  1129        0x80000001 0x76AB
131.99.216.193  131.99.216.193  1129        0x80000001 0x2712
131.99.224.0    131.99.232.225  1215        0x80000001 0xE3ED

                Router Link States (Area 1)

Link ID         ADV Router      Age         Seq#        Checksum Link count
131.99.144.129  131.99.144.129  1080        0x80000003 0x53F     2

                Summary Net Link States (Area 1)

Link ID         ADV Router      Age         Seq#        Checksum
0.0.0.0         131.99.144.129  1080        0x80000001 0xF94B
131.99.0.48     131.99.144.129  1070        0x80000001 0x1D3
131.99.192.0    131.99.144.129  1070        0x80000001 0x742E
131.99.216.193  131.99.144.129  1071        0x80000001 0x2594
131.99.224.0    131.99.144.129  1071        0x80000001 0x136F
routerA#
routerA#show ip ospf
 Routing Process "ospf 100" with ID 131.99.144.129
 Supports only single TOS(TOS0) routes
 Supports opaque LSA
 It is an area border router
 SPF schedule delay 5 secs, Hold time between two SPFs 10 secs
 Minimum LSA interval 5 secs. Minimum LSA arrival 1 secs
 Number of external LSA 0. Checksum Sum 0x0
 Number of opaque AS LSA 0. Checksum Sum 0x0
 Number of DCbitless external and opaque AS LSA 0
 Number of DoNotAge external and opaque AS LSA 0
 Number of areas in this router is 2. 1 normal 1 stub 0 nssa
```

Example 11-4 *The* **show** *and* **debug** *Output Screens for Scenario 11-4, Router A (Continued)*

```
            External flood list length 0
              Area BACKBONE(0)
                  Number of interfaces in this area is 1
                  Area has no authentication
                  SPF algorithm executed 6 times
                  Area ranges are
                  Number of LSA 9. Checksum Sum 0x4BBE8
                  Number of opaque link LSA 0. Checksum Sum 0x0
                  Number of DCbitless LSA 0
                  Number of indication LSA 0
                  Number of DoNotAge LSA 0
                  Flood list length 0
              Area 1
                  Number of interfaces in this area is 2
                  It is a stub area
                    generates stub default route with cost 1
                  Area has no authentication
                  SPF algorithm executed 6 times
                  Area ranges are
                     131.99.128.0/20 Active(1) Advertise
                  Number of LSA 6. Checksum Sum 0x1AD8E
                  Number of opaque link LSA 0. Checksum Sum 0x0
                  Number of DCbitless LSA 0
                  Number of indication LSA 0
                  Number of DoNotAge LSA 0
                  Flood list length 0

          routerA#
          routerA#show ip ospf border routers

          OSPF Process 100 internal Routing Table

          Codes: i - Intra-area route, I - Inter-area route

          i 131.99.232.225 [10] via 131.99.0.51, Ethernet0, ABR, Area 0, SPF 6
          i 131.99.216.193 [10] via 131.99.0.50, Ethernet0, ABR, Area 0, SPF 6
          routerA#show ip ospf interface
          Ethernet0 is up, line protocol is up
            Internet Address 131.99.0.49/28, Area 0
            Process ID 100, Router ID 131.99.144.129, Network Type BROADCAST, Cost: 10
            Transmit Delay is 1 sec, State DROTHER, Priority 1
            Designated Router (ID) 131.99.232.225, Interface address 131.99.0.51
            Backup Designated router (ID) 131.99.216.193, Interface address 131.99.0.50
            Timer intervals configured, Hello 10, Dead 40, Wait 40, Retransmit 5
              Hello due in 00:00:04
            Index 1/1, flood queue length 0
            Next 0x0(0)/0x0(0)
            Last flood scan length is 0, maximum is 1
            Last flood scan time is 0 msec, maximum is 0 msec
```

continues

Example 11-4 *The* **show** *and* **debug** *Output Screens for Scenario 11-4, Router A (Continued)*

```
         Neighbor Count is 2, Adjacent neighbor count is 2
           Adjacent with neighbor 131.99.232.225  (Designated Router)
           Adjacent with neighbor 131.99.216.193  (Backup Designated Router)
         Suppress hello for 0 neighbor(s)
      Ethernet1 is up, line protocol is up
         Internet Address 131.99.136.129/25, Area 1
         Process ID 100, Router ID 131.99.144.129, Network Type BROADCAST, Cost: 10
         Transmit Delay is 1 sec, State DROTHER, Priority 1
         Designated Router (ID) 131.99.232.225, Interface address 131.99.0.51
         Backup Designated router (ID) 131.99.216.193, Interface address 131.99.0.50
         Timer intervals configured, Hello 10, Dead 40, Wait 40, Retransmit 5
           Hello due in 00:00:04
         Index 1/1, flood queue length 0
         Next 0x0(0)/0x0(0)
         Last flood scan length is 0, maximum is 1
         Last flood scan time is 0 msec, maximum is 0 msec
         Suppress hello for 0 neighbor(s)

      Ethernet2 is up, line protocol is up
         Internet Address 131.99.144.129/25, Area 1
         Process ID 100, Router ID 131.99.144.129, Network Type BROADCAST, Cost: 10
         Transmit Delay is 1 sec, State DROTHER, Priority 1
         Designated Router (ID) 131.99.232.225, Interface address 131.99.0.51
         Backup Designated router (ID) 131.99.216.193, Interface address 131.99.0.50
         Timer intervals configured, Hello 10, Dead 40, Wait 40, Retransmit 5
           Hello due in 00:00:04
         Index 1/1, flood queue length 0
         Next 0x0(0)/0x0(0)
         Last flood scan length is 0, maximum is 1
         Last flood scan time is 0 msec, maximum is 0 msec
      Suppress hello for 0 neighbor(s)

      routerA#show ip ospf neighbor

      Neighbor ID      Pri   State          Dead Time    Address        Interface
      131.99.232.225    1    FULL/DR        00:00:39     131.99.0.51    Ethernet0
      131.99.216.193    1    FULL/BDR       00:00:38     131.99.0.50    Ethernet0
      routerA#
      routerA#trace 131.99.232.225

      Type escape sequence to abort.
      Tracing the route to 131.99.232.225

        1 131.99.0.51 4 msec 0 msec *
      routerA#ping 131.99.192.193

      Type escape sequence to abort.
      Sending 5, 100-byte ICMP Echos to 131.99.192.193, timeout is 2 seconds:
      !!!!!
      Success rate is 100 percent (5/5), round-trip min/avg/max = 4/4/4 ms
      routerA#ping
      Protocol [ip]:
      Target IP address: 131.99.224.225
```

Example 11-4 *The* **show** *and* **debug** *Output Screens for Scenario 11-4, Router A (Continued)*

```
Repeat count [5]:
Datagram size [100]:
Timeout in seconds [2]:
Extended commands [n]: y
Source address or interface: 131.99.136.129
Type of service [0]:
Set DF bit in IP header? [no]:
Validate reply data? [no]:
Data pattern [0xABCD]:
Loose, Strict, Record, Timestamp, Verbose[none]:
Sweep range of sizes [n]:
Type escape sequence to abort.
Sending 5, 100-byte ICMP Echos to 131.99.224.225, timeout is 2 seconds:
!!!!!
Success rate is 100 percent (5/5), round-trip min/avg/max = 1/3/
```

Example 11-5 *The* **show** *and* **debug** *Output Screens for Scenario 11-4, Router B*

```
routerB#show version
Cisco Internetwork Operating System Software
IOS (tm) 3600 Software (C3620-JS56I-M), Version 12.0(7)T,  RELEASE SOFTWARE (fc2)
Copyright (c) 1986-1999 by cisco Systems, Inc.
Compiled Wed 08-Dec-99 11:16 by phanguye
Image text-base: 0x600088F0, data-base: 0x612B4000

ROM: System Bootstrap, Version 11.1(20)AA2,
 EARLY DEPLOYMENT RELEASE SOFTWARE (fc1)

routerB uptime is 33 minutes
System returned to ROM by reload
System image file is "flash:c3620-js56i-mz.120-7.T.bin"

cisco 3620 (R4700) processor (revision 0x81) with 59392K/6144K bytes of memory.
Processor board ID 19276633
R4700 CPU at 80Mhz, Implementation 33, Rev 1.0
Bridging software.
X.25 software, Version 3.0.0.
SuperLAT software (copyright 1990 by Meridian Technology Corp).
TN3270 Emulation software.
1 Ethernet/IEEE 802.3 interface(s)
1 Serial network interface(s)
1 ATM network interface(s)
DRAM configuration is 32 bits wide with parity disabled.
29K bytes of non-volatile configuration memory.
16384K bytes of processor board System flash (Read/Write)

Configuration register is 0x2102

routerB#
routerB#show running-config
```

continues

Example 11-5 *The* **show** *and* **debug** *Output Screens for Scenario 11-4, Router B (Continued)*

```
Building configuration...

Current configuration:
!
version 12.0
service timestamps debug datetime msec localtime show-timezone
service timestamps log datetime msec localtime show-timezone
service password-encryption
!
hostname routerB
!
enable password 7 02050D480809
!
!
!
ip subnet-zero
!
cns event-service server
!
!
!
interface Ethernet1
 ip address 131.99.192.193 255.255.255.128
 no ip directed-broadcast
!
interface Ethernet2
 ip address 131.99.216.193 255.255.255.128
 no ip directed-broadcast
!
interface Ethernet0
 ip address 131.99.0.50 255.255.255.240
 no ip directed-broadcast
!
interface Serial0/0
 no ip address
 no ip directed-broadcast
 no ip mroute-cache
 shutdown
 no fair-queue
!
interface ATM1/0
 no ip address
 no ip directed-broadcast
 shutdown
 no atm ilmi-keepalive
!
router ospf 100
 area 2 stub
 area 2 range 131.99.192.0 255.255.240.0
 network 131.99.0.50 0.0.0.0 area 0
 network 0.0.0.0 255.255.255.255 area 2
```

Example 11-5 *The* **show** *and* **debug** *Output Screens for Scenario 11-4, Router B (Continued)*

```
!
ip classless
no ip http server
!
!
!
line con 0
 transport input none
line aux 0
line vty 0 4
 password 7 110A1016141D
 login
!
end

routerB#
routerB#show interface
Ethernet0 is up, line protocol is up
  Hardware is AmdP2, address is 0001.96ea.ca41 (bia 0001.96ea.ca41)
  Internet address is 131.99.0.50/28
  MTU 1500 bytes, BW 10000 Kbit, DLY 1000 usec,
     reliability 255/255, txload 1/255, rxload 1/255
  Encapsulation ARPA, loopback not set
  Keepalive set (10 sec)
  ARP type: ARPA, ARP Timeout 04:00:00
  Last input 00:00:01, output 00:00:02, output hang never
  Last clearing of "show interface" counters never
  Queueing strategy: fifo
Output queue 0/40, 0 drops; input queue 0/75, 0 drops
  5 minute input rate 0 bits/sec, 0 packets/sec
  5 minute output rate 0 bits/sec, 0 packets/sec
     353 packets input, 33544 bytes, 0 no buffer
     Received 340 broadcasts, 0 runts, 0 giants, 0 throttles
     0 input errors, 0 CRC, 0 frame, 0 overrun, 0 ignored
     0 input packets with dribble condition detected
     375 packets output, 48292 bytes, 0 underruns
     0 output errors, 0 collisions, 1 interface resets
     0 babbles, 0 late collision, 0 deferred
     0 lost carrier, 0 no carrier
     0 output buffer failures, 0 output buffers swapped out
Serial0/0 is administratively down, line protocol is down
  Hardware is QUICC Serial
  MTU 1500 bytes, BW 2048 Kbit, DLY 20000 usec,
     reliability 255/255, txload 1/255, rxload 1/255
  Encapsulation HDLC, loopback not set
  Keepalive set (10 sec)
  Last input never, output never, output hang never
  Last clearing of "show interface" counters 00:32:59
  Queueing strategy: fifo
Output queue 0/40, 0 drops; input queue 0/75, 0 drops
  5 minute input rate 0 bits/sec, 0 packets/sec
```

continues

Example 11-5 *The* **show** *and* **debug** *Output Screens for Scenario 11-4, Router B (Continued)*

```
  5 minute output rate 0 bits/sec, 0 packets/sec
     0 packets input, 0 bytes, 0 no buffer
     Received 0 broadcasts, 0 runts, 0 giants, 0 throttles
     0 input errors, 0 CRC, 0 frame, 0 overrun, 0 ignored, 0 abort
     0 packets output, 0 bytes, 0 underruns
     0 output errors, 0 collisions, 1 interface resets
     0 output buffer failures, 0 output buffers swapped out
     0 carrier transitions
     DCD=down  DSR=down  DTR=down  RTS=down  CTS=down

ATM1/0 is administratively down, line protocol is down
  Hardware is RS8234 ATMOC3
  MTU 4470 bytes, sub MTU 4470, BW 155000 Kbit, DLY 80 usec,
     reliability 0/255, txload 1/255, rxload 1/255
  Encapsulation ATM, loopback not set
  Keepalive not supported
  Encapsulation(s): AAL5
  1024 maximum active VCs, 0 current VCCs
  VC idle disconnect time: 300 seconds
  Last input never, output never, output hang never
  Last clearing of "show interface" counters never
  Input queue: 0/75/0 (size/max/drops); Total output drops: 0
  Queueing strategy: Per VC Queueing
  5 minute input rate 0 bits/sec, 0 packets/sec
  5 minute output rate 0 bits/sec, 0 packets/sec
     0 packets input, 0 bytes, 0 no buffer
     Received 0 broadcasts, 0 runts, 0 giants, 0 throttles
     0 input errors, 0 CRC, 0 frame, 0 overrun, 0 ignored, 0 abort
     0 packets output, 0 bytes, 0 underruns
     0 output errors, 0 collisions, 1 interface resets
     0 output buffer failures, 0 output buffers swapped out
Ethernet1 is up, line protocol is up
 Hardware is AmdP2, address is 0001.96ea.ca31 (bia 0001.96ea.ca31)
 Internet address is 131.99.192.193/25
  MTU 1500 bytes, BW 10000 Kbit, DLY 1000 usec,
     reliability 255/255, txload 1/255, rxload 1/255
  Encapsulation ARPA, loopback not set
  Keepalive set (10 sec)
  ARP type: ARPA, ARP Timeout 04:00:00
  MTU 1514 bytes, BW 8000000 Kbit, DLY 5000 usec,
     reliability 255/255, txload 1/255, rxload 1/255
  Encapsulation ARPA
  Last input 00:26:27, output never, output hang never
  Last clearing of "show interface" counters never
  Queueing strategy: fifo
 Output queue 0/0, 0 drops; input queue 0/75, 0 drops
  5 minute input rate 0 bits/sec, 0 packets/sec
  5 minute output rate 0 bits/sec, 0 packets/sec
     0 packets input, 0 bytes, 0 no buffer
     Received 0 broadcasts, 0 runts, 0 giants, 0 throttles
     0 input errors, 0 CRC, 0 frame, 0 overrun, 0 ignored, 0 abort
     3 packets output, 159 bytes, 0 underruns
```

Example 11-5 *The* **show** *and* **debug** *Output Screens for Scenario 11-4, Router B (Continued)*

```
          0 output errors, 0 collisions, 0 interface resets
          0 output buffer failures, 0 output buffers swapped out
      Ethernet2 is up, line protocol is up
        Hardware is AmdP2, address is 0001.96ea.ca71 (bia 0001.96ea.ca71)
        Internet address is 131.99.216.193/25
          MTU 1500 bytes, BW 10000 Kbit, DLY 1000 usec,
            reliability 255/255, txload 1/255, rxload 1/255
          Encapsulation ARPA, loopback not set
          Keepalive set (10 sec)
          ARP type: ARPA, ARP Timeout 04:00:00
        MTU 1514 bytes, BW 8000000 Kbit, DLY 5000 usec,
            reliability 255/255, txload 1/255, rxload 1/255
          Encapsulation ARPA
          Last input 00:26:28, output never, output hang never
          Last clearing of "show interface" counters never
          Queueing strategy: fifo
      Output queue 0/0, 0 drops; input queue 0/75, 0 drops
        5 minute input rate 0 bits/sec, 0 packets/sec
        5 minute output rate 0 bits/sec, 0 packets/sec
          0 packets input, 0 bytes, 0 no buffer
          Received 0 broadcasts, 0 runts, 0 giants, 0 throttles
          0 input errors, 0 CRC, 0 frame, 0 overrun, 0 ignored, 0 abort
          3 packets output, 159 bytes, 0 underruns
          0 output errors, 0 collisions, 0 interface resets
          0 output buffer failures, 0 output buffers swapped out

routerB#show ip interface brief
Interface              IP-Address      OK? Method Status              Protocol
Ethernet0              131.99.0.50     YES manual up                  up

Serial0/0              unassigned      YES unset  administratively down down

ATM1/0                 unassigned      YES unset  administratively down down

Ethernet1              131.99.192.193  YES manual up                  up

Ethernet2              131.99.216.193  YES manual up                  up

routerB#show ip protocols
Routing Protocol is "ospf 100"
  Sending updates every 0 seconds
  Invalid after 0 seconds, hold down 0, flushed after 0
  Outgoing update filter list for all interfaces is
  Incoming update filter list for all interfaces is
  Redistributing: ospf 100
  Routing for Networks:
    131.99.0.50/32
    0.0.0.0
  Routing Information Sources:
    Gateway         Distance      Last Update
    131.99.232.225      110       00:20:43
    131.99.144.129      110       00:20:43
```

continues

Example 11-5 *The* **show** *and* **debug** *Output Screens for Scenario 11-4, Router B (Continued)*

```
        Distance: (default is 110)

routerB#show ip route
Codes: C - connected, S - static, I - IGRP, R - RIP, M - mobile, B - BGP
       D - EIGRP, EX - EIGRP external, O - OSPF, IA - OSPF inter area
       N1 - OSPF NSSA external type 1, N2 - OSPF NSSA external type 2
       E1 - OSPF external type 1, E2 - OSPF external type 2, E - EGP
       i - IS-IS, L1 - IS-IS level-1, L2 - IS-IS level-2, ia - IS-IS inter area
       * - candidate default, U - per-user static route, o - ODR
       P - periodic downloaded static route

Gateway of last resort is not set

     131.99.0.0/16 is variably subnetted, 6 subnets, 4 masks
O IA    131.99.224.0/20 [110/11] via 131.99.0.51, 00:20:53, Ethernet0
O IA    131.99.128.0/20 [110/11] via 131.99.0.49, 00:20:53, Ethernet0
C       131.99.0.48/28 is directly connected, Ethernet0
C       131.99.192.192/25 is directly connected, Ethernet1
O IA    131.99.144.129/32 [110/11] via 131.99.0.49, 00:20:53, Ethernet0
C       131.99.216.192/25 is directly connected, Ethernet2
routerB#
routerB#debug ip ospf events
OSPF events debugging is on
routerB#
*Mar  1 00:35:05.783 UTC: OSPF: Rcv hello from 131.99.232.225
 area 0 from Ethernet0/0 131.99.0.51
*Mar  1 00:35:05.783 UTC: OSPF: End of hello processing
*Mar  1 00:35:06.035 UTC: OSPF: Rcv hello from 131.99.144.129
 area 0 from Ethernet0/0 131.99.0.49
*Mar  1 00:35:06.035 UTC: OSPF: End of hello processing
routerB#
routerB#
routerB#undebug all
All possible debugging has been turned off

routerB#debug ip routing
IP routing debugging is on
routerB#
routerB#debug ip ospf packet
OSPF packet debugging is on
routerB#config t
Enter configuration commands, one per line.  End with CNTL/Z.
routerB(config)#interface lo0
*Mar  1 00:35:35.783 UTC: OSPF: rcv. v:2 t:1 l:52 rid:131.99.232.225
     aid:0.0.0.0 chk:189B aut:0 auk: from Ethernet0
*Mar  1 00:35:36.035 UTC: OSPF: rcv. v:2 t:1 l:52 rid:131.99.144.129
     aid:0.0.0.0 chk:189B aut:0 auk: from Ethernet0o0
routerB(config-if)#shut
*Mar  1 00:35:39.427 UTC: %LINK-3-UPDOWN: Interface Loopback0,
 changed state to up
*Mar  1 00:35:40.427 UTC: %LINEPROTO-5-UPDOWN: Line protocol on
 Interface Loopback0, changed state to up
```

Example 11-5 *The* **show** *and* **debug** *Output Screens for Scenario 11-4, Router B (Continued)*

```
*Mar  1 00:35:45.783 UTC: OSPF: rcv. v:2 t:1 l:52 rid:131.99.232.225
      aid:0.0.0.0 chk:189B aut:0 auk: from Ethernet0
*Mar  1 00:35:46.035 UTC: OSPF: rcv. v:2 t:1 l:52 rid:131.99.144.129
      aid:0.0.0.0 chk:189B aut:0 auk: from Ethernet0
routerB(config-if)#
routerB(config-if)#
routerB(config-if)#no shut
routerB(config-if)#
*Mar  1 00:35:55.783 UTC: OSPF: rcv. v:2 t:1 l:52 rid:131.99.232.225
      aid:0.0.0.0 chk:189B aut:0 auk: from Ethernet0
*Mar  1 00:35:56.035 UTC: OSPF: rcv. v:2 t:1 l:52 rid:131.99.144.129
      aid:0.0.0.0 chk:189B aut:0 auk: from Ethernet0
routerB(config-if)#
routerB(config-if)#
routerB(config-if)#
routerB(config-if)#
routerB(config-if)#no interface lo0
routerB(config)#
*Mar  1 00:36:05.783 UTC: OSPF: rcv. v:2 t:1 l:52 rid:131.99.232.225
      aid:0.0.0.0 chk:189B aut:0 auk: from Ethernet0
*Mar  1 00:36:06.035 UTC: OSPF: rcv. v:2 t:1 l:52 rid:131.99.144.129
      aid:0.0.0.0 chk:189B aut:0 auk: from Ethernet0^Z
routerB#
*Mar  1 00:36:07.459 UTC: %LINK-5-CHANGED: Interface Loopback0,
 changed state to administratively down
*Mar  1 00:36:08.095 UTC: %SYS-5-CONFIG_I: Configured from console by console
*Mar  1 00:36:08.459 UTC: %LINEPROTO-5-UPDOWN: Line protocol on
 Interface Loopback0, changed state to down
routerB#
routerB#
routerB#undebug all
All possible debugging has been turned off

routerB#show ip ospf database
        OSPF Router with ID (131.99.216.193) (Process ID 100)


                Router Link States (Area 0)

Link ID          ADV Router       Age        Seq#        Checksum Link count
131.99.144.129   131.99.144.129   1375       0x80000004 0xEB16    1
131.99.216.193   131.99.216.193   1425       0x80000004 0xE00F    1
131.99.232.225   131.99.232.225   1425       0x80000004 0x296E    1

                Net Link States (Area 0)

Link ID          ADV Router       Age        Seq#        Checksum
131.99.0.51      131.99.232.225   1375       0x80000002 0x516B
```

continues

Example 11-5 *The* **show** *and* **debug** *Output Screens for Scenario 11-4, Router B (Continued)*

```
                        Summary Net Link States (Area 0)

 Link ID          ADV Router        Age        Seq#        Checksum
 131.99.128.0     131.99.144.129    1383       0x80000001 0xB436
 131.99.144.129   131.99.144.129    1383       0x80000001 0x400A
 131.99.192.0     131.99.216.193    1432       0x80000001 0x76AB
 131.99.216.193   131.99.216.193    1432       0x80000001 0x2712
 131.99.224.0     131.99.232.225    1518       0x80000001 0xE3ED

                        Router Link States (Area 2)

 Link ID          ADV Router        Age        Seq#        Checksum Link count
 131.99.216.193   131.99.216.193    1433       0x80000003 0x1B17    2

                        Summary Net Link States (Area 2)

 Link ID          ADV Router        Age        Seq#        Checksum
 0.0.0.0          131.99.216.193    1433       0x80000001 0x7E3E
 131.99.0.48      131.99.216.193    1423       0x80000001 0x85C6
 131.99.128.0     131.99.216.193    1367       0x80000001 0xBB9E
 131.99.144.129   131.99.216.193    1368       0x80000001 0x4772
 131.99.224.0     131.99.216.193    1414       0x80000001 0x9762
 routerB#
 routerB#show ip ospf
  Routing Process "ospf 100" with ID 131.99.216.193
  Supports only single TOS(TOS0) routes
  Supports opaque LSA
  It is an area border router
  SPF schedule delay 5 secs, Hold time between two SPFs 10 secs
  Minimum LSA interval 5 secs. Minimum LSA arrival 1 secs
  Number of external LSA 0. Checksum Sum 0x0
  Number of opaque AS LSA 0. Checksum Sum 0x0
  Number of DCbitless external and opaque AS LSA 0
  Number of DoNotAge external and opaque AS LSA 0
  Number of areas in this router is 2. 1 normal 1 stub 0 nssa
  External flood list length 0
     Area BACKBONE(0)
         Number of interfaces in this area is 1
         Area has no authentication
         SPF algorithm executed 9 times
         Area ranges are
         Number of LSA 9. Checksum Sum 0x4BBE8
         Number of opaque link LSA 0. Checksum Sum 0x0
         Number of DCbitless LSA 0
         Number of indication LSA 0
         Number of DoNotAge LSA 0
         Flood list length 0
     Area 2
         Number of interfaces in this area is 2
         It is a stub area
           generates stub default route with cost 1
         Area has no authentication
         SPF algorithm executed 7 times
```

Example 11-5 *The* **show** *and* **debug** *Output Screens for Scenario 11-4, Router B (Continued)*

```
          Area ranges are
             131.99.192.0/20 Active(1) Advertise
          Number of LSA 6. Checksum Sum 0x2B98D
          Number of opaque link LSA 0. Checksum Sum 0x0
          Number of DCbitless LSA 0
          Number of indication LSA 0
          Number of DoNotAge LSA 0
          Flood list length 0

routerB#show ip ospf border-routers

OSPF Process 100 internal Routing Table

Codes: i - Intra-area route, I - Inter-area route
i 131.99.232.225 [10] via 131.99.0.51, Ethernet0, ABR, Area 0, SPF 9
i 131.99.144.129 [10] via 131.99.0.49, Ethernet0, ABR, Area 0, SPF 9
routerB#show ip ospf interface
Ethernet0 is up, line protocol is up
  Internet Address 131.99.0.50/28, Area 0
  Process ID 100, Router ID 131.99.216.193, Network Type BROADCAST, Cost: 10
  Transmit Delay is 1 sec, State BDR, Priority 1
  Designated Router (ID) 131.99.232.225, Interface address 131.99.0.51
  Backup Designated router (ID) 131.99.216.193, Interface address 131.99.0.50
  Timer intervals configured, Hello 10, Dead 40, Wait 40, Retransmit 5
    Hello due in 00:00:00
  Index 1/1, flood queue length 0
  Next 0x0(0)/0x0(0)
  Last flood scan length is 0, maximum is 1
  Last flood scan time is 0 msec, maximum is 0 msec
  Neighbor Count is 2, Adjacent neighbor count is 2
    Adjacent with neighbor 131.99.144.129
    Adjacent with neighbor 131.99.232.225   (Designated Router)
  Suppress hello for 0 neighbor(s)
Ethernet1 is up, line protocol is up
  Internet Address 131.99.192.193/25, Area 2
  Process ID 100, Router ID 131.99.216.193, BROADCAST, Cost: 10
  Transmit Delay is 1 sec, State BDR, Priority 1
Timer intervals configured, Hello 10, Dead 40, Wait 40, Retransmit 5
    Hello due in 00:00:00
  Index 1/1, flood queue length 0
  Next 0x0(0)/0x0(0)
  Last flood scan length is 0, maximum is 1
  Last flood scan time is 0 msec, maximum is 0 msec
   Suppress hello for 0 neighbor(s)

Ethernet2 is up, line protocol is up
  Internet Address 131.99.216.193/25, Area 2
  Process ID 100, Router ID 131.99.216.193, BROADCAST, Cost: 10
  Transmit Delay is 1 sec, State BDR, Priority 1
  Designated Router (ID) 131.99.232.225, Interface address 131.99.0.51
  Backup Designated router (ID) 131.99.216.193, Interface address 131.99.0.50
```

continues

Example 11-5 *The **show** and **debug** Output Screens for Scenario 11-4, Router B (Continued)*

```
      Timer intervals configured, Hello 10, Dead 40, Wait 40, Retransmit 5
        Hello due in 00:00:00
      Index 1/1, flood queue length 0
      Next 0x0(0)/0x0(0)
      Last flood scan length is 0, maximum is 1
      Last flood scan time is 0 msec, maximum is 0 msec
      Suppress hello for 0 neighbor(s)

   routerB# show ip ospf interface
   Ethernet0 is up, line protocol is up
      Internet Address 131.99.0.50/28, Area 0
      Process ID 100, Router ID 131.99.216.193, Network Type BROADCAST, Cost: 10
      Transmit Delay is 1 sec, State BDR, Priority 1
      Designated Router (ID) 131.99.232.225, Interface address 131.99.0.51
      Backup Designated router (ID) 131.99.216.193, Interface address 131.99.0.50
      Timer intervals configured, Hello 10, Dead 40, Wait 40, Retransmit 5
        Hello due in 00:00:06
      Index 1/1, flood queue length 0
      Next 0x0(0)/0x0(0)
      Last flood scan length is 0, maximum is 1
      Last flood scan time is 0 msec, maximum is 0 msec
      Neighbor Count is 2, Adjacent neighbor count is 2
        Adjacent with neighbor 131.99.144.129
        Adjacent with neighbor 131.99.232.225  (Designated Router)
      Suppress hello for 0 neighbor(s)
   Ethernet1 is up, line protocol is up
      Internet Address 131.99.192.193/25, Area 2
      Process ID 100, Router ID 131.99.216.193, BROADCAST, Cost: 10
      Transmit Delay is 1 sec, State BDR, Priority 1
   Timer intervals configured, Hello 10, Dead 40, Wait 40, Retransmit 5
        Hello due in 00:00:06
      Index 1/1, flood queue length 0
      Next 0x0(0)/0x0(0)
      Last flood scan length is 0, maximum is 1
      Last flood scan time is 0 msec, maximum is 0 msec
   Suppress hello for 0 neighbor(s)

   Ethernet2 is up, line protocol is up
      Internet Address 131.99.216.193/25, Area 2
      Process ID 100, Router ID 131.99.216.193 BROADCAST, Cost: 10
      Transmit Delay is 1 sec, State BDR, Priority 1
   Timer intervals configured, Hello 10, Dead 40, Wait 40, Retransmit 5
        Hello due in 00:00:06
      Index 1/1, flood queue length 0
      Next 0x0(0)/0x0(0)
      Last flood scan length is 0, maximum is 1
      Last flood scan time is 0 msec, maximum is 0 msec
   Suppress hello for 0 neighbor(s)

   routerB# show ip ospf neighbors
```

Example 11-5 *The **show** and **debug** Output Screens for Scenario 11-4, Router B (Continued)*

```
Neighbor ID       Pri   State          Dead Time   Address         Interface
131.99.144.129    1     FULL/DROTHER   00:00:31    131.99.0.49     Ethernet0
131.99.232.225    1     FULL/DR        00:00:31    131.99.0.51     Ethernet0

routerB#ping 131.99.136.129


Type escape sequence to abort.
Sending 5, 100-byte ICMP Echos to 131.99.136.129, timeout is 2 seconds:
!!!!!
Success rate is 100 percent (5/5), round-trip min/avg/max = 4/4/4 ms
routerB#trace 131.99.136.129
Type escape sequence to abort.
Tracing the route to 131.99.136.129
    1 131.99.0.49 4 msec 4 msec *
routerB#ping 131.99.232.225
 Type escape sequence to abort.
Sending 5, 100-byte ICMP Echos to 131.99.232.225, timeout is 2 seconds:
!!!!!
Success rate is 100 percent (5/5), round-trip min/avg/max = 1/2/4 ms
```

Example 11-6 *The **show** and **debug** Output Screens for Scenario 11-4, Router C*

```
routerC#show version
Cisco Internetwork Operating System Software
IOS (tm) C2600 Software (C2600-JS56I-M), Version 12.0(7)T,  RELEASE SOFTWARE (fc2)
Copyright (c) 1986-1999 by cisco Systems, Inc.
Compiled Tue 07-Dec-99 05:53 by phanguye
Image text-base: 0x80008088, data-base: 0x8104B45C

ROM: System Bootstrap, Version 11.3(2)XA4, RELEASE SOFTWARE (fc1)

routerC uptime is 36 minutes
System returned to ROM by reload
System image file is "flash:c2600-js56i-mz.120-7.T.bin"

cisco 2620 (MPC860) processor (revision 0x102) with 39936K/9216K bytes of memory
.
Processor board ID JAD04180F56 (2536534690)
M860 processor: part number 0, mask 49
Bridging software.
X.25 software, Version 3.0.0.
SuperLAT software (copyright 1990 by Meridian Technology Corp).
TN3270 Emulation software.
1 FastEthernet/IEEE 802.3 interface(s)
2 Serial network interface(s)
2 Voice FXS interface(s)
32K bytes of non-volatile configuration memory.
16384K bytes of processor board System flash (Read/Write)
```

continues

Example 11-6 *The* **show** *and* **debug** *Output Screens for Scenario 11-4, Router C (Continued)*

```
Configuration register is 0x2102

routerC#
routerC#show running-config
Building configuration...

Current configuration:
!
version 12.0
service timestamps debug datetime msec localtime show-timezone
service timestamps log datetime msec localtime show-timezone
service password-encryption
!
hostname routerC
!
enable password 7 13061E010803
!
!
!
ip subnet-zero
!
cns event-service server
!
!
!
voice-port 1/0/0
!
voice-port 1/0/1
!
!
!
interface Ethernet1
 ip address 131.99.224.225 255.255.255.128
 no ip directed-broadcast
!
interface Ethernet2
 ip address 131.99.232.225 255.255.255.128
 no ip directed-broadcast
!
interface FastEthernet0/0
 ip address 131.99.0.51 255.255.255.240
 no ip directed-broadcast
 duplex auto
 speed auto
!
interface Serial0/0
 no ip address
 no ip directed-broadcast
 no ip mroute-cache
 shutdown
 no fair-queue
```

Example 11-6 *The* **show** *and* **debug** *Output Screens for Scenario 11-4, Router C (Continued)*

```
!
interface Serial0/1
 no ip address
 no ip directed-broadcast
 shutdown
!
router ospf 100
 area 3 stub
 area 3 range 131.99.224.0 255.255.240.0
 network 131.99.0.51 0.0.0.0 area 0
 network 0.0.0.0 255.255.255.255 area 3
!
ip classless
no ip http server
!
!
!
line con 0
 transport input none
line aux 0
line vty 0 4
 password 7 00071A150754
 login
!
no scheduler allocate
end

routerC# show interface
FastEthernet0/0 is up, line protocol is up
  Hardware is AmdFE, address is 0002.16bb.2fe0 (bia 0002.16bb.2fe0)
  Internet address is 131.99.0.51/28
  MTU 1500 bytes, BW 100000 Kbit, DLY 100 usec,
     reliability 255/255, txload 1/255, rxload 1/255
  Encapsulation ARPA, loopback not set
  Keepalive set (10 sec)
  Full-duplex, 100Mb/s, 100BaseTX/FX
  ARP type: ARPA, ARP Timeout 04:00:00
  Last input 00:00:05, output 00:00:03, output hang never
  Last clearing of "show interface" counters never
  Queueing strategy: fifo
Output queue 0/40, 0 drops; input queue 0/75, 0 drops
  5 minute input rate 0 bits/sec, 0 packets/sec
  5 minute output rate 0 bits/sec, 0 packets/sec
     408 packets input, 36008 bytes
     Received 395 broadcasts, 0 runts, 0 giants, 0 throttles
     0 input errors, 0 CRC, 0 frame, 0 overrun, 0 ignored
     0 watchdog, 0 multicast
     0 input packets with dribble condition detected
     438 packets output, 52473 bytes, 0 underruns
     0 output errors, 0 collisions, 1 interface resets
     0 babbles, 0 late collision, 0 deferred
     0 lost carrier, 0 no carrier
     0 output buffer failures, 0 output buffers swapped out
```

continues

Example 11-6 *The* **show** *and* **debug** *Output Screens for Scenario 11-4, Router C (Continued)*

```
Serial0/0 is administratively down, line protocol is down
  Hardware is PowerQUICC Serial
  MTU 1500 bytes, BW 1544 Kbit, DLY 20000 usec,
     reliability 255/255, txload 1/255, rxload 1/255
  Encapsulation HDLC, loopback not set
  Keepalive set (10 sec)
  Last input never, output never, output hang never
  Last clearing of "show interface" counters 00:35:55
  Queueing strategy: fifo
Output queue 0/40, 0 drops; input queue 0/75, 0 drops
  5 minute input rate 0 bits/sec, 0 packets/sec
  5 minute output rate 0 bits/sec, 0 packets/sec
     0 packets input, 0 bytes, 0 no buffer
     Received 0 broadcasts, 0 runts, 0 giants, 0 throttles
     0 input errors, 0 CRC, 0 frame, 0 overrun, 0 ignored, 0 abort
     0 packets output, 0 bytes, 0 underruns
     0 output errors, 0 collisions, 1 interface resets
     0 output buffer failures, 0 output buffers swapped out
     0 carrier transitions
     DCD=down  DSR=down  DTR=down  RTS=down  CTS=down

Serial0/1 is administratively down, line protocol is down
  Hardware is PowerQUICC Serial
  MTU 1500 bytes, BW 1544 Kbit, DLY 20000 usec,
     reliability 255/255, txload 1/255, rxload 1/255
  Encapsulation HDLC, loopback not set
  Keepalive set (10 sec)
  Last input never, output never, output hang never
  Last clearing of "show interface" counters never
  Input queue: 0/75/0 (size/max/drops); Total output drops: 0
  Queueing strategy: weighted fair
Output queue: 0/1000/64/0 (size/max total/threshold/drops)
     Conversations  0/0/256 (active/max active/max total)
     Reserved Conversations 0/0 (allocated/max allocated)
  5 minute input rate 0 bits/sec, 0 packets/sec
  5 minute output rate 0 bits/sec, 0 packets/sec
     0 packets input, 0 bytes, 0 no buffer
     Received 0 broadcasts, 0 runts, 0 giants, 0 throttles
     0 input errors, 0 CRC, 0 frame, 0 overrun, 0 ignored, 0 abort
     0 packets output, 0 bytes, 0 underruns
     0 output errors, 0 collisions, 12 interface resets
     0 output buffer failures, 0 output buffers swapped out
     0 carrier transitions
     DCD=down  DSR=down  DTR=down  RTS=down  CTS=down

Ethernet1 is up, line protocol is up
  Hardware is AmdP2, address is 0001.96ea.ca41 (bia 0001.96ea.cb41)
  Internet address is 131.99.0.50/25
  MTU 1500 bytes, BW 10000 Kbit, DLY 1000 usec,
     reliability 255/255, txload 1/255, rxload 1/255
  Encapsulation ARPA,
  Keepalive set (10 sec)
  ARP type: ARPA, ARP Timeout 04:00:00
```

Example 11-6 *The* **show** *and* **debug** *Output Screens for Scenario 11-4, Router C (Continued)*

```
       Last input never, output never, output hang never
       Last clearing of "show interface" counters never
       Queueing strategy: fifo
    Output queue 0/0, 0 drops; input queue 0/75, 0 drops
       5 minute input rate 0 bits/sec, 0 packets/sec
       5 minute output rate 0 bits/sec, 0 packets/sec
          0 packets input, 0 bytes, 0 no buffer
          Received 0 broadcasts, 0 runts, 0 giants, 0 throttles
          0 input errors, 0 CRC, 0 frame, 0 overrun, 0 ignored, 0 abort
          0 packets output, 0 bytes, 0 underruns
          0 output errors, 0 collisions, 0 interface resets
          0 output buffer failures, 0 output buffers swapped out
    Ethernet2 is up, line protocol is up
    Hardware is AmdP2, address is 0001.96ea.ca41 (bia 0001.96ea.ca21)
     Internet address is 131.99.232.225/25
       MTU 1514 bytes, BW 8000000 Kbit, DLY 5000 usec,
          reliability 255/255, txload 1/255, rxload 1/255
     Encapsulation ARPA,
       Keepalive set (10 sec)
       ARP type: ARPA, ARP Timeout 04:00:00
       Last input never, output never, output hang never
       Last clearing of "show interface" counters never
       Queueing strategy: fifo
    Output queue 0/0, 0 drops; input queue 0/75, 0 drops
       5 minute input rate 0 bits/sec, 0 packets/sec
       5 minute output rate 0 bits/sec, 0 packets/sec
          0 packets input, 0 bytes, 0 no buffer
          Received 0 broadcasts, 0 runts, 0 giants, 0 throttles
          0 input errors, 0 CRC, 0 frame, 0 overrun, 0 ignored, 0 abort
          0 packets output, 0 bytes, 0 underruns
          0 output errors, 0 collisions, 0 interface resets
          0 output buffer failures, 0 output buffers swapped out
    routerC#
    routerC#show ip interface brief
    Interface              IP-Address      OK? Method Status                Protocol
    FastEthernet0/0        131.99.0.51     YES manual up                    up

    Serial0/0              unassigned      YES unset  administratively down down

    Serial0/1              unassigned      YES unset  administratively down down

    Ethernet1              131.99.224.225  YES manual up                    up

    Ethernet2              131.99.232.225  YES manual up                    up

    routerC#
    routerC#show ip protocols
    Routing Protocol is "ospf 100"
      Sending updates every 0 seconds
      Invalid after 0 seconds, hold down 0, flushed after 0
      Outgoing update filter list for all interfaces is
```

continues

Example 11-6 *The* **show** *and* **debug** *Output Screens for Scenario 11-4, Router C (Continued)*

```
        Incoming update filter list for all interfaces is
        Redistributing: ospf 100
        Routing for Networks:
          131.99.0.51/32
          0.0.0.0
        Routing Information Sources:
          Gateway           Distance       Last Update
          131.99.144.129       110         00:15:22
          131.99.216.193       110         00:15:22
     .  Distance: (default is 110)

     routerC# show ip route
     Codes: C - connected, S - static, I - IGRP, R - RIP, M - mobile, B - BGP
            D - EIGRP, EX - EIGRP external, O - OSPF, IA - OSPF inter area
            N1 - OSPF NSSA external type 1, N2 - OSPF NSSA external type 2
            E1 - OSPF external type 1, E2 - OSPF external type 2, E - EGP
            i - IS-IS, L1 - IS-IS level-1, L2 - IS-IS level-2, ia - IS-IS inter area
            * - candidate default, U - per-user static route, o - ODR
            P - periodic downloaded static route

     Gateway of last resort is not set

          131.99.0.0/16 is variably subnetted, 7 subnets, 4 masks
     O IA    131.99.192.0/20 [110/2] via 131.99.0.50, 00:15:30, FastEthernet0/0
     O IA    131.99.128.0/20 [110/2] via 131.99.0.49, 00:15:30, FastEthernet0/0
     C       131.99.0.48/28 is directly connected, FastEthernet0/0
     C       131.99.224.224/25 is directly connected, Ethernet1
     C       131.99.232.224/25 is directly connected, Ethernet2
     O IA    131.99.144.129/32 [110/2] via 131.99.0.49, 00:15:30, FastEthernet0/0
     O IA    131.99.216.193/32 [110/2] via 131.99.0.50, 00:15:30, FastEthernet0/0
     routerC# debug ip ospf events
     OSPF events debugging is on
     routerC#
     *Mar  1 00:37:38.891 UTC: OSPF: Rcv hello from 131.99.144.129 area 0 from FastEt
     hernet0/0 131.99.0.49
     *Mar  1 00:37:38.891 UTC: OSPF: End of hello processing
     *Mar  1 00:37:47.747 UTC: OSPF: Rcv hello from 131.99.216.193 area 0 from FastEt
     hernet0/0 131.99.0.50
     *Mar  1 00:37:47.747 UTC: OSPF: End of hello processing
     *Mar  1 00:37:48.891 UTC: OSPF: Rcv hello from 131.99.144.129 area 0 from FastEt
     hernet0/0 131.99.0.49
     *Mar  1 00:37:48.891 UTC: OSPF: End of hello processing
     *Mar  1 00:37:57.747 UTC: OSPF: Rcv hello from 131.99.216.193 area 0 from FastEt
     hernet0/0 131.99.0.50
     *Mar  1 00:37:57.747 UTC: OSPF: End of hello processing
     *Mar  1 00:37:58.887 UTC: OSPF: Rcv hello from 131.99.144.129 area 0 from FastEt
     hernet0/0 131.99.0.49
     *Mar  1 00:37:58.891 UTC: OSPF: End of hello processing
     routerC#undebug all
     All possible debugging has been turned off
     routerC#
     *Mar  1 00:38:07.747 UTC: OSPF: Rcv hello from 131.99.216.193 area 0 from FastEt
     hernet0/0 131.99.0.50
```

Example 11-6 *The* **show** *and* **debug** *Output Screens for Scenario 11-4, Router C (Continued)*

```
*Mar  1 00:38:07.747 UTC: OSPF: End of hello processing
routerC#debug ip routing
IP routing debugging is on
routerC#debug ip ospf packet
OSPF packet debugging is on
routerC#
*Mar  1 00:38:27.747 UTC: OSPF: rcv. v:2 t:1 l:52 rid:131.99.216.193
     aid:0.0.0.0 chk:189B aut:0 auk: from FastEthernet0/0
*Mar  1 00:38:28.887 UTC: OSPF: rcv. v:2 t:1 l:52 rid:131.99.144.129
     aid:0.0.0.0 chk:189B aut:0 auk: from FastEthernet0/0

routerC#
*Mar  1 00:38:37.747 UTC: OSPF: rcv. v:2 t:1 l:52 rid:131.99.216.193
     aid:0.0.0.0 chk:189B aut:0 auk: from FastEthernet0/0
*Mar  1 00:38:38.887 UTC: OSPF: rcv. v:2 t:1 l:52 rid:131.99.144.129
     aid:0.0.0.0 chk:189B aut:0 auk: from FastEthernet0/0
routerC#config t
Enter configuration commands, one per line.  End with CNTL/Z.
routerC(config)#interface lo1
routerC(config-if)#shut
routerC(config-if)#no shut
*Mar  1 00:38:47.731 UTC: is_up: 0 state: 6 sub state: 1 line: 0
*Mar  1 00:38:47.747 UTC: OSPF: rcv. v:2 t:1 l:52 rid:131.99.216.193
     aid:0.0.0.0 chk:189B aut:0 auk: from FastEthernet0/0
*Mar  1 00:38:47.831 UTC: RT: interface Ethernet1 removed from routing table
*Mar  1 00:38:47.831 UTC: RT: del 131.99.224.224/28 via 0.0.0.0, connected metri
c [0/0]
*Mar  1 00:38:47.831 UTC: RT: delete subnet route to 131.99.224.224/28t
*Mar  1 00:38:48.887 UTC: OSPF: rcv. v:2 t:1 l:52 rid:131.99.144.129
     aid:0.0.0.0 chk:189B aut:0 auk: from FastEthernet0/0
*Mar  1 00:38:49.731 UTC: %LINK-5-CHANGED: Interface Ethernet1, changed state to
 administratively down
*Mar  1 00:38:49.731 UTC: is_up: 0 state: 6 sub state: 1 line: 0
*Mar  1 00:38:57.743 UTC: OSPF: rcv. v:2 t:1 l:52 rid:131.99.216.193
     aid:0.0.0.0 chk:189B aut:0 auk: from FastEthernet0/0
*Mar  1 00:38:58.887 UTC: OSPF: rcv. v:2 t:1 l:52 rid:131.99.144.129
     aid:0.0.0.0 chk:189B aut:0 auk: from FastEthernet0/0
routerC(config-if)#
*Mar  1 00:39:05.767 UTC: is_up: 1 state: 4 sub state: 1 line: 0
*Mar  1 00:39:05.767 UTC: RT: add 131.99.224.224/28 via 0.0.0.0, connected metri
c [0/0]
*Mar  1 00:39:05.771 UTC: RT: interface Ethernet1 added to routing table^Z
routerC#
*Mar  1 00:39:07.179 UTC: %SYS-5-CONFIG_I: Configured from console by console
*Mar  1 00:39:07.743 UTC: OSPF: rcv. v:2 t:1 l:52 rid:131.99.216.193
     aid:0.0.0.0 chk:189B aut:0 auk: from FastEthernet0/0
*Mar  1 00:39:07.767 UTC: %LINK-3-UPDOWN: Interface Ethernet1, changed state to
up
*Mar  1 00:39:07.767 UTC: is_up: 1 state: 4 sub state: 1 line: 0
*Mar  1 00:39:08.767 UTC: %LINEPROTO-5-UPDOWN: Line protocol on Interface Loopba
ck1, changed state to up
```

continues

Example 11-6 *The* **show** *and* **debug** *Output Screens for Scenario 11-4, Router C (Continued)*

```
*Mar  1 00:39:08.767 UTC: is_up: 1 state: 4 sub state: 1 line: 0
*Mar  1 00:39:08.887 UTC: OSPF: rcv. v:2 t:1 l:52 rid:131.99.144.129
      aid:0.0.0.0 chk:189B aut:0 auk: from FastEthernet0/0
routerC#
*Mar  1 00:39:17.743 UTC: OSPF: rcv. v:2 t:1 l:52 rid:131.99.216.193
      aid:0.0.0.0 chk:189B aut:0 auk: from FastEthernet0/0u
*Mar  1 00:39:18.883 UTC: OSPF: rcv. v:2 t:1 l:52 rid:131.99.144.129
      aid:0.0.0.0 chk:189B aut:0 auk: from FastEthernet0/0 all
All possible debugging has been turned off
routerC#
routerC#show ip ospf database

            OSPF Router with ID (131.99.232.225) (Process ID 100)


                    Router Link States (Area 0)

Link ID          ADV Router       Age       Seq#        Checksum Link count
131.99.144.129   131.99.144.129   1657      0x80000004 0xEB16    1
131.99.216.193   131.99.216.193   1707      0x80000004 0xE00F    1
131.99.232.225   131.99.232.225   1707      0x80000004 0x296E    1

                    Net Link States (Area 0)

Link ID          ADV Router       Age       Seq#        Checksum
131.99.0.51      131.99.232.225   1656      0x80000002 0x516B

                    Summary Net Link States (Area 0)

Link ID          ADV Router       Age       Seq#        Checksum
131.99.128.0     131.99.144.129   1665      0x80000001 0xB436
131.99.144.129   131.99.144.129   1665      0x80000001 0x400A
131.99.192.0     131.99.216.193   1714      0x80000001 0x76AB
131.99.216.193   131.99.216.193   1714      0x80000001 0x2712
131.99.224.0     131.99.232.225   1799      0x80000001 0xE3ED

                    Router Link States (Area 3)

Link ID          ADV Router       Age       Seq#        Checksum Link count
131.99.232.225   131.99.232.225   56        0x80000005 0x2B34    2

                    Summary Net Link States (Area 3)

Link ID          ADV Router       Age       Seq#        Checksum
0.0.0.0          131.99.232.225   1800      0x80000001 0x4D3F
131.99.0.48       131.99.232.225   1698      0x80000003 0xF52D
131.99.128.0     131.99.232.225   1644      0x80000001 0x3003
131.99.144.129   131.99.232.225   1644      0x80000001 0xBBD6
131.99.192.0      131.99.232.225   1694      0x80000001 0x6D85
131.99.216.193   131.99.232.225   1694      0x80000001 0x1EEB
routerC# show ip ospf
 Routing Process "ospf 100" with ID 131.99.232.225
 Supports only single TOS(TOS0) routes
```

Example 11-6 *The* **show** *and* **debug** *Output Screens for Scenario 11-4, Router C (Continued)*

```
        Supports opaque LSA
        It is an area border router
        SPF schedule delay 5 secs, Hold time between two SPFs 10 secs
        Minimum LSA interval 5 secs. Minimum LSA arrival 1 secs
        Number of external LSA 0. Checksum Sum 0x0
        Number of opaque AS LSA 0. Checksum Sum 0x0
        Number of DCbitless external and opaque AS LSA 0
        Number of DoNotAge external and opaque AS LSA 0
        Number of areas in this router is 2. 1 normal 1 stub 0 nssa
        External flood list length 0
            Area BACKBONE(0)
                Number of interfaces in this area is 1
                Area has no authentication
                SPF algorithm executed 11 times
                Area ranges are
                Number of LSA 9. Checksum Sum 0x4BBE8
                Number of opaque link LSA 0. Checksum Sum 0x0
                Number of DCbitless LSA 0
                Number of indication LSA 0
                Number of DoNotAge LSA 0
                Flood list length 0
            Area 3
                Number of interfaces in this area is 2
                It is a stub area
                  generates stub default route with cost 1
                Area has no authentication
                SPF algorithm executed 10 times
                Area ranges are
                    131.99.224.0/20 Active(1) Advertise
                Number of LSA 7. Checksum Sum 0x2E5E9
                Number of opaque link LSA 0. Checksum Sum 0x0
                Number of DCbitless LSA 0
                Number of indication LSA 0
                Number of DoNotAge LSA 0
                Flood list length 0

routerC# show ip ospf border-routers

OSPF Process 100 internal Routing Table

Codes: i - Intra-area route, I - Inter-area route

i 131.99.216.193 [1] via 131.99.0.50, FastEthernet0/0, ABR, Area 0, SPF 11
i 131.99.144.129 [1] via 131.99.0.49, FastEthernet0/0, ABR, Area 0, SPF 11
routerC#show ip ospf interface
FastEthernet0/0 is up, line protocol is up
  Internet Address 131.99.0.51/28, Area 0
  Process ID 100, Router ID 131.99.232.225, Network Type BROADCAST, Cost: 1
  Transmit Delay is 1 sec, State DR, Priority 1
  Designated Router (ID) 131.99.232.225, Interface address 131.99.0.51
  Backup Designated router (ID) 131.99.216.193, Interface address 131.99.0.50
```

continues

Example 11-6 *The* **show** *and* **debug** *Output Screens for Scenario 11-4, Router C (Continued)*

```
        Timer intervals configured, Hello 10, Dead 40, Wait 40, Retransmit 5
          Hello due in 00:00:06
        Index 1/1, flood queue length 0
        Next 0x0(0)/0x0(0)
        Last flood scan length is 1, maximum is 2
        Last flood scan time is 0 msec, maximum is 0 msec
        Neighbor Count is 2, Adjacent neighbor count is 2
          Adjacent with neighbor 131.99.144.129
          Adjacent with neighbor 131.99.216.193  (Backup Designated Router)
        Suppress hello for 0 neighbor(s)
      Ethernet1 is up, line protocol is up
        Internet Address 131.99.224.225/28, Area 3
        Process ID 100, Router ID 131.99.232.225, Network Type BROADCAST, Cost: 1
        Transmit Delay is 1 sec, State DR, Priority 1
        Designated Router (ID) 131.99.232.225, Interface address 131.99.0.51
        Backup Designated router (ID) 131.99.216.193, Interface address 131.99.0.50
        Timer intervals configured, Hello 10, Dead 40, Wait 40, Retransmit 5
          Hello due in 00:00:06
        Index 1/1, flood queue length 0
        Next 0x0(0)/0x0(0)
        Last flood scan length is 1, maximum is 2
        Last flood scan time is 0 msec, maximum is 0 msec
          Suppress hello for 0 neighbor(s)
      Ethernet2 is up, line protocol is up
        Internet Address 131.99.232.225/25, Area 3
        Process ID 100, Router ID 131.99.232.225 Network Type BROADCAST, Cost: 1
        Transmit Delay is 1 sec, State DR, Priority 1
      Timer intervals configured, Hello 10, Dead 40, Wait 40, Retransmit 5
          Hello due in 00:00:06
        Index 1/1, flood queue length 0
        Next 0x0(0)/0x0(0)
        Last flood scan length is 1, maximum is 2
        Last flood scan time is 0 msec, maximum is 0 msec
      Suppress hello for 0 neighbor(s)
      routerC#show ip ospf neighbors

      Neighbor ID    Pri  State        Dead Time  Address         Interface
      131.99.144.129  1   FULL/DROTHER 00:00:37   131.99.0.49     FastEthernet0/
      0
      131.99.216.193  1   FULL/BDR     00:00:36   131.99.0.50     FastEthernet0/
      0

      routerC#ping 131.99.192.193

      Type escape sequence to abort.
      Sending 5, 100-byte ICMP Echos to 131.99.192.193, timeout is 2 seconds:
      !!!!!
      Success rate is 100 percent (5/5), round-trip min/avg/max = 1/2/4 ms
      routerC#trace 131.99.192.193

      Type escape sequence to abort.
```

Example 11-6 *The* **show** *and* **debug** *Output Screens for Scenario 11-4, Router C (Continued)*

```
Tracing the route to 131.99.192.193

 1 131.99.0.50 4 msec 0 msec *
routerC#trace
Protocol [ip]:
Target IP address: 131.99.144.129
Source address: 131.99.232.225
Numeric display [n]:
Timeout in seconds [3]:
Probe count [3]:
Minimum Time to Live [1]:
Maximum Time to Live [30]: 3
Port Number [33434]:
Loose, Strict, Record, Timestamp, Verbose[none]:
Type escape sequence to abort.
Tracing the route to 131.99.144.129

 1 131.99.0.49 0 msec 0 msec *
routerC#trace 131.99.0.49
Type escape sequence to abort.
Tracing the route to 131.99.0.49
 1 131.99.0.49 0 msec 0 msec *
```

Answer the following questions. Use Examples 11-4 through 11-6 as a reference when the question refers directly to this scenario. Although not all of these questions are directly tied to the previous scenario, they all probe foundational knowledge required by the technology examined in this scenario.

1 Which command is used to configure a totally stubby area?

2 What do the letters *ASBR* stand for, and what does this device do?

3 Where is summarization performed in OSPF?

4 Give the command to configure the ASBR to summarize the networks 131.99.224.128, 131.99.224.224, and 131.99.224.0 through 131.99.230.0 for redistribution into the RIP process, using a 20-bit subnet mask.

5 Explain the difference between prefix routing and subnetting.

6 State one consideration when configuring multiarea OSPF across a nonbroadcast multiaccess (NBMA) network.

7 What command is used to turn on OSPF?

8 Explain why OSPF supports VLSM.

9 Explain why all areas must connect through the backbone Area 0.

10 Explain the purpose of the **network** command in OSPF.

11 Which command is used to show a router's internal OSPF routing table?

12 Which command shows the use of VLSM on the OSPF network?

13 Which command verifies the establishment of adjacencies with other routers on the same network?

14 How would you see if there was more than one IP routing protocol running on a router? If more than one IP routing protocol was running, how would you see how redistribution was configured?

15 When troubleshooting an OSPF configuration over an NBMA network, which command shows the network type that has been configured? It is understood that the command **show running** will display this information, but greater analysis of the timers and costs is required.

16 Give the appropriate mask to use on a point-to-point serial interface, where IP unnumbered is not an option.

17 What command would be used to identify that an adjacency could not be formed because one router was configured as a stub, while another was not?

18 Which command is used to ensure that the virtual link is active?

19 What concern should you have when using the **debug** command?

20 What is a floating static route, and when would you use one?

Solutions to Scenario 11-4, Part C—Verification and Questions

The answers to the questions for Scenario 11-4, Part C are as follows:

1 Which command is used to configure a totally stubby area?

The command used to create a totally stubby area is as follows:

```
Router(config-router)# area area-id stub no-summary
```

2 What do the letters *ASBR* stand for, and what does this device do?

The letters ASBR stand for Autonomous System Border Router. This is an OSPF router that connects the OSPF domain to another routing domain. Typically, this is when redistribution is required. The ASBR does not have to be situated in Area 0, although it may be recommended.

3 Where is summarization performed in OSPF?

Summarization is configured on the Area Border Router (ABR) or the Autonomous System Border Router (ASBR).

ABR: Summarization at the ABR creates a network that represents many networks within the area. This summary network is propagated into Area 0 and, from there, into the other areas.

ASBR: Summarization at the ASBR creates a network that represents many networks within the autonomous system. Redistributing this summary network into another routing protocol propagates it to the outside world.

4 Give the command to configure the ASBR to summarize the networks 131.99.224.128, 131.99.224.224, and 131.99.224.0 through 131.99.230.0 for redistribution into the RIP process, using a 20-bit subnet mask.

The command to summarize the networks 131.99.224.128, 131.99.224.224, and 131.99.224.0 through 131.99.230.0 for redistribution into the RIP process is as follows:

```
Router(config-router)#summary-address 131.99.224.0 255.255.240.0
```

Because RIP is using the same NIC address, it is important to note that RIP would need to be using the same mask because it does not support VLSM.

5 Explain the difference between prefix routing and subnetting.

The difference between prefix routing and subnetting is that prefix routing creates supernets for the Internet. That summarizes class addresses—for example, creating one network from 14 Class C addresses. The new mask would be 255.255.240.0 or a prefix of /20.

VLSM is the capability to subnet the class address provided by the Internet, to create smaller subnets.

Prefix routing moves the mask to the left, while subnetting moves the mask to the right.

6 State one consideration when configuring multiarea OSPF across a nonbroadcast multiaccess (NBMA) network.

Considerations when configuring multiarea OSPF across a nonbroadcast multiaccess (NBMA) network include these:

- **The NBMA network can be created as Area 0. The reasoning is that if the NBMA is used to connect all remote sites, all traffic will have to traverse this network. If the remote sites are satellite areas, then all traffic will have to traverse the NBMA, so it makes sense to make it the backbone area. This works well in a full-mesh environment, although it will result in a large number of LSAs being flooded into the WAN and will put extra demands on the routers connecting to the NBMA network.**

- In a hub-and-spoke NBMA network it makes sense to assign the hub network as Area 0 with the other remote sites and the NBMA network as other areas. This is a good design if the satellite areas are stub areas because it means that the routing information, and thus network overhead, is kept to a minimum over the NBMA cloud. Depending on the design, the rest of the network may constitute one other area or multiple areas. This will depend on the size and growth expectations of the OSPF domain.

7   What command is used to turn on OSPF?

The command to turn on OSPF is as follows:

```
Router(config)# Router OSPF process-id
```

The process-id is subtly different from the autonomous system number used in IGRP and EIGRP. The process-id identifies the process. This allows more than one process to be configured on a router. Although unusual, there are instances in which this configuration is appropriate.

8   Explain why OSPF supports VLSM.

OSPF supports VLSM because it carries the subnet mask in the routing updates. Therefore, each router can reference the appropriate mask for each network.

9   Explain why all areas must connect through the backbone Area 0.

Area 0 forms a common path for all areas to connect. Therefore, it ensures that all areas are aware of all networks within the OSPF domain.

10   Explain the purpose of the **network** command in OSPF.

The network command is used to assign an interface or a group of interfaces to an area. When the interfaces are identified, they will participate in the OSPF routing process for the area to which they belong.

11   Which command is used to show a router's internal OSPF routing table?

The command show ip ospf border-routers displays the internal routing table of the OSPF internal router.

12   Which command shows the use of VLSM on the OSPF network?

The show ip route command shows not only all the available routes, but also the masks used. If different masks are used, this command states that the subnet is variably subnetted, with the number of subnets and masks.

13   Which command verifies the establishment of adjacencies with other routers on the same network?

The command show ip ospf neighbor shows the neighbors, the neighbor ID, the connecting interface address of the neighboring router, the outgoing interface on the router to connect to the neighbor, the length of time since the last communication from the neighbor, the connection state, and whether the neighbor is a designated router (DR) or backup designated router (BDR).

14 How would you see if there was more than one IP routing protocol running on a router? If more than one IP routing protocol was running on a router, how would you know how redistribution was configured?

There are a couple of ways to ascertain whether there was more than one routing protocol is running on a router. The first way is by issuing this command:

```
Router# show running
```

Because this command shows the configuration that is currently running, it is easy enough to see if more than one protocol is running and, if redistribution is running, how it is configured. The other and more straightforward method is to issue the following command:

```
Router# show ip protocols
```

This command shows all the IP protocols configured on the router, as well as the details of that configuration, including the redistribution.

15 When troubleshooting an OSPF configuration over an NBMA network, which command shows the network type that has been configured? It is understood that the command **show running** will display this information, but greater analysis of the timers and costs is required.

The command show ip ospf interface will indicate the network type, the delays set for the timers, and the number of neighbors and adjacencies.

16 Give the appropriate mask to use on a point-to-point serial interface, where IP unnumbered is not an option.

The mask to be used in a point-to-point link is 255.255.255.252. This mask allows the allocation of two addresses and is a typical mask for point-to-point networks.

17 What command would be used to identify that an adjacency could not be formed because one router was configured as a stub, while another was not?

The command debug IP ospf adjacency will show that there is a problem in the establishment in an adjacency. The error message would point to a mismatched stub/transit area option bit. You could also do a show ip ospf interface to see that the interface has no neighbors. At this point, it would be wise to check the interface configuration.

18 Which command is used to ensure that the virtual link is active?

The command show IP ospf virtual-links verifies the virtual link configuration.

19   What concern should you have when using the **debug** command?

The debug command is a command that should be used with caution because it can use an enormous amount of system resources. Given priority 1 as a process, it can eventually bring your router to a standstill. It is important to run the utility for a limited time to capture the required output. It is also best not to use the debug command from the console unless logging to the log file only. If the console screen freezes while using debug, there is no recovery other than to reboot the system.

20   What is a floating static route, and when would you use one?

A floating static route is used when a router has a link that is used as a backup using a medium such as a dialup line. The intention is to have no routing protocol running across the link that would keep the link active at a high cost.

The first task is to create a static route so that the routing protocol is not required. Unfortunately, the administrative distance that is used to select the best routes offered by different routing protocols states that a static route is the best route and will use it for all traffic. Thus, despite your best efforts, the backup link becomes a low-bandwidth, expensive primary link. To change the link to take backup status, manually configure the administrative distance to have a higher value than the dynamic routing protocol.

Scenario 11-5

Part A of Scenario 11-5 begins with some planning guidelines that include planning the transition of the network to run EIGRP as the routing protocol. To transition smoothly, the intention is to slowly integrate EIGRP; this requires redistribution between EIGRP and OSPF as well as the filtering of updates between the protocols. After you complete Part A, Part B of the scenario asks you to configure the three routers to implement the planned design and a few other features. Finally, Part C asks you to examine router command output to discover details about the current operation. Part C also lists some questions related to the user interface and protocol specifications.

Scenario 11-5, Part A—Planning

Your job is to deploy a new network with three sites, as shown in Figure 11-7.

Figure 11-7   *Scenario 11-5 Network Diagram*

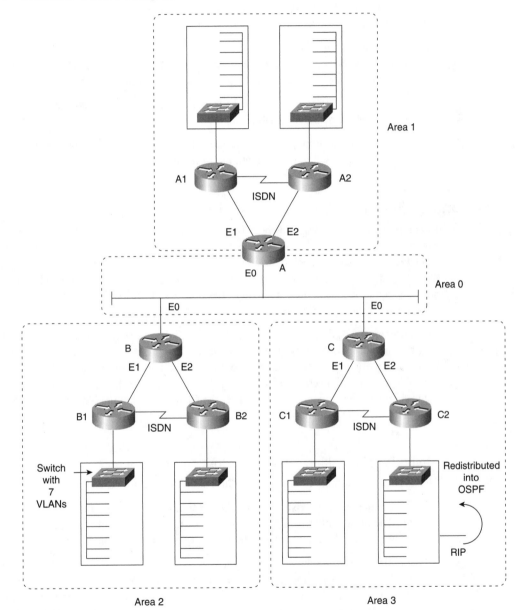

The OSPF network has limitations, and the decision has been made to change the routing protocol to EIGRP. Use the addressing scheme presented in the solutions of Scenario 11-4. For Part A of this scenario, perform the following tasks:

1 The planning committee has stated that the transition to EIGRP should start at the edges of the network and move inward in a controlled manner. Give a brief explanation of how you would implement a transition plan. Is summarization possible?

2 Redistribution is necessary. State the router(s) that would be responsible for redistribution and the nature of the redistribution.

3 To prevent routing loops, it has been decided to implement distribution filters. Plan the content, location, and implementation of the filters.

Solutions to Scenario 11-5, Part A—Planning

Keeping the design as simple as possible, yet not making it so simple that the network cannot evolve, is a good practice. In these suggested answers, remember that many solutions are available. The reasoning behind this planning is to allow the optimum solution while maintaining the strength of the existing network. As in the Scenario 11-4 solution, the addressing scheme allows summarization at the core level of the network. The first few bits in the third octet indicate the summarization bits.

Many organizations decide to transition the network by starting at the outer peripheries of the network to minimize the impact of these changes. The problems that may occur when a change is made to an organization can be catastrophic. Inevitably, something is overlooked, or you have the dubious honor of discovering a new bug. Obviously, if the change is made to a stub network, the problem can be isolated and fixed speedily. Centralized routers with problems tend to share them with the rest of the network.

Alternative Methods of Transition to Another Routing Protocol

The alternative methods of transition include no redistribution at all. For example:

- Each router could be visited in turn, OSPF could be turned off, and EIGRP could be turned on. The disadvantage of this approach is the time that it would take for the network to converge and the capability to troubleshoot any problems that might occur.

- Another solution, which is more practical, is to turn on EIGRP on all the routers and to run both protocols simultaneously. However, because EIGRP has a lower administrative distance than OSPF, routes from EIGRP would be added to the routing table before all the routers were configured. This would create black holes within the network.

- The solution to this is to configure the administrative distance manually, making OSPF preferable to EIGRP. When all the routers have been configured and the network is stable, then it is easy enough to change all the routers to prefer EIGRP by changing the administrative distance back to the default. When the routers have converged, the OSPF protocol can be removed.

- A disadvantage of this solution is that the routers will require extra resources to run both protocols and, inevitably, there is a greater opportunity for black holes and routing loops.

Transitioning to EIGRP from the Outer Edges of the Network

The transition plan is very straightforward because the network in this scenario is very small. However, it reflects the strategy required by any size of network.

The implementation of EIGRP should start in Area 1. The reasoning for this is that there is currently no redistribution in the area, and it has an addressing scheme that is already set up for summarization.

Summarization in EIGRP

Summarization is definitely possible, although EIGRP has no restrictions on summarization in the way OSPF only permits it at the ABR or ASBR. In EIGRP, summarization is configured at the interface level, which allows for great flexibility as well as confusion.

There are two ways to consider summarization in this network. The first is simply to implement the summarization put in place by OSPF. The addressing scheme supports it, and it makes good design sense. The other is necessary during the transition phase. This summarization occurs at the point of redistribution, to the external routes being passed into the new routing protocol.

Router A would be responsible for redistribution at the first level of transition—that would redistribute the routes from A1. If this transition went smoothly, then A2 would be configured for EIGRP. Then Area 2 could be changed to running EIGRP, one router at a time. The most complex redistribution would be in Area 3, which is already redistributing RIP into OSPF. Because RIP is here to stay in Building 2 of Area 3, care must be taken in the transition to EIGRP.

Building C1 would be an easy transition with redistribution on Router C. Router C2 would need to cut over to EIGRP and turn on redistribution immediately.

At this point, the only routers running OSPF are the core routers A, B, and C. The choice is now whether to transition one router at a time or to cut over in one fell swoop. Personally, I would cut over everything. If the transition is done at night, this is the safer method. Only three routers are involved, and the transition of the areas has now proven successful. There is a backup to restore everything to the status quo, in case problems are encountered.

Although this appears rather dangerous, it is much safer and cleaner than configuring further redistribution on the three core routers.

The routers must prevent feedback of routing information during redistribution. This can be done to avoid routing loops, which can result in the death of your network.

The purpose of the distribution lists is to prevent the routing processes telling each other what they already know. We will impose split horizons between the routing protocols manually.

Simply, when Router A is configured to redistribute the EIGRP routes from Router A1 into OSPF, OSPF will have a filter permitting only those routes to be redistributed. In this way, the routes that OSPF sends into EIGRP will not be propagated back into OSPF. Likewise, these filters will be set on routers B and C.

Scenario 11-5, Part B—Configuration

The next step in your job is to deploy the network designed in Scenario 11-5, Part A. Use the solutions for Part A of Scenario 11-5 to direct you in configuring the addressing and summarization at the Area Border Routers. For Scenario 11-5, Part B, perform the following tasks:

1 Configure basic EIGRP for routers A, B, and C based on Scenario 11-5, Part A's design.

2 Configure summarization on routers A, B, and C.

3 Configure redistribution between OSPF and EIGRP on routers A, B, and C.

4 Configure distribution filters on routers A, B, and C.

Solutions to Scenario 11-5, Part B—Configuration

Example 11-7, Example 11-8, and Example 11-9 show the configurations for Scenario 11-5, Part B, given the preceding criteria.

Example 11-7 *Scenario 11-5 Router A Configuration*

```
router eigrp 200
network 131.99.0.0
passive interface e0
!!! This prevents updates from being sent out of interface
!!! E0, which is in the OSPF domain
redistribute ospf 100 metric 1000 100 1 255 1500
!!! Previous configuration
interface e0
ip address 131.99.0.49 255.255.255.240
! 4 bits allows 14 hosts
 interface E1
ip address 131.99.136.129 255.255.255.128
! 7 bits allows 127 hosts
ip summary-address EIGRP 200 131.99.192.0 255.255.240.0
```

Example 11-7 *Scenario 11-5 Router A Configuration (Continued)*

```
ip summary-address EIGRP 200 131.99.224.0.255.255.240.0
! EIGRP summary addresses are interface specific,
! which allows different summarized addresses to be
! advertised out of different interfaces
interface E2
ip address 131.99.144.129 255.255.255.128
! 7 bits allows 127 hosts
ip summary-address eigrp 200 131.99.192.0 255.255.240.0
ip summary-address eigrp 200 131.99.224.0.255.255.240.0
!!
router ospf 100
network 131.99.0.49 0.0.0.0 area 0
! The wildcard mask 0.0.0.0 places the interface E0 into area 0
network 0.0.0.0 255.255.255.255 area 1
! The wildcard mask 255.255.255.255 places all other interfaces into area 1
area 1 range 131.99.128.0 255.255.240.0
! All addresses from area 1 will be summarized into this one network
area 1 stub
! Area 1 is defined as a stub network that will not receive
! network information outside the autonomous system
!!! New OSPF Configuration
redistribute EIGRP 200 metric 50
summary-address 131.99.128.0 255.255.240.0
passive interface e1
passive interface e2
distribute list 101 in
access-list 101 permit ip 131.99.192.0 0.0.15.255 any
access-list 101 permit ip 131.99.224.0 0.0.15.255 any
access-list 101 permit ip 131.99.0.0 0.0.0.255 any
access-list 101 deny   ip any any log
!!! Prevents OSPF networks from being looped back into the OSPF process
```

Example 11-8 *Scenario 11-5 Router B Configuration*

```
router eigrp 200
network 131.99.0.0
passive interface e0
!!! This prevents updates from being sent out of interface E0,
! which is in the OSPF domain
redistribute ospf 100 metric 1000 100 1 255 1500
!
interface e0
ip address 131.99.0.50 255.255.255.240
! 4 bits allows 14 hosts
interface e1
ip address 131.99.192.193 255.255.255.128
! 7 bits allows 127 hosts
ip summary-address eigrp 200 131.99.128.0 255.255.240.0
ip summary-address eigrp 200 131.99.224.0.255.255.240.0
```

continues

Example 11-8 *Scenario 11-5 Router B Configuration (Continued)*

```
! EIGRP summary addresses are interface specific, which allows different
! summarized addresses to be advertised out of different interfaces
interface e2
ip address 131.99.216.193 255.255.255.128
! 4 bits allows 14 hosts
ip summary-address eigrp 200 131.99.128.0 255.255.240.0
ip summary-address eigrp 200 131.99.224.0.255.255.240.0
! EIGRP summary addresses are interface specific, which allows different
! summarized addresses to be advertised out of different interfaces
!!
router ospf 100
network 131.99.0.50 0.0.0.0 area 0
network 0.0.0.0 255.255.255.255 area 2
area 2 range 131.99.192.0 255.255.240.0
area 2 stub
!!! New OSPF Configuration
redistribute eigrp 200 metric 50
summary-address 131.99.192.0 255.255.240.0
passive interface e1
passive interface e2
distribute-list 101 in
access-list 101 permit ip 131.99.128.0 0.0.15.255 any
access-list 101 permit ip 131.99.224.0 0.0.15.255 any
access-list 101 permit ip 131.99.0.0 0.0.0.255 any
access-list 101 deny   ip any any log
!
!!! Prevents OSPF networks from being looped back into the OSPF process
```

Example 11-9 *Scenario 11-5 Router C Configuration*

```
router eigrp 200
network 131.99.0.0
passive interface e0
!!! This prevents updates from being sent out of interface E0,
!!! which is in the OSPF domain
redistribute ospf 100 metric 1000 100 1 255 1500
!
interface e0
ip address 131.99.0.51 255.255.255.240
! 4 bits allows 14 hosts
interface e1
ip address 131.99.224.225 255.255.255.128
! 7 bits allows 127 hosts
ip summary-address eigrp 200 131.99.192.0 255.255.240.0
ip summary-address eigrp 200 131.99.128.0.255.255.240.0
! EIGRP summary addresses are interface specific, which allows different
! summarized addresses to be advertised out of different interfaces
interface e2
ip address 131.99.232.225 255.255.255.240
!7 bits allows 127 hosts
ip summary-address eigrp 200 131.99.192.0 255.255.240.0
ip summary-address eigrp 200 131.99.128.0.255.255.240.0
```

Example 11-9 *Scenario 11-5 Router C Configuration (Continued)*

```
! EIGRP summary addresses are interface specific, which allows different
! summarized addresses to be advertised out of different interfaces)
!!
router ospf 100
network 131.99.0.51 0.0.0.0 area 0
network 0.0.0.0 255.255.255.255 area 3
area 3 range 131.99.224.0 255.255.240.0
!!! New OSPF Configuration
redistribute eigrp 200 metric 50
summary-address 131.99.224.0 255.255.240.0
passive interface e1
passive interface e2
distribute-list 101 in
access-list 101 permit ip 131.99.128.0 0.0.15.255 any
access-list 101 permit ip 131.99.192.0 0.0.15.255 any
access-list 101 permit ip 131.99.0.0 0.0.0.255 any
access-list 101 deny   ip any any log
!!! Prevents OSPF networks from being looped back into the OSPF process
```

Scenario 11-5 Part C—Verification and Questions

The Routing 2.0 exam tests your memory for information that can be found in the output of various **show** commands. Using the output from Examples 11-10 through 11-12, answer the questions that follow.

NOTE   In the network from which these commands were captured, several administrative settings not mentioned in the scenario were configured. For instance, the enable password was configured. Any **show running-config** commands in the examples in this chapter might have other unrelated configuration.

Example 11-10 *The **show** and **debug** Output Screens for Scenario 11-5, Router A*

```
routerA#show version
Cisco Internetwork Operating System Software
IOS (tm) 3600 Software (C3620-JS56I-M), Version 12.0(7)T,  RELEASE SOFTWARE (fc2)
Copyright (c) 1986-1999 by cisco Systems, Inc.
Compiled Wed 08-Dec-99 11:16 by phanguye
Image text-base: 0x600088F0, data-base: 0x612B4000

ROM: System Bootstrap, Version 11.1(20)AA2, EARLY DEPLOYMENT RELEASE SOFTWARE
(fc1)
```

continues

Example 11-10 *The* **show** *and* **debug** *Output Screens for Scenario 11-5, Router A (Continued)*

```
routerA uptime is 2 hours, 8 minutes
System returned to ROM by reload
System image file is "flash:c3620-js56i-mz.120-7.T.bin"

cisco 3620 (R4700) processor (revision 0x81) with 59392K/6144K bytes of memory.
Processor board ID 19276534
R4700 CPU at 80Mhz, Implementation 33, Rev 1.0
Bridging software.
X.25 software, Version 3.0.0.
SuperLAT software (copyright 1990 by Meridian Technology Corp).
TN3270 Emulation software.
1 Ethernet/IEEE 802.3 interface(s)
1 Serial network interface(s)
1 ATM network interface(s)
DRAM configuration is 32 bits wide with parity disabled.
29K bytes of non-volatile configuration memory.
16384K bytes of processor board System flash (Read/Write)

Configuration register is 0x2102

routerA#
routerA#show running-config
Building configuration...

Current configuration:
!
version 12.0
service timestamps debug datetime msec localtime show-timezone
service timestamps log datetime msec localtime show-timezone
service password-encryption
!
hostname routerA
!
enable password 7 1511021F0725
!
!
!
ip subnet-zero
no ip domain-lookup
!
cns event-service server
!
!
!
interface Ethernet1
 ip address 131.99.136.129 255.255.255.128
 no ip directed-broadcast
 ip summary-address eigrp 200 131.99.224.0 255.255.240.0 5
 ip summary-address eigrp 200 131.99.192.0 255.255.240.0 5
!
interface Ethernet2
 ip address 131.99.144.129 255.255.255.128
 no ip directed-broadcast
```

Example 11-10 *The* **show** *and* **debug** *Output Screens for Scenario 11-5, Router A (Continued)*

```
ip summary-address eigrp 200 131.99.224.0 255.255.240.0 5
ip summary-address eigrp 200 131.99.192.0 255.255.240.0 5
!
interface Ethernet0
 ip address 131.99.0.49 255.255.255.240
 no ip directed-broadcast
!
interface Serial0/0
 no ip address
 no ip directed-broadcast
 no ip mroute-cache
 shutdown
 no fair-queue
!
interface ATM1/0
 no ip address
 no ip directed-broadcast
 shutdown
 no atm ilmi-keepalive
!
router eigrp 200
 redistribute ospf 100 metric 1000 100 1 255 1500
 passive-interface Ethernet0
 network 131.99.0.0
!
router ospf 100
 area 1 stub
 area 1 range 131.99.128.0 255.255.240.0
 summary-address 131.99.128.0 255.255.240.0
 redistribute eigrp 200 metric 50
 passive-interface Ethernet1
 passive-interface Ethernet2
 network 131.99.0.49 0.0.0.0 area 0
 network 0.0.0.0 255.255.255.255 area 1
 distribute-list 101 in
!
ip classless
no ip http server
!
access-list 101 permit ip 131.99.192.0 0.0.15.255 any
access-list 101 permit ip 131.99.224.0 0.0.15.255 any
access-list 101 permit ip 131.99.0.0 0.0.0.255 any
access-list 101 deny   ip any any log
!
!
line con 0
 transport input none
line aux 0
line vty 0 4
 password 7 045802150C2E
 login
```

continues

Example 11-10 *The* **show** *and* **debug** *Output Screens for Scenario 11-5, Router A (Continued)*

```
!
end

routerA#
routerA#show ip interface
Ethernet0 is up, line protocol is up
  Internet address is 131.99.0.49/28
  Broadcast address is 255.255.255.255
  Address determined by non-volatile memory
  MTU is 1500 bytes
  Helper address is not set
  Directed broadcast forwarding is disabled
  Multicast reserved groups joined: 224.0.0.5 224.0.0.6 224.0.0.10
  Outgoing access list is not set
  Inbound  access list is not set
  Proxy ARP is enabled
  Security level is default
  Split horizon is enabled
  ICMP redirects are always sent
  ICMP unreachables are always sent
  ICMP mask replies are never sent
  IP fast switching is enabled
  IP fast switching on the same interface is disabled
  IP Flow switching is disabled
  IP Fast switching turbo vector
  IP multicast fast switching is enabled
  IP multicast distributed fast switching is disabled
  IP route-cache flags are Fast
  Router Discovery is disabled
  IP output packet accounting is disabled
  IP access violation accounting is disabled
  TCP/IP header compression is disabled
  RTP/IP header compression is disabled
  Probe proxy name replies are disabled
  Policy routing is disabled
  Network address translation is disabled
  WCCP Redirect outbound is disabled
  WCCP Redirect exclude is disabled
  BGP Policy Mapping is disabled
Serial0/0 is administratively down, line protocol is down
  Internet protocol processing disabled
ATM1/0 is administratively down, line protocol is down
  Internet protocol processing disabled
Ethernet1 is up, line protocol is up
  Internet address is 131.99.136.129/25
  Broadcast address is 255.255.255.255
  Address determined by non-volatile memory
  MTU is 1514 bytes
  Helper address is not set
  Directed broadcast forwarding is disabled
  Multicast reserved groups joined: 224.0.0.5 224.0.0.6 224.0.0.10
  Outgoing access list is not set
  Inbound  access list is not set
```

Example 11-10 *The* **show** *and* **debug** *Output Screens for Scenario 11-5, Router A (Continued)*

```
            Proxy ARP is enabled
            Security level is default
            Split horizon is enabled
            ICMP redirects are always sent
            ICMP unreachables are always sent
            ICMP mask replies are never sent
            IP fast switching is disabled
            IP fast switching on the same interface is disabled
            IP Flow switching is disabled
            IP Fast switching turbo vector
            IP multicast fast switching is enabled
            IP multicast distributed fast switching is disabled
            IP route-cache flags are Fast
            Router Discovery is disabled
            IP output packet accounting is disabled
            IP access violation accounting is disabled
            TCP/IP header compression is disabled
            RTP/IP header compression is disabled
            Probe proxy name replies are disabled
            Policy routing is disabled
            Network address translation is disabled
            WCCP Redirect outbound is disabled
            WCCP Redirect exclude is disabled
            BGP Policy Mapping is disabled
          Ethernet2 is up, line protocol is up
            Internet address is 131.99.144.129/25
            Broadcast address is 255.255.255.255
            Address determined by non-volatile memory
            MTU is 1514 bytes
            Helper address is not set
            Directed broadcast forwarding is disabled
            Multicast reserved groups joined: 224.0.0.5 224.0.0.6 224.0.0.10
            Outgoing access list is not set
            Inbound  access list is not set
            Proxy ARP is enabled
            Security level is default
            Split horizon is enabled
            ICMP redirects are always sent
            ICMP unreachables are always sent
            ICMP mask replies are never sent
            IP fast switching is disabled
            IP fast switching on the same interface is disabled
            IP Flow switching is disabled
            IP Fast switching turbo vector
            IP multicast fast switching is enabled
            IP multicast distributed fast switching is disabled
            IP route-cache flags are Fast
            Router Discovery is disabled
            IP output packet accounting is disabled
            IP access violation accounting is disabled
            TCP/IP header compression is disabled
```

continues

Example 11-10 *The* **show** *and* **debug** *Output Screens for Scenario 11-5, Router A (Continued)*

```
     RTP/IP header compression is disabled
     Probe proxy name replies are disabled
     Policy routing is disabled
     Network address translation is disabled
     WCCP Redirect outbound is disabled
     WCCP Redirect exclude is disabled
     BGP Policy Mapping is disabled
routerA#$
routerA#show ip protocols
Routing Protocol is "ospf 100"
  Sending updates every 0 seconds
  Invalid after 0 seconds, hold down 0, flushed after 0
  Outgoing update filter list for all interfaces is
  Incoming update filter list for all interfaces is 101
  Redistributing: ospf 100, eigrp 200
  Address Summarization:
  Routing for Networks:
    131.99.0.49/32
    0.0.0.0
  Passive Interface(s):
    Ethernet1
    Ethernet2
  Routing Information Sources:
    Gateway          Distance       Last Update
    131.99.232.225       110        00:07:08
    131.99.216.193       110        00:07:08
  Distance: (default is 110)

Routing Protocol is "eigrp 200"
  Outgoing update filter list for all interfaces is
  Incoming update filter list for all interfaces is
  Default networks flagged in outgoing updates
  Default networks accepted from incoming updates
  EIGRP metric weight K1=1, K2=0, K3=1, K4=0, K5=0
  EIGRP maximum hopcount 100
  EIGRP maximum metric variance 1
  Redistributing: ospf 100 (internal, external 1 & 2, nssa-external 1 & 2)

  Redistributing: eigrp 200
  Automatic network summarization is in effect
  Address Summarization:
    131.99.224.0/20 for Ethernet1, Ethernet2
    131.99.192.0/20 for Ethernet1, Ethernet2
  Routing for Networks:
    131.99.0.0
  Passive Interface(s):
    Ethernet0
  Routing Information Sources:
    Gateway          Distance       Last Update
  Distance: internal 90 external 170


routerA# show ip route
```

Example 11-10 *The* **show** *and* **debug** *Output Screens for Scenario 11-5, Router A (Continued)*

```
Codes: C - connected, S - static, I - IGRP, R - RIP, M - mobile, B - BGP
       D - EIGRP, EX - EIGRP external, O - OSPF, IA - OSPF inter area
       N1 - OSPF NSSA external type 1, N2 - OSPF NSSA external type 2
       E1 - OSPF external type 1, E2 - OSPF external type 2, E - EGP
       i - IS-IS, L1 - IS-IS level-1, L2 - IS-IS level-2, ia - IS-IS inter area
       * - candidate default, U - per-user static route, o - ODR
       P - periodic downloaded static route

Gateway of last resort is not set

      131.99.0.0/16 is variably subnetted, 6 subnets, 4 masks
O IA    131.99.224.0/20 [110/11] via 131.99.0.51, 00:08:04, Ethernet0
O IA    131.99.192.0/20 [110/11] via 131.99.0.50, 00:08:04, Ethernet0
C       131.99.0.48/25 is directly connected, Ethernet0
C       131.99.136.128/28 is directly connected, Ethernet1
C       131.99.144.128/28 is directly connected, Ethernet2
O IA    131.99.216.193/32 [110/11] via 131.99.0.50, 00:08:04, Ethernet0
routerA# debug ip ospf events
OSPF events debugging is on
routerA#
*Mar  1 02:11:18.203 UTC: OSPF: Rcv hello from 131.99.216.193 area 0
 from Ethernet0/0 131.99.0.50
*Mar  1 02:11:18.203 UTC: OSPF: End of hello processing
*Mar  1 02:11:19.659 UTC: OSPF: Rcv hello from 131.99.232.225 area 0
 from Ethernet0/0 131.99.0.51
*Mar  1 02:11:19.659 UTC: OSPF: End of hello processing
*Mar  1 02:11:28.203 UTC: OSPF: Rcv hello from 131.99.216.193 area 0
 from Ethernet0/0 131.99.0.50
*Mar  1 02:11:28.203 UTC: OSPF: End of hello processing
*Mar  1 02:11:29.659 UTC: OSPF: Rcv hello from 131.99.232.225 area 0
 from Ethernet0/0 131.99.0.51
*Mar  1 02:11:29.659 UTC: OSPF: End of hello processing
routerA#undebug all
All possible debugging has been turned off

routerA#debug ip routing
IP routing debugging is on
routerA#config t
Enter configuration commands, one per line.  End with CNTL/Z.
routerA(config)#interface lo1
routerA(config-if)#shut
routerA(config-if)#no shut
*Mar  1 02:11:56.263 UTC: is_up: 0 state: 6 sub state: 1 line: 0
*Mar  1 02:11:56.363 UTC: RT: interface Ethernet1 removed from routing table
*Mar  1 02:11:56.363 UTC: RT: del 131.99.136.128/25 via 0.0.0.0, connected metri
c [0/0]
*Mar  1 02:11:56.363 UTC: RT: delete subnet route to 131.99.136.128/25
*Mar  1 02:11:58.263 UTC: %LINK-5-CHANGED: Interface Ethernet1, changed state to
 administratively down
*Mar  1 02:11:58.263 UTC: is_up: 0 state: 6 sub state: 1 line: 0
*Mar  1 02:11:59.263 UTC: %LINEPROTO-5-UPDOWN: Line protocol on
```

continues

Example 11-10 *The* **show** *and* **debug** *Output Screens for Scenario 11-5, Router A (Continued)*

```
Interface Loopback1, changed state to down
*Mar  1 02:11:59.263 UTC: is_up: 0 state: 6 sub state: 1 line: 0
routerA(config-if)#^Z
routerA#
*Mar  1 02:12:04.075 UTC: is_up: 1 state: 4 sub state: 1 line: 0
*Mar  1 02:12:04.075 UTC: RT: add 131.99.136.128/25 via 0.0.0.0, connected
 metric [0/0]
*Mar  1 02:12:04.075 UTC: RT: interface Ethernet1 added to routing table
*Mar  1 02:12:05.307 UTC: %SYS-5-CONFIG_I: Configured from console by console
*Mar  1 02:12:06.071 UTC: %LINK-3-UPDOWN: Interface Ethernet1, changed state to
up
*Mar  1 02:12:06.075 UTC: is_up: 1 state: 4 sub state: 1 line: 0
*Mar  1 02:12:07.071 UTC: %LINEPROTO-5-UPDOWN: Line protocol on
 Interface Loopback1, changed state to up
*Mar  1 02:12:07.071 UTC: is_up: 1 state: 4 sub state: 1 line: 0
routerA#
routerA#undebug all
All possible debugging has been turned off
routerA#debug ip packet
IP packet debugging is on
routerA#
*Mar  1 02:12:18.203 UTC: IP: s=131.99.0.50 (Ethernet0), d=224.0.0.5, len 72,
rcvd 0
*Mar  1 02:12:19.535 UTC: IP: s=131.99.0.49 (local), d=224.0.0.5 (Ethernet0),
len 72, sending broad/multicast
*Mar  1 02:12:19.663 UTC: IP: s=131.99.0.51 (Ethernet0), d=224.0.0.5, len 72,
rcvd 0
*Mar  1 02:12:20.819 UTC: IP: s=131.99.136.129 (local), d=224.0.0.10 (Ethernet1),
 len 60, sending broad/multicast
*Mar  1 02:12:20.819 UTC: IP: s=131.99.136.129 (Ethernet1), d=224.0.0.10, len 60,
rcvd 2
*Mar  1 02:12:20.823 UTC: IP: s=131.99.144.129 (local), d=224.0.0.10 (Ethernet2),
 len 60, sending broad/multicast
*Mar  1 02:12:20.823 UTC: IP: s=131.99.144.129 (Ethernet2), d=224.0.0.10, len 60,
rcvd 2
*Mar  1 02:12:25.691 UTC: IP: s=131.99.136.129 (local), d=224.0.0.10 (Ethernet1),
 len 60, sending broad/multicast
*Mar  1 02:12:25.691 UTC: IP: s=131.99.136.129 (Ethernet1), d=224.0.0.10, len 60,
rcvd 2
*Mar  1 02:12:25.699 UTC: IP: s=131.99.144.129 (local), d=224.0.0.10 (Ethernet2),
 len 60, sending broad/multicast
*Mar  1 02:12:25.699 UTC: IP: s=131.99.144.129 (Ethernet2), d=224.0.0.10, len 60,
rcvd 2
*Mar  1 02:12:28.203 UTC: IP: s=131.99.0.50 (Ethernet0), d=224.0.0.5, len 72,
rcvd 0
*Mar  1 02:12:29.535 UTC: IP: s=131.99.0.49 (local), d=224.0.0.5 (Ethernet0),
len 72, sending broad/multicast
*Mar  1 02:12:29.675 UTC: IP: s=131.99.0.51 (Ethernet0), d=224.0.0.5, len 72,
rcvd 0
*Mar  1 02:12:30.075 UTC: IP: s=131.99.144.129 (local), d=224.0.0.10 (Ethernet2),
 len 60, sending broad/multicast
*Mar  1 02:12:30.075 UTC: IP: s=131.99.144.129 (Ethernet2), d=224.0.0.10, len 60,
rcvd 2
```

Example 11-10 *The* **show** *and* **debug** *Output Screens for Scenario 11-5, Router A (Continued)*

```
*Mar  1 02:12:30.267 UTC: IP: s=131.99.136.129 (local), d=224.0.0.10 (Ethernet1),
len 60, sending broad/multicast
*Mar
routerA#undebug all
 1 02:12:30.267 UTC: IP: s=131.99.136.129 (Ethernet1), d=224.0.0.10, l
en 60, rcvd 2 all
All possible debugging has been turned off
routerA#show ip interface brief
Interface                 IP-Address      OK? Method Status             Protocol
Ethernet0                 131.99.0.49     YES NVRAM  up                      up

Serial0/0                 unassigned      YES NVRAM  administratively down down

ATM1/0                    unassigned      YES NVRAM  administratively down down

Ethernet1                 131.99.136.129  YES NVRAM  up                      up

Ethernet2                 131.99.144.129  YES NVRAM  up                      up

routerA# show ip ospf database

            OSPF Router with ID (131.99.144.129) (Process ID 100)


                   Router Link States (Area 0)

Link ID          ADV Router       Age      Seq#        Checksum Link count
131.99.144.129   131.99.144.129   398      0x80000006 0xED10    1
131.99.216.193   131.99.216.193   1656     0x80000009 0xDC0C    1
131.99.232.225   131.99.232.225   1457     0x80000009 0x256B    1

                   Net Link States (Area 0)

Link ID          ADV Router       Age      Seq#        Checksum
131.99.0.51      131.99.232.225   1977     0x80000008 0x4571

                   Summary Net Link States (Area 0)

Link ID          ADV Router       Age      Seq#        Checksum
131.99.128.0     131.99.144.129   33       0x80000001 0xB436
131.99.144.129   131.99.144.129   1892     0x80000006 0x360F
131.99.192.0     131.99.216.193   382      0x80000003 0x72AD
131.99.216.193   131.99.216.193   885      0x80000006 0x1D17
131.99.224.0     131.99.232.225   1214     0x80000006 0xD9F2

                   Router Link States (Area 1)

Link ID          ADV Router       Age      Seq#        Checksum Link count
131.99.144.129   131.99.144.129   40       0x8000000A 0xFC3E    2
```

continues

Example 11-10 *The* **show** *and* **debug** *Output Screens for Scenario 11-5, Router A (Continued)*

```
                       Summary Net Link States (Area 1)

   Link ID           ADV Router        Age      Seq#        Checksum
   0.0.0.0           131.99.144.129    1893     0x80000004 0xF34E
   131.99.0.48        131.99.144.129   1893      0x80000006 0xF6D8
   131.99.192.0      131.99.144.129    644      0x80000001 0x742E
   131.99.216.193    131.99.144.129    644      0x80000001 0x2594
   131.99.224.0      131.99.144.129    645      0x80000001 0x136F
routerA# show ip ospf
 Routing Process "ospf 100" with ID 131.99.144.129
 Supports only single TOS(TOS0) routes
 Supports opaque LSA
 It is an area border and autonomous system boundary router
 Redistributing External Routes from,
     eigrp 200 with metric mapped to 50
 SPF schedule delay 5 secs, Hold time between two SPFs 10 secs
 Minimum LSA interval 5 secs. Minimum LSA arrival 1 secs
 Number of external LSA 0. Checksum Sum 0x0
 Number of opaque AS LSA 0. Checksum Sum 0x0
 Number of DCbitless external and opaque AS LSA 0
 Number of DoNotAge external and opaque AS LSA 0
 Number of areas in this router is 2. 1 normal 1 stub 0 nssa
 External flood list length 0
    Area BACKBONE(0)
        Number of interfaces in this area is 1
        Area has no authentication
        SPF algorithm executed 38 times
        Area ranges are
        Number of LSA 9. Checksum Sum 0x487F3
        Number of opaque link LSA 0. Checksum Sum 0x0
        Number of DCbitless LSA 0
        Number of indication LSA 0
        Number of DoNotAge LSA 0
        Flood list length 0
    Area 1
        Number of interfaces in this area is 2
        It is a stub area
          generates stub default route with cost 1
        Area has no authentication
        SPF algorithm executed 38 times
        Area ranges are
           131.99.128.0/20 Active(1) Advertise
        Number of LSA 6. Checksum Sum 0x39395
        Number of opaque link LSA 0. Checksum Sum 0x0
        Number of DCbitless LSA 0
        Number of indication LSA 0
        Number of DoNotAge LSA 0
        Flood list length 0

routerA# show ip ospf border-routers

OSPF Process 100 internal Routing Table
```

Example 11-10 *The* show *and* debug *Output Screens for Scenario 11-5, Router A (Continued)*

```
Codes: i - Intra-area route, I - Inter-area route

i 131.99.232.225 [10] via 131.99.0.51, Ethernet0, ABR/ASBR, Area 0, SPF 38
i 131.99.216.193 [10] via 131.99.0.50, Ethernet0, ABR/ASBR, Area 0, SPF 38
routerA# show ip ospf interface
Ethernet0 is up, line protocol is up
  Internet Address 131.99.0.49/28 Area 0
  Process ID 100, Router ID 131.99.144.129, Network Type BROADCAST, Cost: 10
  Transmit Delay is 1 sec, State DROTHER, Priority 1
  Designated Router (ID) 131.99.232.225, Interface address 131.99.0.51
  Backup Designated router (ID) 131.99.216.193, Interface address 131.99.0.50
  Timer intervals configured, Hello 10, Dead 40, Wait 40, Retransmit 5
    Hello due in 00:00:03
  Index 1/1, flood queue length 0
  Next 0x0(0)/0x0(0)
  Last flood scan length is 1, maximum is 2
  Last flood scan time is 0 msec, maximum is 0 msec
  Neighbor Count is 2, Adjacent neighbor count is 2
    Adjacent with neighbor 131.99.232.225  (Designated Router)
    Adjacent with neighbor 131.99.216.193  (Backup Designated Router)
  Suppress hello for 0 neighbor(s)
Ethernet1 is up, line protocol is up
  Internet Address 131.99.136.129/25, Area 1
  Process ID 100, Router ID 131.99.144.129, Network Type BROADCAST, Cost: 10
  Transmit Delay is 1 sec, State DROTHER, Priority 1
    Timer intervals configured, Hello 10, Dead 40, Wait 40, Retransmit 5
    Hello due in 00:00:03
  Index 1/1, flood queue length 0
  Next 0x0(0)/0x0(0)
  Last flood scan length is 1, maximum is 2
  Last flood scan time is 0 msec, maximum is 0 msec
  Suppress hello for 0 neighbor(s)

Ethernet2 is up, line protocol is up
  Internet Address 131.99.144.129/25, Area 1
  Process ID 100, Router ID 131.99.144.129, Network Type BROADCAST, Cost: 10
  Transmit Delay is 1 sec, State DROTHER, Priority 1
    Timer intervals configured, Hello 10, Dead 40, Wait 40, Retransmit 5
    Hello due in 00:00:03
  Index 1/1, flood queue length 0
  Next 0x0(0)/0x0(0)
  Last flood scan length is 1, maximum is 2
  Last flood scan time is 0 msec, maximum is 0 msec
  Suppress hello for 0 neighbor(s)

routerA# show ip ospf neighbor

Neighbor ID      Pri   State        Dead Time   Address        Interface
131.99.232.225    1    FULL/DR      00:00:37    131.99.0.51    Ethernet0
131.99.216.193    1    FULL/BDR     00:00:37    131.99.0.50    Ethernet0
routerA# sh ip eigrp ne
IP-EIGRP neighbors for process 200
```

continues

Example 11-10 *The* **show** *and* **debug** *Output Screens for Scenario 11-5, Router A (Continued)*

```
routerA# show ip eigrp interface
IP-EIGRP interfaces for process 200

                    Xmit Queue   Mean   Pacing Time   Multicast     Pending
Interface    Peers  Un/Reliable  SRTT   Un/Reliable   Flow Timer    Routes
e1           0      0/0          0      0/10          0             0
e2           0      0/0          0      0/10          0             0
routerA# show ip eigrp topology
IP-EIGRP Topology Table for AS(200)/ID(131.99.144.129)

Codes: P - Passive, A - Active, U - Update, Q - Query, R - Reply,
       r - Reply status

P 131.99.224.0/20, 1 successors, FD is 2585600
        via Redistributed (2585600/0)
P 131.99.192.0/20, 1 successors, FD is 2585600
        via Redistributed (2585600/0)
P 131.99.0.48/28, 1 successors, FD is 281600
        via Connected, Ethernet0
        via Rconnected (281600/0)
P 131.99.136.128/25, 1 successors, FD is 128256
        via Connected, Ethernet1
        via Rconnected (128256/0)
P 131.99.144.128/25, 1 successors, FD is 128256
        via Connected, Ethernet2
        via Rconnected (128256/0)
P 131.99.216.193/32, 1 successors, FD is 2585600
        via Redistributed (2585600/0)

routerA# show ip eigrp traffic
IP-EIGRP Traffic Statistics for process 200
  Hellos sent/received: 2862/2861
  Updates sent/received: 0/0
  Queries sent/received: 0/0
  Replies sent/received: 0/0
  Acks sent/received: 0/0
  Input queue high water mark 2, 0 drops

routerA#ping 131.99.216.193

Type escape sequence to abort.
Sending 5, 100-byte ICMP Echos to 131.99.216.193, timeout is 2 seconds:
!!!!!
Success rate is 100 percent (5/5), round-trip min/avg/max = 1/3/4 ms
routerA#ping 131.99.192.193

Type escape sequence to abort.
Sending 5, 100-byte ICMP Echos to 131.99.192.193, timeout is 2 seconds:
!!!!!
Success rate is 100 percent (5/5), round-trip min/avg/max = 4/4/4 ms
routerA#ping 131.99.224.225
```

Example 11-10 *The* **show** *and* **debug** *Output Screens for Scenario 11-5, Router A (Continued)*

```
Type escape sequence to abort.
Sending 5, 100-byte ICMP Echos to 131.99.224.225, timeout is 2 seconds:
!!!!!
Success rate is 100 percent (5/5), round-trip min/avg/max = 1/2/4 ms
routerA#ping 131.99.232.225

Type escape sequence to abort.
Sending 5, 100-byte ICMP Echos to 131.99.232.225, timeout is 2 seconds:
!!!!!
Success rate is 100 percent (5/5), round-trip min/avg/max = 1/3/4 ms
routerA#trace
Protocol [ip]:
routerA#trace
Protocol [ip]:
Target IP address: 131.99.192.193
Source address: 131.99.136.129
Numeric display [n]:
Timeout in seconds [3]:
Probe count [3]:
Minimum Time to Live [1]:
Maximum Time to Live [30]: 3
Port Number [33434]:
Loose, Strict, Record, Timestamp, Verbose[none]:
Type escape sequence to abort.
Tracing the route to 131.99.192.193

  1 131.99.0.50 4 msec *  0 msec

routerA#trace 131.99.232.225

Type escape sequence to abort.
Tracing the route to 131.99.232.225

  1 131.99.0.51 4 msec *  0 msec
```

Example 11-11 *The* **show** *and* **debug** *Output Screens for Scenario 11-5, Router B*

```
routerB#show version
Cisco Internetwork Operating System Software
IOS (tm) 3600 Software (C3620-JS56I-M), Version 12.0(7)T,  RELEASE SOFTWARE
 (fc2)
Copyright (c) 1986-1999 by cisco Systems, Inc.
Compiled Wed 08-Dec-99 11:16 by phanguye
Image text-base: 0x600088F0, data-base: 0x612B4000

ROM: System Bootstrap, Version 11.1(20)AA2, EARLY DEPLOYMENT RELEASE SOFTWARE
 (fc1)

routerB uptime is 5 hours, 43 minutes
System returned to ROM by reload
```

continues

Example 11-11 *The* **show** *and* **debug** *Output Screens for Scenario 11-5, Router B (Continued)*

```
System image file is "flash:c3620-js56i-mz.120-7.T.bin"

cisco 3620 (R4700) processor (revision 0x81) with 59392K/6144K bytes of memory.
Processor board ID 19276633
R4700 CPU at 80Mhz, Implementation 33, Rev 1.0
Bridging software.
X.25 software, Version 3.0.0.
SuperLAT software (copyright 1990 by Meridian Technology Corp).
TN3270 Emulation software.
1 Ethernet/IEEE 802.3 interface(s)
1 Serial network interface(s)
1 ATM network interface(s)
DRAM configuration is 32 bits wide with parity disabled.
29K bytes of non-volatile configuration memory.
16384K bytes of processor board System flash (Read/Write)

Configuration register is 0x2102

routerB# show running-config
Building configuration...

Current configuration:
!
version 12.0
service timestamps debug datetime msec localtime show-timezone
service timestamps log datetime msec localtime show-timezone
service password-encryption
!
hostname routerB
!
enable password 7 02050D480809
!
!
!
ip subnet-zero
no ip domain-lookup
!
cns event-service server
!
!
!
interface ethernet1
 ip address 131.99.192.193 255.255.255.128
 no ip directed-broadcast
!
interface ethernet2
 ip address 131.99.216.193 255.255.255.128
 no ip directed-broadcast
 ip summary-address eigrp 200 131.99.224.0 255.255.240.0 5
 ip summary-address eigrp 200 131.99.128.0 255.255.240.0 5
!
interface Ethernet0
 ip address 131.99.0.50 255.255.255.240
```

Example 11-11 *The **show** and **debug** Output Screens for Scenario 11-5, Router B (Continued)*

```
   no ip directed-broadcast
   ip summary-address eigrp 200 131.99.224.0 255.255.240.0 5
   ip summary-address eigrp 200 131.99.128.0 255.255.240.0 5
   !
  interface Serial0/0
   no ip address
   no ip directed-broadcast
   no ip mroute-cache
   shutdown
   no fair-queue
   !
  interface ATM1/0
   no ip address
   no ip directed-broadcast
   shutdown
   no atm ilmi-keepalive
   !
  router eigrp 200
   redistribute ospf 100 metric 1000 100 1 255 1500
   passive-interface Ethernet0
   network 131.99.0.0
   !
  router ospf 100
   area 2 stub
   area 2 range 131.99.192.0 255.255.240.0
   summary-address 131.99.192.0 255.255.240.0
   redistribute eigrp 200 metric 50
   passive-interface Ethernet1
   passive-interface Ethernet2
   network 131.99.0.50 0.0.0.0 area 0
   network 0.0.0.0 255.255.255.255 area 2
   distribute-list 101 in
   !
  ip classless
  no ip http server
   !
  access-list 101 permit ip 131.99.128.0 0.0.15.255 any
  access-list 101 permit ip 131.99.224.0 0.0.15.255 any
  access-list 101 permit ip 131.99.0.0 0.0.0.255 any
  access-list 101 deny   ip any any log
   !
   !
  line con 0
   transport input none
  line aux 0
  line vty 0 4
   password 7 110A1016141D
   login
   !
  end
```

continues

Example 11-11 *The* **show** *and* **debug** *Output Screens for Scenario 11-5, Router B (Continued)*

```
routerB#show interface
Ethernet0is up, line protocol is up
  Hardware is AmdP2, address is 0001.96ea.ca41 (bia 0001.96ea.ca41)
  Internet address is 131.99.0.50/28
  MTU 1500 bytes, BW 10000 Kbit, DLY 1000 usec,
     reliability 255/255, txload 1/255, rxload 1/255
  Encapsulation ARPA, loopback not set
  Keepalive set (10 sec)
  ARP type: ARPA, ARP Timeout 04:00:00
  Last input 00:00:05, output 00:00:00, output hang never
  Last clearing of "show interface" counters never
  Queueing strategy: fifo
Output queue 0/40, 0 drops; input queue 0/75, 0 drops
  5 minute input rate 0 bits/sec, 0 packets/sec
  5 minute output rate 0 bits/sec, 0 packets/sec
     5759 packets input, 605877 bytes, 0 no buffer
     Received 5142 broadcasts, 0 runts, 0 giants, 0 throttles
     0 input errors, 0 CRC, 0 frame, 0 overrun, 0 ignored
     0 input packets with dribble condition detected
     5467 packets output, 673224 bytes, 0 underruns
     0 output errors, 0 collisions, 2 interface resets
     0 babbles, 0 late collision, 0 deferred
     0 lost carrier, 0 no carrier
     0 output buffer failures, 0 output buffers swapped out
Serial0/0 is administratively down, line protocol is down
  Hardware is QUICC Serial
  MTU 1500 bytes, BW 2048 Kbit, DLY 20000 usec,
     reliability 255/255, txload 1/255, rxload 1/255
  Encapsulation HDLC, loopback not set
  Keepalive set (10 sec)
  Last input never, output never, output hang never
  Last clearing of "show interface" counters 05:43:15
  Queueing strategy: fifo
Output queue 0/40, 0 drops; input queue 0/75, 0 drops
  5 minute input rate 0 bits/sec, 0 packets/sec
  5 minute output rate 0 bits/sec, 0 packets/sec
     0 packets input, 0 bytes, 0 no buffer
     Received 0 broadcasts, 0 runts, 0 giants, 0 throttles
     0 input errors, 0 CRC, 0 frame, 0 overrun, 0 ignored, 0 abort
     0 packets output, 0 bytes, 0 underruns
     0 output errors, 0 collisions, 1 interface resets
     0 output buffer failures, 0 output buffers swapped out
     0 carrier transitions
     DCD=down  DSR=down  DTR=down  RTS=down  CTS=down

ATM1/0 is administratively down, line protocol is down
  Hardware is RS8234 ATMOC3
  MTU 4470 bytes, sub MTU 4470, BW 155000 Kbit, DLY 80 usec,
     reliability 0/255, txload 1/255, rxload 1/255
  Encapsulation ATM, loopback not set
  Keepalive not supported
  Encapsulation(s): AAL5
  1024 maximum active VCs, 0 current VCCs
```

Example 11-11 *The* **show** *and* **debug** *Output Screens for Scenario 11-5, Router B (Continued)*

```
        VC idle disconnect time: 300 seconds
        Last input never, output never, output hang never
        Last clearing of "show interface" counters never
        Input queue: 0/75/0 (size/max/drops); Total output drops: 0
        Queueing strategy: Per VC Queueing
    5 minute input rate 0 bits/sec, 0 packets/sec
        5 minute output rate 0 bits/sec, 0 packets/sec
            0 packets input, 0 bytes, 0 no buffer
            Received 0 broadcasts, 0 runts, 0 giants, 0 throttles
            0 input errors, 0 CRC, 0 frame, 0 overrun, 0 ignored, 0 abort
            0 packets output, 0 bytes, 0 underruns
            0 output errors, 0 collisions, 1 interface resets
            0 output buffer failures, 0 output buffers swapped out
    Ethernet1 is up, line protocol is up
     Hardware is AmdP2, address is 0001.96dc.ba41 (bia 0001.96dc.ba41)
     Internet address is 131.99.192.193/28
     MTU 1500 bytes, BW 10000 Kbit, DLY 1000 usec,
        reliability 255/255, txload 1/255, rxload 1/255
     Encapsulation ARPA, loopback not set
     Keepalive set (10 sec)
     ARP type: ARPA, ARP Timeout 04:00:00
        MTU 1514 bytes, BW 8000000 Kbit, DLY 5000 usec,
            reliability 255/255, txload 1/255, rxload 1/255
     Encapsulation LOOPBACK, loopback not set
     Last input 00:00:01, output never, output hang never
     Last clearing of "show interface" counters never
     Queueing strategy: fifo
    Output queue 0/0, 0 drops; input queue 0/75, 0 drops
        5 minute input rate 0 bits/sec, 0 packets/sec
        5 minute output rate 0 bits/sec, 0 packets/sec
            0 packets input, 0 bytes, 0 no buffer
            Received 0 broadcasts, 0 runts, 0 giants, 0 throttles
            0 input errors, 0 CRC, 0 frame, 0 overrun, 0 ignored, 0 abort
            3223 packets output, 193347 bytes, 0 underruns
            0 output errors, 0 collisions, 0 interface resets
            0 output buffer failures, 0 output buffers swapped out
    Ethernet2 is up, line protocol is up
     Hardware is AmdP2, address is 0001.96ea.ca32(bia 0001.96ea.ca32)
     Internet address is 131.99.216.193/28
     MTU 1500 bytes, BW 10000 Kbit, DLY 1000 usec,
        reliability 255/255, txload 1/255, rxload 1/255
     Encapsulation ARPA, loopback not set
     Keepalive set (10 sec)
     ARP type: ARPA, ARP Timeout 04:00:00
     MTU 1514 bytes, BW 8000000 Kbit, DLY 5000 usec,
        reliability 255/255, txload 1/255, rxload 1/255
        Last input 00:00:04, output never, output hang never
     Last clearing of "show interface" counters never
     Queueing strategy: fifo
    Output queue 0/0, 0 drops; input queue 0/75, 0 drops
        5 minute input rate 0 bits/sec, 0 packets/sec
```

continues

Example 11-11 *The* **show** *and* **debug** *Output Screens for Scenario 11-5, Router B (Continued)*

```
     5 minute output rate 0 bits/sec, 0 packets/sec
        0 packets input, 0 bytes, 0 no buffer
        Received 0 broadcasts, 0 runts, 0 giants, 0 throttles
        0 input errors, 0 CRC, 0 frame, 0 overrun, 0 ignored, 0 abort
        3223 packets output, 193347 bytes, 0 underruns
        0 output errors, 0 collisions, 0 interface resets
        0 output buffer failures, 0 output buffers swapped out
routerB#$
routerB#show ip protocols
Routing Protocol is "ospf 100"
  Sending updates every 0 seconds
  Invalid after 0 seconds, hold down 0, flushed after 0
  Outgoing update filter list for all interfaces is
  Incoming update filter list for all interfaces is 101
  Redistributing: ospf 100, eigrp 200
  Address Summarization:
  Routing for Networks:
    131.99.0.50/32
    0.0.0.0
  Passive Interface(s):
    Ethernet1
    Ethernet2
  Routing Information Sources:
    Gateway          Distance       Last Update
    131.99.232.225        110       02:39:35
    131.99.144.129        110       02:30:36
  Distance: (default is 110)

Routing Protocol is "eigrp 200"
  Outgoing update filter list for all interfaces is
  Incoming update filter list for all interfaces is
  Default networks flagged in outgoing updates
  Default networks accepted from incoming updates
  EIGRP metric weight K1=1, K2=0, K3=1, K4=0, K5=0
  EIGRP maximum hopcount 100
  EIGRP maximum metric variance 1
  Redistributing: ospf 100 (internal, external 1 & 2, nssa-external 1 & 2)

  Redistributing: eigrp 200
  Automatic network summarization is in effect
  Address Summarization:
    131.99.224.0/20 for Ethernet0, Ethernet2
    131.99.128.0/20 for Ethernet0, Ethernet2
  Routing for Networks:
    131.99.0.0
  Passive Interface(s):
    Ethernet0
  Routing Information Sources:
    Gateway          Distance       Last Update
  Distance: internal 90 external 170

routerB# show ip route
```

Example 11-11 *The* **show** *and* **debug** *Output Screens for Scenario 11-5, Router B (Continued)*

```
Codes: C - connected, S - static, I - IGRP, R - RIP, M - mobile, B - BGP
       D - EIGRP, EX - EIGRP external, O - OSPF, IA - OSPF inter area
       N1 - OSPF NSSA external type 1, N2 - OSPF NSSA external type 2
       E1 - OSPF external type 1, E2 - OSPF external type 2, E - EGP
       i - IS-IS, L1 - IS-IS level-1, L2 - IS-IS level-2, ia - IS-IS inter area
       * - candidate default, U - per-user static route, o - ODR
       P - periodic downloaded static route

Gateway of last resort is not set

     131.99.0.0/16 is variably subnetted, 6 subnets, 4 masks
O IA    131.99.224.0/20 [110/11] via 131.99.0.51, 02:39:42, Ethernet0
O IA    131.99.128.0/20 [110/11] via 131.99.0.49, 02:30:43, Ethernet0
C       131.99.192.192/25 is directly connected, Ethernet1
C       131.99.0.48/28 is directly connected, Ethernet0
O IA    131.99.144.129/32 [110/11] via 131.99.0.49, 02:39:42, Ethernet0
C       131.99.216.192/25 is directly connected, Ethernet2
routerB# debug ip ospf events
OSPF events debugging is on
routerB#
*Mar  1 05:46:16.158 UTC: OSPF: Rcv hello from 131.99.144.129 area 0
 from Ethernet0/0 131.99.0.49
*Mar  1 05:46:16.158 UTC: OSPF: End of hello processing
*Mar  1 05:46:16.758 UTC: OSPF: Rcv hello from 131.99.232.225 area 0
 from Ethernet0/0 131.99.0.51
*Mar  1 05:46:16.758 UTC: OSPF: End of hello processing
*Mar  1 05:46:26.158 UTC: OSPF: Rcv hello from 131.99.144.129 area 0
 from Ethernet0/0 131.99.0.49
*Mar  1 05:46:26.158 UTC: OSPF: End of hello processing
*Mar  1 05:46:26.758 UTC: OSPF: Rcv hello from 131.99.232.225 area 0
 from Ethernet0/0 131.99.0.51
*Mar  1 05:46:26.758 UTC: OSPF: End of hello processing
routerB#undebug all
All possible debugging has been turned off
routerB#debug ip routing
IP routing debugging is on
routerB#config t
Enter configuration commands, one per line.  End with CNTL/Z.
routerB(config)#interface lo1
routerB(config-if)#shut
routerB(config-if)#no shut
*Mar  1 05:46:57.786 UTC: is_up: 0 state: 6 sub state: 1 line: 0
*Mar  1 05:46:57.886 UTC: RT: interface Ethernet1 removed from routing table
*Mar  1 05:46:57.886 UTC: RT: del 131.99.192.192/25 via 0.0.0.0,
 connected metric [0/0]
*Mar  1 05:46:57.886 UTC: RT: delete subnet route to 131.99.192.192/25
*Mar  1 05:46:59.786 UTC: %LINK-5-CHANGED: Interface Ethernet1, changed state to
 administratively down
*Mar  1 05:46:59.786 UTC: is_up: 0 state: 6 sub state: 1 line: 0
*Mar  1 05:47:00.786 UTC: %LINEPROTO-5-UPDOWN: Line protocol on
 Interface Loopback1, changed state to down
```

continues

Example 11-11 *The* **show** *and* **debug** *Output Screens for Scenario 11-5, Router B (Continued)*

```
*Mar  1 05:47:00.786 UTC: is_up: 0 state: 6 sub state: 1 line: 0
routerB(config-if)#^Z
routerB#
*Mar  1 05:47:05.030 UTC: is_up: 1 state: 4 sub state: 1 line: 0
*Mar  1 05:47:05.030 UTC: RT: add 131.99.192.192/25 via 0.0.0.0,
 connected metric [0/0]
*Mar  1 05:47:05.034 UTC: RT: interface Ethernet1 added to routing table
*Mar  1 05:47:06.110 UTC: %SYS-5-CONFIG_I: Configured from console by console
*Mar  1 05:47:07.030 UTC: %LINK-3-UPDOWN: Interface Ethernet1,
 changed state to up
*Mar  1 05:47:07.030 UTC: is_up: 1 state: 4 sub state: 1 line: 0
*Mar  1 05:47:08.030 UTC: %LINEPROTO-5-UPDOWN: Line protocol on
 Interface Loopback1, changed state to up
*Mar  1 05:47:08.030 UTC: is_up: 1 state: 4 sub state: 1 line: 0
routerB#
routerB#undebug all
All possible debugging has been turned off
routerB#
routerB#show ip interface brief
Interface                IP-Address      OK? Method Status              Protocol
Ethernet0                131.99.0.50     YES manual up                      up

Serial0/0                unassigned      YES unset  administratively down down

ATM1/0                   unassigned      YES unset  administratively down down

Ethernet1                131.99.192.193  YES manual up                      up

Ethernet2                131.99.216.193  YES manual up                      up

routerB#
routerB#show ip ospf database

        OSPF Router with ID (131.99.216.193) (Process ID 100)


                Router Link States (Area 0)

Link ID         ADV Router      Age         Seq#        Checksum Link count
131.99.144.129  131.99.144.129  1516        0x8000000A  0xE514   1
131.99.216.193  131.99.216.193  765         0x8000000E  0xD211   1
131.99.232.225  131.99.232.225  599         0x8000000E  0x1B70   1

                Net Link States (Area 0)

Link ID         ADV Router      Age         Seq#        Checksum
131.99.0.51     131.99.232.225  1114        0x8000000D  0x3B76

                Summary Net Link States (Area 0)

Link ID         ADV Router      Age         Seq#        Checksum
131.99.128.0    131.99.144.129  1258        0x80000005  0xAC3A
131.99.144.129  131.99.144.129  1258        0x8000000B  0x2C14
```

Example 11-11 *The* **show** *and* **debug** *Output Screens for Scenario 11-5, Router B (Continued)*

```
131.99.192.0    131.99.216.193  19      0x80000001 0x76AB
131.99.216.193  131.99.216.193  1994    0x8000000A 0x151B
131.99.224.0    131.99.232.225  600     0x8000000B 0xCFF7

                Router Link States (Area 2)

Link ID         ADV Router      Age     Seq#       Checksum Link count
131.99.216.193  131.99.216.193  28      0x80000010 0x71C     2

                Summary Net Link States (Area 2)

Link ID         ADV Router      Age     Seq#       Checksum
0.0.0.0         131.99.216.193  1996    0x8000000A 0x6C47
131.99.0.48     131.99.216.193  1996    0x8000000A 0x73CF
131.99.128.0    131.99.216.193  1262    0x80000005 0xB3A2
131.99.144.129  131.99.216.193  1755    0x80000007 0x3B78
131.99.224.0    131.99.216.193  1755    0x8000000C 0x816D
routerB#
routerB#show ip ospf
 Routing Process "ospf 100" with ID 131.99.216.193
 Supports only single TOS(TOS0) routes
 Supports opaque LSA
 It is an area border and autonomous system boundary router
 Redistributing External Routes from,
    eigrp 200 with metric mapped to 50
 SPF schedule delay 5 secs, Hold time between two SPFs 10 secs
 Minimum LSA interval 5 secs. Minimum LSA arrival 1 secs
 Number of external LSA 0. Checksum Sum 0x0
 Number of opaque AS LSA 0. Checksum Sum 0x0
 Number of DCbitless external and opaque AS LSA 0
 Number of DoNotAge external and opaque AS LSA 0
 Number of areas in this router is 2. 1 normal 1 stub 0 nssa
 External flood list length 0
    Area BACKBONE(0)
        Number of interfaces in this area is 1
        Area has no authentication
        SPF algorithm executed 25 times
        Area ranges are
        Number of LSA 9. Checksum Sum 0x44017
        Number of opaque link LSA 0. Checksum Sum 0x0
        Number of DCbitless LSA 0
        Number of indication LSA 0
        Number of DoNotAge LSA 0
        Flood list length 0
    Area 2
        Number of interfaces in this area is 2
        It is a stub area
          generates stub default route with cost 1
        Area has no authentication
        SPF algorithm executed 21 times
        Area ranges are
            131.99.192.0/20 Active(1) Advertise
```

continues

Example 11-11 *The* **show** *and* **debug** *Output Screens for Scenario 11-5, Router B (Continued)*

```
                Number of LSA 6. Checksum Sum 0x253BB
                Number of opaque link LSA 0. Checksum Sum 0x0
                Number of DCbitless LSA 0
                Number of indication LSA 0
                Number of DoNotAge LSA 0
                Flood list length 0

routerB#show ip ospf border-routers

OSPF Process 100 internal Routing Table

Codes: i - Intra-area route, I - Inter-area route

i 131.99.232.225 [10] via 131.99.0.51, Ethernet0, ABR/ASBR, Area 0, SPF 25
i 131.99.144.129 [10] via 131.99.0.49, Ethernet0, ABR/ASBR, Area 0, SPF 25
routerB#sh ip os int
Ethernet0 is up, line protocol is up
  Internet Address 131.99.0.50/28, Area 0
  Process ID 100, Router ID 131.99.216.193, Network Type BROADCAST, Cost: 10
  Transmit Delay is 1 sec, State BDR, Priority 1
  Designated Router (ID) 131.99.232.225, Interface address 131.99.0.51
  Backup Designated router (ID) 131.99.216.193, Interface address 131.99.0.50
  Timer intervals configured, Hello 10, Dead 40, Wait 40, Retransmit 5
    Hello due in 00:00:02
  Index 1/1, flood queue length 0
  Next 0x0(0)/0x0(0)
  Last flood scan length is 1, maximum is 3
  Last flood scan time is 0 msec, maximum is 0 msec
  Neighbor Count is 2, Adjacent neighbor count is 2
    Adjacent with neighbor 131.99.144.129
    Adjacent with neighbor 131.99.232.225   (Designated Router)
  Suppress hello for 0 neighbor(s)
Ethernet1 is up, line protocol is up
  Internet Address 131.99.192.193/25, Area 2
  Process ID 100, Router ID 131.99.216.193, Network Type BROADCAST, Cost: 10
  Transmit Delay is 1 sec, State BDR, Priority 1
  Designated Router (ID) 131.99.232.225, Interface address 131.99.0.51
  Backup Designated router (ID) 131.99.216.193, Interface address 131.99.0.50
  Timer intervals configured, Hello 10, Dead 40, Wait 40, Retransmit 5
    Hello due in 00:00:02
  Index 1/1, flood queue length 0
  Next 0x0(0)/0x0(0)
  Last flood scan length is 1, maximum is 3
  Last flood scan time is 0 msec, maximum is 0 msec
  Suppress hello for 0 neighbor(s)

Ethernet2 is up, line protocol is up
  Internet Address 131.99.216.193/25, Area 2
  Process ID 100, Router ID 131.99.216.193, Network Type BROADCAST, Cost: 10
  Transmit Delay is 1 sec, State BDR, Priority 1
  Designated Router (ID) 131.99.232.225, Interface address 131.99.0.51
  Backup Designated router (ID) 131.99.216.193, Interface address 131.99.0.50
```

Example 11-11 *The* **show** *and* **debug** *Output Screens for Scenario 11-5, Router B (Continued)*

```
      Timer intervals configured, Hello 10, Dead 40, Wait 40, Retransmit 5
        Hello due in 00:00:02
      Index 1/1, flood queue length 0
      Next 0x0(0)/0x0(0)
      Last flood scan length is 1, maximum is 3
      Last flood scan time is 0 msec, maximum is 0 msec
   Suppress hello for 0 neighbor(s)

routerB# show ip ospf neighbor

Neighbor ID      Pri   State          Dead Time   Address        Interface
131.99.144.129    1    FULL/DROTHER   00:00:37    131.99.0.49    Ethernet0
131.99.232.225    1    FULL/DR        00:00:38    131.99.0.51    Ethernet0
routerB#
routerB# show ip eigrp neighbor
IP-EIGRP neighbors for process 200
routerB# show ip eigrp interface
IP-EIGRP interfaces for process 200

                     Xmit Queue   Mean   Pacing Time   Multicast   Pending
Interface   Peers   Un/Reliable   SRTT   Un/Reliable   Flow Timer  Routes
e1           0         0/0          0        0/10           0          0
e2           0         0/0          0        0/10           0          0
routerB# show ip eigrp topology
IP-EIGRP Topology Table for AS(200)/ID(131.99.216.193)

Codes: P - Passive, A - Active, U - Update, Q - Query, R - Reply,
       r - Reply status

P 131.99.224.0/20, 1 successors, FD is 2585600
        via Redistributed (2585600/0)
P 131.99.128.0/20, 1 successors, FD is 2585600
        via Redistributed (2585600/0)
P 131.99.192.192/25, 1 successors, FD is 128256
        via Connected, Ethernet1
        via Rconnected (128256/0)
P 131.99.0.48/25, 1 successors, FD is 281600
        via Connected, Ethernet0
        via Rconnected (281600/0)
P 131.99.144.129/32, 1 successors, FD is 2585600
        via Redistributed (2585600/0)
P 131.99.216.192/25, 1 successors, FD is 128256
        via Connected, Ethernet2
        via Rconnected (128256/0)

routerB# show ip eigrp traffic
IP-EIGRP Traffic Statistics for process 200
  Hellos sent/received: 6551/6550
  Updates sent/received: 0/0
  Queries sent/received: 0/0
  Replies sent/received: 0/0
```

continues

Example 11-11 *The* **show** *and* **debug** *Output Screens for Scenario 11-5, Router B (Continued)*

```
          Acks sent/received: 0/0
          Input queue high water mark 2, 0 drops

     routerB#ping 131.99.136.129

     Type escape sequence to abort.
     Sending 5, 100-byte ICMP Echos to 131.99.136.129, timeout is 2 seconds:
     !!!!!
     Success rate is 100 percent (5/5), round-trip min/avg/max = 1/2/4 ms
     routerB#ping 131.99.144.129

     Type escape sequence to abort.
     Sending 5, 100-byte ICMP Echos to 131.99.144.129, timeout is 2 seconds:
     !!!!!
     Success rate is 100 percent (5/5), round-trip min/avg/max = 1/3/4 ms
     routerB#ping 131.99.232.225

     Type escape sequence to abort.
     Sending 5, 100-byte ICMP Echos to 131.99.232.225, timeout is 2 seconds:
     !!!!!
     Success rate is 100 percent (5/5), round-trip min/avg/max = 1/3/4 ms
     routerB#ping 131.99.224.225

     Type escape sequence to abort.
     Sending 5, 100-byte ICMP Echos to 131.99.224.225, timeout is 2 seconds:
     !!!!!
     Success rate is 100 percent (5/5), round-trip min/avg/max = 1/2/4 ms

     routerB#ping
     Protocol [ip]:
     Target IP address: 131.99.144.129
     Repeat count [5]:
     Datagram size [100]:
     Timeout in seconds [2]: 1
     Extended commands [n]: y
     Source address or interface: 131.99.216.193
     Type of service [0]:
     Set DF bit in IP header? [no]:
     Validate reply data? [no]:
     Data pattern [0xABCD]:
     Loose, Strict, Record, Timestamp, Verbose[none]:
     Sweep range of sizes [n]:
     Type escape sequence to abort.
     Sending 5, 100-byte ICMP Echos to 131.99.144.129, timeout is 1 seconds:
     !!!!!
     Success rate is 100 percent (5/5), round-trip min/avg/max = 4/4/4 ms
     routerB#
     routerB#trace
     Protocol [ip]:
     Target IP address: 131.99.144.129
     Source address: 131.99.216.193
     Numeric display [n]:
     Timeout in seconds [3]:
```

Example 11-11 *The* show *and* debug *Output Screens for Scenario 11-5, Router B (Continued)*

```
Probe count [3]:
Minimum Time to Live [1]:
Maximum Time to Live [30]: 3
Port Number [33434]:
Loose, Strict, Record, Timestamp, Verbose[none]:
Type escape sequence to abort.
Tracing the route to 131.99.144.129

  1 131.99.0.49 4 msec *  0 msec
routerB#ping 131.99.232.225

Type escape sequence to abort.
Sending 5, 100-byte ICMP Echos to 131.99.232.225, timeout is 2 seconds:
!!!!!
Success rate is 100 percent (5/5), round-trip min/avg/max = 1/3/4 ms
```

Example 11-12 *The* show *and* debug *Output Screens for Scenario 11-5, Router C*

```
routerC#show version
Cisco Internetwork Operating System Software
IOS (tm) C2600 Software (C2600-JS56I-M), Version 12.0(7)T,  RELEASE SOFTWARE
 (fc2)
Copyright (c) 1986-1999 by cisco Systems, Inc.
Compiled Tue 07-Dec-99 05:53 by phanguye
Image text-base: 0x80008088, data-base: 0x8104B45C

ROM: System Bootstrap, Version 11.3(2)XA4, RELEASE SOFTWARE (fc1)

routerC uptime is 5 hours, 45 minutes
System returned to ROM by reload
System image file is "flash:c2600-js56i-mz.120-7.T.bin"

cisco 2620 (MPC860) processor (revision 0x102) with 39936K/9216K bytes of memory
.
Processor board ID JAD04180F56 (2536534690)
M860 processor: part number 0, mask 49
Bridging software.
X.25 software, Version 3.0.0.
SuperLAT software (copyright 1990 by Meridian Technology Corp).
TN3270 Emulation software.
1 FastEthernet/IEEE 802.3 interface(s)
2 Serial network interface(s)
2 Voice FXS interface(s)
32K bytes of non-volatile configuration memory.
16384K bytes of processor board System flash (Read/Write)

Configuration register is 0x2102

routerC# show running-config
```

continues

Example 11-12 *The* **show** *and* **debug** *Output Screens for Scenario 11-5, Router C (Continued)*

```
Building configuration...

Current configuration:
!
version 12.0
service timestamps debug datetime msec localtime show-timezone
service timestamps log datetime msec localtime show-timezone
service password-encryption
!
hostname routerC
!
enable password 7 13061E010803
!
!
!
!
!
ip subnet-zero
no ip domain-lookup
!
cns event-service server
!
!
!
!
!
voice-port 1/0/0
!
voice-port 1/0/1
!
!
!
!
interface Ethernet1
 ip address 131.99.224.225 255.255.255.128
 no ip directed-broadcast
 ip summary-address eigrp 200 131.99.192.0 255.255.240.0 5
 ip summary-address eigrp 200 131.99.128.0 255.255.240.0 5
!
interface Ethernet2
 ip address 131.99.232.225 255.255.255.128
 no ip directed-broadcast
 ip summary-address eigrp 200 131.99.192.0 255.255.240.0 5
 ip summary-address eigrp 200 131.99.128.0 255.255.240.0 5
!
interface FastEthernet0
 ip address 131.99.0.51 255.255.255.240
 no ip directed-broadcast
 duplex auto
 speed auto
!
interface Serial0/0
 no ip address
```

Example 11-12 *The* **show** *and* **debug** *Output Screens for Scenario 11-5, Router C (Continued)*

```
                no ip directed-broadcast
                no ip mroute-cache
                shutdown
                no fair-queue
                !
                interface Serial0/1
                no ip address
                no ip directed-broadcast
                shutdown
                !
                router eigrp 200
                redistribute ospf 100 metric 1000 100 1 255 1500
                passive-interface FastEthernet0
                network 131.99.0.0
                !
                router ospf 100
                area 3 stub
                area 3 range 131.99.224.0 255.255.240.0
                summary-address 131.99.224.0 255.255.240.0
                redistribute eigrp 200 metric 50
                passive-interface Ethernet1
                passive-interface Ethernet2
                network 131.99.0.51 0.0.0.0 area 0
                network 0.0.0.0 255.255.255.255 area 3
                distribute-list 101 in
                !
                ip classless
                no ip http server
                !
                access-list 101 permit ip 131.99.128.0 0.0.15.255 any
                access-list 101 permit ip 131.99.192.0 0.0.15.255 any
                access-list 101 permit ip 131.99.0.0 0.0.0.255 any
                access-list 101 deny   ip any any log
                !
                !
                line con 0
                transport input none
                line aux 0
                line vty 0 4
                password 7 00071A150754
                login
                !
                no scheduler allocate
                end

                routerC#show ip route
                Codes: C - connected, S - static, I - IGRP, R - RIP, M - mobile, B - BGP
                       D - EIGRP, EX - EIGRP external, O - OSPF, IA - OSPF inter area
                       N1 - OSPF NSSA external type 1, N2 - OSPF NSSA external type 2
                       E1 - OSPF external type 1, E2 - OSPF external type 2, E - EGP
                       i - IS-IS, L1 - IS-IS level-1, L2 - IS-IS level-2, ia - IS-IS inter area
```

continues

Example 11-12 *The* **show** *and* **debug** *Output Screens for Scenario 11-5, Router C (Continued)*

```
        * - candidate default, U - per-user static route, o - ODR
        P - periodic downloaded static route

Gateway of last resort is not set

     131.99.0.0/16 is variably subnetted, 7 subnets, 4 masks
O IA    131.99.192.0/20 [110/2] via 131.99.0.50, 00:00:56, FastEthernet0
O IA    131.99.128.0/20 [110/2] via 131.99.0.49, 02:34:10, FastEthernet0
C       131.99.224.224/25 is directly connected, Ethernet1
C       131.99.0.48/28 is directly connected, FastEthernet0
C       131.99.232.224/25 is directly connected, Ethernet2
O IA    131.99.144.129/32 [110/2] via 131.99.0.49, 02:44:52, FastEthernet0
O IA    131.99.216.193/32 [110/2] via 131.99.0.50, 02:44:52, FastEthernet0
routerC#
routerC#debug ip ospf events
OSPF events debugging is on
routerC#
*Mar  1 05:52:07.090 UTC: OSPF: Rcv hello from 131.99.216.193 area 0
 from FastEthernet0/0 131.99.0.50
*Mar  1 05:52:07.090 UTC: OSPF: End of hello processing
*Mar  1 05:52:08.442 UTC: OSPF: Rcv hello from 131.99.144.129 area 0
 from FastEthernet0/0 131.99.0.49
*Mar  1 05:52:08.442 UTC: OSPF: End of hello processing
*Mar  1 05:52:17.090 UTC: OSPF: Rcv hello from 131.99.216.193 area 0
 from FastEthernet0/0 131.99.0.50
*Mar  1 05:52:17.090 UTC: OSPF: End of hello processing
routerC#u all
*Mar  1 05:52:18.442 UTC: OSPF: Rcv hello from 131.99.144.129 area 0
 from FastEthernet0/0 131.99.0.49
*Mar  1 05:52:18.442 UTC: OSPF: End of hello processing
All possible debugging has been turned off
routerC#debug ip routing
IP routing debugging is on

routerC#config t
Enter configuration commands, one per line.  End with CNTL/Z.
routerC(config)#interface e1
routerC(config-if)#shut
routerC(config-if)#no shut
*Mar  1 05:52:41.246 UTC: is_up: 0 state: 6 sub state: 1 line: 0
*Mar  1 05:52:41.346 UTC: RT: interface Ethernet1 removed from routing table
*Mar  1 05:52:41.346 UTC: RT: del 131.99.224.224/28 via 0.0.0.0,
 connected metric [0/0]
*Mar  1 05:52:41.346 UTC: RT: delete subnet route to 131.99.224.224/28
*Mar  1 05:52:43.242 UTC: %LINK-5-CHANGED: Interface Ethernet1, changed state to
 administratively down
*Mar  1 05:52:43.242 UTC: is_up: 0 state: 6 sub state: 1 line: 0
*Mar  1 05:52:44.242 UTC: %LINEPROTO-5-UPDOWN: Line protocol on
 Interface Loopback1, changed state to down
*Mar  1 05:52:44.242 UTC: is_up: 0 state: 6 sub state: 1 line: 0
routerC(config-if)#^Z
routerC#
*Mar  1 05:52:47.062 UTC: is_up: 1 state: 4 sub state: 1 line: 0
```

Example 11-12 *The* **show** *and* **debug** *Output Screens for Scenario 11-5, Router C (Continued)*

```
*Mar  1 05:52:47.062 UTC: RT: add 131.99.224.224/28 via 0.0.0.0,
 connected metric [0/0]
*Mar  1 05:52:47.066 UTC: RT: interface Ethernet1 added to routing table
*Mar  1 05:52:48.578 UTC: %SYS-5-CONFIG_I: Configured from console by console
*Mar  1 05:52:49.062 UTC: %LINK-3-UPDOWN: Interface Ethernet1, changed state to
 up
routerC#undebug all
*Mar  1 05:52:49.062 UTC: is_up: 1 state: 4 sub state: 1 line: 0
*Mar  1 05:52:50.062 UTC: %LINEPROTO-5-UPDOWN: Line protocol on
 Interface Loopback1, changed state to up all
*Mar  1 05:52:50.062 UTC: is_up: 1 state: 4 sub state: 1 line: 0
All possible debugging has been turned off
routerC#debug ip ospf packet
OSPF packet debugging is on
routerC#
*Mar  1 05:53:07.090 UTC: OSPF: rcv. v:2 t:1 l:52 rid:131.99.216.193
      aid:0.0.0.0 chk:189B aut:0 auk: from FastEthernet0
*Mar  1 05:53:08.462 UTC: OSPF: rcv. v:2 t:1 l:52 rid:131.99.144.129
      aid:0.0.0.0 chk:189B aut:0 auk: from FastEthernet0
routerC# undebug all
All possible debugging has been turned off
routerC#show ip interface brief
Interface              IP-Address      OK? Method Status           Protocol
FastEthernet0          131.99.0.51     YES manual up                 up

Serial0/0              unassigned      YES unset  administratively down down

Serial0/1              unassigned      YES unset  administratively down down

Ethernet1              131.99.224.225  YES manual up                   up

Ethernet2              131.99.232.225  YES manual up                   up

routerC#
routerC#show ip ospf database

        OSPF Router with ID (131.99.232.225) (Process ID 100)


                Router Link States (Area 0)

Link ID         ADV Router      Age     Seq#       Checksum Link count
131.99.144.129  131.99.144.129  1948    0x8000000A 0xE514   1
131.99.216.193  131.99.216.193  1198    0x8000000E 0xD211   1
131.99.232.225  131.99.232.225  1030    0x8000000E 0x1B70   1

                Net Link States (Area 0)

Link ID         ADV Router      Age     Seq#       Checksum
131.99.0.51     131.99.232.225  1545    0x8000000D 0x3B76
```

continues

Example 11-12 *The* **show** *and* **debug** *Output Screens for Scenario 11-5, Router C (Continued)*

```
                        Summary Net Link States (Area 0)

    Link ID          ADV Router       Age        Seq#        Checksum
    131.99.128.0     131.99.144.129   1690       0x80000005 0xAC3A
    131.99.144.129   131.99.144.129   1690       0x8000000B 0x2C14
    131.99.192.0     131.99.216.193   451        0x80000001 0x76AB
    131.99.216.193   131.99.216.193   420        0x8000000B 0x131C
    131.99.224.0     131.99.232.225   1031       0x8000000B 0xCFF7


                        Router Link States (Area 3)

    Link ID          ADV Router       Age        Seq#        Checksum Link count
    131.99.232.225   131.99.232.225   48         0x80000011 0x1938    2

                        Summary Net Link States (Area 3)

    Link ID          ADV Router       Age        Seq#        Checksum
    0.0.0.0          131.99.232.225   1031       0x8000000B 0x3949
    131.99.0.48       131.99.232.225  532         0x8000000D 0xE137
    131.99.128.0     131.99.232.225   1810       0x80000007 0x2409
    131.99.144.129   131.99.232.225   271        0x80000006 0xB1DB
    131.99.192.0     131.99.232.225   452        0x80000007 0x618B
    131.99.216.193   131.99.232.225   271        0x80000006 0x14F0
    routerC#
    routerC#show ip ospf
     Routing Process "ospf 100" with ID 131.99.232.225
     Supports only single TOS(TOS0) routes
     Supports opaque LSA
     It is an area border and autonomous system boundary router
     Redistributing External Routes from,
        eigrp 200 with metric mapped to 50
     SPF schedule delay 5 secs, Hold time between two SPFs 10 secs
     Minimum LSA interval 5 secs. Minimum LSA arrival 1 secs
     Number of external LSA 0. Checksum Sum 0x0
     Number of opaque AS LSA 0. Checksum Sum 0x0
     Number of DCbitless external and opaque AS LSA 0
     Number of DoNotAge external and opaque AS LSA 0
     Number of areas in this router is 2. 1 normal 1 stub 0 nssa
     External flood list length 0
        Area BACKBONE(0)
            Number of interfaces in this area is 1
            Area has no authentication
            SPF algorithm executed 44 times
            Area ranges are
            Number of LSA 9. Checksum Sum 0x44017
            Number of opaque link LSA 0. Checksum Sum 0x0
            Number of DCbitless LSA 0
            Number of indication LSA 0
            Number of DoNotAge LSA 0
            Flood list length 0
        Area 3
            Number of interfaces in this area is 2
```

Example 11-12 *The* **show** *and* **debug** *Output Screens for Scenario 11-5, Router C (Continued)*

```
                    It is a stub area
                      generates stub default route with cost 1
                    Area has no authentication
                    SPF algorithm executed 39 times
                    Area ranges are
                       131.99.224.0/20 Active(1) Advertise
                    Number of LSA 7. Checksum Sum 0x28017
                    Number of opaque link LSA 0. Checksum Sum 0x0
                    Number of DCbitless LSA 0
                    Number of indication LSA 0
                    Number of DoNotAge LSA 0
                    Flood list length 0

routerC#  show ip ospf border-routers

OSPF Process 100 internal Routing Table

Codes: i - Intra-area route, I - Inter-area route

i 131.99.216.193 [1] via 131.99.0.50, FastEthernet0, ABR/ASBR, Area 0, SPF 44
i 131.99.144.129 [1] via 131.99.0.49, FastEthernet0, ABR/ASBR, Area 0, SPF 44
routerC# sh ip os int
FastEthernet0 is up, line protocol is up
  Internet Address 131.99.0.51/28, Area 0
  Process ID 100, Router ID 131.99.232.225, Network Type BROADCAST, Cost: 1
  Transmit Delay is 1 sec, State DR, Priority 1
  Designated Router (ID) 131.99.232.225, Interface address 131.99.0.51
  Backup Designated router (ID) 131.99.216.193, Interface address 131.99.0.50
  Timer intervals configured, Hello 10, Dead 40, Wait 40, Retransmit 5
    Hello due in 00:00:04
  Index 1/1, flood queue length 0
  Next 0x0(0)/0x0(0)
  Last flood scan length is 0, maximum is 3
  Last flood scan time is 0 msec, maximum is 0 msec
  Neighbor Count is 2, Adjacent neighbor count is 2
    Adjacent with neighbor 131.99.144.129
    Adjacent with neighbor 131.99.216.193  (Backup Designated Router)
  Suppress hello for 0 neighbor(s)
Ethernet1 is up, line protocol is up
  Internet Address 131.99.224.225/25, Area 3
  Process ID 100, Router ID 131.99.232.225, Network Type BROADCAST, Cost: 1
  Transmit Delay is 1 sec, State DR, Priority 1
  Designated Router (ID) 131.99.232.225, Interface address 131.99.0.51
  Backup Designated router (ID) 131.99.216.193, Interface address 131.99.0.50
  Timer intervals configured, Hello 10, Dead 40, Wait 40, Retransmit 5
    Hello due in 00:00:04
  Index 1/1, flood queue length 0
  Next 0x0(0)/0x0(0)
  Last flood scan length is 0, maximum is 3
  Last flood scan time is 0 msec, maximum is 0 msec)
  Suppress hello for 0 neighbor(s)
```

continues

Example 11-12 *The* **show** *and* **debug** *Output Screens for Scenario 11-5, Router C (Continued)*

```
      Ethernet2 is up, line protocol is up
        Internet Address 131.99.232.225/28, Area 3
        Process ID 100, Router ID 131.99.232.225, Network Type BROADCAST, Cost: 1
        Transmit Delay is 1 sec, State DR, Priority 1
        Designated Router (ID) 131.99.232.225, Interface address 131.99.0.51
        Backup Designated router (ID) 131.99.216.193, Interface address 131.99.0.50
        Timer intervals configured, Hello 10, Dead 40, Wait 40, Retransmit 5
          Hello due in 00:00:04
        Index 1/1, flood queue length 0
        Next 0x0(0)/0x0(0)
        Last flood scan length is 0, maximum is 3
        Last flood scan time is 0 msec, maximum is 0 msec)
        Suppress hello for 0 neighbor(s)

      routerC#show ip ospf neighbor

      Neighbor ID      Pri   State          Dead Time   Address          Interface
      131.99.144.129    1    FULL/DROTHER   00:00:38    131.99.0.49      FastEthernet0/
      0
      131.99.216.193    1    FULL/BDR       00:00:36    131.99.0.50      FastEthernet0/
      0
      routerC# show ip eigrp neighbor
      IP-EIGRP neighbors for process 200
      routerC# show ip eigrp interface
      IP-EIGRP interfaces for process 200

                           Xmit Queue    Mean   Pacing Time   Multicast    Pending
      Interface    Peers   Un/Reliable   SRTT   Un/Reliable   Flow Timer   Routes
      E1           0         0/0         0         0/10           0           0
      E2           0         0/0         0         0/10           0           0
      routerC# show ip eigrp topology
      IP-EIGRP Topology Table for AS(200)/ID(131.99.232.225)

      Codes: P - Passive, A - Active, U - Update, Q - Query, R - Reply,
             r - Reply status

      P 131.99.192.0/20, 1 successors, FD is 2585600
             via Redistributed (2585600/0)
      P 131.99.128.0/20, 1 successors, FD is 2585600
             via Redistributed (2585600/0)
      P 131.99.224.224/25, 1 successors, FD is 128256
             via Connected, Ethernet1
             via Rconnected (128256/0)
      P 131.99.0.48/28, 1 successors, FD is 28160
             via Connected, FastEthernet0
             via Rconnected (28160/0)
      P 131.99.232.224/25, 1 successors, FD is 128256
             via Connected, Ethernet2
             via Rconnected (128256/0)
      P 131.99.144.129/32, 1 successors, FD is 2585600
             via Redistributed (2585600/0)
      P 131.99.216.193/32, 1 successors, FD is 2585600
             via Redistributed (2585600/0)
```

Example 11-12 *The* **show** *and* **debug** *Output Screens for Scenario 11-5, Router C (Continued)*

```
routerC#
routerC# show ip eigrp traffic
IP-EIGRP Traffic Statistics for process 200
  Hellos sent/received: 6523/6522
  Updates sent/received: 0/0
  Queries sent/received: 0/0
  Replies sent/received: 0/0
  Acks sent/received: 0/0
  Input queue high water mark 2, 0 drops

routerC#ping 131.99.216.193

Type escape sequence to abort.
Sending 5, 100-byte ICMP Echos to 131.99.216.193, timeout is 2 seconds:
!!!!!
Success rate is 100 percent (5/5), round-trip min/avg/max = 1/3/4 ms
routerC#ping 131.99.192.193

Type escape sequence to abort.
Sending 5, 100-byte ICMP Echos to 131.99.192.193, timeout is 2 seconds:
!!!!!
Success rate is 100 percent (5/5), round-trip min/avg/max = 1/2/4 ms

routerC#ping 131.99.144.129

Type escape sequence to abort.
Sending 5, 100-byte ICMP Echos to 131.99.144.129, timeout is 2 seconds:
!!!!!
Success rate is 100 percent (5/5), round-trip min/avg/max = 1/2/4 ms
routerC#ping 131.99.136.129

Type escape sequence to abort.
Sending 5, 100-byte ICMP Echos to 131.99.136.129, timeout is 2 seconds:
!!!!!
Success rate is 100 percent (5/5), round-trip min/avg/max = 1/3/4 ms
routerC#ping
Protocol [ip]:
Target IP address: 131.99.144.129
Repeat count [5]:
Datagram size [100]:
Timeout in seconds [2]: 1
Extended commands [n]: y
Source address or interface: 131.99.224.225
Type of service [0]:
Set DF bit in IP header? [no]:
Validate reply data? [no]:
Data pattern [0xABCD]:
Loose, Strict, Record, Timestamp, Verbose[none]:
Sweep range of sizes [n]:
Type escape sequence to abort.
Sending 5, 100-byte ICMP Echos to 131.99.144.129, timeout is 1 seconds:
```

continues

Example 11-12 *The* **show** *and* **debug** *Output Screens for Scenario 11-5, Router C (Continued)*

```
!!!!!
Success rate is 100 percent (5/5), round-trip min/avg/max = 1/2/4 ms
routerC#
routerC#trace 131.99.144.129

Type escape sequence to abort.
Tracing the route to 131.99.144.129

  1 131.99.0.49 4 msec *  0 msec
routerC#trace 131.99.192.193

Type escape sequence to abort.
Tracing the route to 131.99.192.193
  1 131.99.0.50 0 msec *  0 msec
```

Answer the following questions. Use Examples 11-10 through 11-12 as a reference when the question refers directly to this scenario. Although not all of these questions are directly tied to the previous scenario, they all probe foundational knowledge required by the technology examined in this scenario.

1 Which command is used to see whether a neighbor adjacency has been created?

2 What is the meaning of the acronym SIA, and where would you see it?

3 What is the difference between the neighbor table and the topology table?

4 How are default routes identified and advertised in EIGRP?

5 What command shows the different IP routing protocols running on a system?

6 How would you detect that an EIGRP neighbor has become unavailable?

7 In redistributing an IP routing protocol, how would you prevent routes from being propagated back into the originating protocol?

8 Which routing protocol supports multilayer protocols?

9 When redistributing OSPF routes into EIGRP, how would you state the metric to be used in the new routing protocol?

10 Where would you see the successors for a route?

11 How would you turn on EIGRP?

12 How would you configure router summarization in EIGRP?

13 What command shows the route summarization configured in EIGRP?

14 What is the purpose of the bandwidth percentage configuration in EIGRP?

15 Where would you see the administrative distance for a route?

16 Which **debug** command is used to identify that there is a problem in creating an adjacency in EIGRP?

17 What is the purpose of the subnet parameter in the EIGRP and OSPF redistribution command?

18 What routes can be redistributed into another routing protocol?

19 What is the difference between the **in** and the **out** parameters when set on a distribute list?

20 What should you consider in configuring EIGRP across an NBMA cloud?

Solutions to Scenario 11-5, Part C—Verification and Questions

The answers to the questions for Scenario 11-5, Part C are as follows:

1 Which command is used to see whether a neighbor adjacency has been created?

The command that shows whether an adjacency has been formed is show ip eigrp topology.

The part of the output from this command that shows the adjacency is seen in the codes.

Codes tell the state of the topology table entry. Passive and active refer to the EIGRP state, with respect to this destination. Update, query, and reply refer to the type of packet that is being sent. The codes are as follows:

- **P—Passive: No Enhanced IGRP computations are being performed for this destination.**

- **A—Active: Enhanced IGRP computations are being performed for this destination.**

- **U—Update: Indicates that an update packet was sent to this destination.**

- **Q—Query: Indicates that a query packet was sent to this destination.**

- **R—Reply: Indicates that a reply packet was sent to this destination.**

- **r—Reply status: Is a flag that is set after the software has sent a query and is waiting for a reply.**

- **successors: Gives the Number of successors. This number corresponds to the number of next hops in the IP routing table.**

- **FD—Feasible distance: This value is used in the feasibility condition check. If the neighbor's reported distance (the metric after the slash) is less than the feasible distance, the feasibility condition is met and that path is a feasible successor. When the software determines it has a feasible successor, it does not have to send a query for that destination.**

- **replies:** Gives the number of replies that are still outstanding (that have not been received) with respect to this destination. This information appears only when the destination is in active state.

- **state:** Gives the exact Enhanced IGRP state that this destination is in. It can be the number 0, 1, 2, or 3. This information appears only when the destination is active.

- **Via:** Gives the IP address of the peer that told the software about this destination. The first *N* of these entries, where *N* is the number of successors, are the current successors. The remaining entries on the list are feasible successors.

2 What is the meaning of the acronym SIA, and where would you see it?

The acronym SIA stands for Stuck in Active, which means that an EIGRP neighbor has not replied to a query that was sent out. If the neighbor does not reply within a limited time, it is presumed dead and is flushed from the tables. This is to prevent a route from being permanently active as an alternative path is sought from unresponsive neighbors.

An error message will be generated to the screen, but it is possible to identify the problem by looking at the log files or issuing commands. In the show ip eigrp topology command, any neighbors that show an R have not yet replied (the active timer shows how long the route has been active) may be Stuck in Active. It is advisable to run this command several times; you begin to see which neighbors are not responding to queries (or which interfaces seem to have a lot of unanswered queries). You should also examine this neighbor to see if it is consistently waiting for replies from any of its neighbors. Repeat this process until you find the router that is consistently not answering queries.

The problems are often on the link to this neighbor, or with memory or CPU utilization with this neighbor.

It is often better to reduce the query range instead of increasing the SIA timer.

3 What is the difference between the neighbor table and the topology table?

The neighbor table holds information about EIGRP neighbors, while the topology table lists all the routes known to have feasible successors.

4 How are default routes identified and advertised in EIGRP?

Answer: Default routes are shown with the address 0.0.0.0 and are advertised as an external address. This affects the administrative distance.

5 What command shows the different IP routing protocols running on a system?

The command that shows all the different IP routing protocol running on a system is show ip protocols.

This shows the protocols, redistribution, and many other details.

6 How would you detect that an EIGRP neighbor has become unavailable?

The command show ip eigrp topology would show that there had not been a reply to packets sent to the neighbor. The command show ip eigrp neighbors shows the neighbors, how long they have been in the table, and the last time they were heard from.

7 In redistributing an IP routing protocol, how would you prevent routes from being propagated back into the originating protocol?

This would be done by creating a distribute list that permits only those routes that did *not* originate from the protocol into which the updates are being redistributed.

8 Which routing protocol supports multilayer protocols?

EIGRP supports IP, AppleTalk, and IPX.

9 When redistributing OSPF routes into EIGRP, how would you state the metric to be used in the new routing protocol?

There are two ways of stating the metric to be used by the redistributed networks. The first is to include the metric on the redistribution command:

```
Router(config-router)#redistribute ospf 200 metric bandwidth delay
reliability load mtu
```

This will give the stated metric to all routes sent to EIGRP from the routing process OSPF 200.

The other method is this command:

```
Router(config-router)# default-metric bandwidth delay reliability load mtu
```

This command assigns the same metric to all routes distributed into EIGRP from any source.

10 Where would you see the successors for a route?

The successors to a route are held in the routing table because it is the current next hop that is being used to forward traffic to the remote destination. The command that shows these successors is as follows:

```
Router# show ip route
```

11 How would you turn on EIGRP?

The command to turn on EIGRP is as follows:

```
Router(config)# router eigrp autonomous-system-number
```

This starts the routing process, while the following command identifies the interfaces that will receive, send, and advertise updates for that process:

```
Router(config-router)# network network number
```

12 How would you configure router summarization in EIGRP?

Route summarization can be configured in one of two ways in EIGRP. The first is to configure summarization within EIGRP. This is achieved at the interface level and allows great flexibility in configuration. The command is as follows:

```
Router(config-if)# ip summary-address eigrp autonomous-system-number network
mask
```

The other method of summarizing routes is done when redistributing routes. The command is as follows:

```
Router(config-router)# ip summary-address eigrp autonomous-system-number
```

This specifies the summary address and mask, as well as the EIGRP process into which the summary is to be advertised.

13 What command shows the route summarization configured in EIGRP?

The command show ip route shows the summarization.

14 What is the purpose of the bandwidth percentage configuration in EIGRP?

The purpose of the bandwidth percentage configuration in EIGRP is to limit the amount of bandwidth that can be taken by EIGRP networking traffic. By default, this is limited to 50 percent of the link. In NBMA clouds—in particular, Frame Relay—it may be advisable to tune this parameter, depending on the CIR of the links.

15 Where would you see the administrative distance for a route?

The administrative distance of a route can be seen in the routing table. It is the second half of the number in brackets. The first number is the metric; the second is the administrative distance.

16 Which **debug** command is used to identify that there is problem in creating an adjacency in EIGRP?

This command

```
Router# debug ip eigrp neighbor autonomous-system-number address
```

adds a filter to this command

```
Router# debug ip eigrp packets
```

and displays only IP packets for the stated process and address.

17 What is the purpose of the **subnet** parameter in the EIGRP and OSPF redistribution command?

The subnet parameter in the EIGRP and OSPF redistribution commands allows the subnets of major networks that are not directly connected to be redistributed into the protocol. Without this, only major networks will be distributed.

18 What routes can be redistributed into another routing protocol?

Static routes, directly connected routes, or routes learned dynamically from another routing protocol can be redistributed.

19 What is the difference between the **in** and the **out** parameters when set on a distribute list?

The in parameter determines routes entering a routing protocol. The out parameter defines the routes that can be redistributed into another routing protocol.

20 What should you consider in configuring EIGRP across an NBMA cloud?

When configuring EIGRP over NBMA clouds, you should consider the nature of the link. Is it point-to-point or multipoint? Also consider overhead traffic associated with EIGRP and bandwidth utilization:

- **Over a point-to-point interface, set the bandwidth to reflect the CIR of the PVC.**

- **Over multipoint Frame Relay, ATM, SMDS, and ISDN PRI, the bandwidth is divided equally among the links. The configuration should reflect the percentage of the available bandwidth.**

- **If the PVCs have different CIRs, then either convert the links to point-to-point or configure the bandwidth to be a multiple of the lowest available CIR by the number of PVCs.**

This appendix contains the answers to the "Do I Know This Already?" quizzes and "Q&A" questions. In some cases, multiple answers are correct. In those cases, the answer listed here is the best possible answer. Note that the answers to the "Scenarios" questions are at the end of each chapter.

Answers to Quiz Questions

Chapter 2

Chapter 2 "Do I Know This Already?" Quiz Answers

1 List two symptoms of network congestion.

Symptoms of network congestion include these:

— **Applications timing out at end stations**

— **Clients not being capable of connecting to network resources**

— **Network death**

The causes of congestion are often the symptoms seen, and they include these:

— **Excessive traffic, seen on the network-management tools**

— **The dropping of packets, seen on the router interfaces**

— **The retransmission of packets, seen on the network-management tools**

— **Incomplete routing tables, seen on the router**

— **Incomplete service tables, seen on servers and routers**

— **Broadcast storms caused by spanning tree**

2 If a switch has redundant links to another switch, what action would be taken if the Spanning-Tree Protocol fails to see a bridge protocol data unit (BPDU) in time (within the MaxAge Timer value)?

If the Spanning-Tree Protocol fails to see the BPDU packet in time, it will unblock the redundant path, in the belief that the primary path is no longer available.

3 How could the dropping of packets cause an increase of traffic on the network?

The dropping of packets could increase the traffic on the network because the applications may request the retransmission of the packet. This is particularly true on a connection-orientated communication.

4 How might network congestion cause a loss of services?

Services may be lost when network congestion is experienced. The reasons include these:

— **The input buffers of the server are overloaded.**

— **The application times out.**

— **The network traffic informing clients of services is lost or delayed sufficiently for the services to be dropped from the server lists.**

5 In Cisco's hierarchical design, what is the function of the core layer?

A layer is created by defining what needs to run through the layer. The core layer is defined by the need for a high-speed backbone linking the different sites, or logical groupings, of the network. It is the central internetwork for the entire enterprise and may include LAN and WAN backbones. The primary function of this layer is to provide an optimized and reliable transport structure.

6 In Cisco's hierarchical design, where is the access layer located?

The access layer is the layer that is the closest to the end stations. The router keeps that local traffic local and therefore prevents unnecessary traffic from traversing the network. The access layer is designed to ensure that LAN traffic can be contained locally and does not travel off the network to create network congestion.

7 In the hierarchical design suggested by Cisco, at which layer are access lists not recommended?

Access lists are not recommended at the core layer because this is where the traffic should switch at the highest speeds. Because access lists are CPU-intensive (adding about 15 percent overhead), they are not recommended for use in the core layer. This is still true, despite the fact that the technology allows the access list to be cached for fast switching, because the general rule is that all decisions are made at the previous layers of the network.

8 What is the function of the distribution layer?

The distribution layer provides the demarcation point between the core and access layers, providing policy-based connectivity and allowing you to do packet manipulation.

9 If an access list is configured as an inbound list, will the packet be sent to the routing process?

The packet from an inbound access list will not be sent to the routing process if a match is found for the access list criteria, and the action is to deny the packet. The packet is discarded before it reaches the routing process.

10 State three uses of access lists.

The following are all valid uses for access lists:

   — Restricting networks sent out in routing updates

   — Restricting connectivity to remote networks

   — Restricting the services advertised in an IPX network

   — Restricting large packet sizes from traversing the network

11 In an IP standard access list, what is the default wildcard mask?

The default wildcard mask in an IP standard access list is 0.0.0.0.

12 If a packet does not match any of the criteria in an access list, what action will be taken?

If the packet being tested against the access list does not match any of the criteria, it will hit the implicit deny all at the bottom of the access list. This results in it being discarded, generating an ICMP message to the sending station.

13 Why does the null interface not report an ICMP message stating that the packet is undeliverable?

The null interface does not report an ICMP message because there is no error to report. From the viewpoint of the routing process, the packet has been successfully routed to the outgoing interface. The routing process is unaware that the outgoing interface is a virtual interface that does not exist. Effectively, the packet has been sent to the dump, thus killing the packet.

14 How would you restrict Telnet connectivity to the router that you were configuring?

To restrict Telnet connections into the router that you are configuring, use access lists that are applied to the terminal lines with the access-class command.

15 Which of the queuing techniques offered by the Cisco IOS are manually configured?

The queuing techniques manually configured on a Cisco system are custom and priority queuing.

16 Explain **ip helper address**. What is its function?

ip helper address is a command that has the router forward User Datagram Protocol (UDP) broadcasts received on an interface to a directed or specific destination on another network.

Combined with the ip forward-protocol global configuration command, the ip helper-address command enables you to control which broadcast packets and which protocols are forwarded. One common application that requires helper addresses is Dynamic Host Configuration Protocol (DHCP). DHCP is defined in RFC 1531. DHCP protocol information is carried inside BOOTP packets. To enable BOOTP

broadcast forwarding for a set of clients, configure a helper address on the router interface closest to the client. The helper address should specify the address of the DHCP server. If you have multiple servers, you can configure one helper address for each server. Because BOOTP packets are forwarded by default, the router can now forward DHCP information. The DHCP server now receives broadcasts from the DHCP clients.

Chapter 2 "Q&A" Answers

1 State two reasons to use an IP tunnel.

The following are reasons to use an IP tunnel:

— To solve problems with discontiguous networks

— To simplify network administration

— To tunnel desktop protocols through an IP-only backbone

2 State instances when access lists may be used for something other than filtering traffic.

Access lists may be used for the following:

— Queuing

— Policy routing

— QoS

— Filtering routing updates

3 In configuring an IP tunnel, how many IP tunnels may be created with the same source and destination address?

By default, only one tunnel is allowed with the same source and destination address.

4 Associate the appropriate IOS feature to solve the network congestion problem experienced on the network in the following table.

Network Congestion Problem	IOS Solution
Clients cannot connect to the centralized servers	Routing access list
Cisco environment in a large network with a large number of WAN connections	Prioritization on the interface
Large routing tables using RIP for IP	Reduction of the size of the broadcast domain by adding a router
Spanning tree is failing	IP helper address
SNA sessions are failing	EIGRP

By matching the numbers in the following list you will have the correct answers:

Network Congestion Problem	IOS Solution
1. Clients cannot connect to the centralized servers	3. Routing access list
2. Cisco environment in a large network with a large number of WAN connections	5. Prioritization on the interface
3. Large routing tables using RIP for IP	4. Reduction of the size of the broadcast domain by adding a router
4. Spanning tree is failing	1. IP helper address
5. SNA sessions are failing	2. EIGRP

5   Which command would prevent the router from forwarding data to a remote network without generating an ICMP message?

The command that would prevent the router from forwarding data to a remote network without generating an ICMP message is the interface null 0 command.

6   Identify two commands that might be used to verify the configuration of an IP access list configuration.

Two commands that might be used to verify the configuration of an IP access list configuration could be taken from the following list:

— **show ip interface**

— **show access-list**

— **show running config**

— **show startup config**

7   What UDP ports will the IP helper address forward automatically?

UDP ports that the IP helper address will forward automatically are TFTP, DNS, BOOTP server, BOOTP client, time, TACACS, NetBIOS name server, and NetBIOS datagram service.

8   If the number of workstations increases on a physical segment, the user may experience delays. Give two reasons why this might occur.

As the number of workstations increases on a physical segment, the user may experience delays because of the following reasons:

— **There are collisions that require retransmission.**

— There is packet loss because buffers on devices are overflowing and require retransmission.

— The end systems could be slowing down because of excessive broadcast traffic.

9 State three considerations when deciding where to place extended IP access lists.

You should consider at least three of the following:

— **Minimize the distance that denied traffic must travel. Place the access list as close to the source as possible.**

— **Keep the denied traffic off the backbone connecting buildings or campuses.**

— **Ensure that the router chosen can deal easily with the additional CPU requirements.**

— **Consider the CPU utilization because an inbound access list does not have to do a routing update on denied traffic. However, the interface may have to match the access list against more traffic.**

— **Consider the number of interfaces affected.**

— **Consider the number of nodes affected. Outbound access lists may afford greater granularity.**

— **Consider access list management.**

— **Consider the network growth and the effect on the management of the interfaces and the changing needs in connectivity.**

10 What is the function of the access layer?

The function of the access layer is to act as the first point of contact for the end devices or workstations. It also acts as a filter layer to ensure that all local traffic stays local and does not unnecessarily clog the network.

11 What is the access list number range for IP extended access lists?

The extended access list number range is 100 to 199.

12 What is priority queuing?

Priority queuing enables network managers to define how they want traffic to be prioritized in the network. By defining a series of filters based on packet characteristics, traffic is placed into a number of queues; the queue with the highest priority is serviced first, and then the lower queues are serviced in sequence. If the highest-priority queue is always full, this queue will continually be serviced, and packets from the other queues will queue up and be dropped. In this queuing algorithm, one particular kind of network traffic can dominate all others. Priority queuing assigns traffic to one of four queues: high, medium, normal, and low.

13 List two symptoms of network congestion.

Symptoms of network congestion include these:

— **Applications timing out at end stations**

— **Clients not being capable of connecting to network resources**

— **Network death resulting**

The causes of congestion are often the symptoms seen, and they include these:

— **Excessive traffic, seen on the network-management tools**

— **Dropped packets, seen on the router interfaces**

— **The retransmission of packets, seen on the network-management tools**

— **Incomplete routing tables, seen on the router**

— **Incomplete service tables, seen on servers and routers**

— **Broadcast storms caused by spanning tree**

14 If a switch has redundant links to another switch, what action would be taken if the Spanning-Tree Protocol fails to see a BPDU in time (within the MaxAge Timer value)?

If the Spanning-Tree Protocol fails to see the BPDU packet in time, it will unblock the redundant path, in the belief that the primary path is no longer available.

15 How could the dropping of packets cause an increase of traffic on the network?

The dropping of packets could increase the traffic on the network because the applications may request the retransmission of the packet. This is particularly true on a connection-orientated communication.

16 How might network congestion cause a loss of services?

Services may be lost when network congestion is experienced. The reasons include these:

— **The input buffers of the server are overloaded.**

— **The application times out.**

— **The network traffic informing clients of services is lost or delayed sufficiently for the services to be dropped from the server lists.**

17 In Cisco's hierarchical design, what is the function of the core layer?

A layer is created by defining what needs to run through the layer. The core layer is defined by the need for a high-speed backbone linking the different sites, or logical groupings, of the network. It is the central internetwork for the entire enterprise and may include LAN and WAN backbones. The primary function of this layer is to provide an optimized and reliable transport structure.

18   In Cisco's hierarchical design, where is the access layer located?

The access layer is the layer that is the closest to the end stations. The router keeps that local traffic local and therefore prevents unnecessary traffic from traversing the network. The access layer is designed to ensure that LAN traffic can be contained locally and does not travel off the network to create network congestion.

19   In the hierarchical design suggested by Cisco, at which layer are access lists not recommended?

Access lists are not recommended at the core layer because this is where the traffic should switch at the highest speeds. Because access lists are CPU-intensive (adding about 15 percent overhead), they are not recommended for use in the core layer. This is still true despite the fact that the technology allows the access list to be cached for fast switching; the general rule is that all decisions are made at the previous layers of the network.

20   What is the function of the distribution layer?

The distribution layer provides the demarcation point between the core and access layers, providing policy-based connectivity and allowing you to do packet manipulation.

21   If an access list is configured as an inbound list, will the packet be sent to the routing process?

The packet from an inbound access list will not be sent to the routing process if a match is found for the access list criteria, and the action is to deny the packet. The packet is discarded before it reaches the routing process.

22   State three uses of access lists.

The following are all valid uses for access lists:

— **Restricting networks sent out in routing updates**

— **Restricting connectivity to remote networks**

— **Restricting the services advertised in an IPX network**

— **Restricting large packet sizes from traversing the network**

23   In an IP standard access list, what is the default wildcard mask?

The default wildcard mask in an IP standard access list is 0.0.0.0.

24   If a packet does not match any of the criteria in an access list, what action will be taken?

If the packet being tested against the access list does not match any of the criteria, it will hit the implicit deny all at the bottom of the access list. This results in it being discarded, generating an ICMP message to the sending station.

25 Why does the null interface not report an ICMP message stating that the packet is undeliverable?

The null interface does not report an ICMP message because there is no error to report. From the viewpoint of the routing process, the packet has been successfully routed to the outgoing interface. The routing process is unaware that the outgoing interface is a virtual interface that does not exist. Effectively, the packet has been sent to the dump, thus killing the packet.

26 How would you restrict Telnet connectivity to the router that you were configuring?

To restrict Telnet connections into the router that you are configuring, use access lists that are applied to the terminal lines with the access-class command.

27 Which of the queuing techniques offered by the Cisco IOS are manually configured?

The queuing techniques manually configured on a Cisco system are custom and priority queuing.

28 Explain **ip helper address**. What is its function?

ip helper address is a command that has the router forward User Datagram Protocol (UDP) broadcasts received on an interface to a directed or specific destination on another network.

Combined with the ip forward-protocol global configuration command, the ip helper-address command enables you to control which broadcast packets and which protocols are forwarded. One common application that requires helper addresses is Dynamic Host Configuration Protocol (DHCP). DHCP is defined in RFC 1531. DHCP protocol information is carried inside BOOTP packets. To enable BOOTP broadcast forwarding for a set of clients, configure a helper address on the router interface closest to the client. The helper address should specify the address of the DHCP server. If you have multiple servers, you can configure one helper address for each server. Because BOOTP packets are forwarded by default, the router can now forward DHCP information. The DHCP server now receives broadcasts from the DHCP clients.

Chapter 3

Chapter 3 "Do I Know This Already?" Quiz Answers

1 If given a Class C address with the requirement to accommodate 14 subnets and 10 hosts on each subnet, what subnet mask would you use?

The mask is 255.255.255.240, or the prefix mask of /28.

2 List the range of hosts available on the 136.122.10.192/28 subnet.

The range of hosts available on the subnet 136.122.10.192 /28 are 136.122.10.193–206.

3 Convert the subnet address 56.98.5.0/24 to binary notation, and state the class to which it belongs.

The Class A subnet 56.98.5.0, when converted to binary notation, is as follows:

00111000.01100010.00000101.00000000

4 Write out the decimal notation of the following subnet mask presented in this binary notation:

11111111.11111111.11111111.11111000

The decimal notation of the subnet mask would be 255.255.255.248.

5 What does VLSM stand for?

VLSM stands for variable-length subnet mask.

6 The Class B network address of 133.222.0.0 has been given a mask of 255.255.255.0. The subnets, 133.222.8.0, 133.222.9.0, 133.222.10.0, 133.222.11.0, 133.222.12.0, 133.222.13.0, and 133.222.14.0 need to be summarized using VLSM. Give the subnet and new mask to achieve this summarization.

The subnet would be 133.222.8.0 with a mask of 255.255.248.0, or /21.

7 Is 201.111.16.0/20 a valid subnet mask?

Yes, this is a valid mask, and it will provide 16 consecutive Class C addresses to the organization.

8 Which routing protocols support VLSM?

RIPv2, OSPF, IS-IS, EIGRP, BGP-4.

9 Briefly define route summarization.

Route summarization is the method of including many subnets in a few routing entries.

10 What sort of design scheme does route summarization require?

Route summarization requires a hierarchical addressing scheme.

11 In route summarization, where is the subnet mask moved?

In route summarization, the subnet mask is moved to the left.

12 How does summarization allow for smaller routing tables?

Summarizing is the consolidation of multiple routes into one single advertisement.

13 Identify two private addresses defined in RFC 1918.

The RFC 1918 addresses that you can use are as follows:

— **Class A: 10.0.0.0**

— **Class B range: 172.16.0.0 through 172.31.0.0**

— **Class C range: 192.168.1.0 through 192.168.254.0**

14 What is a discontiguous network?

In a discontiguous network, a NIC number is bisected by another NIC number.

15 What does CIDR stand for?

CIDR stands for classless interdomain routing.

16 Which RFC is responsible for first describing the use of subnet masking?

RFC 950.

Chapter 3 "Q&A" Answers

1 Identify one criterion to help determine a subnet mask for classful addressing when designing a network-addressing scheme.

Questions to ask include the following:

— **How many networks are there in the network?**

— **How many hosts are there on the largest subnet?**

2 Which command is used to forward broadcast traffic across a router to a particular destination?

The command used to forward broadcast traffic across a router is the ip helper-address.

3 With a classless address of 204.1.64.0/20, what is the range of classful addresses that are included in the address? Write your answer in dotted decimal and the third octet in binary notation.

The address 204.1.64.0 /20 includes the Class C addresses 204.1.64.0 to 204.1.79.0; this is illustrated in both dotted decimal and binary notation in the following table.

Binary Notation	Decimal Notation
01000000	**204.1.64.0**
01000001	**204.1.65.0**
01000010	**204.1.66.0**

continues

(Continued)

Binary Notation	Decimal Notation
01000011	204.1.67.0
01000100	204.1.68.0
01000101	204.1.69.0
01000110	204.1.70.0
01000111	204.1.71.0
01001000	204.1.72.0
01001001	204.1.73.0
01001010	204.1.74.0
01001011	204.1.75.0
01001100	204.1.76.0
01001101	204.1.77.0
01001110	204.1.78.0
01001111	204.1.79.0

4 What is a discontiguous network?

A discontiguous network is a network in which a NIC address is separated by another NIC address. Therefore, the original NIC address is no longer contiguous because an intervening NIC number has interrupted it.

5 For VLSM to be available as a design option in the network, what characteristic must the routing protocol possess?

The routing protocol must send the prefix or subnet mask as part of the routing update.

6 If summarization is to be implemented in the network, name one design criterion for the addressing scheme that must be in place?

For VLSM to work, the addressing scheme must be hierarchical, allowing the upstream devices to share the same high-order bits as the downstream devices.

7 What networks are provided in RFC 1918, and what prefix mask accompanies each network?

The private addresses provided in RFC 1918 are as follows:

— 10.0.0.0 /8 to 255.0.0.0

— 172.16.0.0 /12 to 255.240.0.0

— 192.168.0.0 /16 to 255.255.0.0

8 If the host portion of a subnet has been used to identify end devices, can that subnet be used again for VLSM?

It is not possible to use a subnet for addressing hosts as well as using it to further subnet the network using VLSM. The addresses would be seen as duplicate addresses.

9 Describe the purpose of the **ip forward-protocol** command.

The ip forward-protocol command is used to identify which protocols should be forwarded in reference to the IP helper address.

10 Which command is used on point-to-point lines to conserve IP address space?

The command used is IP unnumbered, and it prevents the use of a subnet of a serial link, which is unnecessary.

11 Give one example of when route summarization would not be a good solution.

Route summarization is not useful in the following circumstances:

— **There are discontiguous networks in the organization.**

— **A specific subnet needs to be seen throughout the network.**

— **The addressing scheme does not support summarization. No common high-order bits are shared in the network-addressing scheme.**

— **Access lists require detailed information.**

12 Give one reason for implementing router summarization.

Route summarization is useful for the following reasons:

— **To keep the routing tables small**

— **To keep the network overhead low**

— **To hide the network details from the rest of the organization**

— **To prevent flapping links from affecting the rest of the network**

13 Given an address of 133.44.0.0 and a prefix mask of /25, how many networks can be addressed, and how many hosts can exist on each network? Write the first and last possible subnets in binary and decimal notation.

For the network address of 133.44.0.0, the subnet mask of 255.255.255.128 would enable you to address 510 subnets with 126 hosts on each subnet. This complies with the subnetting rule of not allocating addresses with all zeros or all ones. The following table illustrates the first and last subnet in their binary and decimal notation formats.

Binary Notation	Decimal Notation
00000000.10000000	133.44.0.128
11111111.00000000	133.44.255.0

14 What class of address is 131.188.0.0, and how many hosts can be addressed if no subnetting is used?

131.188.0.0 is a Class B address and can address more than 65,000 hosts on one network if no subnetting is utilized.

15 If given a Class C address with the requirement to accommodate 14 subnets and 10 hosts on each subnet, what subnet mask would you use?

The mask is 255.255.255.240, or the prefix mask of /28.

16 List the range of hosts available on the 136.122.10.192/28 subnet.

The range of hosts available on the subnet 136.122.10.192 /28 is 136.122.10.193 to 206.

17 Convert the subnet address 56.98.5.0/24 to binary notation, and state the class to which it belongs.

The Class A subnet 56.98.5.0 when converted to binary notation is as follows:

00111000.01100010.00000101.00000000

18 Write out the decimal notation of the following subnet mask presented in the binary notation of 11111111.11111111.11111111.11111000.

The decimal notation of the subnet mask would be 255.255.255.248

19 What does VLSM stand for?

VLSM stands for variable-length subnet mask.

20 The Class B network address of 133.222.0.0 has been given a mask of 255.255.255.0. The subnets 133.222.8.0, 133.222.9.0, 133.222.10.0, 133.222.11.0, 133.222.12.0, 133.222.13.0, and 133.222.14.0 need to be summarized using VLSM. Give the subnet and new mask to achieve this summarization.

The subnet would be 133.222.8.0 with a mask of 255.255.248.0, or /21.

21 Is 201.111.16.0/20 a valid subnet mask?

Yes, this is a valid mask, and it will provide 16 consecutive Class C addresses to the organization.

22 Which routing protocols support VLSM?

RIPv2, OSPF, IS-IS, EIGRP, and BGP-4 support VLSM.

23 Briefly define route summarization.

Route summarization is the method of including many subnets in a few routing entries.

24 What sort of design scheme does route summarization require?

Route summarization requires a hierarchical addressing scheme.

25 In route summarization, where is the subnet mask moved?

In route summarization, the subnet mask is moved to the left.

26 How does summarization allow for smaller routing tables?

Summarizing is the consolidation of multiple routes into a single advertisement.

27 Identify two private addresses defined in RFC 1918.

The RFC 1918 addresses that you can use are as follows:

— Class A: 10.0.0.0

— Class B range: 172.16.0.0 through 172.31.0.0

— Class C range: 192.168.1.0 through 192.168.254.0

28 What is a discontiguous network?

A discontiguous network is a network in which a NIC number is bisected by another NIC number.

29 What does CIDR stand for?

CIDR stands for classless interdomain routing.

30 Which RFC is responsible for first describing the use of subnet masking?

RFC 950 is responsible for this.

Chapter 4

Chapter 4 "Do I Know This Already?" Quiz Answers

1 Cisco distinguishes between the routing and the switching function—what is the difference?

The routing function is how the router learns the logical topology of the network. It decides whether the datagram can be routed, which path to select if there is a choice, and to which outgoing interface to queue the datagram. It operates at Layer 3 of the OSI stack.

The switching function is the forwarding of the frame from the inbound interface to an outbound interface. It operates at Layer 2 of the OSI stack, not at Layer 3, like a router.

A LAN switch connects two or more LAN segments. It uses a table of MAC addresses to determine the segment on which a frame needs to be transmitted; if it is on the interface that the frame received, then the frame is dropped. The switch listens to all

traffic on the interface, at Layer 2, while the router looks at only the MAC address of a multicast group of which it is a member, a broadcast, or its own individual MAC address. Switches operate at much higher speeds than routers, and can support new functionality, such as virtual LANs.

2 State the two ways that an outgoing interface is selected as the preferred path.

An outgoing interface is selected for the following reasons:

— **Because it is the only available path**

— **Because the administrative distance is lower**

— **Because the metric is lower**

3 What is administrative distance?

Administrative distance is the mechanism used by the routing process to select a path offered by two different routing protocols. The administrative distance is a set of values, in which a value is given to each IP routing protocol. This allows a hierarchy to be established so that when multiple protocols offer a path to the same remote network, one path can be chosen. The path that is chosen will be the one offered by the routing protocol with the lowest administrative distance. The administrative distance can be manually configured.

4 If IGRP has three paths to a remote network in which each path has an equal metric, what will happen?

If IGRP sees equal-cost paths to a remote network, it will load balance between those paths by default.

5 Name the interior IP routing protocols that send the mask with the routing update.

The interior IP routing protocols that send the mask with the routing update are EIGRP, OSPF, IS-IS, and RIPv2.

6 Name the interior routing protocol that sends a routing update on a Cisco router every 30 seconds by default.

The routing protocol that sends a routing update every 30 seconds is RIP.

7 Does VLSM require a classful or classless routing protocol, and why?

VLSM requires a classless routing protocol because it needs the subnet mask to be sent with the update.

8 State one of the characteristics of a classful routing protocol.

The characteristics of a classful routing protocol are as follows:

— **It summarizes at the network boundary.**

— **Routes exchanged between foreign networks are summarized to the NIC number.**

— **Within the same network (NIC number), subnet routes are exchanged by routers.**

— **All the interfaces on all the routers within a NIC number must share the same subnet mask.**

— **VLSM is not possible within the network.**

9 A distance vector routing protocol uses the mechanism of poison reverse—what is this?

When the routing process suspects that a route in its routing table is no longer valid, it will set the metric so high for that route that it will render it unusable. This will be propagated in the routing updates to other routers.

10 Name two distance vector routing protocols.

Distance vector routing protocols include RIPv1, RIPv2, IGRP, and EIGRP (an advanced distance vector routing protocol).

11 Name two link-state IP routing protocols.

Link-state IP routing protocols include OSPF, IS-IS, and EIGRP (an advanced distance vector routing protocol with some link-state characteristics).

12 Describe the mechanism of split horizon.

Split horizon is a routing technique in which information about routes is prevented from exiting the router interface through which that information was received. Split-horizon updates are useful in preventing routing loops.

13 What is the command syntax to empty the Cisco routing table of all its routes?

The command syntax to empty the Cisco routing table of all of its routes is as follows:

clear ip route *

(This command must be executed from the privileged EXEC level.)

14 What does 0.0.0.0 signify in an IP routing table?

0.0.0.0 is used to signify the default route in the routing table.

15 What is the command to show whether a specific network, such as 141.131.6.16, is present in the routing table?

The command to show whether a specific network, such as 141.131.6.16, is present in the routing table is as follows:

show ip route 141.131.6.16

16 What is the next logical hop in the routing table?

The next logical hop in the routing table is the address of the interface to which traffic should be sent for it to reach the remote network. The address is taken from the source address of the routing update that provided the remote network.

Chapter 4 "Q&A" Answers

1 Name one routing protocol that sends periodic updates.

RIPv1, RIPv2, and IGRP all send periodic updates.

2 What is an incremental update, and how often is it sent out?

An incremental update is an update that is sent out only when there is a change in the network. It contains only the information about the change. The change could be either the loss of a network or the addition of a network. Protocols that send incremental updates are link-state protocols, such as OSPF, IS-IS, BGP, and EIGRP, although not only link-state protocols will send incremental updates.

3 What is the routing algorithm used in OSPF?

The routing algorithm used in OSPF is the Dijkstra algorithm.

4 State one method by which a link-state routing protocol attempts to reduce the network overhead.

Link-state routing protocols reduce network overhead by sending only incremental updates, or periodic updates with a very long interval. The updates contain information about the links connecting local routers rather than route information that is calculated as part of the routing process.

5 Distance vector routing protocols naturally summarize at which boundary?

Distance vector routing protocols naturally summarize at the NIC or major network boundary. They do this by following the first octet rule.

6 Which routing protocol technology uses the Bellman Ford algorithm?

The routing protocol technology that uses Bellman Ford is distance vector technology.

7   Give three reasons why RIPv1 has problems with working in a large network.

RIPv1 has problems working in a large network because of the following reasons:

— It has a maximum hop count of 15.

— It sends updates of its routing table out of every interface every 30 seconds, which increases the network overhead on a network and leads to link congestion.

— To avoid routing loops, it uses holddown and poison reverse, and thereby increases the time that it takes to propagate the changes in the network.

8   What is the Dijkstra algorithm used for?

The Dijkstra algorithm is used to calculate the shortest path first from the topological database. It examines the topological database and creates the routing table with the best path to each remote subnet. If there is more than one equal-cost path, it will load balance among them.

9   What is the destination address of the distance vector periodic update?

The destination address of the distance vector periodic update is 255.255.255.255 (the broadcast address).

10   State one major difference between a classful and classless routing protocol.

Major differences between a classful and classless routing protocol include these:

— The capability to use VLSM

— The capability to summarize

— The capability to maximize the logical address space

11   In the routing table, a field indicates the source of the routing information. If the field showed the letter C, what would this mean?

A field showing the letter C would mean that the network is directly connected.

12   In the routing table, how is the next logical hop indicated?

In the routing table, the next logical hop is indicated by the word *via* followed by an IP address. This is the address of the next logical hop.

13   Cisco distinguishes between the routing and the switching function—what is the difference?

The routing function is how the router learns the logical topology of the network. It decides whether the datagram can be routed, which path to select if there is a choice, and to which outgoing interface to queue the datagram. It operates at Layer 3 of the OSI stack.

The switching function is the forwarding of the frame from the inbound interface to an outbound interface. It operates at Layer 2 of the OSI stack, not at Layer 3, like a router.

A LAN switch connects two or more LAN segments. It uses a table of MAC addresses to determine the segment on which a frame needs to be transmitted; if it is on the interface that the frame received, then the frame is dropped. The switch listens to all traffic on the interface, at Layer 2, while the router looks at only the MAC address of a multicast group of which it is a member, a broadcast, or its own individual MAC address. Switches operate at much higher speeds than routers and can support new functionality, such as virtual LANs.

14 State the two ways that an outgoing interface is selected as the preferred path.

An outgoing interface is selected for the following reasons:

— **Because it is the only available path**

— **Because the administrative distance is lower**

— **Because the metric is lower**

15 What is administrative distance?

Administrative distance is the mechanism used by the routing process to select a path offered by two different routing protocols. The administrative distance is a set of values, in which a value is given to each IP routing protocol. This allows a hierarchy to be established so that when multiple protocols offer a path to the same remote network, one path can be chosen. The path that is chosen will be the one offered by the routing protocol with the lowest administrative distance. The administrative distance can be manually configured.

16 If IGRP has three paths to a remote network in which each path has an equal metric, what will happen?

If IGRP sees equal cost paths to a remote network, it will load balance between those paths by default.

17 Name the interior IP routing protocols that send the mask with the routing update.

The interior IP routing protocols that send the mask with the routing update are EIGRP, OSPF, IS-IS, and RIPv2.

18 Name the interior routing protocol that sends a routing update on a Cisco router every 30 seconds by default.

The routing protocol that sends a routing update every 30 seconds is RIP.

19   Does VLSM require a classful or classless routing protocol, and why?

VLSM requires a classless routing protocol because it needs the subnet mask to be sent with the update.

20   State one of the characteristics of a classful routing protocol.

The characteristics of a classful routing protocol are as follows:

— **It summarizes at the network boundary.**

— **Routes exchanged between foreign networks are summarized to the NIC number.**

— **Within the same network (NIC number), subnet routes are exchanged by routers.**

— **All the interfaces on all the routers within a NIC number must share the same subnet mask.**

— **VLSM is not possible within the network.**

21   A distance vector routing protocol uses the mechanism of poison reverse—what is this?

When the routing process suspects that a route in its routing table is no longer valid, it sets the metric so high for that route that it renders it unusable. This will be propagated in the routing updates to other routers.

22   Name two distance vector routing protocols.

Distance vector routing protocols include RIPv1, RIPv2, IGRP, and EIGRP (an advanced distance vector routing protocol).

23   Name two link-state IP routing protocols.

Link-state IP routing protocols include OSPF, IS-IS, and EIGRP (an advanced distance vector routing protocol, with some link-state characteristics).

24   Describe the mechanism of split horizon.

Split horizon is a routing technique in which information about routes is prevented from exiting the router interface through which that information was received. Split-horizon updates are useful in preventing routing loops.

25   What is the command syntax to empty the Cisco routing table of all its routes?

The command syntax to empty the Cisco routing table of all its routes is as follows:

clear ip route *

(This command must be executed from the privileged EXEC level.)

> **26**   What does 0.0.0.0 signify in an IP routing table?
>
> **0.0.0.0 is used to signify the default route in the routing table.**
>
> **27**   What is the command to show whether a specific network, such as 141.131.6.16, is present in the routing table?
>
> **The command to show whether a specific network, such as 141.131.6.16, is present in the routing table is as follows:**
>
> **show ip route 141.131.6.16**
>
> **28**   What is the next logical hop in the routing table?
>
> **The next logical hop in the routing table is the address of the interface to which traffic should be sent for it to reach the remote network. The address is taken from the source address of the routing update that provided the remote network.**

Chapter 5

Chapter 5 "Do I Know This Already?" Quiz Answers

> **1**   How often, by default, does OSPF send out hello packets on a broadcast multiaccess link?
>
> **By default, OSPF sends out hello packets every 10 seconds on a broadcast network.**
>
> **2**   What is a neighbor in OSPF?
>
> **A neighbor is a router on the same network link.**
>
> **3**   What is an adjacency in OSPF?
>
> **An adjacency is the state that two neighbors can achieve after they have synchronized their OSPF databases.**
>
> **4**   If the network is stable and sees no changes, how often will it send LSAs? Why are these updates sent out periodically?
>
> **If the network is stable, OSPF will still send out LSAs every 30 minutes by default. This is to ensure the integrity of the topological databases.**
>
> **5**   If a router has an OSPF priority set to 0, what does this indicate?
>
> **A router with the OSPF priority set to 0 is one that cannot participate in the election of a designated router. It can become neither a designated nor a backup designated router.**
>
> **6**   What does NBMA stand for?
>
> *NBMA* **stands for nonbroadcast multiaccess**

7 RFC 2328 describes the operation of OSPF in two modes across an NBMA cloud. What are they?

The two modes of operation across a NBMA cloud as described in RFC 2328 are nonbroadcast multiaccess and point-to-multipoint operation.

8 The Cisco solution point-to-point mode does not require the configuration of DR and BDR. Explain briefly why.

The Cisco solution point-to-point mode does not require the election of either a designated router or a backup designated router because there are only two nodes on the network. They will form an adjacency directly.

9 The address 192.100.56.10 has been allocated to an interface on the router. This interface alone is to be included in the OSPF process. State the command that would start the process on this interface.

There are several ways to configure the process to include the interface. The command network *network number wildcard mask* area *area number* would be a subcommand to the global command router ospf *process-id*. The network command is used in both possible solutions; the difference is in the wildcard mask.

network 192.100.56.10 0.0.0.0 area 2—This will match every bit in the interface address.

network 192.100.56.10 0.0.7.255 area 2—This will also match the interface because it will resolve to the subnet assigned to the wire connected to the interface. This bit allocation was chosen merely to demonstrate the technique. The allocation assumed is the subnet mask of 255.255.248.0. Note that the wildcard mask is the inverse of the subnet mask, ensuring that the individual subnet is selected for the interface.

10 What command would identify the designated router for your LAN?

The command show ip ospf interface shows the designated and backup designated routers.

11 The metric used by OSPF is cost. How would you change the default setting on an interface?

Underneath the appropriate interface, issue the command ip ospf cost *cost*. The value for *cost* is an unsigned integer value expressed as the link-state metric. It can be a value in the range 1 to 65535.

12 If the command **ip ospf network non-broadcast** is used, what additional statement is necessary?

If the command ip ospf network non-broadcast is used, the additional statement that is required is the neighbor statement. Because the network is a nonbroadcast network that cannot see its neighbors, they are to be manually configured.

13 What command shows which router on a LAN is the BDR?

The show ip ospf neighbor command shows the designated router and the backup router. Another command that will show the designated router is the show ip ospf interface command.

14 Explain briefly what **show ip ospf database** will reveal.

The command show ip ospf database shows the contents of the topology database and gives a status on the LSAs that have been sent and received, including how long it has been since the last LSA was received.

15 What command is used to show the state of adjacencies?

The command show ip ospf interface shows the adjacencies that exist with neighbors.

16 It is possible to have more than one OSPF process on a router. Which command would achieve this?

It is possible to have more than one process, although it is rarely configured. The process ID in the command router ospf *process id* not only starts the process, but it also identifies the process; repeating the command with another ID number will create another process. One possible scenario for this configuration is at a service provider that wants to separate its OSPF domain from its customer.

Chapter 5 "Q&A" Answers

1 What information is held in the topology table?

The topology table holds a map of every link in the area. Every topology table in the area is the same. This is sometimes referred to as the link-state database.

2 What command is used to manually determine which router on a LAN will become the DR?

The priority command is used to manually determine the DR. The higher the priority, the greater the likelihood is of success.

3 What details are used to determine the metric of a route in OSPF by default on a Cisco router?

The bandwidth is used to determine the default cost or the value of the path with the lowest cost.

4 It is possible to have more than one OSPF process on a router—how would this be achieved?

The router command creates the OSPF process with an ID number to identify it. To create another process on the same router, issue the same command again with a different ID number. There are design issues to consider, and this configuration should not be implemented lightly.

5 Which RFC identifies the use of OSPF over an NBMA cloud?

RFC 2338 explains the use of OSPF in a point-to-multipoint and NBMA environment.

6 State the different types of packets used to build a routing table for the first time.

Five packets are used to build the routing table for the first time:

— **The Hello protocol—This is used to find neighbors and to determine the designated and backup designated router. The continued propagation of the Hello protocol maintains the transmitting router in the topology database of those that hear the message.**

— **The database descriptor—This is used to send summary information to neighbors to synchronize topology databases.**

— **The link-state request—This is a request for more detailed information, which is sent when the router receives a database descriptor that contains new information.**

— **The link-state update—This is the link-state advertisement (LSA) packet issued in response to the request for database information in the link-state request packet.**

— **The link-state acknowledgement—This acknowledges the link-state update.**

7 In creating an adjacency, what is the exstart state?

The exstart state is a stage in the forming of an adjacency between neighbors. This stage is the stage when the DR and the BDR have been elected. The master/slave relationship has been established, as has the initial sequence number of the DDP packets.

8 Explain the command **ip ospf network non-broadcast**.

The ip ospf network non-broadcast command is the RFC-compliant mode for NBMA. It is the default mode for interfaces and point-to-point subinterfaces. It is used in a full or partial meshed network, and OSPF operates as if on a nonbroadcast network. It is necessary to manually define the DR to be a hub router that is connected to all the other routers. Neighbors must be defined manually.

9 In which of the NBMA configuration choices is it necessary to manually state the neighbors? Why is this necessary?

It is necessary to manually configure the neighbors in the industry-standard NBMA mode and in the Cisco point-to-point nonbroadcast mode.

It is necessary to define the neighbors to the network because the network believes that it is a nonbroadcast medium, so it cannot send out the multicast traffic to ascertain the neighbors.

10 In a Frame Relay environment, which is fully meshed, which OSPF configurations might be chosen? Give reasons for your choice.

The industry-standard NBMA configuration may be chosen in a fully meshed environment. It requires an additional manual configuration of the neighbors, but the network will elect the DR and the BDR. There may be some design concerns about running this mode in an unstable network, which could burden the CPU and the WAN links.

It is possible to use point-to-point subinterfaces without worrying about the OSPF network type because they will become neighbors.

The other alternative is the Cisco broadcast mode, which does not require the manual configuration of neighbors.

11 How often by default does OSPF send out hello packets on a broadcast multiaccess link?

By default, OSPF sends out hello packets every 10 seconds on a broadcast network.

12 What is a neighbor in OSPF?

A neighbor is a router on the same network link.

13 What is an adjacency in OSPF?

An adjacency is the state that two neighbors can achieve after they have synchronized their OSPF databases.

14 If the network is stable and sees no changes, how often will it send LSAs? Why are these updates sent out periodically?

If the network is stable, OSPF will still send out LSAs every 30 minutes by default. This is to ensure the integrity of the topological databases.

15 If a router has an OSPF priority set to 0, what does this indicate?

A router with the OSPF priority set to 0 is one that cannot participate in the election of a designated router. It can become neither a designated nor a backup designated router.

16 What does NBMA stand for?

NBMA **stands for nonbroadcast multiaccess.**

17 RFC 2328 describes the operation of OSPF in two modes across an NBMA cloud. What are they?

The two modes of operation across a NBMA cloud as described in RFC 2328 are nonbroadcast multiaccess and point-to-multipoint.

18 The Cisco solution point-to-point mode does not require the configuration of DR and BDR. Explain briefly why.

The Cisco solution point-to-point does not require the election of either a designated or a backup designated router because there are only two nodes on the network. They will form an adjacency directly.

19 The address 192.100.56.10 has been allocated to an interface on the router. This interface alone is to be included in the OSPF process. State the command that would start the process on this interface.

There are several ways to configure the process to include the interface. The command network *network number wildcard mask* **area** *area number* **would be a subcommand to the global command router ospf** *process-id.* **The network command is used in both possible solutions; the difference is in the wildcard mask.**

network 192.100.56.10 0.0.0.0 area 2—This will match every bit in the interface address.

network 192.100.56.10 0.0.7.255 area 2—This will also match the interface because it will resolve to the subnet assigned to the wire connected to the interface. This bit allocation was chosen merely to demonstrate the technique. The allocation assumed is the subnet mask of 255.255.248.0. Note that the wildcard mask is the inverse of the subnet mask, ensuring that the individual subnet is selected for the interface.

20 What command would identify the designated router for your LAN?

The command show ip ospf interface shows the designated and backup designated routers.

21 The metric used by OSPF is cost. How would you change the default setting on an interface?

Underneath the appropriate interface, issue the command ip ospf cost *cost.* **The value for** *cost* **is an unsigned integer value expressed as the link-state metric. It can be a value in the range 1 to 65,535.**

22 If the command **ip ospf network non-broadcast** is used, what additional statement is necessary?

If the command ip ospf network non-broadcast is used the additional statement that is required is the neighbor statement. Because the network is a nonbroadcast network that cannot see its neighbors, they are to be manually configured.

23 What command shows which router on a LAN is the BDR?

The show ip ospf neighbor command will show the designated router and the backup router. Another command that will show the designated router is the show ip ospf interface command.

24 Explain briefly what **show ip ospf database** will reveal.

The command show ip ospf database shows the contents of the topology database and gives a status on the LSAs that have been sent and received, including how long it has been since the last LSA was received.

25 What command is used to show the state of adjacencies?

The command show ip ospf interface shows the adjacencies that exist with neighbors.

26 It is possible to have more than one OSPF process on a router. Which command would achieve this?

It is possible to have more than one process, although it is rarely configured. The process ID in the command router ospf *process id* not only starts the process, but it also identifies the process; repeating the command with another ID number will create another process. One possible scenario for this configuration is at a service provider that wants to separate its OSPF domain from its customer.

Chapter 6

Chapter 6 "Do I Know This Already?" Quiz Answers

1 A virtual link in OSPF is used to solve what problem?

The virtual link will provide the disconnected area a logical path to the backbone. The virtual link has to be established between two ABRs that have a common area, with one ABR connected to the backbone. It can also be used to connect two area 0s together. This may be necessary when two companies merge, each with its own area 0, or if, due to the loss of a link, the area 0 becomes bisected.

2 State one disadvantage for making an NBMA Frame Relay cloud Area 0.

Creating the Frame Relay cloud as a one OSPF area, preferably Area 0, causes summary LSAs to be flooded throughout the Frame Relay network. This results in a large number of routers recalculating whenever there is a change that requires the topology table to be updated, and the Frame Relay cloud may become saturated. If the Frame Relay cloud has a problem, then the entire network may well suffer.

3 State one advantage in making the centralized routers and network resources dwell in Area 0 while the Frame Relay cloud and the stub remote LANs reside in satellite stub areas.

One advantage of this design is that any flooding of external LSAs is prevented from entering the Frame Relay network because it is a stub network. This reduces the network overhead.

4 How does creating the number of areas in OSPF reduce the number of SPF calculations?

The number of SPF calculations is reduced because the size of the topology table is reduced. This lessens the likelihood of a change in the network and, thus, SPF calculations.

5 How does a stub area differ from the backbone area?

A stub area differs from the backbone area in that it does not propagate external routes into its area. The backbone is obliged to forward these LSAs to ensure connectivity throughout the network.

6 How does a totally stubby area differ from a stub area?

A totally stubby area differs from a stub area in that it propagates neither external routes nor summary routes from other areas. This is a Cisco solution to minimize the amount of CPU and memory required of the routers within the area. Connectivity is achieved by the use of default routes, which are advertised to the internal routers.

7 State the different LSA types.

The different LSA update types are as follows:

— **Router link—Sent by the router, stating the links directly connected. These are flooded through the area. This update is identified by the type code Type 1.**

— **Network link—Sent by the designated router, stating the links for the LAN for which it is the designated router. These LSAs are flooded throughout the area. This update is identified by the type code Type 2.**

— Summary link—Sent by the ABR into the backbone. It states the IP subnets within the area that are to be advertised into other areas. This is where summarization would be configured. This update is identified by the type code Type 3.

— Summary link (to an ASBR)—Sent from an ABR to a router that connects to the outside world (ASBR). It contains the metric cost from the ABR to the ASBR. This update is identified by the type code Type 4.

— External link—Sent to the ASBRs to which the organization is directly connected. This update is identified by the type code Type 5.

8 Where does the backbone router reside, and what is its function?

OSPF has special restrictions when multiple areas are involved. If more than one area is configured, one of these areas must be Area 0. This is called the backbone. When designing networks, it is good practice to start with Area 0 and then expand into other areas later.

The backbone must be at the center of all other areas—that is, all areas must be physically connected to the backbone. The reasoning behind this is that OSPF expects all areas to inject routing information into the backbone; in turn, the backbone will disseminate that information into other areas.

9 Are there any considerations for OSPF configured with VLSM sending routing updates into RIPv1?

If OSPF sends updates into RIPv1 and those updates include routes with VLSM, all the mask information will be lost. This is because the routing protocol RIPv1 has no concept of VLSM and does not propagate the subnet mask. Static routes will have to be configured for the RIPv1 process to understand these routes. It should also be understood that the routes sent into RIPv1 will have to summarize into one classful mask.

10 There are two types of summarization. What are they?

The two types of summarization are these:

Interarea route summarization—These routes are sent between areas. The ABR will summarize routes if the network within the area was designed using contiguous addresses, conforming to both a physical and a logical hierarchy.

External route summarization—These are routes sent into OSPF from another routing protocol. This summarization also demands a hierarchical design using contiguous addresses. This is employed at the ASBR.

11 Can the following subnets with a mask of 255.255.255.0 be summarized? If so, state the subnet and mask that can be used.

19.44.16.0	19.44.24.0
19.44.17.0	19.44.25.0
19.44.18.0	19.44.26.0
19.44.19.0	19.44.27.0
19.44.20.0	19.44.28.0
19.44.21.0	19.44.29.0
19.44.22.0	19.44.30.0
19.44.23.0	19.44.31.0

The subnets can be summarized to 19.44.16.0/20 with a mask of 255.255.240.0 or /20.

12 Why can interarea summarization be configured only on ABRs?

Interarea summarization can be configured only on ABRs because of the topology table. Every router within an area knows of every link and, therefore, every network within the area. Every router shares the same topology table; they are identical. Therefore, it is not possible to summarize within an area because the process of summarization subsumes subnets. The ABR is the only router that has knowledge of several areas and thus that is capable of summarizing among them.

13 What command would be used to create a totally stubby area?

The command area *area-id* stub no-summary will create a totally stubby area. This is a subcommand to the router ospf *process-id* command. It is necessary only on the ABR.

14 What is a virtual link, and what command would be used to create it?

A virtual link is a link that creates a tunnel through an area to the backbone (area 0). This allows an area that cannot connect directly to the backbone to do so virtually. The command to create the link is area *area-id* virtual-link *router-id*. Note, the *area-id* that is supplied is that of the transit area and the *router-id* is that of the router at the other end of the link. The command needs to be configured at both ends of the tunnel.

15 Where would you issue the command to summarize IP subnets? State the command that would be used.

Summarization is done at area boundaries. The command to start summarization is the area range command, with the syntax area *area-id* range *address mask*.

16 How would you summarize external routes before injecting them into the OSPF domain?

The command summary-address *address mask* is the command that would be used.

Chapter 6 "Q&A" Answers

1 In a totally stubby area, which routes are not propagated into the area?

There will be no summary or external routes propagated by the ABR into the area.

2 Where would you see whether a learned network was within the same area as the router you were looking at?

The show ip route command identifies how the route was learned. If it is a network from another area, it will have the code IA next to it.

3 An Area Border Router must be resident in which area?

An Area Border Router must be resident in Area 0 as well as the area that is connecting to the backbone area. It will have two topological databases, one for each area it is resident in, so that it knows how to forward traffic.

4 What does ABR stand for, and what LSAs will it forward?

***ABR* stands for Area Border Router, and it forwards summary LSAs. It forwards both Type 3 LSAs and Type 4 LSAs. Type 3 LSAs are forwarded to the other ABRs, and Type 4 LSAs are forward to the ASBRs. ABR also forwards Type 3 LSAs from other areas into its own area.**

5 State two advantages in creating areas in OSPF.

The advantages in creating areas in OSPF include these:

— **It is easier to manage and administrate.**

— **It uses a smaller topology table, which reduces the CPU, memory, and network bandwidth consumption.**

— **Fewer SPF calculations are involved because the topology table is smaller and there is less likelihood of change in the network.**

— **It uses a smaller routing table if summarization is in operation.**

6 What is an external route, and on which type of router will this route be introduced?

An external route is a route that did not originate in the OSPF domain. It has been redistributed from another routing protocol or static routing. An external route is introduced into the OSPF domain by an Autonomous System Boundary Router (ASBR).

7 Which command in OSPF shows the network LSA information?

The command show ip ospf [*process-id area-id*] database network displays the network link state information.

8 Why is the use of VLSM important in the design of OSPF?

VLSM is important in the design of OSPF because it supports a hierarchical design and allows for the summarization of IP subnets between areas.

9 Given the networks 144.12.8.0 and 144.12.12.0, both with the mask of 255.255.255.0, is it possible to summarize these into one subnet? If so, state the new subnet and mask.

The new subnet and mask will be 144.12.8.0, with a mask of 255.255.248.0 or /21.

10 What is a discontiguous network?

A discontiguous network is a network with a major network number (NIC number) that has a different NIC number dividing it. For example, consider the network 131.10.1.0 appearing on a LAN in San Francisco and the network 131.10.2.0 appearing on a network in San Jose. These are both subnets of the major network 131.10.0.0. If these subnets are connected over a Frame Relay link that has the address of 10.10.10.0, the network number 131.10.0.0 would be discontiguous because it is not configured contiguously. This is not a problem for routing protocols that carry the subnet mask.

11 A virtual link in OSPF is used to solve what problem?

The virtual link provides the disconnected area with a logical path to the backbone. The virtual link must be established between two ABRs that have a common area, with one ABR connected to the backbone. It can also be used to connect two area 0s together. This may be necessary when two companies merge, each with its own area 0, or if, due to the loss of a link, the area 0 becomes bisected.

12 State one disadvantage for making an NBMA Frame Relay cloud Area 0.

Creating the Frame Relay cloud as one OSPF area, preferably Area 0, causes summary LSAs to be flooded throughout the Frame Relay network. This results in a large number of routers recalculating whenever there is a change that requires the topology table to be updated, and the Frame Relay cloud may become saturated. If the Frame Relay cloud has a problem, then the entire network may well suffer.

13 State one advantage in making the centralized routers and network resources dwell in Area 0 while the Frame Relay cloud and the stub remote LANs reside in satellite stub areas.

One advantage of this design is that any flooding of external LSAs is prevented from entering the Frame Relay network because it is a stub network. This reduces the network overhead.

14 How does creating the number of areas in OSPF reduce the number of SPF calculations?

The number of SPF calculations is reduced because the size of the topology table is reduced. This lessens the likelihood of a change in the network and, thus, SPF calculations.

15 How does a stub area differ from the backbone area?

A stub area differs from the backbone area in that it does not propagate external routes into its area. The backbone is obliged to forward these LSAs to ensure connectivity throughout the network.

16 How does a totally stubby area differ from a stub area?

A totally stubby area differs from a stub area in that it propagates neither external routes nor summary routes from other areas. This is a Cisco solution to minimize the amount of CPU and memory required of the routers within the area. Connectivity is achieved by the use of default routes, which are advertised to the internal routers.

17 State the different LSA types.

The different LSA update types are as follows:

— **Router link—Sent by the router, stating the links directly connected. These are flooded through the area. This update is identified by the type code Type 1.**

— **Network link—Sent by the designated router, stating the links for the LAN for which it is the designated router. These LSAs are flooded throughout the area. This update is identified by the type code Type 2.**

— **Summary link—Sent by the ABR into the backbone. It states the IP subnets within the area that are to be advertised into other areas. This is where summarization would be configured. This update is identified by the type code Type 3.**

— **Summary link (to an ASBR)—Sent from an ABR to a router that connects to the outside world (ASBR). It contains the metric cost from the ABR to the ASBR. This update is identified by the type code Type 4.**

— **External link—Sent to the ASBRs to which the organization is directly connected. This update is identified by the type code Type 5.**

18 Where does the backbone router reside, and what is its function?

OSPF has special restrictions when multiple areas are involved. If more than one area is configured, one of these areas must be Area 0. This is called the backbone. When designing networks, it is good practice to start with Area 0 and then expand into other areas later.

The backbone must be at the center of all other areas—that is, all areas must be physically connected to the backbone. The reasoning behind this is that OSPF expects all areas to inject routing information into the backbone; in turn, the backbone will disseminate that information into other areas.

19 Are there any considerations for OSPF configured with VLSM sending routing updates into RIPv1?

If OSPF sends updates into RIPv1 and those updates include routes with VLSM, all the mask information will be lost. This is because the routing protocol RIPv1 has no concept of VLSM and does not propagate the subnet mask. Static routes will have to be configured for the RIPv1 process to understand these routes. It should also be understood that the routes sent into RIPv1 will have to summarize into one classful mask.

20 There are two types of summarization. What are they?

The two types of summarization are these:

Interarea route summarization—These routes are sent between areas. The ABR will summarize routes if the network within the area was designed using contiguous addresses, conforming to both a physical and a logical hierarchy.

External route summarization—These are routes sent into OSPF from another routing protocol. This summarization also demands a hierarchical design using contiguous addresses. This is employed at the ASBR.

21 Can the following subnets with a mask of 255.255.255.0 be summarized? If so, state the subnet and mask that can be used.

19.44.16.0	19.44.24.0
19.44.17.0	19.44.25.0
19.44.18.0	19.44.26.0
19.44.19.0	19.44.27.0
19.44.20.0	19.44.28.0
19.44.21.0	19.44.29.0
19.44.22.0	19.44.30.0
19.44.23.0	19.44.31.0

The subnets can be summarized to 19.44.16.0/20, with a mask of 255.255.240.0 or /20.

22 Why can interarea summarization be configured only on ABRs?

Interarea summarization can be configured only on ABRs because of the topology table. Every router within an area knows of every link and, therefore, every network within the area. Every router shares the same topology table; they are identical. Therefore, it is not possible to summarize within an area because the process of summarization subsumes subnets. The ABR is the only router that has knowledge of several areas and thus that is capable of summarizing among them.

23   What command would be used to create a totally stubby area?

The command area *area-id* stub no-summary will create a totally stubby area. This is a subcommand to the router ospf *process-id* command. It is necessary only on the ABR.

24   What is a virtual link, and what command would be used to create it?

A virtual link is a link that creates a tunnel through an area to the backbone (area 0). This allows an area that cannot connect directly to the backbone to do so virtually. The command to create the link is area *area-id* virtual-link *router-id*. Note, the *area-id* that is supplied is that of the transit area and the *router-id* is that of the router at the other end of the link. The command needs to be configured at both ends of the tunnel.

25   Where would you issue the command to summarize IP subnets? State the command that would be used.

Summarization is done at area boundaries. The command to start summarization is the area range command, with the syntax area *area-id* range *address mask*.

26   How would you summarize external routes before injecting them into the OSPF domain?

The command summary-address *address mask* is the command that would be used.

Chapter 7

Chapter 7 "Do I Know This Already?" Quiz Answers

1   EIGRP may be used to send information about which three routing protocols?

EIGRP can be used as a routing protocol for IP, IPX, and AppleTalk.

2   Which EIGRP packets are sent reliably?

The packets that EIGRP sends reliably are updates, queries, and replies. It uses the Reliable Transport Protocol (RTP). This is necessary because EIGRP does not send out periodic updates, and this mechanism ensures a loop-free synchronized network.

3   In what instances will EIGRP automatically redistribute?

EIGRP will automatically redistribute between itself and IGRP as long as both processes are running the same autonomous system number.

EIGRP also automatically redistributes between the LAN protocol and EIGRP. EIGRP for IPX automatically redistributes into IPX for RIP/SAP and EIGRP for AppleTalk; it similarly redistributes automatically into RTMP.

4 How long is the holdtime, by default?

The holdtime is three times the Hello timer, which is 15 seconds or 180 seconds, depending on the medium.

5 What is an EIGRP topology table, and what does it contain?

The topology table contains every network and every path to every network in the domain. The metric for every path is held, as is the metric from the next logical hop or neighbor. The table contains the outgoing interface on the router through which to reach the remote network and the IP address of the next-hop address. The status of the route (passive or active) is also recorded. The topology table also keeps track of the routing packets that have been sent to the neighbors.

6 What is the advertised distance in EIGRP, and how is it distinguished from the feasible distance?

Advertised distance is the metric that is reported by the neighbor router(s). Feasible distance is the metric that is reported by neighbor router(s), plus the cost associated with the forwarding link from the local interface to the neighbor router(s).

7 What EIGRP algorithm is run to create entries for the routing table?

The Diffusing Update Algorithm (DUAL) is run on the topology table. It is used to determine the best path and so build the routing table.

8 When does EIGRP place a network in active mode?

EIGRP places a network into active mode when there is no feasible successor in its topology table.

9 By default, EIGRP summarizes at which boundary?

By default, EIGRP summarizes at the NIC or major network boundary.

10 What is Stuck in Active?

Stuck in Active (SIA) is a state in which a router will place a route after it has failed to hear a reply to a query that was sent to a neighbor.

EIGRP sends a query when a route is lost and another feasible route doesn't exist in the topology table. The SIA is caused by two sequential events: First, a route has gone away. Second, an EIGRP neighbor (or neighbors) has not replied to the query for that route. When the SIA occurs, the router clears the neighbor that has not replied to the query. When this happens, it is necessary to determine which neighbor has been cleared, keeping in mind that this router could be many hops away.

11 What is the **variance** command used for?

The variance command is used to determine additional paths to be included in load balancing traffic to remote networks. The command is used in conjunction with the multiplier number. This number multiplies the path with the best (lowest) metric by the number stated as the multiplier. Any paths that the router knows of that have a metric value less than the result of the multiplier are included in the paths for load balancing. The amount of traffic sent across each path will be proportional to the metric value of the path.

12 State two factors that influence EIGRP scalability.

A hierarchical tiered design and contiguous addressing are both critical to being able to scale an EIGRP network. If these are in place, it is possible to summarize the network, which reduces the network resources needed for large tables and limits the query range of the router. It is also important to ensure that the router has sufficient memory, that the network has sufficient bandwidth on its WAN links, and that, where appropriate, the bandwidth command has been configured.

13 What command is used to display which routes are in passive or active mode?

The command show IP EIGRP topology shows the passive and active state of the routes that are contained in the table. The route is passive if the route is operational; it is in an active state if the router must query its neighbors for alternative paths to a network. This command also shows the number of successors and the neighbors and distance information.

14 What command is used in EIGRP to perform manual summarization?

It is first necessary to turn off automatic summarization. This is achieved with the router command no auto-summary. Then the interface command IP summary-address *as number address mask* is used to define the summary address to be used.

15 For Frame Relay, when would you configure the physical interface (as opposed to a subinterface) with the **bandwidth** command?

If all the circuits have the same CIR, the bandwidth command may be used on the physical interface. The interface will divide the available bandwidth set on the command by the number of circuits.

16 Which command is used to display all types of EIGRP packets that are both received and sent by a router?

The command debug eigrp packet displays the types of EIGRP packets that are both sent and received by the router.

Chapter 7 "Q&A" Answers

1 If a router does not have a feasible successor, what action will it take?

If the router does not have a feasible successor in its topology table, it sends a query packet to its neighbors asking whether they have a feasible successor.

2 When does EIGRP need to be manually redistributed into another EIGRP process?

EIGRP needs to be manually redistributed into another EIGRP process when the autonomous system number is different.

3 Which timers are tracked in the neighbor table?

The timers that the neighbor table keeps track of are the holdtime, the SRTT, and the RTO.

4 What is the difference between an update and a query?

An update is the routing information packet that a router will send out to inform its neighbors of a change in the network. In a query, the router has no feasible successor in its topology table for a network that is down. At this point, it queries its neighbors to ascertain whether they have a feasible successor. If they do, this route becomes the feasible successor for the original router.

5 When does EIGRP recalculate the topology table?

Enhanced IGRP recalculates the topology table whenever it receives a change input to the topology table. This could be a change of metric for a physically connected link, a change of status of a physically connected link, or an EIGRP routing packet, either an update, a query, or a reply packet.

6 EIGRP has a default limit set on the amount of bandwidth that it can use for EIGRP packets. What is the default percentage limit?

The default percentage limit of bandwidth allocated to EIGRP packets is 50 percent.

7 State two rules for designing a scalable EIGRP network.

The rules for scaling an EIGRP network include these:

— **Allocation of addresses should be contiguous to allow summarization.**

— **A hierarchical tiered network design should be used, to allow summarization.**

— **Summarization should be used.**

— **Sufficient network resources (both H/W and S/W) should be used on network devices.**

— **Sufficient bandwidth should be used on WAN links.**

— **Appropriate EIGRP configuration should be used on WAN links.**

— **Filters should be used.**

— **Network monitoring should be used.**

8   What is the preferred configuration for a hybrid multipoint NBMA network when one VC has a CIR of 56 kbps and the other five VCs each have a CIR of 256 kbps?

The preferred configuration for a multipoint NBMA network, in which one circuit is lower than the other circuits, is to create a point-to-point subinterface for the lower circuit and then to configure the bandwidth to reflect the CIR of the link. Another subinterface should be created as a multipoint interface with a configured bandwidth that equals the aggregate CIR of all the circuits in this instance 5×256 kbps, or 1280 kbps.

9   With four Frame Relay circuits in a multipoint solution and a bandwidth configuration of 224, what is the allocation per circuit, and where would the **bandwidth** command be configured?

The command would be configured on the physical interface. The CIR of each circuit is 56 kbps.

10   Explain the purpose of the command **no auto-summary**.

The command no auto-summary is used to turn off automatic summarization, which in EIGRP happens at the NIC or major network boundary. This command is necessary in manual summarization and precedes the summarization commands.

11   Explain the meaning of the command **ip bandwidth-percent eigrp 63 100**.

This command overrides the default bandwidth of 50 percent that is allocated to EIGRP for network overhead. This command sets the bandwidth allocation to be 100 percent of the link for the EIGRP AS of 63 on the interface upon which it is configured. This command would be used if the bandwidth command had set the logical bandwidth of the link to be artificially low.

12   EIGRP may be used to send information about which three routing protocols?

EIGRP can be used as a routing protocol for IP, IPX, and AppleTalk.

13   Which EIGRP packets are sent reliably?

The packets that EIGRP sends reliably are updates, queries, and replies. It uses the Reliable Transport Protocol (RTP). This is necessary because EIGRP does not send out periodic updates, and this mechanism ensures a loop-free synchronized network.

14   In what instances will EIGRP automatically redistribute?

EIGRP will automatically redistribute between itself and IGRP as long as both processes are running the same autonomous system number.

EIGRP also automatically redistributes between the LAN protocol and EIGRP. EIGRP for IPX automatically redistributes into IPX for RIP/SAP and EIGRP for AppleTalk; it similarly redistributes automatically into RTMP.

15   How long is the holdtime, by default?

The holdtime is three times the Hello timer, which is 15 seconds or 180 seconds, depending on the medium.

16   What is an EIGRP topology table, and what does it contain?

The topology table contains every network and every path to every network in the domain. The metric for every path is held along with the metric from the next logical hop or neighbor. The table contains the outgoing interface on the router through which to reach the remote network and the IP address of the next-hop address. The status of the route (passive or active) is also recorded. The topology table also keeps track of the routing packets that have been sent to the neighbors.

17   What is the advertised distance in EIGRP, and how is it distinguished from the feasible distance?

Advertised distance is the metric that is reported by the neighbor router(s). Feasible distance is the metric that is reported by neighbor router(s), plus the cost associated with the forwarding link from the local interface to the neighbor router(s).

18   What EIGRP algorithm is run to create entries for the routing table?

The Diffusing Update Algorithm (DUAL) is run on the topology table. It is used to determine the best path and to build the routing table.

19   When does EIGRP place a network in active mode?

EIGRP places a network into active mode when there is no feasible successor in its topology table.

20   By default, EIGRP summarizes at which boundary?

By default, EIGRP summarizes at the NIC or major network boundary.

21   What is Stuck in Active?

Stuck in Active (SIA) is a state in which a router will place a route after it has failed to hear a reply to a query that was sent to a neighbor.

EIGRP sends a query when a route is lost and another feasible route doesn't exist in the topology table. The SIA is caused by two sequential events: First, a route has gone away. Second, an EIGRP neighbor (or neighbors) has not replied to the query for that route. When the SIA occurs, the router clears the neighbor that has not replied to the query. When this happens, it is necessary to determine which neighbor has been cleared, keeping in mind that this router could be many hops away.

22   What is the **variance** command used for?

The variance command is used to determine additional paths to be included in load balancing traffic to remote networks. The command is used in conjunction with the multiplier number. This number multiplies the path with the best (lowest) metric by the number stated as the multiplier. Any paths that the router knows of that have a metric value less than the result of the multiplier are included in the paths for load balancing. The amount of traffic sent across each path will be proportional to the metric value of the path.

23   State two factors that influence EIGRP scalability.

A hierarchical tiered design and contiguous addressing are both critical to being able to scale an EIGRP network. If these are in place, it is possible to summarize the network, which reduces the network resources needed for large tables and limits the query range of the router. It is also important to ensure that the router has sufficient memory, that the network has sufficient bandwidth on its WAN links, and that, where appropriate, the bandwidth command has been configured.

24   What command is used to display which routes are in passive or active mode?

The command show IP EIGRP topology shows the passive and active state of the routes that are contained in the table. The route is passive if the route is operational; it is set in an active state if the router must query its neighbors for alternative paths to a network. This command also shows the number of successors and the neighbors and distance information.

25   What command is used in EIGRP to perform manual summarization?

It is first necessary to turn off automatic summarization. This is achieved with the router command no auto-summary. Then the interface command IP summary-address *as number address mask* is used to define the summary address to be used.

26   For Frame Relay, when would you configure the physical interface (as opposed to a subinterface) with the **bandwidth** command?

If all the circuits have the same CIR, the bandwidth command may be used on the physical interface. The interface will divide the available bandwidth set on the command by the number of circuits.

27   Which command is used to display all types of EIGRP packets that are both received and sent by a router?

The command debug eigrp packet displays the types of EIGRP packets that are both sent and received by the router.

Chapter 8

Chapter 8 "Do I Know This Already?" Quiz Answers

1 What type of routing protocol is BGP-4 classified as, and what does this mean?

BGP-4 is classified as an External Gateway Routing (EGP) as opposed to OSPF, EIGRP, RIP and so on, which are known as Interior Gateway Protocols (IGPs). If required, it can send a summary of the networks known within an organization to maximize security and minimize bandwidth overhead. It is used to convey routing information between autonomous systems.

2 What is a static route?

A static route is a route that has been manually configured. It has the lowest administrative distance of either 0 or 1, depending on the configuration. This means that it will always take precedence and that it must be redistributed into a routing protocol for other routers to make use of it.

3 What is the transport protocol for BGP-4?

The transport protocol for BGP-4 is TCP 2. It uses TCP port 179.

4 What is a default route?

A default route is a route used when there is no entry for the remote network in the routing table. It is used to connect to the Internet and other routing domains when it is not practical to know all the available networks. It is sufficient to have an exit point from your network identified.

5 State two attributes of BGP-4.

The following are BGP-4 attributes: next hop, AS Path, local preference, Multiple Exit Discriminator (MED), community, atomic aggregate, aggregator, and origin.

6 State four message types of BGP-4.

The four message types of BGP-4 are these:

— **Update messages: Contain paths to destination networks and their attributes. Routes that are no longer available or withdrawn routes are included in updates.**

— **Open messages: Used to establish connections with peers.**

— **Keepalives: Sent periodically between peers to maintain connections and verify paths held by the router sending the keepalive.**

— **Notification: Used to inform the receiving router of errors.**

7 What is policy-based routing?

Policy-based routing is the means by which traffic may be forced to take a different route from that determined by the dynamic routing protocol. It is defined on a hop-by-hop basis, in that the policy is stated on a router and determines which next hop will be used. The decisions may be based on source and/or destination.

8 What do the letters MED represent? Give a brief explanation of what this does.

The Multiple Exit Discriminator is an optional, nontransitive attribute. It is sent only to external BGP-4 peers and is used to influence routers in another autonomous system on the path to take into the autonomous system if multiple paths are available. The lower the value of the attribute, the higher the likelihood that the path will be chosen. By default, a router will compare only the MED from routers that are in the same autonomous system as each other but in a different autonomous system from the determining router.

9 What is a community in BGP-4?

A community is a group of networks that share a common property. The commonality is defined by the optional transitive attribute, and it has no physical boundaries. A network can be a member of more than one community. When the community is defined, decisions or filtering can be made based on the group instead of the individual.

10 Give two reasons why peer groups are useful.

Peer groups are useful because this simplifies the configurations when they are shared by a group of peers. They are also more efficient because updates are generated once per peer group instead of on a per-router (peer) basis.

11 Explain the term "third-Party next hop."

When a router sends an update onto a multiaccess (MA) link such as Ethernet, all routers on the link will hear the update and will propagate their own updates. When propagating a network heard from another router on the MA link, the router should keep the IP address of the source router and should not substitute its IP address. If every router substituted its address as the next-hop router, a packet would have to visit many routers on the same link instead of directing traffic to the router that first sent out the update.

12 What is the difference between a peer and a neighbor?

In external BGP-4, there is no difference between a neighbor and a peer. A peer is the BGP-4 term for a neighbor. Both terms refer to a router that is directly connected, with whom routing information is exchanged. In internal BGP-4 these routers are not necessarily physically adjacent, but they are the next logical-hop router running the BGP-4.

13 Explain briefly the synchronization rule.

The synchronization rule states that the BGP-4 router cannot advertise a route to a neighbor unless the route that it is advertising is known by the interior routing protocol—that is, until both the interior routing protocol and BGP-4 have synchronized, no route will be advertised. The reason for this rule is that it could cause problems to advertise a route to another autonomous system if the advertised route was not in the routing table of every router within the advertising autonomous system. The result could be that a router from another autonomous system sends data to a remote network advertised by BGP-4, and although the data safely reaches the advertising autonomous system, an ignorant router within the autonomous system will drop the packet because it has no knowledge of the advertised network. This rule ensures that traffic can be directed to all destinations that are advertised outside the autonomous system.

14 In BGP-4, describe the purpose of the **network** command.

The network command permits BGP-4 to advertise a network if it is present in the routing table. It is not responsible for starting the BGP-4 process on an interface; instead, it identifies which networks the router originates.

15 Explain the command **neighbor** {ip-address | peer-group-name} **next-hop-self**.

On a broadcast multiaccess network such as Ethernet, the next-hop address will be the IP address of the advertising router. This command forces BGP-4 to advertise itself as the next-hop router instead of letting the protocol determine the address to be used. This avoids problems seen on NBMA networks or nonmeshed environments, such as X.25 and Frame Relay.

16 Which command is used to show all BGP-4 connections?

The command show ip bgp summary shows BGP-4 connections.

Chapter 8 "Q&A" Answers

1 If the weight attribute is used, is a higher or lower weight preferred?

The weight attribute is proprietary to Cisco and is an attribute that is determined locally on the router. The preference in selection is to the highest weight on the router.

2 When would you use external BGP-4 as opposed to internal BGP-4?

External BGP-4 is used to connect different autonomous systems, and the routers are usually neighbors. Internal BGP-4 is used within the same autonomous system to communicate information that has been learned from the external BGP-4 processes.

External BGP-4 is used between the organization and the ISP or the Internet, and internal BGP-4 is used within the ISP or the Internet.

3   What is an alternative to using BGP-4 as the method of connection to the ISP?

The alternative method, suggested by Cisco, is to use a default route into the ISP and for the ISP to configure static routes into your autonomous system.

4   State two reasons for the synchronization rule.

The synchronization rule states that a route will neither be used nor advertised if the advertising router does not have the path in its internal routing table. This prevents black holes. The second reason for the synchronization rule is that it ensures consistency by eliminating router loops.

5   What does the command **clear ip bgp *** achieve, and why should it be used cautiously?

The command resets BGP peer associations, clears the BGP routing table, and re-establishes BGP connections to the neighbors. It should be used cautiously because the loss of connections will drop packets.

6   Give three reasons why you should not use BGP-4 to connect to the Internet.

It is ill-advised to use BGP-4 in certain conditions:

- When the company has only one connection into the Internet

- When there are limited resources on the network

- When the user is not familiar with BGP-4 configurations or policy routing

- When the routers do not understand or need to have greater understanding of each other

7   Explain the use of the command **neighbor 10.10.10.10 remote-as 250.**

The command tells the router, the IP address of the BGP neighbor and the autonomous system to which the neighbor belongs. This information allows the router to create a TCP session with the neighboring router and exchange BGP routing information.

8   Explain briefly the purpose of the community attribute.

The community attribute is used to identify routers, without regard to geographic location, that have some common similarity.

9   In the route selection process, place the following in order of preference: origin code, highest weight, local preference, and MED. State the method of selection for the individual attributes themselves.

The correct order is: highest weight, highest local preference, lowest origin code, and lowest MED.

10 What command is used to enable the BGP-4 process?

The command used to enable the BGP-4 process is router bgp *autonomous system* **number.**

11 Which command is used to show the BGP-4 connections between peers?

The command show ip bgp neighbor is used for this.

12 What is a mandatory attribute?

A mandatory attribute is an attribute that is well known. It contains information required in BGP messages in order to maintain the BGP network.

13 What type of routing protocol is BGP-4 classified as, and what does this mean?

BGP-4 is classified as an External Gateway Protocol (EGP), as opposed to OSPF, EIGRP, RIP, and so on, which are known as Interior Gateway Protocols (IGPs). If required, it can send a summary of the networks known within an organization to maximize security and minimize bandwidth overhead. It is used to convey routing information between autonomous systems.

14 What is a static route?

A static route is a route that has been manually configured. It has the lowest administrative distance of either 0 or 1, depending on the configuration. This means that it will always take precedence and that it must be redistributed into a routing protocol for other routers to make use of it.

15 What is the transport protocol for BGP-4?

The transport protocol for BGP-4 is TCP 2. It uses TCP port 179.

16 What is a default route?

A default route is a route used when there is no entry for the remote network in the routing table. It is used to connect to the Internet and other routing domains when it is not practical to know all the available networks. It is sufficient to have an exit point from your network identified.

17 State two attributes of BGP-4.

The following are BGP-4 attributes: next hop, AS Path, local preference, Multiple Exit Discriminator (MED), community, atomic aggregate, aggregator, and origin.

18 State four message types of BGP-4.

The four message types of BGP-4 are these:

— **Update messages: Contain paths to destination networks and their attributes. Routes that are no longer available or withdrawn routes are included in updates.**

— Open messages: Used to establish connections with peers.

— Keepalives: Sent periodically between peers to maintain connections and verify paths held by the router sending the keepalive.

— Notification: Used to inform the receiving router of errors.

19   What is policy-based routing?

Policy-based routing is the means by which traffic may be forced to take a different route from that determined by the dynamic routing protocol. It is defined on a hop-by-hop basis in that the policy is stated on a router and determines which next hop will be used. The decisions may be based on source and/or destination.

20   What do the letters MED represent? Give a brief explanation of what this does.

The Multiple Exit Discriminator is an optional, nontransitive attribute. It is sent only to external BGP-4 peers and is used to influence routers in another autonomous system on the path to take into the autonomous system if multiple paths are available. The lower the value of the attribute, the higher the likelihood that the path will be chosen. By default, a router compares only the MED from routers that are in the same autonomous system as each other, but a different autonomous system from the determining router.

21   What is a community in BGP-4?

A community is a group of networks that share a common property. The commonality is defined by the optional transitive attribute, and it has no physical boundaries. A network can be a member of more than one community. When the community is defined, decisions or filtering can be made based on the group instead of the individual.

22   Give two reasons why peer groups are useful.

Peer groups are useful because this simplifies the configurations when they are shared by a group of peers. They are also more efficient because updates are generated once per peer group instead of on a per-router (peer) basis.

23   Explain the term "third-party next hop."

When a router sends an update onto a multiaccess (MA) link such as Ethernet, all routers on the link will hear the update and will propagate their own updates. When propagating a network heard from another router on the MA link, the router should keep the IP address of the source router and should not substitute its IP address. If every router substituted its address as the next-hop router, a packet would have to visit many routers on the same link instead of directing traffic to the router that first sent out the update.

24 What is the difference between a peer and a neighbor?

In external BGP-4, there is no difference between a neighbor and a peer. A peer is the BGP-4 term for a neighbor. Both terms refer to a router that is directly connected, with whom routing information is exchanged. In internal BGP-4 these routers are not necessarily physically adjacent, but they are the next logical hop router running the BGP-4.

25 Explain briefly the synchronization rule.

The synchronization rule states that the BGP-4 router cannot advertise a route to a neighbor unless the route that it is advertising is known by the interior routing protocol—that is, until both the interior routing protocol and BGP-4 have synchronized, no route will be advertised. The reason for this rule is that it could cause problems to advertise a route to another autonomous system if the advertised route was not in the routing table of every router within the advertising autonomous system. The result could be that a router from another autonomous system sends data to a remote network advertised by BGP-4, and although the data safely reaches the advertising autonomous system, an ignorant router within the autonomous system will drop the packet because it has no knowledge of the advertised network. This rule ensures that traffic can be directed to all destinations that are advertised outside the autonomous system.

26 In BGP-4, describe the purpose of the **network** command.

The network command permits BGP-4 to advertise a network if it is present in the routing table. It is not responsible for starting the BGP-4 process on an interface; instead, it identifies which networks the router originates.

27 Explain the command **neighbor** {ip-address | peer-group-name} **next-hop-self.**

On a broadcast multiaccess network such as Ethernet, the next-hop address will be the IP address of the advertising router. This command forces BGP-4 to advertise itself as the next-hop router instead of letting the protocol determine the address to be used. This avoids problems seen on NBMA networks or nonmeshed environments, such as X.25 and Frame Relay.

28 Which command is used to show all BGP-4 connections?

The command show ip bgp summary shows BGP-4 connections.

Chapter 9

Chapter 9 "Do I Know This Already?" Quiz Answers

1 Why does IBGP-4 need to be fully meshed?

IBGP-4 needs to be fully meshed because IBGP-4 has a fundamental rule that states that IBGP-4 will not propagate back into IBGP-4 a route that it has learned from IBGP-4. The reasoning is that this is the only way to prevent routing loops. If each router is connected to every other router (fully meshed), the updates come directly from the source, which removes the need for a router to propagate any updates that it has received.

2 How is a fully meshed network avoided in IBGP-4?

A fully meshed network can cause some problems to the routers because they have a great deal of information to deal with from every directly connected router. To avoid this intensity of bandwidth, CPU, and memory, an alternative is the configuration of route reflectors. Route reflectors allow the router to pass routes onto its peers.

3 What is the formula to determine the number of sessions needed in a fully meshed BGP-4 network?

The equation for determining the number of sessions required is $n\ (n-1)\ /\ 2$, where n is the number of routers. Thus, 10 routers would mean $10\ (10-1)\ /\ 2 = 10 \times 9\ /\ 2 = 45$ sessions.

4 Why does a fully meshed network in IBGP-4 cause problems?

A fully meshed network in IBGP-4 causes problems because the network has to accommodate a large number of TCP connections, and this can eat up memory, CPU, and eventually bandwidth.

5 State two benefits to using route reflectors.

Route reflectors have many benefits:

— **The use of a router reflector means that fewer TCP peer connections are needed. This streamlines the network traffic and solves the excessive use of network resources sometimes incurred with a fully meshed network.**

— **The design and configuration are very straightforward, which means that it is easy to implement and thus to migrate an existing network, particularly because path attributes are not affected by them.**

— Despite the fact that the route reflectors are straightforward, the flexibility in the design means that it is possible to become very sophisticated, using redundant route reflectors and even multiple levels of route reflectors. Complex solutions are possible using router reflectors.

6 Can the next-hop-self option be used between EBGP-4 peers?

No, the next-hop-self option is used only with IBGP-4. It is used on a broadcast multiaccess link and ensures that the appropriate source address for the update is provided in the message header. In EBGP-4, this is not relevant because the next hop is always that of the EBGP-4 neighbor.

7 Explain the difference between a cluster-ID and an originator-ID.

The cluster-ID is an optional, nontransitive BGP-4 attribute (type code 10). A cluster is the route reflector and its clients. If a cluster has more than one route reflector, it needs to be identified by a cluster-id. This is listed in the update; if a router receives an update with its own cluster-ID, it will be ignored, thus preventing routing loops. An originator-ID is the ID given to a route reflector when there is only one route reflector in the cluster. It serves the same purpose as the cluster-ID in that it prevents routing loops because a router that receives an update that contains its own originator-id will ignore the update. Therefore, the difference between the two is one of scale. The originator-ID is used for one route reflector in a cluster, whereas the cluster-ID is used when there are multiple route reflectors in the cluster.

8 State two advantages in using prefix lists over access lists.

The advantages of using prefix lists are the same as those of access lists. The advantages of using prefix lists instead of access lists include the following;

— **They have better performance than access lists.**

— **They allow editing of the lists so that additional lines of code can be inserted anywhere in the list.**

— **The user interface is easier to use.**

— **They are more flexible.**

9 If the ISP has provided a default route, how will the router within the autonomous system select the exit path in a multihomed environment?

The IGP within the autonomous system will use the metric associated with that routing protocol. The router running EIGRP, for example, will select the nearest router based on the composite metric of bandwidth and delay (by default).

10 What is a disadvantage of an autonomous system receiving full routing updates from all providers?

The disadvantage is that a great deal of network resources, such as memory and CPU, is required.

11 What is the danger of redistributing BGP-4 into the IGP?

The danger is that the autonomous system routers receiving the BGP-4 updates will be overwhelmed by the amount of routing information that they receive. This could result in an unstable network or even a network exhausted unto death.

12 What are the advantages of a fully meshed IBGP-4 network?

The advantage of a fully meshed network is that the network will receive full routing information from the directly connected peers. This means that the IGP does not need to carry routing information to the BGP-4 peers, and this means that no redistribution is necessary. This does not run the risk of overloading the IGP. It also means that the network will converge more quickly and that synchronization can be turned off, which will also improve performance.

13 In configuring a route reflector, how is the client configured?

The client of a route reflector is configured at the same time as the route reflector. The command issued on the router that is to become the route reflector identifies the router that is to become the client. The following command is the syntax issued at the router reflector:

neighbor *ip address* route-reflector-client

14 What command is used to display the route reflector clients?

The command show ip bgp neighbor is used.

15 What commands are used to display the BGP-4 router ID that identifies the router that is sending the updates and peering with its neighbor?

The commands that display the BGP-4 router ID are show ip bgp neighbor or show ip bgp ip address.

16 Which command is used to display the AS path?

The command used to display the AS path is show ip bgp.

Chapter 9 "Q&A" Answers

1 If a route reflector hears an update from a nonclient, what action will be taken?

If a route reflector hears an update from a nonclient, it will reflect the update to clients only.

2 In version 11.0 of the Cisco IOS, what method would be used to restrict routing information from being received or propagated?

Distribute lists would be used to restrict BGP-4 routing updates in version 11.0 of the Cisco IOS. Prefix lists became available to ISPs in 11.2 of the IOS and in 12.0 to the general public.

3 Explain the purpose and use of the command **show ip prefix-list name** [**seq** seq-number].

This command displays the entry prefix list with a given sequence number.

4 How and why would you redistribute static routes into BGP-4?

Static routes would be redistributed into BGP-4 with these commands:

```
router bgp 100
redistribute static
ip route 201.33.0.0 255.255.0.0 null 0
```

The static routes are forwarded to the nonexistent interface null 0 to aggregate the routes to create a supernet. This is then redistributed to the BGP process instead of the hundreds of routes that exist. Because any route redistributed into BGP-4 must be in the IP routing table, this is a way of creating a supernet and having it redistributed.

A static route to null 0 is not needed if the network command is used and no address aggregation is performed.

5 Give the command that would change the weight attribute for the path to the next hop 192.16.5.3.

The command to change the weight attribute for the path to the next hop to be 48 is as follows:

```
neighbor 192.16.5.3 weight 48
```

6 Why do route reflectors have to be fully meshed with IBGP-4?

Although clients are not fully meshed within a cluster, it is important that the route reflectors are fully meshed. This is to ensure that the routers pass routing information to each other. Remember that IBGP-4 does not propagate routing information; it generates information only based on the network command.

7 Why is filtering often required when redistributing BGP-4 into an IGP?

Filtering is often required when redistributing BGP-4 into an IGP because the routing tables can become overwhelmed by the number of routes that are imported.

8 What are the advantages of multihoming?

Multihoming allows for redundancy, which is important when the link is into the Internet and may well carry crucial business information for the company. Multihoming also increases performance by allowing the selection of the better paths.

9 What are the two most common forms of multihoming?

The most common forms of multihoming include these:

- **The ISPs send default routes into the autonomous system.**
- **The default routes and some selected routes are sent by the ISP into the autonomous system.**
- **All routes known by the ISP are sent into the autonomous system.**

10 Which command will show the local preference and weight attribute values?

The command that shows the local preference and weight attribute values is show ip bgp.

11 Why does IBGP-4 need to be fully meshed?

IBGP-4 needs to be fully meshed because IBGP-4 has a fundamental rule that states that IBGP-4 will not propagate back into IBGP-4 a route that it has learned from IBGP-4. The reasoning is that this is the only way to prevent routing loops. If each router is connected to every other router (fully meshed), the updates come directly from the source, which removes the need for a router to propagate any updates that it has received.

12 How is a fully meshed network avoided in IBGP-4?

A fully meshed network can cause some problems to the routers because they have a great deal of information to deal with from every directly connected router. To avoid this intensity of bandwidth, CPU, and memory, an alternative is the configuration of route reflectors. Route reflectors allow the router to pass routes on to its peers.

13 What is the formula to determine the number of sessions needed in a fully meshed BGP-4 network?

The equation for determining the number of sessions required is $n\,(n-1)\,/\,2$, where n is the number of routers. Thus, 10 routers would mean $10\,(10-1)\,/\,2 = 10 \times 9\,/\,2 = 45$ sessions.

14 Why does a fully meshed network in IBGP-4 cause problems?

A fully meshed network in IBGP-4 causes problems because the network has to accommodate a large number of TCP connections, and this can eat up memory, CPU, and eventually bandwidth.

15 State two benefits to using route reflectors.

Route reflectors have many benefits:

- **The use of a router reflector means that fewer TCP peer connections are needed. This streamlines the network traffic and solves the excessive use of network resources sometimes incurred with a fully meshed network.**

— The design and configuration are very straightforward, which means that it is easy to implement and thus to migrate an existing network, particularly because path attributes are not affected by them.

— Despite the fact that the route reflectors are straightforward, the flexibility in the design means that it is possible to become very sophisticated using redundant route reflectors and even multiple levels of route reflectors. Complex solutions are possible using router reflectors.

16 Can the next-hop-self option be used between EBGP-4 peers?

No, the next-hop-self option is used only with IBGP-4. It is used on a broadcast multiaccess link and ensures that the appropriate source address for the update is provided in the message header. In EBGP-4, this is not relevant because the next hop is always that of the EBGP-4 neighbor.

17 Explain the difference between a cluster-ID and an originator-ID.

The cluster-ID is an optional, nontransitive BGP-4 attribute (type code 10). A cluster is the route reflector and its clients. If a cluster has more than one route reflector, it needs to be identified by a cluster-id. This is listed in the update; if a router receives an update with its own cluster-ID, it will be ignored, thus preventing routing loops. An originator-ID is the ID given to a route reflector when there is only one route reflector in the cluster. It serves the same purpose as the cluster-ID in that it prevents routing loops because a router that receives an update that contains its own originator-id will ignore the update. Therefore, the difference between the two is one of scale. The originator-ID is used for one route reflector in a cluster, whereas the cluster-ID is used when there are multiple route reflectors in the cluster.

18 State two advantages in using prefix lists over access lists.

The advantages of using prefix lists are the same as those of access lists. The advantages of using prefix lists instead of access lists include the following;

— **They have a better performance than access lists.**

— **They allow editing of the lists so that additional lines of code can be inserted anywhere in the list.**

— **The user interface is easier to use.**

— **They are more flexible.**

19 If the ISP has provided a default route, how will the router within the autonomous system select the exit path in a multihomed environment?

The IGP within the autonomous system will use the metric associated with that routing protocol. The router running EIGRP, for example, will select the nearest router based on the composite metric of bandwidth and delay (by default).

20 What is a disadvantage of an autonomous system receiving full routing updates from all providers?

The disadvantage is that a great deal of network resources, such as memory and CPU, is required.

21 What is the danger of redistributing BGP-4 into the IGP?

The danger is that the autonomous system routers receiving the BGP-4 updates will be overwhelmed by the amount of routing information that they receive. This could result in an unstable network or even a network exhausted unto death.

22 What are the advantages of a fully meshed IBGP-4 network?

The advantage of a fully meshed network is that the network will receive full routing information from the directly connected peers. This means that the IGP does not need to carry routing information to the BGP-4 peers, and this means that no redistribution is necessary. This does not run the risk of overloading the IGP. It also means that the network will converge more quickly and that synchronization can be turned off, which will also improve performance.

23 In configuring a route reflector, how is the client configured?

The client of a route reflector is configured at the same time as the route reflector. The command issued on the router that is to become the route reflector identifies the router that is to become the client. The following command is the syntax issued at the router reflector:

neighbor *ip address* route-reflector-client

24 What command is used to display the route reflector clients?

The show ip bgp neighbor command is used for this.

25 What commands are used to display the BGP-4 router ID that identifies the router that is sending the updates and peering with its neighbor?

The commands that display the BGP-4 router ID are show ip bgp neighbor or show ip bgp ip address.

26 Which command is used to display the AS path?

The command used to display the AS path is show ip bgp.

Chapter 10

Chapter 10 "Do I Know This Already?" Quiz Answers

1 Give two reasons for using multiple routing protocols.

The main reasons for multiple protocols existing within an organization are as follows:

— **The organization is transitioning from one routing protocol to another because the network has grown and there is a need for a more sophisticated protocol that will scale.**

— **Although a vendor solution is preferred, there is a mix of different vendors within the network, so the vendor solution is used in the areas available. This is particularly true in client/server networks.**

— **Historically, the organization was a series of small network domains that have recently been tied together to form one large enterprise network. The company may well have plans to transition to a single routing protocol in the future.**

— **Often after a merger or a takeover, when several companies become one, it takes planning, strategy, and careful analysis to determine the best overall design for the network.**

— **Politically, there are ideological differences among the different network administrators, which until now have not been resolved.**

— **In a very large environment, the various domains may have different requirements, making a single solution inefficient. A clear example is in the case of a large multinational corporation, where EIGRP is the protocol used at the access and distribution layer, but BGP is the protocol connecting the core.**

2 How many IP routing tables are there?

There is one IP routing table, and all the routes from all the different routing protocol are held in the one table. If a route has multiple paths from multiple protocols, one path will be selected based on the administrative distance.

3 When implementing redistribution, state one possible problem that you might experience, and explain why it is a problem.

The problems experienced as a result of multiple routing processes and their redistribution include the following:

— **The wrong or less efficient routing decision being made, referred to as the** *suboptimal path.*

— A routing loop occurring, where the data traffic is sent in a circle without ever arriving at the destination.

— The convergence time of the network increasing because of the different technologies involved. If the routing protocols converge at different rates, this may also cause problems. In some cases, this may result in timeouts and the temporary loss of networks.

4 Which has a lower administrative distance, IGRP or OSPF?

IGRP has an administrative distance of 100, while OSPF has an administrative distance of 110. The IGRP path will be entered into the routing table if there are paths offered to the same destination from both protocols.

5 What command is used to configure an outbound route filter?

The command for configuring a route filter is as follows:

```
distribute list {access-list-number | name} out
[interface-name | routing process | autonomous-system number]
```

6 What is a passive interface?

A passive interface is an interface that will listen to routing updates but that will not propagate any updates for the protocol configured. It is used to prevent unnecessary traffic from being sent out of an interface. Usually a passive interface is configured when there are no routers to hear the updates on that network.

7 What is the purpose of administrative distance?

When the routing table is populated with networks that are provided by multiple routing protocols, the administrative distance is used to choose the best path to the remote network.

8 What is the concern of redistributing into a redundant network?

The concern with redistributing into a redundant network is that it is possible to select suboptimal routes. That is, if two routing protocols both have a path to the same destination, the path for the routing table will be selected based on administrative distance. This is a blanket solution that does not always render the best decision.

9 What is a default network?

A default network is a route used when there is no entry for the remote network in the routing table. It is used to connect to the Internet and other routing domains when it is not practical to know all the available networks. It is sufficient to have an exit point from your network identified.

10 Why is it necessary to configure a default metric when redistributing between routing protocols?

The metric is used within a routing protocol to select the best path to a remote network when there are multiple paths. When redistributing, it is not always possible to port the metric across because the metric is protocol-specific. The default metric throws the original metric away and substitutes a new metric for the new routing protocol.

11 Which command is used to modify the administrative distance of a route?

The command to configure the administrative distance of a route is as follows:

```
distance weight [address mask [access-list-number | name]] [ip]
```

A different command is used for EIGRP and BGP-4. The EIGRP command to change the administrative distance is as follows:

```
distance eigrp internal-distance external-distance
```

12 What is the difference in processing for an inbound and an outbound route filter?

If a filter is applied to an incoming interface, the routing table is not checked unless the route is permitted. However, the router has to examine every incoming packet, which is expensive in resources. The outbound filter must go through the routing decision process the first time, after which the result is cached.

Inbound filters are wider-ranging because they prevent routes from entering the router instead of filtering on each outgoing interface that is affected.

13 State two benefits of using policy-based routing.

The benefits of policy-based routing include the following:

— **Organizations can determine traffic flow based on the origin of the traffic. They can send traffic owned by different groups across different paths.**

— **Quality of service (QoS) can be set in the IP header using the precedence or TOS bits. This allows certain traffic to be prioritized through the network.**

— **High-cost links can be raised on more specific criteria, which allows an efficient use of the resources available.**

— **Traffic can be sent across multiple paths based on traffic characteristics.**

14 How are matching routes modified in a route map?

Using the set commands modifies matching routes. If the criteria is met in the match command and the action was to permit, then the set criteria is initiated to control the routing as specified.

15 Explain the command **set ip default-next-hop** [ip-address...ip-address].

This command provides a list of IP addresses if there is no explicit route in the routing table for a destination. These addresses are those of next-hop routers or of the interfaces of adjacent routers. If multiple next-hop addresses are listed, then the first address is tried and the others are tried in turn.

16 Which command displays route maps that are configured on interfaces?

The command show ip policy displays the route maps used for policy routing on the router's interfaces. The command show route-map [*map-name*] displays the route maps.

Chapter 10 "Q&A" Answers

1 State two of the methods that Cisco recommends for controlling routing traffic.

The methods that Cisco discusses as useful methods of controlling routing updates are as follows:

— **Passive interfaces: Prevent network communication and thus an adjacency from being formed with neighboring routers.**

— **Changing the administrative distance on the route: Changes the natural order as laid down by Cisco on which routing protocol is more plausible than the others. A scale of weighting is applied to the protocols.**

— **Default routes: Instruct the interface on where to send the destination traffic if the routing table had no entry for that destination.**

— **Static routes: Offers the ability to manually configure the path to a destination network.**

— **Route update filtering: Offers the use of access lists to configure.**

2 What is the administrative distance for RIP?

The administrative distance for RIP is 120; it has the highest distance of interior routing protocols and is therefore the least likely to be selected.

3 State two instances when you do not want routing information propagated.

The two occasions that you do not want routing information to be propagated are as follows:

— **If there is a WAN link where the cost of the link is based on network traffic. This may also have the added disincentive of being a WAN link that is a dial-on-demand link, which is raised and maintained by the presence of traffic attempting to flow across the interface.**

— The other situation in which you should prevent routing updates from being propagated is when you are trying to prevent routing loops. If the routing domain has redundant paths that will be learned by different routing protocol, it is advisable to filter the propagation of one of the paths.

4 In what instances will Enhanced IGRP automatically redistribute?

Enhanced IGRP will automatically redistribute between itself and IGRP as long as both processes are running the same autonomous system number.

Enhanced IGRP also automatically redistributes between the LAN protocol and Enhanced IGRP. EIGRP for IPX automatically redistributes; IPX for RIP/SAP and Enhanced IGRP for AppleTalk similarly redistribute automatically into RTMP.

5 Which command is used to view the administrative distance on a route?

The command show ip route displays the administrative distance for each route; the number is in brackets, coupled with the metric for the route.

6 When is redistribution required?

Redistribution is required when there is more than one routing protocol for IP running within the organization and when every part of the network needs connectivity to all the networks.

7 Why does Cisco recommend that you not overlap routing protocols?

The reason not to overlap routing protocols is that it will increase network traffic, router CPU processing, and memory because of the additional protocol updates. This additional traffic and CPU and memory requirements complicate the routing process. Now, the decision is not simply between multiple paths, but also between the various routing protocols that are advertising them.

8 Why would you want to prevent routing updates across an on-demand WAN link?

A WAN link that is a dial-on-demand link is raised and maintained by the presence of traffic attempting to flow across the interface. Thus, every time a RIP update was sent, the path would be raised—or, more likely, kept up all the time.

9 What is the metric used for in a routing protocol?

The metric is used to select the best path when multiple paths are available to a remote network.

10 Explain the command **match** ip-address {access-list-number | name} [access-list number | name].

The command is used to match criteria in establishing the policy-based routing. Access lists are used to specify the addressing of the packets to be affected.

11 Explain the command **ip-route-cache policy.**

This command is set on an incoming interface and enables the fast switching of policy routing. Before version 11.2 of the Cisco IOS, policy routing was process-switched. This caused some applications to time out, but the problem has now been resolved. Fast switching of policy routing is disabled by default. Therefore, it is necessary to manually configure it.

12 Give two reasons for using multiple routing protocols.

The main reasons for multiple protocols existing within an organization are as follows:

— **The organization is transitioning from one routing protocol to another because the network has grown and there is a need for a more sophisticated protocol that will scale.**

— **Although a vendor solution is preferred, there is a mix of different vendors within the network, so the vendor solution is used in the areas available. This is particularly true in client/server networks.**

— **Historically, the organization was a series of small network domains that have recently been tied together to form one large enterprise network. The company may well have plans to transition to a single routing protocol in the future.**

— **Often after a merger or a takeover, when several companies become one, it takes planning, strategy, and careful analysis to determine the best overall design for the network.**

— **Politically, there are ideological differences among the different network administrators, which until now have not been resolved.**

— **In a very large environment, the various domains may have different requirements, making a single solution inefficient. A clear example is in the case of a large multinational corporation, where EIGRP is the protocol used at the access and distribution layer, but BGP is the protocol connecting the core.**

13 How many IP routing tables are there?

There is one IP routing table, and all the routes from all the different routing protocol are held in the one table. If a route has multiple paths from multiple protocols, one path will be selected based on the administrative distance.

14 When implementing redistribution, state one possible problem that you might experience, and explain why it is a problem.

The problems experienced as a result of multiple routing processes and their redistribution include the following:

— **The wrong or a less efficient routing decision being made, referred to as the** *suboptimal path.*

— **A routing loop occurring, in which the data traffic is sent in a circle without ever arriving at the destination.**

— **The convergence time of the network increasing because of the different technologies involved. If the routing protocols converge at different rates, this may also cause problems. In some cases, this may result in timeouts and the temporary loss of networks.**

15 Which has a lower administrative distance, IGRP or OSPF?

IGRP has an administrative distance of 100, while OSPF has an administrative distance of 110. The IGRP path will be entered into the routing table if there are paths offered to the same destination from both protocols.

16 What command is used to configure an outbound route filter?

The command for configuring a route filter is as follows:

```
distribute list {access-list-number | name} out
[interface-name | routing process | autonomous-system number]
```

17 What is a passive interface?

A passive interface is an interface that will listen to routing updates but that will not propagate any updates for the protocol configured. It is used to prevent unnecessary traffic from being sent out of an interface. Usually a passive interface is configured when there are no routers to hear the updates on that network.

18 What is the purpose of administrative distance?

When the routing table is populated with networks that are provided by multiple routing protocols, the administrative distance is used to choose the best path to the remote network.

19 What is the concern of redistributing into a redundant network?

The concern with redistributing into a redundant network is that it is possible to select suboptimal routes. That is, if two routing protocols both have a path to the same destination, the path for the routing table will be selected based on administrative distance. This is a blanket solution that does not always render the best decision.

20 What is a default network?

A default network is a route used when there is no entry for the remote network in the routing table. It is used to connect to the Internet and other routing domains when it is not practical to know all the available networks. It is sufficient to have an exit point from your network identified.

21 Why is it necessary to configure a default metric when redistributing between routing protocols?

The metric is used within a routing protocol to select the best path to a remote network when there are multiple paths. When redistributing, it is not always possible to port the metric across because the metric is protocol-specific. The default metric throws the original metric away and substitutes a new metric for the new routing protocol.

22 Which command is used to modify the administrative distance of a route?

The command to configure the administrative distance of a route is as follows:

```
distance weight [address mask [access-list-number | name]] [ip]
```

A different command is used for EIGRP and BGP-4. The EIGRP command to change the administrative distance is as follows:

```
distance eigrp internal-distance external-distance
```

23 What is the difference in processing for an inbound and an outbound route filter?

If a filter is applied to an incoming interface, the routing table is not checked unless the route is permitted. However, the router has to examine every incoming packet, which is expensive in resources. The outbound filter must go through the routing decision process the first time, after which the result is cached.

Inbound filters are wider-ranging because they prevent routes from entering the router instead of filtering on each outgoing interface that is affected.

24 State two benefits of using policy-based routing.

The benefits of policy-based routing include the following:

— **Organizations can determine traffic flow based on the origin of the traffic. They can send traffic owned by different groups across different paths.**

— **Quality of service (QoS) can be set in the IP header using the precedence or TOS bits. This allows certain traffic to be prioritized through the network.**

— **High-cost links can be raised on more specific criteria, which allows an efficient use of the resources available.**

— **Traffic can be send across multiple paths based on traffic characteristics.**

25 How are matching routes modified in a route map?

Using the set commands modifies matching routes. If the criteria is met in the match command and the action was to permit, then the set criteria is initiated to control the routing as specified.

26 Explain the command **set ip default-next-hop** [ip-address...ip-address].

This command provides a list of IP addresses if there is no explicit route in the routing table for a destination. These addresses are those of next-hop routers or of the interfaces of adjacent routers. If multiple next-hop addresses are listed, then the first address is tried and the others are tried in turn.

27 Which command displays route maps that are configured on interfaces?

The command show ip policy displays the route maps used for policy routing on the router's interfaces. The command show route-map [*map-name*] displays the route maps.

Sample Configurations

This appendix contains two live configurations taken from companies that are currently using them in their networks. (The names and addresses have been changed.) The comment sections of the configurations clarify major topics covered in this book and appear with a gray background.

This appendix is included because it can be very helpful to see the configuration of a particular topic in context, to see the wider picture that an entire configuration provides, and to dissect a real configuration that is up and running in a very large company.

Configuration 1—OSPF and Dialup Links

Figure B-1 illustrates the wider network topology of the organization.

Figure B-1 *Configuration Map of the Organization in Example B-1*

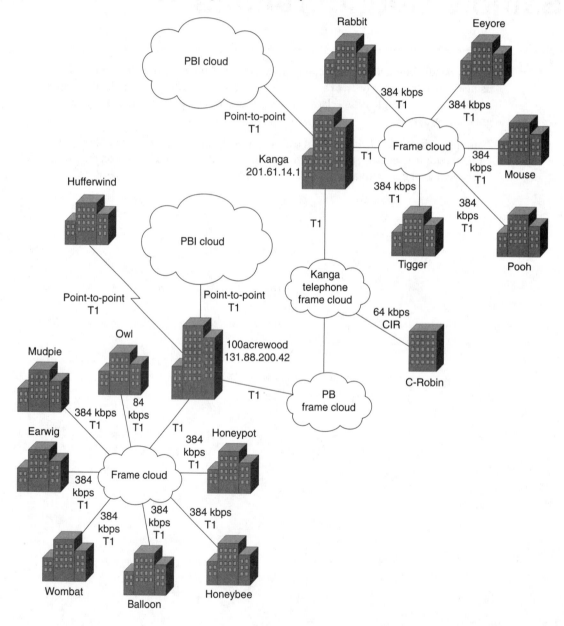

Example B-1 *OSPF and Dialup Links*

```
Tigger#show running
Building configuration...
Current configuration:
!
version 11.2
service timestamps debug datetime msec
service password-encryption
service udp-small-servers
service tcp-small-servers
!
hostname Tigger
!
aaa new-model
aaa authentication login default tacacs+ none
aaa authentication login no_tacacs enable
aaa authentication ppp default tacacs+ local
aaa authorization exec if-authenticated tacacs+ none
aaa authorization network if-authenticated tacacs+ none
aaa accounting exec start-stop tacacs+
aaa accounting commands 15 start-stop tacacs+
aaa accounting network start-stop tacacs+
enable secret 5 VerySecretIndeed
enable password 7 Reallyverysecret
!
username Tigger password 7 Hiddenfromview
username Piglet password 7 Nottoknow
username Roo password 7 Nevertosee
ip tacacs source-interface Ethernet0
ip host Kanga 201.61.14.1
ip name-server 201.61.0.10
!
interface Ethernet0
 description Tigger Administrative Subnet
 ip address 201.61.12.1 255.255.255.0
!
interface Ethernet1
 description Tigger Finance Segment
 ip address 201.61.13.1 255.255.255.0
!
interface Serial0
 description WAN frame-relay / Circuit ID: 16453
 no ip address
 encapsulation frame-relay IETF
 bandwidth 128
 frame-relay lmi-type ansi
!
interface Serial0.1 point-to-point
 description Home to 100acrewood DLCI 16
 ip address 131.88.200.42 255.255.255.252
```

continues

Example B-1 *OSPF and Dialup Links (Continued)*

```
 bandwidth 384
 shutdown
 frame-relay interface-dlci 16
!
interface Serial0.2 point-to-point
 description FRAME TO Kanga dlci 20
 ip address 131.88.240.17 255.255.255.252
 bandwidth 1544
 frame-relay interface-dlci 20
!
interface Serial1
 description ISDN redundant route
ip unnumbered Ethernet0
 encapsulation ppp
 ip ospf network point-to-multipoint
```
The configuration is stating that it is a NMBA cloud that needs to propagate updates
```
ip ospf cost 20000
```
The cost of the link is so high as to render it unusable unless there is no alternative. Similar to a floating static route
```
bandwidth 128
 dialer in-band
 dialer map ip 201.61.0.2 name Roo broadcast 14152274113
 dialer-group 1
 no fair-queue
 no cdp enable
 ppp authentication chap
 pulse-time 1
!
router ospf 1
network 0.0.0.0 255.255.255.255 area 0
```
This router is a backbone router as all interfaces are in area 0
```
!
ip classless
ip default-network 0.0.0.0
```
The default route is defined
```
ip route 0.0.0.0 0.0.0.0 201.61.0.2 200
ip route 201.61.0.2 255.255.255.255 Serial1 200
logging buffered 50000 debugging
no logging console
access-list 111 deny    ospf any any
access-list 111 permit ip any any
tacacs-server host 201.61.0.4
tacacs-server host 201.61.0.40
tacacs-server key 666
snmp-server community public RO
snmp-server community private RW
snmp-server location Tigger - Circuit #
snmp-server contact PC Coordinator/Director (222)555-1212
dialer-list 1 protocol ip list 111
```
Prevents OSPF updates from raising the line

Example B-1 *OSPF and Dialup Links (Continued)*

```
!
line con 0
 password 7 jollysecret
 login authentication no_tacacs
line aux 0
 exec-timeout 5 0
 password 7 dontlook
modem InOut
 transport input all
 flowcontrol hardware
line vty 0 4
 password 7 minetoknow
!
end
```

Figure B-2 illustrates the network topology of the router.

Figure B-2   *Example B-1 Network Topology of the Router*

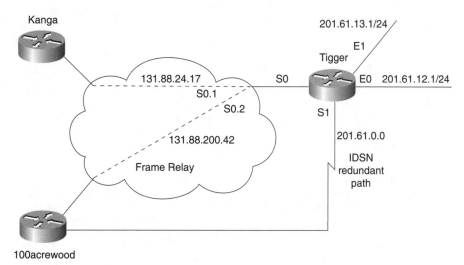

Commands Showing the Configuration 1 Working Network

Example B-2 *Commands Showing the Working Network*

```
TIGGER#show ip protocols
Routing Protocol is "ospf 1"
  Sending updates every 0 seconds
  Invalid after 0 seconds, hold down 0, flushed after 0
  Outgoing update filter list for all interfaces is not set
  Incoming update filter list for all interfaces is not set
  Redistributing: ospf 1
  Routing for Networks:
    0.0.0.0
  Routing Information Sources:
    Gateway          Distance      Last Update
    10.10.3.2           110        00:01:15
    201.61.25.1         110        00:01:15
    201.61.27.1         110        00:01:15
    201.61.29.1         110        00:01:15
    201.61.31.1         110        00:01:15
    201.61.17.1         110        00:01:16
    201.61.23.1         110        00:01:16
    201.61.9.1          110        00:01:16
    201.61.11.1         110        00:00:19
    201.61.0.1          110        00:01:16
    201.61.1.1          110        3w0d
    207.183.0.1         110        00:01:16
    201.61.3.1          110        00:01:16
    Gateway          Distance      Last Update
    201.61.5.1          110        00:01:18
    201.61.7.1          110        00:01:18
    201.61.200.1        110        00:01:18
    201.33.143.1        110        00:01:18
    201.61.1.129        110        00:01:18
  Distance: (default is 110)
TIGGER#show ip route
Codes: C - connected, S - static, I - IGRP, R - RIP, M - mobile, B - BGP
       D - EIGRP, EX - EIGRP external, O - OSPF, IA - OSPF inter area
       N1 - OSPF NSSA external type 1, N2 - OSPF NSSA external type 2
       E1 - OSPF external type 1, E2 - OSPF external type 2, E - EGP
       i - IS-IS, L1 - IS-IS level-1, L2 - IS-IS level-2, * - candidate default
       U - per-user static route, o - ODR
 Gateway of last resort is 131.88.240.18 to network 0.0.0.0
      144.144.0.0/24 is subnetted, 1 subnets
O        144.144.0.0 [110/399] via 131.88.240.18, 00:01:22, Serial0.2
      10.0.0.0/8 is variably subnetted, 5 subnets, 2 masks
O        10.10.3.0/24 [110/74] via 131.88.240.18, 00:01:22, Serial0.2
O        10.9.9.0/24 [110/139] via 131.88.240.18, 00:01:22, Serial0.2
O        10.1.1.0/24 [110/389] via 131.88.240.18, 00:01:22, Serial0.2
O E2     10.4.4.0/24 [110/10] via 131.88.240.18, 00:01:22, Serial0.2
O        10.4.4.1/32 [110/75] via 131.88.240.18, 00:01:22, Serial0.2
O     201.61.25.0/24 [110/142] via 131.88.240.18, 00:01:22, Serial0.2
      201.61.24.0/26 is subnetted, 1 subnets
```

Example B-2 *Commands Showing the Working Network (Continued)*

```
O         201.61.24.64 [110/142] via 131.88.240.18, 00:01:22, Serial0.2
O       201.61.27.0/24 [110/399] via 131.88.240.18, 00:01:22, Serial0.2
O       201.61.26.0/24 [110/399] via 131.88.240.18, 00:01:22, Serial0.2
O       201.61.29.0/24 [110/142] via 131.88.240.18, 00:01:22, Serial0.2
O       201.61.28.0/24 [110/142] via 131.88.240.18, 00:01:25, Serial0.2
O       201.61.31.0/24 [110/142] via 131.88.240.18, 00:01:25, Serial0.2
O       201.61.30.0/24 [110/142] via 131.88.240.18, 00:01:25, Serial0.2
O       201.61.17.0/24 [110/203] via 131.88.240.18, 00:01:25, Serial0.2
O       201.61.16.0/24 [110/203] via 131.88.240.18, 00:01:25, Serial0.2
O       201.61.23.0/24 [110/399] via 131.88.240.18, 00:01:25, Serial0.2
O       201.61.22.0/24 [110/399] via 131.88.240.18, 00:01:25, Serial0.2
O       201.61.9.0/24 [110/204] via 131.88.240.18, 00:01:25, Serial0.2
O       201.61.8.0/24 [110/204] via 131.88.240.18, 00:01:25, Serial0.2
          201.61.11.0/24 is variably subnetted, 5 subnets, 2 masks
O E2      201.61.11.40/32 [110/10] via 131.88.240.18, 00:00:03, Serial0.2
O E2      201.61.11.41/32 [110/10] via 131.88.240.18, 00:00:29, Serial0.2
O E2      201.61.11.44/32 [110/10] via 131.88.240.18, 00:01:25, Serial0.2
O E2      201.61.11.0/24 [110/10] via 131.88.240.18, 00:01:25, Serial0.2
O         201.61.11.1/32 [110/140] via 131.88.240.18, 00:01:25, Serial0.2
C       201.61.13.0/24 is directly connected, Ethernet1
C       201.61.12.0/24 is directly connected, Ethernet0
O       201.61.15.0/24 [110/74] via 131.88.240.18, 00:01:25, Serial0.2
O       201.61.14.0/24 [110/74] via 131.88.240.18, 00:01:25, Serial0.2
          201.61.1.0/26 is subnetted, 1 subnets
O         201.61.1.64 [110/142] via 131.88.240.18, 00:01:25, Serial0.2
O       207.183.0.0/24 [110/74] via 131.88.240.18, 00:01:25, Serial0.2
          201.61.0.0/24 is variably subnetted, 2 subnets, 2 masks
O         201.61.0.0/24 [110/139] via 131.88.240.18, 00:01:25, Serial0.2
S         201.61.0.2/32 is directly connected, Serial1
O       201.61.3.0/24 [110/399] via 131.88.240.18, 00:01:25, Serial0.2
O       201.61.2.0/24 [110/399] via 131.88.240.18, 00:01:25, Serial0.2
O       201.61.5.0/24 [110/920] via 131.88.240.18, 00:01:25, Serial0.2
O       201.61.4.0/24 [110/920] via 131.88.240.18, 00:01:25, Serial0.2
O       201.61.7.0/24 [110/399] via 131.88.240.18, 00:01:25, Serial0.2
O       201.61.6.0/24 [110/399] via 131.88.240.18, 00:01:25, Serial0.2
O       201.61.200.0/24 [110/139] via 131.88.240.18, 00:01:25, Serial0.2
          131.88.0.0/16 is variably subnetted, 16 subnets, 2 masks
O         131.88.200.0/24 [110/257] via 131.88.240.18, 00:01:26, Serial0.2
O         131.88.200.8/30 [110/389] via 131.88.240.18, 00:01:26, Serial0.2
O         131.88.200.16/30 [110/910] via 131.88.240.18, 00:01:26, Serial0.2
C         131.88.240.16/30 is directly connected, Serial0.2
O         131.88.240.20/30 [110/132] via 131.88.240.18, 00:01:26, Serial0.2
O         131.88.240.8/30 [110/132] via 131.88.240.18, 00:01:26, Serial0.2
O         131.88.240.12/30 [110/132] via 131.88.240.18, 00:01:26, Serial0.2
O         131.88.240.0/30 [110/129] via 131.88.240.18, 00:01:26, Serial0.2
O         131.88.200.56/30 [110/389] via 131.88.240.18, 00:01:26, Serial0.2
O         131.88.244.0/30 [110/454] via 131.88.240.18, 00:01:26, Serial0.2
O         131.88.244.0/24 [110/194] via 131.88.240.18, 00:01:26, Serial0.2
O         131.88.240.4/30 [110/132] via 131.88.240.18, 00:01:26, Serial0.2
O         131.88.200.72/30 [110/389] via 131.88.240.18, 00:01:26, Serial0.2
```

continues

Example B-2   *Commands Showing the Working Network (Continued)*

```
O        131.88.200.88/30 [110/389] via 131.88.240.18, 00:01:26, Serial0.2
O        131.88.200.108/30 [110/129] via 131.88.240.18, 00:01:26, Serial0.2
O        131.88.200.124/30 [110/193] via 131.88.240.18, 00:01:26, Serial0.2
O    201.33.143.0/24 [110/399] via 131.88.240.18, 00:01:26, Serial0.2
O*E2 0.0.0.0/0 [110/10] via 131.88.240.18, 00:01:26, Serial0.2
TIGGER#show access-list
Extended IP access list 111
    deny   ospf any any (161738 matches)
    permit ip any any (24923 matches)
```

Configuration 2—BGP-4 and Route Maps

Example B-3   *BGP-4 and Route Maps*

```
Faraday#show config
Using 3262 out of 30712 bytes
!
! Last configuration change at 11:15:41 EDT Fri May 5 2000
! NVRAM config last updated at 11:15:43 EDT Fri May 5 2000
!
version 11.2
no service finger
no service pad
service timestamps log datetime localtime
service password-encryption
no service udp-small-servers
no service tcp-small-servers
!
hostname FARADAY-gw
!
enable secret 5 $1$Pleasedontpeak.
enable password 7 thisisprivate
!
ip subnet-zero
ip domain-name Rufus.NET
ip name-server 218.12.211.11
ip name-server 190.121.50.2
clock timezone EST -5
clock summer-time EDT recurring
!
interface Ethernet0/0
 ip address 200.172.136.21 255.255.255.0
 ip broadcast-address 200.172.136.255
!
interface Serial0/0
 ip address 144.39.228.50 255.255.255.252
 ip access-group 101 in
 bandwidth 1536
 fair-queue 256 256 0
 hold-queue 1000 out
```

Example B-3 *BGP-4 and Route Maps (Continued)*

```
!
interface Ethernet0/1
 no ip address
 shutdown
!
interface Serial0/1
 description ### T1 Link to VERDI
 ip address 155.94.83.2 255.255.255.252
 ip access-group 101 in
 bandwidth 1536
 fair-queue 256 256 0
 hold-queue 1000 out
!
router rip
 redistribute connected
```
Redistributes connected interfaces into RIP
```
 passive-interface Serial0/0
```
Prevents RIP updates being sent out of S10/0
```
 passive-interface Ethernet0/1
```
Prevents RIP updates being sent out of E0/1
```
 passive-interface Serial0/1
```
Prevents RIP updates being sent out of S10/1
```
 network 200.172.136.0
 network 144.39.0.0
!Start the BGP-4 process and identify neighbors
router bgp 13462
 bgp dampening
 network 200.172.136.0
 neighbor 155.94.83.1 remote-as 2914
```
Identifies the router address and Autonomous System
```
neighbor 155.94.83.1 route-map limit-VERDI in
```
Prevents updates from entering the process
```
 neighbor 155.94.83.1 filter-list 1 out
```
Prevents the process from sending updates
```
 neighbor 144.39.228.49 remote-as 701
 neighbor 144.39.228.49 route-map limit-MEMENET in
 neighbor 144.39.228.49 filter-list 1 out
 no auto-summary
!
ip classless
ip route 0.0.0.0 0.0.0.0 144.39.228.49
```
Creates a default route
```
ip route 0.0.0.0 0.0.0.0 155.94.83.1
ip route 111.193.48.0 255.255.255.0 Null0
```
Sends traffic for this network to a black hole
```
ip route 140.98.0.0 255.255.0.0 200.172.136.5
```
Static route
```
ip route 218.215.175.0 255.255.255.0 Null0
ip route 218.215.176.0 255.255.255.0 Null0
ip route 218.215.249.0 255.255.255.0 Null0
ip route 220.99.235.0 255.255.255.0 155.94.83.1
```

continues

Example B-3 *BGP-4 and Route Maps (Continued)*

```
ip route 193.48.67.0 255.255.255.0 Null0
ip as-path access-list 1 permit ^$
Checks the attribute AS-Path
logging buffered 4096 debugging
no logging console
access-list 5 permit 166.6.0.0 0.0.255.255
access-list 5 permit 200.172.136.0 0.0.0.255
access-list 54 permit 0.0.0.0 63.255.255.255
access-list 54 permit 190.0.0.0 63.255.255.255
access-list 54 permit 218.0.0.0 15.255.255.255
access-list 55 permit 13.0.0.0 0.255.255.255
access-list 55 permit 111.0.0.0 63.255.255.255
access-list 55 permit 193.0.0.0 15.255.255.255
access-list 101 deny    ip 166.6.0.0 0.0.255.255 any
access-list 101 permit tcp any host 200.172.136.14 eq smtp
access-list 101 permit tcp any host 200.172.136.22 eq smtp
access-list 101 deny    tcp any host 200.172.136.14 eq 18000
access-list 101 deny    tcp any 200.172.136.0 0.0.0.255 eq smtp
access-list 101 deny    tcp any host 200.172.136.3 eq 1555
access-list 101 deny    tcp any host 200.172.136.10 eq 1555
access-list 101 deny    ip 200.172.136.0 0.0.0.255 any
access-list 101 permit ip any any
route-map limit-MEMENET permit 10
 match ip address 54
!
route-map limit-VERDI permit 10
 match ip address 55
!
!
line con 0
 exec-timeout 0 0
 password 7 **************
 login
 transport preferred none
line aux 0
 password 7 **********************
 login
 transport preferred none
line vty 0 4
 access-class 5 in
 password 7 ***********************
 login
 transport preferred none
!
end
FARADAY-gw#
```

Commands Showing the Configuration 2 Working Network

Figure B-3 illustrates the wider network topology of the organization.

Figure B-3 *Wider Network Topology of the Organization*

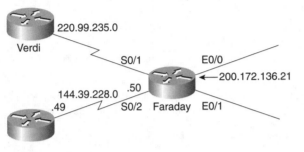

Example B-4 *Commands Showing the Working Network*

```
FARADAY-gw#show ip route summary
Route Source    Networks    Subnets     Overhead    Memory (bytes)
connected       1           3           168         752
static          7           1           504         1556
rip             0           0           0           0
bgp 13462       13468       1013        791000      2800992
  External: 14481 Internal: 0 Local: 0
internal        36                      .           5184

Total           13512       1017        791672      2808484
FARADAY-gw#show ip bgp neighbor
BGP neighbor is 155.19.83.1,  remote AS 2914, external link
  Index 1, Offset 0, Mask 0x2
    BGP version 4, remote router ID 129.250.116.16
    BGP state = Established, table version = 171471, up for 3d18h
    Last read 00:00:25, hold time is 180, keepalive interval is 60 seconds
    Minimum time between advertisement runs is 30 seconds
    Received 855482 messages, 0 notifications, 0 in queue
    Sent 8988 messages, 1 notifications, 0 in queue
    Inbound path policy configured
    Outbound path policy configured
    Outgoing update AS path filter list is 1
    Route map for incoming advertisements is limit-VERDI
    Connections established 29; dropped 28
    Last reset 3d18h, due to : User reset request
    No. of prefix received 12053
Connection state is ESTAB, I/O status: 1, unread input bytes: 0
Local host: 155.94.83.2, Local port: 11081
Foreign host: 155.94.83.1, Foreign port: 179

Enqueued packets for retransmit: 0, input: 0  mis-ordered: 0 (0 bytes)
```

continues

Example B-4   *Commands Showing the Working Network (Continued)*

```
Event Timers (current time is 0xEF5F2918):
Timer          Starts    Wakeups         Next
Retrans          5501        52          0x0
TimeWait            0         0          0x0
AckHold         25556     18990          0x0
SendWnd             0         0          0x0
KeepAlive           0         0          0x0
GiveUp              0         0          0x0
PmtuAger            0         0          0x0
DeadWait            0         0          0x0

iss: 2045856199  snduna: 2045959755  sndnxt: 2045959755    sndwnd:  15244
irs: 3226467718  rcvnxt: 3240164488  rcvwnd:       15773  delrcvwnd:   611

SRTT: 305 ms, RTTO: 697 ms, RTV: 43 ms, KRTT: 0 ms
minRTT: 4 ms, maxRTT: 964 ms, ACK hold: 300 ms
Flags: higher precedence, nagle

Datagrams (max data segment is 1460 bytes):
Rcvd: 34130 (out of order: 0), with data: 28736, total data bytes: 13696769
Sent: 33048 (retransmit: 52), with data: 5448, total data bytes: 103555

BGP neighbor is 144.39.228.49,  remote AS 701, external link
 Index 2, Offset 0, Mask 0x4
  BGP version 4, remote router ID 144.39.3.104
  BGP state = Established, table version = 171471, up for 3d19h
  Last read 00:00:09, hold time is 180, keepalive interval is 60 seconds
  Minimum time between advertisement runs is 30 seconds
  Received 89083 messages, 0 notifications, 0 in queue
  Sent 72512 messages, 0 notifications, 0 in queue
  Inbound path policy configured
  Outbound path policy configured
  Outgoing update AS path filter list is 1
  Route map for incoming advertisements is limit-MEMENET
  Connections established 15; dropped 14
  Last reset 3d19h, due to : User reset request
  No. of prefix received 1418
Connection state is ESTAB, I/O status: 1, unread input bytes: 0
Local host: 144.39.228.50, Local port: 179
Foreign host: 144.39.228.49, Foreign port: 12971

Enqueued packets for retransmit: 0, input: 0  mis-ordered: 0 (0 bytes)

Event Timers (current time is 0xEF5F31B4):
Timer          Starts    Wakeups         Next
Retrans          5478         6          0x0
TimeWait            0         0          0x0
AckHold          6486      3848          0x0
SendWnd             0         0          0x0
KeepAlive           0         0          0x0
GiveUp              0         0          0x0
PmtuAger            0         0          0x0
DeadWait            0         0          0x0
```

Example B-4 *Commands Showing the Working Network (Continued)*

```
iss:  661369547  snduna:  661473540  sndnxt:  661473540   sndwnd:   16270
irs:  514995089  rcvnxt:  515155949  rcvwnd:        15478 delrcvwnd:    906

SRTT: 317 ms, RTTO: 759 ms, RTV: 62 ms, KRTT: 0 ms
minRTT: 4 ms, maxRTT: 948 ms, ACK hold: 300 ms
Flags: passive open, nagle, gen tcbs

Datagrams (max data segment is 1460 bytes):
Rcvd: 10743 (out of order: 0), with data: 6490, total data bytes: 160859
Sent: 9437 (retransmit: 6), with data: 5471, total data bytes: 103992
FARADAY-gw#show ip bgp
BGP table version is 457017, local router ID is 199200.172.136.21
Status codes: s suppressed, d damped, h history, * valid, > best, i - internal
Origin codes: i - IGP, e - EGP, ? - incomplete

   Network          Next Hop         Metric LocPrf Weight Path
*> 97.2.0.0/16      144.39.228.49                       0 701 i
*> 17.4.126.0/24    144.39.228.49                       0 701 i
*> 17.96.91.0/24    144.39.228.49                       0 701 i
*> 33.48.2.0/23     144.39.228.49                       0 701 i
*> 33.48.7.0/2424   144.39.228.49                       0 701 i
*> 33.48.8.0/24     144.39.228.49                       0 701 i
*> 33.48.14.0/24    144.39.228.49                       0 701 i
*> 33.48.123.0/24   144.39.228.49                       0 701 i
*> 33.48.124.0/23   144.39.228.49                       0 701 i
*> 33.48.176.0/20   144.39.228.49                       0 701 i
*> 33.49.32.0/23    144.39.228.49                       0 701 i
*> 33.49.35.0/24    144.39.228.49                       0 701 i
*> 33.49.36.0/23    144.39.228.49                       0 701 i
*> 33.96.0.0/18     144.39.228.49                       0 701 i
*> 33.143.24.0/21   144.39.228.49                       0 701 i
*> 33.154.0.0/18    144.39.228.49                       0 701 i
*> 33.216.0.0/24    144.39.228.49                       0 701 i
*> 33.216.0.0/19    144.39.228.49                       0 701 i
   Network          Next Hop         Metric LocPrf Weight Path
*> 33.216.0.0/16    144.39.228.49                       0 701 i
*> 33.216.1.0/24    144.39.228.49                       0 701 i
*> 33.216.2.0/24    144.39.228.49                       0 701 i
*> 33.216.2.0/23    144.39.228.49                       0 701 i
*> 33.216.3.0/24    144.39.228.49                       0 701 i
*> 33.216.4.0/23    144.39.228.49                       0 701 i
*> 33.216.6.0/24    144.39.228.49                       0 701 i
*> 33.216.7.0/24    144.39.228.49                       0 701 i
*> 33.216.8.0/23    144.39.228.49                       0 701 i
*> 33.216.11.0/24   144.39.228.49                       0 701 i
*> 33.216.14.0/24   144.39.228.49                       0 701 i
*> 33.216.14.0/23   144.39.228.49                       0 701 i
*> 33.216.15.0/24   144.39.228.49                       0 701 i
*> 33.216.16.0/24   144.39.228.49                       0 701 i
*> 33.216.16.0/23   144.39.228.49                       0 701 i
*> 33.216.18.0/24   144.39.228.49                       0 701 i
*> 33.216.19.0/24   144.39.228.49                       0 701 i
```

continues

Example B-4 *Commands Showing the Working Network (Continued)*

```
*> 33.216.20.0/24     144.39.228.49                         0 701 i
*> 33.216.21.0/24     144.39.228.49                         0 701 i
*> 33.216.22.0/24     144.39.228.49                         0 701 i
*> 33.216.23.0/24     144.39.228.49                         0 701 i
*> 33.216.25.0/24     144.39.228.49                         0 701 i
*> 13.93.29.0/24      144.39.228.49                         0 701 i
*> 13.93.64.0/19      155.94.83.1        20                 0 2914 3356 15206 i
*> 13.93.96.0/20      155.94.83.1        20                 0 2914 701 15206 i
*> 13.93.212.0/22     144.39.228.49                         0 701 i
*> 13.93.243.0/24     144.39.228.49                         0 701 i
*> 13.94.92.0/23      155.94.83.1        20                 0 2914 14717 i
*> 13.94.94.0/23      155.94.83.1        20                 0 2914 14717 i
*> 13.95.10.0/24      144.39.228.49                         0 701 i
*> 13.95.128.0/19     155.94.83.1        20                 0 2914 701 13878 i
*> 13.95.173.0/24     155.94.83.1        20             0 2914 6993 6993 6993 6
993 6993 6993 14241 i
   Network             Next Hop          Metric LocPrf Weight Path
*> 13.95.174.0/23      155.94.83.1        20             0 2914 6993 6993 6993 6
993 6993 6993 14241 i

*> 13.96.0.0/13       144.39.228.49                         0 701 i
*> 13.96.95.0/24      144.39.228.49                         0 701 i
*> 13.96.96.0/20      155.94.83.1        20                 0 2914 3561 15245 i
*> 13.96.201.0/24     155.94.83.1        20                 0 2914 15265 i
*> 13.98.1.0/24       144.39.228.49                         0 701 i
*> 13.98.128.0/24     144.39.228.49                         0 701 i
*> 13.98.171.0/24     144.39.228.49                         0 701 i
*> 13.99.8.0/24       144.39.228.49                         0 701 i
*> 13.99.36.0/24      155.94.83.1        20             0 2914 12179 12179 1217
9 12179 12179 12179 12179 15280 i
*> 13.99.192.0/19     155.94.83.1        20             0 2914 701 11486 i

*> 13.99.192.0/18     155.94.83.1        20             0 2914 701 11486 i
*> 13.100.43.0/24     144.39.228.49                         0 701 i
*> 13.100.104.0/24    144.39.228.49                         0 701 i
*> 13.100.155.0/24    144.39.228.49                         0 701 i
*> 13.101.8.0/24      144.39.228.49                         0 701 i
*> 13.101.19.0/24     155.94.83.1        20                 0 2914 13615 i
*> 13.101.128.0/20    155.94.83.1        20                 0 2914 11908 12127 ?
*> 13.102.112.0/20    155.94.83.1        20                 0 2914 701 14434 i

*> 13.102.223.0/24    144.39.228.49                         0 701 i
*> 13.103.9.0/24      144.39.228.49                         0 701 i
*> 13.103.24.0/22     144.39.228.49                         0 701 i
   Network             Next Hop          Metric LocPrf Weight Path
*> 13.103.35.0/24     144.39.228.49                         0 701 i
*> 13.103.81.0/24     155.94.83.1        20                 0 2914 15265 i
*> 13.104.0.0/13      144.39.228.49                         0 701 i
*> 13.104.71.0/24     144.39.228.49                         0 701 i
*> 13.104.164.0/22    144.39.228.49                         0 701 i
*> 13.104.184.0/23    155.94.83.1        20                 0 2914 14796 i
```

Example B-4 *Commands Showing the Working Network (Continued)*

```
FARADAY-gw#show ip route summary
Route Source    Networks     Subnets     Overhead     Memory (bytes)
connected       1            2           168          564
static          7            5           728          2296
rip             0            0           0            0
bgp 13462       13608        1474        844592       2934888
  External: 15082 Internal: 0 Local: 0
internal        49                                    7056
Total           13665        1481        845488       2944804
FARADAY-gw#
FARADAY-gw#show ip bgp ?
  A.B.C.D          Network in the BGP routing table to display
  cidr-only        Display only routes with non-natural netmasks
  community        Display routes matching the communities
  community-list   Display routes matching the community-list
  dampened-paths   Display paths suppressed due to dampening
  filter-list      Display routes conforming to the filter-list
  flap-statistics  Display flap statistics of routes
  inconsistent-as  Display only routes with inconsistent origin ASs
  neighbors        Detailed information on TCP and BGP neighbor connections
  paths            Path information
  peer-group       Display information on peer-groups
  regexp           Display routes matching the AS path regular expression
  summary          Summary of BGP neighbor status
```

Glossary

This glossary assembles and defines the terms and acronyms used in this book and used in the internetworking industry. Many of the definitions have yet to be standardized, and many terms have several meanings. Multiple definitions and acronym expressions are included where they apply. These definitions can be found on CCO at www.cisco.com under the title "Internetworking Terms and Acronyms."

10BaseT. 10-Mbps baseband Ethernet specification using two pairs of twisted-pair cabling (Category 3, 4, or 5): one pair for transmitting data and the other for receiving data. 10BaseT, which is part of the IEEE 802.3 specification, has a distance limit of approximately 328 feet (100 meters) per segment.

802.x. Set of IEEE standards for the definition of LAN protocols.

A

AAA. Authentication, authorization, and accounting (pronounced "triple a").

ABR. Area Border Router. A router located on the border of one or more OSPF areas that connects those areas to the backbone network. ABRs are considered members of both the OSPF backbone and the attached areas. Therefore, they maintain routing tables describing both the backbone topology and the topology of the other areas.

access layer. Layer in a hierarchical network that provides workgroup/user access to the network.

access list. List kept by routers to control access to or from the router for a number of services (for example, to prevent packets with a certain IP address from leaving a particular interface on the router).

access method. Generally, the way in which network devices access the network medium.

access server. Communications processor that connects asynchronous devices to a LAN or WAN through network and terminal emulation software. Performs both synchronous and asynchronous routing of supported protocols. Sometimes called a *network access server (NAS).*

accounting management. One of five categories of network management defined by ISO for management of OSI networks. Accounting management subsystems are responsible for collecting network data relating to resource usage.

accuracy. The percentage of useful traffic that is correctly transmitted on the system, relative to total traffic, including transmission errors.

ACF. Advanced Communications Function. A group of SNA products that provides distributed processing and resource sharing.

ACK. 1. Acknowledgment bit in a TCP segment. 2. See *acknowledgment.*

acknowledgment. Notification sent from one network device to another to acknowledge that some event (for example, receipt of a message) occurred. Sometimes abbreviated *ACK.* Compare with *NAK.*

ACL. See *access list.*

ACS. Access control server. This is a centralized security server that includes individual access control through network access servers and firewalls. It can also simultaneously control management access to routers and switches.

CiscoSecure Access Control Server is one of Cisco's specialized security software soulutions for Authentication, Authorization, and Accounting (AAA). This range of servers provide TACACS+ or RADIUS-based AAA services, while leveraging Cisco IOS functionality for smooth interoperation.

active. Route state when a network change is seen but, on interrogation of the topology table, there is no FC. The router queries its neighbors for alternative routes.

address. A data structure or logical convention used to identify a unique entity, such as a particular process or network device.

address mapping. A technique that allows different protocols to interoperate by translating addresses from one format to another. For example, when routing IP over X.25, the IP addresses must be mapped to the X.25 addresses so that the IP packets can be transmitted by the X.25 network. See also *address resolution.*

algorithm   **769**

address resolution. Generally, a method for resolving differences between computer addressing schemes. Address resolution usually specifies a method for mapping network layer (Layer 3) addresses to data link layer (Layer 2) addresses.

adjacency. A relationship formed between selected neighboring routers and end nodes for the purpose of exchanging routing information. Adjacency is based on the use of a common media segment.

adjacent neighbors. A neighbor is a router that is directly connected to another router. Both neighbors must also have the same mask and hello parameters. An adjacent router is a router that has exchanged routing information with its neighbor.

administrative distance. A rating of the trustworthiness of a routing information source. The higher the value, the lower the trustworthiness rating. Used when multiple routing protocol are updating the IP routing table and another method than metric is required to select the best route.

ADSL. Asymmetric digital subscriber line. One of four DSL technologies. ADSL is designed to deliver more bandwidth downstream (from the central office to the customer site) than upstream. Downstream rates range from 1.5 to 9 Mbps, while upstream bandwidth ranges from 16 to 640 kbps. ADSL transmissions work at distances up to 18,000 feet (5,488 meters) over a single copper twisted-pair wire.

advertised distance (AD). The cost of the path to the remote network from the neighbor (the metric from the next-hop router).

agent. 1. Generally, software that processes queries and returns replies on behalf of an application. 2. In NMSs, a process that resides in all managed devices and reports the values of specified variables to management stations.

aggregated route. The consolidation of advertised addresses in a routing table. The use of summarizing routes reduces the number of routes in the routing table, the routing update traffic, and overall router overhead. Also called route summarization.

aggregation. See *route summarization.*

alarm. A message notifying an operator or administrator of a network problem.

algorithm. Well-defined rule or process for arriving at a solution to a problem. In networking, algorithms are commonly used to determine the best route for traffic from a particular source to a particular destination.

analog. An electrical circuit that is represented by means of continuous, variable physical quantities (such as voltages and frequencies), as opposed to discrete representations (such as the 0/1, off/on representation of digital circuits).

analog transmission. Signal transmission over wires or through the air in which information is conveyed through variation of some combination of signal amplitude, frequency, and phase.

ANSI. American National Standards Institute. Voluntary organization composed of corporate, government, and other members that coordinates standards-related activities, approves U.S. national standards, and develops positions for the United States in international standards organizations. ANSI helps develop international and U.S. standards relating to, among other things, communications and networking. ANSI is a member of the IEC and the ISO.

API. Application programming interface. A specification of function-call conventions that defines an interface to a service.

APPC. Advanced Program-to-Program Communications. IBM SNA system software that allows high-speed communication between programs on different computers in a distributed computing environment. APPC runs on LU 6.2 devices.

AppleTalk. A series of communications protocols designed by Apple Computer. Two phases currently exist. Phase 1, the earlier version, supports a single physical network that can have only one network number and can be in one zone. Phase 2, the more recent version, supports multiple logical networks on a single physical network and allows networks to be in more than one zone. See also *zone*.

application layer. Layer 7 of the OSI reference model. This layer provides services to application processes (such as electronic mail, file transfer, and terminal emulation) that are outside the OSI model. The application layer identifies and establishes the availability of intended communication partners (and the resources required to connect with them), synchronizes cooperating applications, and establishes agreement on procedures for error recovery and control of data integrity. It corresponds roughly with the transaction services layer in the SNA model.

ARAP. AppleTalk Remote Access Protocol. Protocol that provides Macintosh users direct access to information and resources at a remote AppleTalk site.

area. A logical set of network segments and their attached devices. Areas are usually connected to other areas via routers, making up a single autonomous system. See also *AS*. Used in DECnet, IS-IS, and OSPF.

ARP. Address Resolution Protocol. An Internet protocol used to map an IP address to a MAC address. It is defined in RFC 826.

ARPA. Advanced Research Projects Agency. Research and development organization that is part of the United States Department of Defense. ARPA is responsible for numerous technological advances in communications and networking. ARPA evolved into DARPA and then back into ARPA again (in 1994). It is responsible for Ethernet II and the frame structure.

ARPANET. Advanced Research Projects Agency Network. Landmark packet-switching network established in 1969. ARPANET was developed in the 1970s by BBN and was funded by ARPA (and later DARPA). It eventually evolved into the Internet. The term ARPANET was officially retired in 1990.

AS. Autonomous system. A collection of networks under a common administration sharing a common routing strategy. Autonomous systems may be subdivided into areas.

ASA. Adaptive security algorithm used in Cisco's PIX firewall.

ASBR. Autonomous System Boundary Router. An ABR located between an OSPF autonomous system and a non-OSPF network. ASBRs run both OSPF and another routing protocol, such as RIP. ASBRs must reside in a nonstub OSPF area.

ASCII. American Standard Code for Information Interchange. An 8-bit code for character representation (7 bits plus parity).

assigned numbers. RFC [STD2] documents the currently assigned values from several series of numbers used in network protocol implementations. This RFC is updated periodically, and current information can be obtained from IANA. If you are developing a protocol or application that will require the use of a link, socket, port, protocol, and so forth, contact IANA to receive a number assignment.

asynchronous transmission. Term describing digital signals that are transmitted without precise clocking. Such signals generally have different frequencies and phase relationships. Asynchronous transmissions usually encapsulate individual characters in control bits (called start and stop bits) that designate the beginning and end of each character.

ATM. Asynchronous Transfer Mode. An international standard for cell relay in which multiple service types (such as voice, video, or data) are conveyed in fixed-length (53-byte) cells. Fixed-length cells allow cell processing to occur in hardware, thereby reducing transit delays. ATM is designed to take advantage of high-speed transmission media, such as E3, SONET, and T3.

attribute. The metric used by BGP-4.

AUI. Attachment unit interface. IEEE 802.3 interface between an MAU and a NIC. The term AUI can also refer to the rear panel port to which an AUI cable might attach.

authentication. In security, the verification of the identity of a person or process.

autonomous switching. Feature on Cisco routers that provides faster packet processing by allowing the ciscoBus to switch packets independently without interrupting the system processor.

autonomous system. Term that defines the organizational boundary. Within the terminology of the routing protocols, it defines all the routers within an administrative domain, where each router has full knowledge of the subnets within the domain. This becomes confused with the introduction of summarization within an autonomous system. If you are connecting directly to the Internet using BGP, the autonomous system number must be unique and obtained from the Internet addressing committees.

average rate. Average rate, in kilobits per second (kbps), at which a given virtual circuit will transmit.

B

backbone. Part of a network that acts as the primary path for traffic that is most often sourced from and destined for other networks.

backward explicit congestion notification. See *BECN*.

bandwidth. Difference between the highest and lowest frequencies available for network signals. The term is also used to describe the rated throughput capacity of a given network medium or protocol.

bandwidth reservation. Process of assigning bandwidth to users and applications served by a network. It involves assigning priority to different flows of traffic based on how critical and delay-sensitive they are. This makes the best use of available bandwidth; if the network becomes congested, lower-priority traffic can be dropped. This sometimes is called bandwidth allocation.

Basic Rate Interface. See *BRI*.

baud. Unit of signaling speed equal to the number of discrete signal elements transmitted per second. Baud is synonymous with bits per second (bps) if each signal element represents exactly 1 bit.

Bc. Committed burst. Negotiated tariff metric in Frame Relay internetworks. The maximum amount of data (in bits) that a Frame Relay internetwork is committed to accept and transmit at the CIR.

B channel. Bearer channel. This is an ISDN communication channel that bears or carries voice, circuit, or packet conversations. The B channel is the fundamental component of ISDN interfaces. It carries 64,000 bps in either direction. See also *bearer channel*.

BDR. Backup designated router. Used in OSPF as a backup to the designated router.

Be. Excess burst. Negotiated tariff metric in Frame Relay internetworks. This is the number of bits that a Frame Relay internetwork will attempt to transmit after Bc is accommodated. Be data, in general, is delivered with a lower probability than Bc data because Be data can be marked as DE by the network. See also *Bc* and *De*.

Bearer channel. See *B channel*.

BECN. Backward explicit congestion notification. A bit set by a Frame Relay network in frames traveling in the opposite direction of frames encountering a congested path. DTE receiving frames with the BECN bit set can request that higher-level protocols take flow control action as appropriate. Compare with *FECN*.

Bellman-Ford routing algorithm. See *distance vector routing protocol*.

best-effort delivery. Delivery in a network system that does not use a sophisticated acknowledgment system to guarantee reliable delivery of information.

BGP. Border Gateway Protocol. An interdomain routing protocol that replaces EGP. BGP exchanges reachability information with other BGP systems. It is defined in RFC 1163. See also *BGP-4* and *EGP*.

BGP-4. BGP version 4. This is version 4 of the predominant interdomain routing protocol used on the Internet. BGP-4 supports CIDR and uses route aggregation mechanisms to reduce the size of routing tables. See also *BGP*.

BIA. Burned-in address; another name for a MAC address.

binary. Numbering system characterized by 1s and 0s (1 = on, 0 = off).

bit. Binary digit used in the binary numbering system. This can be 0 or 1.

BOD. Bandwidth on demand.

BRI. Basic Rate Interface. The most common kind of ISDN interface available in the United States. BRI contains two B channels, each with a capacity of 64 kbps, and a single D channel (with a capacity of 16 kbps) that is used for signaling and call progress messages. Compare with *PRI*.

broadcast. Data packet that will be sent to all nodes on a network. Broadcasts are identified by a broadcast address. Compare with *multicast* and *unicast*.

BSD (Berkeley Standard Distribution). Term used to describe any of a variety of UNIX-type operating systems based on the UC Berkeley BSD operating system.

buffer. Storage area used for handling data in transit. Buffers are used in internetworking to compensate for differences in processing speed between network devices. Bursts of data can be stored in buffers until they can be handled by slower processing devices. This sometimes is referred to as a packet buffer.

byte. Term used to refer to a series of consecutive binary digits that are operated upon as a unit (for example, an 8-bit byte).

C

cable. Transmission medium of copper wire or optical fiber wrapped in a protective cover.

CCITT. Consultative Committee for International Telegraph and Telephone. International organization responsible for the development of communications standards. It is now called the ITU-T. See *ITU-T*.

CCO. Cisco Connection Online. Cisco's web site.

channel. Communication path. Multiple channels can be multiplexed over a single cable in certain environments.

Channelized E1. Access link operating at 2.048 Mbps that is subdivided into 30 B channels and 1 D channel. It supports DDR, Frame Relay, and X.25.

Channelized T1. Access link operating at 1.544 Mbps that is subdivided into 24 channels (23 B channels and 1 D channel) of 64 kbps each. The individual channels or groups of channels connect to different destinations. It supports DDR, Frame Relay, and X.25. It is also referred to as fractional T1.

CHAP. Challenge Handshake Authentication Protocol. Security feature supported on lines using PPP encapsulation that prevents unauthorized access. CHAP does not itself prevent unauthorized access; it merely identifies the remote end. The router or access server then determines whether that user is allowed access. Compare to *PAP*.

chat script. String of text that defines the login "conversation" that occurs between two systems. Consists of expect-send pairs that define the string that the local system expects to receive from the remote system and then determine what the local system should send as a reply.

checksum. Method for checking the integrity of transmitted data. A checksum is an integer value computed from a sequence of octets taken through a series of arithmetic operations. The value is recomputed at the receiving end and is compared for verification.

CIDR (classless interdomain routing). The means by which the Internet assigns blocks of addresses, typically Class C addresses, and summarizes them by using the prefix mask.

CIR. Committed information rate. Rate at which a Frame Relay network agrees to transfer information under normal conditions, averaged over a minimum increment of time. CIR, measured in bits per second, is one of the key negotiated tariff metrics. See also *Bc*.

circuit. Communications path between two or more points.

Cisco Express Forwarding (CEF). Advanced, Layer 3 IP switching technology. CEF optimizes network performance and scalability for networks with large and dynamic traffic patterns, such as the Internet, on networks characterized by intensive web-based applications or interactive sessions.

CiscoSecure. A complete line of access-control software products that complement any dial network solution, enabling the centralization of security policies.

classful routing protocols. Routing protocols that do not transmit any information about the prefix length. Examples are RIP and IGRP.

classless routing protocols. Routing protocols that include the prefix length with routing updates; routers running classless routing protocols do not have to determine the prefix themselves. Classless routing protocols support VLSM.

CLI. Command-line interface. An interface that enables the user to interact with the operating system by entering commands and optional arguments.

client. A node or software program that requests services from a server. See also *server*.

client/server computing. Computing (processing) network systems in which transaction responsibilities are divided into two parts: client (front end) and server (back end). Both terms (*client* and *server*) can be applied to software programs or actual computing devices. This is also called distributed computing (processing).

cluster-ID. The cluster-ID is another attribute used in configuring route reflectors. If the cluster has more than one route reflector, the cluster-ID is used to recognize updates from other route reflectors within the cluster.

collapsed backbone. A nondistributed backbone in which all network segments are interconnected by way of an internetworking device. A collapsed backbone might be a virtual network segment existing in a device such as a hub, a router, or a switch.

collision. In Ethernet, the result of two nodes transmitting simultaneously. The frames from each device impact and are damaged when they meet on the physical media.

committed burst. See *Bc*.

committed information rate. See *CIR*.

common carrier. Licensed, private utility company that supplies communication services to the public at regulated prices.

common transport semantic. Clear To Send signal. Circuit in the EIA/TIA-232 specification that is activated when the DCE is ready to accept data from the DTE.

connection-orientated. When the software on two end nodes guarantees the transmission of network traffic, because a circuit setup is established before sending any data. It requires the use of sequencing, windowing, and acknowledgements.

convergence. Speed and capability of a group of internetworking devices running a specific routing protocol to agree on the topology of an internetwork after a change in that topology.

cost. An arbitrary value, typically based on hop count, media bandwidth, or other measures, that is assigned by a network administrator and used to compare various paths through an internetwork environment. Cost values are used by routing protocols to determine the most favorable path to a particular destination: The lower the cost, the better the path. In OSPF, this is the value assigned to a link. This metric is based on the speed of the media. It is sometimes called path cost.

count to infinity. Problem that can occur in routing algorithms that are slow to converge, in which routers continuously increment the hop count to particular networks. Typically, some arbitrary hop-count limit is imposed to prevent this problem.

CPE. Customer premises equipment. Terminating equipment, such as terminals, telephones, and modems, supplied by the telephone company, installed at customer sites, and connected to the telephone company network.

CR. Carriage return.

CRC. Cyclic redundancy check. Error-checking technique in which the frame recipient calculates a remainder by dividing frame contents by a prime binary divisor and then comparing the calculated remainder to a value stored in the frame by the sending node.

CSU. Channel service unit. Digital interface device that connects end-user equipment to the local digital telephone loop. It is often referred to, together with DSU, as CSU/DSU. See also *DSU*.

customer premises equipment. See *CPE*.

cyclic redundancy check. See *CRC*.

D

DARPA. Defense Advanced Research Projects Agency. U.S. government agency that funded research for and does experimentation with the Internet. It evolved from ARPA and then, in 1994, back to ARPA.

Data Encryption Standard. See *DES*.

Data Network Identification Code. See *DNIC*.

data terminal equipment. See *DTE*.

datagram. Logical grouping of information sent as a network layer unit over a transmission medium without prior establishment of a virtual circuit. IP datagrams are the primary information units in the Internet. The terms *cell, frame, message, packet,* and *segment* are also used to describe logical information groupings at various layers of the OSI reference model and in various technology circles.

data-link connection identifier. See *DLCI*.

DB. Data bus connector. Type of connector used to connect serial and parallel cables to a data bus. DB connector names are in the format DB-*x*, where *x* represents the number of wires within the connector. Each line is connected to a pin on the connector, but in many cases, not all pins are assigned a function. DB connectors are defined by various EIA/TIA standards.

DCE. Data circuit-terminating equipment (ITU-T expansion). Devices and connections of a communications network that comprise the network end of the user-to-network interface. The DCE provides a physical connection to the network, forwards traffic, and provides a clocking signal used to synchronize data transmission between DCE and DTE devices. Modems and interface cards are examples of DCE. Compare with *DTE*.

DDR. Dial-on-demand routing. Technique whereby a router can automatically initiate and close a circuit-switched session as transmitting stations demand. The router spoofs keepalives so that end stations treat the session as active. DDR permits routing over ISDN or telephone lines using an external ISDN terminal adapter or modem.

DE. Discard eligible indicator. When the router detects network congestion, the FR switch will drop packets with the DE bit set first. The DE bit is set on the oversubscribed traffic—that is, the traffic that was received after the CIR was sent.

decryption. Reverse application of an encryption algorithm to encrypted data, thereby restoring that data to its original, unencrypted state. See also *encryption*.

dedicated line. Communications line that is indefinitely reserved for transmissions rather than switched as transmission is required. See also *leased line*.

default route. A routing table entry that is used to direct packets for which a next hop is not explicitly listed in the routing table.

default router. The router to which frames are directed when a next hop is not explicitly listed in the routing table. Also called a default gateway.

delay. Time between the initiation of a transaction by a sender and the first response received by the sender. Also, the time required to move a packet from source to destination over a given path.

demarc. Demarcation point between carrier equipment and CPE.

DES. Data Encryption Standard. Standard cryptographic algorithm developed by the U.S. National Bureau of Standards.

destination address. Address of a network device that is receiving data. See also *source address*.

DHCP (Dynamic Host Configuration Protocol). Provides a mechanism for allocating IP addresses dynamically so that addresses can be reused when hosts no longer need them.

dial backup. Feature that provides protection against WAN downtime by allowing the network administrator to configure a backup serial line through a circuit-switched connection.

dial-on-demand routing. See *DDR*.

dialup line. Communications circuit that is established by a switched-circuit connection using the telephone company network.

Diffusing Update Algorithm (DUAL). An algorithm performed on the topology table to converge the network. It is based on a router detecting a network change within a finite time, with the change being sent reliably and in sequence. Because the algorithm is calculated simultaneously, in order, and within a finite time frame on all affected routers, it ensures a loop-free network.

digital. The use of a binary code to represent information, such as 0/1 or on/off.

Dijkstra algorithm. Routing algorithm that iterates on length of path to determine a shortest-path spanning tree. Commonly used in link-state routing algorithms. Sometimes called shortest path first algorithm.

distance vector routing protocol. Class of routing algorithms that iterate on the number of hops in a route to find a shortest-path spanning tree. Distance vector routing algorithms call for each router to send its entire routing table in each update, but only to its neighbors. Distance vector routing algorithms can be prone to routing loops, but they are computationally simpler than link-state routing algorithms. These routing protocols are also called Bellman-Ford routing algorithms.

distribute list. An access list that is applied to the routing protocol. It is used to control routing updates by filtering out those updates that are not to be propagated. This is particularly useful in preventing routing loops in redistributed networks.

DLCI. Data-link connection identifier. Value that specifies a PVC or an SVC in a Frame Relay network. In the basic Frame Relay specification, DLCIs are locally significant (connected devices might use different values to specify the same connection). In the LMI extended specification, DLCIs are globally significant (DLCIs specify individual end devices). See also *LMI*.

DNIC. Data Network Identification Code. Part of an X.121 address. DNICs are divided into two parts, with the first specifying the country in which the addressed PSN is located, and the second specifying the PSN itself.

DNS (Domain Name System). System used in the Internet for translating names of network nodes into addresses.

DoD. Department of Defense. U.S. government organization that is responsible for national defense. The DoD has frequently funded communication protocol development.

domain. In the Internet, a portion of the naming hierarchy tree that refers to general groupings of networks based on organization type or geography.

Domain Name System. See *DNS*.

dot address. Refers to the common notation for IP addresses in the form n.n.n.n, where each number *n* represents, in decimal, 1 byte of the 4-byte IP address. This is also called dotted notation or four-part dotted notation.

dotted decimal notation. Syntactic representation for a 32-bit integer that consists of four 8-bit numbers written in base 10 with periods (dots) separating them. It is used to represent IP addresses in the Internet, as in 192.67.67.20. This is also called dotted quad notation.

DR. Designated router. Used in OSPF on multiaccess links. The router is responsible for maintaining the routing tables of the other OSPF routers on the same link. All the routers on the link form an adjacency with the designated router.

DS. Digital signal.

DS0. Digital signal level 0. Framing specification used in transmitting digital signals over a single channel at 64 kbps on a T1 facility. Compare with *DS1* and *DS3*.

DS1. Digital signal level 1. Framing specification used in transmitting digital signals at 1.544 Mbps on a T1 facility (in the United States), or at 2.108 Mbps on an E1 facility (in Europe). Compare with *DS0* and *DS3*.

DS3. Digital signal level 3. Framing specification used for transmitting digital signals at 44.736 Mbps on a T3 facility. Compare with *DS0* and *DS1*.

DSL. Digital subscriber line. Public network technology that delivers high bandwidth over conventional copper wiring at limited distances. There are four types of DSL: ADSL, HDSL, SDSL, and VDSL. All are provisioned via modem pairs, with one modem located at a central office and the other at the customer site. Because most DSL technologies do not use the whole bandwidth of the twisted pair, there is room remaining for a voice channel. See also *ADSL* and *HDSL*.

DSU. Data service unit. Device used in digital transmission that adapts the physical interface on a DTE device to a transmission facility such as T1 or E1. The DSU is also responsible for such functions as signal timing. It is often referred to, together with CSU, as CSU/DSU. See also *CSU*.

DTE. Data terminal equipment. Device at the user end of a user-network interface that serves as a data source, a destination, or both. DTE connects to a data network through a DCE device (for example, a modem) and typically uses clocking signals generated by the DCE. DTE includes such devices as computers, protocol translators, and multiplexers. Compare with *DCE*.

DUAL. See *Diffusing Update Algorithm*.

dynamic address resolution. Use of an address resolution protocol to determine and store address information on demand.

dynamic routes. Automatic rerouting of traffic based on sensing and analyzing current actual network conditions, not including cases of routing decisions taken on predefined information.

E

E1. Wide-area digital transmission scheme used predominantly in Europe that carries data at a rate of 2.048 Mbps. E1 lines can be leased for private use from common carriers. Compare with *T1*. See also *DS1*.

EGP. Exterior Gateway Protocol. An Internet protocol for exchanging routing information between autonomous systems. It is documented in RFC 904. This is not to be confused with the general term exterior gateway protocol; EGP is an obsolete protocol that has been replaced by BGP.

EIA/TIA. Electronic Industries Association/Telecommunications Industry Association.

EIA/TIA-232. Common physical layer interface standard, developed by EIA and TIA, that supports unbalanced circuits at signal speeds of up to 64 kbps. It closely resembles the V.24 specification. It was formerly called RS-232.

EIGRP. Enhanced Interior Gateway Routing Protocol. An advanced version of IGRP developed by Cisco. It provides superior convergence properties and operating efficiency, and combines the advantages of link-state protocols with those of distance vector protocols.

e-mail. Electronic mail. Widely used network application in which text messages are transmitted electronically between end users over various types of networks using various network protocols.

encapsulation. Wrapping of data in a particular protocol header. For example, Ethernet data is wrapped in a specific Ethernet header before network transit. Also, when bridging dissimilar networks, the entire frame from one network is simply placed in the header used by the data link layer protocol of the other network.

encryption. Application of a specific algorithm to data to alter the appearance of the data, making it incomprehensible to those who are not authorized to see the information. See also *decryption*.

end node. A device that is connected to the network.

Enhanced IGRP. See *EIGRP*.

excess burst. See *Be*.

Extended Super Frame. ESF. Framing type used on T1 circuits that consists of 24 frames of 192 bits each, with the 193rd bit providing timing and other functions. ESF is an enhanced version of SF.

Exterior Gateway Protocol (EGP). Protocol that runs between autonomous systems. A protocol with this name was the precursor to BGP.

exterior routing. A routing protocol used to exchange information between autonomous systems or organizations, used to connect organizations into the Internet. BGP and EGP are examples of exterior routing protocols.

exterior routing protocols. See *Exterior Gateway Protocol*.

external BGP. BGP is used to connect different autonomous systems.

F

fast switching. A cache in the Cisco router that contains routing decisions. When the routing decision for a packet has been made, it can be cached in any one of a variety of caches. This means that the forwarding of traffic throughout the router is greatly enhanced.

FCC. Federal Communications Commission. U.S. government agency that supervises, licenses, and controls electronic and electromagnetic transmission standards.

FCS. Frame check sequence. Extra characters added to a frame for error control purposes. This is used in HDLC, Frame Relay, and other data link layer protocols.

feasible condition (FC). When a neighbor reports a path (AD) that is lower than the router's FD to a network, the neighbor's (next-hop router's) path has a lower metric than the router's path.

feasible distance (FD). The lowest-cost distance (metric) to a remote network.

feasible successor (FS). The neighbor reporting the AD that is lower than the router's FD becomes the feasible successor. This is the next-hop router that meets the FC.

FECN. Forward explicit congestion notification. Bit set by a Frame Relay network to inform the DTE receiving the frame that congestion was experienced in the path from the source to the destination. The DTE receiving frames with the FECN bit set can request that higher-level protocols take flow-control action as appropriate. Compare with *BECN.*

FIFO. First in, first out. With FIFO, transmission occurs in the same order as messages are received.

filter. Generally, a process or device that screens network traffic for certain characteristics, such as source address, destination address, or protocol, and determines whether to forward or discard that traffic based on the established criteria.

firewall. Router or access server, or several routers or access servers, designated as a buffer between any connected public networks and a private network. A firewall router uses access lists and other methods to ensure the security of the private network.

first octet rule. The mechanism by which the Layer 3 device identifies the class of IP address. If the protocol is a classful address, it is the only means available to determine the network portion of an address to which it is not directly connected.

flapping. Intermittent interface failures.

flash update. A routing update sent asynchronously in response to a change in the network topology. Compare with *routing update*.

floating static route. A static route that has a higher administrative distance than a dynamically learned route so that it can be overridden by dynamically learned routing information. Used to create a DDR backup to an existing link.

flood. A term that refers to network information. When it is flooded, it is sent to every network device in the domain.

flooding. A traffic-passing technique used by switches and bridges in which traffic received on an interface is sent out to all the interfaces of that device, except the interface on which the information was originally received.

flow. Stream of data traveling between two endpoints across a network (for example, from one LAN station to another). Multiple flows can be transmitted on a single circuit.

flow control. Technique for ensuring that a transmitting entity, such as a modem, does not overwhelm a receiving entity with data. When the buffers on the receiving device are full, a message is sent to the sending device to suspend the transmission until the data in the buffers has been processed.

FR. See *Frame Relay.*

fragmentation. Process of breaking a packet into smaller units when transmitting over a network medium that cannot support the original size of the packet.

frame. Logical grouping of information sent as a data link layer unit over a transmission medium. This often refers to the header and trailer, used for synchronization and error control, that surround the user data contained in the unit. The terms *cell, datagram, message, packet,* and *segment* are also used to describe logical information groupings at various layers of the OSI reference model and in various technology circles.

Frame Relay. Industry-standard, switched data link layer protocol that handles multiple virtual circuits using HDLC encapsulation between connected devices. Frame Relay is more efficient than X.25, the protocol for which it is generally considered a replacement. See also *X.25.*

frequency. Number of cycles, measured in hertz, of an alternating current signal per unit time.

FTP. File Transfer Protocol. Application protocol, part of the TCP/IP protocol stack, used for transferring files between network nodes. FTP is defined in RFC 959.

full duplex. Capability for simultaneous data transmission between a sending station and a receiving station.

full mesh. Term describing a network in which devices are organized in a mesh topology, with each network node having either a physical circuit or a virtual circuit connecting it to every other network node. A full mesh provides a great deal of redundancy, but because it can be prohibitively expensive to implement, it is usually reserved for network backbones. See also *mesh* and *partial mesh*.

fully adjacent. When the routing tables of the two neighbors are fully synchronized, with exactly the same view of the network.

G - H

gateway. In the IP community, an older term referring to a routing device. Today, the term *router* is used to describe nodes that perform this function, and *gateway* refers to a special-purpose device that performs an application layer conversion of information from one protocol stack to another.

half duplex. Capability for data transmission in only one direction at a time between a sending station and a receiving station.

HDLC. High-Level Data Link Control. Bit-oriented synchronous data link layer protocol developed by ISO. Derived from SDLC, HDLC specifies a data encapsulation method on synchronous serial links using frame characters and checksums.

HDSL. High data-rate digital subscriber line. One of four DSL technologies. HDSL delivers 1.544 Mbps of bandwidth each way over two copper twisted-pair wires. Because HDSL provides T1 speed, telephone companies have been using HDSL to provision local access to T1 services whenever possible. The operating range of HDSL is limited to 12,000 feet (3658.5 meters), so signal repeaters are installed to extend the service. HDSL requires two twisted-pair wires, so it is deployed primarily for PBX network connections, digital loop carrier systems, interexchange POPs, Internet servers, and private data networks. Compare with *ADSL*.

header. Control information placed before data when encapsulating that data for network transmission.

hello. Hellos are used to find and maintain neighbors in the topology table. They are sent periodically and are sent reliably.

Hello protocol. A protocol used by OSPF systems for establishing and maintaining neighbor relationships.

High-Speed Serial Interface. See *HSSI*.

holddown. A state into which a route is placed so that routers will neither advertise the route nor accept advertisements about the route for a specific length of time (the holddown period); in this way, the entire network has a chance to learn about the change. Holddown is used to flush bad information about a route from all routers in the network. A route is typically placed in holddown when a link in that route fails.

holdtime. The holdtime is sent in the hello packet. It determines how long the router waits for hellos from a neighbor before declaring it unavailable. This information is held in the neighbor table.

hop. The passage of a data packet between two network nodes (for example, between two routers). See also *hop count*.

hop count. A routing metric used to measure the distance between a source and a destination. IP RIP uses hop count as its sole metric.

HSRP. Hot Standby Router Protocol. Provides a way for IP workstations to keep communicating on the internetwork even if their default router becomes unavailable, thereby providing high network availability and transparent network topology changes.

HSSI. High-Speed Serial Interface. Network standard for high-speed (up to 52-Mbps) serial connections over WAN links.

hub. Hardware or software device that contains multiple independent but connected modules of network and internetwork equipment. Hubs can be active (when they repeat signals sent through them) or passive (when they do not repeat, but merely split signals sent through them).

I

I/O. Input/output. Typically used when discussing ports on a device where data comes in or goes out.

IANA (Internet Assigned Numbers Authority). Responsible for address allocation in the Internet.

ICMP. Internet Control Message Protocol. Network layer Internet protocol that reports errors and provides other information relevant to IP packet processing. It is documented in RFC 792.

IDN. International data number. ITU-T standard describing an addressing scheme used in X.25 networks. X.121 addresses are sometimes called IDNs.

IEEE. Institute of Electrical and Electronic Engineers. Professional organization whose activities include the development of communications and network standards. IEEE LAN standards are the predominant LAN standards today.

IETF. Internet Engineering Task Force. Task force consisting of more than 80 working groups responsible for developing Internet standards. The IETF operates under the auspices of ISOC.

IGP. Interior Gateway Protocol. An Internet protocol used to exchange routing information within an autonomous system. Examples of common Internet IGPs include IGRP, OSPF, and RIP.

IGRP. Interior Gateway Routing Protocol. An IGP developed by Cisco to address the problems associated with routing in large, heterogeneous networks. Compare with *Enhanced IGRP.*

incremental update. A routing update that is sent only when there is a change in the topology, not periodically when a timer expires.

Integrated Services Digital Network. See *ISDN.*

Interior Gateway Protocol (IGP). In the past, the term *gateway* was used to define a router. This is a routing protocol that runs within an autonomous system.

interior routing protocols. Routing protocols used by routers within the same autonomous system, such as RIP, IGRP, and Enhanced IGRP.

internal BGP. BGP used to connect routers resident in the same autonomous system.

Internet. A term that refers to the largest global internetwork, connecting tens of thousands of networks worldwide and having a "culture" that focuses on research and standardization based on real-life use. Many leading-edge network technologies come from the Internet community. The Internet evolved in part from ARPANET. At one time, it was called the DARPA Internet. This is not to be confused with the general term *internet*.

internet. Short for internetwork. Not to be confused with the Internet. See also *internetwork*.

internetwork. A collection of networks interconnected by routers and other devices that functions (generally) as a single network. It is sometimes called an internet, which is not to be confused with the Internet.

internetworking. The industry that has arisen around the problem of connecting networks. The term can refer to products, procedures, and technologies.

intranet. A network, internal to an organization, based on Internet and World Wide Web technology, that delivers immediate, up-to-date information and services to networked employees.

IOS. Internetwork Operating System.

IP. Internet Protocol. A network layer protocol in the TCP/IP stack offering a connectionless internetwork service. IP provides features for addressing, type-of-service specification, fragmentation and reassembly, and security. It is documented in RFC 791.

IP address. A 32-bit address assigned to hosts using TCP/IP. An IP address belongs to one of five classes (A, B, C, D, or E) and is written as four octets separated with periods (dotted decimal format). Each address consists of a network number, an optional subnetwork number, and a host number. The network and subnetwork numbers together are used for routing, and the host number is used to address an individual host within the network or subnetwork. A subnet mask is used to extract network and subnetwork information from the IP address. It is also called an Internet address.

IP multicast. A routing technique that allows IP traffic to be propagated from one source to a number of destinations or from many sources to many destinations. Rather than send one packet to each destination, one packet is sent to a multicast group identified by a single IP destination group address.

IPSec. Standards-based method of providing privacy, integrity, and authenticity to information transferred across IP networks. It provides IP network layer encryption.

IPv6. IP version 6. Replacement for the current version of IP (version 4). IPv6 includes support for flow ID in the packet header, which can be used to identify flows. It formerly was called IPng (IP next generation).

IPX. Internetwork Packet Exchange. A NetWare network layer (Layer 3) protocol used for transferring data from servers to workstations.

IPX address. An IPX address is 80 bits long, with 32 bits for the network number and 48 bits for the node number.

IS. Information systems. A broad term used to describe the use of information technology in organizations. This includes the movement, storage, and use of information.

ISDN. Integrated Services Digital Network. Communication protocol offered by telephone companies that permits telephone networks to carry data, voice, and other source traffic.

IS-IS. Intermediate System-to-Intermediate System. An OSI link-state hierarchical routing protocol based on DECnet Phase V routing whereby ISs (routers) exchange routing information based on a single metric to determine network topology.

ISO. International Organization for Standardization. International organization that is responsible for a wide range of standards, including those relevant to networking. The ISO developed the OSI reference model, a popular networking reference model.

ISOC. Internet Society. International nonprofit organization, founded in 1992, that coordinates the evolution and use of the Internet. In addition, ISOC delegates authority to other groups related to the Internet, such as the IAB. ISOC is headquartered in Reston, Virginia (United States).

ISP. Internet service provider. Company that provides Internet access to other companies and individuals.

ITU-T. International Telecommunication Union–Telecommunication Standardization Sector. International body that develops worldwide standards for telecommunications technologies. The ITU-T carries out the functions of the former CCITT.

J - K

jitter. Analog communication line distortion caused by the variation of a signal from its reference timing positions. Jitter can cause data loss, particularly at high speeds.

Kb. Kilobit. Approximately 1,000 bits.

kbps. Kilobits per second.

keepalive. Message sent by one network device to inform another network device that the virtual circuit between the two is still active.

keepalive message. A message sent by one network device to inform another network device that the circuit between the two is still active.

Kerberos. Developing standard for authenticating network users. Kerberos offers two key benefits: It functions in a multivendor network, and it does not transmit passwords over the network.

L

LAN. Local-area network. High-speed, low-error data network covering a relatively small geographic area (up to a few thousand meters). LANs connect workstations, peripherals, terminals, and other devices in a single building or other geographically limited area. LAN standards specify cabling and signaling at the physical and data link layers of the OSI model. Ethernet, FDDI, and Token Ring are widely used LAN technologies. Also see *MAN* and *WAN*.

LAPB. Link Access Procedure, Balanced. Data link layer protocol in the X.25 protocol stack. LAPB is a bit-oriented protocol derived from HDLC.

LAPD. Link Access Procedure on the D channel. ISDN data link layer protocol for the D channel. LAPD was derived from the LAPB protocol and is designed primarily to satisfy the signaling requirements of ISDN basic access. It is defined by ITU-T recommendations Q.920 and Q.921.

Layer 3 switching. Used in the context of VLANs, the mechanism by which a switch will route between VLANs. It also refers to routers, when the routing decision has been made and the result has been cached. The subsequent lookup involves switching (such as fast switching), but on a Layer 3 decision.

leased line. Transmission line reserved by a communications carrier for the private use of a customer. A leased line is a type of dedicated line. See also *dedicated line*.

LED. Light emitting diode. Semiconductor device that emits light produced by converting electrical energy. Status lights on hardware devices are typically LEDs.

link. Network communications channel consisting of a circuit or transmission path and all related equipment between a sender and a receiver. It is most often used to refer to a WAN connection and sometimes is referred to as a line or a transmission link.

link-state routing algorithm. A routing algorithm in which each router broadcasts or multicasts information regarding the cost of reaching each of its neighbors to all nodes in the internetwork. Compare with *distance vector routing protocol*.

LMI. Local Management Interface. Set of enhancements to the basic Frame Relay specification. LMI includes support for a keepalive mechanism, which verifies that data is flowing; a multicast mechanism, which provides the network server with its local DLCI and the multicast DLCI; global addressing, which gives DLCIs global rather than local significance in Frame Relay networks; and a status mechanism, which provides an ongoing status report on the DLCIs known to the switch. It is known as LMT in ANSI terminology.

load balancing. In routing, the capability of a router to distribute traffic over all its network ports that are the same distance from the destination address. Good load-balancing algorithms use both line speed and reliability information. Load balancing increases the use of network segments, thus increasing effective network bandwidth.

loading state. During the process whereby two routers are creating an adjacency, if the receiving router requires more information, it will request that particular link in more detail, using the link-state request packet (LSR). The LSR will prompt the master router to send the link-state update packet (LSU). This is the same as a link-state advertisement (LSA) used to flood the network with routing information. While the receiving is awaiting the LSUs from its neighbor, it is in the loading state.

local loop. Also known as "the last mile." Line from the premises of a telephone subscriber to the telephone company central office.

logical AND. The mechanism by which a subnet is derived from an IP host address. The router maps the subnet mask, in binary, onto the host address, in binary. The result of the logical AND is the subnet address.

loopback interface. A virtual interface that does not exist physically. This characteristic makes it very powerful: If it does not exist, it can never go down.

LSA (link-state advertisement). Broadcast packet used by link-state protocols that contains information about neighbors and path costs. LSAs are used by the receiving routers to maintain their routing tables. Sometimes called an LSP.

M

MAN. Metropolitan-area network. Network that spans a metropolitan area. Generally, a MAN spans a larger geographic area than a LAN but a smaller geographic area than a WAN. Compare with *LAN* and *WAN*.

maximum transmission unit. See *MTU*.

MD5. Message digest algorithm 5. Algorithm used for message authentication. MD5 verifies the integrity of the communication, authenticates the origin, and checks for timeliness.

mesh. A network topology in which devices are organized in a manageable, segmented manner with many often redundant interconnections strategically placed between network nodes. See also *full mesh* and *partial mesh*.

message. An application layer (Layer 7) logical grouping of information, often composed of a number of lower-layer logical groupings such as packets.

metric. A standard of measurement, such as performance, that is used for measuring whether network management goals have been met.

modem. Modulator-demodulator. Device that converts digital and analog signals. At the source, a modem converts digital signals to a form suitable for transmission over analog communication facilities. At the destination, the analog signals are returned to their digital form. Modems allow data to be transmitted over voice-grade telephone lines.

modulation. Process by which the characteristics of electrical signals are transformed to represent information. Types of modulation include AM, FM, and PAM.

MP. Multilink Point-to-Point Protocol. Defined in the RFC 1717, it is sometimes referred to as MLPPP. It takes advantage of the ability of switched WAN services to open multiple virtual connections between devices to give users extra bandwidth as needed. This allows access devices to combine multiple PPP links into one logical data pipe.

MTU. Maximum transmission unit. Maximum packet size, in bytes, that a particular interface can handle.

multiaccess network. Network that allows multiple devices to connect and communicate simultaneously.

multicast. Single packets copied by the network and sent to a specific subset of network addresses. These addresses are specified in the Destination Address field. Compare with *broadcast* and *unicast*.

multiplexing. Scheme that allows multiple logical signals to be transmitted simultaneously across a single physical channel.

N

NAK. Negative acknowledgment. Response sent from a receiving device to a sending device indicating that the information received contained errors. Compare to *acknowledgment*.

NAS. See *access server*.

NAT. Network Address Translation. Mechanism for reducing the need for globally unique IP addresses. NAT allows an organization with addresses that are not globally unique to connect to the Internet by translating those addresses into globally routable address space. Also known as Network Address Translator.

NBMA. Nonbroadcast multiaccess. Term describing a multiaccess network that does not support broadcasting (such as X.25) or in which broadcasting is not feasible (for example, an SMDS broadcast group or an extended Ethernet that is too large).

neighbor. A router running EIGRP that is directly connected.

neighbor table. A list of every neighbor, including the IP address, the outgoing interface, the holdtime, SRTT, and uptime, or how long since the neighbor was added to the table. The table is built from information on hellos received from adjacent routers (neighbors).

neighboring router. In OSPF or EIGRP, two routers that have interfaces to a common network.

NetBEUI. NetBIOS Extended User Interface. Enhanced version of the NetBIOS protocol used by network operating systems such as LAN Manager, LAN Server, Windows for Workgroups, and Windows NT. NetBEUI formalizes the transport frame and adds additional functions. NetBEUI implements the OSI LLC2 protocol.

NetFlow. A Cisco solution that enhances the speed of transmission by caching routing decisions.

network. Collection of computers, printers, routers, switches, and other devices that are capable of communicating with each other over some transmission medium.

network congestion. When excessive traffic on the network is the cause of delays and packet loss.

NNI. The standard interface between two Frame Relay switches meeting the same criteria.

nonstub area. A resource-intensive OSPF area that carries a default route, static routes, intra-area routes, interarea routes, and external routes. Compare with *stub area*. See also *ASBR*.

NVRAM. Nonvolatile random access memory.

O

OC. Optical carrier. Series of physical protocols (OC-1, OC-2, OC-3, and so forth) defined for SONET optical signal transmissions. OC signal levels put STS frames onto multimode fiber-optic line at a variety of speeds. The base rate is 51.84 Mbps (OC-1); each signal level thereafter operates at a speed divisible by that number (thus, OC-3 runs at 155.52 Mbps).

octet. Eight bits. In networking, the term *octet* is often used (rather than *byte*) because some machine architectures employ bytes that are not 8 bits long.

ODBC. Open database connectivity.

OLE. Object linking and embedding. Compound document standard developed by Microsoft Corporation. It enables creating objects with one application and then linking or embedding them in a second application. These objects keep their original format and links to the application that created them.

originator-ID. A BGP-4 attribute. It is an optional nontransitive attribute that is created by the route reflector. The attribute contains the router ID of the router that originated the route in the update. The purpose of this attribute is to prevent a routing loop. If the originating router receives its own update, it ignores it.

OSI. Open System Interconnection. International standardization program created by ISO and ITU-T to develop standards for data networking that facilitate multivendor equipment interoperability.

OSI reference model. Open System Interconnection reference model. Network architectural model developed by ISO and ITU-T. The model consists of seven layers, each of which specifies particular network functions such as addressing, flow control, error control, encapsulation, and reliable message transfer. The lowest layer (the physical layer) is closest to the media technology. The lower two layers are implemented in hardware and software, while the upper five layers are implemented only in software. The highest layer (the application layer) is closest to the user. The OSI reference model is used universally as a method for teaching and understanding network functionality.

OSPF. Open Shortest Path First. A link-state, hierarchical IGP routing algorithm proposed as a successor to RIP in the Internet community. OSPF features include least-cost routing, multipath routing, and load balancing. OSPF was derived from an early version of the IS-IS protocol. See also *EIGRP, IGP, IGRP, IS-IS,* and *RIP.*

OUI. Organizationally unique identifier. Three octets assigned by the IEEE, used in the 48-bit MAC addresses.

P

packet. Logical grouping of information that includes a header containing control information and (usually) user data. Packets are most often used to refer to network layer units of data. The terms *datagram, frame, message,* and *segment* are also used to describe logical information groupings at various layers of the OSI reference model and in various technology circles. See also *PDU.*

packet switching. Networking method in which nodes share bandwidth with each other by sending packets.

PAP. Password Authentication Protocol. Authentication protocol that allows PPP peers to authenticate one another. The remote router attempting to connect to the local router is required to send an authentication request. Unlike CHAP, PAP passes the password and host name or username in the clear (unencrypted). PAP does not itself prevent unauthorized access, but it merely identifies the remote end. The router or access server then determines whether that user is allowed access. PAP is supported only on PPP lines. Compare with *CHAP.*

partial mesh. Network in which devices are organized in a mesh topology, with some network nodes organized in a full mesh, but with others that are connected to only one or two other nodes in the network. A partial mesh does not provide the level of redundancy of a full-mesh topology, but it is less expensive to implement. Partial-mesh topologies are generally used in the peripheral networks that connect to a fully meshed backbone. See also *full mesh* and *mesh.*

passive. An operational route is passive. If the path is lost, the router examines the topology table to find an FS. If there is an FS, it is placed in the routing table and the router does not query the others, which would send it into active mode.

PAT. Port Address Translation. A subset of NAT.

payload. Portion of a cell, frame, or packet that contains upper-layer information (data).

PDN. Public data network. Network operated either by a government (as in Europe) or by a private concern to provide computer communications to the public, usually for a fee. PDNs enable small organizations to create a WAN without all the equipment costs of long-distance circuits.

PDU. Protocol data unit. OSI term for *packet*.

peak rate. Maximum rate, in kilobits per second, at which a virtual circuit can transmit.

permanent virtual circuit (PVC). See *PVC*.

ping. Packet Internet groper. ICMP echo message and its reply. This is often used in IP networks to test the reachability of a network device.

PIX. Cisco's Private Internet Exchange firewall. See also *firewall*.

playback. Reuse of a packet captured from a line by a sniffer.

point of demarcation. The physical point at which the phone company ends its responsibility with the wiring of the phone line.

poison reverse. Routing updates that specifically indicate that a network or subnet is unreachable, rather than implying that a network is unreachable by not including it in updates.

POP. Point of presence. A long-distance carrier's office in your local community. A POP is the place where your long-distance carrier, or IXC, terminates your long-distance lines just before those lines are connected to your local phone company's lines or to your own direct hookup. Each IXC can have multiple POPs within one LATA. All long-distance phone connections go through the POPs.

POTS. Plain old telephone service. See *PSTN*.

PPP. Point-to-Point Protocol. Successor to SLIP that provides router-to-router and host-to-network connections over synchronous and asynchronous circuits. Whereas SLIP was designed to work with IP, PPP was designed to work with several network layer protocols, such as IP, IPX, and ARA. PPP also has built-in security mechanisms, such as CHAP and PAP. PPP relies on two protocols: LCP and NCP. See also *CHAP* and *PAP*.

prefix list. These replace distribute lists for BGP-4. The prefix list is used to control how BGP-4 learns or advertises updates.

prefix mask. Identifies the number of bits in the subnet mask. It is written in the /xx format after the address. It is used in supernetting and router aggregation.

PRI. Primary Rate Interface. ISDN interface to primary rate access. Primary rate access consists of a single 64-Kbps D channel plus 23 (T1) or 30 (E1) B channels for voice or data. Compare with *BRI*.

private addressing. The means by which an organization can address its network without using a registered address from the Internet. This saves considerable address space in the Internet and eases restrictions within the organization.

process switching. The routing process within the Cisco router. This is resource-intensive.

PSTN. Public Switched Telephone Network. General term referring to the variety of telephone networks and services in place worldwide. Sometimes called POTS.

PTT. Poste, Telephone, Telegramme.

PVC. Permanent virtual circuit. Virtual circuit that is permanently established. PVCs save bandwidth associated with circuit establishment and teardown in situations in which certain virtual circuits must exist all the time. In ATM terminology, this is called a permanent virtual connection. See also *SVC*.

Q

QoS. Quality of service. A measure of performance for a transmission system that reflects its transmission quality and service availability.

query. Sent from the router when it loses a path to a network. If there is no alternate route (feasible successor), the router will send out queries to neighbors inquiring whether they have a feasible successor. This makes the route state change to active. The queries are sent reliably.

query scoping. Another term for SIA.

queue. 1. Generally, an ordered list of elements waiting to be processed. 2. In routing, a backlog of packets waiting to be forwarded over a router interface.

R

RADIUS. Database for authenticating modem and ISDN connections and for tracking connection time.

rate enforcement. See *traffic policing*.

redistribution. Exchanging routing updates between different routing protocols. This can be done only between protocols that support the same protocol suite at Layer 3—for example EIGRP and OSPF for TCP/IP. Redistribution cannot happen between Layer 3 protocols such as AppleTalk and IPX.

Reliable Transport Protocol (RTP). Requires that the packets be delivered in sequence and guaranteed.

reply. A response to the query. If a router has no information to send in a reply, it will send queries to all its neighbors. A unicast is sent reliably.

Retransmission Timeout (RTO). Timer calculated in reference to the SRTT. RTO determines how long the router waits for an ACK before retransmitting the packet.

RIP. 1. Routing Information Protocol. A distance vector IGP, RIP uses hop count as a routing metric. See also *Enhanced IGRP, hop count, IGP, IGRP,* and *OSPF.* 2. IPX Routing Information Protocol. A distance vector routing protocol for IPX.

RJ-45. Registered jack connector. Standard connectors used for 10BaseT and other types of network connections.

route reflector. The router that is configured to forward routes from other identified IBGP-4 clients. This removes the necessity for a fully meshed IBGP-4 network, which preserves network resources.

route reflector client. A client is a router that has a TCP session with its IBGP-4 peer. It forwards routes to the route reflector, which propagates these on to other routers. The client does not have peer connections with other clients.

route reflector cluster. A cluster is the group of route reflector and clients. There can be more than one route reflector in a cluster.

route summarization. The consolidation of advertised addresses in a routing table. Summarization of routes reduces the number of routes in the routing table, the routing update traffic, and overall router overhead. Also called route aggregation.

routed protocol. Protocol that can be routed by a router. A router must be capable of interpreting the logical internetwork as specified by that routed protocol. Examples of routed protocols include AppleTalk, DECnet, and IP.

router. A network layer device that uses one or more metrics to determine the optimal path along which network traffic should be forwarded. Routers forward packets from one network to another based on network layer information. It is occasionally called a gateway (although this definition of gateway is becoming increasingly outdated).

routing. The process of finding a path to a destination host. Routing is complex in large networks because of the many potential intermediate destinations that a packet might traverse before reaching its destination host. Routing occurs at Layer 3, the network layer.

routing domain. A group of end systems and intermediate systems operating under the same set of administrative rules.

routing loop. Occurs when routers have misinformation about the network and, instead of sending traffic to the destination, pass the packets between themselves in the belief that the other router knows the path.

routing metric. A standard of measurement, such as path length, that is used by routing algorithms to determine the optimal path to a destination. This information is stored in routing tables. Metrics include bandwidth, communication cost, delay, hop count, load, MTU, path cost, and reliability. It is sometimes referred to simply as a metric.

routing protocol. Supports a routed protocol by providing mechanisms for sharing routing information. Routing protocol messages move between the routers. A routing protocol allows the routers to communicate with other routers to update and maintain routing tables. Routing protocol messages do not carry end-user traffic from network to network. A routing protocol uses the routed protocol to pass information between routers. Examples of routing protocols are IGRP, OSPF, and RIP.

routing table. A table stored in a router or some other internetworking device that keeps track of routes to particular network destinations and metrics associated with those routes.

routing update. A message sent from a router to indicate network reachability and associated cost information. Routing updates are typically sent at regular intervals and after a change in network topology. Compare with *flash update*.

runaway congestion. When the results of network congestion cause the network to generate more traffic and compound the problem.

S

SA. Source address.

SAP. Service access point; also Service Advertising Protocol (Novell).

SAPI. Service access point identifier.

SDLC. Synchronous Data Link Control. SNA data link layer communications protocol. SDLC is a bit-oriented, full-duplex serial protocol that has spawned numerous similar protocols, including HDLC and LAPB.

seed metric. The metric that is given to a route when it enters the routing protocol. Most routes start with a metric of 0 because they first become known to the routing protocol to which they are directly connected. However, if they are redistributed into the routing protocol, there is no starting point from which to increment the route metric. Therefore, the default metric is configured to provide a seed metric for the redistributed routes.

server. Node or software program that provides services to clients. See also *client*.

setup script. This is a question-and-answer dialogue that is offered by the Cisco router. If the router is booted without an existing configuration, it will ask you if you want to enter the setup script to create a basic configuration.

ships in the night (SIN). See *SIN*.

shortest path first (SPF). The same as the Dijkstra algorithm, which is the algorithm used to find the shortest path.

SIA. Stuck in Active (EIGRP).

silicon switching. Switching based on the silicon switching engine (SEE), which allows the processing of packets independent of the Silicon Switch Processor (SSP) system processor. Silicon switching provides high-speed, dedicated packet switching.

SIN. Ships-in-the-night. This type of routing advocates the use of a completely separate and distinct routing protocol for each network protocol so that the multiple routing protocols essentially exist independently.

Smooth Round Trip Time (SRTT). The time that the router waits after sending a packet reliably to hear an acknowledgment. This is held in the neighbor table and is used to calculate the RTO.

SMTP. Simple Mail Transfer Protocol. Internet protocol providing e-mail services.

SNA. Systems Network Architecture.

SNAP. SubNetwork Access Protocol.

SNMP. Simple Network Management Protocol.

SOF. Start of frame.

SOHO. Small office, home office. Networking solutions and access technologies for offices that are not directly connected to large corporate networks.

SONET. Synchronous Optical Network. High-speed (up to 2.5-Gbps) synchronous network specification developed by Bellcore and designed to run on optical fiber. STS-1 is the basic building block of SONET. It was approved as an international standard in 1988.

source address. Address of a network device that is sending data. See also *destination address*.

SPF. Shortest path first.

SPID. Service profile identifier. Number that some service providers use to define the services to which an ISDN device subscribes. The ISDN device uses the SPID when accessing the switch that initializes the connection to a service provider. The ISDN switch needs to have a unique identification number for each ISDN set to which it sends calls and signals.

split horizon rules. Routing technique in which information about routes is prevented from exiting the router interface through which that information was received. Split-horizon updates are useful in preventing routing loops.

spoofing. Scheme used by routers to cause a host to treat an interface as if it were up and supporting a session. The router spoofs replies to keepalive messages from the host to convince the host that the session still exists. Spoofing is useful in routing environments such as DDR, in which a circuit-switched link is taken down when there is no traffic to be sent across it to save toll charges.

SPP. Sequenced Packet Protocol (Vines).

SPX. Sequenced Packet Exchange (Novell).

SQL. Structured Query Language.

SRAM. Static RAM.

SRTT. Smooth Round-Trip Timer (EIGRP).

SS7. Signaling System 7. Standard CCS system developed by Bellcore and used with BISDN and ISDN.

SSAP. Source service access point (LLC).

SSE. Silicon switching engine.

SSP. Silicon Switch Processor.

static route. A route that is explicitly configured and entered into the routing table.

STP. Shielded twisted-pair; also Spanning-Tree Protocol.

stub area. An OSPF area that carries a default route, intra-area routes, and inter-area routes, but that does not carry external routes. Compare with *nonstub area*.

stub network. Part of an internetwork that can be reached by only one path; a network that has only a single connection to a router.

Stuck in Active (SIA). When a router has sent out network packets and is waiting for ACKs from all its neighbors. The route is active until all the ACKs have been received; if they do not appear after a certain time, the router is Stuck in Active for the route.

subinterface. One of a number of virtual interfaces on a single physical interface.

subnet. See *subnetwork*.

subnet mask. A 32-bit number that is associated with an IP address; each bit in the subnet mask indicates how to interpret the corresponding bit in the IP address. In binary, a subnet mask bit of 1 indicates that the corresponding bit in the IP address is a network or subnet bit; a subnet mask bit of 0 indicates that the corresponding bit in the IP address is a host bit. The subnet mask then indicates how many bits have been borrowed from the host field for the subnet field. It sometimes is referred to simply as mask.

subnetwork. In IP networks, a network sharing a particular subnet address. Subnetworks are networks arbitrarily segmented by a network administrator to provide a multilevel, hierarchical routing structure while shielding the subnetwork from the addressing complexity of attached networks. It is sometimes called a subnet.

suboptimal path. A path that is not the best path. Sometimes a path that is less desirable is chosen.

successor. The next-hop router that passes the FC. It is chosen from the FSs as having the lowest metric to the remote network.

supernet. A summarization of class addresses given out by the Internet community. For example, the group of Class C addresses 200.100.16.0 through 200.100.31.0 could be summarized into the address 200.100.16.0 with a mask of 255.255.224.0 (/19).

SVC. Switched virtual circuit. Virtual circuit that is dynamically established on demand and is torn down when transmission is complete. SVCs are used in situations in which data transmission is sporadic. It is called a switched virtual connection in ATM terminology. Compare with *PVC.*

switch. 1. A network device that filters, forwards, and floods frames based on the destination address of each frame. The switch operates at the data link layer of the OSI model. 2. An electronic or mechanical device that allows a connection to be established as necessary and terminated when there is no longer a session to support.

switching function. Forwarding packets from an inbound interface to an outbound interface.

SYN. Synchronize (TCP segment).

synchronization. Establishment of common timing between sender and receiver.

synchronization rule. Rule stating that a router cannot forward a route to an EBGP-4 peer unless the route is in the IP routing table. This requires the IGP and BGP-4 routing tables to be synchronized. This is to prevent BGP-4 from advertising routes that the autonomous system cannot direct to the destination.

T

T1. Digital WAN carrier facility. T1 transmits DS-1-formatted data at 1.544 Mbps through the telephone-switching network using AMI or B8ZS coding.

TA. Terminal adapter (ISDN).

TAC. Technical Assistance Center (Cisco).

TACACS. Terminal Access Controller Access Control System.

TCP. Transmission Control Protocol. Connection-oriented transport layer protocol that provides reliable full-duplex data transmission. TCP is part of the TCP/IP protocol stack. See also *TCP/IP*.

TCP/IP. Transmission Control Protocol/Internet Protocol. Common name for the suite of protocols developed by the U.S. DoD in the 1970s to support the construction of worldwide internetworks. TCP and IP are the two best-known protocols in the suite. See also *IP*, *TCP*, and *UDP*.

TDM. Time-division multiplexing.

Telco. Telephone company.

TFTP. Trivial File Transfer Protocol.

TIA. Telecommunications Industry Association.

topology table. Used by EIGRP and OSPF, this is the table that records all the routes in the network before determining which will be entered into the routing table.

ToS. Type of service.

traffic policing. Process used to measure the actual traffic flow across a given connection and then compare it to the total admissible traffic flow for that connection. Traffic outside the agreed-upon flow can be tagged (where the CLP bit is set to 1) and can be discarded en route if congestion develops. Traffic policing is used in ATM, Frame Relay, and other types of networks.

traffic shaping. The use of queues to limit surges that can congest a network. Data is buffered and then sent into the network in regulated amounts to ensure that the traffic will fit within the promised traffic envelope for the particular connection. Traffic shaping is used in ATM, Frame Relay, and other types of networks. It is also known as metering, shaping, and smoothing.

transit autonomous system. This is an autonomous system that is used to carry BGP-4 traffic across it to another autonomous system. None of the traffic is destined for any router within the autonomous system, it is simply being routed through it.

Transmission Control Protocol. See *TCP.*

triggered update. See *flash update*

TTL. Time To Live. A field in an IP header that indicates how long a packet is considered valid.

tunneling. An architecture that provides a virtual data link connection between two like networks through a foreign network. The virtual data link is created by encapsulating the network data inside the packets of the foreign network.

twisted pair. Two insulated wires, usually copper, twisted together and often bound into a common sheath to form multipair cables. In ISDN, the cables are the basic path between a subscriber's terminal or telephone and the PBX or the central office.

two-way state. During the process whereby two routers are creating an adjacency, the router reaches a stage called the two-way state. This is when the new router sees its own router ID in the list of neighbors, and a neighbor relationship is established. This is the stage before routing information is exchanged.

U

UDP. User Datagram Protocol. Connectionless transport layer protocol in the TCP/IP protocol stack. UDP is a simple protocol that exchanges datagrams without acknowledgments or guaranteed delivery, requiring that error processing and retransmission be handled by other protocols.

UNC. Universal Naming Convention or Uniform Naming Convention. A PC format for specifying the location of resources on a local-area network (LAN). UNC uses the following format: \\server-name\shared-resource-pathname.

UNI. User-Network Interface.

unicast. Message sent to a single network destination. Compare with *broadcast* and *multicast*.

update. An EIGRP packet containing change information about the network. It is sent reliably. It is sent only when there is a change in the network to affected routers: when a neighbor first comes up, when a neighbor transitions from active to passive for a destination, or when there is a metric change for a destination.

URL. Uniform resource locator.

UTC. Coordinated Universal Time (same as Greenwich Mean Time).

UTL. Utilization.

UTP. Unshielded twisted-pair wire.

V

V.35. ITU-T standard describing a synchronous, physical layer protocol used for communications between a network access device and a packet network. V.35 is most commonly used in North America and in Europe, and is recommended for speeds up to 48 Kbps.

VC. See *virtual circuit*.

VIP. Versatile Interface Processor.

virtual circuit. Logical circuit created to ensure reliable communication between two network devices. A virtual circuit is defined by a VPI/VCI pair and can be either permanent (PVC) or switched (SVC). Virtual circuits are used in Frame Relay and X.25. In ATM, a virtual circuit is called a virtual channel. It is sometimes abbreviated VC.

VLAN (virtual LAN). A logical grouping devices, identified on switch ports instead of a physical segment attached to a router. This means that the devices associated with the logical network do not have to be geographically local to one another.

VLSM (variable-length subnet mask). The capability to specify a different subnet mask for the same network number on different subnets. VLSM can help optimize available address space. Some protocols do not allow the use of VLSM. See also *classless routing protocols*.

VPN. Virtual private network. Enables IP traffic to travel securely over a public TCP/IP network by encrypting all traffic from one network to another. A VPN uses tunneling to encrypt all information at the IP level.

vty. Virtual terminal line.

W

WAIS. Wide Area Information Server. Distributed database protocol developed to search for information over a network. WAIS supports full-text databases, which allow an entire document to be searched for a match (as opposed to other technologies that allow only an index of key words to be searched).

WAN. Wide-area network. Data communications network that serves users across a broad geographic area and that often uses transmission devices provided by common carriers. Frame Relay, SMDS, and X.25 are examples of WANs.

watchdog packet. Used to ensure that a client is still connected to a NetWare server. If the server has not received a packet from a client for a certain period of time, it sends that client a series of watchdog packets. If the station fails to respond to a predefined number of watchdog packets, the server concludes that the station is no longer connected and clears the connection for that station.

watchdog spoofing. Subset of spoofing that refers specifically to a router acting especially for a NetWare client by sending watchdog packets to a NetWare server to keep the session between client and server active. It is useful when the client and server are separated by a DDR WAN link.

watchdog timer. 1. Hardware or software mechanism used to trigger an event or an escape from a process unless the timer is periodically reset. 2. In NetWare, a timer that indicates the maximum period of time that a server will wait for a client to respond to a watchdog packet. If the timer expires, the server sends another watchdog packet (up to a set maximum).

weighted fair queuing. Abbreviated as WFQ. Congestion-management algorithm that identifies conversations (in the form of traffic streams), separates packets that belong to each conversation, and ensures that capacity is shared fairly between these individual conversations. WFQ is an automatic way of stabilizing network behavior during congestion, and it results in increased performance and reduced retransmission.

wildcard mask. A 32-bit quantity used in conjunction with an IP address to determine which bits in an IP address should be ignored when comparing that address with another IP address. A wildcard mask is specified when setting up access lists.

window. The number of data segments that the sender is allowed to have outstanding without yet receiving an acknowledgment.

windowing. A method to control the amount of information transferred end to end, using different window sizes.

WINS. Windows Internet Name Service. Allows clients on different IP subnets to dynamically register and browse the network without sending broadcasts.

workgroup. A collection of workstations and servers on a LAN that are designed to communicate and exchange data with one another.

World Wide Web. See *WWW.*

WWW. World Wide Web. A large network of Internet servers providing hypertext and other services to terminals running client applications such as a WWW browser.

WWW browser. A GUI-based hypertext client application, such as Mosaic, used to access hypertext documents and other services located on innumerable remote servers throughout the WWW and the Internet. See also *Internet* and *WWW.*

X

X.25. ITU-T standard that defines how connections between DTE and DCE are maintained for remote terminal access and computer communications in PDNs. X.25 specifies LAPB, a data link layer protocol, and PLP, a network layer protocol. To some degree, Frame Relay has superseded X.25.

xDSL. Group term used to refer to ADSL, HDSL, SDSL, and VDSL. All are emerging digital technologies using the existing copper infrastructure provided by the telephone companies. xDSL is a high-speed alternative to ISDN.

XNS. Xerox Network Systems.

XOT. X.25 over TCP.

Z

ZIP. Zone Information Protocol. AppleTalk session layer protocol that maps network numbers to zone names. ZIP is used by NBP to determine which networks contain nodes that belong to a zone.

ZIT. Zone Information Table (AppleTalk).

zone. In AppleTalk, a logical group of network devices.

zone multicast address. Data link-dependent multicast address at which a node receives the NBP broadcasts directed to its zone.

INDEX

A

ABR (Area Border Router), 290
    LSA propagation, 292
access, 32
access-class, 50
access-group, 50
Access layer, hierarchical designs, 40
access lists, 43-44. *See also* IP access lists
    BGP-4, 471
    guidelines for writing, 46-47
    prioritization, 52–53
    security, 49
        controlling terminal access, 49–50
accessibility, network requirements, 32
ACRC (Advanced Cisco Router Configuration), 5
    how to use this book if you've taken this course, 17–18
AD (advertised distance), 353
adaptability, network requirements, 32
adding networks to topology tables, 357
address exhaustion, summarization, 111
addresses
    class addresses, 90
    Internet addresses, 90
    IP addresses. *See* IP addresses
    major addresses, 90
    network addresses, 90
    NIC addresses, 89
    supernet addresses, 90
    translating, 123–124
    VLSM addresses, allocating, 105–106
addressing networks, 87–89
addressing schemes, case studies, 86
adjacent neighbors, 178
    OSPF, 215
administrative distance
    configuring, 533–534
    path selection between routing protocols, 524-526
    routing protocols, path selection, 179, 181
Advanced Cisco Router Configuration. *See* ACRC
advantages
    of CIDR, 99, 101
    of neighbors, OSPF, 216
    of policy routing, 551–552
    of summarization, 110, 130
    synchronization rule, BGP-4, 408
    of VLSM, 102
        allocating VLSM addresses, 106
        bit allocation, 105

        VLSM addresses, 105
advertised distance, 353
advertising routes
    from BGP-4 to IGP, 485–486
    from IGP to BGP-4, 485
aggregate-address command, 485
aggregated routes, 107
aggregating routes, autonomous systems, 423
Aggregator, BGP-4 attributes, 416
alleviating network congestion, 41
allocating VLSM addresses, 105–106
alternative methods
    for connecting ISP, 427
    for connecting to ISP, 426
alternatives to summarization, 113
and, 3
answers
    to scenario 11-1, 585, 587
    to scenario 11-2, 587–588
    to scenario 11-3, 589, 591
    to scenario 11-4 Part A, 597, 599–600
    to scenario 11-4 Part B, 602–603
    to scenario 11-4 Part C, 634, 636–638
    to scenario 11-5 Part A, 640–642
    to scenario 11-5 Part B, 642, 644–645
    to scenario 11-5 Part C, 679, 680-683
AppleTalk, configuring EIGRP for, 376
applications, delays in, 38
Area 0, 290
Area Border Router. *See* ABR
area boundaries, multiple areas, 288
area range command, 302
    configuring multiarea OSPF networks, 303
    configuring OSPF multiarea networks, 302
areas
    backbone areas, 296
    NSSA, 296
    stub area, 296
    stubby areas, 296
    types of, OSPF, 295-297
AS external ASBR summary link, LSAs, 292
AS_Path, BGP-4 attributes, 416
ASBR (Autonomous System Boundary Router), 290
    LSA propagation, 292
    OSPF summarization command, 303
assigning IP VLSM subnets
    for WAN connections, 114
    to WAN connections, 115
Atomic Aggregate, BGP-4 attributes, 416

C

D

E

J-K

L

P

Cisco Press

Committed to being your **long-term** resource as you grow as a **Cisco Networking professional**

Help Cisco Press **stay connected** to the issues and challenges you face on a daily basis by registering your product and filling out our brief survey. Complete and mail this form, or better yet ...

Register online and enter to win a **FREE** book!

Jump to **www.ciscopress.com/register** and register your product online. Each complete entry will be eligible for our monthly drawing to win a FREE book of the winner's choice from the Cisco Press library.

May we contact you via e-mail with information about **new releases, special promotions** and customer benefits?

❏ Yes ❏ No

E-mail address _____

Name _____

Address _____

City _____ State/Province _____

Country _____ Zip/Post code _____

Where did you buy this product?

❏ Bookstore ❏ Computer store/electronics store
❏ Online retailer ❏ Direct from Cisco Press
❏ Mail order ❏ Class/Seminar
❏ Other_____

When did you buy this product? _____ Month _____ Year

What price did you pay for this product?

❏ Full retail price ❏ Discounted price ❏ Gift

How did you learn about this product?

❏ Friend ❏ Store personnel ❏ In-store ad
❏ Cisco Press Catalog ❏ Postcard in the mail ❏ Saw it on the shelf
❏ Other Catalog ❏ Magazine ad ❏ Article or review
❏ School ❏ Professional Organization ❏ Used other products
❏ Other_____

What will this product be used for?

❏ Business use ❏ School/Education
❏ Other_____

Cisco Press
201 West 103rd Street
Indianapolis, IN 46290
ciscopress.com

Place
Stamp
Here

Cisco Press
Customer Registration—CP0500227
P.O. Box #781046
Indianapolis, IN 46278-8046

CCNP Routing Exam Certification Guide (1-58720-001-5)
Thank you for completing this survey and registration. Please fold here, seal, and mail to Cisco Press.

_____

_____

Do you have any additional comments or suggestions?

_____

_____

On what topics would you like to see more coverage?

☐ Yes ☐ No
Have you purchased a Cisco Press product before?

☐ College degree ☐ Masters degree ☐ Professional or Doctoral degree
☐ High school ☐ Vocational/Technical degree ☐ Some college
What is your formal education background?

☐ Professor/Teacher ☐ Other
☐ Marketing/Sales ☐ Consultant ☐ Student
☐ Network Design ☐ Network Support ☐ Webmaster
☐ Corporate Management ☐ Systems Engineering ☐ IS Management
Which best describes your job function?

☐ 2 years or less ☐ 3-5 years ☐ 5+ years
How many years have you been employed in a computer-related industry?

Cisco Press
c i s c o p r e s s . c o m